CW01646705

International Communism and the Spanish Civil War

Solidarity and Suspicion

LISA A. KIRSCHENBAUM
West Chester University, West Chester, PA

CAMBRIDGE
UNIVERSITY PRESS

CAMBRIDGE
UNIVERSITY PRESS

University Printing House, Cambridge CB2 8BS, United Kingdom

One Liberty Plaza, 20th Floor, New York, NY 10006, USA

477 Williamstown Road, Port Melbourne, VIC 3207, Australia

314-321, 3rd Floor, Plot 3, Splendor Forum, Jasola District Centre, New Delhi-110025, India

79 Anson Road, #06-04/06, Singapore 079906

Cambridge University Press is part of the University of Cambridge.

It furthers the University's mission by disseminating knowledge in the pursuit of education, learning and research at the highest international levels of excellence.

www.cambridge.org
Information on this title: www.cambridge.org/9781107514058

First published 2015
First paperback edition 2018

A catalogue record for this publication is available from the British Library

Library of Congress Cataloging in Publication data
Kirschenbaum, Lisa A.
International communism and the Spanish Civil War : solidarity and suspicion / Lisa A. Kirschenbaum (West Chester University, West Chester, PA).
pages cm
Includes bibliographical references and index.
ISBN 978-1-107-10627-7 (hardback)
1. Communists – History – 20th century. 2. Internationalism – Political aspects – History – 20th century. 3. Solidarity – Political aspects – History – 20th century. 4. Suspicion – Political aspects – History – 20th century. 5. Communists – Spain – History – 20th century. 6. Communists – Soviet Union – History – 20th century. 7. Spain – History – Civil War, 1936–1939 – Political aspects. 8. Spain – Relations – Soviet Union. 9. Soviet Union – Relations – Spain. I. Title.
HX40.K517 2015
335.4309′043–dc23 2015010668

ISBN 978-1-107-10627-7 Hardback
ISBN 978-1-107-51405-8 Paperback

For John

Contents

Illustrations

Acknowledgments

It is a pleasure to acknowledge the many people and institutions that helped make this book possible. I am indebted to the librarians and archivists who facilitated my work at the Russian State Archive of Socio-Political History; the Russian State Archive of Literature and Art; the National Historical Archive in Madrid; the National Archive of Catalonia; the Historical Archive of the Communist Party of Spain; the National Archives at College Park, Maryland; the Library of Congress; the Hoover Institution; the Bancroft Library at the University of California, Berkeley; the University of Illinois Rare Book and Manuscript Library; the Tamiment Library at New York University; the New York Public Library; the Columbia University Rare Book and Manuscript Library; the University of Pennsylvania Rare Book and Manuscript Library; and the West Chester University Library.

I thank the Kennan Institute for Advanced Russian Studies and its then-director Blair Ruble for two timely short-term grants. A short-term grant from the International Research and Exchanges Board funded my research in Moscow. West Chester University provided generous and essential research funding. In 2008–9 I was named a Penn Humanities Forum Mellon Regional Faculty Research Fellow. I thank the forum's organizers Peter Struck and Wendy Steiner for facilitating a wonderful year-long interdisciplinary discussion of "change." The 2009 National Endowment for the Humanities Summer Institute,"America Engages Russia," hosted by the New York Public Library and organized by Edward Kasinec and Robert H. Davis, provided an ideal environment in which to learn from colleagues in American and Russian history and to explore the library's resources.

I thank all the friends and colleagues who read parts of the manuscript, provided excellent questions, or offered crucial pieces of information and advice; they include Choi Chatterjee, Gina Herrmann, Alastair Kocho-Williams, Daniel Kowalsky, Adele Lindenmeyr, Elizabeth McGuire, Benjamin Nathans, Cynthia

Paces, Karl Qualls, Marci Shore, the late Richard Stites, Gerald D. Surh, and Glennys Young. Special thanks go to Bob Weinberg and the participants in his invaluable Delaware Valley Seminar for their careful and generous readings. I thank Ben Nathans and Peter Holquist for the invitation to present a chapter at a session of the Penn Kruzhok – and the *kruzhovtsy* for their helpful and illuminating feedback. Mark D. Steinberg provided critical support and advice as well as the opportunity to present my work at the Russian, East European, and Eurasian Center at University of Illinois at Urbana-Champaign. Nancy M. Wingfield once again went above and beyond in her willingness to read everything I sent her. My trip to Moscow would have been far less enjoyable and productive without Julia Mickenberg's comradeship. I thank her for her responses to my work and for sharing her work in progress with me.

It has been a pleasure to work again with Cambridge University Press. I thank Lew Bateman for his early and unfailing support of this project.

With permission of the publisher, the book includes parts of the article "Exile, Gender, and Communist Self-Fashioning: Dolores Ibárruri (La Pasionaria) in the Soviet Union," which appeared in *Slavic Review,* the journal of the Association for Slavic, East European, and Eurasian Studies, 71, no. 3 (Fall 2012): 566–89. I thank the Bancroft Library for permission to publish quotations from the Veterans of the Abraham Lincoln Brigade Bay Area Post records, and the Tamiment Library at New York University for permission to publish photographs from the Harry Randall collection.

None of this would have been possible without the support and love of my family. My parents Diane and Barry Kirschenbaum inspire me with their curiousity and enjoyment of life. My mom, as always, is my first and most enthusiastic reader; I hope she is happy with "our" book. I thank John Conway for sharing the journey with me. This book is dedicated to him.

A Note on Transliteration and Translation

In the text and notes, I use the Library of Congress system of transliteration, except in the case of well-known names, such as Ehrenburg. Where the sources transliterated Spanish or English names into Cyrillic, I tried to restore the original language's spelling conventions. Where I was unable to confirm the original spelling, I included a direct transliteration of the Cyrillic in the notes. All translations are my own, except where noted.

Introduction

Being Communist

In a letter marked "urgent" sent in 1937 to Mikhail Kalinin, the nominal head of the Soviet state, Spanish communist Adela Rivera Sánchez told an intimate story of war. A party member since 1930, Rivera Sánchez wrote that she had recently arrived in the Soviet Union from Asturias with three small children, the youngest of whom was two. Because the Spanish party required her "immediate return to work in Spain," she wrote that she was planning "to leave my three children in the Soviet Union and return as soon as possible."[1] Such a decision was not uncommon among international communists, who viewed the Soviet Union as a safe haven for their children.[2] What complicated her return – and the reason for her appeal to Kalinin – was that she was two-and-a-half-months pregnant. The "situation in Spain and the conditions of my work," she explained, "do not permit me to have another child at this time (I am 26 and this is my sixth child)." Thus she asked Kalinin to intervene on her behalf and permit her to have an immediate abortion, "so that I can return to my country and take an active part in the struggle of the Spanish people."[3]

Rivera Sánchez needed special dispensation to terminate her pregnancy because abortion had been prohibited in the Soviet Union in June 1936. (The

[1] "Predsedateliu VTsIK Tov. Kalininu," Rossiiskii gosudarstvennyi arkhiv sotsial'no-politicheskoi istorii (RGASPI), f. 531, op. 1, d. 186, l. 3. Her name appears in Cyrillic as Adela Rovira Sanches.

[2] Mariia Minina-Svetlanova, "Two Motherlands Are Mine, and I Hold Both Dear in My Heart: Upbringing and Education in the Ivanovo Interdom," *Russian Studies in History* 48, no. 4 (Spring 2010): 75; Huang Jian, "A Chinese Student in the USSR," in Glennys Young, ed., *The Communist Experience in the Twentieth Century: A Global History through Sources* (New York: Oxford University Press, 2012), 264–9; Immaculada Colomina Limonero, *Dos patrias, tres mil destinos: Vida y exilo de los niños de la Guerra de España refugiados en la Unión Soviética* (Madrid: Ediciones Cinca, 2010); A. V. Elpat'evskii, *Ispanskaia emigratsiia v SSSR: Istorigrafiia i istochniki, popytka interpretatsii* (Tver: Izdatel'stvo "GERS," 2002), 13–37.

[3] RGASPI, f. 531, op. 1, d. 186, l. 3.

Spanish Republic never fully decriminalized abortion.[4]) The Soviet legislation justified the abortion ban as a means of combating "a frivolous attitude toward the family and family responsibility."[5] Rivera Sánchez, however, presented her reasons as anything but frivolous. Rather, she invoked earlier revolutionary norms that called on exemplary communists to subordinate the satisfactions of family life to the needs of the revolution, while also underscoring the fact that she already had five children.[6] In response to her request, she received a note instructing her to report on 13 December 1937 to the Secretariat of the President of the Central Executive Committee to "discuss your matter."[7] The archive contains no information regarding the outcome of that meeting.

Rivera Sánchez's request allows us to see how, for the most committed, international communism was not only a political movement; it was also a way of life. Her appeal dramatizes the personal sacrifices that communists made for the cause. It also suggests how a "good" communist might understand and enact the connection between her political duty and her personal life – indeed she might not consider herself to be making a sacrifice at all as she left her children thousands of miles from home and petitioned to end her pregnancy in order to participate in "the struggle of the Spanish people." Her determination to join the struggle in Spain demanded the perhaps temporary abandonment of her maternal role. At the same time, her individual circumstances encouraged her to challenge, however implicitly, the Stalinist sanctification of the family. Thus her story – and others like it told in this book – illustrates the ways in which communist commitments shaped personal lives and personal relationships influenced political understandings.

Focusing on the everyday lives of international communists, this book offers a grassroots history of international communism. Transnational interactions among communists occurred, as Rivera Sánchez's story illustrates, in the context of norms and institutions largely established by the Soviet party. But although such interactions were unequal, they were also messy, unpredictable, emotionally charged, and ultimately productive. This book thus explores the transnational exchanges that occurred in Soviet-structured spaces – from clandestine schools for training international revolutionaries in Moscow to the International Brigades in Spain – as a means of tracing the everyday practices of being communist. It analyzes the appeal of communism, specifically Soviet

[4] Richard Cleminson, "Beyond Tradition and 'Modernity': The Cultural and Sexual Politics of Spanish Anarchism," in Helen Graham and Jo Labanyi, eds., *Spanish Cultural Studies: An Introduction: The Struggle for Modernity* (New York: Oxford University Press, 1995), 121–2.

[5] Cited in Wendy Z. Goldman, *Women, the State, and Revolution: Soviet Family Policy and Social Life, 1917–1936* (New York: Cambridge University Press, 1993), 331.

[6] Jeffrey Brooks, "Revolutionary Lives: Public Identities in *Pravda* during the 1920s," in Stephen White, ed., *New Directions in Soviet History* (Cambridge: Cambridge University Press, 1992), 34; Elizabeth A Wood, *The Baba and the Comrade: Gender and Politics in Revolutionary Russia* (Bloomington: Indiana University Press, 1997), 47.

[7] RGASPI, f. 531, op. 1, d. 186, l. 5.

communism for those outside of the Soviet Union, by taking it seriously not only as a revolutionary political creed but also as a way of understanding (and remaking) both the world and the self, the self in the world.

International Communism and Individual Lives

When the Bolsheviks seized power in Petrograd in October 1917, they aimed not only, or even primarily, to remake the Russian empire and the Russian people. They intended to shake the world: to spark a global transformation of political and human relations. This Bolshevik sense of world historical mission took the institutional form of the Third or Communist International (Comintern), founded in Moscow in 1919 as the headquarters of world revolution.[8] Even now, from the vantage of our thoroughly globalized world, the breadth of the Comintern's revolutionary ambition is impressive; by 1935, it operated on six continents and had sixty-five member parties. Working in well over a dozen languages, Comintern agents and functionaries collected information and issued directives on topics as diverse as strike activity, the agrarian question, women's activism, youth mobilization, regional party organizations, the labor press, clandestine operations, the celebration of communist holidays, and the training of new cadres – to provide only a very partial list.[9] The Comintern, in short, can be understood as an enormous fact-finding and policy-making operation run out of Moscow, structured largely by the shifting needs and interests of the Soviet leadership.

Thus histories of international communism are often organized around the important question of the extent to which "central authorities in Moscow" controlled "national communist parties."[10] The so-called traditionalists in this debate focus on local parties' subservience to Moscow. In this vein, some

[8] "Manifesto of the Communist International to the Workers of the World," *Communist International*, no. 1 (May 1919): 5–10. There is a vast literature on the institutional history of the Comintern. See for example, Aleksandr Vatlin, *Komintern: idei, resheniia, sud'by* (Moscow: ROSSPEN, 2009); Norman LaPorte, Kevin Morgan, and Matthew Worley, eds., *Bolshevism, Stalinism, and the Comintern: Perspectives on Stalinization, 1917–53* (Basingstoke: Palgrave Macmillan, 2008); Carlos Díaz, *Tercera Internacional (Comunista): De la Revolución Rusa a la dictadura de Franco* (Madrid: Fundación Emmanuel Mounier, 2003); A. O. Chubarin, ed., *Istoriia kommunisticheskogo internatsionala, 1919–1943: Dokumental'nye ocherki* (Moscow: Nauka, 2002); Tim Rees and Andrew Thorpe, eds., *International Communism and the Communist International, 1919–43* (Manchester: Manchester University Press, 1998); Pierre Broué, *Histoire de l'Internationale communiste: 1919–1943* (Paris: Fayard, 1997); Kevin McDermott and Jeremy Agnew, *The Comintern: A History of International Communism from Lenin to Stalin* (Basingstoke: Palgrave Macmillan, 1996); E. H. Carr, *The Twilight of the Comintern* (London: Macmillan, 1982); Fernando Claudín, *The Communist Movement from Comintern to Cominform*, trans. Brian Pearce and Francis MacDonagh (New York: Monthly Review Press, 1975).

[9] An inventory of the Comintern archive was available at http://www.comintern-online.com/ (accessed 11 April 2013).

[10] McDermott and Agnew, *Comintern*, xx.

scholars of the British party emphasize the degree to which study at the International Lenin School, the Comintern's most prestigious institution devoted to training foreign communists, forged strong bonds between British communists and the Soviet regime – in some cases ties so close that British communists became Soviet spies.[11] So-called revisionists, by contrast, emphasize the social histories of local parties and the dynamism and at least partial autonomy of the communist grassroots.[12] From this perspective another study of British students at the Lenin School emphasizes the "limited and ephemeral" influence of the school and the "resilience" of "prior cultural formations" even in the face of "intense conditioning."[13]

Recent transnational and cultural studies of international communism have complicated this traditionalist-revisionist dichotomy. In an essay collection on *Bolshevism, Stalinism, and the Comintern,* editors Norman LaPorte, Kevin Morgan, and Matthew Worley propose expanding the "centre-periphery debate" via transnational comparisons of the extent to which the Soviets controlled a range of national parties.[14] Brigitte Studer and Heiko Haumann's multilingual collection on Stalinist subjects emphasizes that Soviet control was as much cultural and subjective as political.[15] In his contribution to a collection of essays on British communists, Kevin Morgan emphasizes the variety of communists' relationships with Moscow. He suggests that exploring the diversity and idiosyncrasy of communist biographies – paying attention to "personal centres" rather than institutional ones – offers a "possible route out of the recent impasse of the centre-periphery dichotomy" and what he calls the "fixation" on questions of control.[16]

[11] John McIlroy et al., "Forging the Faithful: The British at the International Lenin School," *Labour History Review* 68, no. 1 (April 2003): 99, 113; see also Harvey Klehr, John Earl Haynes, and Fridrikh Igorevich Firsov, *The Secret World of American Communism* (New Haven: Yale University Press, 1995), 18; Ronald Radosh, Mary R. Habeck, and Grigory Sevostianov, eds., *Spain Betrayed: The Soviet Union in the Spanish Civil War* (New Haven: Yale University Press, 2001), xviii; John McIlroy and Alan Campbell, "A Peripheral Vision: Communist Historiography in Britain," *American Communist History* 4, no. 2 (2005): 125–57.

[12] Fraser M. Orttanelli, *The Communist Party of the United States from the Depression to World War II* (New Brunswick, NJ: Rutgers University Press, 1991), 4; Randi Storch, *Red Chicago: American Communism at its Grassroots, 1928–35* (Urbana: University of Illinois Press, 2007); Helen Graham, *The Spanish Republic at War, 1936–1939* (Cambridge: Cambridge University Press, 2002), 296, 287.

[13] Gidon Cohen and Kevin Morgan, "Stalin's Sausage Machine: British Students at the International Lenin School, 1926–1937," *Twentieth Century British History* 13, no. 4 (2002): 330, 328–9.

[14] Norman LaPorte, Kevin Morgan, and Matthew Worley, "Introduction: Stalinization and Communist Historiography," in *Bolshevism, Stalinism and the Comintern*, 1–21.

[15] Brigitte Studer and Heiko Haumann, "Introduction," in Studer and Haumann, eds., *Stalinistische Subjekte: Indivduum und System in der Sowjetunion und der Komintern, 1929–1953* (Zurich: Chronos, 2006), 39–64.

[16] Kevin Morgan, "Parts of People and Communist Lives," in John McIlroy, Kevin Morgan, and Alan Campbell, eds., *Party People, Communist Lives: Explorations in Biography* (London: Lawrence & Wishart, 2001), 23, 24.

Drawing on the cultural and biographical strands of this recent work, this book focuses on the everyday work of creating a transnational revolutionary network. Looking at sites of transnational exchange it emphasizes the complex webs of interaction, at once personal and political, that linked international communists not only to Moscow but also to one another. Part I (Chapters 1–2) focuses on Americans and Spaniards who studied and worked in Moscow in the 1930s and introduces several individuals whose trajectories I follow throughout the book. Places like the International Lenin School functioned as points of connection between center and periphery, sites of everyday interactions among communists, both international and Soviet. As they interacted in institutions structured by the "center," mobile communists from the "periphery" lived and made international communism, although never just as they pleased.

Part II (Chapters 3–5) follows to Spain a number of Lenin School alumni and others who worked or studied in the Soviet Union and explores the transnational contacts central to the experiences of so many who participated in the International Brigades. Initiated in Moscow and managed on a day-to-day basis largely by Western European communists, many of whom were trained in the Soviet Union, the International Brigades brought about thirty-five thousand volunteers to Spain: It constituted the largest and most ambitious, although ultimately unsuccessful, international operation orchestrated by the Comintern. I pay particular attention to the American volunteers in Spain (widely known as the Abraham Lincoln Brigade), who included large numbers of foreign-born or first-generation Americans and were thus a notably transnational and multilingual contingent.

Part III (Chapters 6–7) tracks the personal and institutional connections among those who participated in the Spanish war through World War II and the early years of the cold war. I focus on both Spanish exiles in the Soviet Union, who saw the Soviet war against Germany as an extension of "our war," and on American communists, who unlike many of their European comrades, had no later story of local resistance to Nazism to overshadow or compete with the (often mythologized) memory of the Spanish war. The book concludes with a discussion of the impact of the cold war and of de-Stalinization on international communists' connections to one another and the cause.

The Spanish Civil War and the Culture of International Communism

The conflict that came to be known as the Spanish civil war began as a military coup on 17–18 July 1936. Deeply rooted in the social, economic, and political upheavals that shook Spain in the early twentieth century and that in 1931 gave rise to the Spanish Republic, the insurgency aimed to halt change and to overturn Republican reforms that challenged the traditional authority of large landowners, the Catholic Church, and the army.[17] Initiated by

[17] For introductions to very different assessments of the origins of the war, see Helen Graham, *The Spanish Civil War, A Very Short Introduction* (New York: Oxford University Press, 2005),

soldiers in Spain's Army of Africa, the coup achieved rapid success in the Protectorate of Morocco. However, on the peninsula supporters of the Popular Front government that had been elected in February 1936 offered strong, if not always well-coordinated, resistance. Thus "despite the support of many officers, the uprising in Spain" was "largely unsuccessful," taking control of only about one-third of the country.[18] The situation initially seemed to favor the Republic.

What turned the attempted coup into a civil war and an international cause célèbre on the left was the provision of German and Italian military aid to the rebels. By the end of July, Benito Mussolini and Adolf Hitler were dispatching weapons, planes, and troops to Spain. In August 1936 German and Italian planes ferried General Francisco Franco and some fourteen thousand Spanish and Moroccan troops across the Straits of Gibraltar to Spain. On the mainland the Army of Africa launched a ruthless campaign through western Andalusia and Extremadura to Madrid, employing the tactics that colonial officers had developed as a response to guerrilla warfare in the Rif: "sporadic, mobile warfare, executed on a number of fronts" coupled with "systematic ethnic cleansing as a means of ensuring order."[19] Ultimately, Italy contributed more than seventy thousand troops, and both Germany and Italy sent hundreds of artillery pieces, tanks, planes, and pilots, including the infamous German Condor Legion responsible for the April 1937 destruction of Guernica.[20] In August 1936, the French government, hoping to undercut aid to the insurgents, proposed a ban on all intervention in Spain that won the support of Britain and the Soviet Union, as well as of Italy and Germany, even as the latter two violated it.[21] Thus as the rebels built their forces, the nonintervention agreement denied arms to the Republic.

1–19, and Stanley G. Payne, *The Spanish Civil War* (New York: Cambridge University Press, 2012), 5–81. Graham argues that the Republic's "failure was a quite specific one: It proved unable to prevent sectors of the officer corps from making a coup" and that it was the insurgents' "original act of violence" that "killed off the possibility of other forms of peaceful political evolution" (18); Payne argues that "political violence was initiated primarily by the left" (45) and that the insurgents acted only "when they judged that it literally would be more dangerous not to rebel than to rebel" (68).

18 Sebastian Balfour, *Deadly Embrace: Morocco and the Road to the Spanish Civil War* (Oxford: Oxford University Press, 2002), 271. See also María Rosa de Madariaga, "The Intervention of Moroccan Troops in the Spanish Civil War: A Reconsideration," *European History Quarterly* 22 (1992): 67, 78.

19 Balfour, *Deadly Embrace,* 290–1, and more generally 286–96; Madariaga, "Intervention," 80; Paul Preston, *The Spanish Holocaust: Inquisition and Extermination in Twentieth-Century Spain* (New York: W. W. Norton, 2012).

20 Michael Alpert, "The Clash of Spanish Armies: Contrasting Ways of War in Spain, 1936–1939," *War in History* 6, no. 3 (July 1999): 331–51; Robert H. Whealey, *Hitler and Spain: The Nazi Role in the Spanish Civil War* (Lexington: University of Kentucky Press, 1989), 44–51; Brian R. Sullivan, "Fascist Italy's Military Involvement in the Spanish Civil War," *Journal of Military History* 59, no. 4 (October 1995): 697–727.

21 Michael Alpert, *A New International History of the Spanish Civil War* (New York: St. Martin's Press, 1994), 40–64; Enrique Moradiellos, "The Allies and the Spanish Civil War," in Sebastian

Airlifted across the strait, the brutally effective Army of Africa saved the insurgency from defeat, while the arrival of German and Italian bombers and tanks firmly linked it to fascism and Nazism, not least of all in the Soviet media. Less than two weeks after the rebellion began, *Izvestiia* carried reports of German and Italian military aid to the rebels and, like Comintern propaganda, characterized the struggle in Spain as a link in the chain of international fascist aggression. A photo that ran in *Pravda* of a downed rebel airplane with a swastika on its tail made the connection between German fascism and the war in Spain unmistakable.[22] By contrast, the Soviet press emphasized that the Loyalist cause was the "cause of all advanced and progressive humanity" (*delo vsego peredovogo i progressivnogo chelovechestva*), as Stalin declared in a telegram to the Spanish communist leader José Díaz that appeared in the 16 October 1936 issue of *Pravda*.

From the beginning, this image of the Soviet Union as committed to defending democracy against fascism was both pervasive and contested. Soviet antifascism galvanized many international volunteers, but others saw it as a smokescreen. Among the earliest and certainly best-known critics of Soviet propaganda and actions in Spain was George Orwell, who in *Homage to Catalonia* documented his military service in Spain as a member of a militia affiliated with the POUM (Partit Obrer d'Unificació Marxista), an anti-Stalinist Marxist party. For Orwell, vociferous Soviet antifascism effectively obscured the fact that the "whole Comintern policy is now subordinated (excusably, considering the world situation) to the defense of the USSR." Concerned only about ensuring their own security via cooperation with France, the Soviets, he argued, were more interested in quashing the revolution in Spain than in winning the war.[23] On the other side, the rebels represented communists – Francoist shorthand for all who supported the Republic – as irredeemable infidels, foreign agents of Moscow against whom it was reasonable and necessary to employ "Nationalist" Moroccan troops and German bombs.[24]

The opening of the Soviet archives after 1991 has done little to resolve or substantially reframe debates on the sincerity of Soviet antifascism. Ronald Radosh, Mary R. Habeck, and Grigory Sevostianov, the editors of *Spain Betrayed*, a collection of Soviet military and Comintern documents published in English translation in 2001, argue that the newly accessible materials verify the "duplicitous maneuvers of the Soviet Union in the Spanish Republic."[25] Particularly controversial is their claim that the archives demonstrate that the

Balfour and Paul Preston, eds., *Spain and the Great Powers in the Twentieth Century* (London: Routledge, 1999), 105–7.

22 On early coverage in *Izvestiia* of German and Italian intervention see David E. Allen, "The Soviet Union and the Spanish Civil War" (PhD diss., Stanford University, 1952), 431. "Samolet fashistskikh miatezhnikov," *Pravda*, 29 August 1936; Mikhail Kol'tsov, "Germanskaia pomoshch' ispanskim miatezhnikam," *Pravda*, 31 August 1936.

23 George Orwell, *Homage to Catalonia* (1938; reprint, San Diego: Harvest/HBJ, 1980), 56.

24 Balfour, *Deadly Embrace*, 286.

25 Radosh et al., *Spain Betrayed*, xxii.

real Soviet mission was not to save the Republic or combat fascism but rather "to 'Sovietize' Spain and to turn it into what would have been one of the first 'People's Republics,' with a Stalinist-style economy, army, and political structure."[26] From their perspective, the documents indisputably debunk the "compelling legend" that the Soviet effort to stop fascism in Spain constituted "one of the noblest and most selfless undertakings of the international communist movement."[27] They thus raise what historian Tony Judt called "the most delicate question" of whether "the International Brigades and their supporters were duped." Judt for one was ready to agree that the international volunteers "*were* duped," dismissing the communist rhetoric of antifascism and defense of democracy as a "fairy tale."[28]

For other historians, however, the claim that the newly opened archives clearly and incontrovertibly demolish the supposed "legend" of the Spanish civil war is itself a fairy tale. Historian Peter Carroll, best known for his work on the Abraham Lincoln Brigade, argues that two recent document collections including *Spain Betrayed* willfully misuse historical evidence to replace the "honorable legend of the Lincoln Brigade" with "the myths of the Moscow archives."[29] Helen Graham, a prominent British historian of the war, characterizes *Spain Betrayed* as an exemplar of "the new historical McCarthyism."[30] She finds "nothing" in the documents presented to sustain the editors' assumption that "all Soviet actions in Spain were designed to achieve" – and in fact did achieve – "total control of the Republican government and army."[31] To make their case, she argues, the editors left "entirely out of account the broader picture of Republican Spain at war."[32] Historians attending to the "broader historical context" often understand the Soviets as opportunistic – but not necessarily insincere – antifascists: Providing military aid to the Republic served Soviet efforts to prevent "German aggression from turning eastward."[33] Historian Daniel Kowalsky notes that for its part the Republic accepted the Soviet aid only "grudgingly," recognizing that "Communist participation and assistance,

26 Ibid., xxiii. See also Stanley Payne, *The Spanish Civil War, the Soviet Union, and Communism* (New Haven: Yale University Press, 2004), 137–8.

27 Radosh et al., *Spain Betrayed*, xvi.

28 Emphasis in original. Tony Judt, "Rehearsal for Evil," *New Republic* 225, no. 11 (10 September 2001): 33, 34.

29 Carroll also reviews Klehr et al., *The Secret World of American Communism*; Peter Carroll, "The Myth of the Moscow Archives," *Science and Society* 68, no. 3 (Fall 2004): 337, 338.

30 Helen Graham, "Spain Betrayed? The New Historical McCarthyism," *Science and Society* 68, no. 3 (Fall 2004): 364–9.

31 Ibid., 366. Judt makes a similar point, "Rehearsal," 32.

32 Graham, "Spain Betrayed?" 367.

33 Ibid., 367, 365. See for example Ángel Viñas, *La soledad de la República: El abandono de los democracias y el viraje hacia la Unión Soviética* (Barcelona: Crítica, 2006), 282–3; Geoffrey Roberts, "Soviet Foreign Policy and the Spanish Civil War, 1936–1939," in Christain Leitz and David J. Dunthorn, eds., *Spain in an International Context, 1936–1959* (New York; Berghahn, 1999), 81–103.

which could not reasonably be refused, was as likely to doom the Loyalist cause as save it," by "completing its alienation from the West."[34] He also emphasizes that Soviet control of "events on the ground in Spain was always severely limited."[35] From this perspective, the argument that the Soviets were working effectively to transform Spain into a "people's democracy" on the (later) East European model seems at best "questionable."[36]

If the war in Spain is no longer, as Christopher Hitchens claimed in 2001, "probably the one argument from the age of twentieth-century ideology that is still alive," its historiography remains polarized, a high-stakes "take no prisoners" affair.[37] Thus it is worth emphasizing that this book puts the Spanish civil war at the center of a history of international communism in order to understand the importance of Spain as a personal and political point of reference for individual communists, not to argue that the Republic was dominated by communists.[38] The emphasis here is less on high politics than on understanding the meanings and political and emotional appeal of communism for individuals. Indeed the book does not intervene directly in the polemics over alleged Soviet manipulation or control of the Spanish Popular Front government and the international volunteers.[39] It does not assess Soviet motives or track the impacts of Soviet military and political intervention.[40]

34 Daniel Kowalsky, "The Soviet Union and the International Brigades, 1936–1939," *Journal of Slavic Military Studies* 19 (2006): 681, 682.

35 Ibid., 703.

36 Mike Gonzalez, "Review of *Spain Betrayed*,"*European Legacy* 8, no. 5 (October 2003): 666. See also Ruth MacKay, "History on the Line: The Good Fight and Good History in the Spanish Civil War," *History Workshop Journal*, no. 70 (2010): 203.

37 Christopher Hitchens, "Who Lost Spain?" *Wilson Quarterly* 25, no. 3 (Summer 2001): 106–7; Ichiro Takayoshi, "The Wages of War: Liberal Gullibility, Soviet Intervention, and the End of the Popular Front," *Representations* 115, no. 1 (Summer 2011): 106. See also George Esenwein, "The Persistence of Politics: The Impact of the Cold War on Anglo-American Writings on the Spanish Civil War," *Bulletin of Spanish Studies: Hispanic Studies and Researches on Spain, Portugal and Latin America* 91, no. 1–2 (2014): 115–35.

38 The case for Soviet domination is made by Burnett Bolloten, *The Spanish Civil War: Revolution and Counterrevolution* (Chapel Hill: University of North Carolina Press, 1991); Viñas, *Soledad*, challenges this interpretation. Daniel Kowalsky emphasizes the limits of communist control, "Operation X: Soviet Russia and the Spanish Civil War," *Bulletin of Spanish Studies: Hispanic Studies and Researches on Spain, Portugal and Latin America* 91, no. 1–2 (2014): 174.

39 On Spanish relations with the Comintern and Soviet Union, see Antonio Elorza and Marta Bizcarrondo, *Queridos camaradas: La Internacional Comunista y España, 1919–1939* (Barcelona: Editorial Planeta, 1999); M.T. Meshcheriakov, *Ispanskaia respublika i Komintern: Natsional'no-revoliutsionnaia voina ispanskogo naroda i politika kommunisticheskogo internatsionala, 1936–1939 gg.* (Moscow: Mysl', 1981); Denis Smyth, "'We Are with You': Solidarity and Self-Interest in Soviet Policy towards Republican Spain," in Paul Preston and Ann L. Mackenzie, eds., *The Republic Besieged: Civil War in Spain, 1936–1939* (Edinburgh: Edinburgh University Press, 1996), 53–86.

40 On Soviet intervention, see Kowalsky, "Operation X,"159–78; Ángel Viñas, *El escudo de la República: El oro de España, la apuesta soviética y los hechos de mayo de 1937* (Barcelona: Crítica, 2007); Daniel Kowalsky, *Stalin and the Spanish Civil War* [electronic resource]

Nor does it raise the "delicate question" of whether the volunteers were duped.[41]

The book links international communism to the Spanish civil war because so many communists reported, then and later, that in Spain they lived their ideals more intensely, passionately, and fully than they had anywhere else. Even for those who eventually left the party, the Spanish civil war often remained a defining moment of their own life stories and personal networks – something that they often separated (or tried to separate) from the larger Stalinist context. Thus the focus is on Spain as a critical, but not isolated, moment in the history of international communism and international communist lives.

To get at the role of Spain in communists' life histories and communist culture, the book sets the International Brigades in the context of the understandings, experiences, and identities that communists brought with them to Spain. It begins in Moscow with an examination of everyday life at the Lenin School and in the offices of the English-language *Moscow News*. In both places, remarkably transnational groups of communists worked to define and live lives of Bolshevik "virtue," not only in politics but also in the realms of gender and

(New York: Columbia University Press, 2004), http://www.gutenberg-e.org/kodo1/index.html (accessed 6 November 2014); Iurii E. Ribalkin, *Operatsiia "X": Sovetskaia voennaia pomoshch' respublikanskoi Ispanii (1936–1939)* (Moscow: AIRO-XX, 2000); Pierre, Broué, *Staline et la révolution: le cas espagnol* (Paris: Fayard, 1993); Juan García Durán, "La intervención soviética en la guerra civil," *Historia 16*, no. 103 (November 1984): 11–22; David Cattell, *Soviet Diplomacy and the Spanish Civil War* (Berkeley: University of California Press, 1957).

41 For an introduction to the contentious historiography see George Esenwein, "Freedom Fighters or Comintern Soldiers? Writing about the 'Good Fight' during the Spanish Civil War," *Civil Wars* 12, no. 1–2 (March-June 2010): 156–66. Many accounts focus on particular national contingents: Michael Petrou, *Renegades: Canadians in the Spanish Civil War* (Vancouver: University of British Columbia Press, 2008); Peter Carroll, *The Odyssey of the Abraham Lincoln Brigade: Americans in the Spanish Civil War* (Stanford: Stanford University Press, 1994); John Gerassi, *The Premature Anti-Fascists: North American Volunteers in the Spanish Civil War, 1936–1939* (New York: Praeger 1986); Cecil Eby, *Between the Bullet and the Lie: American Volunteers in the Spanish Civil War* (New York: Rhinehart, 1969); Richard Baxell, *British Volunteers in the Spanish Civil War: The British Battalion in the International Brigades, 1936–1939* (London: Routledge 2004); James K. Hopkins, *Into the Heart of Fire: The British in the Spanish Civil War* (Stanford: Stanford University Press 1998); R. A. Stradling, *The Irish and the Spanish Civil War* (Manchester: Manchester University Press 1999); Hywel Francis, *Miners against Fascism: Wales and the Spanish Civil War* (London: Lawrence & Wishart 1984); Rémi Skoutelsky, *L'espoir guidait leurs pas: les volontaires française dans les Brigades internationales, 1936–1939* (Paris: B. Grasset, 1998). On the brigades as a whole, see Manuel Requena Gallego, ed., *Las Brigadas Internacionales* (Madrid: Marcial Pons, 2004); Ricardo de la Cierva, *Brigadas Internacionales, 1936–1996: La verdadera historia: Mentira histórica y error de Estado* (Madrid: Editorial Fénix, 1997); Michael Jackson, *Fallen Sparrows: The International Brigades and the Spanish Civil War* (Philadelphia: American Philosophical Society 1994); Dan Richardson, *Comintern Army: The International Brigades and the Spanish Civil War* (Lexington: University of Kentucky Press 1982); Verle Johnston, *Legions of Babel: The International Brigades in the Spanish Civil War* (University Park: Pennsylvania State University Press, 1967).

sexuality. Chapter 1 focuses on the Lenin School, where students were supposed to live according to strict rules mandating political and personal discipline. However, as records of their disputes and disciplinary violations reveal, students did not always live according to the rules – or agree on a single consistent "Bolshevik" norm. In Chapter 2 attention turns to the *Moscow News*, a newspaper controlled by the Soviet party and geared toward raising the political consciousness of English-speaking workers in the Soviet Union. Focusing on how international communists managed the mismatch between what they had imagined the Soviet Union to be and what they experienced, the chapter emphasizes their emotional responses, their sense of themselves in the Soviet Union, and their sense of participating in an international cause.

The three chapters centered on the Spanish civil war analyze how experiences in Spain reinforced or reconfigured understandings of the cause and the communist self. These chapters draw on letters home and the volunteers' wartime cultural productions – poems, songs, and holiday celebrations – as well as later memoirs and official Comintern documents. Chapter 3 examines whether and how participants understood the abstraction "international solidarity" to operate on the ground in Spain. Although the volunteers often represented the immediately salient fact of linguistic diversity as offering powerful evidence of international solidarity and the world historical significance of their cause, commissars' reports documented serious problems, including low morale, desertion, drunkenness, and strained relations between the volunteers and Spanish troops assigned to the International Brigades.

Chapter 4 focuses on wartime cultural exchanges. The war in Spain generated models of communist behavior as well as symbols and narratives of the "good fight" against fascism that circulated internationally, reinvigorating and redefining revolutionary idealism and resonating with communists within and beyond the Soviet Union. At the same time, Soviet and Stalinist cultural products and practices – films, political education, the hunt for Trotskyites – shaped everyday life in Spain.

Chapter 5 returns to the question of Bolshevik "virtue" raised in Part I, exploring volunteers' relationships with their wives and one another. Drawing on intimate stories of communists in love and war, the chapter traces the connections between political convictions and individual responses to the wartime disruption of personal life and traditional gender roles.

The final part tracks the experiences of international communists as World War II eclipsed the Revolution as the Soviet state's central legitimizing myth and as wartime antifascism gave way to cold war anti-Americanism. Chapter 6 investigates the echoes of the Spanish civil war in Soviet coverage of World War II and in the wartime experiences of Spanish exiles in the Soviet Union and of American veterans of the Spanish war. It argues that the war in Spain remained a vital element of the Stalinist cultural landscape, shaping representations and understandings of the Great Fatherland War that ultimately overshadowed it. Chapter 7 analyzes the early cold war as a turn against internationalism and border crossers, a cultural shift illustrated by the prominence of Spanish war veterans among the victims of the spy mania that gripped governments on both sides of the iron curtain.

Solidarity and Suspicion

Placing the years 1936–9 – the years of the Spanish civil war and of the Stalinist terror – at the heart of a history of international communism calls attention to a central paradox of Stalinism: the simultaneous celebration and suspicion of transnational interactions. This paradoxical combination is visible in the lives of students at Comintern schools, where the curriculum encouraged identification with Soviet life while the rules prohibited casual contacts with Soviet citizens. It emerged with particularly clarity in the Soviet media during the Spanish civil war, which covered the heroic antifascist struggle alongside stories that explained setbacks in Spain as the work of the same agents of a worldwide "Trotskyite-fascist" conspiracy that threatened the Soviet Union and justified the purges. A similar blend of ecstatic and conspiratorial thinking is visible in contemporary letters home from Spain, which combined paeans to international solidarity with denunciations of Trotskyite enemies.

In retrospective accounts, solidarity often trumped suspicion, as communists forgot, effaced, minimized, or excused the denunciations and purges that had accompanied expressions of international solidarity. Such omissions and evasions are often taken as evidence of communist duplicity and self-deception. The "legend" of the noble and selfless cause may also, however, suggest the depth and persistence of communist commitments. Here the issue is less one of accuracy than identity. In the wake of public revelations of Stalin's crimes, communists and former communists alike sought means of distancing themselves from Stalinism while continuing to express pride in their actions as communists – and especially their service in Spain. Thus rather than attempting to debunk or substantiate the legend of the noble and selfless cause, the book seeks to locate its sources in communist life histories and everyday practices. It tells the often intimate stories of individual communists as a means of illuminating the daily, situated work of interpreting and applying norms of communist behavior, of making communism a way of life that might outlast political affiliations.

PART I

INTERNATIONAL COMMUNISTS AND THE SOVIET UNION, 1930–1936

1

Learning to Be Bolshevik

In 1926, a first class of seventy students entered the International Lenin School in Moscow. The following September, British communist J. T. Murphy provided a rare contemporary public description of the clandestine school. It was, according to Murphy, a "direct sequel" to the resolutions of the Fifth Comintern Congress in 1924 that called on each national party to become a "genuine Bolshevik party" – "revolutionary, Marxist in nature, working undeviatingly towards its goal."[1] Conceptualized as the "highest Marxist educational institution for qualified Party workers," the Lenin School aimed to achieve the "bolshevisation of the Communist Parties in the capitalist countries" by turning international communists into Bolsheviks.[2]

The school's program, as Murphy emphasized, was quite "ambitious" and intensive. The syllabus changed over time, but generally emphasized political economy, philosophy, history, and strategies of organizational and party work.[3] By 1930 the school also provided students with instruction in underground work, including the use of safe houses, aliases, codes, "secret ink,"

[1] J. T. Murphy, "The First Year of the Lenin School," *Communist International,* 30 September 1927, 267; "Theses on Tactics, Adopted by the Fifth Congress, July 1924," in Kevin McDermott and Jeremy Agnew, *The Comintern: A History of International Communism from Lenin to Stalin* (Basingstoke: Palgrave Macmillan, 1996), 232. See also Harvey Klehr, John Earl Haynes, and Fridrikh Igorevich Firsov, eds., *The Secret World of American Communism* (New Haven: Yale University Press, 1995), 202.

[2] Murphy, "First Year," 267.

[3] Ibid.; "Ob"iasnitel'naia zapiska k planu uchebnoi i partiino-vospitatel'noi raboty MLSh," 1933–4, Rossiiskii gosudarstvennyi arkhiv sotsial'no-politicheskoi istorii (RGASPI), f. 531, op. 1, d. 41, ll. 21–60b; "Plan uchebnoi i part. vospitatel'noi raboty MLSh," 1933–4, ibid., d. 43, l. 85; "Ob"iasnitel'naia zapiska k planu uchebnoi i partino-vospitatel'noi raboty MLSh," 1934–5, ibid., ll. 89–100; "Programma po istorii mezhdunarodnogo rabochego dvizheniia i Kominterna," 7 May 1937, ibid., d. 118, ll. 50–69; Harry Wicks, *Keeping My Head: The Memoirs of a British Bolshevik* (London: Socialist Platform, 1992), 88–91.

and a variety of print technologies.[4] Students attended lectures and undertook many independent research projects on which they reported back to their groups during regular discussion sections. During the summer, they engaged in "practical" work, visiting Soviet factories, collective farms, and construction sites where they met with workers, made speeches, and wrote articles for the communist press in their home countries.[5] In 1936 and perhaps earlier, some of the male students participated in two weeks of military training during the summer, during which they learned jiu-jitsu, map reading, and the basics of shooting and street fighting.[6]

The Lenin School also represented an ambitious exercise in institution building. Although it was not, as Murphy claimed, a wholly unprecedented "attempt to draw together leading cadres of the working class parties of the world," its purview was broader and its program more prestigious than that of two earlier schools, both founded in 1921: the Communist University of Toilers of the East (KUTV) and the Communist University of National Minorities of the West (KUMNZ).[7] By the mid-1920s, KUTV had recruited African, Asian, and African American students. KUMNZ initially taught Lithuanian, Jewish, Latvian, Polish, German, Romanian, Estonian, and Finnish students in their native languages.[8] In 1926, the Lenin School's first class of seventy included students from twenty-two countries, and the curriculum was taught in three languages: German, French, and English. By the 1931–2 academic year, the school attracted about six hundred students from more than fifty countries.[9]

[4] "Skhema: Programmy po izucheniiu opyta podpol'nom raboty," 1930, RGASPI, f. 531, op. 1, d. 26, ll. 167–76.

[5] "Otchet o rabote komissii po priemu novykh studentov," [1930], RGASPI, f. 531, op. 1, d. 21, ll. 14–23ob; "Otchet o letnei praktike," July–August 1931, ibid., d. 33, ll-29–44; "Dokladnaia zapiska o rabote sektora 'D' v vostochnoi sibiri," 28 August 1934, ibid., d. 166, ll. 19–22.

[6] Resolutions on work in the camp, June 1936, RGASPI, f. 531, op. 1, d. 136, ll. 10–24; "Taktika ulichnogo boia po opytu revoliutsionnykh vosstanii," ibid., d. 254, ll. 152–9; on military training see also Klehr et al., *Secret World,* 202–4. On military training at KUTV, see "Uchebnyi plan Sektora A," 1931–2, RGASPI, f. 532, op. 1, d. 101, ll. 1, 5–50b.

[7] Murphy, "First Year," 267. On the school's prestige see Wicks, *Keeping,* 84.

[8] Murphy, "First Year," 267, 268. On other schools see Woodford McClellan, "Africans and Black Americans in the Comintern Schools, 1925–1934," *International Journal of African Historical Studies* 26, no. 2 (1993): 372; Irina Filatova, "Indoctrination or Scholarship? Education of Africans at the Communist University of the Toilers of the East in the Soviet Union, 1923–1937," *Paedagogica historica* 35, no. 1 (1999): 42–6; E. V. Panin, "Kommunisticheskii Universitet Natsional'nykh Men'shinstv Zapada imeni Iu. Iu. Markhlevskogo," *Platonovskie chteniia: XVI Vserossiiskaia konferentsiia molodykh istorikov* (Samara: Izdatel'stvo "Samarskii universitet," 2010),177–8.

[9] "Ob"iasnitel'naia zapiska o sostave studentov, prokhodiashchikh uchebu v MLSh," 27 November 1933, RGASPI, f. 531, op. 1, d. 47, l. 46; Brigette Studer, *Un parti sous influence: Le Parti communiste suisse, une section du Komintern, 1931 à 1939* (Lausanne: L'Age d'Homme, 1994), 234; Julia Köstenberger puts the number of countries at twenty-three, "Die Internationale Leninschule (1926–1936)," in Michael Buckmiller and Klaus Meschkat, eds., *Biographisches Handbuch zu Geschichte der Kommunistischen Internationale: Ein deutsche-russisches Forschungsprojekt* (Berlin: Academie Verlag, 2007),290; Alexander V. Pantsov and Daria A.

Admissions criteria required that they be able to study in one of seven languages: German, French, English, Spanish, Chinese, Hungarian, or Russian.[10] The students themselves spoke perhaps a dozen additional languages, including Italian, Czech, Polish, Greek, Bulgarian, Romanian, Finnish, and Korean.[11] All told, between 1926 and 1938 the school graduated roughly three thousand students from fifty-nine countries.[12] Thus the Lenin School, along with other schools organized by the Comintern, not only trained students but also provided officials with experience meeting the challenges of incorporating diverse, multilingual, multinational cadres into disciplined, unified, bolshevized institutions.

The process of bolshevization that inspired the founding of the Lenin School was directed by officials in Moscow, but often coincided with the interests and identities of international communists for whom the Russian revolutionaries provided powerful and appealing role models.[13] Defining bolshevization as "a trend towards Russian dominance of the Comintern," historians Kevin McDermott and Jeremy Agnew emphasize that Bolshevik ideological "intransigence," however constraining, was often welcomed because it effectively "tapped into a rich vein of 'leftist' communist culture common to all national parties."[14] Moreover, Soviet efforts to control national parties were nothing new. The "Theses on the Conditions for Admission" to the Comintern, which was promulgated in 1920, directed member parties to remake themselves in the Bolshevik image: "organized in the most centralized way possible and governed by iron discipline."[15] Implicit in this directive was the requirement that international communists themselves become more like Bolsheviks – reliable, unsentimental, uncompromising. Many international communists embraced

Spichak, "New Light from the Russian Archives: Chinese Stalinists and Trotskyists at the International Lenin School in Moscow, 1926–1938," *Twentieth Century China* 33, no. 2 (April 2008):31–3.

10 "Instruktsiia ob usloviiakh priema v Mezhdunarodnuiu Leninskuiu Shkolu," 31 March 1930, RGASPI, f. 531, op. 1, d. 18, l. 13.

11 "Svedeniia o natsional'nom sostave sektorov v1931–1932 uch. godu," 15 February 1933, RGASPI, f. 531, op. 1, d. 47, ll. 22–20b.

12 Köstenberger, "Internationale," 287; Barry McLoughlin, "Proletarian Academics or Party Functionaries? Irish Communists at the International Lenin School," *Saothar* 22 (1997): 64.

13 Tim Rees, "Deviation and Discipline: Anti-Trotskyism, Bolshevization, and the Spanish Communist Party, 1924–34," *Historical Research* 82, no. 215 (February 2009): 132–3, 155; Eric Hobsbawm, *Interesting Times: A Twentieth-Century Life* (New York: New Press, 2002), 140, 201–2; Joni Krekola, "The Finnish Sector at the International Lenin School," in Kevin Morgan, Gidon Cohen, and Andrew Flinn, eds., *Agents of the Revolution: New Biographical Approaches to the History of International Communism in the Age of Lenin and Stalin* (Bern: Peter Lang, 2005), 296.

14 McDermott and Agnew, *Comintern*, 42–3.

15 "Theses on the Conditions for Admission," in John Riddell, ed., *Workers of the World and Oppressed Peoples, Unite! Proceedings and Documents of the Second Congress, 1920* (New York: Pathfinder Press, 1991), vol. 2, 769; McDermott and Agnew, *Comintern*, 46.

this sort of transformation, attracted to the idea, as Spanish communist Manuel Tagüeña Lacorte recalled in his 1978 memoir, of reaching "utopia" by the road of "organization and discipline."[16]

The announcement at the Sixth Comintern Congress in 1928 that a "Third Period" in the crisis of capitalism had opened – a phase that would be characterized by "gigantic class battles" and a worldwide resurgence of revolutionary activity – marked an intensification of bolshevization and of its appeal.[17] Hopeful that their own parties stood on the verge of "armed uprising," many international communists embraced Bolshevik methodology with renewed urgency.[18] Historians generally understand the ultra-leftist Third Period line, with its slogan of "class against class" and attacks on social democrats as "social fascists," as "disastrous" for communist parties. The line arguably facilitated the Nazis' rise to power and resulted everywhere in declining party membership, declines that were reversed only with the introduction of the Popular Front at the Comintern's Seventh Congress in 1935.[19] Yet however unwise as a means of attracting new members, and however ineffective on the ground, the radical line, as historian Tim Rees points out, effectively "united communists around the renewal of their special revolutionary mission and helped define their political identity"[20]

Even where its prescriptions proved impractical or counterproductive and generated some measure of local resistance, the Third Period line – and its consequences, such as arrests – often confirmed communists' belief in the power and correctness of Bolshevik predictions and practices.[21] Thus in April 1931, an American party circular analyzing recent events in light of Comintern categories interpreted "the rising wave of militancy on the part of the unemployed and long suffering masses" along with the "vicious attacks against the working class" by capitalist governments and "their allies, the fascists and social fascists" as "unmistakable signs" of imminent revolutionary upheaval. Party leaders warned that each local district must be "prepared *now*" for

[16] Quoted in Rees, "Deviation," 136.

[17] "Thesis on the International Situation and the Tasks of the Communist International, Adopted by the Sixth Congress, 29 August 1928," in McDermott and Agnew, *Comintern*, 235.

[18] "Rech' tov. Dolores," *XIII Plenum IKKI: Stenograficheskii otchet* (Moscow: Partizdat, 1934), 531.

[19] McDermott and Agnew, *Comintern*, 81; William J. Chase, *Enemies within the Gates? The Comintern and the Stalinist Repression, 1934–1939* (New Haven: Yale University Press, 2001), 13–14; Fernando Claudín, *The Communist Movement from Comintern to Cominform: Part One, The Crisis of the Communist International*, trans. Brian Pearce (New York: Monthly Review Press, 1967), 159–66.

[20] Tim Rees, "The 'Good Bolsheviks': The Spanish Communist Party and the Third Period," in Matthew Worley, ed., *In Search of Revolution: International Communist Parties in the Third Period* (New York: I. B. Tauris, 2004), 183. See also John Manley, "Moscow Rules? 'Red' Unionism and 'Class against Class' in Britain, Canada, and the United States, 1928–1935," *Labour/Le Travail* 56 (Fall 2005): 23–8.

[21] Manley, "Moscow Rules?" 35–6.

"raids upon its officers and leading functionaries" that would necessitate the American party's transformation into a clandestine revolutionary organization.[22] From this perspective, learning to be Bolshevik appeared imperative and desirable. The Bolsheviks, after all, offered a tested path to what appeared to be successful revolution.

The Lenin School provided international communists an opportunity to learn Bolshevik methods. Because Moscow controlled the terms of that education, studies of the school often situate it within the broader debate on the relationship between the Comintern and its member parties. When assessing the extent of Moscow's control over national sections, historians have raised the critical questions of how effectively the school created bolshevized cadres and how much influence those cadres had on their home parties.[23] In this chapter, I shift the perspective, approaching the school not as an agent of the center working to mold communists from the periphery, but as a point of connection between center and periphery, a site of everyday interactions among communists, both international and Soviet. Such interactions were necessarily unequal, because the Comintern built the structure and set the rules. Nonetheless, as students and teachers entered those structures and attempted to live by those rules, they became to some degree co-constructors of the school.[24] Thus rather than focusing on the school's long-term impact on individuals or member parties, the chapter examines the relationships that constituted its everyday life.

Becoming Bolshevik required adhering to rigid norms of everyday behavior that made little distinction between the political and the personal. Students came to the school for a variety of reasons, but once there all were expected to obey clearly specified "rules of conspiracy" that limited students' contacts with outsiders and of personal comportment – to be disciplined, sober, chaste

[22] Emphasis in original."To All District Organizers," 1 December 1931, RGASPI, f. 515, op. 1, d. 2264, l. 95. See also "How to Act under Arrest and Police Terrorism," April 1931, ibid., d. 2268, ll. 24–8.

[23] For an extended debate on these matters see Gidon Cohen and Kevin Morgan, "Stalin's Sausage Machine: British Students at the International Lenin School, 1926–37," *Twentieth Century British History* 13, no. 4 (2002): 327–55; John McIlroy et al., "Forging the Faithful: The British at the Lenin School," *Labour History Review* 68, no. 1 (April 2003): 99–128; Gidon Cohen and Kevin Morgan, "British Students at the International Lenin School, 1926–37: A Reaffirmation of Methods, Results, and Conclusions," *Twentieth Century British History* 15, no. 1 (2004): 77–107; Alan Campbell et al., "The International Lenin School: A Response to Cohen and Morgan," *Twentieth Century British History* 15, no. 1 (2004): 51–76; Gidon Cohen and Kevin Morgan, "The International Lenin School: A Final Comment," *Twentieth Century British History* 18, no. 1 (March 2007): 129–33. Other studies focus on education and indoctrination: McLoughlin, "Proletarian Academics," 63–79; Filatova, "Indoctrination."

[24] Yves Cohen, "La co-construction de la personne et de la bureaucratie: Aspects de la subjectivé de Staline et des cadres soviétiques (années 30)," in Brigitte Studer and Heiko Haumann, eds., *Stalinistische Subjekte: Individuum und System in der Sowjetunion und der Komintern, 1929–1953* (Zurich: Chronos, 2006), 175–96.

Bolsheviks. Disciplinary investigations reveal that students did not always meet these standards – or agree on a single consistent "communist" norm. A dispute over "white chauvinism" in the American sector illustrates how the communist commitment to racial equality clashed with concerns about maintaining respectable white womanhood and Soviet strictures against political "fractions." Accusations of political weakness were sometimes verified with evidence of an ostensibly personal nature such as drunkenness. Even those students who did not internalize Bolshevik norms understood that they entailed the equation of personal and political purity – or personal and political deviance.

Examining how Bolshevik values were taught, contested, violated, and (mis)understood at the school, this chapter provides a view of international communism at its grassroots. Although the school was conceived as a tool of the Soviet party, offering "indoctrination not education,"[25] it can also be understood as a site of complicated and perhaps unanticipated transnational interactions. Such an approach to the school allows us to assess Murphy's claim, which on its face may seem like sheer propaganda or wishful thinking, that indoctrination was not always unidirectional: that "much has been learned by everybody – teachers and students alike."[26] In exchanges with one another and their Soviet comrades, international communists learned and, to some extent, shaped Stalinist norms and practices.

Building an Institution for Raising Bolsheviks

Despite dramatic changes in the Comintern line occurring between the Lenin School's founding in 1926 and its demise in 1938, the school's primary mission remained remarkably stable. In 1930, teachers who were preparing a history of the school underscored that, in establishing it, the Fifth Comintern Congress had been responding to the then current "stabilization of capitalism" and had thus ignored the "practical side of things" that acquired new importance in the revolutionary Third Period.[27] Still, if the methods established in the earlier period had to be rejected as too "theoretical," the goal was very much the same: to "reveal the inner life of each student . . . to bolshevize each individual comrade."[28] In 1930 Lev Khonanovich Segal', a teacher of economics, characterized the school as "the only institution, the only place, where western European comrades are taken out of their daily routine for a long period and are placed in laboratory conditions, where it is possible to identify their deficiencies, in the sense of various remnants" of non-Bolshevik ways of thinking

[25] McIlroy et al., "Forging," 100.

[26] Murphy, "First Year," 269.

[27] "Stenogramma zasedaniia po voprosu o podgotovke raboty po istorii sozdaniia i razvitiia mezhdunarodnoi leninskoi shkoly," 6 March 1930, RGASPI, f. 531, op. 1, d. 20, l. 60b.

[28] "Soveshchanie po podgotovke i razrabotke materialov po istorii MLSh," 27 March 1930, RGASPI, f. 531, op. 1, d. 20, l. 35.

and acting.[29] As the school's director Klavdiia Ivanovna Kirsanova asserted, the students left as "different people."[30] In 1936, in the wake of yet another shift in the Comintern line, this time toward the antifascist Popular Front, the school remained committed to "raising Bolsheviks."[31] Those who worked there still described it as a unique and transformative environment where "the remains of arrogance and national narrow-mindedness melt away" as communists from the "advanced capitalist countries of the West" and the "semi-colonial countries of the East" lived, worked, and struggled side by side.[32]

The "conditions of admission" that Lenin School authorities sent to national parties in 1930 suggest that they had a clear vision of the sort of raw material on which they could work this transformation. First and foremost, they wanted workers, especially in heavy industry, who had been active party members "NO LESS THAN 3 YEARS." For nonworkers, the requirement was at least five years of party membership. The conditions admitted no potential conflict between the demand that candidates for admission be workers and that they be "capable of theoretical work," "oriented to current politics," and "certainly literate." If the school's examination commission determined that a potential student lacked adequate preparation, he or she would be sent home at the home party's expense. Likewise, students had to be healthy and were subject to "medical inspection" on arrival. A detailed list of suspect behaviors precluding enrollment included voluntarily taking up arms against the Red Army; serving in the police or militia of a "bourgeois government;" and exhibiting "insufficient revolutionary restraint" when arrested by, for example, betraying comrades or showing "cowardice" at trial. Party members who had engaged in active "fractional struggle" with the Comintern or their own party's leaders could be admitted only after demonstrating that they "stood with the Comintern line"for a minimum of three years.[33] Committed to raising Bolsheviks, the school required that member parties send their most active, politically reliable, theoretically oriented, and healthy cadres.

The conditions for admission also offer a clear sense of the school's atmosphere – serious, rigorous, and austere, not to say ascetic. Students received dormitory housing, food, and bedding, but not "clothing, footwear, or underwear;" they also were given a "stipend sufficient for minimal needs" such as buying books. The school offered a small allowance to dependent wives and children, who remained at home, but recommended that member parties send single, childless comrades. In any case, family members were prohibited from visiting students during the course of their studies, and students were not

29 Ibid., l. 40b.

30 Ibid., l. 30.

31 "Stenogrammy torzhestvennykh zasedanii v MLSh," December 1936, RGASPI, f. 531 op. 1 d. 92, l. 17.

32 Ibid., l. 18.

33 Emphasis in original."Instruktsiia ob usloviiakh priema," l. 13; Studer, *Parti,* 235.On the exam and medical inspection, see Wicks, *Keeping,* 73, 85.

allowed to leave the school during the academic year.[34] A draft version of the conditions for admission offered the "conspiratorial character" of the school as the rationale for these restrictions.[35] In 1935, current students took a dimmer view, likening the school to a prison.[36]

Despite the clear instructions, less than ideal candidates often arrived in Moscow. In response, the school's administrators frequently reiterated but rarely loosened their requirements and repeatedly complained that national parties failed to comply with them. The British party in particular acquired a reputation for using the school as a "dumping ground" for problem comrades, but it was hardly alone.[37] Reviewing the poor crop of students sent in 1932, the school authorities complained that the Italian, Romanian, Latvian, Estonian, French, and American contingents reflected party leaders' "insufficiently careful selection of students, in the sense of party consistency, political and educational preparedness, health conditions, [and] ability to return" to their country of origin. Instructions for choosing students for the coming year reminded national party leaders that they "under no circumstances" should send candidates who had participated in "fractions or groups opposed to the Comintern line" – the three-year probationary period apparently having been eliminated – or those who were physically ill.[38] Such reminders notwithstanding, the admissions committee rejected almost 10 percent of the students who arrived for the 1935–6 school year, primarily because they were judged politically "doubtful" or "suspicious." The school warned member parties that they had to fully document the political reliability of their candidates along with their ability to return to their own countries after completing the course of study.[39]

Difficulties meeting the admissions requirements stemmed in part from their rigidity and specificity. The standards set in 1932 for the Spanish party's allotment of five graduate students were typical. The school expected qualified candidates to demonstrate "political firmness" and sound "theoretical preparation;" have a minimum of five years of party experience, including two years working at a regional party school, with no history of involvement in fractional struggle; "suffer from no illness that would prevent their study (tuberculosis,

34 "Instruktsiia ob usloviiakh priema," l. 14; Studer, *Parti*, 236.

35 "Instruktsiia ob usloviiakh priema," l. 12.

36 "Protokol'naia zapis' o soveshchanii kollektiva sektora 'D' s amerikanskoi delegatsiei 7 kongressa Kominterna o rabote MLSh," May 1935, RGASPI, f. 531, op. 1, d. 165, l. 15.

37 Cohen and Morgan, "British Students," 336. McIlroy et al. take issue with this characterization, "Forging," 106. "Stenogramma: Soveshchaniia po voprosu o uchebnom plane MLSh na 1934 g.," 23 December 1933, RGASPI, f. 531, op. 1, d. 43, l. 2; "Report of Work – Sector D," [1933?], ibid., d. 167, l. 43.

38 "Postanovlenie politkomissii po dokladu MLSh ob itogakh komplektovaniia shkoly v 1932–1933 uchebnom godu," RGASPI, f. 531, op. 1, d. 41, l. 19.

39 "Instruktsii, predlozheniia i razverstka po priema v MLSh," 13 May 1936, RGASPI, f. 531, op. 1, d. 103, l. 31.

venereal diseases);" be prepared to spend two years in Moscow without their families; and "know French well enough to follow the course."[40] The Spanish party also received specific instructions regarding its contingent of forty students in the basic course: it was to include at least three Catalans, three to four Basques, two to three Asturian miners, a minimum of six women, and six Young Communists, who had been members for at least six months. Lists of students from the 1932–3 school year provide no information on nationality, but suggest that these goals were not met with regard to miners, women, or Young Communists.[41]

The American party found it difficult to meet similar demands that it send minimum numbers of African American and female students. Noting that in August 1931 the party had fewer than one thousand African American members (approximately 7 percent of the total membership), most of whom had been in the party for less than a year, and unwilling to send "out all our developed Negro comrades," the party leaders identified eleven candidates, most of whom in some way violated Comintern guidelines.[42] Mack Coad (aka Jim Wright), whom the party characterized as "our best southern organizer both capable and reliable," was nonetheless a "special case," "very poor at reading and writing" and nursing a "physical ailment" that was "neither contagious nor dangerous" – "traces" of gonorrhea. Although party leaders judged William Odell Nowell, a Ford worker for ten years, to have "many bourgeois ideas in his head from previous education" and to be lacking in "initiative," they decided that "his earnestness, loyalty, and desire to be with the Party will enable him to overcome these weaknesses in school." Other African American candidates had been in the party less than six months or had taken positions opposed to the Central Committee. Still, party leaders noted that the "weakest element is among the women comrades." They could not locate a "single Negro woman" to send to the Lenin School in 1931 and deemed only a handful of white women to be "strong." The American cohort also lacked participants in "our strike struggles," as the local "Districts refused to leave a single comrade go."[43]

Competing pressures on national parties also worked against the school's efforts to enforce admissions standards. Facing both the wrath of Moscow when they failed to show sufficient evidence of revolutionary organization and outcries from local leaders who hated to lose their most effective organizers,

40 "Au C. C. du P.C. Espagne," [1932], RGASPI, f. 531, op. 1, d. 183, l. 5.

41 "Instructions concernant l'admission a l'ecole [sic] Leniniste Internationale," RGASPI, f. 531, op. 1, d. 183, l. 1; "Spisok studenov MLSh KP Isp," ibid., d. 185, ll. 47–9; "Spisok studentov komsomol'tsev Leninskoi shkolu s 1930–1937 gg.," ibid., d. 230, l. 103.

42 Letter to Clarence Hathaway, 19 August 1931, RGASPI, f. 515, op. 1, d. 2225, l. 71. Harvey Klehr, *Communist Cadre: The Social Background of the American Communist Party Elite* (Stanford: Hoover Institution Press, 1978), 57.

43 Letter to Hathaway. On Coad see Robin D. G. Kelley, *Hammer and Hoe: Alabama Communists during the Great Depression* (Chapel Hill: University of North Carolina Press, 1990), 40–2.

national leaders might be tempted to preserve their best people for work at home. Such concerns may explain why, for example, the British party, which was allotted twenty-two places in the incoming class of 1935–6, sent only six students. Indeed at least ten parties, notably the Polish, German, and Chinese, substantially underfulfilled their norms that year.[44] As noted earlier, local district leaders in the United States managed to veto plans to send strike organizers to Moscow. American party leaders in New York apparently shared the locals' concerns, bemoaning the loss of cadres, particularly Russian Americans, who overstayed leaves in the Soviet Union to work or study. Their plan to stem the tide of emigration with an "ideological campaign inside the Party...on the necessity of Communists remaining for the struggle in the United States" suggests that they may have resented sending a dozen or more comrades each fall to the Lenin School for terms ranging from nine months to two or three years.[45] Yet unlike their British comrades, the Americans sent their quota of students, although not necessarily with great enthusiasm.[46] For example in 1930, the party selected Steve Nelson (born Stjepan Mesaroš), a Croatian American organizer in the coalfields, for the Lenin School; however, "problems in southern Illinois" prevented his departure. When he finally left for Moscow a year later, the local district leaders complained bitterly.[47] That the Comintern often recruited students from legal parties to work as international operatives added to national leaders' incentives to keep them home. Neither the American leadership nor local organizers were likely to have been pleased when, after completing a year of study, Nelson undertook courier missions to Germany, Switzerland, and China, returning to the anthracite only in late 1933.[48]

Additionally, the composition of communist parties and the hostility of the states in which they operated complicated the school's recruitment efforts. The fact that the American party was a "party of immigrants"[49]– coupled with the

[44] Cohen and Morgan, "British Students," 336; McLoughlin, "Proletarian Academics," 74; "Svedeniia o prieme studentov 1935–1936 uch. goda," 5 October 1935, RGASPI, f. 531, op. 1, d. 84, l. 9. The British party left only two places unfilled in the 1931–2 school year, "Statistika priema studentov 1931–32 uch. goda," ibid., d. 38, l. 1, ch. 1; "Stenogrammy zasedanii v MLSh o podgotovke rabote o MLSh 1930," ibid., d. 21, l. 8.

[45] "Memorandum to Comrade Browder from Comrade Weinstone," 24 June 1931, RGASPI, f. 515, op. 1, d. 2268, l. 74. Randi Storch, *Red Chicago: American Communism at its Grassroots, 1928–35* (Urbana: University of Illinois Press, 2007), 68. For a case of overstaying a leave see RGASPI, f. 515, op. 1, d. 1646, ll. 15–19. On terms of study at the school see McLoughlin, "Proletarian Academics," 64; Pantsov and Spichak, "New Light," 32.

[46] "Svedeniia o prieme studentov 1935–1936 ," l. 9; "Statistika priema studentov 1931–32," ch. 1.

[47] Steve Nelson, James R. Barrett, and Rob Ruck, *Steve Nelson, American Radical* (Pittsburgh: University of Pittsburgh Press, 1982), 126; Philadelphia District to Secretariat, Central Committee, 12 September 1931, RGASPI, f. 515, op. 1, d. 2272, l. 43.

[48] Nelson et al., *American Radical,* 132–56; Will Paynter, *My Generation* (London: Allen & Unwin, 1972), 55–9.

[49] Klehr, *Communist Cadre,* 35.

U.S. government's unwillingness to renew the passports of immigrants who had traveled, often illegally, to Moscow – meant that some American communists found themselves stranded in the Soviet Union. (Before the establishment of formal diplomatic ties in 1933, the United States did not issue passports good for travel to the Soviet Union.[50])For example, in November 1931 the American party confronted the "serious problem" of two Chinese and two Japanese students who were unable to return to the United States after completing their courses of study. William Randolph, the American party's representative in Moscow, informed leaders in New York that he could arrange passage for the Japanese students to Berlin "provided you can arrange to get them to the States from there." Although they decided that the students "cannot be used anywhere else except in the United States," the Soviet authorities offered no assistance and planned to place them in a factory "if a method is not found for their return."[51] The problem of reentry into the United States was especially acute in the case of Russian-born communists, the largest foreign-born contingent in the American party.[52] The most reliable solution open to the American party – sending only American-born comrades to Moscow – would have dramatically reduced the pool of candidates for the school.[53]

Repatriation also posed a problem for students who faced arrest or prison on their return. Ignoring such concerns, the Spanish party sent comrades needing safe haven to the school – and the school admitted them. Thus among the new arrivals in 1931 was Jesús Hernández, described in his school evaluation as a "former pistolero" (gunman), who was sent by the Spanish party to Moscow as a means of evading a threatened thirty-year prison term for the murder of two "social-fascists."[54] The brutal repression that followed the so-called Asturian October, a 1934 uprising in Spain's northern coal-mining region, brought some two hundred Spaniards to the Soviet Union, many of whom were socialists and anarchists.[55] Many of the communists ended up at the Lenin School. Indeed

50 Loy W. Henderson, *A Question of Trust: The Origins of US-Soviet Diplomatic Relations: The Memoirs of Loy W. Henderson* (Stanford: Hoover Institution Press, 1986), 369.

51 Wm. Randolph to Secretariat, Communist Party U.S.A., 11 November 1931, RGASPI, f. 515, op. 1, d. 2225, l. 89.

52 Klehr, *Communist Cadre,* 27; K. E. Heikkinen to Secretariat, CP USA, 12 May 1931 (two letters), RGASPI, f. 515, op. 1, d. 2225, ll. 40, 41.

53 A list of American students from 1930 includes twenty "American-born" party members and sixteen "foreign-born" (one Russian, one Italian, and fourteen Jews, who were likely born in the Russian Empire), RGASPI, f. 531, op. 1, d. 168, l. 17.

54 "Spisok studentov MLSh KP Isp," l. 45; Fernando Hernández Sánchez, "Jesús Hernández, pistolero, ministro, espía y renegado," *Historia 16,* no. 368 (2006): 81; Ángel Ruiz Ayúcar, *El partido comunista: Treinta y siete años de clandestinidad* (Madrid: Liberia Editorial San Martín, 1976), 367.

55 On the uprising and its aftermath see Helen Graham, *Socialism and War: The Spanish Socialist Party in Power and Crisis, 1936–1939* (New York: Cambridge University Press, 1991), 16–19. On the repression in Asturias, see Sebastian Balfour, *Deadly Embrace: Morocco and the Road to the Spanish Civil War* (Oxford: Oxford University Press, 2002), 252–6. On emigration see

most of the sixty-four Spaniards whose biographies were prepared for the school in 1935 had participated in the 1934 uprising, many fighting on the barricades. One, Francisco Cordero Bazaga, was described as "arrested and exiled." Another, Ángel Vega, had, on orders of the party organization, killed a "provocateur" and thus needed to flee the country.[56] In these sorts of cases, the party – and the Spanish party was hardly unique – could not guarantee that the students would be able to return home after completing their studies. Much to the chagrin of the school's director, many students remained in the dormitories eight months or longer after their courses ended.[57]

Such complaints suggest the director's frustration with the school's dependence on both member parties and the Comintern. Whatever pressure they might, as representatives of the center, bring to bear on national parties, administrators and teachers ultimately had to operate the school and attempt to fulfill Comintern directives with the students they were sent. Indeed the arrival of unqualified students – or at least complaints about unqualified students – can be considered a fundamental, if unintentional, feature of the school: It necessarily functioned without sufficient numbers of ideal candidates. At the same time, the school had to cope with Comintern demands that, like the dispatch of students, were largely beyond its control. While the general mission of raising Bolsheviks remained constant, changes in the Comintern line – and in the Soviet Union more broadly – transformed both the national composition of the student body and students' concerns and needs.

The arrival of exiles from Spain illustrates the degree to which the composition of the school shifted over time as Comintern leaders reassessed the world revolutionary situation and got caught up in the vicious contemporary battles between Josef Stalin and his opponents for dominance within the Soviet party.[58] In the first years of its existence (1926–30), more than a third of the Lenin School's 903 students came from Czechoslovakia (138), Germany (106 students), and Poland (85).[59] Logistics – the relative ease of reaching

A. V. Elpat'evskii, *Ispanskaia emigratsiia v SSSR: Istoriografiia i istochniki, popytka interpretatsii* (Tver: Izdatel'stvo "GERS," 2002), 22–37; Margarita Nelken, "Un héroe español del ejército rojo: Santiago de Paúl Nelken," Archivo de Margarita Nelken, Archivo Histórico Nacional, Madrid, Legajo 3245; Gabriel Jackson, *Juan Negrín: Spanish Republican War Leader* (Portland, OR: Sussex Academic Press, 2010), 54; Paulina Abramson and Adelina Abramson, *Mosaico Roto* (Madrid: Compañía Literaria, 1994), 94–7; Mikhail Kol'tsov, *Ispanskii dnevnik* (Moscow: Grifon, 2005), 131.

[56] "Biograficheskie dannye o sostave sektora 'L' za 1935 g.," 1 June 1935, RGASPI, f. 531, op. 1, d. 184, ll. 36–47; quotations, 39, 40. Both were accepted as students, "Spisok studentov MLSh KP Isp," l. 51. For a similar example see Krekola, "Finnish Sector," 300.

[57] Hernández (as Juan Ventura) apparently returned on a Paraguayan passport, "Dopolnitel'nye dannye," 2 August 1932, RGASPI, f. 531, op. 1, d. 183, l. 13. Director of the Lenin School Kirsanova to com. Manuil'skii, 28 February 1936, ibid., d. 112, l. 6.

[58] McDermott and Agnew, *Comintern,* 54.

[59] "Svedeniia o studentakh po stranam v 1926–1930 uch. god.," RGASPI, f. 531, op. 1, d. 47, l. 17.

Moscow from Prague, Berlin, or Warsaw – may account for the predominance of students from these parties. However, it is not surprising that the large, legal Czechoslovak and German parties, which were relatively successful at the polls (winning between 11 and 13 percent of the vote), attracted Soviet attention.[60] The pro-Soviet Polish party was illegal in this period, but nonetheless won parliamentary seats, polling as high as 10 percent.[61]

Between 1926 and 1930, large numbers of students also came from China (65), England (57), and the United States (52). Here the appeal for the Comintern was less the parties' electoral successes than their presumed importance to revolutionary struggles in the colonies and the West. In the case of China, the Comintern's assessment of the revolutionary situation was closely connected to concurrent disputes in the Soviet party between Stalin and Nikolai Bukharin (the Comintern's leader) on one side and the United Opposition of Lev Trotsky, Lev Kamenev, and Grigorii Zinoviev (the Comintern's former leader) on the other.[62] The Nationalists' violent repression of their erstwhile Chinese communist allies in 1927 became evidence of the need, as the 1928 "Theses on the Revolutionary Movements in Colonial and Semi-Colonial Countries" emphasized, to make "every effort to create a cadre of party functionaries from the ranks of the working class itself." Largely co-opting the policy advocated by the defeated Trotsky, the theses called for training communists to undertake "the immediate practical task of preparing for and carrying through armed insurrection" in China.[63] The Lenin School, one of a number of institutions in the Soviet Union that trained Chinese cadres for this task, added a Chinese-language section to meet the new demand.[64]

The British and American parties were likewise, as Stalin declared in 1929, "among those very few Communist parties of the world that are entrusted by history with tasks of decisive importance from the point of view of the revolutionary movement."[65] Moreover, the American party, which included Chinese, Japanese, and African Americans, appealed to Comintern officials as

60 Vít Hloušek and Lubomír Kopeček, *Origin, Ideology, and Transformation of Political Parties: East-Central and Western Europe Compared* (Burlington, VT: Ashgate, 2010), 51, 50. McDermott and Agnew, *Comintern*, 110; Eberhard Kolb, *The Weimar Republic*, 2nd ed. (New York: Routledge, 2005), 79.

61 Jeffrey S. Kopstein and Jason Wittenberg, "Who Voted Communist? Reconsidering the Social Bases of Radicalism in Interwar Poland," *Slavic Review* 62, no. 1 (Spring 2003): 88; Marci Shore, *Caviar and Ashes: A Warsaw Generation's Life and Death in Marxism, 1917–1968* (New Haven: Yale University Press, 2006), 67–8.

62 Bruce Elleman, *Moscow and the Emergence of Communist Power in China: The Nanchang Rising and the Birth of the Red Army* (New York: Routledge, 2009), 72–3, 100, 122–3; McDermott and Agnew, *Comintern*, 54–5.

63 "Theses on the Revolutionary Movements in Colonial and Semi-Colonial Countries, Adopted by the Sixth Congress, 1 September 1928," in McDermott and Agnew, *Comintern*, 236, 237.

64 Pantsov and Spichak, "New Light," 29.

65 Quoted in Manley, "Moscow Rules?"15.

a potential strategic asset in anticolonial struggles.[66] (Before the school added a Chinese-language course in 1928, Chinese students studied in English.[67]) By contrast, in these same years, the small, fragmented, underground Spanish Communist Party sent a total of only eleven students to the Lenin School, including the party's future secretary-general José Díaz.[68]

The Comintern's proclamation at its Sixth Congress in 1928 that circumstances were once again ripe for proletarian revolution, coupled with the founding of the Republic in 1931, raised Spain's revolutionary profile in Moscow. In the 1931–2 academic year, the number of Spanish students arriving at the Lenin School jumped from 3 (of a total of 349) in the 1929–30 academic year to 30 (of 633), among them the former pistolero Hernández.[69] In June 1935, just two months before the Seventh Comintern Congress ratified another shift in the Comintern line, this time in favor of the antifascist Popular Front, the Spanish party sent the largest single national contingent, 70 students, many of whom had participated in the uprising in Asturias, of a total entering class of 313.[70]

As the national composition of the student body shifted, Lenin School administrators continued to struggle with the complexities of building an international institution for raising Bolsheviks. The "language difficulty" that Murphy highlighted as a feature of the school's first year remained a problem ten years later. Although Russian language was often included in the curriculum, the process of bolshevization usually took place through translators, who frequently were in short supply and sometimes lacked the necessary technical vocabulary.[71] Some groups, such as the Spaniards, were particularly poorly served, as the school's practice of corresponding with the Spanish party in

[66] Josephine Fowler, *Japanese and Chinese Immigrant Activists: Organizing in American and International Communist Movements, 1919–1933* (New Brunswick, NJ: Rutgers University Press, 2007), 2–3, 105; Jonathan Derrick, *Africa's "Agitators": Militant Anti-Colonialism in Africa and the West, 1918–1939* (New York: Columbia University Press, 2008), 121; Kate A. Baldwin, *Beyond the Color Line and the Iron Curtain: Reading Encounters between Black and Red, 1922–1963* (Durham, NC: Duke University Press, 2002), 45–51.

[67] Pantsov and Spichak, "New Light," 34.

[68] "Svedeniia o studentakh po stranam v 1926–1930," l. 17.On the situation of the Spanish party in this period, see Rees, "Deviation," 138–44. Díaz questionnaire, Archivo Histórico del Partido Comunista Española (AHPCE), Dirigentes PCE, Sig. 8/2.1.

[69] "Sostav studentov mezhd. Leninsk. skholy za 1929/30 g," RGASPI, f. 531, op. 1, d. 22, l. 14, ch. 1; "Statistika priema studentov 1931–32," ch. 1. Tim Rees, "Living Up to Lenin: Leadership Culture and the Spanish Communist Party, 1920–1939," *History* 97, no. 326 (April 2012): 237. On the new importance of Spain within the Comintern, see Stanley G. Payne, *The Spanish Civil War, the Soviet Union, and Communism* (New Haven: Yale University Press, 2004), 29.

[70] "Svedeniia o prieme studentov 1935–36," l. 9.

[71] "Otchet o letnei praktike," ll. 7, 42; "Struktura sektora 'A' KUTV programmy, uchebnye plany," RGASPI, f. 532, op. 1, d. 101, l. 1; "Resolution on Practical Work of Sector 'D,' 1934," 3 November 1934, RGASPI, f. 531, op. 1, d. 166, l. 9; "Soveshchanie v Uchebnom Otdele," 22 March 1937, ibid., d. 118, l. 6; Pantsov and Spichak, "New Light," 33, 37, 39; Nelson et al., *American Radical*, 129; Harry Haywood, *Black Bolshevik: Autobiography of an*

French suggests.[72] As more and more Spanish speakers filled the Lenin School's classrooms and the number of party members purged from the Comintern apparatus began to mount after 1933, the school's staff, which included only a relatively small number of Spanish-speaking teachers and translators, was stretched thin.[73]

By 1937, the school was swept up into the atmosphere of denunciation and terror that decimated the Comintern in the late 1930s. Stalin and the NKVD viewed the Comintern and its associated institutions as a nest of terrorists, Trotskyites, and spies masked as members of fraternal parties.[74] In these conditions, pedagogical deficiencies that hindered the Lenin School's efforts to meet central directives became dangerous political problems. Thus at a meeting in March 1937 teachers blamed both themselves and the lack of translations (especially Spanish and German) of essential texts for their students' incorrect understandings of Trotskyism, among other critical issues.[75] As a solution, teachers proposed that new students immediately take up the study of Stalin's speeches.[76] In late 1937, at the height of the purges, such problems were "solved" with the dismissal of the school's director Kirsanova, the arrests of at least twenty-eight teachers, and the preemptive firing of some thirty more. By then, the school had only 111 students, 62 of whom had completed their course and were awaiting repatriation, and 32 graduate students.[77] Nonetheless, the arrests and firings left the school hopelessly shorthanded. Hardest hit was the South American sector, which emerged from the purge without a single Spanish-speaking teacher, without any translators, and without Spanish-language materials.[78]

In addition to disrupting instruction, the purge undermined the school as a cohesive community. In early December 1937, the acting director reported that a group of German students, who had finished their studies but still lived

Afro-American Communist (Chicago: Liberator, 1978), 160. The Finnish Sector was unique in having courses taught primarily by native Finns. Krekola, "Finnish Sector," 295.

72 RGASPI, f. 531, op 1, d. 183.

73 "Pis'ma MLSh v TsK i MK VKP(b) o studentakh i kadrakh MLSh," 1934, RGASPI f. 531, op. 1, d. 51, ll. 5–6, 20, 36; "Rabota otdela Kadrov Mezhdunarodnoi Leninskoi Shkoli," ibid., d. 53, l. 23; "Apparat Uchebnogo Otdela," [1937], ibid., d. 124, l. 29; ibid., d. 45 (Statistical information on teachers, 1933–34); "Stenogramma obshchego sobraniia kollektiva MLSh po chistke partii," 1 October 1933, ibid., op. 2, d. 22, l. 29.

74 Chase, *Enemies,* 7–9, 263–4; McDermott and Agnew, *Comintern,* 145–6.

75 "Soveshchanie v Uchebnom Otdele," 22 March 1937, RGASPI, f. 531, op. 1, d. 118, ll. 6, 9.

76 RGASPI, f. 531, op. 1, d. 118, l. 26 (Pedagogical materials).

77 "Protokol obshchego sobraniia studentov Leninskoi Shkoly," 22–23 November 1937, RGASPI, f. 531, op. 1, d. 120, ll. 1–14; Acting Director of the Lenin School Chervenkov to Deputy Director of the TsK VKP(b) Department of Agitation and Propaganda, com. Rubenshtein, 2 December 1937, ibid., d. 125, ll. 86–87; "Spisok na uvolennykh sotrudnikov Leninskoi Shkoly s 9/XII-37-g," ibid., d. 124, l. 68; On Kirsanova, see Branko Lazitch, *Biographical Dictionary of the Comintern: New, Revised, and Expanded Edition* (Stanford: Hoover Institution Press, 1986), 216–17.

78 Acting Director of the Lenin School Chervenkov," l. 86.

in a dormitory at 14 Gogolovskii Boulevard that also housed families of those arrested by the NKVD, had engaged in "blatant" but unspecified violations of the school's conspiratorial rules. Transgressions also occurred among students living in the dormitory at 51 Herzen Street, where they came into contact with a number of Chinese comrades excluded from the party, including one "clearly suspicious type."[79] Although the students' motives and the nature of the disturbances remain obscure, the memo conveys a sense of the school's inability to control its students, indeed to control its affairs at all. A few weeks later, the school's cadres department reported that well-known teachers, who had been dismissed from the school but continued to live alongside students in the school's dormitories, created an "intolerable situation" and had an "undesirable impact" on students.[80] Again, the picture is necessarily fuzzy. The head of the cadres department was hardly likely to raise the issue of students' potential sympathy for their former – perhaps beloved – teachers or the question of students' own fears, disillusionment, or bewilderment. Nonetheless the report hints at the degree to which raising Bolsheviks had depended on or engendered shared understandings among student and teachers – understandings stressed if not destroyed by the terror. The deputy director grimly predicted a much reduced enrollment for the coming school year, and the acting director wondered what to do with the belongings of former students who had been arrested. In spring 1938, the school was formally "liquidated"[81]

Student Life: Secrets, Solidarity, and Suspicion

When students entered the Lenin School they entered a new, clandestine, and predominantly male world. Each chose an alias, and in theory students knew one another only by their assumed names.[82] Whether or not students

79 Ibid., l. 88.

80 Lenin School Department of Cadres to Com. Shvartsman, 20 December 1937, RGASPI, f. 531, op. 1, d. 124, l. 71.

81 Deputy Director of the Lenin School Bogomolov to IKKI, 14 May 1938, RGASPI, f. 531, op. 1, d. 138, l. 110; Vladimirov to Cadres Department, ibid., l. 115; Acting Director of the Lenin School Chervenkov," l. 88.

82 "Instruktsii po provedeniiu konspiratsii v M.L.Sh," [1930], RGASPI, f. 531, op. 1, d. 18, l. 39; "Pravila Konspiratsii," [1933], ibid., d. 52, l. 37; "Prikazy Direktsii MLSh," ibid., d. 142, l. 22. Records for the American and Spanish sectors and work on other sectors suggest that Arvo Tuominen's claim that the student body was "about equally divided" between men and women, although perhaps true of the Finnish or Scandinavian sectors, does not hold for the school as a whole. In 1930, 87.3 percent of students were male. A schedule of student allotments for 1932–3 noted a specific quota of women only for the American party, which was allocated a total of forty-five places, including fifteen blacks and four women. Arvo Tuominen, *The Bells of the Kremlin: An Experience in Communism*, trans. Lily Leino (Hanover, NH: University Press of New England, 1983), 81; "Studentcheskii sostav M.L.Sh. priema 1930 goda," RGASPI, f. 531, op. 2, d. 18, l. 44; "Razverstka studentov MLSh na 32/33 uch. god," ibid., op. 1 d. 47, l. 58.

understood their aliases in terms of the "rebirth"[83] of a revolutionary self, adopting the pseudonym, like the review by the examination commission and the medical inspection, initiated the student into the school. The fact that students generally reverted to their real names when they returned home may have reinforced the sense of the school as a place apart. Moreover, in coming to Moscow, students agreed to cut themselves off from their former selves. Students might tell family members that they were leaving for the Soviet Union, but they were not to mention the Lenin School. Particularly after 1930 school authorities strictly enforced rules of conspiracy and largely barred communication between students and their friends and families.[84] Some, like Nelson, managed to evade the restriction on spouses accompanying students to Moscow; his wife Margaret found employment with the Comintern that "alternated between clerical work and activities cloaked with a certain sensitivity." Still, given the strict visiting rules at the Hotel Lux where she was housed, spending the night together, he recalled, "would have been easier to arrange at an exclusive girls' school."[85]

While in Moscow, students were required to hide their affiliation with the Lenin School and to obey rigid limits on their social contacts and activities. The 1934 "rules of conspiracy" that students affirmed in writing required them to exercise extreme caution with acquaintances, "especially women" with whom they entered into "intimate relations" – a regulation that underscores the degree to which, for all the efforts to recruit women, the Lenin School remained an overwhelmingly male environment. To prevent the unwitting revelation of secrets, students were required to report their friends' addresses and "data on their social situation" to the cadres department. Students were further instructed to "avoid meeting with foreigners" – presumably those not associated with the school – and to avoid locations frequented by émigrés and foreign tourists. A list of off-limits hotels and restaurants was helpfully appended. When going to the movies, the theater, museums, or other public places students had to try to blend in, refraining from wearing foreign clothing that might attract attention, from speaking loudly in their native languages, and from starting conversations.[86]

Long after they returned home, many former students continued to respect the security measures that protected the secret world of the school. Relatively few later described the school or their experiences there in detail.[87] For the

83 Cohen and Morgan are skeptical that the names were meaningful, "Stalin's Sausage," 332; McIlroy et al. less so, "Forging," 107.

84 McLoughlin, "Proletarian Academics," 70. Studer, *Parti*, 236; "Pravila Konspiratsii," [1933], l. 38.

85 Nelson et al., *American Radical*, 130. Margaret Yeager [Eger] personnel file, RGASPI, f. 495, op. 261 d. 5293, ll. 1–3. For other exceptions, see Harry Pollitt to the Administration, 22 September 1933, RGASPI, f. 531, op. 1, d. 169, l. 5.

86 "Pravila Konspiratsii," [1933], ll. 38–40.

87 McIlroy et al., "Forging," 125 n. 13; Studer, *Parti*, 236.

historian, the pledge of secrecy complicates efforts to get at students' perspectives on the school. Autobiographies prepared by those seeking admission to evening classes and memoirs offer only a fragmentary sense of students' experiences. At the same time, the reticence of former students suggests the interpretive potential of approaching the school as a close and closed community, a place where not only new individuals but also new relationships were forged.

Although the relatively small number of contemporary autobiographies and memoirs do not allow the reconstruction of a "typical" school experience, they offer a suggestive complement to the institutional sources, which include student voices primarily in the act of criticism and self-criticism, privileging moments of suspicion. The "correct" application of self-criticism, as André Marty, a member of the Comintern's executive committee, explained to French students in 1933, required comrades "to give up ideas of 'tolerance' and to forget about group loyalties."[88] By contrast, the memoirs suggest how, at least for some students, personal connections shaped the life of the school – or memories of the life of the school – and created a sense of becoming not only a genuine Bolshevik but also a vital participant in an international movement.[89] Of course, such a sense of solidarity did not rule out suspicion and self-criticism, and indeed it often united students against perceived enemies. The "deviation hunting" that Fred Douglas, a graduate student from Edinburgh, remembered as being "carried to the point of dementia," relied on, perhaps perverted, a perceived need to defend the international cause and community of communists to which students felt connected.[90]

The autobiographies of foreigners resident in Moscow who applied individually for admission to evening classes at the Lenin School constitute one of the few contemporary sources offering a view, albeit a formulaic one clearly tailored to a specific audience, of the hopes and understandings that potential students brought to the school. As noted earlier, urgent individual considerations such as escaping a long prison term might determine who ended up on national parties' lists of candidates. However, because the school was shrouded in secrecy and because students were prohibited from discussing it, little contemporary evidence documents their motivations and expectations.

88 Berthold Unfried, "Foreign Communists and the Mechanisms of Soviet Cadre Formation in the USSR," in Barry McLoughlin and Kevin McDermott, eds., *Stalin's Terror: High Politics and Mass Repression in the Soviet Union* (Basingstoke: Palgrave Macmillan, 2003), 183.

89 In addition to the memoirs discussed later, see Tuominen, *Bells of the Kremlin;* Wicks, *Keeping;* Heinz Hoffmann, *Mannheim-Madrid-Moskau* (Berlin: Militärverlag der Deutschen Demokratischen Republik, 1981); Zhang Guotao, *The Rise of the Chinese Communist Party, 1928–1938: Volume Two of the Autobiography of Chang Kuo-t'ao* (Lawrence: University Press of Kansas, 1972); Afanasii G. Krymov, *Istoriko-memuarnyie zapiski kitaiskogo revoliutsionera* (Moscow: Nauka, 1989). For additional memoirs that contain brief mentions of the school see McIlroy et al., "Forging," 125 n. 13.

90 Quoted in McIlroy et al., "Forging," 109.

Retrospective sources suggest that most did not actively seek admission – they were not supposed to know about the school – but went, as Nelson recalled in his 1981 memoir, "because the National Office chose me to go."[91] How resident foreigners learned of the "secret" school remains unclear, but the school's files include a number of their applications.

For those who decided on their own to apply, and perhaps also for those who were chosen, part of the school's appeal seems to have been its emphasis on joining a transnational community of revolutionaries. In his 1933 application for evening classes at the Lenin School, Jacob Axelbaum presented himself as already a very international communist. An immigrant and an inveterate border crosser, Axelbaum was born in Bobruisk (Belorussia) in 1899 and emigrated to the United States in 1909 with his mother and brothers. He joined the American party in 1925 and visited the Soviet Union in 1928. From there he went to Germany, where he worked for the German party, and then to France, where in 1929 he distributed "contraband literature" to the French army of occupation on the Rhine and studied at the University of Strasbourg.[92] In 1930 Axelbaum returned to the United States, where he worked as an automobile mechanic and became the "unit organizer" of a party cell in the Bronx.[93]

Axelbaum returned to the Soviet Union in 1931, apparently for economic reasons. With the West mired in depression, jobs in the Soviet Union had tremendous appeal. In 1931, the Soviet hiring agency in New York reported that the announcement of 40,000 jobs for skilled foreign technicians and engineers brought 100,000 applications in just eight months.[94] Axelbaum accepted an invitation from the Grain Trust to work as a mechanic on a state farm. By 1933, he was working as a "chief executive" (*otvetstvennogo ispolnitelia*) at Metrostroi, managing foreign Metro workers – quite a promotion for an auto mechanic from the Bronx.[95] Yet Axelbaum was something of an anomaly. In 1932, there were approximately 42,000 foreign workers in Soviet industry, only about 1,464 of whom, including Axelbaum, were card-carrying communists.[96] No doubt fewer still had worked in the American, French, and German parties. The autobiography and questionnaire he submitted to the school suggests that

91 Nelson et al., *American Radical,* 93. See also Haywood, *Black Bolshevik,* 148; Wicks, *Keeping,* 73.

92 "Avtobiografiia," RGASPI, f. 531, op. 1, d. 242, ll. 73–4.

93 "Questionnaire," 21 September 1933, RGASPI, f. 531, op. 1, d. 242, l. 78.

94 Andrea Graziosi, "Foreign Workers in Soviet Russia, 1920–40: Their Experience and Their Legacy," *International Labor and Working-Class History* 33 (Spring 1988): 41. Sergei Zhuravlev, "American Victims of the Stalin Purges, 1930s," in *Stalinistische Subjekte,* 399; Tim Tzouliadis, *The Forsaken: An American Tragedy in Stalin's Russia* (New York: Penguin, 2008), 6. Ruth Kennell and Milly Bennett, "American Immigrants in Russia," *American Mercury* 25, no. 100 (April 1932): 463–4.

95 "Avtobiografiia," l. 74; "Kharakteristika," 23 August 1933, RGASPI, f. 531, op. 1, d. 242, l. 72.

96 Andrea Graziosi, "'Visitors from Other Times': Foreign Workers in the Prewar *Piatletki,*" *Cahiers du monde russe et soviétique* 29, no. 2 (April–June 1988): 162; "Avtobiografiia," l. 75.

Axelbaum viewed political education not only as a means of advancement at work but also as vital to a vision of himself as a professional international revolutionary – a vision supported by his ability to speak English, German "quite well," French "enough so that I can be understood," and "Jewish – very good."[97]

Whereas Axelbaum presented himself as a participant in an international struggle, seventeen-year-old Morris Rosenblatt, another applicant for evening classes, underscored the powerful draw of the Soviet Union as the place to become a real and effective revolutionary. In his autobiography Rosenblatt explained that his father, a Russian immigrant to the United States, had been blacklisted in 1929 after serving as his trade union's delegate to a meeting in the Soviet Union. Unable to find employment, the father arranged in early 1932 "to come to the Soviet Union to work."[98] More intriguing than the father's decision to escape unemployment by leaving for the Soviet Union is the son's decision, despite his "poor knowledge of Russian," to join him. Less than a semester away from graduating high school, Rosenblatt might have found a way to stay in the United States. But whereas his father was not a party member, he was a Young Communist League (YCL) activist, proud of organizing a Pioneer troop in Passaic, New Jersey. In the Soviet Union, he found work at the Stalin Auto Plant as a mechanic, transferred his YCL membership to the Komsomol, and was applying to study at the Lenin School. Hoping to return to the United States "in a few years," he believed he could "be of greater use to the Young Communist League and the revolutionary movement if I were to return with an advanced political education."[99] That his father was able to solve his "difficulties" only in the Soviet Union may have persuaded the young Rosenblatt of both the dangers of reformism at home and the necessity of learning Bolshevik methods of revolution and bringing them back to the United States. (Axelbaum's and Rosenblatt's fates after their applications to the Lenin School are unclear. I have found no evidence that either returned to the United States. Like many foreign workers who remained after 1934, they may have fallen victim to the purges.[100])

Rosenblatt's case highlights the overlap of personal and political commitments and ties in bringing students to the school – a dynamic also visible in retrospective accounts. In his autobiography, Rosenblatt scarcely distinguished between family and party loyalty. Both encouraged him to emigrate to the Soviet Union; although if his father had found work in the United States, he was unlikely to have left – or to have attended the Lenin School. Personal

97 "Questionnaire," l. 76.

98 "Autobiography," nd, RGASPI, f. 531, op. 1, d. 246, l. 104.

99 "Application," nd, RGASPI, f. 531, op. 1, d. 246, l. 103.

100 Graziosi, "Visitors," 162; Tzouliadis, *Forsaken*.Their names do not appear in the database "Zhertvy politicheskogo terrora v SSSR" maintained by Memorial, http://lists.memo.ru/index1.htm (accessed 6 November 2014).

ties might also influence the selection of cadres by their national parties. Thus in his memoir Nelson guessed that it "was probably Rudy Baker" (Randolph Blum) – an old friend with shared roots in Philadelphia's Croatian community, who also happened to be an alumnus of the school and the party's current organizational secretary – "who suggested I attend the Lenin School."[101] An invitation to attend the prestigious school, delivered, as Harry Haywood's was, in an intimate setting over vodka, offered a potentially powerful means of conflating and cementing personal and party relationships.[102]

In his 1978 memoir, Haywood (born Haywood Hall; he adopted his school pseudonym as a permanent name) described his experiences at KUTV and the Lenin School in the late 1920s in terms more personal than institutional or ideological. Still proud of his Stalinism – "history," he believed, had largely proven Stalin "correct"[103] – Haywood structured his remembrances of the school around brief renderings of the people he met there, both true believers and eventual renegades, who linked him to struggles of world historical importance. Typical of Haywood's approach is the account of the course on Leninism and the history of the Soviet party, which he deemed "perhaps our most interesting and stimulating course." To describe the course and its importance, Haywood described its teacher, the historian Isaak Izrailevich Mints, "a young Ukrainian Jew, a soft-spoken and mild-mannered little man," who had participated in the civil war. Particularly memorable was the lesson on "Bolshevik agrarian policy during the Civil War," during which Mints "told us of his involvement in the settling of the question of land redistribution in a Ukrainian district."[104] Haywood similarly recalled fellow students in terms of their past and future contributions to (or deviations from) the revolution.

Haywood's biographical sketches create the impression that the shared school experience generated long-lasting, transnational bonds among Bolsheviks. The story of Haywood's bond with his "special friend" among the British students, his roommate Dave (Douglas) Springhall, "Springy," illustrates his approach. The narrative begins with the gossipy recollection that Springhall was "popular with everybody, particularly among the women on the technical staff." However, Haywood quickly moves from his own memories of Springhall to a dry summary of his political biography: "After leaving the Lenin School, [Springhall] returned to England where he rose rapidly in Party leadership. He also fought in Spain as a member of the Fifteenth International Brigade and was wounded at Jarama."[105] Haywood further recounts Springhall's conviction during World War II for spying, his postwar sojourn to China,

[101] Nelson et al., *American Radical*, 28, 51, 125 (quotation). On Baker see Klehr et al., *Secret World*, 83–95, 119–21.

[102] Haywood, *Black Bolshevik*, 188, 200.

[103] Ibid., 184.

[104] Ibid., 209.

[105] Ibid., 202–3.

and his death in a Moscow hospital.[106] Both Springhall and Haywood served in Spain, and their paths may have crossed again there. Yet Haywood does not mention such a meeting or any detail of his relationship with Springhall that might explain why he considered him a "special friend."[107] Attending the school together was apparently enough to link them irrevocably to the cause and to one another.

Steve Nelson's 1981 memoir takes a rather more critical view of Stalin and the party – which he left in 1957 – than Haywood's, but shares its emphasis on the long-term importance of the personal connections made at the Lenin School. For Nelson, as for Haywood, the most memorable lessons involved listening "to men and women who had participated in these revolutionary movements," including "a man past eighty who had been a drummer boy in the Paris Commune of 1871."[108] Nelson, too, had fond memories of his roommates, with whom he recalled passing "many an evening sprawled on our beds exchanging stories and arguing politics." The roommates came from across the English-speaking world – an Indian who had escaped a British prison, a "working-class intellectual" from Australia, "some Scottish and Cockney" comrades. Looking back, Nelson averred, "I learned as much from them as I did from my classes."[109] Housing international comrades four or eight to a room, the school authorities created, consciously or not, an atmosphere that, as Nelson remembered with perhaps a degree of nostalgia, "really made me feel part of a movement in which solidarity on a global scale was more than an abstraction." The power and concreteness of that solidarity may have been particularly clear in retrospect. Nelson concluded the story of his roommates with the observation, "I met some of them again on the battlefields of Spain," where he saw some of his school friends die.[110]

The school's structure – its polyglot students and teachers, its insistence on the need for conspiracy – made international revolutionary solidarity a lived political and emotional reality. While the school fostered a sense of participation in a global network, it also reminded students that they belonged to an embattled minority. The school's regime of conspiracy was not merely a practical response to the fact that comrades returning from Moscow faced potential

106 Haywood makes some errors in this biography, *Black Bolshevik,* 203. McIlroy et al., "Forging," 113; Nigel West, "Dave Springhall," *Mask: MI5's Penetration of the Communist Party of Great Britain* (London: Routledge, 2005), 219–27; "Douglas Springhall Dies," *New York Times,* 8 September 1943.

107 Haywood, *Black Bolshevik,* 467–89; Richard Baxell, *British Volunteers in the Spanish Civil War: The British Battalion in the International Brigades, 1936–1939* (London: Routledge, 2004), 88.

108 Nelson et al., *American Radical,* 129. On Nelson's decision to leave the party, see ibid., 380–98. On meeting eyewitnesses to revolution, see also "Dokladnaia zapiska o rabote sektora 'D' v vostochnoi sibiri," l. 14; "Otchet o provedennoi praktike s gruppoi sektora 'L,'" 6 March 1935, RGASPI, f. 531, op. 1, d. 184, l. 31.

109 Nelson et al., *American Radical,* 130.

110 Ibid., 130–1.

repression at home: It was a central feature of the school's institutional culture. Nelson conveyed the jittery mood in his account of the one incident that "troubled" his recollections of the school – the frantic revision of the curriculum on the eve of the new term to excise material related to Trotsky's role in 1917 that had suddenly become "counterrevolutionary."[111] The mimeograph machines humming through the night impressed the lesson that truths learned and friends made might, without warning, turn out to be false.

White Chauvinism: Race, Gender, and Trotskyism

The clandestine lives of the American students who entered the Lenin school in fall 1931 got off to a rather inauspicious start. Conflict began soon after they steamed out of New York harbor bound for London on the first leg of their journey to Moscow. Nelson remembered that the party's leaders had instructed the group to limit contact across racial lines during the trip in order to remain "inconspicuous" – a directive, he noted, that "pretty well ostracized" the black comrades. Indeed several students who "felt we had to bend a little or we would be letting our comrades down" apparently engaged in interracial socializing on board the ship.[112] Precisely what sort of socializing occurred, what steps some white comrades had taken to prevent it – and whether those steps constituted "white chauvinism" – became the subject of a lengthy investigation that began with self-critical discussions on the ship. It culminated in a three-day session of self-criticism held in December 1931, a session important enough to draw party leader Earl Browder, then visiting Moscow, to the Lenin School for the proceedings.

In March 1932, the Communist Party of the United States officially resolved the issue, which it characterized as an "extremely serious situation" among the American students enrolled in the Comintern's International Lenin School in Moscow. An early draft of the resolution described the students as having become divided into "two main warring groups, with the principal dividing line the white versus the Negro."[113] The final resolution depicted the problem less dramatically as a "politically unhealthy atmosphere developing among the American group of the ILS as a result of concrete manifestations of the remnants of white chauvinism."[114] The resolution defined "white chauvinism" as a "weapon" wielded by the American bourgeoisie "to isolate the Negro masses from the white workers" through "propaganda of white superiority and Jim Crowism," and it declared "OUR FIGHT AGAINST INCREASED

111 Ibid., 131, 132.

112 Ibid., 126.

113 "Draft Resolution on the Situation which Developed in the American Lander Group of the I. L. S.," 25 January 1932, RGASPI, f. 515, op. 1, d. 2602, l. 60.

114 "Resolution of the Situation in the American Lander Group of the I.L.S.," 11 March 1932, RGASPI, f. 515, op. 1, d. 2602, l. 44.

BOURGEOIS OPPRESSION OF THE NEGRO MASSES" to be the "MOST IMPORTANT TASK of the American Party and above all the first duty of white comrades."[115]

From this perspective, the problems in the school were ones of political understanding and practice. The "situation," according to the party resolution, stemmed from the failure of white comrades "to understand the whole political importance of cleansing themselves first of all from all the traces of this arrogance toward the Negroes . . . that stinks of the disgusting atmosphere of the old slave market."[116] More specifically, the final resolution traced the origins of the conflict to the "mechanical application of certain necessary" but unspecified "conspirative [sic] directives" designed to allow the students to blend in on the ship to London.[117] Thus a lack of political understanding led to a clumsy effort at maintaining party discipline and secrecy. After outlining errors made not only by the white students, but also by school officials and black students, the resolution concluded that through a process of "Bolshevik self-criticism" the "divergencies [sic] in the American group of the ILS, are definitely liquidated."[118] The "situation" appeared to be neatly and definitively resolved.

However, the transcripts of the investigations and self-criticism sessions in Moscow offer a more complicated picture of both the dispute itself and the sometimes tense relationships among students and teachers at the school. The actual conspiratorial directive, which went unmentioned in the final resolution, was, as reported during the course of the investigation in Moscow, that "the girls [*devushki*] among our comrades weren't to communicate with the Negro comrades, so as not to attract too much attention."[119] (Approximately three women students sailed for London aboard the *Majestic* in late summer 1931; all were white. The group also included about six African American men and seven white men.[120]) Although the transcripts clearly suggest the gendered dimensions of the "white chauvinism" debate, neither the investigators in Moscow nor party authorities in New York seemed to have noticed that the "necessary" ban on "conspicuous" interracial socializing between black men and white women might help account for the sharpness of the conflict, because it both interfered

[115] Emphasis in original. Ibid., ll. 44–5.

[116] Ibid., l. 45.

[117] Ibid.

[118] Ibid., l. 47.

[119] "Protokol: Sobraniia amerikanskoi lendergruppy ot 19 IX-31 g.," RGASPI, f. 531, op. 2, d. 56, ll. 19, 4. The archive does not include the English (original?) of this protocol. The 1931 cohort traveled in two separate ships. Comrade Dennis who traveled on the second ship reported receving the same instruction "that the white girls should not speak to the Negro comrades," "American Landergroup Meeting, December 24, 1931," ibid., d. 56a, l. 91.

[120] Estimates based on lists of the overall cohort, internal evidence from the various meetings, and Nelson's memoir. "Spisok studentov," RGASPI, f. 531, op. 1, d. 106, l. 71; Letter to Hathaway, l. 71; Nelson et al., *American Radical*, 125.

with and suggested the illegitimacy of interracial male-female relationships. The rule not only directly contradicted the party's commitment to extending "black-white unity . . . into the sphere of personal relations," but also effectively perpetuated "the disenfranchisement of blacks" and "the marginalization of women."[121]

The rule proved particularly toxic because the student group included an interracial married couple, William Odell Nowell (known at the school as Cooper), an African American auto worker from Detroit, and his Ukrainian American wife Pearl Demery (Paign). Testifying in Moscow, Nowell emphasized that he felt "a strong undercurrent throughout the trip, that is, of tense feeling. It apparently centered around the relations between myself and Paign, who happens to be my wife. We were completely isolated from the group. I noticed *concealed* chauvinism on the part of a large number of comrades in the group."[122] Leonard Patterson (Terry) an African American shipyard worker from Baltimore, drew attention to the fears of miscegenation implicit in the instruction. Recalling suggestions that Nowell and Demery not walk together in London, he observed, "Some of the white comrades, jealous, still having this prejudice in them, hate to see a Negro comrade married to a white comrade. Is this an isolated case? No."[123]

The most public incident of alleged racism occurred in the ship's dance hall. Enjoined from dancing with the white women, two black men apparently began dancing together.[124] Rose Riley (one of the few students always referred to by her school name rather than her real name, Rose Cohen or Clark) motioned for them to leave the dance floor. Because, as a number of both white and black students testified, there had been no sign of discrimination on the part of the ship's staff or other passengers, her action was deemed a "mechanical" application of the rule and thus a manifestation of white chauvinism.[125] Riley

121 On "unity," see Mark Naison, *Communists in Harlem during the Depression* (Urbana: University of Illinois Press, 1983), 36, 47; Baldwin, *Beyond*,67.

122 Emphasis in original. "Meeting of Special Commission to Investigate Situation in American Lander-Group, held Nov. 14, 1931," RGASPI, f. 531, op. 2, d. 56, l. 56; Angela D. Dillard, *Faith in the City: Preaching Radical Social Change in Detroit* (Ann Arbor: University of Michigan Press, 2007), 56. *Hearings before a Special Committee on Un-American Activities, House of Representatives, Seventy-fifth Congress, Third Session*, vol. 2 (Washington, DC: U.S. Government Printing Office, 1938), 1334.

123 "Meeting of Special Commission," l. 162.

124 The dancers are variously identified as Jacoby (Dzhakobi) and Shoemaker (Shumaker) and Brown (Braun) and White (Uait) ("Protokol," ll. 3, 8). On the basis of internal evidence, Shoemaker appears to be the school name of Charles H. White, a member of the Young Communist League, who later became a witness against the party in House Un-American Activities Committee hearings. Thomas Sakmyster, *Red Conspirator: J. Peters and the American Communist Underground* (Urbana: University of Illinois Press, 2011), 34. Jacoby appears to be "Brown" (no first name given), who was listed among "our oldest [black] comrades" in a letter describing the students to be sent to the school (Letter to Hathaway).

125 "Protokol," ll. 2, 8, 10, 16, 27.

explained her behavior as a response to the sex, not the race, of the dancers: "It was just a matter of seeing two boys dance together.... Even at the Party affairs, we told the boys to split up."[126] Another student contested this explanation of her motives – but not the larger point that "boys" should be "split up."[127]

In the final resolution, there is no indication of the gender anxieties visible in the transcripts of the meetings in Moscow. Comrade Cooper (Nowell) appears in a draft version of the resolution not in the context of the difficulty, indeed the possible "white chauvinism," of applying a ban on interracial socializing in a group that included an interracial married couple, but as an example of a comrade "insufficiently armed against the influence of Negro bourgeois nationalism."[128] Likewise, there is no indication of Riley's appeal to ostensibly acceptable homophobia. Instead the resolution castigates a mistaken (and genderless) "barring of Negro comrades from the dance floors by some white comrades."[129] By ignoring the connections between racial and sexual liberation, both school officials and party leaders in New York implicitly endorsed stereotypes of dangerous black male sexuality and (white) female purity. Indeed they seemed to view such endorsement as unproblematic, never considering how the personal relationships among the students on the ship – most notably the presence of an interracial married couple – shaped and exacerbated the "political" conflict that they sought to resolve. Yet it seems clear that the "political" debate was hardly separable from the deeply personal and painful effects of the "conspiratorial" ban on interracial socializing.

The transcripts also illustrate how the failure of the school's Soviet leadership to understand the dynamics of race relations in the United States – or, perhaps more accurately, their dogged insistence on fitting American problems into Soviet categories – could undermine their efforts to promote both the Comintern line and the racial equality that they themselves set as the "most important task" of the U.S. party.[130] After the publication in late October 1931 of Stalin's letter to the editor of the historical journal *Proletarskaia revoliutsiia,* concerns about Trotskyism became an increasingly visible part of the discussions of white chauvinism. An attack on Trotskyite falsifications of history, Stalin's letter set off a far-reaching – and, historian John Barber argues, largely unintended – "campaign against ideological unorthodoxy" that brought Soviet intellectual life to a virtual standstill.[131] The controversy hit the

126 "Meeting of Special Commission," l. 149. See also "Protokol," ll. 5, 9

127 "Protokol," l. 16.

128 "Draft Resolution on the Situation which Developed in the American Landergroup of the I.L.S," 3 February 1932, RGASPI, f. 515, op. 1, d. 2602, l. 81.

129 "Resolution of the situation," l. 45. In his 1981 memoir, Nelson recalled that one of the black men asked a white woman to dance. The testimony in Moscow does not support this version. Nelson et al., *American Radical,* 126.

130 Naison, *Communists in Harlem,*16–18; Letter to Hathaway; L. Pokrowsky to Comrade Randolph, 13 March 1930, RGASPI, f. 515, op. 1, d.869, l. 27.

131 John Barber, "Stalin's Letter to the Editors of *Proletarskaya Revoliutsiya,*" *Soviet Studies* 28, no. 1 (January 1976): 23 (quotation), 22.

American section of the school particularly hard because Haywood's fondly remembered professor Mints (or Mintz), who taught the English-language seminar on Leninism at the school, was among the contributors to the official *History of the Communist Party* in which Stalin had detected "a number of errors."[132]

The fevered unmasking, criticism, self-criticism, firing, and in some cases expulsion from the party of "Trotskyite falsifiers" reached a climax in December 1931 just as the Lenin students were undertaking three days of intensive self-criticism.[133] At the Institute of Red Professors' tenth anniversary celebration in December, Stalin's right-hand man Lazar' Kaganovich openly charged Mints with taking a Trotskyite approach to history.[134] At the Lenin School, as noted earlier, the students frantically revised the curriculum on the eve of the new term to excise material related to Trotsky's role in 1917. Not surprisingly perhaps, rooting out Trotskyism also became part of the white chauvinism investigation. The perceived necessity of linking the issue of white chauvinism to this prominent Soviet campaign emerges most poignantly in Mack Coad's only recorded intervention in the December meeting. The African American steel worker from Birmingham, whom the American party had characterized as "our best southern organizer" but "very poor at reading and writing," confessed that "Stalin's letter is a hard language, but I can understand a few words in it. I never knew there was anything like it in the world. I am scuffling over it."[135]

The speeches at the meeting illustrate how the Soviet directive that the American party fight "remnants of white chauvinism" interacted with the equally insistent Soviet directive to root out factions and Trotskyites. Although more politically sophisticated than Coad, the school officials also seemed to struggle with how to connect the letter and its concerns about Trotskyism to the matter at hand. In his questioning of Nowell in November, Dmitrii Matveevich Evtushenko, a school official, attempted to develop a connection between Nowell's "disagreement with the instructions of the C[entral] C[ommittee] in America regarding the trip" and his alleged political "differences with the policy of the CC of the Party" on the Negro question that in turn appeared "similar to the opposition which was inside" the Soviet party.[136] Evtushenko appeared unable to grasp the meaning of the "*concealed* chauvinism" – more a feeling of isolation than concrete political acts – that Nowell emphasized existed on the ship and seemed to view the charge of white chauvinism as merely a clever means of deflecting (perhaps legitimate)

132 Ibid., 21, 22; Elaine MacKinnon, "Writing History for Stalin: Isaak Izrailevich Mints and the *Istoriia grazhdanskoi voiny*," *Kritika* 6, no. 1 (Winter 2005): 14. "Spisok: Studentov II kursa i prepodovatelei M.L.K," 5 March 1928, RGASPI, f. 531, op. 1, d. 13, l. 5.

133 Barber, "Stalin's Letter," 22–3.

134 MacKinnon, "Writing History," 16.

135 "American Landergroup Meeting, December 24, 1931," l. 65.

136 "Meeting of Special Commission," ll. 65, 67, 68.

charges of factionalism and Trotskyism.[137] Likewise, Mints, questioning Arthur Murphy (Jacobs), an African American steelworker from Pennsylvania, could not or would not distinguish Murphy's complaints about white chauvinism on the ship from a general political opposition – framed as opposition to "white chauvinism" – that constituted some sort of "propagandistic" effort on the part of black students to "isolate themselves from the whites."[138] Unable to understand how attitudes or words might be offensive and painful, the Soviet teachers and administrators took the black students' complaints about the behavior of their white comrades as a form of fractional politics.

The American students, both black and white, by and large rejected or perhaps did not understand the effort to connect the campaigns against Trotskyism and white chauvinism. At the December session, a white student emphasized that "if the Negro comrades isolated themselves [from the white comrades], we are the cause, we gave them the basis for their isolation," and regretted that "if you speak or are sociable with a Negro comrade you are [seen as] the leader of the Negro comrades and you have groupings with them."[139] Patterson made the firmest and clearest objection to understanding the black students' concerns through the lens of factionalism, asserting that "If the comrades try to connect this question with the Trotsky question, I don't think there is any comparison."[140]

The American party's final resolution echoed Patterson's objections, chiding the "ILS leadership" for formulations such as those suggested by Evtushenko and Mints that "tried to create a certain balance" between the "manifestations of remnants of white chauvinism" on the part of some white comrades and the political errors of some black comrades exercising their "political right" to condemn such behavior.[141] In short, the Americans managed to define the collective complaints of black comrades – even when they (mistakenly, in the party's view) charged Soviet comrades with white chauvinism – as something other than the organization of a "fraction," the primary way in which the Soviets understood such complaints. Instead, they were asserting their legitimate rights to be treated as equal members of the communist community.

Clearly the American students and the American party leaders in New York were learning and applying Stalinist categories. But neither the debate within the school nor the final resolution revealed a straightforward or unidirectional process of indoctrination. Although all could agree that excising the remnants of "white chauvinism" in personal relations was a "political duty," Stalin's letter made "Trotskyism" the preferred framework for understanding the issue

137 Ibid., ll. 61, 62.

138 Ibid., l. 140.

139 "American Landergroup Meeting, December 24, 1931," ll. 106, 107.

140 "Meeting of Special Commission," l. 159.

141 "Resolution of the Situation," l. 46; "Meeting of Special Commission," l. 166.

of white chauvinism.[142] However, the letter offered few guidelines as to how to proceed. At a moment when "practically every established authority was being subjected to violent criticism,"[143] the representatives of the "center" struggled to construct, let alone inculcate, a monolithic "Stalinist" approach to the American party's problems. Not only students – the ostensible objects of indoctrination – but also their teachers found it difficult to fit U.S. race relations, especially as they played out in personal and intimate relations among communists, into Soviet and specifically Stalinist categories. Fifty years later, Nelson summed up the incident as a "conflict of Party discipline vs. the Negro question in America."[144] In contrast to the party's resolution, he characterized the conflict as at once political and emotionally charged, and as never really resolved. If the "divergencies" were liquidated, the difficulty of building a communist community and establishing and enforcing communist norms of behavior in personal relationships remained.

"Not a School of Monks": Political Health and Bolshevik Norms

A February 1933 report on the Lenin School's American sector makes it clear that white chauvinism had not been the only "difficulty" faced the previous year: The "school also had to struggle against" drunkenness, antisemitism, and social democratic "deviations on questions of socialist construction."[145] The equation of the seemingly incommensurate issues of drunkenness and social democratic "deviations" reflected the long-standing communist practice of establishing and enforcing normative codes that defined ostensibly private behaviors as politically meaningful. Drunkenness, no less than an incorrect attitude toward black or Jewish comrades or socialist construction, carried serious political implications, because it demonstrated an un-Bolshevik lack of discipline and often led to breaches of conspiracy.[146]

The Soviet conflation of personal and political unreliability often "perplexed" and discomfited foreign communists, for whom, as historian Berthold Unfried emphasizes, the practice "seemed to violate Western notions of individuality and ignore the boundaries between private and public domains."[147] In his 1972 memoir *My Generation*, Welsh communist Will Paynter's primary recollection of the school was of an incident that suggested precisely the strangeness, even – at least in retrospect – the absurdity, of finding political meaning in apparently innocent, apolitical behavior. He recounted that a

142 On interracial socializing as a "political duty," see Naison, *Communists in Harlem*, 47.

143 Barber, "Stalin's Letter," 40.

144 Nelson does not mention the Browder meeting, *American Radical*, 126.

145 "Otchet o nabore studentov sektora 'D,'" 15 February 1933, RGASPI, f. 531, op. 1, d. 164, l. 3.

146 "Stenogramma obshchego sobraniia kollektiva MLSh po chistke partii," ll. 46–47; "Prikaz," June 1934, RGASPI, f. 531, op. 1, d. 53, l. 58.

147 Unfried, "Foreign," 175.

simple "frolic"– a boisterous "booze up" with two roommates that involved "bawling rude parodies on some of the current popular songs" – resulted in "a special party meeting the following morning of the English-speaking group, where we were condemned and classified as 'petty bourgeois degenerates.'"[148] Indeed not only Westerners were perplexed by the linkage of political and personal behavior. A Chinese comrade, who observed the director of the Lenin School's "self-criticism" in 1929, remembered that "in the course of her hour-long confession [Kirsanova] even made mention of her private life during her younger days, which astonished foreign Communist Party members."[149] The necessity of scrutinizing a communist's personal behavior in order to assess political "health" constituted a central lesson of the Lenin School.

Although the general tendency to blur the borders of public and private life may have astonished foreign communists, it was the school's rigid, abstinent code of conduct that, as Paynter's story suggests, often became the flashpoint in conflicts between students and administrators. Nelson, who, unlike Paynter, seems to have complied with the rules, remembered that "some students rebelled against the strict discipline and regimentation, but," he insisted, "only a handful."[150] In his 1935 address to incoming students, Marty sought to preempt any possible tensions by emphasizing that the school's rules allowed and encouraged students to enjoy themselves in healthy communist ways. Assuring the students that the school was not a "school of monks," Marty urged them to "absolutely mix in all the life of the Soviet country and follow it" by reading the English-language *Moscow Daily News* and participating in "winter and summer sports as much as possible." He also called on students to emulate the wholesome habits of Soviet youth and "go to the theaters and the pictures." He recommended that students see the film *Chapaev* (1934) about the legendary Russian civil war commander Vasilii Chapaev, not in order to model themselves on the swashbuckling hero, but rather to learn from the political commissar portrayed in the film – the disciplined, authoritative embodiment of party consciousness.[151]

When violations of Bolshevik norms of behavior occurred, the school addressed them with tools borrowed from the Soviet party: criticism and self-criticism and the related production of "characterizations" or evaluations (*kharakteristiki*).[152] Hence a drunken spree resulted in an impromptu meeting called to label the offenders "petty bourgeois degenerates." The case of Jack Larkin (probably a school alias) offers a fuller illustration of the process of self-criticism. In June 1932, Larkin sent an eight-page letter to the

[148] Paynter, *My Generation*, 54.
[149] Zhang, *The Rise of the Chinese Communist Party*, 98; Wicks, *Keeping*, 94.
[150] Nelson et al., *American Radical*, 129.
[151] "The Main tasks of Students in Party Schools: Scheme of the speech of Comrade Marty," 8 October 1935, RGASPI, f. 531, op. 1, d. 72, ll. 11ob, 20.
[152] Unfried, "Foreign," 180–1. On "characterizations," see Krekola, "Finnish," 296–9.

Anglo-American Sector Bureau that defended his remark, made in a speech before the sector, to the effect that "in every American City where there is a Party Unit, the Party is run by a bunch of Jewish Comrades who think they own the Party." The remark, he argued, constituted a legitimate, if inelegant, protest against "Petty Bourgeois Jewish Chauvinism."[153] Less than a week later, after the sector meeting that heard his case, Larkin was contrite, confessing that "I came to the conclusions that were wrong, anti-Communist, and anti-Semetic [sic]." He now understood that in such cases a comrade had to "fully realize the seriousness of my mistakes and repudiate them."[154] Such criticism and self-criticism constituted a crucial feature of periodic and, until the terror of 1936–8, nonlethal purge (*chistka*) proceedings designed to rid the Soviet party of "unworthy elements." The process was, according to Unfried, "more an educational measure than a tool of political repression."[155]

By the mid-1930s, however, the balance in the Soviet party began to shift from education to repression. Responding to the December 1934 murder of Leningrad party boss Sergei Kirov, the Soviet party and the Comintern began in early 1935 an intense "vigilance campaign against 'Trotskyites.'" Officially blamed on a treasonous conspiracy linked to the exiled Trotsky, as well as to Zinovev and Kamenev, who were duly arrested, the murder fed "mounting suspicion of foreigners, spy mania, and xenophobia."[156] Ironically, the stepped-up vigilance coincided with the Comintern's adoption of a more moderate line, the "united front against fascism" that called for an end to sectarian attacks on "social fascism" in favor of "unity of action" among "all sections of the working class, irrespective of what organization they belong to"[157] – except, of course, Trotskyite organizations. The Comintern's new flexibility succeeded in sparking the growth of communist parties in many places; however, these very successes ended up stoking fears that spies and Trotskyites were increasingly infiltrating national parties and making their way to Moscow disguised as political émigrés or students.[158]

Anxiety ran high at the Lenin School, where the class entering in 1935 included students who only a year or two earlier had been social democrats or anarchists. Addressing a meeting of Lenin School teachers in December 1935, Italian communist and member of the Comintern's executive committee Palmiro Togliatti (aka Ercoli) emphasized the success of the Popular Front line

153 I have been unable to identify Larkin's real name. Jack Larkin to Sector Buro, 15 June 1932, RGASPI, f. 531, op. 2, d. 56v, ll. 20, 21.

154 Jack Larkin to Sector Buro, 21 June 1932, RGASPI, f. 531, op. 2, d. 56v, l. 23.

155 Unfried, "Foreign," 177, 186.

156 Chase, *Enemies*, 5, 37–8; Matthew Lenoe, *The Kirov Murder and Soviet History* (New Haven: Yale University Press, 2010).

157 Chase, *Enemies*, 5; "Resolution on Fascism, Working-Class Unity, and the Tasks of the Comintern, Adopted by the Seventh Congress, 20 August 1935," in McDermott and Agnew, *Comintern*, 243.

158 McDermott and Agnew, *Comintern*, 121.

in France, where the party had rapidly grown from about 40,000 to almost 100,000 members. However, he warned the gathered teachers, impressive as this growth appeared, most of these new party members were not yet "real communists." The teachers, therefore, had to be alert for signs of Trotskyism among their students, and carefully train the new cadres in the "foundations of our politics, of our tactics, and, especially the fight against Trotskyism."[159] He located the greatest dangers among the "young people" from France, Spain, Belgium, and the "Latin countries in general, where there are strong remnants of anarchism and anarcho-syndicalism."[160] Although neither the Italian nor Belgian parties sent large numbers of students to the school in 1935, the French and Spanish parties overfilled their enrollment allotments, sending, respectively, thirty-two and seventy students.[161] Given the national composition of the student body, Lenin School teachers had their work cut out for them.

Yet even as Togliatti emphasized the dangers, he remained unwilling to assume that the school was honeycombed with Trotskyites, insisting that the means of combating Trotskyism among international communists necessarily differed from those employed in the Soviet party. Togliatti proposed that, rather than simply condemning Trotskyism, teachers explain the dangers it posed in specific countries. The students, he reminded their teachers, "come from capitalist countries, social democratic parties, they are ideologically weak."[162] Moreover, Togliatti argued, Trotskyism was more dangerous inside the Soviet Union, where "the question of Trotskyism... is a question of struggle against counterrevolution," than in the students' home countries, where it was a "question of the correct policy of the united front."[163] Here Togliatti ignored the danger to the Soviet Union – perhaps far-fetched but frequently invoked – of foreign Trotskyites hidden in Moscow.

In his speech to the students, Marty similarly underscored the necessity of fighting against "enemies" and "deviations" while advocating gentle, pedagogical correction. He asked the students, "So when a comrade makes a mistake, should we say to him 'you are an opportunist,' or should we show him what his mistake consists of without wounding him?... It is necessary to eliminate mistakes from the minds of comrades but without sticking a label on them."[164] To become real Bolsheviks, to develop a "Communist mentality," required training, not punishment.[165]

159 "Stenogramma," 13 December 1935, RGASPI, f. 531, op. 1 d. 72, ll. 21, 22. Togliatti's figure of 40,000 members in 1934 squares with that of M. Adereth, *The French Communist Party: A Critical History (1920–1984)* (Manchester: Manchester University Press, 1984), 291. McDermott and Agnew provide a figure of 87,000 for 1935, *Comintern,* 137

160 "Stenogramma," 13 December 1935, l. 26.

161 RGASPI, f. 531, op. 1, d. 84, l. 9.

162 "Stenogramma," 13 December 1935, l. 31, 61.

163 Ibid., l. 27.

164 "Main tasks of Students," l. 17ob.

165 Ibid., l. 11ob.

By contrast, the teachers gathered in December 1935, while agreeing that they needed to tailor their struggle with Trotskyism to each particular national group, suggested that they saw a greater Trotskyite menace than did Togliatti or Marty. To Togliatti's question of the sorts of "Trotskyite arguments" they heard among the students, teachers responded with specific examples, such as the American Trotskyites' contention that "in the Soviet Union there is a dictatorship of the party at the head of which stands Stalin," an argument that proved difficult to combat even when teachers took into account "national peculiarities."[166] In answer to Togliatti's question about whether students "valued Stalin enough," teachers again provided concrete evidence of apparently dangerous misunderstandings, including one student's quip that the posters of Stalin in workers' clubs reminded him of the "advertisement of [President Paul von] Hindenburg in Germany."[167] The most alarming language came from Kirsanova, who concluded the teachers' session with the unsubtle reminder that Kirov's murder had proved that Trotskyites are capable of anything and that "we need vigilance" because they may be "masked."[168]

Reports compiled by the Lenin School's cadres department in 1936 found evidence of Trotskyite influence throughout the school, in large part because the compilers employed an extremely broad and vague definition of Trotskyism. Organized by national sector, the summaries documented classroom exchanges, overheard conversations, articles in wall newspapers, and letters that allegedly demonstrated Trotskyite attitudes and activities. Seemingly any "incorrect" statement or action could be labeled "Trotskyite." Thus Spanish, Danish, and German students, who were puzzled by claims that Trotsky had played no positive role in the revolution or civil war, along with British students, who were "surprised" that it had taken so long to exclude Trotsky from the party, appeared equally suspicious. Some students made the mistake of comparing Trotsky and Stalin, for example, a student in the Scandinavian sector who granted that "Stalin is a great man, he's done a lot for the workers," but who also believed "we cannot say that Trotsky did nothing... Trotsky was a great man after Lenin."[169]

Many of the reports' examples of "Trotskyism" documented not opposition views, but rather ignorance of Bolshevik norms of vigilance and toughness. Some students appeared potentially dangerous because they had no understanding of the matter that so preoccupied their Soviet comrades. Thus the report suggested something ominous in the fact that when the examination commission posed questions about Trotskyism to students in the French sector they answered, "I don't know" or "There aren't any Trotskyites in our region." Also problematic were students who had some understanding of Trotskyism, but saw no real danger in it. A Scandinavian student, sounding very much like

166 "Stenogramma," 13 December 1935, l. 23, 55.

167 Ibid., ll. 32,49–50.

168 Ibid., l. 64.

169 "O Trotskizme," [1936], RGASPI, f. 531, op. 1, d. 94, ll. 51, 52.

Togliatti, affirmed that although Trotskyism in the Soviet Union "is a counter-revolutionary movement" in "capitalist countries" it is merely an "opposition within the workers' movement." The lack of Bolshevik toughness was particularly clear in the case of a French student who admitted that the Trotskyites "are politically and theoretically stronger than us, and we just avoid discussions with them." The report also found evidence of Trotskyite influence in comments critical of Bolshevik discipline, such as a Greek Young Communist's complaint that there was "no difference between the school and prison in a capitalist country."[170]

Like the surveillance reports, the characterizations of forty-eight Spanish students, apparently prepared near the end of the 1935–6 academic year, suggest that "Trotskyism" functioned, despite Marty's injunction, more as a label than a precise diagnosis. The characterizations were essentially collages of set phrases – "incomplete political formation," "anarchist and social democratic remnants," "a healthy comrade" – and rarely included evidence that supported the choice of a particular label.[171] "Trotskyite" was one of a number of general political descriptors that could be attributed to the students – perhaps the most damning – but one employed sparingly. Only three of the forty-eight students manifested Trotskyite "remnants" or "ties."[172]

Such assessments were usually prepared by the teachers in conjunction with the student party organizers.[173] In this case, the evaluators appeared to understand the seriousness of the charge of "Trotskyism" and the importance of identifying it, but seemed unwilling or unable to define it precisely or condemn it strongly in the Spanish context. Telling a more cryptic story than the transcripts of the white chauvinism dispute, the evaluations from the Spanish sector likewise hint at the complexity and difficulty of political indoctrination. The evaluations tended to offset even the most negative statements with some redeeming feature, often the assertion that a comrade was politically "healthy." Apparently still committed to pedagogical correction, evaluators wrote off only the most undisciplined and disruptive students. The characterization of Gonzalo López, a thirty-three-year-old metalworker who had been a party member since 1922, illustrates how a series of epithets might be integrated into an ultimately sympathetic evaluation: "Strong resistance to discipline and in constant disagreement with the rules and work norms of the Sector. Little political firmness, with Trotskyite remnants . . . contributed to fomenting indiscipline and bad relations with the leadership of the Sector. We believe that, despite everything, he is an honest and healthy element."[174] "Health" in

[170] Ibid., ll. 52, 53.

[171] "Cándido ALVAREZ," RGASPI, f. 531, op. 1, d. 184, l. 94.

[172] "Kharakteristiki na slushat. ispan.sektora MLSh, 1934–1935 g.g.," RGASPI, f. 531, op. 1, d. 184, ll. 93, 94, 96.

[173] Krekola, "Finnish Sector," 297; Wicks, *Keeping*, 123.

[174] "GONZALEZ," RGASPI, f. 531, op. 1, d. 184, l. 94; "Spisok studentov MLSh KP Isp," l. 52; "Destacados comunistas asturianos," http://elcieluporasaltu.blogspot.com/2008/10/destacados-comunistas-asturianos.html (accessed 6 November 2014).

this and other cases was compatible with breaches of discipline, undisciplined work habits, and even "political weakness." More a disposition than a behavior, "health" correlated with honesty and loyalty to the party that evaluators suggested would allow comrades to overcome or compensate for even serious faults.[175]

Although they obscured the meanings that evaluators attributed to political labels, the characterizations offer a relatively sharp picture of their understandings of appropriately Bolshevik personal behavior. A December 1934 memo on the need to strengthen conspiracy had noted that students "routinely" stayed out until three or four o'clock and sometimes six or seven o'clock in the morning. When asked "where they were that they're getting home so late," they answered, "I was walking around the city and got lost" or "I spent the night with my girlfriend."[176] Traces of such escapades made their way into characterizations as "errors" in conspiracy connected to "relations with women," frequent drinking, a "scandal," and lost school passes.[177]

In condemning such behavior, the evaluations drew on a clear vision of Bolshevik masculine toughness. Abstentious and ascetic, the ideal student was not a monk, but a healthy revolutionary. A true Bolshevik demonstrated neither a "liberal" squeamishness that put friendships before party loyalty nor an "excessive modesty" that made a comrade "weak in the face of his supposed superiors." When a woman embraced such norms, she might be criticized as excessively "brusque."[178] However, few such comrades existed. Only four of the forty-eight Spanish students evaluated in 1936 were women. The one deemed "brusque," Luisa Pérez, a twenty-four-year old domestic worker who had been a Young Communist for five years and had recently joined the party, was the only one judged to have a "high level" of political development.[179]

By the end of 1936, most of these students had returned to Spain. In April 1936, the first group of eleven Spaniards, including Pérez, prepared to leave Moscow. Perhaps in response to the February 1936 election of the Popular Front government in Spain, a "special decision" of the Comintern's executive committee sent them home before the end of the term.[180] In the wake of the July 1936 coup that launched the Spanish civil war and the first of the great show trials in August that marked the ratcheting up of terror and xenophobia

175 "Kharakteristiki," ll. 88, 90, 91, 95 ("good disposition"), 96.

176 "Nasha zadacha usilit' konspiratsii i podniat' revoliutsionuiu biditel'nost," 12 December 1934, RGASPI, f. 531, op. 1, d. 52, l. 58.

177 "Kharakteristiki," ll. 97, 96, 92, 94. Similar behavior appeared in characterizations of students in the American sector, "Dokladnaia zapiska o rabote sektora 'D' v vostochnoi siberi," ll. 21–2.

178 "Kharakteristiki," ll. 89, 90, 97, 96 (weak), 98 (brusque).

179 "Spisok studenov MLSh KP Isp," l. 49; "CARMEN," RGASPI, f. 531, op. 1, d. 184, l. 98. In the Russian version she was described as using "command methods" (*metody komandovaniia*), "Karmen," ibid., d. 185, l. 30.

180 "OO GUGB [Special Sections of the Main Directorate of State Security] NKVD," 13 April 1936, RGASPI, f. 531, op. 1, d. 112, l. 7.

in the Soviet Union, nearly all the remaining students in the Spanish sector left the school.[181] This exodus was followed in 1937 by the departure of most of the students from legal parties. Thus few students from Spain or other western democracies remained to witness or fall victim to the terror.[182]

As the frontline of the international struggle shifted to Madrid, many who had been associated with the Lenin School made their way to Spain. Of the approximately three thousand students who graduated from the school between 1926 and 1936, perhaps several hundred participated in the Spanish civil war. A contemporary accounting of Spanish party members and Young Communists who had attended the Lenin School listed a total of 148 students.[183] Some, like José Díaz, the leader of the Spanish party, and Jesús Hernández, who became minister of public instruction in 1936, were among the most prominent communists in Spain. Others, such as Juan José Manso, who was elected as a parliamentary deputy from Asturias in 1936, and Laureano Argüelles, a teacher and wartime mayor killed by the Francoists, played important local roles.[184] After the formation of the International Brigades in September 1936, a dozen or more current students from a number of national sectors made their way from Moscow to Madrid to join the war effort.[185] Large numbers of Lenin School alumni likewise went to Spain, often serving as political commissars. The American party sent both Nelson and Haywood as commissars in 1937. Dozens of others, notably Springhall and Paynter, served as commissars or, like Mack Coad, as regular troops.[186] Togliatti and Marty, who had both been involved in the life of the school, also served in Spain, the former as the Comintern's representative in the Spanish party, the latter as commander of the International Brigades.

Although the number of students and alumni who contributed to the war effort in Spain pales beside the tens of thousands of primarily communist volunteers who joined the International Brigades, the school nonetheless provided crucial organizing experience and a shared frame of reference for communists in Spain. In assembling the International Brigades, national parties and the Comintern drew on a decade of experience vetting candidates and transporting them, often illegally, to Moscow and on the lessons learned in organizing a multilingual, multinational institution. Political commissars and rank-and-file

181 "Spisok studentov MLSh KP Isp," ll. 48–53. Chase, *Enemies*, 146–7.

182 McLoughlin, "Proletarian Academics," 65; "Sektor 'D,'" 1936, RGASPI, f. 531, op. 1, d. 106, l. 4; "Spisok studentov komsomol'tsev," ll. 98–106; Unfried, "Foreign," 188.

183 "Spisok studentov MLSh KP Isp," ll. 44–53.

184 "Destacados comunistas asturianos"; Valentín Brugos, et al., *Los comunistas en Asturias (1920–1982)* (Gijón: Ediciones TREA, 1996), 76.

185 "Spisok studentov LSh, sluzhivshikh na voennoi sluzhbe," RGASPI, f. 531, op. 1, d. 106, l. 157; "Zav. Otdelom kadrov IKKI," 16 February 1937, ibid., d. 134, l. 1. I have found no evidence to substantiate Tuominen's claim that "all male students should leave for the front," *Bells*, 87.

186 On British alumni in Spain, see McIlroy et al., "Forging," 121–4.

comrades brought an awareness of Bolshevik norms and of the need for discipline, vigilance, and perhaps a "'healthy' hatred of Trotskyism."[187] On the battlefields of Spain, communists already linked by connections to one another and the school, might feel, even more profoundly than in Moscow, a sense of global solidarity.

187 "Kharakteristiki," l. 96.

2

Imagining, Seeing, Feeling the Revolution

Almost thirty years after her first visit to the Soviet Union in 1933, Spanish communist Dolores Ibárruri remembered viewing Moscow "with her heart" and seeing it as the "most marvellous city in the world."[1] As a delegate to the Comintern's Thirteenth Plenum, Ibárruri followed a carefully managed itinerary of meetings and excursions and witnessed a parade in Red Square during which, as she wrote her Spanish comrades, she felt herself reborn (*resucita*).[2] She was apparently sheltered from the realities – severe shortages of food and housing, not to mention of "luxuries" such as soap and shoes – that made 1933 "the worst year of the decade" in the Soviet Union.[3] But even if she noticed the ubiquitous queues that gave public form to shortages, they apparently had no impact on what she remembered seeing "with her heart": "socialism being constructed" and the Soviet people "marching toward Communism." She saw, she suggested in retrospect, the city of the future, not the city before her eyes. In her speech to the plenum, she emphasized her own identification with that future as she set before the delegates a "vivid picture of the Spanish revolution" or, what amounted to virtually the same thing, the "armed uprising [that] could erupt at any moment."[4]

Ibárruri was hardly the only foreign visitor to the Soviet Union to see (or remember seeing) what she was predisposed to see. This tendency can be understood in terms of a more general process of "suspending disbelief" that historian

[1] Dolores Ibárruri, *They Shall Not Pass: The Autobiography of La Pasionaria* (New York: International Publishers, 1976), 128.

[2] As quoted in Juan Avilés Farré, *Pasionaria: La mujer y el mito* (Barcelona: Random House Mondadori, 2005), 78.

[3] Sheila Fitzpatrick, *Everyday Stalinism: Ordinary Life in Extraordinary Times: Soviet Russia in the 1930s* (New York: Oxford University Press, 1999), 41, 97.

[4] "Rech' tov. Dolores," *XIII Plenum IKKI: Stenograficheskii otchet* (Moscow: Partizdat, 1934), 525, 531.

Stephen Kotkin argues was vital to Stalinism. He characterizes workers in Magnitogorsk as living a "dual reality: observational truth based on experience, and a higher revolutionary truth based partly on experience and ultimately on theory."[5] To explain the power of revolutionary truth in the face of the evidence of experience, Kotkin evokes workers' variable but powerful "willingness to suspend disbelief," a willingness shored up by the fact that in the closed world of Stalinist Russia, "few could imagine alternatives."[6] Historian Michael David-Fox identifies a similar process at work among fellow travelers who visited the Soviet Union. Rather than understanding prominent Western visitors, who were wined, dined, chaperoned, and flattered by their hosts, as "manipulated" into supporting the Soviet Union, David-Fox emphasizes that even the most carefully staged visits depended on visitors' "willing or eager suspension of disbelief."[7] In the case of fellow travelers, distance from the Soviet Union – not immersion in it – seems to have facilitated the voluntary forgetting of observed facts. Visitors such as Theodore Dreiser made pronouncements about Soviet Russia after returning home, where a declaration to the effect that "nowhere in Russia . . . will you find men without coats standing in bread lines waiting for a hand-out" constituted a criticism of "rich" America circa 1928 as much as praise of – or a suspension of disbelief in – the Soviet system.[8]

Although rank-and-file international communists, who lived for extended periods in the Soviet Union, might also be understood as "suspending disbelief," the term hardly captures the political and psychological complexities of their situation. They differed from both Soviet workers, who could not easily imagine alternatives to a system in which they were enmeshed, and from short-term visitors from the West, who were willing to ignore deficiencies of the Soviet system in order to imagine an alternative to their own. Because long-term international communist residents had not merely a frame of reference beyond the Soviet Union but also a store of experiences that had somehow led them to identify with "revolutionary truth," everyday "observational truth" potentially challenged their most fundamental – and freely chosen – understandings of the world and their place in it. Rather than simply overlooking unpleasant or dissonant realities, communists maintained their identities by learning to observe in particular, mediated ways. As Eugene Lyons, the United Press (UP) wire service's correspondent in Moscow, remarked of foreign communists,

[5] Stephen Kotkin, *Magnetic Mountain: Stalinism as a Civilization* (Berkeley: University of California Press, 1995), 228–9.

[6] Ibid., 358.

[7] On manipulation and "manufacturing support," see Ludmila Stern, *Western Intellectuals and the Soviet Union, 1920–1940* (New York: Routledge, 2007), 4,105–7, 120–2. Michael David-Fox, *Showcasing the Great Experiment: Cultural Diplomacy and Western Visitors to the Soviet Union* (New York: Oxford University Press, 2012), 112.

[8] "Dreiser Home, Sees Soviet Aims Gaining," *New York Times* (*NYT*), 22 February 1928. Thomas P. Riggio makes a similar point, "Introduction," in Thomas P. Riggio and James L. W. West III, eds., *Dreiser's Russian Diary* (Philadelphia: University of Pennsylvania Press, 1996), 12–13.

"Their minds become finely adjusted instruments for selecting impressions in harmony with their exalted state. The validity of their life's work, their sufferings, and their sacrifices is at stake."[9] Thus revolutionary truth structured their observational truth. Or, to borrow Ibárruri's metaphor, they saw not with their eyes, but with their hearts.

The literal impossibility of "seeing with the heart" highlights the degree to which becoming communist – or remaining a communist in a new context – required learning how to view (or, more precisely, interpret) the world. Moscow could be "seen" in its "marvelous" form only if the true communist heart somehow filtered the raw data captured by the speciously accurate eye. The ability to distinguish deceptively "transparent vision" from authentic "subjective perceptual clarity" marked an individual as a communist.[10] Thus when a comrade who had arrived in the Soviet Union full of passion for the new Russia later left, as one African American communist did in 1931, "completely demoralized" and spouting what a party official in New York characterized as "crazy slanders," the simplest explanation seemed to be that the dissident had been "an undercover agent of counter-revolutionary forces from the beginning."[11] How else to explain such a failure to "see" the Soviet Union properly?

The offices of the English-language *Moscow News*, a newspaper geared toward raising the political consciousness of English-speaking workers in the Soviet Union, offer a particularly rich site for a case study of international communists' ways of seeing and explaining the Soviet Union. Founded in 1930 by American journalist and fellow traveler Anna Louise Strong, but controlled by the Soviet party, the paper employed both communists and those attracted to the possibility of becoming communists. In 1935, the American party's leader Earl Browder accepted a check from Strong for membership dues, but never issued her a party card.[12] As Strong noted in her 1935 memoir, her journalistic instincts often "raged" against the "suppression of truth" required by the party line. At the same time, her commitment to the cause allowed her to see the logic, as the paper's editor-in-chief Mikhail Borodin explained to Strong, of understanding "truth" to mean "a clear description of the general line of our struggle" rather than "sensational unanalyzed 'facts,'" such as the number of people dying of famine in Ukraine, "from which no good can come."[13] Living in many cases for years in the Soviet Union, witnessing party purges and the arrests of Russian friends and lovers, the staff members of the *Moscow*

[9] Eugene Lyons, *Assignment in Utopia* (New York: Harcourt Brace, 1937), 95.

[10] Joan W. Scott, "The Evidence of Experience," *Critical Inquiry* 17, no. 4 (Summer 1991): 794.

[11] C. Dirba to Comrade Randolph, 23 October 1931, Rossiiskii gosudarstvennyi arkhiv sotsial'no-politicheskoi istorii (RGASPI), f. 515, op. 1, d. 2225, l. 86.

[12] Tracy B. Strong and Helene Keyssar, *Right in Her Soul: The Life of Anna Louise Strong* (New York: Random House, 1983), 163.

[13] Anna Louise Strong, *I Change Worlds: The Remaking of an American* (1935; reprint, Seattle: Seal Press, 1979), 371, 375.

News were well positioned to see the "facts," sensational or otherwise, but nonetheless endured hardships and deprivations to produce an increasingly stilted propaganda sheet.

This chapter examines international communists' management of the mismatch between what they had imagined and the realities they encountered by analyzing how they represented the Soviet Union to the world and themselves; in other words, their strategies for "seeing" and "feeling" Soviet reality. Efforts to distinguish truth from "sensational" fact are visible in the newspaper itself and in the reports of Lenin School students who, much like *Moscow News* reporters, visited construction sites, factories, and collective farms and worked to interpret what they saw in "correct" ways. Drawing on contemporary letters and memoirs, the chapter also analyzes international communists' emotional responses, their sense of themselves in the Soviet Union, and their sense of participating in an international cause. I focus on the case of Milly Bennett (born Mildred Bremler, aka Milly Mitchell), who began working at the *Moscow News* in early 1931. In 1934, shortly after the Soviet state recriminalized sodomy, her Russian husband was arrested for homosexuality, as was the Russian lover of another *Moscow News* staffer, British communist Harry Whyte.[14] Nonetheless, Bennett remained on the paper's staff until at least mid-1935 and in the Soviet Union until the end of 1936, when she left for Spain. Her story illustrates the ways in which commitment to revolutionary truth could be as much personal – a component of self-identity, a means of being reborn– as ideological.

Political Commitments and Personal Ties

The complicated life stories of the *Moscow News*'s largely communist and strikingly transnational staff underscore the importance of personal ties in forging and shaping international communist identities and institutions. In her 1935 account of the paper's founding, Strong traced the rekindling of her interest in starting an English-language newspaper to Borodin. The two met briefly in 1918 in Seattle, reconnected in Moscow in the early 1920s, and became close during Strong's two trips to China in the mid-1920s, when Borodin was serving as the Bolsheviks' advisor to the Chinese Nationalists. In 1931, Strong found Borodin back in Moscow, in the lower profile post of deputy director of the paper and lumber trust. Remembering her earlier interest in "starting an American newspaper in Moscow," Borodin told her that if she "tried now" she would likely "find support."[15] Drawing on personal contacts at the Supreme Council of the National Economy (VSNKh) and among the

[14] Dan Healey, *Homosexual Desire in Revolutionary Russia: The Regulation of Sexual and Gender Dissent* (Chicago: University of Chicago Press, 2001), 188.

[15] Strong, *I Change*, 300; on her earlier contacts with Borodin, 188, 231–5; Strong and Keyssar, *Right in Her Soul*, 95–6; 107, 125, 130–3, 140.

American émigré community in Moscow, Strong obtained official permission, hired a staff, and quickly produced the first issue.[16]

In the premier issue of 5 October 1930, Strong described the paper as targeting "English-speaking specialists working in the Soviet Union, Russian students of English, and interested persons living abroad."[17] As Milly Bennett told the story of the paper's founding, Strong had "'sold' the Soviet government the idea of backing a newspaper . . . to be distributed abroad . . . the paper to propagandize . . . or 'sell' the idea of Soviet Russia in a 'subtle, witty, amusing manner.'"[18] After 1932, when Borodin became the *Moscow News*'s editor-in-chief and the paper merged with the *Workers' News*, it became notably less subtle, witty, and amusing.[19] As noted in Chapter 1, by 1935 the *Moscow News* was recommended reading for English-speaking students at the Lenin School.[20]

This official endorsement notwithstanding, the staffers were brought together as much by personal connections and circumstances as political commitment. Bennett, for example, joined the paper in 1931 at the invitation of Strong, whom she knew from her time in China in the mid-1920s, where both had worked as journalists. Bennett had been in China from 1926 to 1927, "mak[ing] propaganda for Chiang Kai-shek," until the violent end of his alliance with the Chinese Communist Party.[21] Not a communist but always on the verge of joining the party, Bennett accepted Strong's job offer, she told George Kennan, then the third secretary of the Riga legation, out of boredom with her life in San Francisco.[22] However, boredom may not fully account for her decision. Once she was in Moscow she took, as she wrote a friend, "three separate classes in politics." She deemed the first (on communism) and third (on dialectic materialism) "knockouts," while characterizing the instructor of

[16] Strong, *I Change*, 301–3.

[17] "Representatives of Many Organizations Hail Opening of *Moscow News*,"*Moscow News* (*MN*), 5 October 1930; M. Timothy O'Keefe, "The *Moscow News:* Russia's First English Language Newspaper," *Journalism Quarterly* 50, no. 3 (Autumn 1973): 463.

[18] Milly Bennett to Dear Fred, 8 April [1931?], Milly Bennet Papers, Box 1, Folder 21, Hoover Institution Archives.

[19] Strong, *I Change*, 338. Sylvia R. Margulies, *The Pilgrimage to Russia: The Soviet Union and the Treatment of Foreigners, 1924–1937* (Madison: University of Wisconsin Press, 1968), 101. The paper became a daily, *The Moscow Daily News;* the *Moscow News* continued to appear as a weekly supplement.

[20] "The Main tasks of Students in Party Schools: Scheme of the speech of Comrade Marty," 8 October 1935, RGASPI, f. 531 op. 1 d. 72, l. 190b; "Resolution of Group II," [June 1936], ibid., d. 136, l. 11.

[21] Milly Bennett, *On Her Own: Journalistic Adventures from San Francisco to the Chinese Revolution, 1917–1927*, ed. A. Tom Grunfeld (Armonk, NY: M. E. Sharpe, 1993), 74; on Bennett and Strong's less than cordial relations see, 259–64.

[22] Bennett, *On Her Own*, xi; "Interview with Milly Bennett in Riga prepared by George Kennan," 17 February 1933, National Archives College Park, Maryland (NACP), Record Group (RG) 59, 861.911/1403.

the course on Leninism as having a "mean disposition, and no talent whatsoever as a teacher."[23] She had come to Moscow to work, but was also drawn, as she wrote in a contemporary letter, to the vision of a "beautiful socialist world."[24]

In Moscow Bennett reunited with other acquaintances and friends from China, most notably Borodin, who, in 1928, after the Nationalist government's purge of its erstwhile communist allies, escaped to Moscow via the Gobi Desert.[25] The other Chinese exiles on the staff, Jack and Percy Chen, likewise spoke English (and French), not Chinese. The Chen brothers, who, along with Strong, had fled China with Borodin, were the sons of Eugene Chen, the Nationalist government's former foreign minister; their father had been the first Chinese lawyer in Trinidad, where the brothers were born.[26] In Moscow, Percy occasionally wrote articles for the paper, and Jack wrote and contributed cartoons.[27] In contemporary notes, Bennett characterized Jack as "a great joy to my souring heart. He's joined the Communist party – but managed to keep his sophisticated and charming sense of humor."[28]

In addition to the Chinese refugees, the staff included a large number of returning Russian immigrants, who had both personal and political connections to one another and to the Soviet Union. Borodin (aka Michael Gruzenberg) was himself a re-emigrant, an Old Bolshevik, who had gone into political exile after the Revolution of 1905. Having lived for a decade in Chicago where he ran an English-language school for immigrants on the city's West Side, he spoke English, as journalist Louis Fischer remembered, "intermixed with American slang."[29] Morris (Moshe) Stolar, who had left Russia in 1909, knew Borodin from Chicago, where Stolar, a printer, was a communist activist dubbed the "Chicago Lenin." Returning to Moscow, he became a "responsible secretary" at the paper. His family eventually joined him in the Soviet Union; his son Abe, his daughter Eva, and her husband all found work at the *Moscow News*.[30]

23 Bennett to Marjory, 26 November [1932?], Bennett Papers, Box 2, Folder 1.

24 Bennett to David, 13 May [1931?], Bennett Papers, Box 1, Folder 21.

25 Percy Chen, *China Called Me: My Life inside the Chinese Revolution* (Boston: Little Brown, 1979), 125–77; Strong and Keyssar, *Right in Her Soul*, 130–6.

26 Chen, *China*, 6.

27 Ibid., 224; O'Keefe, "*Moscow News*," 464.

28 Bennett to Peggy Taren, 4 May [1932?], Bennett Papers, Box 1, Folder 21.

29 Louis Fischer, *Men and Politics: An Autobiography* (1941; reprint, Westport, CT: Greenwood Press, 1970), 139; Max Lippett interview, 6 November 1951, Michael Gruzenberg, Federal Bureau of Investigation 65-HQ-58053 (FBI/Gruzenberg); Lydia Holubnychy, *Michael Borodin and the Chinese Revolution, 1923–1925* (Ann Arbor: University Microfilms for the East Asia Institute, Columbia University, 1979), 18.

30 "Report made by L. Hoyt McGuire," 21 February 1952, FBI/Gruzenberg; Meyer Zolotareff, "Imprisonment, Loss of Rights Revealed by Red Refugee," *Chicago Herald American*, 28 January 1938 (clipping in ibid.); Thom Shanker, "Refusenik's Dream Died in USSR," *Chicago Tribune*, 1 January 1989.

If Morris Stolar and Borodin returned as dedicated communists, other re-emigrants on the staff had somewhat more complicated stories in which the personal and the political were deeply entangled. In 1989 when he finally returned to Chicago, Abe Stolar, the only member of the family to survive the purges, remembered that he had emigrated to the Soviet Union as much or more for personal as political reasons. He recalled that at nineteen he had followed his Russian-born father to the Soviet Union because "my family were communists. I felt communism was natural, the right thing to be." In retrospect, he also emphasized that because he was a "youngster," he "had to go, although I didn't want to."[31] Stolar, like others who spent many years trying to return to the United States, may have exaggerated his reservations.[32] Nonetheless, his story highlights the ways in which personal ties might make political commitments "natural," even irresistible.

Some members of the staff, again for both personal and political reasons, had even less choice in the matter of emigration. Bennett described Rosie Prokofiev, the office secretary, as "brought from England, where she was born, by her [R]ussian parents when she was 13."[33] Whether she was enthusiastic about the move is unclear. Her "sweetheart" Ed Falkowski, who wrote for the paper, was more clearly committed to the cause. Bennett described him as "an ascetic young coal miner, with an extraordinary instinct for writing." The son of Polish immigrants, he had arrived in Moscow from the coal country of Pennsylvania via Berlin, where he wrote in German for the *Die Linkskurve*, the magazine of the Association of Proletarian Writers of Germany.[34] When he departed the Soviet Union in 1937, he left Rosie and a child behind.[35]Max Halff, a Russian-born Jew deported from England in 1928 as "a very dangerous communist," had studied at the Lenin School before finding a position at the *Moscow News*.[36] Bennett characterized him as the "gentlest and sweetest young thing you ever saw, all fresh and brand new out of the Communist

[31] Bill Peterson, "After 58 Years in U.S.S.R., American Comes Home," *Washington Post*, 6 July 1989.

[32] Mary M. Leder, *My Life in Stalinist Russia: An American Woman Looks Back*, ed. Laurie Bernstein (Bloomington: Indiana University Press, 2001), 1–2.

[33] "It is raining heavily," nd, Bennett Papers, Box 1, Folder 21.

[34] Douglas Wixson, *Worker-Writer in America: Jack Conroy and the Tradition of Midwestern Literary Radicalism, 1898–1990* (Urbana: University of Illinois Press, 1994), 200–9.

[35] Rose Prokofiev correspondence, Edward Falkowski Papers, TAM 120, Box 3, Tamiment Library/Robert F. Wagner Labor Archives, New York University. Jenny [Miller] to Milly Bennett, 1 September 1938, Bennett Papers, Box 4, Folder 2; Jenny to Bennett, 10 July 1939, ibid.

[36] Steve Cohen, *No One Is Illegal: Asylum and Immigration Control Past and Present* (London: Trentham Books, 2003), 180; John McIlroy et al., "Forging the Faithful: The British at the International Lenin School," *Labour History Review* 68, no. 1 (April 2003): 103, 113; Harry Haywood places Halff at the Communist University of Toilers of the East (KUTV), *Black Bolshevik: Autobiography of an Afro-American Communist* (Chicago: Liberator, 1978), 165. He may be the Max described by Strong in *I Change*, 312–13.

academy, with per[f]ect petty bourgeo[i]s standards of behavior," a description that complicates the notion that he was a single-minded revolutionary.

For others, the possibility of dispensing with petty bourgeois standards constituted a prime attraction of Soviet Russia. Lyons, who in 1932 became an unwilling neighbor of the *Moscow News* when the paper's operations took over space previously occupied by the UP, remembered the staff as a "bevy of oversexed American females and homosexual Englishmen" apparently seeking liberation in a land that, in the words of an enraptured visitor quoted by Lyons, had "liquidated sex bugaboos."[37] He may have been including Bennett among the oversexed. Described by friends as "far from beautiful – in fact, almost ugly" but at the same time "evidently a most attractive or sexually desirable woman," Bennett characterized herself as "sprung right into the mad, mad postwar business, when all of us were supposed to be flinging at life."[38] Bennett described the paper's first associate editor, British communist Charles Ashleigh, as "an emasculated IWW [Industrial Workers of the World] (in other words an IWW turned Communist.)"[39] In Borodin's FBI file, two anonymous informants interviewed in the early 1950s described Ashleigh as a "homosexual," who, along with two other homosexuals, Hillary Brown and Harry Whyte, also British communists who worked at the paper, became involved in a scandal and returned to England in 1934 or 1935.[40] In May 1934, Whyte wrote a now well-known letter to Stalin protesting the recriminalization of male homosexuality. In the letter, Whyte compared the persecution of homosexuals to "the persecution of any social group subject to exploitation and persecution in conditions of capitalist hegemony," an understanding that perhaps contributed to his 1932 decision to move to the Soviet Union.[41]

[37] Lyons, *Assignment in Utopia*, 510. 511, 331. See also James E. Abbe, *I Photograph Russia* (London: G.G. Harrap, 1935), 183–4.

[38] Freda Utley, *Odyssey of a Liberal: Memoirs* (Washington, DC: Washington National Press, 1970), 246; Bennett to Rosie [Elmer Roessner], [1934], Bennett Papers, Box 4, Folder 22. See also Marion Merriman and Warren Lerude, *American Commander in Spain: Robert Hale Merriman and the Abraham Lincoln Brigade* (Reno: University of Nevada Press, 1986), 41, 151.

[39] Bennett, "It is raining." Ashleigh is best known for his novel about the IWW, *Rambling Kid* (London: Faber and Faber, 1930). On Ashleigh see, Patrick Renshaw, "The IWW and the Red Scare, 1917–24," *Journal of Contemporary History* 3, no. 4 (October 1968): 68, 71; Gene D. Overstreet and Marshall Windmiller, *Communism in India* (Berkeley: University of California Press 1959), 42, 50.

[40] Wixson, *Worker-Writer*, 207; O'Keefe, "*Moscow News*," 464. "Report made by L. Hoyt McGuire," 30 October 1952, FBI/Gruzenberg; Ashleigh is identified as "Ashly" in the report; Whyte as "White." Ashleigh's name disappeared from the masthead in April 1934; Whyte continued contributing articles until November 1935.

[41] Healey, *Homosexual Desire*, 188–92; "Harry Whyte, a British Communist, Challenges Stalin on Homosexuality," in Glennys Young, ed., *The Communist Experience in the Twentieth Century: A Global History through Sources* (New York: Oxford University Press, 2012), 88–98, quotation: 90–1.

In the heady days of the early 1930s, when the whole of the Soviet Union appeared to be one vast construction site and capitalism seemed to be experiencing a decisive crisis, communists emigrated to the Soviet Union for a wide range of reasons: to build socialism, to find employment, to become "real" revolutionaries in the Bolshevik mold, to escape prison and persecution.[42] Motivations might overlap in a single individual or among seemingly similarly situated immigrants, as was the case at the *Moscow News*. For many, personal and political motivations and understandings were tightly intertwined, as immigrants imagined themselves participating in the construction of a beautiful socialist world. Although such expectations were often tragically betrayed, they nonetheless remained defining points of reference in communists' life histories.

"There Are No More Queues": Communist Ways of Seeing

For those struggling to find housing, food, and clothing in the Soviet capital, the vision of marvelous Moscow could seem very much like a lie. Such was, at least on occasion, Bennett's perspective. In a letter apparently written shortly after her arrival, she pronounced herself unwilling to "pass out the sunshine in pound rolls the way the professional sovietis do." As a professional reporting facts, she distanced herself from the "professional sovietis," among whom she included two prominent journalists, Strong and *The Nation's* Soviet correspondent Louis Fischer, who sometimes contributed to the *Moscow News*. Although it took the cover-up of the 1932–3 famine to elicit Strong's rage against the suppression of truth, Bennett fumed at Fischer and Strong's claim that "'there are no more orcherids' [*ocheredi*] (queues waiting for food, clothing). The truth being that Anna Louise has a servant to stand in ocherids for her, and Fischer a devoted wife to stand in line for him ... and so these two talented people, neither of whom has ever waited in line four hours for meat ... sit down and write that there are no ocherids. Although, either, by a short, observing stroll down any [M]oscow shopping street, could count 10 or 20 ocherids – or [I]'m a damned liar.... AND I'M NOT."[43]

For Bennett, a plausible picture of the Soviet Union had to include some measure of criticism. Ironically, she identified the *New York Times*'s correspondent Walter Duranty, best known for denying the extent and severity of the 1932–3 famine, as someone who reported truthfully – if not always the whole truth. In a contemporary letter to another newspaperwoman (probably Ethel

[42] Sergei Zhuravlev, "American Victims of the Stalin Purges, 1930s," in Brigitte Studer and Heiko Haumann, eds., *Stalinistische Subjekte: Individuum und System in der Sowjetunion und der Komintern, 1929–1953* (Zurich: Chronos, 2006), 397–400.

[43] Emphasis in original. Bennett to George, [193?], Bennett Papers, Box 1, Folder 21. Lyons, *Assignment in Utopia*, 510; Louis Fischer, *Soviet Journey* (1935; reprint, Westport, CT: Greenwood Press, 1972), 132–3; Strong, *I Change*, 368.

Bogardus), Bennett described Duranty as "notoriously pro-Soviet... but pro-Soviet in a way that you and all of us... (I mean tough-minded American newspaper birds) would like. He pokes fun at them... never hesitates to criticize, etc. when he sees cause... and surveys objectively."[44] Tempering sunshine with mockery, Duranty remained, from Bennett's perspective, a "tough-minded" journalist even as he left much out of his Soviet reporting.

The *Moscow News* initially operated or tried to operate along similar lines, criticizing deficiencies but representing them as transitory inconveniences that paled beside the shimmering essence of the Soviet Union: the heroic effort to build socialism. Indeed, notwithstanding Bennett's sense that Strong failed to observe accurately, Strong herself understood that Soviet officials had taken an interest in the paper as a means of "handling complaints of Americans" working in the Soviet Union.[45] However, detailing such complaints "accurately" – that is, in terms acceptable to the censor and the paper's Soviet editors – proved difficult. In the paper's first issue, Falkowski attempted a humorous take on Moscow's intractable housing shortage, citing, for example, the case of a doctor who married in order to obtain a room.[46] The censor flagged the article as "slander," completely missing, according to Strong, the effectiveness of satire as a means of simultaneously broaching and minimizing the housing problem. Only after Strong "furiously" telephoned everyone she knew late into the night did the censor relent and agree to the cutting of only "two short paragraphs which even [Strong] admitted might be misunderstood."[47] In later articles, Falkowski adopted a more cheerful and earnest tone, noting, for example, that, although the basement cafeteria in one Moscow factory was poorly ventilated, the "food was good" and the "manager explained that a new restaurant will soon be constructed."[48] Apparently skeptical that she would be doing much "tough-minded" reporting, Bennett admitted in another letter to Bogardus that "I'm not using a bi-line in the paper for very obvious reasons."[49] She did, however, often publish under the name "Milly B. Mitchell" (Mike Mitchell was her ex-husband) or the initials M. M. So identified, she passed out a good bit of sunshine, writing features with titles such as "You Can Eat in Moscow," extolling "co-operative feeding" as the "new way of life." Occasionally her articles addressed circumscribed complaints, such as the

44 Bennett to Ethel [Bogardus?], [1931?], Bennett Papers, Box 1, Folder 21. On Duranty's reporting on the famine, see David C. Engerman, "Modernization from the Other Shore: American Observers and the Cost of Soviet Economic Development," *American Historical Review* 105, no. 2 (April 2000): 390–1; S. J. Taylor, *Stalin's Apologist: Walter Duranty: The New York Times's Man in Moscow* (New York: Oxford University Press, 1990), 210–23.

45 Strong, *I Change*, 301; "Representatives of Many Organizations."

46 E[d] F[alkowski], "Moscow Nomads," *MN*, 5 October 1930.

47 Strong, *I Change*, 305.

48 Ed Falkowski, "What's for Dinner in the Factory," *MN*, 28 June 1931.

49 Bennett to Ethel [Bogardus?], 4 May [1931?], Bennett Papers, Box 1, Folder 21.

shortage of nails among otherwise enthusiastic Finnish American immigrants in Karelia.[50]

A comparison of Bennett's reporting for the American press and for the *Moscow News* suggests how she learned to "see" – if not necessarily believe – like a communist. With coauthor Ruth Kennell, an American who had emigrated to the Soviet Union in 1922 and had recently returned to the United States, Bennett published two articles in *American Mercury* that, she wrote a friend, made her "proud fit to burst."[51] The first, published in December 1931, was poorly received in Moscow. Indeed in the 1932 interview conducted by Kennan, Bennett reported that the article had resulted in her being "dropped" from the paper's staff; only the "combined efforts" of Borodin and Strong got her reinstated.[52] The situation may explain Bennett's "request" that the *Moscow News* publish a letter she had sent to the *American Mercury*'s editor H. L. Mencken clarifying her intentions. Noting that the article "They All Come to Moscow" "has been interpreted as an attack on the Soviet Union," Bennett emphasized that "I wrote the sketches in no such spirit, but as satirical portraits of a few Americans who had come under my observation and who were by no means intended to be representative of the American worker who comes to Moscow." She regretted "if anyone has sought to use this material against either the USSR or the many fine Americans who seek work here" and asked Mencken to publish a disclaimer, stating "that no attack was intended." For their part, the *Moscow News*'s editors published her letter, but appended a postscript to it noting their "disapproval of the article mentioned and also of the mention of 'Moscow News' in that connection."[53]

In the same issue of the *Moscow News* in which Bennett's letter was published, "Moscow Mike" provided a point-by-point refutation of Bennett and Kennell's 1931 article. "Moscow Mike" was a (probably fictional) plain-spoken Midwesterner long resident in Moscow whose homey wisdom as offered to *Moscow News* reporters appeared in the regular column "Moscow Mike Tells Us." In this case the unnamed author of the column, perhaps Bennett herself, reported Mike's observation that most of the American immigrants he met in the Soviet Union "don't whine if conditions isn't always just perfect right away.... Not like the people I've been readin' about in a high-class intellectual American magazine, called 'American Mercury,' in an article

[50] M. M., "You Can Eat in Moscow," *MN*, 17 April 1931; Milly B. Mitchell, "Karelian Timber Trade Must Be 100 Percent Mechanized," *MN*, 25 August 1932.

[51] Bennett to Marj[ory McKillop], 24 March [1932], Bennett Papers, Box 2, Folder 1.

[52] "Interview with Milly Bennett in Riga," p. 3; "Report made by Donald G. Hanning," 30 July 1951, Mildred Bremler [Milly Bennett] Federal Bureau of Investigation file HQ 100–124391/SF 100–12592 (FBI/Bennett).

[53] "Statement re: 'American Mercury,'" *MN*, 18 December 1931. Ruth Kennell and Milly Bennett, "They All Come to Moscow," *American Mercury* 24, no. 96 (December 1931): 394–401. Bennett wrote the third and fourth sketches; Bennett to Brook, December 28 [1931], Bennett Papers, Box 1, Folder 21.

written by two ladies named Ruth Kennell and Milly Bennett."[54] Mike took particular issue with the fact that "sex plays a big part in the story these ladies has supplied to the 'Mercury' for the titillation of superior readers," adding "this sort of stuff disgusts me." The article was, he argued, "sneakily anti-Soviet," as "all the characters described is freaks, eccentrics, sex-hungry." Although he admitted that "such birds... blowed into this town some time or another," he insisted that they were "very exceptional. But there ain't a word in the article to indicate that. You'd think that we're runnin' a nut-house here, instead of a mighty vigorous work-shop for the buildin' of socialism."[55]

Bennett and Kennell's second article for *American Mercury*, published in April 1932, rectified many of the errors identified by Moscow Mike. The authors now focused on Americans who came to build blast furnaces and automobiles, lauding what Mike had characterized as "the real immigration;" that is, family men "mighty keen" to "get right down to work." They cautioned that the American worker who went to the Soviet Union with "ideas of making his fortune must be disappointed." To succeed in the Soviet Union, American immigrants had to be true pioneers, "who would rather have jobs in a land where poverty is general and hope is boundless – even standing in long lines to receive the food they pay for – than be idle in a land of plenty and despair."[56] The real heroes of the piece were the Finnish re-emigrants from the United States, who had established a commune alongside the Ford plant in Nizhnii Novgorod where they lived "in a two-story, box-like community house, eating at a common table, paying equally and sharing the expense of wives and children."[57] Indeed their story had been told in much the same terms in the *Moscow News*, although that paper's more didactic version had explicitly drawn the desired conclusion that the "commune is one of the best groups of foreign workers in the Soviet Union," who "did not allow itself to be discouraged or cast down by difficulties and hardships encountered in its work."[58] Moreover, the second article completely lacked the sex element. Moscow Mike registered no complaint.

Highlighting ambitious construction projects and hardy "pioneers" building the socialist future, Bennett and Kennell's second article adapted a fundamental communist way of seeing: measuring the bright Soviet future against both the backward Russian past and the grim capitalist present. Acknowledging the "discomforts and irritations" endured by many Americans in the Soviet Union,

54 "Moscow Mike Tells Us: Why They All Come to Moscow," *MN*, 18 December 1931. I found only one Moscow Mike column with a byline, CA (likely Charles Ashleigh), "Moscow Mike Tells Us: How to Pay Europe's War Debts," *MN*, 1 November 1931. The column ran from late 1931 to mid-1932 and varied somewhat in tone, language, and style.

55 "Moscow Mike Tells Us: Why They All Come to Moscow."

56 Ruth Kennell and Milly Bennett, "American Immigrants in Russia," *American Mercury* 25, no. 100 (April 1932): 468.

57 Ibid., 470.

58 "'Cement': The Finnish-American Commune at Autostroy," *MN*, 28 July 1931.

Bennett and Kennell described how those able to withstand the rigors were "inspired by the size of the job" and appreciative of the special treatment accorded skilled foreign workers. To explain and excuse current hardships, they invoked Russia's status as a "backward, Asiatic country."[59] The industrializing Soviet Union, they suggested, was analogous to the old American frontier, a savage, wild land full of hope and possibility.[60] They offered less a "romance of economic development" that "valued the fruits of rapid industrialization above its costs" than an adventure for the "true pioneer, for the fellow who gets a kick out of hardship."[61] Only the Soviet Union, they emphasized, offered such opportunities for heroic action.

In her later reporting for *Moscow News*, Bennett demonstrated that she had learned the importance of "seeing" the radiant future – and of getting her readers to see it as well – even if she also still observed plenty of queues. In a series of articles on Karelia and the Soviet northeast that ran in the summer of 1932, Bennett superimposed a vision of the wondrous future on the rather bleak present. "Murmansk today," she admitted, was a pitiful, backward place: "Pigs root along the sandy stretches . . . , goats are tethered to fences. Women haul water from street wells, carry it along, balanced on sticks swinging from their shoulders. It is a wild, ugly little frontier town, and not a pavement in the place." But a visit to the office of the secretary of the regional planning commission opened her eyes to "a vision of the Murmansk of tomorrow." On the rough-hewn pine wall hung a "gaudy, futuristic map" that offered a "dream of a City Beautiful." The enthusiastic secretary detailed spending for vast industrial projects. Thus, Bennett assured her readers, "When you leave that office, a new vision of Murmansk crowds your eyes." She now "saw" not the pigs and goats and unpaved roads, but "the tall, white, modern planned port city, greater than Leningrad, they'll tell you, that is just beginning to rise on the sandy wastes."[62] Bennett presented the builders of this future as exemplars of a communist way of seeing. Thus, she reported that Alexander Leskov, the director the Karelia Timber Trust, told her, "'I like to sit at this window . . . like to sit and watch the gradual mechanization of Karelia.' And when an overburdened Ford truck lumbered past, as if Leskov had conjured this bit of mechanization with his talk, he beamed. (Nor, I might add, did he seem to see the long, tedious, dusty horse-drawn wagon train which followed close behind.)"[63] The future materializing before her readers' eyes was, Bennett

59 Kennell and Bennett, "American Immigrants," 463, 471, 468.

60 Ibid.," 465.

61 Engerman, "Modernization," 383; the phrase "romance of economic modernization" is George Kennan's; Kennell and Bennett, "American Immigrants," 468. On foreign workers' living conditions, see Elena Osokina, *Our Daily Bread: Socialist Distribution and the Art of Survival in Stalin's Russia, 1927–1941*, trans. Kate Transchel and Greta Bucher (Armonk, NY: M. E. Sharpe, 2001), 46–52.

62 Milly B. Mitchell, "American-Finns Help Build Socialist Karelia," *MN*, 10 August 1932.

63 Mitchell, "Karelian Timber Trade."

suggested, the sight that mattered, even if they could still glimpse the less lovely present.

Rather than simply ignoring the deficiencies of the Soviet present, reporters in the *Moscow News* explained them as the vestiges of the past destined to be obliterated by the First Five-Year Plan. Thus, for example, Moscow Mike granted what his readers surely knew: Moscow's street cars were uncomfortably overcrowded. However, he argued that the discomforts had to be understood in context. Those foreigners who complained about the overcrowding failed to appreciate that it was "unavoidable," the consequence both of the "backward transportation system Moscow inherited from the old days" and of the city's rapid growth. Soviet citizens, by contrast, were "patient because they know we've had to go heavy on the basic industries first, in our Five-Year Plan.... Then, after that, we can go ahead – as we are now goin' ahead – to provide more of the amenities of life."[64]

Evidence that the promissory notes would be paid came in articles that described the progress already achieved and represented the West as stagnant and hopeless. Headlines, such as "No Hope for Solution of World Wide Crisis: Soviet Union Alone Faces Year 1931 with Confidence," effectively captured a central comparison that structured the paper's reporting of topics as diverse as unemployment, marriage law, race relations, and prisons.[65] Moscow Mike, for example, asserted that whereas the Moscow metro would soon solve the local transit problem, the London and New York subways were doomed to remain "crowded in order to make profit." When Ashleigh joined the staff in September 1931, among his early contributions was an article describing his "first impressions" on returning to Europe after eight years. Stopping in Germany on his way to Moscow, he saw, he emphasized "no difference": "Hunger and unemployment press upon the workers.... Men sleep in old hulks in the harbour for want of better shelter." By contrast, Moscow had been transformed. He saw not cobblestones and droshkies, but paved streets and shiny new cars. Although he heard of shortages, people appeared better dressed; houses had been repaired and repainted. Most of all he noticed order: "Out of the chaos left by civil war, up from the starvation and blockade and the struggle for power, there has come order – the planned co-ordination of the

64 "Moscow Mike Tells Us: A Sure Way of Solving Traffic Problems," *MN*, 22 November 1931. See also "Moscow Mike Tells Us: When, and When Not to Say 'Zavtra,'" *MN*, 22 January 1932; Eugene Lyons, "Nations Build New Life Along Ancient Volga," *MN*, 20 October 1930; Anna Louise Strong, "Sleeping to Berlin," *MN*, 26 November 1930.

65 *MN*, 11 January 1931. "Unemployment Depopulating Europe whilst USSR Adds 3 Million Yearly" and "'Communism the Only Hope of the Negro People,'" *MN*, 17 September 1931; "May Day Delegates, Welcome to the USSR! How You May Judge What You See Here," *MN*, 28 April 1932; "Marriage Law in Old England Still Medieval" and "Birth Control Scientifically Handled by Soviet State," *MN*, 30 October 1930; "Moscow Mike Tells Us: Where Brides Are for Sale," *MN*, 7 January 1932; Anna Louise Strong, "Sunny California Hell for Workers," *MN*, 6 February 1931.

resources of a vast land." The revolution, he concluded, "has gone forward. There is still a great territory to be conquered, but the troops are fit and new strength comes at every step."[66]

Thus the *Moscow News*'s reporting of the First Five-Year Plan, like the reporting in the central Soviet press, prefigured the aesthetic of socialist realism. Systematized only in 1934, socialist realism, as summed up by central committee member Andrei Zhdanov, combined "the most matter-of-fact, everyday reality with the most heroic prospects."[67] In his study of the prehistory of socialist realism in Soviet mass journalism, historian Matthew Lenoe emphasizes that "journalists, literati, and agitprop [agitation and propaganda] officials strove to develop print genres that would *both* convey a political message *and* galvanize young male activists" by drawing on the "perceived preferences of these activists for narratives of heroism, adventure, and military glory."[68] The *Moscow News*, with its stories of rough and ready pioneers and its use of language, such as Ashleigh's quoted earlier, that turned workers into "troops," appeared to fit this mold.However, because its imagined readers were not Soviet "activists," but were English-speaking engineers initially and, after its May 1932 merger with the *Workers' News*, all English speakers in Soviet industry, the *Moscow News*, which often published translations from the Soviet press, also provided instruction on how foreigners should "see" the Soviet Union. The "Moscow Mike" column that ran until mid-1932 and stories such as Bennett's on Karelia explained to readers, who, unlike their Soviet counterparts, had very clear pictures of alternative systems, how to make sense of the hardships and shortages they saw around them.

By 1933 and the beginning of the Second Five-Year Plan, both the *Moscow News*'s audience and its tone had shifted. With the completion of the First Five-Year Plan, the Soviets had stopped paying skilled foreign workers in hard currency; many left and few arrived to take their places. Those foreign workers who remained were often political refugees, predominantly communists, from Germany, Austria, and Spain.[69] In 1934, Borodin told Strong that as

[66] Charles Ashleigh, "First Impressions after Eight Years," *MN*, 2 October 1931. See also Anna Louise Strong, "Thirteen Years of Building Socialism Progresses with Unchanging Purpose Conditioned by Four Major Epochs," *MN*, 5 November 1930.

[67] Zhdanov quoted in Katerina Clark, *The Soviet Novel: History as Ritual* (Chicago: University of Chicago Press, 1981), 34.

[68] Emphasis in original; Matthew Lenoe, *Closer to the Masses: Stalinist Culture, Social Revolution, and Soviet Newspapers* (Cambridge, MA: Harvard University Press, 2004), 71. See also Jeffrey Brooks, *Thank You, Comrade Stalin: Soviet Public Culture from Revolution to Cold War* (Princeton: Princeton University Press, 2000), 109–10.

[69] Andrea Graziosi, "Foreign Workers in Soviet Russia, 1920–40: Their Experience and Their Legacy," *International Labor and Working-Class History* 33 (Spring 1988): 41; Sergei Zhuravlev, "Inostrannaia koloniia v Sovetskoi Rossii v 1920–1930-e gody (Postanovka problemy i metody issledovaniia)," *Otechestvennaia istoriia*,1994, no. 1: 181; Andrea Graziosi, "'Visitors from Other Times': Foreign Workers in the Prewar *Piatletki*," *Cahiers du monde russe et soviétique* 29, no. 2 (April-June 1988): 162.

the *Moscow News*'s readers changed, "we change ourselves to fit them. The valuta [hard currency] specialists go and we drop the fluffy stuff that amused them." Those who stayed had different needs; indeed, he warned her that they might not need an English-language paper at all. Borodin related that when he attended "factory meetings of 'Readers of *Moscow Daily News*' I ask what language I shall use and they tell me Russian!" The workers themselves were "neither Russian nor American: they are Pole, Jugo-Slav, Hungarian, Finn, the nomad workers of the world," who "are Americans to us because they learned to read in America," but who "understand Russian because it is spoken around them." Their readers, Borodin argued, needed not "clever writing" but help to "function efficiently in Soviet enterprises" – hence his willingness to "take some Russian articles;" that is, translations from the Soviet press.[70] By 1935 the paper carried regular columns of statistics lauding the successes of the Second Five-Year Plan along with more reporting of high culture – such as Bennett's review of a new production of *Carmen* – and less humor and international news than it had a few years earlier.[71]

Even as it provided fewer of the "snappy American articles" favored by Strong and more Soviet-style analysis, the *Moscow News* continued to publish articles that depicted Americans in the act of observing the Soviet Union.[72] After she returned from a book tour in the United States to promote her memoir *I Change Worlds*, a work structured in large part around explaining her realization that "party membership had begun to seem inevitable," Strong contributed sunny articles on the state of collective farming.[73] She emphasized her personal observations of Soviet progress, of obstacles decisively overcome, as in this passage:

> Five years ago [1930], when I traversed the southern steppe lands of the Ukraine, the soil was criss-crossed by a hundred narrow strips of privately owned land, separated from each other by boundary ridges of weeds. Three years ago, though the boundary ridges were broken, the weeds, encouraged by inefficient farming and sabotage, had filled large areas with their waist-high growth. Today the weeds have been beaten back to the gutters of the roadways.... Green shoots of winter wheat breaking from black soil sweep unchecked to the horizon, in undulating prairies marked by no fence or boundary ridge.[74]

In such articles she offered a glorious view of the successes of collectivization, reflected in the eyes of the first graduates from the collective farm's seven-year

70 Strong, *I Change*, 408–10.

71 Milly B. Mitchell, "A New Version of 'Carmen' by Stanislavski," *MN*, 9 May 1935. Much of the article was reprinted in "Four Carmens in Moscow," *NYT*, 2 June 1935.

72 Strong, *I Change*, 406.

73 Ibid., 414; Strong and Keyssar, *Right in Her Soul*, 163.

74 Anna Louise Strong, "I Visit a Collective Farm in the Ukraine," *MN*, 7 November 1935. See also, Strong, "Pioneers Hew Collective Farms out of Birobijan Wilderness," *MN*, 30 May 1935.

school that "seemed to sparkle with an even livelier electricity than that which came by wire from Dnieper Dam to the streets of the village."

A series of articles on collective farming by Robert Merriman, a graduate student in economics at the University of California at Berkeley, who traveled to the Soviet Union in 1934 to study the Soviet economy, similarly emphasized eyewitness observation of Soviet achievements. Adopting a more detached and scientific tone than Strong, Merriman reported both statistics and conversations with "the more enlightened collective farmers" that verified his picture of collective farming as a successful "agricultural system which is more revolutionary than any previously known."[75] In a memoir published in 1986, Merriman's widow Marion represented Bennett as skeptical of such absolute claims, and her husband, whom she quoted speaking in terms that echoed his articles in the *Moscow News*, as an objective observer, who merely reported "what I saw as an economist."[76] She explicitly denied that he was a communist – a denial that does not square with the autobiography Merriman wrote when he joined the International Brigades.[77] Indeed the articles' unremitting optimism, not to mention their publication in the *Moscow News*, suggests that Merriman saw not only as an economist but also as a communist.

In his contribution to *The God that Failed* (1950), the by then disillusioned Fischer described himself and, by extension, his journalism in the 1930s as looking at the Soviet Union "through the magnifying glass of hope." The metaphor suggested that he and others who trumpeted Soviet achievements saw clearly but partially and with a good measure of exaggeration. Drawing, as did Strong, on powerful personal observations, Fischer recalled his visits to the Dnieprostroi Dam: "With the chief Soviet engineer I climbed over the boulders on the river-bed when the water was first pumped away, and five years later I drove in a car over the mighty concrete wall, more than a hundred feet high and a third of a mile long, which rested on those boulders." Fischer contrasted such emotionally charged and authentic memories to socialist realism, which he defined as "the Soviet device for distorting the truth." Yet, as Fischer himself implied, the two instruments – his magnifying glass and the Soviet truth-distorting device – had more in common than he might care to admit. Both worked by "treat[ing] the present as though it did not exist" – or as though it were unimportant – "and the future as if it had already arrived."[78] The difference was that the Soviet device could work on

75 R. H. Merriman, "Among Collective Farmers in the Tatar Republic," *MN*, 24 October 1935; Merriman, "Some Collective Farm Problems and How They're Being Solved," *MN*, 14 November 1935.

76 Merriman and Lerude, *American Commander*, 55. John Scott represents Merriman in similar terms, *Behind the Urals: An American Worker in Russia's City of Steel* (1942; reprint, Bloomington: Indiana University Press, 1989), 209.

77 See Chapter 4.

78 Louis Fischer in Richard Crossman, ed., *The God that Failed* (1950; reprint, New York: Bantam Books, 1965), 186–7.

observations resistant to Fischer's magnifying glass, namely the 1939 Nazi-Soviet Pact, which he viewed as the "gravestone of Bolshevik internationalism."[79] "Seeing" with the heart – or through the magnifying glass of hope – was not always easy or natural, but was essential and compelling to people such as Bennett, who refused to understand themselves as liars, while seeking to reconcile the observed "ragged, filthy child, about 10" begging in central Moscow with the conviction that "the 140,000,000 workers and peasants are better off now than they've been before – and in many ways better off than the same class of any country on earth."[80]

"Karl Meredith Did Not Feel Fully at Home in the USSR"

Learning how to see "correctly" constituted a central component of the Lenin School curriculum. Students, like *Moscow News* reporters, visited factories and collective farms and were expected to describe what they saw in articles both for the Soviet press and for communists back home. They also engaged in propaganda work, describing for sometimes skeptical Soviet workers the (wretched) conditions and revolutionary struggles of the working class in the West. In both cases, their pictures had to magnify the right details and put them in the proper context. Students had to learn, as the American communist Karl Meredith, who was ultimately expelled from the Lenin School, did not, to view the Soviet Union from the perspective of a "proletarian revolutionary" rather than a "bourgeois statistician."[81]

In 1930, incoming Lenin School students participated in "practical work," visiting factories in Moscow, Leningrad, Nizhnii Novgorod, and Ivanovo-Voznesensk even before classes started. The program of excursions aimed to "acquaint students with concrete examples of the practice of socialist construction in the USSR."[82] Factory tours began with a sixty- or ninety-minute discussion with a representative of the factory's party committee, after which students examined the production process, engaged in conversations with workers, and listened to prepared talks over lunch. While traveling in the Soviet Union, the students, divided into language groups, also undertook an extensive program of "international propaganda."[83] In the course of their two-week excursion, the French group, for example, made eighty-two speeches in factories, clubs,

79 Fischer, *God*, 201.

80 Bennett to Esther [Johnson?], 25 April [1931?], Bennett Papers, Box 1, Folder 21; Bennett to Ethel [Bogardus?], 23 May [1931?], ibid.

81 "Resolution on the Expulsion of Karl Meredith from the L. S.," 14 May 1936, RGASPI, f. 531, op. 1, d. 167, l. 11.

82 "Otchet o rabote komissii po priemu novykh studentov," [1930], RGASPI, f. 531, op. 1, d. 31, ll. 15–15ob.

83 Ibid., ll. 16ob, 18ob. See also, "Ob"iasnitel'naia zapiska k planu uchebnoi i partiino-vostpitatel'noi raboty MLSh," 1933–4, RGASPI, f. 531, op. 1, d. 43, ll. 80–1; "Ob"iasnitel'naia zapiska k planu uchebnoi i partiino-vostpitatel'noi raboty MLSh," 1934–5, ibid., ll. 91ob–2ob.

and Red Army units, reaching twenty thousand people. One of the English-language groups organized fifty-five speeches and wrote twenty-two articles for the local press and twenty-three for the foreign press. The talks reportedly inspired Soviet workers to undertake shock work and engage in socialist competition – both heavily promoted work speedups during the First Five-Year Plan – as well as to contribute funds to aid political prisoners in capitalist countries.[84]

When students visited Soviet factories and met Soviet workers, they gained a new and, the report on the 1930 excursions suggested, generally "accurate" view of Soviet life. For example, the German group that visited Nizhnii Novgorod affirmed that the trip had allowed them "to see that socialist construction is the flesh and blood of Soviet workers, that, as shown by the facts, the Five-Year Plan in four years is carried out by the real enthusiasm of the working class."[85] The Russian-speaking group had "clearly seen how local party organizations struggle against difficulties," which they attributed to the negative influence of "kulaks," "right and left opportunists," and "conciliators." The report concluded that the excursions offered a powerful means of helping students "to overcome incorrect representations of Soviet reality," including the "very negative impression" of Moscow that a few comrades had formed when they observed queues for food in the capital.[86]

The emphasis on the difficulty of overcoming "backwardness" that figured so prominently in the *Moscow News*'s coverage of industrialization and collectivization also appeared in reports on "practical work" at the Lenin School, often explicitly attached to concerns about identifying – and quashing – political opponents. When some workers in Leningrad told the recently arrived students to "let workers overseas know that Russian workers are dying of starvation," the students were allegedly "able to discern . . . the impact of kulak ideology on some unstable elements among the workers." Moreover, they recognized the "unstable" workers as "newly arrived from the village;" that is, scarcely distinguishable from (backward) peasants.[87] The students' "discernment" can be understood as the result of the fact that they "succumbed" to the justifications "cogently presented" by their Soviet minders, as the disillusioned communist Fred Beal – one of the organizers of the 1929 Gastonia, North Carolina, textile strike, who had jumped bail and fled to the Soviet Union– argued in his 1937 memoir.[88] The instructors, however, took the students' conclusions as evidence that their charges "saw" clearly. When students themselves demonstrated "unhealthy attitudes" – asserting, for example, that

84 "Otchet o rabote," ll. 19, 20. See also "Resolution on Practical Work of Sector 'D,' 1934," 3 September 1934, RGASPI, f. 531, op. 1, d. 166, l. 7.

85 "Otchet o rabote, " ll. 21ob-2.

86 Ibid., l. 22ob.

87 Ibid., l. 23.

88 Fred E. Beal, *Proletarian Journey: New England, Gastonia, Moscow* (New York: Hillman-Curl, 1937), 243. Beal briefly attended the Lenin School, ibid., 263.

Czechoslovak workers and Spanish peasants were more politically developed than their Soviet counterparts or that "Russian workers live in awful conditions" – they were met with their peers' sharp rebukes. The report on the 1930 excursions noted that students who made inaccurate observations "recognized their errors – although how sincerely must be verified."[89]

Students had greater opportunity to observe "backward" Russia when they undertook summer practical work outside the major industrial centers, often visiting collective farms. On such visits students were supposed to gain practical experience in "mobilizing the masses" and refuting, as one 1934 report put it, "the false theories, lies, and slanders of the bourgeoisie and their allies, the social-fascists."[90] Their reports often emphasized that foreign communists' descriptions of the capitalist West motivated Soviet workers. Among the most effective speakers were African American students, who described American racism.[91] Students who paid too much attention to Soviet shortcomings, such as an American comrade who was disturbed by the sight of armed Red Army soldiers in the countryside and who expressed – in Russian – his judgment that workers' apartments were "very bad," risked aligning themselves with "antiproletarian" and anti-Soviet elements.[92] On the other hand, students who went too far in the direction of exaggerating Soviet achievements and criticizing the West, as did Spanish students visiting the Tatar Republic in 1934 who claimed that Spain had neither hospitals nor labor laws, risked undermining their credibility with Soviet workers.[93]

The theme of "backwardness" comes out more forcefully in retrospective accounts of students' practical work in the countryside. British communist Harry Wicks, looking back on the youthful communist commitment that he had long since renounced, remembered the summer of 1929, when he visited Dagestan in the North Caucasus, as a rude awakening: "With our heads full of Socialism in One Country, our eyes showed us social relations which were pre-feudal," particularly with regard to the treatment of women. He described the shock among the visiting students as mutual and deeply felt; "no discussion was necessary, we could see each other's faces."[94] Although Wicks seemed to take the experience, at least in anticommunist retrospect, as an indicator of the failure, if not futility, of the Soviet project, Steve Nelson, a less bitter former communist who visited collective farms in the summer of 1932, remembered learning a more hopeful lesson. Recalling the "unsettling" observation that

89 "Otchet o rabote," l. 23.

90 "Resolution on Practical Work of Sector 'D,'" l. 1.

91 "Dokladnaia zapiska o rabota sektora 'D' v vostochnoi sibiri," 28 August 1934, RGASPI, f. 531, op. 1, d. 166, l. 13.

92 Ibid., l. 15.

93 "Otchet o letnei praktike (sektora 'L')," 2 November 1934, RGASPI, f. 531, op. 1, d. 183, l. 63.

94 Harry Wicks, *Keeping My Head: The Memoirs of a British Bolshevik* (London: Socialist Platform, 1992), 117.

collective farm leaders "packed pistols," Nelson, even in 1981, seemed ready to take at face value their explanation that "there are still White Guards and counterrevolutionaries around."[95] He also remembered seeing such disturbing details as evidence of the "contradictions that arose from the efforts to build an industrialized society out of an underdeveloped agrarian country."[96] He "saw this inefficiency – you couldn't help but see it – but side by side with it I saw an effort to do something great."[97]

A student who proved unable or unwilling to see at least the beginnings of "something great" might be deemed, as Karl Meredith (school pseudonym, possibly for Karl Lochner) was in May 1936, "unfit to be a student at the Lenin School."[98] Although the charges leveled against Meredith included holding himself "aloof" from the collective, violating party discipline, and having a "very irresponsible attitude to Party assignments," his fundamental transgression was a desire to return home. Summarizing "the reasons for his request to leave for the United States," the resolution expelling him from the school emphasized that "*Karl Meredith did not feel fully at home in the USSR.*"[99] He had, according to the resolution, developed an unhealthy "attitude to socialist construction in the USSR." The root of the problem was his "mechanical, typically bourgeois method of comparison of figures," which allowed him to reach the "erroneous conclusion that the standard of living in the USSR is lower than in the USA." In short, he did not know or refused to learn how to view the Soviet Union correctly: "Declaring that he was 'looking at the USSR *objectively*,' he began looking for shortcomings."[100] Moreover, he persisted in his incorrect "views of the Soviet Union," despite opportunities, notably in the course of practical work in the Donbas, "to convince himself by seeing for himself."[101]

Foreign communists who lived, often for many years, in the Soviet Union had ample opportunity to see all kinds of inefficiencies and failures, not to mention evidence of political repression. For Lenin School students, "practical work" provided an essential test of their commitment to the cause, one that went well beyond a commitment to ideological principles. Confronted with difficult observed truths, international communists had to find ways of seeing something great and feeling at home in the Soviet Union.

95 Steve Nelson, James R. Barrett, and Rob Ruck, *Steve Nelson, American Radical* (Pittsburgh: University of Pittsburgh Press, 1981), 134.

96 Ibid., 135.

97 Ibid., 135–6.

98 "Resolution on the Expulsion," l. 10. On Lochner, see "Spisok: Studentov po stranam," 7 April 1936, RGASPI, f. 531, op. 1, d. 106, l. 35.

99 Emphasis in original. "Resolution on the Expulsion," ll. 10, 11. For his request see Karl Meredith to Comrade Griffin, 21 January 1935, ibid., l. 14.

100 Emphasis in original. "Resolution on the Expulsion," l. 11.

101 Ibid., l. 12.

"Rationalizing Works on Me like an Acid": Feeling the Revolution

In an 18 April 1934 letter to an old friend, Bennett recounted the arrest of her Russian husband of about two years, Evgenii Vasilevich Konstantinov. By the time she wrote the letter, Konstantinov, an actor, was "on his way to Siberia under a three year sentence in a concentration camp." The Soviet political police (OGPU), she wrote, had "found him guilty of homosexuality." Bennett took the precaution of having Duranty mail the letter for her from Berlin.[102]

In the letter, Bennett described walking into Konstantinov's apartment just after midnight on 27 February to find a search already underway. Her first thought "was confusion." Perhaps "the agents were guests, friends of [Z]henya's." When she asked "what's this... what does this mean?" and her husband replied, "an [OGPU] search," they were warned against speaking "any foreign language." The agent, "with what he seemed to think was a bright smile," told her they were looking for guns. The search went on until three o'clock in the morning, with Bennett apparently wisecracking throughout. When one of the agents took an interest in a *New Yorker* magazine, for example, she "assured him that it was an [A]merican humorous magazine, much like the soviet 'Crocodile,' except that as he could see it was printed on much better paper."[103]

Not until early April was Bennett able to confirm the reason for her husband's arrest. As she explained in her letter, on 8 March "the press carried a *new law*, the crime of being a homosexual, (mind, there was no law against this practice previously)."[104] At the same time she heard of the arrests of one Victor Pavilovich [sic], presumably someone associated with the *Moscow News*, and of two homosexual men who worked at the Bolshoi Theater. She thus initially concluded that her husband, who had told her about earlier affairs "some with women and some with *men*," was "being held as a witness." Only a month later did she manage to arrange a meeting with the prosecutor, who informed her that Konstantinov had been found guilty of homosexuality. When Bennett protested that "he's been living with me for two years," the prosecutor produced a statement signed by her husband confessing to have "taken part in homosexual evenings in 1933." Whether a "homosexual evening," as Bennett rather indelicately put it, "meant an evening at which homos were present, or whether [Z]henya actually committed acts of homosexuality" she was never able to learn. She did, however, get permission to visit him in exile north of Novosibirsk in July.

Although Bennett often affected a hard-boiled tone in her letters about the arrest, it seems to have struck a deep blow, posing a far greater challenge to

102 Bennett to Marjory [McKillop], 18 April [1934], Bennett Papers, Box 1, Folder 21.

103 On Bennett's penchant for wisecracking, see Si-lan Chen Leyda, *Footnote to History* (New York: Dance Horizons, 1984), 70.

104 Emphasis in original. Bennett to Marjory [McKillop], 18 April [1934].

her faith in the revolution than the material hardships of Soviet life. For all her bluster, Bennett characterized herself to friends as someone who "feels first and thinks after."[105] Freda Utley, a British communist then living in Moscow, remembered finding Bennett after the arrest "in tears in her hotel room," a description that rings true despite the fact by the time she wrote her memoir, Utley was a vocal anticommunist.[106] Before her husband's arrest, Bennett described her strategy for coping with all that was "bitter . . . and dark, past understanding" in the Soviet Union: The "thing you have to do about Russia," she advised in a letter, "is what you do about any other 'faith.' You set your heart to know they are right . . . and then, when you see things that shudder your bones, you close your eyes and say . . . 'facts are not important.'"[107] After Konstantinov's arrest, setting her heart apparently became more punishing. In an August 1934 letter to a friend, Bennett introduced her situation with typical bravado, writing, "Well, the boy friend falls into the hands of the law six months ago . . . and then one rationalizes." However, she confessed, "Rationalizing works on me like an acid. It eats away my flesh while blanching my mind. Is that right? Blanching? Bleaching, perhaps."[108]

Harry Whyte, the other *Moscow News* staffer who left a detailed rumination on the new law recriminalizing homosexuality, likewise emphasized that it was eating away at his sense of himself in the Soviet Union. Writing to Stalin in May 1934, Whyte began with a question that he deemed "of great importance for a large number of communists in the USSR and other countries as well": "Can a homosexual be considered a person worthy of becoming a member of the Communist Party?" Concluding that the "law just published about criminal sodomy . . . obviously means that a homosexual cannot be considered worthy," Whyte, who described himself as "personally interested in this question," produced a lengthy analysis, running to well over three thousand words, of the law's flimsy "theoretical basis." The personal pain was clearest in Whyte's admission that he had "visited two psychiatrists to ask them if it is possible to 'cure' homosexuality" because he needed "some way out of this damned dilemma."[109]

Both Bennett and Whyte struggled to maintain faith in communism and deference to Bolshevik understandings of the best interests of the revolution as they worked to make sense of the arrests of their lovers. Bennett seemed to accept at face value the notion that the arrest served some larger, if murky, political purpose. In the letter she entrusted to Duranty, she explained that her

[105] Bennett to Esther [Johnson?], 26 April [1931?], Bennett Papers, Box 1 Folder 21; see also Bennett to Blake, 21 April [1931?], ibid.
[106] Freda Utley, *Lost Illusion* (Philadelphia: Fireside Press, 1948), 238.
[107] Bennett to Florence, 27 January [1932?], Bennett papers, Box 2 Folder 1.
[108] Bennett to Lionel [Houser?], 18 August 1934, Bennett Papers, Box 2 Folder 2.
[109] Whyte, "Letter," 89, 90, 95.

situation had to be understood "in the light of the Revolution . . . they have decided that homosexuality is a threatening evil . . . and thus, they set about stamping out homosexuality."[110] An article she contributed to the *New York Times* in 1935 offers an oblique view of how she may have explained the Soviet decision to recriminalize homosexuality. Outlining the "stricter social laws" that redefined the place of Soviet women, Bennett denied that the new emphasis on family life marked a "return to Philistine morals." Rather, she described the "struggle for a healthy family life" – potentially including the recriminalization of sodomy, which the article did not mention –as "a struggle for the continuation of the species."[111]

Even if she did not fully understand or embrace the supposed logic of these "stricter social laws," Bennett represented herself in her letters as remaining, or trying to remain, emotionally committed to the Soviet project. After visiting Konstantinov in Siberia, Bennett was still able to declare, "There is no answer . . . except scientific socialism." She had, she reported, found her husband "in splendid health . . . sunburned and with fine muscles . . . and in cheerful spirits."[112] The former actor and "dancer of small parts at the Grand Opera House" was a "member of the Agitation Propaganda Brigade," traveling "throughout the Siberian countryside giving programs aimed at raising the spirits of collective farmers."[113] She knew "full well," she wrote another friend, "that it was necessary for him to have experienced some such realities as he has seen." Nonetheless, with "friends" who insisted that "'it will do him good,' [I] am restrained, by heaven knows only what inner strength, from clouting in the nose."[114]

The more politically sophisticated Whyte attempted to reconcile the emerging communist equation of fascism with homosexuality with the promise of a communist private sphere. As historian Dan Healey notes, the "virulent propaganda war" between fascism and communism that followed Adolf Hitler's rise to power "significantly contributed to justifications for the decision to recriminalize sodomy" in the Soviet Union.[115] *The Brown Book of the Hitler Terror and the Burning of the Reichstag*, written by a collective of German communists in exile – which was published in 1933, translated into twenty languages, and distributed in large print runs in twenty-six countries – constituted a particularly prominent weapon in this propaganda war. Debunking the myth of the Reichstag fire as the result of a communist conspiracy, the book, which Whyte referenced, proposed instead "a conspiracy of homosexual

110 Bennett to Marjory, 18 February [1934], Bennett Papers, Box 1, Folder 21.

111 Bennett, "Soviet Russia Discovers 'Home, Sweet, Home,'" *NYT*, 10 November 1935.

112 Bennett to Esther [Johnson?], 3 October [1934], Bennett Papers, Box 2, Folder 2. See also Bennett to Bill, 3 October [1934], ibid.

113 Bennett to Cleo, 20 June [1934], Bennett Papers, Box 1, Folder 21.

114 Bennett to Grace [Gould], [September 1934], Bennett Papers, Box 2, Folder 42.

115 Healey, *Homosexual Desire*, 182.

Nazis."[116] It asserted that inquiries into the arsonist Marinus van der Lubbe's life in his hometown of Leyden "have definitely established the fact that he was homosexual" and alleged that he had had homosexual relations with, among other Nazis, Ernst Röhm. It was precisely these "homosexual connections with National Socialist leaders and his material dependence on them [that] made him obedient and willing to carry out the incendiary's part."[117] Whyte endorsed this conclusion, but also called attention to the book's condemnation of the Nazis' attack on Magnus Hirschfeld, the "'liberator' of the homosexual movement."[118] Attempting to find an acceptable theoretical basis for his defense of homosexuality, he emphasized that Friedrich Engels had attacked homosexuality only when "it took the form of a political organization by specific bourgeois elements." Moreover, because psychiatrists had informed him that homosexuality was often "incurable," Whyte concluded that there was "no justification for making these people criminals on the basis of their distinguishing features, which they are in no way responsible for creating, which they cannot change, even if they wanted to."[119] His logic failed to impress Stalin, who noted the following in the letter's margin: "To the archives. An idiot and a degenerate."

Whyte ultimately left the Soviet Union, probably in late 1935 or early 1936. However, until November 1935, he was still contributing pieces on Soviet theater, his usual subject, to the *Moscow News*.[120] After his departure, he seems to have remained a communist or was aligned with the Communist Party at least for a time, contributing in 1936 to *Left Review*, the journal of the British branch of the Writers' International.[121] In the years of the Popular Front against fascism, the Soviet Union's relatively quiet "proscription of male homosexuality" perhaps appeared a lesser evil when contrasted with "Hitler's loud and crude antihomosexual campaigning."[122]

For reasons both personal and political, Bennett remained in Moscow until late 1936, when she left to join the antifascist struggle in Spain. In the April 1934 letter carried out of the Soviet Union by Duranty, Bennett wrote that she planned to stay to the end of her husband's term "unless the bolos give

116 Harry Oosterhuis, "The 'Jews' of the Antifascist Left: Homosexuality and Socialist Resistance to Nazism," *Journal of Homosexuality* 29, no. 2/3 (1995): 233. On the writing of the book, see Gustav Regler, *The Owl of Minerva*, trans. Norman Denny (London: Rupert Hart-Davis, 1959), 162–4.

117 World Committee for the Victims of German Fascism, *The Brown Book of the Hitler Terror and the Burning of the Reichstag* (New York: A. A. Knopf, 1933), 46, 48, 52.

118 Whyte, "Letter," 92.

119 Ibid., 97.

120 H. O. Whyte, "Chelyuskin Epic Now a Play," *MN*, 21 November 1935.

121 H. O. Whyte, "Goodbye to a' That!," *Left Review* 2, no. 14 (November 1936): 790–1. Ashleigh was also a contributor: "Fred Ellis in London: Famous Revolutionary Artist Interviewed by Charles Ashleigh," *Left Review* 2, no. 12 (September 1936): 608–12; Charles Ashleigh, "It Mustn't Happen Here," *Left Review* 2, no. 4 (January 1936): 188–91.

122 Healey, *Homosexual Desire*, 183.

me an unrequested exit visa."[123] Also keeping her in Moscow, at least for a time, was an intense and ultimately unhappy affair with Lindsay Parrott, the head of the Moscow bureau of the International News Service (INS). When Parrott's wife, Marian Moore, who was apparently having an affair of her own, refused to agree to a divorce, Parrott ended the relationship with Bennett. In a letter with no date and the time "2 am," she accused Parrott of trying "to salve what appears to be your conscience about me with 'jobs'" for the *New York Times*, "a fair swap of course for having the correspondent's colony of [M]oscow... believe that while being [M]arion [M]oore's 'best friend' [I] was stealing or trying to steal her husband."[124] In 1935, Bennett did begin to work as a "correspondent for the capitalist press," writing for the *New YorkTimes* when Duranty was out of the country, although she contined to contribute to the *Moscow News* until at least mid-1935.[125]

By early 1936, Bennett was apparently working exclusively for the "capitalist press," having taken over what was left of the INS's Moscow operation after Parrott's departure in December 1935. Parrott, she reported, had left her exactly "1 rubber stamp" and "200 sheet of letter head paper."[126] He had also passed the apartment assigned to the agency "to an undersecretary of the Chinese embassy," leaving Bennett to operate the bureau from her apartment, from which she was subsequently evicted.[127] Bennett seems to have understood her work for INS, which she called "the lousey [H]earst outfit," as to some degree an abandonment of her ideals, but as preferable to writing the "sob stuff rubbish" that a job in America would require.[128]

Bennett's decision to take a position with the Spanish Republic's foreign propaganda service can thus be understood as allowing her both to reclaim her ideals and to satisfy her professional interest in reporting on "this war business."[129] She apparently divorced Konstantinov in late 1936, amending

[123] Bennett to Marjory [McKillop], 18 April [1934].

[124] Bennett to Lindsay [Parrott], [1935?], 2 am, Bennett Papers, Box 2, Folder 3. Parrott published under the name "Lindsay," but also used "Lindesay." His wife's name was spelled "Marian."

[125] Utley, *Odyssey of a Liberal*, 246; Bennett, "Soviet Russia"; Milly Bennett, "Russia's New Hero Sticks to Mine," *NYT*, 8 December 1935; Milly B. Mitchell, "Preserving an Ancient Folk Art," *MN*, 6 June 1935.

[126] Bennett to [Elmer Roessner], [1936], Bennett Papers, Box 4, Folder 22; Bennett to William Hillman, 17 September 1936, Bennett Papers, Box 2, Folder 51.

[127] Bennett to International News Service, 2 March 1936, Bennett Papers, Box 2, Folder 51; Loy W. Henderson, Chargé d'Affaires ad Interim to Secretary of State, 18 January 1936, NACP, RG 59, 811.91261/137; Milton K. Wells, American Vice Consul, Valencia to Secretary of State, 7 November 1937, NACP, RG 59, 800.00B Mitchell, Mildred B./1.

[128] Bennett to [Elmer Roessner], [1936], Bennett Papers, Box 4, Folder 22; See also Falkowski's account of a meeting with her in October 1936, Falkowski Papers, Box 1, Folder 5.

[129] Bennett to [Elmer Roessner], [1936]; "Ministerio del Estado, El Jefe de la Oficina de Prensa," 19 January 1937, Bennett Papers, Box 1, Folder 17.

her U.S. passport in November to reflect a change in marital status.[130] By January 1937, his three-year term would have been nearing an end. Some fifty years later, Marion Merriman, who also made her way to Spain in 1937, remembered that Bennett "had left her Russian ballet-dancing husband, though she continued to send money to his family in Moscow."[131] A year or so after she left for Spain, Bennett told the story of her departure in her signature hard-boiled style, emphasizing less professional ambition, political ideals, or personal entanglements than simple adventure. She recalled that William Bullitt, the American ambassador to the Soviet Union, had said to her when she presented her papers, "My God, girl, dont [sic] go to Spain. After six years in Russia! Go somewhere and relax. Bermuda where the sands are white and the seas are blue." And she had replied, "You'd go yourself, Bill, if you could.... Bullitt signed my papers."[132]

Although largely invisible in Bennett's contemporary letters and stories, the sense of fear and hope that looms so large in other foreigners' retrospective accounts of 1936 in Moscow may also have contributed to her decision to leave for Spain. In his *God that Failed* essay, Fischer recalled that even before the first of the great show trials in August 1936, he had vaguely perceived that a "black plague cast its shadows" over Moscow, and he "gladly left Russia to be near the battle" in Spain, the "front line against Fascism." He welcomed the prospect of an open struggle:"Death stalked Russia in the cellar. Death came to Spain in open combat in the sun." Like "innumerable persons in the Soviet Union," Fischer "hoped that Spain would be a spiritual blood transfusion for the prostrate élan of Bolshevism."[133] The German communist Gustav Regler, a contributor to *The Brown Book*, remembered the Moscow mood in remarkably similar terms. In retrospect he characterized his reaction to the news of war in Spain as one of "grotesque" joy: "I felt as though the grey sky overhanging the Russian town had suddenly cleared." He, too, saw in Spain the revolutionary spirit that had once drawn him to the Soviet Union, and he, too, looked forward to the "obvious dangers" that he would face there.[134]

Bennett's contemporary letters and stories lack this retrospective coherence. Nonetheless, her writing hinted at the sense that Spain represented a place to recapture the idealism and internationalism of the Russian Revolution. In a story she sent to her agent Hal Matson she described a rooftop gathering in Madrid of a cosmopolitan group of writers – Nordahl Grieg from Norway, Martin Andersen Nexø from Denmark, Jef Last from the Netherlands, Ludwig

130 "Report made by Francis Butterworth, Jr.," 5 October 1942, FBI/Bennett; Wells to Secretary of State, 7 November 1937.

131 Merriman and Lerude, *American Commander*, 151.

132 "I couldn't say," Bennett Papers, Box 9, Folder 5.

133 Fischer, *God*, 196, 197, 199. Arthur Koestler makes a similar point, ibid., 55.

134 Regler, *Owl*, 258, 271; Katerina Clark, *Moscow, the Fourth Rome: Stalinism, Cosmopolitanism, and the Evolution of Soviet Culture, 1931–1941* (Cambridge, MA: Harvard University Press, 2011), 243, 254–5.

Renn from Germany, and Aleksander Fadeev from the Soviet Union. Grieg, who Bennett knew from her days in China, had just returned to Madrid from the front, "heartsick" that the "iron ring" around the city "would not be broken." Renn "who hates war, but fights this one, is telling someone why." Fadeev was singing in a "deep bass" that made Bennett "think of the voices of the Russian deacons in the dim, little incense filled orthodox churches on Easter midnight," except that Fadeev "was singing of the 'Red Partisan' soldier who died on the taiga in the long ago Soviet Civil War."[135] In Spain, Bennett suggested, one felt the moving and heroic emotions of the Russian Revolution. And it was in Spain that she finally decided to apply for membership in the Communist Party.

135 "milly bennett for hal matson," [1938?], Bennett Papers, Box 9, Folder 5.

PART II

BEING BOLSHEVIK: MAKING HISTORY IN SPAIN, 1936–1939

3

"All Advanced and Progressive Humanity"

During the civil war, one of the first things that new arrivals in Republican Spain noticed was, as Finnish American volunteer Ranse Edward Arvola wrote in a letter home, "This thing sure is International." The mix of languages in the air and on posters was breathtaking. Arvola, a working-class communist from Michigan who spoke English and Finnish, wished that "I knew a dozen languages now."[1] In Paris on his way to Spain, William Sennett wrote his wife, "I have been trying to talk in so many different languages that by the time I come home I'll be talking broken English. I get along best speaking German. It's somewhat like Yiddish," his first language as the child of Russian Jewish immigrants in Chicago.[2] In the first pages of the journal he kept in Spain, American novelist Alvah Bessie described the International Brigades' base at Figueras in early 1938 as a "babble of tongues." He saw "notices posted in every language, publications ditto" and transcribed the slogan "Workers of the World, Unite!" displayed in Spanish, German, French, Polish, and Italian. He concluded that "comradeship between these men, young and old, of every land, real and touching."[3]

1 Ranse Edward Arvola to H[elen Kruth] and F[annie Arvola], 3 June 1937, Mito Kruth Papers, ALBA 240, Box 1, Folder 1, Tamiment Library/Robert F. Wagner Labor Archives, New York University.

2 William Sennett to Gussie [Machen], 5 March 1937, Veterans of the Abraham Lincoln Brigade, Bay Area Post, (VALB), BANC MSS 71/105 z, Container 1, Bancroft Library, University of California, Berkeley. Sennett and Augusta (Gussie) Machen were married in October 1938, William Sennett, "Communist Functionary and Corporate Executive," an oral history conducted 1981 and 1982 by Marshall Windmiller, Regional Oral History Office, The Bancroft Library, University of California, Berkeley, 1984, 42; on his experiences in Paris, see ibid., 67–70.

3 Alvah Bessie, *Alvah Bessie's Civil War Notebooks*, ed. Dan Bessie (Lexington: University of Kentucky Press, 2002), 2.

Such impressions of "a babble of tongues" accurately reflected the makeup of the International Brigades. Over the course of the war, perhaps thirty-five thousand volunteers from fifty-three countries, speaking about twenty different languages, served in Spain. Although they constituted only a small fraction of the Republic's military forces – about 2 percent – they had great symbolic and often military significance.[4] The first international volunteers were people who happened to be in Spain in July 1936 at the time of the military uprising against the Republic. The International Brigades themselves had their origin in the 18 September 1936 decision of the Comintern's executive committee to "recruit volunteers having military experience among workers of all countries, with the purpose of sending them to Spain."[5] Paris emerged as the key center of recruitment and transport to Spain; the critical organizing role of the Comintern and communist parties was largely hidden. That many leading communists took noms de guerre in Spain added to the conspiratorial atmosphere. The Soviets worked to recruit foreigners resident in the Soviet Union, ultimately sending about 589 to Spain.[6] Almost immediately after the decision to organize the Brigades, the authorities at the Lenin School began compiling information on current students with military experience who might serve in Spain.[7] In February 1937, about thirty students – Swedish, Norwegian, British, Canadian, American, Czech, and Slovak – were recommended for "use."[8]

In October 1936, the first five hundred international volunteers arrived at the training base in Albacete, a small town about 250 kilometers (155 miles) southeast of Madrid on the plain of La Mancha. The base, like the Brigades themselves, was a Comintern – and thus ultimately Soviet – operation run on a day-to-day basis largely by West European communists. French communist André Marty, the first base commander, was succeeded by another French communist Vital Gayman (known as "Vidal"), who ran the base at Albacete from October 1936 until his removal in July 1937, the period of most

4 M. T. Meshcheriakov, "Sud'ba interbrigad v Ispanii po novym dokumentom," *Novaia i noveiashaia istoriia*,1993, no. 5: 20; Helen Graham, *The Spanish Republic at War, 1936–1939* (New York: Cambridge University Press, 2002), 175–7, 201, 356; Verle B. Johnston, *Legions of Babel: The International Brigades in the Spanish Civil War* (University Park: Pennsylvania State University Press, 1969), 56, 88–9.

5 Daniel Kowalsky, "The Soviet Union and the International Brigades, 1936–1939," *Journal of Slavic Military Studies* 19 (2006): 687; on the early volunteers, see Johnston, *Legions of Babel*, 28–32.

6 Meshcheriakov, "Sud'ba," 20.

7 "Svedeniia o studentakh leninskoi shkoly," 22 September 1936, Rossiiskii gosudarstvennyi arkhiv sotsial'no-politicheskoi istorii (RGASPI), f, 531, op. 1, d. 106, l. 101; "Spisok studentov LSh, sluzhivshikh na voennoi sluzhbe," 22 December 1936, ibid., l. 157. The identification of students' prior military experience suggests that the military training provided by the Lenin School was not the totality of graduates' "preparation for military service" in Spain as suggested in Harvey Klehr, John Earl Haynes, and Fridrickh Firsov, eds., *The Secret World of American Communism* (New Haven: Yale University Press, 1995), 204.

8 "Zav. Otdelom kadrov IKKI," 19 February 1937, RGASPI, f. 531, op. 1, d. 134, l. 1.

concentrated Soviet aid to the Republic.[9] In December 1936, Italian communist Luigi Longo (known as "Gallo"), who had served on the Madrid front, became Gayman's assistant as the base's general inspector.[10] The languages of business on the base – at least as reflected in the reports preserved in the archives – appear to have been French and Spanish. Working in this polyglot environment, the troops communicated in a mix of languages, perhaps something like what Finnish American volunteer Mito Kruth described as an "international jargon which slightly resembles French or Spanish."[11] As Wilfred Mendelson noted in a 1938 letter, Yiddish was the "real international language" among "Jews from Germany, France, England, Poland, Czech [sic], Hungary, Rumania."[12]

Although establishing the reality of the "babble" is relatively straightforward, assessing the level and reality of "comradeship" is more complicated. Despite the tendency of contemporaries and historians to describe battalions or brigades as, for example, "English" or "German," there was a great deal of linguistic and national diversity in most units. Such diversity, as Bessie's notebook and volunteers' letters home often attested, could create a "real and touching" sense of international solidarity. The very fact of linguistic diversity seemed to offer powerful evidence of international solidarity. However, what Longo tactfully characterized as "differences in language, military experience, and customs"[13] could also, as commissars' reports frequently noted, produce frictions within and between units, occasionally with unpleasant if not disastrous results.

Much of the early organization of the International Brigades was improvised and unsystematic as the base administration worked quickly to establish units able to assist in the critical defense of Madrid from Francisco Franco's advancing Nationalists. Between October and December 1936, brigade officials hastily organized battalions, primarily but not strictly on the basis of language. The Eleventh Brigade, which was dispatched to the Madrid front in the first week of

9 Meshcheriakov, "Sud'ba," 22; Kowalsky, "Soviet Union," 686, 687. The Bulgarian Georgii Damianov (known as Lt. Colonel Belov in Spain) succeeded Gayman on 1 August 1937; Wilhelm Zeisser (known as Gómez in Spain) took over on 15 November 1937; see Gómez's report of July 1938, in Ronald Radosh, Mary R. Habek, and Grigory Sevostianov, eds., *Spain Betrayed: The Soviet Union in the Spanish Civil War* (New Haven: Yale University Press, 2001), 465, 466. On Belov, see Fridrikh I. Firsov, "Dimitrov, the Comintern, and Stalinist Repression," in Barry McLoughlin and Kevin McDermott, eds., *Stalin's Terror: High Politics and Mass Repression in the Soviet Union* (Basingstoke: Palgrave Macmillan, 2003), 71.

10 Biographies of personnel in Brigades' commissariat, 29 October 1938, RGASPI, f. 545, op. 1, d. 61, l. 40: Gallo autobiography, 26 April 1938, ibid., ll. 1–4.

11 Mito Kruth to Helen [Kruth], 2 May 1937, Kruth Papers, Box 1, Folder 9.

12 Wilfred Mendelson to Folks, 22 June 1938, in Cary Nelson and Jefferson Hendricks, eds., *Madrid 1937: Letters of the Abraham Lincoln Brigade from the Spanish Civil War* (New York: Routledge, 1996), 40; see also William Herrick, *Jumping the Line: Adventures and Misadventures of an American Radical* (Madison: University of Wisconsin Press, 1998), 139.

13 "Doklad Voennogo komissariata interbrigad," RGASPI, f. 545, op. 1, d. 2, l. 3.

November 1936 and provided timely military and moral support to Republican forces, was quite heterogeneous in terms of both language and nationality. It brought together the mostly Austro-German Edgar André battalion; a company of British gunners; the predominantly Franco-Belgian Commune de Paris battalion; and the mostly Polish Dąbrowski battalion, which also included Bulgarians and Ukrainians.[14]

Until they were reorganized in August 1937, all the brigades were similarly mixed. The Twelfth Brigade, which was also rapidly set up and sent to defend Madrid in November, as well as the Thirteenth and Fourteenth Brigades established in December 1936, included diverse international assortments of troops, described in one report as "French or Franco-Belgians, Italians, Germans, or Slavs (Polish, Balkan)," with "Balkan" itself denoting diverse backgrounds and languages.[15] The Fifteenth International Brigade organized in February 1937 likewise included an English battalion, a French battalion, two companies of Slavs, an Italian battalion, and a Spanish battalion. The Americans arriving in January and February were formed into what they decided to call the "Abraham Lincoln battalion." The battalion joined the Fifteenth Brigade already deployed at the Jarama front, where the rebels were attempting to take the Madrid-Valencia road.[16]

In propaganda spread in the United States and Canada, the entire Fifteenth Brigade was often referred to as the "Abraham Lincoln Brigade," a situation that "created resentment among the comrades of other nationalities," who believed that "the Americans were seeking the hegemony of the Brigade."[17] In general, the naming of battalions after foreign heroes – imprisoned German communists Ernst Thälmann and Edgar André; Jarosław Dąbrowski, a Pole who died defending the Paris Commune; the Italian nationalist Giuseppe Garibaldi – had a strong negative "effect on the Spanish comrades," who from at least early 1937 participated in every International Brigade.[18] More Spaniards joined the Internationals in the autumn of 1937, when the brigades were incorporated into the Republican Army. Indeed by 1938 a combination of

[14] "La formation de la XVè Brigade," RGASPI, f. 545, op. 2, d. 32, l. 105; Nikolai Platoshkin, *Grazhdanskaia voina v Ispanii, 1936–1939 gg.* (Moscow: Olma Press, 2005), 221–2; Richard Baxell, *British Volunteers and the Spanish Civil War: The British Battalion in the International Brigades, 1936–1939* (New York: Routledge, 2004), 52; Johnston, *Legions of Babel*, 45–6; Burnett Bolloten, *The Spanish Civil War: Revolution and Counterrevolution* (Chapel Hill: University of North Carolina Press, 1991), 288–9; Hugh Thomas, *The Spanish Civil War: Revised Edition* (New York: Modern Library, 2001), 465–70.

[15] "La formation de la XVè Brigade," l. 105. See also Johnston, *Legions of Babel*, 59–64; Michael W. Jackson, *Fallen Sparrows: The International Brigades in the Spanish Civil War* (Philadelphia: American Philosophical Society, 1994), 18.

[16] "La formation de la XVè Brigade," ll. 107–9.

[17] "Report on the political development of the XV International Brigade," RGASPI, f. 545, op. 6, d. 21, l. 22.

[18] Ibid.

high losses and slowed recruitment from abroad made Spaniards the majority throughout the "International" Brigades.[19]

Although differences of both language and nationality could cause problems within the brigades, exactly what counted as a "national" group was not always clear. An analysis conducted in December 1937 of the Anglo-American group, for example, identified three "nationality" groups in the American section: "U.S." (2287), "Negro" (74), and "Latin" (110). The "U.S." group was further broken down into "Native American Born" (1252) and "Foreign Born" (1035). The English-speaking group also included British and Canadian volunteers, who were both "native" and "foreign born" and might be subdivided as such.[20] A later report on "two years of political and military work in the 15th Brigade" also described the brigade as nationally heterogeneous, but cataloged "five national groups": Cuban, Canadian, British, Spanish, and North American – a catchall term for those from the United States.[21] The African Americans were now apparently subsumed into "North American" – although "Canadian" remained a distinct nationality. Members of both groups, however, complained about "chauvinism" and being excluded from key posts in the unit.[22]

In conformity with the Popular Front line, the International Brigades were not an exclusively communist organization. They were open to all representatives of "advanced and progressive humanity," to quote Joseph Stalin's characterization of the supporters of the Loyalist cause who wished to fight fascism.[23] Indeed when they compiled statistics on the brigades, Comintern functionaries did not always include party affiliation.[24] Still, communists predominated. By one count 75 percent of the American contingent were party members or members of the Young Communist League (YCL).[25] In some cases people who had long been sympathizers joined or attempted to join the party in Spain. In this chapter I focus on communists, particularly those of long standing or those who had also worked or studied in the Soviet Union – groups with considerable overlap – as a means of examining how experiences in Spain interacted with earlier experiences and understandings of the cause.

The least visible group among the Internationals were Soviet citizens, although Spaniards and Internationals saw plenty of evidence of Soviet support

[19] On growing percentages of Spaniards in the Brigades see Mershcheriakov, "Sud'ba," 28–9; "Otchet nachal'nika Bazy interbrigad Vidalia o strukture i deiatel'nosti Bazy za period oktribria 1936 g. po 1937 g.," [report in French], RGASPI, f. 545, op. 2, d. 32, ll. 366–73.

[20] "Anglo-American Group Analysis: Personnel Section," 22 December 1937, RGASPI, f. 545, op. 6, d. 5, l. 10. Myron Momryk, "Hungarian Volunteers from Canada in the Spanish Civil War, 1936–1939," *Hungarian Studies Review* 24 (Spring 1997): 3–14; Myron Momryk, "Ukrainian Volunteers from Canada in the International Brigades, Spain, 1936–1939," *Journal of Ukrainian Studies* 16 (June 1991): 181–94.

[21] "Report on Two Years of Political and Military Work," RGASPI, f. 545, op. 2, d. 75a, l. 21.

[22] Ibid.; "Interview with Thomas Page," 16 December 1937, RGASPI f. 545, op. 3, d. 469, l. 2.

[23] *Pravda*, 16 October 1936.

[24] See statistics on volunteers arriving in 1938, RGASPI, f. 545, op. 6, d. 6.

[25] "Anglo-American Group Analysis," l. 10.

for the Republic – and Loyalists' enthusiasm for the Soviet Union. When he arrived in Spain from Moscow in 1937, what caught Robert Merriman's eye was an "interesting poster" in Barcelona featuring the Russian alphabet and advertising a "Course in Russian" sponsored by the socialist-affiliated Unión General de Trabajadores (UGT). At the International Brigades' base in Albacete he noted more posters drawing comparisons to the civil war in Russia and lauding Soviet aid.[26] Volunteers exulted over "our Soviet anti-aircraft guns giving the fascists' planes hell!"[27] They often, and sometimes with great enjoyment, watched Soviet films.[28] However, they saw few Soviet people. As American volunteer Don MacLeod observed in a letter home, "There are practically no Russian soldiers here," adding, "yet we all know that without Russia we would not be in the advantageous position we hold today."[29] Actually, about 2,200 Soviet military personnel – tank crews, pilots, and advisors – were active in Spain, but they were not integrated into the International Brigades. Rather, the Soviets remained under the aegis of a separate Red Army military mission known as "Operation X."[30]

The low profile of Soviet personnel allowed the Soviet Union to aid the Republic while publicly maintaining that it was honoring the Nonintervention Agreement. Sponsored by France and Britain in the summer of 1936, the agreement prohibited signatories, including the Soviet Union, Germany, and Italy, from intervening in the civil war, although neither the Germans nor the Italians allowed it to curtail their aid to the rebels. Some historians have also understood the secrecy of Soviet military involvement in Spain as evidence that the Soviet goal was not, as Stalin claimed, to defeat fascism, but rather to turn Spain into a Soviet satellite.[31] From this perspective the Internationals were Stalin's "Comintern soldiers," at best "duped" by Soviet professions of antifascism, at worst "spies in the making" – but certainly not the "freedom fighters" conjured in paeans to international solidarity in the fight against fascism.[32]

[26] Robert H. Merriman diary, vol. 1, 1 enero [1937], 5 diciembre (I refer to entries by the dates printed in the diary; however, the printed dates do not always correspond to the date of entry), Robert Merriman Papers, ALBA 191, Box 1, Folder 3.

[27] Ben Gardner [to Alice Gardner], 30 August 1937, VALB, Container 1.

[28] See Chapter 4. Mikhail Kol'tsov, *Ispankii dnevnik* (Moscow: Grifon, 2005), 27–8. Julian Graffy, *Chapaev* (London: I.B. Tauris, 2009), 88–90; José Cabeza San Deogracias, "Buscando héroes: La historia de Antonio Col como ejemplo del uso de la narrativa como propaganda durante la Guerra Civil española," *Revista Historia y Comunicación Social* 10 (2005): 37–50.

[29] Don McLeod to Stuart, 8 June 1937, VALB, Container 1. See also John Tisa, *Recalling the Good Fight: An Autobiography of the Spanish Civil War* (South Hadley, MA.: Bergin and Garvey, 1985), 117.

[30] Kowalsky, "Soviet Union," 686, 689; Iurii E. Ribalkin, *Operatsiia "X": Sovetskaia voennaia pomoshch' respublikanskoi Ispanii (1936–1939)* (Moscow: AIRO-XX, 2000).

[31] Radosh et al., *Spain Betrayed*, xxiii.

[32] George Esenwein, "Freedom Fighters or Comintern Soldiers? Writing about the 'Good Fight' during the Spanish Civil War," *Civil Wars* 12, no. 1–2 (March–June 2010): 156–66; Richard Baxell, "Myths of the International Brigades," *Bulletin of Spanish Studies: Hispanic Studies*

To debunk the "myth" of the "good fight" historians have emphasized that political rivalries – especially the feverish hunt to unmask Trotskyites – often overwhelmed the celebrated comradeship of the cause and that Comintern officials executed an "untold number of... alleged subversives" as a means of disciplining troops.[33]

By contrast, this chapter aims not to debunk myths but rather to examine the everyday lives of the International brigadistas to get a sense of whether and how participants understood the abstraction "international solidarity" to operate on the ground in Spain. It sets the less than mythic realities of the International Brigades in the larger contexts of Republican Spain and international communism. As historian Helen Graham argues, all actors in Spain were limited by the brutal and changing realities of the war. To focus narrowly on the question of whether the Internationals were freedom fighters or Stalinist dupes risks treating Spain as "a blank screen waiting to be written on by Soviet and Comintern players."[34] It also risks ignoring the understandings, experiences, and identities that volunteers brought with them to Spain and that circumstances there might challenge, reinforce, or perhaps remake. This chapter thus explores how the volunteers' ideas of themselves, their cause, and the Soviet Union interacted with the unanticipated and often poorly understood military, political, and social context in which they operated. What did the "good fight" mean to the undersupplied, multinational, often poorly trained, multilingual, mostly communist volunteers in Spain?

Language Barriers, International Solidarity, and the *Internationale*

In 1937, Lini De Vries (aka Lee Moerkirk Fuhr), a Dutch American nurse volunteering with the Medical Bureau to Aid Spanish Democracy, began a letter home with a description of the sounds of Spain. From her office in the hospital, she could hear French troops "practicing French revolutionary songs," apparently "copying the plan of the Germans who are putting on a chorus." She wrote that on the previous evening, 14 April, in honor of the anniversary of the Spanish Republic, several people, whom she described as a Greek, a Spanish anarchist, and a Spanish communist, had collaborated on writing a speech that was then translated into German, French, English, and Italian. After the speech, the "Spaniards sang "rev.[olutionary] songs, then the

and Researches on Spain, Portugal and Latin America 91, no. 1–2 (2014): 11–24; Chris Ealham argues against the view of Internationals as "spies" in "'Myths' and the Spanish Civil War: Some Old, Some Exploded, Some Clearly Borrowed and Some Almost 'Blue,'" *Journal of Contemporary History* 42, no. 2 (2007): 372; Dan Richardson, *Comintern Army: The International Brigades and the Spanish Civil War* (Lexington: University of Kentucky Press, 1982).

33 Esenwein, "Freedom Fighters," 163. Both Mershcheriakov and Kowalsky argue that the number was likely low, "Sud'ba," 25; "Soviet Union," 696. See Chapter 4.

34 Helen Graham, "Spain Betrayed? The New Historical McCarthyism," *Science and Society* 68, no. 3 (Fall 2004): 367.

girls, then me solo & then there was group singing. It was very moving." Later in the letter, describing her daily routine, she provided a long and diverse list of non-nursing, organizational, and political duties and concluded, "I can't walk 5 ft. without some one stopping me to ask something or settle something – & this in about 10 different languages."[35] For De Vries, Spain was a place where everyone spoke a different language, yet no one had trouble communicating. In her telling, the "babble of tongues" produced not "legions of Babel,"[36] but an international chorus singing revolutionary songs.

De Vries may well have minimized the difficulties of dealing with patients and staff who often lacked a common language. As cultural historian and World War II veteran Paul Fussell notes, letters home from war "are composed largely to sustain the morale of the folks at home, to hint as little as possible at the real, worrisome circumstance of the writer."[37] De Vries may also have hoped to shore up faith in the possibility and power of international solidarity. She had joined the Communist Party in 1934 – she is best known as the woman whom confessed spy Elizabeth Bentley named as recruiting her into the party – and offered in her letter to send a copy of the anniversary speech for use in the party's *Daily Worker*.[38] Finally, her letter was no doubt written with the understanding that it would have to clear the censor.

Still, the insistence that the diversity of languages spoken (and sung) by the volunteers constituted a defining feature of the brigades – if not always an unproblematic one – is significant. It shows up in letters home and in later reminiscences, as well as in the reports generated by commissars and commanders. The administrative records often emphasized the problems caused by linguistic diversity, but always with the hope of finding ways of overcoming language barriers and achieving the promise of international solidarity.

The multiple languages spoken in the brigades had the most serious potential consequences at the front. In the Twelfth Brigade, for example, the Soviet-trained Hungarian commander Máté Zalka (known as "Pavol Lukács") gave commands in Russian that an adjutant translated into French so others could then translate them into German, Spanish, and Italian.[39] Unsurprisingly, commands often got muddled in the course of multiple translations; language and communications problems contributed to severe losses in the battle for Madrid.[40] At Jarama in February 1937, the main communication problem

35 Lini De Vries to Max, 15 April [1937], Fredericka Martin Papers, ALBA 001, Box 6, Folder 19.

36 Johnston, *Legions of Babel.*

37 Paul Fussell, *Wartime: Understanding and Behavior in the Second World War* (New York: Oxford University Press, 1990), 145.

38 On Bentley see Chapter 7.

39 Mershcheriakov, "Sud'ba," 27.

40 Robert G. Colodny, *The Struggle for Madrid: The Central Epic of the Spanish Conflict, 1936–1937* (New York: Transaction Publishers, 2009), 74; Antony Beevor, *The Spanish Civil War*

was the lack of working field telephones between the battalions and Fifteenth Brigade headquarters. Still, in a May 1937 report, Merriman, who had served as the commander of the Abraham Lincoln battalion at Jarama, emphasized that language barriers contributed to the confusion and lack of coordination that marked the battle as a whole. He blamed difficulties communicating with the French drivers of the convoy that brought the Lincolns to the front for the loss of "3 trucks with very important materiel and 20 men."[41] In the aftermath of the battle in which the Lincolns sustained more than one hundred casualties, a result, they believed, of poor command decisions, the brigade commissar, French communist Jean Chaintron (known as "Barthel"), struggled to appease the near-mutinous men through a translator, who, according to the brigade's history, "knew very little French and consequently added to the difficulties of the argument, since the Commissar neither understood English, nor the comrades French."[42] Language barriers thus appear to have added to the human costs of the successful defense of Madrid.

Multilingual brigadistas, including the large foreign-born contingent among the Americans, both facilitated and complicated communication across languages. As translators, they were "worth their weight in gold."[43] For Robert Gladnick, a Russian-born American in the Fifteenth Brigade, his native knowledge of Russian, along with an ability to speak German and an apparent facility for picking up other languages including Spanish and French, fundamentally transformed his service in Spain. As Gladnick tells the story in his memoir – a self-aggrandizing and not always reliable source – Russian general Dmitrii Grigorevich Pavlov for whom he acted as an impromptu translator recognized him as "one of us" and saw to his transfer (as Roman Gladnik) to the Soviet tank corps. His language skills would have been particularly useful there, because tank crews might include a Soviet commander, an International technician – mostly members of the Czechoslovak, Austrian, German, and Bulgarian parties – and a Spanish gun loader.[44] Ultimately, Gladnick was transferred to the tank school at Archena as a translator.[45] More commonly, bilingual troops provided a convenient source of casual translators. For example, although there was far less demand for Finnish than Russian translators, Arvola occasionally

(New York: Penguin, 1982), 136. On similar language problems at Fuentes de Ebro, see John Gates, *The Story of an American Communist* (New York: Thomas Nelson, 1958), 51.

41 "La Bataille du Jarama," RGASPI, f. 545, op. 2, d. 32, l. 426. See also "A Documentary History of the XV Brigade," ibid., op. 3, d. 471, l. 25, 30.

42 "Documentary History of the XV Brigade," l. 35.

43 Mershcheriakov, "Sud'ba," 27.

44 Robert Gladnick memoirs, chapter 3, pp. 4, 13–15, Hoover Institution Archives; Kowalsky, "Soviet Union," 694; "Spisok Internatsionalistov rabotavshikh tankovykh chastiakh Respublikanskoi Armii," RGASPI, f. 545, op. 2, d. 120, ll. 15–19. On Gladnick's language skills, see Herrick, *Jumping the Line*, 137–8.

45 "Spisok Internatsionalistov," l. 16ob. Gladnick describes himself as an "instructor" at the school, not a translator, Gladnick memoirs, chapter 9, p. 4.

found himself pulled away from other tasks to translate for the Scandinavian political commissar.[46]

At the same time, troops speaking and writing their "own" languages could to some degree escape the scrutiny of political commissars and superior officers. At Brunete in July 1937, American officers Steve Nelson and Mirko Markovicz consulted with the commander of the Fifteenth Brigade, Lieutenant Colonel Klaus Becker, through a translator who spoke English and German. Taken aback by what seemed to him an impossible order, Markovicz expressed his doubts to Nelson in their native Croatian, a language neither Becker nor his translator understood. The irritated colonel demanded that his subordinates speak English. As soon as he understood Markovicz's objections, Becker relieved him of command.[47] In a similar vein, the base inspector Longo reported that one of the early problems facing his office was the lack of "personnel necessary to censor all the letters, especially those in lesser-known languages."[48] The problem was well known enough for Mito Kruth to warn his wife that the Finnish letters he sent to his mother would take longer to arrive than the letters in English he wrote to her.[49]

Thus even away from the front, where translation had somewhat less urgency than under fire, translators were in great demand. Longo viewed effective translation as essential not only to censorship but also to maintaining morale. Worrying that failing to provide necessary translations would create "manifestations of wounded national pride," he asked for authorization to make sure his office had a staff able to translate into every possible language.[50] Language skills thus became a key qualification for brigade functionaries. When Robert Merriman, still recovering from the wounded shoulder he suffered at Jarama, tried to find employment in the brigades for his wife Marion, recently arrived from Moscow, he received the reply that an assignment would depend on "what languages she knows."[51] Underscoring the importance of language, lists of military instructors at the base specified not their party affiliation – which may have been uniformly communist –but rather the language or languages they spoke.[52]

[46] Ranse Edward Arvola to Comrade Helen [Kruth], 16 July 1937, Kruth Papers, Box 1, Folder 1.

[47] Peter N. Carroll, *The Odyssey of the Abraham Lincoln Brigade: Americans in the Spanish Civil War* (Stanford: Stanford University Press, 1994), 143–4. R. H. Merriman to Comrade Bielov, 4 August 1937, RGASPI, f. 545, op. 6, d. 947, l. 52. Markovicz's Croatian was apparently better than his English, see Cecil Eby, *Between the Bullet and the Lie: American Volunteers in the Spanish Civil War* (New York: Holt, Rinehart and Winston, 1969),142.

[48] "Doklad Voennogo komissariata," l. 50.

[49] Mito Kruth to Helen, 25 June [1937], Kruth Papers, Box 1, Folder 10.

[50] "Doklad Voennogo komissariata," l. 53.

[51] Estado Mayor to Merriman, 21 March [1937] as copied by Merriman into his diary, vol. 1, 27 septiembre, Merriman Papers, Box 1, Folder 3.

[52] "2nd Battalion of Instruction, Tarazona," 21 September 1937, RGASPI, f. 545, op. 2, d. 65, l. 23.

The reorganization of the brigades undertaken in August 1937 in the wake of the costly and failed Brunete offensive aimed to "reduce the difficulties of language that exist in the different brigades" by reducing the number of languages spoken in each unit.[53] As Longo and the base commander Gayman recognized, it was the heavy casualties suffered in July, along with the almost total lack of leaves from the front – not concerns about language barriers – that constituted the root causes of demoralization and desertions.[54] Still, Longo suggested that the reorganization along linguistic lines – something in which troops had expressed interest and that had begun before the offensive – would help restore morale.[55] Moreover, separating the brigades according to language conformed to standard Comintern practice, visible, for example, in the organization of Comintern schools into language sections.

However, even after the reorganization, the brigades were not linguistically homogeneous. Because all brigades included large numbers of Spaniards, the reorganization produced a "Spanish-Italian" Twelfth Brigade, a "Spanish-French" Fourteenth, and a "Spanish-English" Fifteenth Brigade. The Eleventh was designated the "Spanish-German" Brigade, but also included Dutch speakers and speakers of various Scandinavian languages. The Thirteenth "Spanish-Slavic" Brigade included speakers of Polish as well as a number of other Slavic languages.[56]

To facilitate better relations between the brigadistas and Spanish troops, Longo's office advocated and organized Spanish-language instruction for the Internationals and literacy courses for the Spanish conscripts. Commissars regularly reported organizing language instruction.[57] Among Lini De Vries's hospital duties was organizing a Spanish class for hospital personnel.[58] Propaganda among the troops also encouraged language learning. A collection of materials for publication in the Fifteenth Brigade's newspaper and bulletin includes the

53 "Informe sobre la acción y la situación de las Brigadas Internacionales," 11 August 1937, RGASPI, f. 545, op. 1, d. 4, l. 24.

54 Ibid., ll. 15–19 ; "Conclusions au mémorandum sur la situation des Brigades Internationales," 11 August 1937, RGASPI, f. 545, op. 2, d. 32, l. 386.

55 "Informe sobre la acción ," ll. 17, 25 ; "Informe sobre el trabajo del comisariado político de la XV Brigada," 16 April 1937, RGASPI, f. 545, op. 4, d. 435, l. 21; Mershcheriakov, "Sud'ba," 28.

56 "Conclusions au mémorandum," l. 388; Mershcheriakov, "Sud'ba,"29 ;"Informe sobre la acción ," l. 23. Soviet officers Manfred (Moshe) Stern (known as Emilio Kléber in Spain) and Karol Świerczewski (or Sverchevskii, known as Walter in Spain) disagree on the details of the reorganization: "An account by M. Fred [Manfred Stern] on work in Spain," 14 December 1937, in *Spain Betrayed*, 346; "Notes on the Situation in the International Units in Spain Report by Colonel Com. Sverchevsky (Walter)," 14 January 1938, in ibid., 437.

57 On language and literacy see "Informe sobre el trabajo del comisariado," l. 19; "The Meeting of the Political Commissars held May 10th [1937]," RGASPI, f. 545, op. 4, d. 435, l. 30; "Informe sobre las 35 y 45 Divisiones y otras unidades internacionales durante el periodo del 2 al 7 de julio de 1938," ibid., op. 1, d. 3, l. 313; "Informe sobre las divisiones 35 y 45," 16–22 July 1938, ibid., l. 325.

58 Lini De Vries to Max, 15 April [1937], Martin Papers, Box 6, Folder 19.

song "La Joven Guardia" (The Young Guard), the anthem of the Juventudes Socialistas Unificadas (JSU, the communist youth organization), accompanied by a note instructing as follows: "COMRADE: YOU ARE ENCOURAGED TO COPY THIS SONG AND LEARN IT AT YOUR LEISURE. IT WILL NOT ONLY HELP YOU TO LEARN SPANISH, BUT ALSO A POPULAR REVOLUTIONARY SONG."[59] The troops were also encouraged to learn the *Internationale*, "the communist hymn," in Spanish and to attend a Spanish class that met "at 2 everyday."[60]

Whether or not brigadistas actually learned much Spanish is another question. One Irish volunteer claimed that few learned the language because "there was a superstition that anyone who started to study Spanish grammar got killed," which provided a convenient "excuse for not doing it."[61] Italian communist and Comintern representative Palmiro Togliatti (known in Spain as "Alfredo") considered the failure of the Internationals to learn Spanish and read the Spanish press as evidence of "inadequate" political work. With what sounds like some exaggeration, he claimed that it was "easier to find a brigade of Spaniards who can read some Polish or German than the other way around."[62] Cecil Cole, a twenty-four-year-old Berkeley graduate from Oakland wrote home that "it's really lots of fun to learn the language" by conversing with the locals; however, he noted, "most of the men don't care to learn the language, ... so I do speak almost fluently in comparison to the majority of men here."[63] Steve Nelson judged intensive language study unnecessary. Imprisoned in France on the way to Spain, he wrote to his wife, "I am learning German, Italian, Spanish & French at the same time. Not making much progress but can get along with all."[64] Ben Gardner, a party organizer born in the town of Uman in Ukraine, followed a similar strategy, noting, "I speak English, Yiddish, Rus. & Spanish combined to some of our Internationals. It's a regular riot. But somehow I make out."[65]

Others reported making serious, if sometimes frustrating, attempts to master Spanish. Kruth, a long-time communist organizer and teacher, began trying to learn Spanish almost as soon as he arrived. In the hospital in August 1937, he wrote his wife that he had again picked up a Spanish grammar book,

59 Emphasis in original."La Joven Guardia," 2 August 1937, RGASPI f. 545, op. 3, d. 473, l. 83; *Canciones de las Brigadas Internacionales* (1938, reprint, Seville: Renacimiento, 2007), xiii, 19.

60 RGASPI, f. 545, op. 3, d. 473, ll. 96, 183 (Notes, poems, lyrics, slogans, drawings for Fifteenth Brigade newspapers and bulletins).

61 Joe Monks quoted in Baxell, *British Volunteers*, 146.

62 Untitled report, 29 August 1937, in *Spain Betrayed*, 256.

63 C. M. Cole to Jeff, 1 January 1938, VALB, Container 1.

64 Steve Nelson to Maggie [Nelson], from Perpignan, France, nd, Steve Nelson Papers ALBA 008, Box 1, Folder 8.

65 Ben Gardner to Alice [Gardner], 6 January 1938, VALB, Container 1.

"trying to master the verbs enough to get along." The process reminded him of his experiences studying in Moscow in the early 1930s: "Remember the old Russky? Well it's the same old ground all over again."[66] At the end of October, unsatisfied with his progress, he wrote, "I hope the next war is in a country where I can speak the language. It makes it so much easier."[67] Merriman did not detail his learning process, but noted in his diary that he knew enough Spanish to give the morning drill in Spanish. (He also prided himself on his ability to participate in party meetings in Russian.[68])

Ignoring or minimizing the practical difficulties of learning Spanish and of working in a multilingual environment, many volunteers in their letters, diaries, and reminiscences idealized the literal and metaphorical music of the many languages heard in Spain. Some, such as Nelson and Gardner, suggested that the ease and naturalness of communication across language barriers demonstrated the reality of international solidarity. With relatively little effort, they could "get along with all" in whatever language they happened to speak. Arvola emphasized the odd and wonderful mix of languages and nationalities possible only in Spain. In the field kitchen he ran in Teruel, he found a new world in the making: "The Spanish comrade is singing songs. The Negro comrade telling (interrupting) us with stories and I have to join in."[69] Similarly, for Gene Wolman, a volunteer from New York, among the "rural joys" of being at the front was seeing "some 'foreign' bunch go marching gaily past us singing their national songs. The best singers, in my opinion, are the Germans, Slavs, and Italians."[70] Such unexpected and harmonious combinations of languages appeared to provide vivid proof that the brigades were successful in what Giuseppe Di Vittorio (known as "Nicoletti"), the chief political commissar of the Albacete base, deemed their "role and aim": "symbolizing the unity of all workers, and the union of all the peoples of Europe in the fight for bread, peace, and liberty."[71]

Those volunteers who emphasized the moving sense of solidarity they felt in Spain often illustrated it with examples both of the pervasiveness of communal singing and the possibility of hearing songs and conversation in an astonishing range of languages. Collective singing – and adding new songs inspired by Spain to the national "revolutionary repertoire" – was, as Josie McLellan emphasizes

[66] Mito Kruth to Helen, 30 August [1937], Kruth Papers, Box 1, Folder 11. See also, Mito to Helen, 18 April [1937], 25 April [1937], Box 1, Folder 9; 20 June 1937, Box 1, Folder 10; 2 September [1937], Box 1, Folder 11.

[67] Mito Kruth to Helen, 31 October 1937, Kruth Papers, Box 1, Folder 12.

[68] Merriman diary, vol. 1, Merriman papers, Box 1, Folder 3, 1 junio (Russian), 3 junio (Spanish); Merriman diary, vol. 2, ibid. p. 59.

[69] Arvola to Sis and Helen, 26 January 1938, Kruth Papers, Box 1, Folder 1. See also Merriman diary, vol. 2, 30 October 1937, Merriman Papers, Box 1, Folder 3.

[70] Gene Wolman to Family, Letter no. 3, nd, VALB, Container 1.

[71] "Doklad Voennogo komissariata," l. 19.

FIGURE 1. Ranse (Frank) Edward Arvola, chief cook in the Auto Park, Alcover. Courtesy Tamiment Library, New York University (ALBA Photo 11–0334 [Series E])

in her study of German volunteers, "a powerful symbol" of solidarity among German communists.[72] In his memoirs, Gladnick suggests a similar impulse to forge and mark solidarity across national lines through singing. On the train from Paris to the Spanish border, the volunteers "began asking one another 'Votre Nationalite' in reply we got Pollonaise, Bulgar, Hungoire, Italienne." When Joe Gordon (born Joseph Mendelowitz) "was asked he replied Juif des Etats Unis – all of a sudden the Pollonaise, Hungoise said 'Vis send oich Yidden' (We too are Jews) so Joe proposed that instead of singing the International we should sing the Hatikva [the Zionist anthem] – the Poles & Hungarians knew the words. Most of us had to hum along."[73] That they needed to sing something together went without saying.

The *Internationale*, a song that virtually all the volunteers knew, even if in different languages, provided for many a particularly emotional means of bridging language divides. The song itself, and especially repeated communal

[72] Josie McLellan, "'I Wanted To Be a Little Lenin': Ideology and the German International Brigade Volunteers," *Journal of Contemporary History* 41, no. 2 (2006): 301.

[73] All spelling as in original. Gladnick memoirs, chapter 5, p. 5. On Joe Gordon see Daniel Czitrom, "Volunteers for Liberty: Letters from Joe and Leo Gordon, Americans in Spain, 1937–38," *Massachusetts Review* 25 (Fall 1984): 348–54.

FIGURE 2. Soldier playing mandolin and singing with group. Courtesy Tamiment Library, New York University (ALBA Photo 177–177080)

singing of it, underscored shared allegiances without specifying them too precisely. After all, the song was at once familiar from home, the international anthem of the proletarian cause, and the Soviet national anthem. In Republican Spain, it echoed everywhere. Volunteers sang it on the train from Paris to Perpignan on the Mediterranean near the Spanish border.[74] They sang it on reaching Spain after crossing the Pyrenees.[75] They sang it on the march and at the front.[76] In June 1937, political commissar Frederick Lutz, enjoying a rare leave from the front, described the sounds reaching him through the window: "The propaganda loud speaker is playing the ever-thrilling 'Internationale' and the townspeople and the troops are all singing. You know I can't get over the thrill of hearing the 'Internationale' and the 'Youthful Guardsman'

74 Beevor, *Spanish Civil War*, 126.

75 Steve Nelson, James R. Barrett, and Rob Ruck, *Steve Nelson, American Radical* (Pittsburgh: University of Pittsburgh Press, 1982), 202; Cary Nelson and Jefferson Hendricks, *Edwin Rolfe: A Biographical Essay and Guide to the Rolfe Archive at the University of Illinois at Urbana-Champaign* (Urbana: University of Illinois Press, 1990), 23.

76 Steve Nelson, *The Volunteers* (New York: Masses and Mainstream, 1953), 160; Bessie, *Civil War Notebooks*, 13; Marcel Acier, *From Spanish Trenches: Recent Letters from Spain* (New York: Modern Age, 1937), 35, 117, 156; Alexander Szurek, *The Shattered Dream*, trans. Jacques Grunblatt and Hilda Grunblatt (Boulder, CO: East European Monographs, 1989), 22, 174, 229; William Rust, *Britons in Spain: The History of the XVth International Brigade* (London: Lawrence and Wishart, 1939), 134.

sung by everyone everywhere I go."[77] According to Harry Meloff (aka Malofsky), a composer and playwright killed in action in 1937, the sound of the *Internationale* in Spain moved his friend, fellow New Yorker Abe Harris, to tears.[78]

A poem submitted to the Fifteenth Brigade's newspaper provides a glimpse of how the brigadistas imagined and mythologized themselves, as well as the importance of song and language in this process. The poem emphasized both the diversity of the soldiers and their unity in struggle and in song. "Men from the Nazi dungeons,/ Scots from the Glasgow slums,/ Frenchmen, Dutchmen, Irish,/ What is the host that comes?/ Speaking a score of lingoes,/ Dirty and ill-arrayed." A subsequent stanza expanded the "host" to include "Bulgars, Chinese, and Negroes,/ Men of a myriad hues,/ Danes, and Italians, and Lascars [sailors from the Indian subcontinent],/ Slovaks, Englishmen, Jews." Yet they were all united, "Singing into the battle" – perhaps songs in a dozen languages, perhaps the *Internationale*.[79] Song here functioned as a bridge across "a score of lingoes." Despite all the difficulties and confusion caused by language, simply hearing so many languages resound could nonetheless function as thrilling proof of international solidarity in Spain. In this way, the fact of linguistic diversity contributed to the production and power of the "myth" of the brigades.

Cigarettes, Shortages, and the Limits of International Solidarity

If the sounds of Republican Spain announced the unprecedented international scope of the cause, the smells confirmed the ugly and prosaic realities of war. Moving into battle with a reserve unit, Bessie was overwhelmed by the "sudden, sickening smell of the dead."[80] Life in the trenches had its own "characteristic smell" – in George Orwell's "experience a smell of excrement and decaying food."[81] Judging from the incessant references to cigarettes and smoking in diaries, letters, and reports on troop morale, the "constant scent of cigarettes" was, as Fussell noted about World War II, "part of the unique atmosphere of the war" along with "the automatic, ubiquitous actions of deep inhaling, borrowing, and offering smokes."[82] "Tobacco helps you remain sane," Bessie noted

77 Frederick Lutz to Shirley [Gottlieb], JunJl26e 16 '37 [sic], in *Madrid 1937*, 104–5.

78 Harry Meloff to Mim, 16 May 1937, in *Madrid 1937*, 148. See also Gustav Regler, *The Owl of Minerva*, trans. Norman Denny (London: Rupert Hart-Davis, 1959), 309.

79 "International Brigades," RGASPI, f. 545, op. 3, d. 473, l. 54.

80 Bessie, *Civil War Notebooks*, 88.

81 George Orwell, *Homage to Catalonia* (1938; reprint, San Diego: Harcourt Brace Jovanovich, 1980), 16. Orwell served in a POUM (Partido Obrero de Unificación Marxista) militia unit, but his description squares with conditions found in the People's Army. Michael Seidman, "Quiet Fronts in the Spanish Civil War," *Historian* 61, no. 4 (Summer 1999): 827.

82 Fussell, *Wartime*, 145. Michael Seidman, *Republic of Egos: A Social History of the Spanish Civil War* (Madison: University of Wisconsin Press, 2002), 110.

FIGURE 3. Three soldiers, one handing a cigarette to another. Courtesy Tamiment Library, New York University (ALBA Photo 177–178023)

during the terrifying 1938 offensive on the Ebro, "but it's not enough . . . – you smoke like a house afire."[83] "War," wrote poet and volunteer Edwin Rolfe, "is your comrade struck dead beside you, his shared cigarette still alive in your lips."[84]

In Spain, where cigarettes were always in short supply and everyone smoked, sharing cigarettes could be an act of profound solidarity. As in World War I, the war in which smoking and cigarettes had become ubiquitous, the tobacco ration never seemed to be sufficient.[85] Ben Gardner provided his wife a list of key items difficult to find in Spain: soap, soft drinks, and "good cigarettes." Perhaps hoping to inspire folks at home to send care packages, he added,

83 Bessie, *Civil War Notebooks*, 92.

84 Edwin Rolfe, "City of Anguish," in *First Love, and Other Poems* (Los Angeles: L. Edmunds Book Shop, 1951), 19, quoted in Carroll, *Odyssey*, 91.

85 On World War I see Chris Wrigley, "Soldiers and Cigarettes: Smoking for King and Country," *History Today* 64, no. 4 (April 2014): 24–30; Allan Brandt, *The Cigarette Century: The Rise, Fall and Deadly Persistence of the Product that Defined America* (New York: Basic Books, 2007), 51–4.

"Boy if our comrades and friends could only see how much it means to our fighters to get American cigarettes!"[86] Volunteers obsessively managed their cigarette ration – which Bessie described as "1 pack French Gaulois[es] blue or American Twenty Grand a week."[87] Hank Rubin, a college student turned political commissar, remembered "how carefully we had hoarded our tobacco. On the rare occasions we got a real cigarette, we often cut it in two and rerolled the parts to make two cigarettes. At the very least, we saved the cigarette butts."[88] In these circumstances, the sharing of cigarettes could cement personal and political bonds. When Arvola received a letter with cigarettes, he shared them all, save one, with his comrades "from Fascist or Semi-Fascist countries" who had no hope of receiving any from home.[89] For Bessie, the emblem of "comradeship and generosity" at the front was a "man who received 2 cartons of Camels today, has given them all away."[90]

A "tobacco famine" could quickly demoralize troops.[91] American commissar DeWitt Parker looked forward to the arrival of packages from the United States containing chocolate and tobacco, noting "a cigarette becomes a very important political instrument sometimes."[92] Longo's early 1938 report on morale within the brigades similarly noted that a several week hiatus in the distribution of cigarettes to the troops – they were being held up in Spanish customs – "has created a malaise that will be aggravated if the situation continues."[93] He deemed the "fact that package service from abroad functions very badly and that many packages don't arrive at their destinations" as having "a negative influence on the men."[94]

Although the volunteers may have griped most about cigarettes, tobacco was hardly the only item in short supply in Republican Spain. According to a documentary history of the Fifteenth Brigade, at the time of its formation, "the men were poorly clothed and poorly armed;" of the roughly one hundred Italians in the Dimitrov battalion, "there were still about 30 who were in civilian clothes, had their suitcases, and were without military knapsacks."[95]

86 Ben Gardner [to Alice Gardner], 24 July 1937, VALB, Container 1. For a similar hint, see Lloyd to Pop [F. J. Edmonds], 24 June 1937, in Lloyd Edmonds, *Letters from Spain*, ed. Amirah Inglis (Sydney: George Allen & Unwin, 1985), 110.

87 Bessie, *Civil War Notebooks*, 4.

88 Hank Rubin, *Spain's Cause Was Mine: A Memoir of an American Medic in the Spanish Civil War* (Carbondale: Southern Illinois University Press, 1997), 148; Bessie, *Civil War Notebooks*, 4.

89 Ranse Edward Arvola to Helen [Kruth], 4 October 1937, Kruth Papers, Box 1, Folder 1. Nearly all of Arvola's letters make reference to cigarettes.

90 Bessie, *Civil War Notebooks*, 17.

91 The phrase "tobacco famine" is from Bessie, *Civil War Notebooks*, 59.

92 DeWitt Parker to Funny, 26 October 1937, in *Madrid 1937*, 177.

93 "Informe sobre la situación de las brigadas internacionales," 1 January 1938, RGASPI, f. 545, op. 1 d. 3, ll. 80–1.

94 Ibid., ll. 80 (quotation), 333, 334.

95 "Documentary History of the XV International Brigade," l. 3.

The situation never improved appreciably; by the last year of the war, when less military aid was arriving from the Soviet Union, it had deteriorated. In a confidential memo written in July 1937, on the eve of his dismissal from the command of the Albacete base for alleged embezzlement, Gayman reported "demoralization" brought on by the difficulty of obtaining "authorizations for the purchase of provisions, and for the supply of equipment and clothing."[96] Laurie Lee, a British volunteer who arrived in the winter of 1937, described the brigades as armed with "antique muskets and jamming machine guns."[97] In January 1938, Longo reported acute shortages of pants and shoes (*alpargatas*, espadrilles) and recommended the regular distribution of tobacco, short leaves from the front, better clothing, and the provision of necessary gear, including entrenchment tools, helmets, and gas masks, as essential to maintaining morale.[98] When Bessie arrived at the front in March 1938 in the wake of the Nationalist breakthrough in Aragon, he found the men without "decent clothes, shoes, or even blankets; few have mess kits – we use tin cans and fingers. Tin cans are hard to come by."[99] In July 1938, Longo's office was still reporting that "there are many comrades, especially in the 15th Brigade, who are completely barefoot" and thus unable to participate in military exercises.[100]

Such shortages, which constituted a defining feature of life in Republican Spain, were a consequence of the August 1936 Nonintervention Agreement. As Helen Graham argues in her history of the Spanish civil war, the British and French refusal to sell arms or make loans "placed the Republic . . . at an enormous material disadvantage."[101] The effects of nonintervention were felt first in the military sphere. While Nazi Germany and fascist Italy violated the agreement with impunity, supplying men and material to the Nationalists, the agreement effectively barred the Republic from "normal channels for buying modern military weaponry."[102] In the face of the arms embargo, the Republic was forced to "procure arms at extortionate prices on the black market" and

[96] Translation from "Confidential Note on the Situation of the International Brigades at the End of July 1937," in *Spain Betrayed*, 247. *Spain Betrayed* includes part of the memo, as held in the Russian State Military Archives (RGVA, f. 35082, op. 1, d. 90, ll. 539–5[sic]33), 241–8. The 453-page "Otchet nachal'nika Bazy" is held at RGASPI, f. 545, op. 2, d. 32 (quotation l. 383). On deliveries of Soviet hardware to Spain, see Daniel Kowalsky, *Stalin and the Spanish Civil War* [electronic resource] (New York: Columbia University Press, 2004), chapter 10.

[97] Laurie Lee, *Moment of War: A Memoir of the Spanish Civil War* (New York: New Press, 1991), 46.

[98] "Informe sobre la situación," ll. 79, 87.

[99] Bessie, *Civil War Notebooks*, 17. On the retreats, see Carroll, *Odyssey*, 171–88.

[100] "Informe Sobre las 35 y 45 Divisiones," l. 316.

[101] Graham, *Spanish Republic*, xi. Michael Seidman argues that the Nationalists used foreign aid more effectively, *Victorious Counterrevolution: The Nationalist Effort in the Spanish Civil War* (Madison: University of Wisconsin Press, 2011), 6.

[102] Kowalsky, "Soviet Union," 681. On German and Italian military aid to the insurgents, see Michael Alpert, *An International History of the Spanish Civil War* (New York: St. Martin's Press, 1994), 78, 82–6, 90–4.

ultimately to rely on a frequently disrupted flow of Soviet military aid of uneven quality and insufficient quantity.[103] Paying "crippling prices" for arms meant that the Republic struggled to purchase other necessary goods, such as foreign wheat, when in 1937 it faced a crisis of grain production at home.[104] As the war dragged on and more and more territory was lost to the Nationalists, the costs of economic isolation increased, producing shortages throughout the economy. Spanish troops in the People's Army, no less than the brigades, often lacked food, coats, shoes, and arms; they, too, smoked cigarettes "as thin as toothpicks."[105]

However, this larger context hardly figured in the explanations of shortages, especially of cigarettes, proposed by the Internationals or their commanders and commissars. From the brigadistas' perspective, shortages resulted not from the international situation facing the Republic, but rather from, at best, inefficiency or inadequate political work or, at worst, from corruption or even sabotage. Emphasizing bureaucratic inefficiencies, Longo granted that some measure of blame for the poor mail delivery might fall to the brigades, but insisted that much depended on the Customs Service; he had therefore "solicited and obtained the intervention of superior authorities"[106] In his July 1937 memo, Gayman identified a "provocation" in the director of the tobacco monopoly's use of "his pen to transform these two million individual cigarettes" sent by Belgian and Dutch branches of the International Red Aid "*into two million packs*, which allowed him to invite all branches of the army – ground, air, and sea – to ask the International Brigades for these cigarettes."[107] At the same time, Gayman faulted the British and Americans for failing to share their cigarettes and care packages with the other Internationals, noting that donations "sent by French organizations were distributed in all international units, while those which came from America or England were reserved exclusively to the British and Americans."[108] The English-speaking brigadistas themselves complained that their cigarettes were (mis)directed to Spanish troops. They blamed the American party, which raised funds for Spain "on a basis of misrepresentation – that these funds buy comforts for 'the American boys in Spain,' which the A. b. in Spain never see (or rarely) since these comforts go to the General

[103] Graham, *Spanish Republic*, 150, 157; Kowalsky, "Soviet Union," 682; Klement Voroshilov to the Politburo of the CC VKP(b), 16 February 1939, in *Spain Betrayed*, 512.

[104] Graham, *Spanish Republic*, 158; Seidman, *Republic of Egos*, 167, 82. On food aid, see [Pedro] Checa and Luis [Comintern representative Vittorio Codovilla] to G. Dimitrov, 11 September 1937, in *Spain Betrayed*, 380.

[105] Lluís Montagut quoted in James Matthews, *Reluctant Warriors: Republican Popular Army and Nationalist Army Conscripts in the Spanish Civil War, 1936–1939* (Oxford: Oxford University Press, 2012), 112; Seidman, *Republic of Egos*, 178.

[106] "Informe sobre la situación," ll. 80–1.

[107] Emphasis in original.Translation from "Confidential Note" in *Spain Betrayed*, 245, with slight modification; "Otchet nachal'nika," ll. 380–1.

[108] "Otchet nachal'nika," l. 450.

FIGURE 4. Soldiers distributing mail. Courtesy Tamiment Library, New York University (ALBA Photo 11–1463 [Series E])

Intendencia [Quartermaster] of the army and are distributed among the entire Spanish army."[109] That morale among the rest of the army might also be suffering because of a lack of cigarettes – or that solidarity might require sharing the Internationals' cigarettes and "comforts" more broadly – seems to have occurred to very few members of the brigades.[110]

The commissars' tendency to attribute shortages (and the resultant demoralization) to inefficiency or insufficient political work grew out of their more general conviction that all problems facing the brigades could be solved with enough vigilance, persistence, and education. The history of the Fifteenth Brigade noted that initially "each particular national group complained about the other National groups." Complaints ranged from "being neglected and kept away from all Battalion activities" to "not being told when foods were distributed, military orders given," or being "assigned to the worst place."[111]

109 Bessie, *Civil War Notebooks*, 51.
110 Świerczewski makes a similar point in "Notes on the Situation," in *Spain Betrayed*, 449, 453.
111 "Documentary History of the XV International Brigade," l. 3.

However, the report did not conclude that scarcity fueled charges of "neglect" or lack of access to food distribution. Rather, it argued, "This misunderstanding among different national groups was chiefly due to the difficulties arising out of the inability to communicate properly because of the language impediments," suggesting that with better communication, national tensions would disappear.[112]

Yet despite the commissars' efforts, the "political error" of each national group focusing on its own interests persisted. Gayman's 1937 memo, for example, noted that the German volunteers, mostly political émigrés, had nothing but contempt for the more numerous and less politically homogeneous French volunteers, whom the Germans viewed as "drinkers, quarrelsome, and sometimes sloppy."[113] The Austrians, Scandinavians, and German speakers from Czechoslovakia in battalions dominated by Germans "complained" in turn "that they were 'oppressed' by the Germans who reserved all the officer and political commissar positions for themselves."[114] Karol Świerczewski (or Sverchevskii, known as "General Walter"), a Polish Red Army officer who commanded the Internationals, noted that "anti-Semitism flourished" in the early days of the brigades and as late as early 1938 "still has not been completely extinguished" – this despite the fact that Jews, at about 18 percent of the brigades, constituted the largest "national" group.[115] Gayman concluded that the failure to resolve "frequent conflicts between different nationalities" required heightened vigilance, because such conflicts provided "fertile ground for enemy agents."[116]

It was, as Gayman's warning suggests, often a short step from explaining conflicts and shortages as the result of political errors to understanding such problems as an opening to, or even as evidence of, sabotage. Bessie's summary of the troops' "dissatisfaction" described the "mail and package situation" as "badly handled and possibly even the object of definite sabotage," although he gave no specific evidence to support his conclusion.[117] In a March 1938 letter to the central committee of the Spanish Communist Party (Partido Comunista de España, PCE), Marty, likewise citing no specific evidence, suggested that delays in the delivery of tobacco and care packages to the Internationals might be the work of a "5th column agent" exploiting "bureaucratic formalities to stop packages sent from abroad."[118] Marty may have used the suggestion of

112 Ibid.
113 "Otchet nachal'nika," ll. 448, 449.
114 Ibid., l. 449.
115 "Notes on the Situation," in *Spain Betrayed*, 448. Hywel Francis, "'Say Nothing and Leave in the Middle of the Night': The Spanish Civil War Revisted," *History Workshop Journal*, no. 32 (Autumn 1991): 71.
116 "Otchet nachal'nika," l. 449.
117 Bessie, *Civil War Notebooks*, 51.
118 André Marty to Secretariado del C. C. del P.C.E., 28 March 1938, RGASPI, f. 545, op. 1, d. 11, l. 35.

sabotage as a crude means of motivating prompt action on behalf of the Internationals. At the same time, the easy recourse to "sabotage" as an explanation on the part of both brigadistas and their commander suggests a shared tendency to attribute any and all problems and mistakes to hidden "enemies" – a clear echo of the contemporary purges in the Soviet Union that aimed to "unmask" enemies.

A similar conspiratorial frame of mind shaped efforts to explain the Republic's failed July 1937 offensive at Brunete, about thirty kilometers (nineteen miles) west of Madrid. The operation had been designed to relieve pressure on the capital and to hasten a negotiated end to the war by demonstrating the Republic's strength. Fought in scorching heat, it was one of the deadliest battles of the war, in which the brigades provided the Republic's shock troops. Their initial gains proved unsustainable, because they were not backed by sufficient reserves of men or arms, due to delays at the French frontier and an effective blockade of Republican ports.[119] The Internationals suffered heavy casualties, with the Fifteenth Brigade the hardest hit, its strength reduced from 2,144 to 885 men – with 293 dead, 735 wounded, and 167 missing.[120]

Unsurprisingly, the battle left the troops badly demoralized. As an early August report on morale in the Fifteenth Brigade noted, "even the most tried and reliable [comrades] began to think 'the end of this war is so far off now that we shall never come out alive.'"[121] Thus the brigades' commissars' reports focused less on explaining the failures at Brunete than on restoring morale. Indeed getting the troops to see Brunete as a "significant," if not entirely successful, operation constituted an important part of their morale-building work.[122] The commissars also proposed the provision of longer and more frequent leaves for the troops, some of whom had been on the lines for 150 days with scarcely a break.[123]

When they did turn to the sources of problems within the brigades, the commissars highlighted the action of "fifth column agents" and "masked" fascists among the new Spanish recruits. They reported, for example, that when two Spanish battalions in the Thirteenth Brigade violated orders and abandoned the front, they did so with "perfect order, which proved that the action had been organized by enemy agents." In the Fourteenth Brigade, the commissars' "vigilance" led to the detention of a Spanish recruit who turned out to be a "fascist," and to uncovering "shady elements in other

[119] Graham, *Spanish Republic*, 318–19; Beevor, *Spanish Civil War*, 197–201; Carroll, *Odyssey*, 140–5.

[120] "Informe sobre la acción," l. 17. See also, Baxell, *British Volunteers*, 88. After the losses at Brunete, the two American battalions were merged into a single Lincoln-Washington battalion, Carroll, *Odyssey*, 142; on deserters, see ibid., 147–51.

[121] "Report on Morale of XV Brigade," 8 August 1937, RGASPI, f. 545, op. 4, d. 35, l. 172.

[122] Ibid., l. 173.

[123] "Mémorandum sur quelques questions concernant les Brigades Internationales," 19 May 1937, RGASPI, f. 545, op. 2, d. 32, ll. 357–8.

Brigades."[124] Only after detailing similar incidents in all the International Brigades did the report turn to what appears to be a simpler explanation for the self-inflicted wounds and desertions noted among the (probably quite young) recruits: their near-total lack of military training. Many came to the front without ever having seen a rifle; some "died without ever having fired a shot in their whole lives, and some fired on our men out of inexperience or treason." Moreover, "in general they were not prepared to withstand strong artillery fire or strong bombardment" – all of which, the report concluded, "demonstrated the new recruits' lack of military and political education."[125]

This conflation of political and military errors is telling. Presenting themselves as unable to discern whether the recruits "fired on our men out of inexperience or treason," the commissars effectively downplayed the consequences of poor training – and the lack of arms and ammunition that made live fire training impossible. Instead they took betrayal and sabotage as essentially indistinguishable from and even directly linked to the inexperienced soldiers' inability to hold up under fire. Even as they objected to the "savage and unjustified criticism of Spanish troops [that] was heard, particularly from the weakest comrades,"[126] the commissars themselves made the political unreliability of Spanish troops central to their account of military failures.

In his memo assessing the situation of the brigades after Brunete, Gayman emphasized that the Internationals felt betrayed by the Spanish leadership and that such charges had merit. He reported that the "great majority of officers, noncommissioned officers and volunteers in the International Brigades... are consumed by the idea that the International Brigades are considered a foreign body, a band of intruders – I will not say by the Spanish people as a whole, but by the vast majority of political leaders, soldiers, civil servants, and political parties in Spain."[127] Gayman thus distinguished the "Spanish people," whom the brigadistas often romanticized (a point taken up later), from Spanish "political leaders, soldiers, civil servants, and political parties," whom the Internationals, correctly in his view, deemed enemies of the brigades. Among the "facts" Gayman marshaled to support this view was the "patently clear" "prevailing opinion among high officers in the Spanish army, more or less regardless of political affiliation, that the International Brigades are nothing but a foreign legion, an army of mercenaries fighting for money."[128]

124 "Informe sobre la acción," l. 21; see also "Informatsiia komissar-inspektora interbrigad L. Gallo,"RGASPI, f. 545, op. 1, d. 1, l. 8; "Doklad Voennogo komissariata," ll. 173–4.

125 "Informe sobre la acción," l. 22. On the recruits' lack of training and youth, see Matthews, *Reluctant Warriors*, 60–1, 189.

126 "Report on Morale of XV Brigade," l. 172; see also "Notes on the Situation," in *Spain Betrayed*, 449–50.

127 Quotation from "Confidential Note" with slight changes, in *Spain Betrayed*, 241, 234; "Otchet nachal'nika," l. 374.

128 Quotation from "Confidential Note" with slight changes, in *Spain Betrayed*, 241; "Otchet nachal'nika," ll. 374–5.

Gayman's charges echoed and endorsed the views of the men themselves who, according to a commissar's report, understood their losses at Brunete to be the result of the failures, if not betrayals, of vaguely specified authorities. The commissars described the men as expressing "something like contempt for the 'Power' or 'Higher Command.'" As evidence, the report recounted that, when a number of long-serving American volunteers were finally reassigned to the rear guard, even the noncommunist brigadistas explained the release of men from the front as the result of the pressure put on the Spanish authorities by the American party, which defended them "whatever the Spanish Government does."[129]

Gayman's brief against the Spanish authorities ignored the shortages and dislocations that plagued the Republic as a whole, blaming the high casualties suffered by the brigades instead on a presumed "concerted effort to annihilate and sacrifice the international contingents."[130] He found proof of contempt for the brigades in the alleged "unequal treatment" they received: They were allotted inferior, obsolete arms; denied leaves; and "entrusted with the most difficult sector in every battle."[131] In some matters, the brigades did suffer "unequal treatment." Until they were incorporated into the People's Army, for example, they received lower pay (seven versus ten pesetas per day) than Spanish troops.[132] However, complaints about the lack of leaves, rifles, and food could be heard throughout the People's Army. Entrusting the brigades with "the most difficult" sectors may not, as Gayman argued, have been an "honor," but may have been a necessity. Even if military historian Gabriel Cardona overstates the matter when he argues that the Brigades, predominantly Spanish by the time of the final Loyalist offensive at the Ebro in 1938, constituted "the only Republican troops capable of sustaining serious offensive combat," their heavy casualties likely reflected less a desire on the part of Republican leaders to destroy them than their vital military role.[133]

A similar readiness on the part of the Internationals to understand losses as the result of sabotage reappeared after the failure of the Teruel offensive. Launched in the midst of a fierce blizzard, the offensive – initially an all-Spanish operation – captured Teruel in late December 1937. The Internationals joined

129 "Report on Morale of XV Brigade," l. 174.

130 "Confidential Note" in *Spain Betrayed*, 242; "Otchet nachal'nika ," l. 376.

131 "Confidential Note" in *Spain Betrayed*, 242; "Otchet nachal'nika, l. 375." For a contrary view see Longo, *Las Brigadas Internacionales en España*, trans. Victor Flores Olea (Mexico City: Ediciones Era, 1966), 200.

132 Gallo to Estimados Camaradas, 1 March 1937, RGASPI, f. 545, op. 1, d. 9, l. 21.

133 "Confidential Note" in *Spain Betrayed*, 242; "Otchet nachal'nika," l. 376; Gabriel Cardona, "El Ejercito Popular y las Brigadas Internacionales ¿Cúal fue la importancia de las Brigadas?" in Manuel Requena Gallego and Rosa Mª Sepúlveda Losa, eds., *Las Brigadas Internacionales: El contexto internacional, los medidos de propaganda, literatura y memorias* (Cuenca: Ediciones de la Universidad de Castilla-La Mancha, 2003), 43. On the offensive capability of the People's Army, see Seidman, "Quiet Fronts," 821–41.

the fighting in January, just as the counterattack began; the Nationalists recaptured Teruel in late February 1938. Just two weeks later, the rebels launched a surprise offensive along almost the entire Aragon front. The Loyalist retreat turned into a rout (the so-called Great Retreats). In April 1938, the Nationalists reached the Mediterranean, establishing a corridor that separated Catalonia from the rest of Republican Spain. Bessie noted rumors circulating among the troops in March 1938 that "sabotage apparently accounted for the loss of Teruel and Belchite."[134] A month later he recorded that the troops understood the decimation of the International Brigades during the Great Retreats as due in large part to the "definite sabotage by Spanish officers who hated 'Reds' ([former War Minister Indalecio] Prieto) or were jealous of IB reputation, or both."[135] Such explanations ignored the Nationalists' distinct advantages, including trained reserves, superior artillery, and the Nazi Condor Legion's devastating air strikes.

The volunteers' suspicions of Spanish leaders dovetailed with their concerns about the loyalty and ability of Spanish soldiers and officers. In an early 1938 report, Soviet advisor Świerczewski deplored the Internationals' continuing and, from his point of view, baseless, tendency to blame military failures on Spanish recruits.[136] More broadly he faulted the Internationals' "stubborn refusal to face the fact that we are on Spanish soil, we are subordinate to the Spanish army." Drawing on statistics detailing the overrepresentation of Internationals in the "key command and political positions" of the Eleventh and Fifteenth Brigades, Świerczewski pointed out that, even as the number of Spaniards in the brigades increased, the Internationals allowed only a few "the right and the honor to lead their own compatriots."[137] A contemporary commissar's report, which concluded that Internationals took the appointment of Spanish commissars or officers as a "hostile" act, appears to confirm Świerczewski's sense of the patronizing and distrustful mood in the brigades.[138]

The Republic's low level – and perhaps inefficient use – of foreign aid sentenced it to a "hand-to-mouth" existence.[139] Yet the Internationals and their leaders, as if unaware of the problems of supply facing the Republic, often explained setbacks ranging from tobacco famines to Nationalist victories as the work of so-called fifth-column agents and saboteurs. However, the tendency to turn "problems caused by shortage and dislocation ... into accusations of

[134] Bessie, *Civil War Notebooks*, 17.

[135] Ibid., 34. He recognized that "incompetence or inexperience" also played a role. On Prieto see Graham, *Spanish Republic*, 360–1.

[136] "Notes on the Situation," in *Spain Betrayed*, 436.

[137] Ibid., 450. Somewhat different figures (also from December 1937) corroborate the tendency of Spaniards to be concentrated in the lower ranks, in "Anglo-American Group Analysis," ll. 25–6.

[138] "Informe sobre la situación," ll. 81, 77.

[139] Graham, *Spanish Republic*, 318.

treason and crypto-fascism," although prevalent among the Internationals, was not necessarily a foreign import; it can be understood as rooted to some degree in the fact that the civil war itself had begun with a conspiracy of military officers.[140] Who could tell if other conspirators remained hidden in the ranks of the Republic's army? This interpretive framework can also be understood as a corollary to the faith voiced, for example, by Kruth on his arrival in Spain, in "the invincible character of the advanced farsighted people."[141] The sense that they stood on the side of history could raise unrealistic expectations among the Internationals, even those who recognized the very real obstacles to victory. As British volunteer Laurie Lee remembered the winter of 1937, "Perilous as the situation may have been, it was a time of crazy optimism, too, and all the talk was of an offensive.... It would be an Olympian battle to turn the war."[142] When the "Olympian battle" ended in the defeat of the "advanced farsighted people," a nefarious network of "hidden fascists" may have seemed a reasonable explanation.[143]

The Cause, the Spanish People, and the "Legend" of the Brigades

General Świerczewski did not doubt the pervasiveness of the brigadistas' sense that their cause was the cause of "all advanced and progressive humanity." Yet, from his perspective, this conviction made them an often undisciplined and unreliable fighting force. In an early 1938 review of the situation in the International Brigades, he complained that the Internationals, unlike the best Spanish units, did a poor job of caring for their weapons and carrying out their officers' instructions because, rather than concerning themselves "only with matters entrusted to them," they took on the "key problems of immediately reconstructing the world and saving Spain, about which our internationalists love to argue all the time." He disapproved in particular of the of the Internationals' conviction that "being an 'antifascist revolutionary' allows you to argue and debate with the commander, as a rule, using the familiar 'tú' with your hands in your pockets and a cigarette in you mouth."[144] American commissar Steve Nelson took a more generous view of the same behavior, explaining in his memoir that "blind discipline to authority might work in some armies, but it was out of the question in the International Brigades." He understood the commissar's job as explaining "every situation, to see that military decisions and objectives are understood." Thus when he was told to prepare his exhausted

140 Ibid., 144.

141 Mito Kruth to Helen, April 1937, Kruth Papers, Box 1, Folder 9.

142 Lee, *Moment of War*, 73. See also Mito Kruth to Helen, 2 May [1937], Kruth Papers, Box 1, Folder 9; Bessie, *Civil War Notebooks*, 46.

143 Radosh et al. make a similar point, *Spain Betrayed*, 474–5.

144 "Notes on the Situation," in *Spain Betrayed*, 445, 446. On Świerczewski's dim view of British informality, see Len Crome, "Walter (1897–1947): A Soldier in Spain," *History Workshop Journal*, no. 9 (Spring 1980): 124.

men to return to the lines in Brunete, Nelson held a meeting in which he got them to agree to the order – which fortunately was rescinded.[145]

In their letters home, volunteers often emphasized the antifascist political commitments that brought them to Spain. Writing home about a month after his arrival, Arvola captured the politically charged atmosphere in the brigades, describing how he and a "comrade from Finland" had discussed the workers' role "in the present world situation, late into the night." In Spain, he concluded, one could see more clearly than elsewhere the role of the party and the working class.[146] Volunteers attempting to convince their families of the justice of the cause, as well as those whose spouses shared their convictions, wrote letters that echoed the party press's insistence that "to defeat fascism in Spain was to defend democracy everywhere."[147] In May 1938, Cecil Cole explained to his family, "Even tho [sic] you are not in sympathy with communism, remember we are not fighting for a communistic state in Spain but for a democracy.... We are fighting as you in the states would fight against a forced dictatorship."[148] Gene Wolman likewise explained to his skeptical family, "Sure life is sweet at twenty four and it is just for this reason that we are fighting. We are battling to prevent it from becoming the sour stench that Fascism brings." On the "positive side," he added, "We are fighting to make life much sweeter. Under Capitalism life with its worries, pettiness, meanness is none too sweet. Under the modified Capitalism toward which Spain is driving, life will indeed be *muy dulce*."[149] (Both Cole and Wolman were killed in action in Spain.) In remarkably similar language, Ben Gardner explained to his wife, who was working for the North American Committee to Aid Spanish Democracy, the thrill of being on guard duty, when he had "the wonderful feeling of holding a rifle with a bayonet, guarding Democracy."[150]

Many volunteers linked the cause in Spain to the Soviet Union – as a model for the future, a source of aid, and a guarantor of victory. In a diary entry written on the eve of the battle at Jarama, Merriman prepared himself to die for the cause, justifying his actions in terms at once heartfelt and bombastic: "About to lead first Battalion of Americans in this war.... Long Live Communism! Long live the Soviet Union!... Men die and mean to die (if necessary) so that the revolution may live on. They may stop us today but tomorrow we still

[145] Nelson et al., *American Radical*, 203, 224–5; "Report on Morale of XV Brigade," l. 72 largely confirms Nelson's account.

[146] Ranse Edward Arvola to Helen, 16 July 1937, Kruth Papers, Box 1, Folder 1.

[147] Steve Nelson, "We Sailed on Christmas," 1937 clipping from party press held in Nelson Papers, Box 1, Folder 13.

[148] C. M. Cole to Family, 19 May [1938], VALB, Container 1.

[149] Gene Wolman to Family, Letter # 6, 10 June 1937, VALB, Container 1.

[150] Ben Gardner [to Alice Gardner], 5 July 1937, VALB, Container 1. See also Don MacLeod to Stuart, 8 June 1937, VALB Container 1; Mito Kruth to Helen, 2 May [1937], Kruth Papers, Box 1, Folder 9.

FIGURE 5. Portraits of president of the Spanish Republic Manuel Azaña, Vladimir Lenin, Josef Stalin, and Karl Marx hang over soldier working at a typewriter. Courtesy Tamiment Library, New York University (ALBA Photo 177–178068)

take up the march."[151] Letters home tended to be less dramatic. Kruth, who often took a didactic tone in letters to his wife, explained in April 1937 that "without the S.[oviet] U.[nion] Spain would today be a fascist country."[152] Don MacLeod likewise affirmed in a letter home that "the very existence of the strong & powerful working class government of the USSR is the greatest assurance we have that the Spanish loyalists will be victorious."[153]

Defending Spain with the assistance of the Soviet Union, the volunteers identified themselves with an international cause. This sense of connection via the Soviet Union to a global movement appears most clearly in Internationals' accounts of the celebration of Soviet holidays in Spain.[154] On the eve of the

[151] Merriman Diary, vol. 1, 17 febrero, Merriman Papers, Box 1, Folder 3.

[152] Mito Kruth to Helen, 25 April 1937, Kruth Papers, Box 1, Folder 9; see also Mito to Helen, 21 August 1937, 23 August [1937], Box 1, Folder 10.

[153] Don MacLeod to Stuart, 8 June 1937, VALB, Container 1.

[154] On the celebration of Soviet holidays in Spain see Kowalsky, *Stalin and the Spanish Civil War*, chapter 7.

1 May holiday in 1937, William Sennett described the celebration planned in Spain as part of an international event. He sent his wife the program for the local observance, directing her to "notice the evening discussions in an educational form in three different languages. I am leading the one in English." He then immediately connected this local event to the one he was missing in Chicago, along with the one he imagined was happening in New York. He hoped, he wrote, "to hear of the biggest Chicago demonstration ever with the most colorful parade ever seen. New York I know will come through."[155] Likewise, on the eve of the twentieth anniversary of the Bolshevik revolution in November 1937, Gardner described his local "little celebration" as both uniquely Spanish with its "young workers mandolin orchestra" and – with its hour-and-a-half speech that is "killing the whole program," its stage adorned with Republican flags and "pictures of Lenin, Marx & Engels," as well as Spanish communist Dolores Ibárruri and the Republic's president Manual Azaña – as not so very different from the much larger gathering he was missing in Philadelphia.[156] Communists everywhere celebrated the same heroes, heard the same speeches, and sang the *Internationale*. The holiday in a Spanish village was connected to those in Philadelphia, Chicago, and New York and resembled, or so Kruth imagined in a letter home, "celebrations in the Russian villages."[157]

Such letters, as a number of the volunteers' wives complained, sounded very much like party propaganda. Responding to criticism of his letters, Gardner wrote, "Alice dear, you say that I don't write anything but an agitation letter." He was, he admitted, constrained, although whether by the censor or a self-imposed need to maintain morale is unclear: "In war time lots of things cannot be written, so at certain moments one just feels empty." He pledged to try to make his letters "as concrete & full of actual events as possible."[158] Helen Kruth likewise complained about Mito's "stereotypical letters," and he too promised to do better.[159]

However unsatisfying they may have been to receive, "stereotypical" letters stuffed with party rhetoric were not necessarily insincere or mere propaganda. For Kruth, the language of the party seemed to be a primary mode of expression. In a 1935 letter to Helen written when he was in Michigan on party business, Mito tried to cheer her up with Friedrich Engels' "adage that beaten armies learn well."[160] In Spain, he framed his efforts to produce more personal letters in political terms, vowing to do "some real self criticism."[161] Two months later he finally succeeded in surprising Helen "as well as myself by writing a

155 William Sennett to Gussie [Machen], 30 April 1937, VALB, Container 1.

156 Ben Gardner to Elky [Alice Gardner], 6 November 1937, VALB, Container 1. See also Mito Kruth to Helen, 9 November 1937, Kruth Papers, Box 1, Folder, 12.

157 Mito Kruth to Helen, 25 April 1937, Kruth Papers, Box 1, Folder 9.

158 Ben Gardner [to Alice Gardner], 8 September 1937, VALB, Container 1.

159 Mito Kruth to Helen, 19 February [1938], Kruth Papers, Box 1, Folder 13.

160 Mito Kruth to Helen, 27 February 1935, Kruth Papers, Box 1, Folder 8.

161 Mito Kruth to Helen, 19 February [1938].

whole letter without politics."[162] In some cases political clichés could carry strong emotional content. Thus Ben Gardner also offered comfort in the form of a slogan, writing to his wife Alice in June 1938 as he neared the one-year anniversary of his service in Spain, "I suffer & feel guilty when I read how much you have to go thru, but at the same time I feel that I have & am doing my little share in this great & historic struggle of the Spanish people."[163] In the same month, William Sennett wrote his partner Gussie, "So many things are happening throughout the world [China, Spain, Czechoslovakia, Britain, France, etc.] that if a person were not a Communist he would be in despair."[164]

As Sennett's lumping together of China, Spain, Czechoslovakia, etc., suggests, the volunteers often had little specific knowledge of the Spain that they imagined themselves to be saving. They relied on often schematic, idealized, and sometimes condescending notions of the "Spanish people." Laurie Lee, who had traveled in Spain before the war, was able to see the "empty villages that seem to have had their eyes put out" as evidence "of the gaseous squalor of a country at war."[165] But other volunteers assumed that what they were seeing was the eternal backwardness of Spain. In a letter home, Kruth described an unnamed village as "of course... very backward. The people must have lived this way 1,000 years ago."[166] In a letter to his wife Marion, then still in Moscow, Robert Merriman detailed with ethnographic exactness the customs of the local family that had him to dinner: "No plates or knives and forks are used at all. Each person is given some flat tough bread with which he scoops up his food from the main pot and places it on another piece of this bread which serves as a plate." Ever concerned with the agricultural issues that had brought him to the Soviet Union three years earlier, Merriman peppered his hosts with questions "about the land problem here" and concluded that collectivization would be premature because "the material conditions are not yet ripe for such a thing."[167]

Such understandings of Spanish "backwardness" coexisted with and perhaps reinforced both warm feelings for the Spanish people and a desire to help them. Kruth decided that "there is nothing like the Spanish people for kindness and consideration."[168] The volunteers seem to have taken up with enthusiasm the programs designed by their commissars to cultivate good relations with Spanish civilians. When on leave in small villages, they organized fiestas, passed out candy and gifts to the children, provided basic medical care, and "helped" with

[162] Mito Kruth to Helen, 19 April 1938, Kruth Papers, Box 1, Folder 13.

[163] Ben Gardner [to Alice Gardner], 14 June 1938, VALB, Container 1.

[164] William Sennett to Gussie, 9 June 1938, VALB, Container 1; see also William Sennett to Gussie, 14 July 1937; William Sennett to Gussie, 14 September 1937, ibid.

[165] Lee, *Moment of War*, 49.

[166] Mito Kruth to Helen, 18 April [1937], Kruth Papers, Box 1, Folder 9.

[167] Robert Merriman to Marion Merriman, 13 February 1937, Merriman Papers, Box 1, Folder 2.

[168] Mito Kruth to Helen, 18 April [1937]. See also Mito to Helen, 9 May 1937, ibid.

the harvest; Nelson related that the brigadistas, most of whom grew up in cities, "wasted so much barley that the farmers, with the utmost tact and delicacy, asked them not to trouble themselves further in the matter."[169] (On leave they also might get drunk, fight, bust up wine shops, and carouse.[170]) Alongside their hospitals, the Internationals organized homes for refugee children; volunteers contributed funds for books, clothing, and food.[171]

Even as they "helped" the civilian population, the volunteers, as noted earlier, often resented, denigrated, and distrusted Spanish "political leaders, soldiers, civil servants, and political parties." Of course, such feelings were not universal. Cecil Cole, for example, noted in a letter home that "they're a swell people taken individually or collectively. I'm working now to have more Spanish added to my group."[172] Cole, however, spoke more Spanish than most of his fellow brigadistas – enough to realize that people in Spain spoke "four distinct languages"[173] – and thus may have been able to make a more sophisticated evaluation than most Internationals of both his Spanish comrades and the situation in Spain. Indeed Świerczewski, who picked up a "rough and ready" Spanish and also learned French "tolerably well" in the short time he commanded the Fourteenth Brigade, deemed the ability to speak Spanish a vital qualification for all Soviet advisors in Spain precisely because it allowed them to make independent assessments and to meet their Spanish comrades as equals.[174] Świerczewski advocated "quickly eliminating the condescension and the patronizing tone" that characterized the Internationals' interactions with the Spaniards.[175] Thus when Len Crome, a Russian who had emigrated to Scotland as a teenager and served as the chief medical officer of Świerczewski's Thirty-Fifth Division, failed to punish a drunk Irish driver who, in his eagerness to evacuate a field hospital, threatened a Spanish surgeon with a gun, Świerczewski accused him of behaving like a "British soldier in India."[176] The same could perhaps be said of many of the Internationals, who devoutly wished to save Spain, but were also ready to judge the "natives" as ignorant and incompetent if not traitorous.

[169] "Informe sobre la situación," l. 83; "Informe sobre la 35 y 45 división durante el periodo del 9 al 15 de julio de 1938," 21 July 1938, RGASPI, f. 525, op. 1, d. 3, l. 325; Nelson et al., *American Radical*, 212.

[170] Nelson et al., *American Radical*, 210; "Perepiska iuridicheskoi komissii shtaba XV brigady," RGASPI, f. 545, op. 3, d. 451, ll. 41–53.

[171] "Doklad Voennogo komissariata," l. 386. George Foucek to Folks, 3 October 1937, VALB, Container 1; Lini De Vries to Max, 15 April [1937], Martin Papers, Box 6, Folder 19; Johnston, *Legions of Babel*, 92.

[172] C. M. Cole to Family, 22 November 1937, VALB, Container 1.

[173] C. M. Cole to Jeff, 1 January [1938], VALB, Container 1.

[174] On Świerczewski's language skills see Crome, "Walter," 121; "About the work of our people in Spain," undated memorandum, in *Spain Betrayed*, 495–6.

[175] "About the work," in *Spain Betrayed*, 492.

[176] Crome, "Walter," 116, 125; Szurek, *Shattered Dream*, 231.

Still, the brigadistas' love for the kind and hospitable Spanish people, however abstract or tinged with condescension, was often sincere, widespread and, long lasting. In a 1937 letter, Lini De Vries gushed, "And the Spanish people – words can't describe them – there they are in a society semi-feudalistic – yet so much higher on the thinking political level than the American proletariat – alert, sensitive, and intelligent. I love them!"[177] In a letter written as he prepared to leave Spain in 1938, Canute Frankson, a skilled machinist who had emigrated from Jamaica to the United States in 1917 and joined the Communist Party in 1934, asked, "I wonder will we ever forget the tears of Spain? The pictures of the dead mothers and the little hands of their children wounded, and dead, clinging to their breasts. I doubt it very much.... There will be many of us who will want to return to Spain. Because we love the Spanish people."[178] In 1939, William Rust, a British communist who served as the *Daily Worker*'s correspondent in Spain, emphasized the mutuality of that love: "Received into families, the Internationals made warm friendships and were loved by the children, for whom they bought toys and sweets out of their scanty pay of ten pesetas a day." He also emphasized that "between the British and Spanish soldiers there exists a mutual love and respect."[179] Even those who ultimately renounced communism, such as Robert Gladnick, often retained a fondness for the Spanish people. In his 1996 memoir, he described his service in the Soviet tank corps as a pivotal moment: "I was to serve with the Spaniards whom I learned to love & the Russians with the exception of a few – I learned to hate."[180]

In October 1938, at an impressive farewell celebration in Barcelona, Dolores Ibárruri, the legendary communist orator better known as La Pasionaria, codified the sentimental story of solidarity with the Spanish people for the brigadistas. The farewell came in the wake of the Internationals' participation in the Republic's last great offensive, a surprise attack across the Ebro River in July 1938. As in previous offensives, initial gains, made at great cost, were turned back. But in this case, the problem was less the shortage of arms and reserves – and they were quite scarce – than international events, namely the Munich Agreement signed in September 1938 as Loyalist troops were retreating in the face of Nationalist counterattacks. The British and French decision to appease Adolf Hitler clearly spelled the failure of the offensive to achieve its aim of persuading the democracies to lift the arms embargo. In a September address to the League of Nations, Juan Negrín, the Republic's prime minister, offered to withdraw the International Brigades in hopes of creating pressure for the withdrawal of the Italian and German troops aiding the rebels. On 29 October 1938, perhaps two hundred thousand people lined the streets of Barcelona to

[177] Lini Fuhr [De Vries] to Ida, 15 March 1937, in *Madrid 1937*, 242.

[178] Canute Frankson to My dear, 10 May 1938, in *Madrid 1937*, 134.

[179] Rust, *Britons in Spain*, 19, 154.

[180] Gladnick memoirs, chapter 5, p. 11.

cheer the departing volunteers.[181] Gardner, who was among the six thousand Internationals there that day, wrote, "It wasn't just a show like in a capitalist country a parade. You could see & feel it that the people love the internationals from the bottom of their hearts.... It was the highest expression of the unity of the international proletariat & the Spanish people."[182]

Ibárruri's speech at the farewell celebration emphasized precisely the love and solidarity that Gardner felt. She spoke, she said, with "anguish and infinite sorrow." She appealed to the mothers and women of Spain to tell their children how the volunteers "came to our country as crusaders for liberty... they sacrificed everything – their loves, countries, homes, fortunes, mothers, wives, brothers and sisters, children – and they came to us and said, 'We are here! Your cause, Spain's cause, is our cause, the cause of all advanced and progressive humanity.'" To the departing brigadistas, she declared, "You can go proudly. You are history. You are legend."[183] With profound emotion, Ibárruri thus summed up everything many believed or wanted to believe about the reality of international solidarity in Spain: the great cause of progressive humanity united people across language and nationality. The mothers of Spain would remember the departing heroes and the heroes "shrouded in the Spanish earth."

For many of the volunteers the legend long remained powerful and persuasive. On the one hand, it elevated and celebrated their often deeply felt experiences of sacrifice in the name of a great cause and the thrilling feeling of working in a truly international environment. On the other hand, the story Ibárruri sent them off with simultaneously obscured or minimized the limits of international solidarity. Her assertion that "Communists, socialists, anarchists, republicans, men of every color, of differing ideologies, of antagonistic religions... came and offered themselves unconditionally" glided over not only national animosities – within the brigades and between the Internationals and the "natives" they both loved and distrusted – but also the fears of hidden "enemies" so central to the way many volunteers understood the war. The Internationals' tendency to explain failures as the work of saboteurs and "wreckers" grew in part out of the conviction that they stood on the side of progress. It also linked them to the culture of Stalinism – which encompassed not only denunciations, purges, and terror but also the rituals, symbols, heroes, and narratives cherished by international communists.

181 On Munich, see Alpert, *International History*, 165–7. On the Ebro and the withdrawal of the Brigades, see Johnston, *Legions of Babel*, 135–43; Graham, *Spanish Republic*, 382–4; G. Dimitrov and D. Manuilsky to Voroshilov, 29 August 1938, in *Spain Betrayed*, 469.

182 Ben Gardner to Elky [Alice Gardner], 1 November 1938, VALB, Container 1.

183 Dolores Ibárruri, "Hasta pronto, hermanos: Mensaje de despedida a los voluntarios de las Brigades Internacionales," in Manuel Vásquez Montalbán, *Pasionaria y los siete enanitos* (Barcelona: Random House Mondadori, 2005), 407–9.

4

True Bolsheviks and Trotskyite Bastards

On 29 September 1937, fourteen men arrested for desertion were returned to the Fifteenth International Brigade, then in Aragon.[1] Over the course of two days, on 4 and 5 October, twelve of them stood for trial. Henry Shapiro, who had arrived in Spain only two months before and "never saw action" was sentenced to be shot. He had, according to the laconic trial report, "organised stealing of [the American-Canadian] battalion's only ambulance... and worked out the route through Spain" that he and his co-conspirators would take to the French border. Robert W. Isenberg, a seaman from New York, was also "sentenced to be shot" for participating in stealing the ambulance. He had been in Spain only two weeks longer than Shapiro and likewise "never saw action." They received death sentences because both "lied continuously throughout the trial, showed no antifascist conduct, both are lumpen elements."[2]

By contrast, Richard deWitt Brown, a seaman from Kansas City, Missouri, who also "participated in deserting with the ambulance," received a one-year prison term "because he took a more sincere stand at the trial, exposed the plot... and also because he had already seen service at the front and asked for a chance to redeem himself in coming operations." The rest, who apparently deserted in separate incidents, were sentenced to prison terms ranging from one month to "the duration of the war." The lightest sentence went to Henry Plotnick, a nineteen-year-old communist who "cracked under strain of battle;" the longest to Nelson Fishnelson, a communist who was unwilling "to help

[1] "Etat Major de la 15° Brigade," 29 September 1937, Rossiiskii gosudarstvennyi arkhiv sotsial'no-politicheskoi istorii (RGASPI), f. 545, op. 3, d. 451, l. 86.

[2] "Report on the Trials of 12 Deserters," 9 October 1937, RGASPI, f. 545, op. 3, d. 435, l. 81. The Abraham Lincoln Brigade Archives (ALBA) database, www.alba-valb.org, identifies Shapiro as a traveling salesman from Roxbury, Massachusetts. Michael Petrou identifies him as from Montreal, *Renegades: Canadians in the Spanish Civil War* (Vancouver: University of British Columbia Press, 2008), 231.

in the proceedings of the trial," and to Murray Krangle [Morris or Murray Krangel], also a communist, who had been to officers' training school and "deserted once before."[3]

On their face, the death sentences handed down to raw recruits appear to confirm dark conclusions about the pervasiveness of Stalinist terror in Spain. Drawing on similar evidence, historians Harvey Klehr, John Earl Haynes, and Fridrikh Igorevich Firsov argue that the archives document "ideological warfare and personal terror directed at some volunteers by their own comrades."[4] As proof they present a letter describing the October 1937 trials that "does not, however, confirm the executions," along with a long list of "suspicious individuals and deserters" from the Fifteenth Brigade, which includes the name of a volunteer whom several veterans claimed was executed. They acknowledge that estimates of the "number of American volunteers executed for desertion vary from none to several score."[5] Still, they agree with historian Stanley Payne that, even if "the total number of victims was not particularly great," the recourse to the "liquidation" of deserters verifies a deep penetration of Stalinist practices.[6]

The importation into Spain of the culture of Stalinism is often understood as the work of Soviet NKVD agents and the Republic's military intelligence service, which was organized with assistance from the NKVD.[7] The June 1937 arrest and execution of Andreu Nin, the leader of the POUM (Partit Obrer d'Unificació Marxista, Workers' Party of Marxist Unity), who in the 1920s had lived in Moscow and worked as Lev Trotsky's secretary, was almost certainly an NKVD operation.[8] The NKVD was also likely responsible for the disappearance and death of José Robles, a Spanish-born, Russian-speaking Johns Hopkins professor who had served as a translator for top Soviet advisors.[9]

3 "Report on the Trials of 12 Deserters," ll. 81–2. Corrected spellings of names from ALBA database.

4 Harvey Klehr, John Earl Haynes, and Fridrikh Igorevich Firsov, *The Secret World of American Communism* (New Haven: Yale University Press, 1995), 186, 187.

5 Ibid., 160.

6 Stanley G. Payne, *The Spanish Civil War, the Soviet Union, and Communism* (New Haven: Yale University Press, 2004), 205.

7 Ronald Radosh, Mary R. Habeck, and Grigory Sevostianov, eds., *Spain Betrayed: The Soviet Union in the Spanish Civil War* (New Haven: Yale University Press, 2001), xvii–iii, 106–7, 208–9, 372–3, 476; Klehr et al., *Secret World*, 151–87; Pedro Corral, *Desertores: La Guerra Civil que nadie quiere contar* (Barcelona: Random House Mondadori, 2006), 218–28.

8 Ángel Viñas, *El escudo de la República: El oro de España, la apuesta soviética y los hechos de mayo de 1937* (Barcelona: Crítica, 2007), 605–27; Payne, *Spanish Civil War*, 227–30; Helen Graham, *The Spanish Republic at War, 1936–1939* (Cambridge: Cambridge University Press, 2002), 287–90, 344–6. Víctor Alba and Stephen Schwartz, *Spanish Marxism versus Soviet Communism: A History of the POUM* (New Brunswick, NJ: Transaction Books, 1988). José María Zavala, *En busca de Andreu Nin: Vida y muerte de un mito silenciado de la Guerra Civil* (Barcelona: Plaza & Janés, 2005).

9 Enric Ucelay Da-Cal, "La 'Traición revolucionaria': Los escándalos soviéticos en la guerra civil española y los orígenes de la 'guerra fría,'" in *Los rusos en la guerra de España, 1936–1939* (Madrid: Fundación Pablo Iglesias, 2009), 110–11. Another contested example is the death of

Yet for all its documented horrors, the "terror" in Spain never operated on the Soviet scale. Even if Soviet agents aimed to approximate domestic practice more closely – advocating, for example, the dissolution of the "counterrevolutionary officer corps" – they were to some degree constrained by the larger Spanish context.[10] As one Soviet advisor, a Comrade Kachelin, noted in an October 1937 report to military intelligence in Moscow, Soviet personnel, unable to "even imagine" the sort of contentious, multiparty political environment in which they found themselves, acted in inappropriate and counterproductive ways. In general, Kachelin complained, Soviets in Spain "really overdo it with tacking on labels; they say that this one is a 'fascist,' that one is a 'wrecker,' and so on."[11] Applying Stalinist labels in Spain signaled Stalinist ways of thinking, but Soviet expectations notwithstanding, such labels did not "work" as they did in the Soviet Union to justify and drive mass terror.

In the cases tried in October 1937, the convicted deserters seem to have escaped execution. Robert Merriman, then the Fifteenth Brigade's chief of staff, recorded in his diary that he had quarreled with brigade commander Vladimir Ćopić over the suggestion made by division commander General Walter (Karol Świerczewski) "about even shooting a few if necessary." The unit, Merriman noted, was "demanding tough sentences even death." But he also suggested his own uneasiness with such extreme measures: "In the evening, some drinking took place. I helped myself heavily."[12] Ćopić's own journal notes that shortly after the trial the two condemned men "were pardoned and later they held up well."[13] Shapiro, who was sentenced to death in 1937, was listed as "missing"

Bob Smillie, who served in the POUM militia. Tom Buchanan, "The Death of Bob Smillie, the Spanish Civil War, and the Eclipse of the Independent Labour Party," *Historical Journal* 40, no. 2 (June 1997): 435–61; John Newsinger and George Kopp, "The Death of Bob Smillie," *Historical Journal* 41, no. 2 (June 1998): 575–8; Tom Buchanan, "The Death of Bob Smillie: A Reply," *Historical Journal* 43, no. 4 (December 2000): 1009–112.

[10] "Letter of Comrade Donizetti [Yan Berzin] from 22/2/37," in *Spain Betrayed*, 150. On constraints see Graham, *Spanish Republic*, 284–6.

[11] "Report of Com. Kachelin," in *Spain Betrayed*, 293. See also Karl Schlögel, *Moscow, 1937*, trans. Rodney Livingstone (Malden, MA: Polity, 2012), 103–8.

[12] Robert Merriman diary, vol. 2, p. 19, Robert Merriman Papers, ALBA 191, Box 1, Folder 3, Tamiment Library/Robert F. Wagner Labor Archives, New York University. On Lincoln veterans' support for shooting repeat deserters see John Dollard, *Fear in Battle* (Washington, DC: Infantry Journal, 1944), 37. In a January 1938 report, Świerczewski could not recall a single case of "punishment for desertion by an internationalist." "Notes on the Situation in the International Units in Spain, Report by Colonel Com. Sverchevsky (Walter)," 14 January 1938, in *Spain Betrayed*, 455. Other sources claim that Świerczewski carried out harsh penalties, including execution, for desertion. Richard Baxell, *British Volunteers and the Spanish Civil War: The British Battalion in the International Brigades, 1936–1939* (New York: Routledge, 2004),140; Alexander Szurek, *The Shattered Dream*, trans. Jacques Grunblatt and Hilda Grunblatt (Boulder, CO: Eastern European Monographs, 1985), 105. On executions in the Republic's Army see Matthews, *Reluctant Warriors*, 196–7, 211.

[13] John Peter Kraljic, "The War Diary of Vladimir Copic," *The Volunteer: Journal of the Veterans of the Abraham Lincoln Brigade* 24, no. 3 (September 2002): 8.

in 1938, presumably killed in action or captured and executed at Teruel. I have found no trace in the archives of Isenberg's fate.[14]

The apparently nonlethal outcome of these and other trials[15] points to the importance of distinguishing the culture of Stalinism from a particular set of deadly results. Understanding NKVD agents as the primary carriers of Stalinism in Spain cannot help us explain why, as Merriman noted in his diary, some brigadistas demanded death sentences for deserters. Likewise, emphasizing that the Soviets sought to "manipulate and control events" discourages an analysis of how and why, in reporting the trial of the deserters, political commissar Dave Doran, a communist trade union organizer from upstate New York, without any apparent prompting or pressure from Soviet agents, used classic Stalinist formulas: Deserters wished to "redeem" themselves in combat; "every battalion and unit sent in resolutions passed by the men calling for the death penalty."[16] A focus on Soviet agents' manipulation and on the egregious instances of political terror that they perpetrated risks ignoring the everyday meanings and operation of Stalinist culture in Spain and the question of how – through films and the press, as well as through political education and the hunt for Trotskyites – Stalinism shaped the lives and understandings of rank-and-file international communists, who were themselves neither victims nor perpetrators of terror.

Little Chapaevs in Spain

Even for many noncommunists in Spain, the Soviet Union – specifically the October Revolution and the Russian civil war – provided models of revolutionary behavior that shaped, if not their own conduct, then their aspirations. George Orwell, whose *Homage to Catalonia* published in 1938 became both one of the most celebrated and one of the most explicitly anti-Soviet memoirs of the war, joined the anti-Stalinist POUM militia, whose members trained at the Lenin Barracks in Barcelona and fought in the Lenin Division.[17] Of course, Orwell and his comrades, whether Spanish or British, may have had something different in mind when they invoked Lenin than did the German volunteer in the International Brigades, who went to Spain because "I wanted to be a little

[14] Petrou, *Renegades*, 133. The ALBA database lists Shapiro as "killed in action" in 1938. Mark Zuehlke concludes that Shapiro was executed and was reported missing as part of a cover-up, *The Gallant Cause: Canadians in the Spanish Civil War 1936–1939* (Mississauga, Ontario: Wiley & Sons Canada, 2007), 181. Other sources conclude that no one was executed. Peter N. Carroll, *The Odyssey of the Abraham Lincoln Brigade: Americans in the Spanish Civil War* (Stanford: Stanford University Press, 1994), 165; Cecil Eby, *Between the Bullet and the Lie: American Volunteers in the Spanish Civil War* (New York: Holt, Rinehart, and Winston, 1969), 174.

[15] Peter Carroll, "The Myth of the Moscow Archives," *Science and Society* 68, no. 3 (Fall 2004): 339.

[16] Radosh et al., *Spain Betrayed*, xxx; "Report on the Trials of 12 Deserters," ll. 81, 82.

[17] George Orwell, *Homage to Catalonia* (1938; reprint, San Diego: Harcourt Brace Jovanovich, 1980), 6–7, 112.

Lenin."[18] But they, too, would likely have taken as a compliment the praise recorded by Merriman in his diary: "Bill and Gall said I knew how to work like a Bolshevik."[19] As historian Tom Buchanan notes, even the anti-Stalinist leftists respected the "authority of Lenin and the Bolshevik revolution."[20]

Long-standing respect for the Bolshevik revolution among the noncommunist left in Spain intensified during the civil war. In 1921, when the Spanish Socialist Party (Partido Socialista Obrero Español) voted against affiliation with the Third International, its executive committee explained that the rejection of the Comintern's Twenty-one Conditions did not mean the rejection of the Revolution: "We are with the Russian Revolution; and to our Party we say, as always, that we consider ourselves obliged to defend it."[21] More broadly, in the 1920s and 1930s, the Spanish middle classes saw in the Soviet Union an "icon of modernity."[22] On the eve of the civil war, more than thirty chapters of the Friends of the Soviet Union operated in the Republic, distributing Spanish-language propaganda shipped from Moscow that promoted Soviet economic and cultural "advances."[23] Francisco Largo Caballero, a prominent and quite moderate socialist in the 1920s, was hailed after the Popular Front victory in 1936 as the "Spanish Lenin."[24] The sense that an association with Lenin and the Bolshevik revolution, however inappropriate, added a gloss of revolutionary modernity grew in tandem with the arrival of much-needed Soviet aid in the wake of the military rebellion. As Orwell grimly noted, "The Russian arms and the magnificent defense of Madrid by troops mainly under Communist control had made the Communists heroes in Spain.... Every Russian aeroplane that flew over our heads was Communist propaganda."[25] Soviet arms and the International Brigades provided a boost to Republican morale and produced a "sudden craze" for all things Soviet – from hats to films.[26]

And the Soviets were happy to indulge the craze. Along with military and humanitarian aid, the Soviet Union supplied cultural products – literature, magazines, records, posters, and especially films – to the Republic.[27] The

[18] Quoted in Josie McLellan, "'I Wanted To Be a Little Lenin': Ideology and the German International Brigade Volunteers," *Journal of Contemporary History* 41, no. 2 (2006): 292.

[19] Bill is probably Bill Lawrence, the American party's representative in Albacete. Gall (or Gal) is Janos Galicz, the Hungarian Red Army officer who commanded the Fifteenth Brigade. Merriman diary, vol. 1, 31 mayo, Merriman Papers, Box 1, Folder 3.

[20] Tom Buchanan, "The Death of Bob Smillie," 458.

[21] Quoted in Gerald H. Meaker, *The Revolutionary Left in Spain, 1914–1923* (Stanford: Stanford University Press, 1974), 370, see also 103, 209.

[22] Graham, *Spanish Republic*, 18, 181.

[23] Daniel Kowalsky, *Stalin and the Spanish Civil War* [electronic resource] (New York: Columbia University Press, 2004), chapter 6, paragraphs 9, 12.

[24] Hugh Thomas, *The Spanish Civil War: Revised Edition* (New York: Modern Library, 2001), 155.

[25] Orwell, *Homage*, 63.

[26] Graham, *Spanish Republic*, 174.

[27] Kowalsky, *Stalin and the Spanish Civil War*, chapter 7.

Russian civil-war-themed films *We're from Kronstadt* (My iz Kronshtadta, 1936) and *Chapaev* (1934) were widely screened in the Republican zone. Billeted in the small town of Villanueva de la Jara in early 1937, the Lincoln battalion ran films three times a day, including one showing for the townspeople who apparently enjoyed "equally well" *We're from Kronstadt*, which was about the 1919 defense of Petrograd during the Russian civil war, and *How to Operate a Maxim Machinegun*.[28] Still, when given the option, civilians clearly preferred Hollywood films, which dominated Madrid's movie houses. The musical *Circus* (Tsirk, 1936) was the only Soviet production among the fifty films most widely viewed in the city during the war.[29]

Loyalist troops, both Spanish and International, provided the largest and most enthusiastic audiences for Soviet films. *Chapaev*, the story of the legendary civil war commander Vasilii Chapaev, appears to have been particularly popular. Mikhail Kol'tsov, *Pravda*'s correspondent in Spain, attributed the film's popularity to the soldiers' identification with the heroic Bolshevik fighting a familiar (if anachronistic) "fascist" enemy along the "Ural River, so like the Ebro River."[30] Kol'tsov's emphasis notwithstanding, such identification was not necessarily ideological. Soldiers might see in Soviet civil war films a reflection – however idealized and romanticized – of their own experiences or expectations of combat. When in October 1937 American volunteer Mito Kruth saw *Chapaev* for at least the second time since his arrival in Spain, he likened the experience to watching a "wild west" picture: "When the enemy gets licked a great cheer goes up."[31] After viewing *We're from Kronstadt* for the fourth time in mid-September 1937, during the Aragon offensive, Ben Gardner took a more somber view, writing that this time, "Certain scenes looked like the ones we went thru. Watching our Russian comrades in the picture we felt we are participating in the picture."[32]

Chapaev himself offered soldiers a charismatic and unpretentious role model. Dedicated to the cause and confident of victory, Chapaev was nonetheless unsure about whether there was a difference between Bolsheviks and

[28] Eby, *Between the Bullet*, 28–9.

[29] José Cabeza San Deogracias, *El descanso del guerrero: El cine en Madrid durante la Guerra Civil española (1936–1939)* (Madrid: Ediciones Rialp, 2005), 17, 44.

[30] Mikhail Kol'tsov, *Ispankii dnevnik* (Moscow: Grifon, 2005), 27–8. See also Colonel Simonov to Kliment Voroshilov, 21 August 1937, in *Spain Betrayed*, 249; Alfred Kantorowicz, *Chapaev – batal'on dvadtsati odnoi natsional'nosti* (Moscow: Khudozhestvennaia literatura, 1939); Thomas, *Spanish Civil War*, 494; Julian Graffy, *Chapaev* (London: I. B. Tauris, 2009), 88–90; Vsevolod Vishnevskii, "Nash fil'm v Madride," in *Stat'i, dnevniki, pis'ma: O literature i iskusstve* (Moscow: Sovetskii pisatel', 1961), 192–3.

[31] Mito Kruth to Helen [Kruth], 31 October 1937, Mito Kruth Papers, ALBA 240, Box 1, Folder 12. See also Mito Kruth to Helen, 21 August 1937, Box 1, Folder 11.

[32] Ben Gardner to Elky [Alice Gardner], 13 September 1937, Veterans of the Abraham Lincoln Brigade, Bay Area Post, (VALB), BANC MSS 71/105 z, Container 1, Bancroft Library, University of California, Berkeley.

communists.[33] If, as Julian Graffy argues in his study of the film, Chapaev's description of himself as having "only known how to read for two years" was "calculated to endear him to those large sections of the [Soviet] audience who have themselves only recently become literate," his recently attained literacy – along with his political ignorance – was also well suited to audiences of Spanish recruits, who often learned how to read in the army.[34] The historian Richard Stites describes the character of Chapaev, although based on a real commander, as "folkloric." Chapaev and his men returned from battle on the steppe "like cowboys back from the range: tough, dirty, rude, even menacing, but also humorous, brave, loyal, and egalitarian except in their universal deference to the leader."[35] It was with this Chapaev that American volunteer Alvah Bessie identified not himself but his company's acting commander, Pavlos Fortis, whom he described as "like Chapayev in many ways." Although Bessie did not specify the similarity, his earlier description of Fortis as a "crack machine-gunner," a "swell, big-hearted guy – but not having the attributes of a commander – language difficulty also" suggests an immigrant Greek cowboy, a down-to-earth and idealized volunteer for liberty.[36]

Republican journalists and propagandists expected that Spanish troops would not only identify with the revolutionary heroes on screen but would also imitate them. After observing an open-air screening of a Soviet film, journalist and novelist Clemente Cimorra had no doubt that the hundreds of soldiers in the audience would follow the example set by the celluloid combatants. He reported that Spanish soldiers who viewed a film about the Red Army went on to undertake the "most successful operations in the history of the division."[37] To make sure that soldiers understood the films correctly, commissars organized "explanatory conversations" after the screenings.[38]

The most remarkable case of life imitating art was that of Antonio Col, a native of Madrid whose marine unit had taken the name "Sailors of Kronstadt." In November 1936, less than one month after the first Madrid screening of *We're from Kronstadt* (the Spanish title was *Los marinos de Cronstadt*), six local newspapers reported that Col heroically destroyed four enemy tanks with hand grenades and then sacrificed his life in defense of Madrid: He was either

33 Denise Youngblood, *Russian War Films: On the Cinema Front* (Lawrence: University of Kansas Press, 2010), 43.

34 Graffy, *Chapaev*, 38; Matthews, *Reluctant Warriors*, 98–9.

35 Richard Stites, *Russian Popular Culture: Entertainment and Society since 1900* (New York: Cambridge University Press, 1992), 45. See also John Haynes, *New Soviet Man: Gender and Masculinity in Stalinist Soviet Cinema* (Manchester: Manchester University Press, 2003), 164.

36 Alvah Bessie, *Alvah Bessie's Civil War Notebooks*, ed. Dan Bessie (Lexington: University of Kentucky Press, 2002), 48, 43.

37 Quoted in José Cabeza San Deogracias, "Buscando héroes: La historia de Antonio Col como ejemplo del uso de la narrativa como propaganda durante la Guerra Civil española," *Revista Historia y Comunicación Social* 10 (2005): 47.

38 Ministry of War pamphlet as quoted in Cabeza San Deogracias, "Buscando," 48.

gunned down by a fifth tank or killed a few days later in a different battle. Although accounts of his exploits varied, all narrated Col's acts in terms that conjured the brief scene in the film *We're from Kronstadt* in which a lone soldier immobilizes a tank. One newspaper added an additional detail that paralleled the action in the film: "Our troops advanced singing the Internationale."[39] Col's widely publicized heroism quickly inspired others, whose actions in turn were also widely publicized. A 1937 Republican manual on methods of propaganda advised publicizing examples of those who fought tanks with grenades as a practical means of teaching young people how they could destroy tanks and become heroes.[40]

Chapaev – as did the soldier in *Kronstadt* who stops the tank, shoots its occupants through a small gun embrasure, and then nonchalantly rolls a cigarette while sitting on the turret – provided compelling, if ruthless, images of Bolshevik masculinity. As Kruth wrote to his wife after seeing *Chapaev* for the first time in Spain, "We too will be little Chapayevs in our small way."[41] In her study of German volunteers, Josie McLellan suggests that the "wish to be a 'little Lenin' was an ideological one, but it also expressed a yearning for a purposeful, active masculinity."[42] A similar argument could be made more forcefully for Chapaev or the sailors from Kronstadt, whose militarized masculinity was more directly relevant to soldiers.

The masculinity modeled in Soviet civil war films – at once rough-edged and loyal to the cause – may have been particularly important in the People's Army. Historian James Matthews argues that the Republic worked to transform constructions of gender. Reacting "against the ultra-masculine and rigidly hierarchical version manifested by their enemies," Republican propagandists promoted ideals of masculinity – for example, in mobilization campaigns – that fused traditional bravery, sacrifice, and dedication to the expectation that the soldier be "literate, educated, and freethinking."[43] In the film, Chapaev becomes more disciplined under the tutelage of his commissar who, to quote Stites, "harnesses the energy of the steppe warrior to the cause of Bolshevism."[44] The presence in the film of a female soldier – the highly skilled Anka, the machine gunner – also signals a revolutionary transgression and reconfiguration of traditional gender identities.[45] Still, Chapaev's steppe

39 Cabeza San Deogracias, "Buscando," 38–40; *Ahora*, 9 November 1936, as quoted in ibid., 40. The film is available online; see http://video.mail.ru/list/negativa.net/RETROFILM4/22686.html (*Internationale* at the 2:00 minute mark; tank sequence 6:35), accessed 6 November 2014.

40 Cabeza San Deogracias, "Buscando," 42–3.

41 Mito Kruth to Helen, 21 August 1937 (second letter), Kruth Papers, Box 1, Folder 11.

42 McLellan, "'I Wanted To Be,'" 303.

43 Matthews, *Reluctant Warriors*, 94. See also Mary Vincent, "The Martyrs and the Saints: Masculinity and the Construction of the Francoist Crusade," *History Workshop Journal*, no. 47 (Spring 1999): 68–98.

44 Stites, *Russian Popular Culture*, 45.

45 Anna Krylova, *Soviet Women in Combat: A History of Violence on the Eastern Front* (New York: Cambridge University Press, 2010), 67–68, 200–201; Graham Dawson, *Soldier Heroes:*

masculinity – humorous, spontaneous, irreverent – is never fully tamed in the film, making him a less ideologically motivated and more appealing character than the smug commissar.

Soviet propaganda in Spain inserted Stalinist symbols, images, and heroes into new and unexpected contexts, where they potentially acquired new meanings and associations. Spanish conscripts – often young, poorly educated, and noncommunist – and the predominantly communist international volunteers viewed the same films, but likely came away with different understandings of Chapaev and the sailors from Kronstadt as models for male (communist) behavior in war. *We're from Kronstadt*'s lesson in antitank warfare may have resonated more strongly for some than the implied analogy between the Russian and Spanish civil wars. The aspiration to be a "little Chapaev" might have more to do with the attractions of a certain kind of larger-than-life masculinity than with a desire to achieve greater political consciousness. The ubiquity of Chapaev as a point of reference in Spain highlights not only the international reach of Stalinist culture but also the ways in which Soviet cultural products might be transformed as they crossed into more open political cultures.

La Pasionaria in the Soviet Union

The circulation of images of true Bolsheviks (or true antifascists, at a time when international communists understood the two as synonymous) was not unidirectional. In the Soviet Union, the media encouraged Soviet people to identify with the "heroic Spanish people" and especially the "fiery" communist orator Dolores Ibárruri (better known as *La Pasionaria*, the passion flower) as actors in a great international struggle against fascism.[46] Briefly pushed off the front pages of Soviet newspapers by the first of the show trials in mid-August 1936, the Spanish civil war received substantial, if diminishing, coverage to the end of the conflict.[47] By early August 1936, the war and especially the massive campaign to raise money for humanitarian aid to "heroic Spain" dominated the Soviet press.[48] In late August, Il'ia Ehrenburg joined Kol'tsov in Spain as

British Adventure, Empire and the Imagining of Masculinities (London: Routledge, 1994), 13.

46 Olga Novikova, "Las visiones de España en la Unión Soviética durante la guerra civil española," *Historia del presente*, no. 11 (2008): 9–44; Kowalsky, *Stalin and the Spanish Civil War*, chapter 8; Timur Mukhamatulin, "'Prisvoenie Ispanii': Ispaniia v sovetskom obshchestve v 1936–1939 godakh," *Bulletin des DHI Moskau* Band 6 (2012): 113–27 (Perspectivia.net).

47 Jeffrey Brooks finds that, in *Pravda*, coverage of the trials overshadowed the war, *Thank You, Comrade Stalin! Soviet Public Culture from Revolution to Cold War* (Princeton: Princeton University Press, 2000), 151. A wider survey of the Soviet media makes clear that editors continued to pay attention to the story. See also Schlögel, *Moscow, 1937*, 95–8.

48 On early coverage in *Izvestiia* see David E. Allen, "The Soviet Union and the Spanish Civil War" (PhD diss., Stanford University, 1952), 431. Allen reviewed virtually every issue of *Izvestiia* for the duration of the war, pp. 419–39. Examples of early coverage in *Pravda* include "Voenno-fashistskii miatezh v Ispanii," 20 July 1936; "Deistviia fashistskikh interventov," 11 August

Izvestiia's correspondent. *Izvestiia*'s coverage of the war peaked in October 1936, when it devoted approximately a quarter of its column inches to events in Spain. As late as February 1939, by which time Soviet intervention had largely ended and the war was all but lost, events in Spain still claimed about 6 percent of the paper's space.[49] Coverage of events in Spain appeared – if not always on the front page – in nearly every issue of *Pravda* to March 1939, often accompanied by a map and, until November 1937, a feature article by Kol'tsov. Writing in *Leningradskaia pravda* in October 1936, the poet Nikolai Tikhonov described, or perhaps prescribed, the mood of the moment: "Every morning we awake with one thought: What's new in Spain?"[50]

Soviet coverage of Spain was hardly limited to the newspapers. The filmmakers Roman Karmen and Boris Makaseev arrived in Spain in late August 1936, and their first newsreels of the conflict appeared in Moscow theaters in early September, a remarkably fast turnaround. Their feature-length documentary *Madrid Defends Itself* (Madrid oboroniaetsia) was released in December 1936. The two remained in Spain for eleven months, shooting almost forty thousand meters of film for the documentary series "K sobytiiam v Ispanii" (On Events in Spain). The film *Ispaniia*, directed by Esfir' Shub with footage by Karmen, premiered in Moscow months after the war ended, in the summer of 1939.[51]

During the war, a craze for all things Spanish overtook Soviet mass culture. Soviet radio broadcast Spanish revolutionary songs. Soviet theaters staged Spanish plays, notably, Frederico García Lorca's 1933 tragedy *Bodas de sangre* and Lope de Vega's *Fuente Ovejuna*, a story of a fifteenth-century peasant revolt. A review described the latter play as providing an "unforgettable picture of a Spanish woman in which the spectator sees a forerunner of the fiery Dolores Ibárruri."[52] Translations of Spanish literature, Soviet literature honoring Spain, and accounts of the war and of key figures – especially Ibárruri, the only Spanish communist whose picture appeared fairly regularly in the Soviet

1936; "Fashistskii terror," 19 August 1936; Mikhail Kol'tsov, "Germanskaia pomoshch' ispanskim miatezhnikam," 31 August 1936; V. Rudol'f, "Molodye antifashisty," 1 September 1936; "Zverstva ispanskikh fashistov," 13 September 1936; "Ispanskaia kompartiia v bor'be protiv fashizma," 14 September 1936; "Ispanskie pisatel'i – zhertvy fashizma," 26 September 1936.

49 Allen provides a monthly tabulation of the "Percentage of space in *Izvestiia* devoted to the Spanish story," in "The Soviet Union and the Spanish Civil War," 437–8.

50 N. Tikhonov, "Ne zakhlestnut' dozhdem pulemetov muzhestvo ispanskikh rabochikh," *Leningradskaia pravda*, 10 October 1936.

51 Daniel Kowalsky, "The Soviet Cinematic Offensive in the Spanish Civil War," *Film History: An International Journal* 19, no. 1 (2007): 10–19. Allen, "The Soviet Union," 439. For announcements of the films see *Pravda*, 5 September 1936; *Izvestiia*, 12 December 1936. R. Karmen, "Odinnadtsat' mesiatsev na frontakh v Ispanii," *Literaturnaia gazeta*, 5 August 1937. L. Arnshtam, "Kino: 'Ispaniia,'" *Pravda*, 7 June 1939.

52 "Chronicle," *International Literature* 1938, no. 9: 98. Allen, "The Soviet Union," 440. *Krovavaia svad'dba*, trans. F. V. Kel'in (verse) and A. V. Febral'skii (prose), *Internatsional'naia literatura* 1938, no. 8: 101–24.

press – were published in large press runs as late as January 1939.[53] Adapting the tradition of naming children after revolutionary heroes – or simply attracted to the exoticism of Spanish names in the news – Soviet parents made Dolores and José (after José Díaz, secretary-general of the Spanish Communist Party) popular children's names in the mid-1930s.[54]

Whereas in Spain Chapaev provided a model of Bolshevik masculinity, in the Soviet Union, coverage of the Spanish civil war offered influential and to some degree competing models of militarized and maternal communist womanhood. The "rifle-toting militiawoman dressed in dungarees" became in the Soviet Union, as in Spain, a symbol of the war.[55] The young Spanish women with guns who appeared in the Soviet press dramatically illustrate the Stalinist state's continuing use of the new woman as a revolutionary icon – its "resurrection of the family," notably 1936 legislation outlawing abortion and restricting divorce, notwithstanding.[56] Young Soviet women for whom Anka the machine gunner was an "obsession" could look to accounts of the Spanish civil war for real-world inspiration and validation.[57] This is not to say that women's emancipation constituted a Spanish or a Soviet reality. When in the fall of 1936 the Republic's People's Army replaced the hastily organized militias, women largely disappeared from the front and were officially banned from combat units.[58] In the Soviet Union, women who actually "penetrated the bastions of male primacy" were often resented, marginalized, or demeaned – by both men and more traditional women – for crossing still powerful gender divides.[59]

53 Allen, "The Soviet Union," 440–4. *Geroicheskaia Ispaniia* (Moscow: Partizdat TsK VKP(b), 1936) had a pressrun of 300,000; for a review see *Pravda*, 7 October 1936. Dolores Ibárruri, *Rechi i stat'i 1936–1938 gg.* (Moscow: Gosudarstvennoe izdatel'stvo politicheskoi literatury, 1938) had a pressrun of 90,000; for a review, see *Pravda*, 25 August 1938. Mikhail Kol'tsov, *Ispanskii dnevnik* was serialized in *Novyi mir* in April to September 1938. For favorable reviews see V. Aleksandrov, "Pervaia kniga 'Ispanskogo dnevnika,'" *Literaturnyi kritik* 1938, no. 6: 132–47; A. Tolstoi and A. Fadeev, "'Ispanskii dnevnik,'" *Pravda*, 4 November 1938.

54 Ales' Adamovich and Daniil Granin, eds., *Blokadnaia kniga* (Moscow: Sovetskii pisatel', 1982), 12. *Izvestiia*, 14 October 1936, 9 May 1937, cited in Allen, "The Soviet Union," 448. On naming practices see Richard Stites, *Revolutionary Dreams: Utopian Vision and Experimental Life in the Russian Revolution* (New York: Oxford University Press, 1989), 111–12.

55 Frances Lannon, "Women and Images of Women in the Spanish Civil War," *Transactions of the Royal Historical Society*, 6th Ser., vol. 1. (1991): 217. Militia women appeared regularly in the Soviet press in the first months of the war: *Pravda*, 12 August 1936, 17 September 1936, 20 September 1936, 28 September 1936, 30 October 1936; *Komsomol'skaia pravda*, 24 September 1936; Krylova, *Soviet Women in Combat*, 65.

56 Wendy Z. Goldman, *Women, the State, and Revolution: Soviet Family Policy and Social Life, 1917–1936* (New York: Cambridge University Press, 1993), 296–336.

57 Krylova, *Soviet Women in Combat*, 68.

58 Lannon, "Women and Images of Women," 221–2; "Decisiones del Secretariado," 12 January 1938, RGASPI, f. 545, op. 6, d. 7, l. 3.

59 The quotation is from Choi Chatterjee, "Soviet Heroines and the Language of Modernity, 1930–39," in Melanie Ilič, ed. *Women in the Stalin Era* (Basingstoke: Palgrave, 2001), 54. Melanie Ilič, "*Traktoristka:* Representations and Realities," in ibid., 121–2; Wendy Goldman, "*Babas* at the Bench: Gender Conflict in Soviet Industry in the 1930s," in ibid., 85–6; Mary Buckley,

Indeed, Soviet coverage of the war in Spain, and specifically of Ibárruri, did much to popularize a compelling image of fierce communist motherhood. Even as the Soviet media publicized Spanish militia women in arms, they added mothers and housewives to the Bolshevik "visual lexicon."[60] Ibárruri's self-presentations and representations of her in the Soviet press evoked these more traditional models. La Pasionaria, the nom de plume Ibárruri chose in 1918, when she published her first political article during Holy Week, drew on her recently abandoned faith to evoke "the Passion of Christ and the sorrows of his mother."[61] Effectively fusing Catholic imagery with her own biography – dire poverty, the deaths of four children – she emphasized her intimate and painfully won understanding of the suffering of Spanish mothers. Ibárruri thus constructed a place for herself as an orator and propagandist, particularly on women's issues, in the male-dominated and profoundly masculinist culture of the Spanish Communist Party.[62] In the mid-1930s, around the time of her fortieth birthday, Ibárruri began appearing always in widow's black.[63] The costume disguised the fact that she was separated from her husband Julián Ruiz and allowed her to project an "asexual maternity," simultaneously "feminine and ferocious."[64]

"The Stalinist Subject and Gender Dimensions," in Brigitte Studer and Heiko Haumann, eds., *Stalinistische Subjekte: Indivduum und System in der Sowjetunion und der Komintern, 1929–1953* (Zurich: Chronos, 2006), 348–55; Pasha Angelina, "The Most Important Thing," in Sheila Fitzpatrick and Yuri Slezkine, eds., *In the Shadow of Revolution: Life Stories of Russian Women from 1917 to the Second World War* (Princeton: Princeton University Press, 2000), 312.

60 Victoria Bonnell, *Iconography of Power: Soviet Political Posters under Lenin and Stalin* (Berkeley: University of California Press, 1999), 10 ("visual lexicon"). On mothers and housewives see Victoria Bonnell, "The Peasant Woman in Stalinist Political Art in the 1930s," *American Historical Review* 98 (February 1993): 63, 75; Susan E. Reid, "All Stalin's Women: Gender and Power in Soviet Art in the 1930s," *Slavic Review* 57, no. 1 (Spring 1998): 136. On women as icons of the Stalinist revolution see Ilič, "*Traktoristka*," 110–12; Chatterjee, "Soviet Heroines," 54–9. On women aviators and other role models, see Krylova, *Soviet Women in Combat*, 75–83; Stites, *Russian Popular Culture*, 68–72; Karen Petrone, *Life Has Become More Joyous, Comrades: Celebrations in the Time of Stalin* (Bloomington: Indiana University Press, 2000), 46–84; Reina Pennington, *Wings, Women, and War: Soviet Airwomen in World War II Combat* (Lawrence: University Press of Kansas, 2007),14–17.

61 Gina Herrmann, *Written in Red: The Communist Memoir in Spain* (Urbana: University of Illinois Press, 2010), 26. See also Juan Avilés Farré, *Pasionaria: La mujer y el mito* (Barcelona: Random House Mondadori, 2005), 29, 100.

62 Gregorio Morán, *Miseria y grandeza del Partido Comunista de España, 1939–1985* (Barcelona: Planeta, 1986), 23; Herrmann, *Written in Red*, 27; Lannon, "Women and Images," 220; Kol'tsov, *Ispanskii dnevnik*, 47.

63 Avilés, *Pasionaria*, 74; Carrie Hamilton, "Activism and Representations of Motherhood in the Autobiography of Dolores Ibárruri, *Pasionaria*," *Journal of Romance Studies* 1, no. 1 (2001): 18.

64 Gina Herrmann, "The Hermetic Goddess: Dolores Ibárruri as Text," *Letras Peninsulares* 11 (Spring 1998): 196, 194. Hamilton makes a similar point, "Activism and Representations," 18. See also Mary Nash, *Defying Male Civilization: Women in the Spanish Civil War* (Denver: Arden Press, 1995), 54–7.

During the civil war, beginning with her call to arms "*¡No pasarán!*" (They shall not pass!), broadcast by radio on 19 July 1936, just two days after Spanish troops in Morocco launched the military coup against the Republic, Ibárruri's popular influence and appeal had less to do with a specifically communist message than with her powerful and profoundly gendered performance of defiance and self-sacrifice. The emotional intensity of her September 1936 speech in Paris, where she introduced the slogan, "Better to die on your feet than live on your knees," was clear, or so observers and later biographers claimed, even to those who did not speak Spanish, and it made her an international icon.[65] In mid-October, with Nationalist forces threatening Madrid, she proclaimed, "Better the widow of a hero than the wife of a coward!" Throughout the dangerous and difficult defense of the city, she was regularly photographed "digging trenches, haranguing the troops, and consoling soldiers."[66] Her austere beauty visible in the photographs from the period amplified her message.

In Soviet accounts, Ibárruri came to embody the nobility and pathos of the Spanish people and their cause. In one of his earliest columns from Spain, Kol'tsov described her as a "daughter of the people – yesterday a simple, illiterate worker, today one of the leaders of the Spanish communist party . . . a simple Spanish woman in a black housedress."[67] Writing in *Izvestiia* Ehrenburg described for Soviet readers the physical presence that made it so easy to imagine her as a symbol: "exacting eyes, silver hair, traditional earrings, in a long black dress – this is Spain."[68] In a letter published in *Pravda*, addressing the Soviet actress who had played her in Aleksandr Afinogenov's play *Salut, Ispanii!*, Ibárruri attributed her success as an orator to her ability to express – to become – the suffering and courage of the Spanish people: "My voice is the outraged cry of a people that does not wish to be enslaved. . . . In my voice sounds the cry of mothers, the lament of women in bondage, demeaned and scorned."[69] By 1939, the "woman-revolutionary Dolores Ibárruri" constituted an "ideal" of Soviet youth.[70] She also prefigured the real and symbolic mothers who became so central to Soviet propaganda during the Great Fatherland War.

Although it is of course impossible to say how the "average" Soviet citizen responded to this coverage, anecdotal evidence suggests that at least some

65 Eric Hobsbawm, *Interesting Times: A Twentieth-Century Life* (New York: Pantheon, 2003), 133. See also Paul Preston, *¡Comrades! Portraits from the Spanish Civil War* (London: Harper Collins, 1999), 291; Vásquez, *Pasionaria*, 93–94; Herrmann, *Written in Red*, 36–37. "Paris Plea Made by La Pasionaria," *New York Times* (*NYT*), 3 September 1936.

66 Preston, *¡Comrades!* 293; Herrmann, *Written in Red*, 28.

67 Mikhail Kol'stov, "Dolores na fronte," *Pravda*, 22 August 1936.

68 Il'ia Erenburg, "Zhenshchiny Ispanii," *Izvestiia*, 8 March 1937. On the identification of Ibárruri with Spain see Herrmann, *Written in Red*, 37.

69 Dolores Ibárruri, "Pis'mo Dolores Ibarruri," *Pravda*, 9 February 1937. On the playwright, who became a target of the great purge, see Jochen Hellbeck, *Revolution on My Mind: Writing a Diary Under Stalin* (Cambridge, MA: Harvard University Press, 2006), 303–45.

70 Tamara Sycheva as quoted in Krylova, *Soviet Women in Combat*, 87.

Soviet people identified strongly with the official accounts of the war in Spain. In December 1936, during the crucial battle to defend Madrid, Vladimir Zhelezniakov, the chairman of a remote village soviet, recorded in his diary that he had dreamed of bayoneting fascists in Spain. Awakened mid-dream, he wrote, "You, Wife, be more careful when turning over tomorrow night. I will be fighting fascism."[71] In December 1939, nine months after the Republic's defeat, Nina Khor'uptenko, a "simple woman" from Khar'kov, wrote to Ibárruri and José Díaz to express her great joy that they were in Moscow. Suggesting a profound, almost pathological commitment to Spain, she wrote, "For so many months (even years) have I, together with the whole Soviet people, watched with worry and joy the heroic struggle of the Spanish people under the direction of the Communist Party.... How much I have suffered! It is enough to note that at one time, the doctors prohibited me from reading about events in Spain."[72]

Encountering Spain only through the Soviet media, many Soviet citizens seem to have internalized a political and emotional identification with the Republic. In the 1960s, the fiction writer and literary historian Lidia Libedinskaia, who was fifteen in 1936, recalled that she and her friends had "dreamed of going" to Spain.[73] In a 1991 reminiscence Grigorii Brailovskii recalled how during the Spanish civil war he and his young friends "wore blue forage caps with tassels and tossed around Spanish words: 'viva,' 'salud,' and 'no pasarán.' We fiercely hated Franco, and worried grimly about the republicans."[74]

Such emotional reactions – dreams, worry, suffering, hatred – perhaps went beyond official intentions. To take one example, the changes made to the poet Rafael Alberti's account of his 1937 visit to Moscow suggest a concern with moderating the identification of the Soviet Union – and especially Josef Stalin – with the Spanish cause. The article as it appeared in *Izvestiia* omitted Alberti's assertion that in Moscow he felt as if he were still in Spain because he found Spain "in all Soviet hearts." Tellingly, in the Spanish manuscript version, Alberti remembered the two hours he and his wife, the author María Teresa León, shared with Stalin as filled with "acute emotion for Spain." The Russian version, by contrast, emphasized acute emotion for Stalin, noting that the meeting with the leader "left a deep impression in our memory."[75]

71 Diary entry for 13 December 1936 as quoted in Hellbeck, *Revolution on My Mind*, 92–3. See also Kowalsky, *Stalin and the Spanish Civil War*, chapter 4; Mary M. Leder, *My Life in Stalinist Russia: An American Woman Looks Back*, ed. Laurie Bernstein (Bloomington: Indiana University Press, 2001), 130–1; Stephen Kotkin, *Magnetic Mountain: Stalinism as a Civilization* (Berkeley: University of California Press, 1995), 228.

72 Nina Khor'uptenko to Dolores Ibárruri and José Díaz, 24 December 1939, Russian original and Spanish translation, Arxiu Nacional de Catalunya, El fons centro español de Moscú (ANC), sig. 202.

73 Lidia Libedinskaia, "The Green Lamp," in *In the Shadow of Revolution*, 300.

74 Grigorii Brailovskii, "Minuty molchaniia," *Nevskoe vremia*, 22 June 1991.

75 Rafael Alberti, "Mi tercera visita a Moscú. Mi tercera despedida," Rossiiskii gosudarstvennyi arkhiv literatury i isskustva, f. 2555, op. 1, d. 316 R, ll. 13, 14; Rafael Alberti, "Moia Moskva,"

The Soviet media also encouraged, or anticipated, pragmatic responses to campaigns to raise money for the women and children of Spain. In addition to lauding Soviet citizens' generosity, the press emphasized the material benefits, often measured in citrus fruit, of Soviet aid. The papers provided regular updates on the number of crates of lemons, tangerines, and oranges arriving at Soviet ports from republican Spain – extraordinary luxuries in the Soviet economy of scarcity. Alongside stories on the heroism of Spanish workers, Soviet newspapers carried advertisements advising mothers that "for the health of daughters and sons there is nothing better than a SPANISH ORANGE."[76] The actual appearance of oranges in the stores in 1937 significantly enhanced the media message.[77]

These reactions in the Soviet Union to the Spanish civil war – and the enthusiasm for Soviet heroes in faraway Spain – both suggest how the war worked to internationalize Stalinist culture and offer a useful reminder of the paradoxes of that culture. The mid-1930s in the Soviet Union have been described as a moment of "Great Retreat" marked by the increasing prominence of Russian nationalism in Soviet propaganda, the growing xenophobia that accompanied the purges, and a new emphasis on motherhood and family.[78] To some degree, the Soviet media's coverage of the Spanish cause and of Spanish heroes challenged these trends, reviving at least rhetorical commitments to both internationalism and a revolution in gender roles. Increasingly marginalized in dominant Soviet discourses, older revolutionary values remained visible in accounts of the Spanish civil war; they remained part of the Stalinist cultural landscape.

Real War, Real Enemies: The Spanish Civil War as Escape from the Purges

In 1932, Argentine-born Adelina Abramson, fourteen years old and speaking no Russian, emigrated to the Soviet Union with her family. Her father, an "eternal Don Quixote" who had left Russia in 1910 to escape a death sentence, decided to return to the USSR despite the warnings of friends in Buenos Aires

Izvestiia, 23 March 1937. For an account of the meeting see *The Diary of Georgi Dimitrov, 1933–1939*, Ivo Banac, ed. (New Haven: Yale University Press, 2003), 60.

76 The advertisement ran in *Izvestiia*, 16 May 1937, as translated in Allen, "The Soviet Union," 417. See also *Izvestiia*, 9 January 1937, 11 January 1937, 24 January 1937, 27 March 1937, 6 April 1937, 17 April 1937, and 3 January 1939.

77 Valentina Bogdan, "Memoirs of an Engineer," in *In the Shadow of Revolution*, 400.

78 Nicholas S. Timasheff, *The Great Retreat: The Growth and Decline of Communism in Russia* (New York: E. P. Dutton, 1946); David Brandenberger, *National Bolshevism: Stalinist Mass Culture and the Formation of Modern Russian National Identity, 1931–1956* (Cambridge, MA: Harvard University Press, 2002); William J. Chase, *Enemies within the Gates? The Comintern and the Stalinist Repression, 1934–1939* (New Haven: Yale University Press, 2001), 45–6, 226; David L. Hoffman, "Was There a 'Great Retreat' from Soviet Socialism? Stalinist Culture Reconsidered," *Kritika* 5, no. 4 (Fall 2004): 651–74; Matthew E. Lenoe, "In Defense of Timasheff's *Great Retreat*," *Kritika* 5, no. 4 (Fall 2004): 721–30.

that "things seem rosy at a distance, but black up close."[79] In a 1994 memoir written with her older sister Paulina, Adelina remembered that in Moscow the family was immediately "suspect" because half of its members (she and her sister) were "foreigners" and half Russians who had lived "many years outside the country." To avoid "tragic consequences," they broke all ties with friends and family in Argentina.[80] Adelina was denied membership in the Komsomol (Young Communist League) because she was "considered the daughter of a Trotskyite with the aggravating circumstance of having been born in Buenos Aires."[81] Then, as she tells the story, the war in Spain broke the spell, at least temporarily:

> At school, the students were electrified by events in distant Spain, and undertook projects to offer immediate aid; some, the most daring, quietly swore that they would volunteer to fight fascism. It seemed that the atmosphere had been purified: ... From the first days of July '36, people at solidarity rallies raised their fists and shouted *¡No pasarán!*[82]

Both sisters, who by then spoke Russian, went to Spain as translators. Their participation was invaluable, as the Soviets never had "sufficient personnel trained in Castilian."[83] Paulina interpreted for Kol'tsov and Karmen and later Aleksandr Orlov, the NKVD chief in Spain; Adelina for Soviet advisors to the Republic's armed forces.[84] In early 1938, Adelina returned to Moscow and an atmosphere of "anxiety, uncertainty, and fear."[85] Writing in the 1990s, neither she nor her sister harbored illusions about the dark side of Soviet intervention. Paulina held Orlov responsible for the murder of Andreu Nin; both saw the grim toll the purges took on those, including Kol'tsov and Vladimir Ćopić, the commander of the Fifteenth Brigade, who had been in Spain. Nonetheless, they looked back on Spain as a light in the Stalinist night, underscoring the dignity and honor of the "volunteers for liberty," as well as the friendship and camaraderie of Soviet and Spanish pilots, engineers, and mechanics.[86]

Even for those who remained in the Soviet Union, Spain as covered in the Soviet media could appear as a counterpoint to the terror and disruption of the contemporaneous purges. Certainly the oranges were a bright spot in an otherwise bleak landscape. Daniel Kowalsky argues that the "cheery" story of Spanish children evacuated to the safe and happy Soviet Union had particularly high domestic propaganda value as "a foil to the general gloom that enveloped

79 Paulina Abramson and Adelina Abramson, *Mosaico Roto* (Madrid: Compañía Literaria, 1994), 34.
80 Ibid., 12.
81 Ibid., 13.
82 Ibid., 13, 14.
83 Kowalsky, *Stalin and the Spanish Civil War*, chapter 7, paragraph 25; chapter 13.
84 Abramson and Abramson, *Mosaico Roto*, 47, 162, 67. Kol'tsov, *Ispanskii dnenvik*, 123–36.
85 Abramson and Abramson, *Mosaico Roto*, 113.
86 Ibid., 52, 186, 73, 103.

Soviet society."[87] Spain, of course, was not the only "cheery" news in the Soviet media. During the Spanish civil war and the purges, the press offered a constant round of joyous stories ranging from accounts of astounding record-breaking long-distance flights and polar expeditions to prodigious feats of industrial and agricultural production and celebrations of the poetic genius of Aleksandr Pushkin.[88]

What set the Spanish story apart from these other happy stories of Soviet accomplishment was the element of idealistic, even revolutionary, struggle against real and overt enemies. On returning to Moscow from Spain in late 1936, journalist Louis Fischer found that "everybody talked Spain... At least eight Soviet friends asked me how they could go and fight in Spain." To his questions about the Soviet Union his friends replied, "Spain is more important.... If we win in Spain we will be happy here."[89] Libedinskaia's remembered dreams of joining the "valiant Spanish Revolution... struggling and bleeding" underscore the attraction for at least some Soviet citizens of imagining themselves as idealistic, self-sacrificing revolutionaries.[90] Updating the children's game of playing at being partisans in Chapaev's legendary civil war detachment, the Leningrad boys in forage caps, who hailed one another in Castilian, found in the story of Spain the romance of fighting for a grand international cause. For all their daring, even the Soviet test pilots could not match the élan of the Spanish volunteers fighting the fascist enemy.

Robert Merriman's decision to leave Moscow for Madrid in early 1937 suggests the power of the struggle in Spain to (re)ignite revolutionary fervor and idealism. In her rather hagiographic reminiscences, Merriman's widow Marion described a trip in the summer of 1936 to Budapest, Vienna, and Prague as "a turning point" in her husband's shift from "observer to activist," because in Eastern Europe "we began to feel the threat of war."[91] Asserting that his previous interest in the Soviet Union had been purely academic, she insisted that he went to Spain as an "idealist," not a party member.[92] These assertions understate her husband's earlier communist activism and contradict clear evidence – in the autobiography he prepared in Spain and in evaluations of his work there – that he was a member of the Communist Party, probably before

87 Kowalsky, "Soviet Cinematic Offensive," 13. Immaculada Colomina Limonero, *Dos patrias, tres mil destinos: Vida y exilio de los niños de la guerra de España refugiados en la Unión Soviética* (Madrid: Ediciones Cinca, 2010).

88 Petrone, *Life Has Become*. For examples see: *Pravda*, 12 August 1936, 14 September 1936, 17 June 1937 (long-distance flights); 8 December 1936 (Stalin constitution); 8 February 1937 (Pushkin); 7 October 1937, 29 December 1937 (Stakhanovites); 21 September 1938 (polar expedition).

89 Louis Fischer, *Men and Politics: An Autobiography* (1941; reprint, Westport, CT: Greenwood Press, 1970), 403.

90 Libedinskaia, "The Green Lamp," 300.

91 Marion Merriman and Warren Lerude, *American Commander in Spain: Robert Hale Merriman and the Abraham Lincoln Brigade* (Reno: University of Nevada Press, 1986), 63, 66.

92 Ibid., 80.

he left for the Soviet Union in 1934 and certainly after he arrived in Spain. In his autobiography, Merriman described himself as "in Party Nucleus" while working in 1934 as a body polisher and carpenter at the Ford assembly plant in Richmond, California. (This piece of information is difficult to reconcile with the marginal note, in Merriman's handwriting: "Not Party member – have applied 1/1937 since being in Spain.") He also described himself as an "organizer" for the International Labor Defense in San Francisco and Oakland, a position that implied party membership – all this while also being a graduate student in economics at the University of California, Berkeley. In the Soviet Union, he noted, he spent a year at the Communist Academy, a prestigious research institution closely associated with the party.[93] In a May 1937 letter, a State Department observer emphasized "that the longer Mr. Merriman stayed in the Soviet Union the more violently pro-Soviet he became in language and action."[94] When Marion herself arrived in Spain from Moscow, she, too, became a party member.[95] Clearly, the Merrimans were not, as she insisted, simply nonparty "idealists."

However, although Spain was not the first communist cause Merriman was involved in, it may have been the one to which he was committed most fully and emotionally. It is entirely possible that, as Marion claimed, it was the experience of "having seen for himself the spreading power of Hitler," rather than any previous work for the party, that inspired Bob to fight in what he assured her would be a short war.[96] Fischer recounts that some time after he returned to Moscow, Merriman, his erstwhile tennis partner, "phoned to find out how he could get to Spain."[97] Unfortunately, Fischer provides no further information about either his own assistance in the matter – having worked to organize the International Brigades, he was likely in a position to help – or Merriman's reasons for going, which he seemed to assume were self-evident.[98] Writing in 1986, Marion rather understandably denied Bob's communism and emphasized his idealism. But there is no reason to doubt her claim that the struggle in Spain renewed his – and perhaps her – sense of (communist) idealism.

93 "Merriman," RGASPI, f. 545, op. 6, d. 947, l. 31. "Characteristics of Chief of Brigade, War Commissars and Chiefs of Estado Mayor," describes Merriman as "Member of C.P.U.S.A." and as "organiser for I.L.D. in California," ibid., l. 34. Ćopić's characterization of Merriman describes him as joining the Communist Party in Spain, ibid., l. 29. On the Institute of Red Professors and the Communist Institute where Merriman worked (albeit later) see Michael David-Fox, "Symbiosis to Synthesis: The Communist Academy and the Bolshevization of the Russian Academy of Sciences, 1918–1929," *Jahrbücher für Geschichte Osteuropas*, Neue Folge, Bd. 46, H. 2 (1998): 219–43.

94 Elbridge Durbrow to Secretary of State, 13 May 1937, National Archives College Park, Maryland (NACP), Record Group (RG) 59, 852.2221 Merriman, Robert H./1.

95 Robert Merriman diary, vol., 1, 9 junio, Merriman Papers, Box 1, Folder 3.

96 Merriman and Lerude, *American Commander*, 66, 72.

97 Fischer, *Men and Politics*, 403.

98 Ibid., 386; Luigi Gallo [Longo] to Louis Fischer, 20 September 1937, RGASPI, f. 545, op. 1, d. 11, l. 30.

FIGURE 6. Marion Merriman and Robert Merriman (center) with officers. Courtesy Tamiment Library, New York University. (ALBA Photo 177-177027)

Participating in the Spanish civil war also offered a politically acceptable way out for resident foreigners who wanted or needed to leave the Soviet Union while remaining publicly supportive of it. Thus, for example, more than 200 Austrian exiles applied to serve, of whom more than 150 were permitted to go to Spain.[99] A letter apparently from Henry Shapiro, the United Press correspondent in Moscow, that Merriman copied into his Spanish diary hints that he may also have made this more complicated type of exit. Adopting a joking tone – and signed "Henrico (not Shapiro)" – the letter alluded to some sort of political trouble or misunderstanding that had prompted Merriman to leave Moscow without a forwarding address: "I know how you must have felt you and many of your best friends going around wearing an artificial 'filthy mug' or safety mask, largely the result of sticking your nose into something

[99] Barry McLoughlin, "Proletarian Cadres En-route: Austrian NKVD Agents in Britain, 1941–1943," *Labour History Review* 62, no. 3 (Winter 1997): 304. See also Andrea Graziosi, "Foreign Workers in Soviet Russia, 1920–40: Their Experience and Their Legacy," *International Labor and Working-Class History* 33 (Spring 1988): 48; Gleb J. Albert, "'To Help the Republicans Not Just by Donations and Rallies, but with the Rifle': Militant Solidarity with the Spanish Republic in the Soviet Union, 1936–1937," *European Review of History* 21, no. 4 (2014): 504–12.

you ordinarily wouldn't go near – and where you are now you have at least the one advantage of knowing who's who."[100]

The letter specified neither what Merriman was "sticking his nose into" nor exactly how he now knew "who's who." However, its assertion – "It must be wonderful to be in such good company as you are, for a change – really good people, unselfish, willing to sacrifice all (if necessary) not just for a cause but to *the real* cause, scientifically sound and historically progressive" – suggests a contrasting state of affairs in Moscow. Spain offered an appropriately idealistic reason for leaving an unpleasant, perhaps dangerous, situation, although the fact that Marion remained in the Soviet Union until Bob was wounded at Jarama in February 1937 implies a rather low level of fear.

The case of Hermann Muller, a prominent American geneticist who had been working in the Soviet Union since 1933 and who socialized in the same expatriate circles as the Merrimans, offers a clearer example of how Spain functioned as a politically acceptable escape from the terror. Muller's leftist involvements had begun at the University of Texas, which he left in 1932 when his participation in a communist student organization came to the attention of the FBI. In 1933, Muller was a fellow at the Kaiser Wilhelm Institute for Brain Research in Berlin. The Nazi seizure of power and a subsequent physical attack on the institute and some of its scientists persuaded Muller to accept an invitation to direct a genetics lab in the Soviet Union. However, by 1936 the rise of Lysenkoism made the Soviet Union an increasingly dangerous place for a classical geneticist. Moreover, Muller, perhaps unaware of the stakes, became one of Trofim Lysenko's most outspoken opponents.[101] He also incurred Stalin's displeasure with his advocacy of a program of "Bolshevik" eugenics.[102] By March 1937, a number of prominent Soviet geneticists had been arrested on charges of holding fascist or Trotskyite views, and Muller himself became the target of what he characterized as "scurrilous and insipid attacks." He decided that he needed to leave, but as historian Peter Kuznick notes, he wanted to do so without creating "the impression that he had gone over to the enemy camp" or putting his Soviet colleagues at further risk.[103] Muller's solution was to go to Spain, where he served in the Instituto Hispano-Canadiense de Transfusión de Sangre (Spanish-Canadian Blood Transfusion Institute) organized by Canadian surgeon Norman Bethune. Muller, whose research on genetic mutations

100 "First outside letter received in Spain. Moscow Jan. 14, 1936," Merriman diary, vol., 1, 29 octubre, Merriman Papers, Box 1, Folder 3. On news of arrests in Moscow, see 19 septiembre.

101 Peter J. Kuznick, *Beyond the Laboratory: Scientists as Political Activists in 1930s America* (Chicago: University of Chicago Press, 1987), 121, 122. See also Elof Axel Carlson, *Hermann Joseph Muller, 1890–1967* (Washington, DC: National Academy of Sciences, 2009), 12, 14, 16–20.

102 "Pis'mo Germana Mellera – I. V. Stalinu," ed. I. A. Zakharov, *Voprosy istorii estestvoznaniia tekhniki*, 1997, no. 1: 65–76.

103 Kuznick, *Beyond the Laboratory*, 136. "Moscow Cancels Genetics Parley," *NYT*, 14 December 1936; the *Times* erroneously reported N. I. Vavilov's arrest.

in fruit flies earned him a Nobel Prize in 1946, arrived in Spain as an expert on Soviet techniques for preserving the blood of the dead for transfusion. He stayed only eight weeks – long enough to make service in Spain a plausible reason for his decision to leave his post in the Soviet Union.[104]

In the Soviet Union, the official call to join "all advanced and progressive humanity" in the fight against overt fascist aggression made possible figurative and literal escapes from Stalinist terror. The fight in Spain seemed to offer a purifying alternative to hunting for hidden enemies and Trotskyite plots – or to being hunted. Yet the escape was never complete, because the press explained setbacks in Spain as the work of the same agents of a worldwide "Trotskyite-fascist" conspiracy that threatened the Soviet Union. A good communist like Mito Kruth might at the same time aspire to participate in the pure cause as a "little Chapaev" and subscribe to the notion that defeats in Spain were the work of Trotskyite "rats" and "traitors."[105]

Trotskyites Everywhere: The Spanish Civil War as Part of the Story of the Purges

From the perspective of high politics, the Spanish civil war appears closely connected to the development of the "Great Terror" in the Soviet Union. Historian Oleg Khlevniuk argues that, although events in Spain did not necessarily cause the terror, Stalin understood them as demonstrating "the need for a policy of repression."[106] As a Soviet trade representative reported from Spain in December 1936, "it is not out of the question that amongst the highest [Republican] officers there exists a Fascist organization which is engaged in sabotage and, of course, spying."[107] That explanation effectively captures the way in which the Soviet leadership filtered information through a distinctive worldview. Such "evidence" that Republican defeats could be attributed to traitorous officers may have confirmed for Stalin the wisdom of preparations already being made to purge allegedly Trotskyite Red Army commanders.[108]

104 On Bethune see Petrou, *Renegades*, 158–68. On Muller's blood transfusion expertise see "A new technique of blood transfusion," [c. 1939–40], Milly Bennett Papers, Box 9, Folder 6, Hoover Institution Archives; Hermann Muller to Milly Bennett, 11 May 1937, ibid., Box 4, Folder 6. On Soviet experiments in blood banking see Douglas Starr, *Blood: An Epic History of Medicine and Commerce* (New York: Alfred A. Knopf, 1998), 67–70.

105 Mito Kruth to Helen, 9 May 1937, Kruth Papers, Box 1, Folder 9.

106 Oleg Khlevniuk, "The Reasons for the 'Great Terror': The Foreign-Political Aspect," in Silvo Pons and Andrea Romano, eds., *Russia in the Age of Wars, 1914–1945* (Milan: Feltrinelli, 2000), 163. See also Hiroaki Kuromiya, "Accounting for the Great Terror," *Jahrbücher für Geschichte Osteuropas*, Neue Folge, Bd. 53, H. 1 (2005): 86–101.

107 Khlevniuk, "The Reasons," 164.

108 Robert Conquest, *The Great Terror: A Reassessment* (New York: Oxford University Press, 2008), 190–1; Robert W. Thurston, *Life and Terror in Stalin's Russia, 1934–1941* (New Haven: Yale University Press, 1996), 50–7.

From the perspective of readers of Soviet newspapers, the story of the heroic battle against fascism in Spain could simultaneously validate and provide a kind of escape from the domestic "reign of the lie."[109] Whether or not reports from Spain drove decision making at the highest levels, the Soviet media's representations of the situation in Spain made terror at home thinkable, even reasonable. Measuring the column inches devoted to news from Spain versus accounts of show trials, although analytically useful, obscures the ways in which both were part of the same story: awe-inspiring achievements threatened by shadowy enemies, an unholy alliance of Lev Trotsky and the Gestapo dedicated to assassinating the leaders of the All-Union Communist Party (Bolshevik) and abetting the spread of fascism.[110]

For all its unique features, Spain fit quite well into the Stalinist political culture of "omnipresent conspiracy."[111] In the Soviet media's telling, the "heroic Spanish people" faced not only open German and Italian intervention but also, and perhaps more ominously, disguised "accomplices in the murder of Spanish children" – the "traitors, spies, and saboteurs" of the allegedly Trotskyite-fascist POUM.[112] In an article on "Trotskyite agents in Spain," Kol'tsov accused the POUM militias of abandoning the front and the POUM press of spreading anti-Soviet lies about famine in Leningrad, the liquidation of the Comintern, and the arrest of its leader Georgi Dimitrov.[113] The Soviet press characterized the street fighting that broke out in Barcelona in May 1937 as a Trotskyite-fascist "putsch" orchestrated by the POUM with the aim of aiding Francisco Franco and his German and Italian allies.[114]

Such charges of collusion with the enemy had little connection to reality: The violence in Barcelona is more convincingly explained as a result of "the social and political protests of radicalized workers and the urban poor."[115] But there was enough substance to Soviet charges of sabotage and spying in Spain to give them a whiff of plausibility. The war, after all, had begun with an uprising of traitorous officers supported by Nazi Germany and fascist Italy. Opponents operating within the Republic and engaging in activities ranging from spying

109 Boris Pasternak, *Doctor Zhivago*, trans. Max Hayward and Manya Harrari (New York: Pantheon, 1958), 507.

110 "Trotskii-Zinov'ev-Kamenev-Gestapo," *Pravda*, 22 August 1936. See also *Pravda*, 16 September 1937; Schlögel, *Moscow, 1937*, 101.

111 Gábor Tamás Rittersporn, "The Omnipresent Conspiracy: On Soviet Imagery of Politics and Social Relations in the 1930s," in J. Arch Getty and Roberta Manning, eds., *Stalinist Terror: New Perspectives* (New York: Cambridge University Press, 1993), 99–115.

112 "Inostrannaia pechat' o protsesse antisovestskogo 'pravo-trotskistskogo bloka,'" *Pravda*, 7 March 1938. See also, "Trotskistskie shpiony na sluzhbe u Franko,"*Pravda*, 21 June 1937.

113 Mikhail Kol'tsov, "Agentura Trotskogo v Ispanii," *Pravda*, 22 January 1937. See also Kol'tsov, "Raskrytie trotskistskoi shpionskoi organizatsii v Barselone,"*Pravda*, 25 October 1937.

114 B. Mikhailov, "Trotskistsko-fashistskii putch v Barselone,"*Pravda*, 11 May 1937.

115 Graham, *The Spanish Civil War*, 63. George Orwell suggested a possible communist provocation, Orwell, *Homage to Catalonia*, 157. Payne deems a communist provocation "likely," *Spanish Civil War*, 217; Viñas disagrees, *Escudo*, 541–8.

to spreading demoralizing rumors constituted a real and "serious problem" for the Republic that "expanded as the war went on" – even if they lacked the level of coordination implied by the label "fifth column."[116] International espionage was not merely a figment of the fevered Stalinist imagination. The Italian secret police and the Gestapo really had agents active in Republican Spain.[117] The U.S. government really convicted a "ring" of German spies in 1938.[118] For those fighting in Spain, the "reality" of such plots was palpable. As noted in the previous chapter, both the Internationals and their commanders often understood everything from tobacco shortages to military defeats as the result of the fascist "fifth column." From there it was a short step to the conclusion that (complicated and poorly understood) political rivalries on the Republican side disguised particularly insidious fascist agents.

If the Spanish plots were plausible – and they might seem so particularly at a distance and to people with little knowledge of Spanish politics – and if the vipers were truly everywhere, then the alleged crimes of erstwhile Bolshevik leaders were perhaps not so fantastic after all.[119] The stories of Gestapo agents operating everywhere from New York to Madrid, from Finland to Bulgaria, had the cumulative effect of both explaining the rebels' successes in Spain and lending a certain credibility to the conspiracies uncovered at home. In the Soviet media the domestic hunt for "enemies of the people" was thus fundamentally inseparable from the valiant struggle in Spain to defeat fascist aggression and unmask Trotskyite-fascists. The insistence that the Soviet Union fought on the side of all progressive humanity did not rule out, but rather shored up, conspiracy theories.

Ultimately, Stalinist charges of "Trotskyite fascism" relied on the claim that the Soviet Union alone represented all progressive humanity and that only its leaders knew the best path to the radiant future. George Orwell, an eyewitness to the May Days in Barcelona, was willing to grant that a case could be made – although he ultimately did not agree with it – for the communist contention that the POUM's revolutionary agitation "weakened the Government forces and thus endangered the war" effort. What he could not tolerate, and what from his point of view revealed the true face of Stalinism, was the communist attack on the POUM as "a gang of disguised Fascists, in the pay of Franco and Hitler." Writing before the war ended, Orwell correctly noted that this mendacious "story was spread all over Spain ... and repeated over and over in

116 Graham, *Spanish Republic*, 342. José Luis Rodríguez Jiménez, "La 'Quinta Columna' en la Guerra Civil," *Historia y vida* 20, no. 226 (1987): 116–25. The term "fifth column" is usually attributed to General Emilio Mola; Payne argues that it was an "invention of Communist propaganda," *Spanish Civil War*, 88 n. 2.

117 Graham, *Spanish Republic*, 295–6, 342.

118 V. Minaev, "Raskrytie germanskogo shpionskogo tsentra v SShA," *Pravda*, 23 July 1938. "Nazis Seized Here in Spy Ring Case," *NYT*, 7 April 1938; "Prison Sentences Given Three Spies Here," *NYT*, 3 December 1938.

119 John Gates, *The Story of an American Communist* (New York: Thomas Nelson, 1958), 54.

the Communist and pro-Communist press of the whole world."[120] For Orwell, such accusations aimed to disguise the fact that the Comintern was concerned only with Soviet security and that in Spain the Soviet Union was an "anti-revolutionary" force.[121]

It was precisely this paradox of (perhaps temporarily) nonrevolutionary communism in Spain that turned some international communist participants in the war – particularly those who had joined the party during the Comintern's revolutionary Third Period and still defined themselves in terms of its radicalism – against the Soviet Union. Robert Gladnick, who joined the party in the early 1930s in Texas, remembered being greeted at the Spanish border by an anarchist militia, whose frontier post flew not the Republic's red, gold, and violet tricolor but "the anarchist Red & Black Flag." When the anarchists responded to the volunteers' "Viva la república" and "Viva el frente popular" with "Viva la revolución proletaria," Gladnick "as an old Third Period Communist" was "thrilled but most of the men were Popular Front recruits – did not understand the subtlety of this."[122] Firsthand experiences with Russian antisemitism in Spain further soured him on the notion that the Soviets were revolutionaries.[123] Gladnick's buddy William Herrick was likewise an old Third Period communist who eventually repudiated the party. In his 1998 memoir, he remembered sympathizing with the POUM and the anarchists who "socialized factories and formed voluntary communes," who made *señor* "taboo" and replaced it with "*compañero*, friend."[124] By contrast, "my Party called for bourgeois democracy, and lowered the red flag. I couldn't understand it." In retrospect he explained the Popular Front as pure cynicism: "We really were for the revolution, but not yet; only when *we*, the vanguard of the proletariat, were prepared to take power ourselves."[125] At the time, however, he may have been upset primarily by the betrayal of his sense of what it meant to be a communist.

For those international communists willing to accept that the Soviet Union was, as the Comintern often reminded them, the only country to have made a socialist revolution and thus the legitimate leader of the world proletarian movement,[126] Stalinist "explanations" provided a means of making sense of events about which they often knew very little. As Australian volunteer Lloyd

[120] Orwell, *Homage*, 64.
[121] Ibid., 56.
[122] Robert Gladnick memoirs, chapter 5, pp. 5–6, Hoover Institution Archives.
[123] Ibid., chapter 3, p. 16.
[124] William Herrick, *Jumping the Line: Adventures and Misadventures of an American Radical* (Madison: University of Wisconsin Press, 1998), 120.
[125] Emphasis in original. Ibid., 121. Payne makes a similar argument, *Spanish Civil War*, 137–8.
[126] Fernando Claudín, *The Communist Movement: From Comintern to Cominform*, trans. Brian Pearce (New York: Monthly Review Press, 1975), pt.1, 75–7; Kevin McDermott and Jeremy Agnew, *The Comintern: A History of International Communism from Lenin to Stalin* (Basingstoke: Palgrave Macmillan, 1996), 51, 79–80.

Edmonds noted in a 1983 interview, "I was very ignorant about Spain.... You see we were concerned in those days – and I'm sure this applies to most people who went to Spain – primarily with the fight against fascism. After you hit Spain, you suddenly gathered that this was a Spanish war really."[127] Or as Herrick put it more bluntly, "we knew and learned little about [Spain], except what our ignorant and biased commissars told us."[128] It may be the case, as historian Michael Petrou argues in relation to the Canadians, that the "concept of Trotskyism" "meant little to the average" volunteer.[129] However, many among the communists, notably but not only the alumni of the International Lenin School, had long familiarity with this potent epithet. By the mid-1930s, Trotskyism was a catchall term that covered the behavior of all manner of alleged enemies, traitors, wreckers, undisciplined elements, and spies.[130]

The volunteers' use of "Trotskyism" and "Trotskyites" to explain the situation in Spain to friends and family back home suggests that they viewed these terms as offering understandable explanations or at least explanations likely to sustain home-front morale – and pass the censor. The vehemence with which they used the terms points to their own investment in these explanations. In a mid-May 1937 letter, written just after the uprising in Barcelona had been put down, Jack Friedman, the commissar of the transport division, explained to his comrade Joe Freedman,

> In one of our truck convoys we had to guard ourselves with guns, not against the fascists – but against the Trotskyites. You see Trotskyism is no longer a theoretical question to us, it is real, and any bastard that tries to discuss and uphold the theory of it is quite apt to get the butt of my gun over his fucking head as a most convincing argument.[131]

The letter may not demonstrate a high-level understanding of Trotskyism as a "concept," but Friedman took up the attack on Trotskyites with enthusiasm and real Bolshevik style as a question of practice not theory.

Other volunteers were equally emphatic if also equally vague in their attacks on Trotskyites. William Sennett wrote to his partner Gussie, a Young Communist activist in Chicago, that they could learn from the Youth movement

[127] Lloyd Edmonds, *Letters from Spain*, ed. Amirah Inglis (Sydney: George Allen & Unwin, 1985), 86; Jack Taylor to the Commission of Work among Internationals, CC, CPS [Central Committee of PCE], 20 February 1938, RGASPI, f. 545, op. 6, d. 11, l. 2.

[128] Herrick, *Jumping the Line*, 220.

[129] Petrou, *Renegades*, 113.

[130] On "Trotskyite" behaviors see ibid., 113–19.

[131] Jack Friedman to Joe [Freeman], 13 May 1937 in Cary Nelson and Jefferson Hendricks, eds., *Madrid 1937: Letters of the Abraham Lincoln Brigade from the Spanish Civil War* (New York: Routledge, 1996), 349. See also Jack Friedman to George, 27 February [1937], ibid., 64; Carl Geiser to Impy, 3 June 1937, ibid., 158; Leon Rosenthal to Lee, 2 August 1937, ibid., 166; Lawrence Kleidman to Family, 18 December 1937, ibid., 122; Lini De Vries to Evelyn, 27 June 1937, Fredericka Martin Papers, ALBA 001, Box 6, Folder 19.

in Spain whose newspaper "has come out openly against Trotskyism and... is carrying on a consistent campaign for the extermination of this evil force."[132] Having heard that his sister was a Trotskyite, Ralph Fasanella, an Italian American from the Bronx who served in the transport division, threatened to throw her out a window if he returned from Spain, explaining, "Mom, there is [sic] only two sides today and that is Democracy or fascism. These ultra lefts are a bunch of bastards." Fasanella did return home, becoming an artist known for his labor-themed paintings, but apparently never carried out his threat.[133]

Indeed the brigadistas were familiar enough with the term "Trotskyite" and with the conventions of Stalinist discourse more generally that they were able to parody it. At the front, where the distance between the cheery news carried in the *Volunteer for Liberty* and military realities was particularly clear – and might have been funny had the reality been less grim – the Anglo-American troops dubbed their political commissars "comic stars."[134] In letters home and in their submissions to company or battalion publications, the men demonstrated a keen ear for the slogans that at once endowed their decision to fight in Spain with world historical significance and, under their current circumstances, sounded a little absurd. Sennett, whose letters to Gussie Machen were often full of earnest political arguments and lessons, treated her in a September 1937 letter to a "satire" by Dave Thompson, a communist who was the scion of a wealthy California family:

> Dialectically, from a true Marxian standpoint, an analysis of the political and general internal situation on the Iberian peninsula, is... a source wherein an unbiased student of world affairs is able to better understand, and appreciate to a fuller degree, the struggle not only here, now, but everywhere, anytime. It's overwhelming! It's collossal! [sic] You'll laugh, you'll cry. You'll have the bestest fun EVER![135]

In an October letter, Jack Friedman enclosed a clipping from the transport division's newspaper of perhaps the same "satirical article by Dave Thompson," whom he described as a "swell guy with plenty of wit."[136]

A handwritten submission to an unspecified Fifteenth Brigade publication illustrates the degree to which Stalinist political discourse pervaded the brigadistas' everyday life and thus their senses of humor. Beginning with the assertion, "Someone should teach the facts of life to the young men of Company One," the story equated sexual and political immaturity. The hardened veterans of Company Two pointed out that the "lads of Company One unblushingly indicated their ignorance of this advanced subject of nature when they organized a strident snake dance through neighboring barracks the other night loudly

[132] William Sennett to Gussie [Machen], 3 June 1937, VALB, Container 1.
[133] Ralph Fasanella to Mom, 20 April 1938, VALB, Container 1. Roberta Smith, "Ralph Fasanella, 83, Primitive Painter Dies," *NYT*, 18 December 1997.
[134] Bessie, *Civil War Notebooks*, 31; Eby, *Between the Bullet*, 31, 53, 117, 227.
[135] William Sennett to Gussie, 16 September 1937, VALB, Container 1.
[136] Jack Friedman to Esther, 8 October 1937, in *Madrid 1937*, 174.

proclaiming that [the company dog] Minnie had pups." They lectured, "Oh dear children, the stork must have notification months in advance," and also pointed out that "the potential father of the pups must be old enough to have adult proclivities. (That means: You must become a man, my son.)" The story then took a strangely politically turn, as the men of Company Two deemed it "our duty" to reveal – "And remember, you youths approaching manhood, this hurts us more than it does you" – that "the Company Two Gay Pay OO" (GPU, the Soviet political police, later known as the NKVD) had "conclusive proof" that Minnie "belongs to the secret organization of the MOUP – (the POUM is just against the anti-fascist united front, the Soviet Union and 183½ other things. MOUP is against *everything*!)" The proof of her political transgressions came in the form of a letter in which she credited a patent medicine with giving her the energy to "sleep with anybody's husband" – a parody that relied on familiarity with the Stalinist habit of conflating political and personal failings. The story's conclusion offered at once good political and sexual advice: "the young men of Co. 1 must be much more careful of both the company they keep and the way they pop off prematurely."[137]

Yet the brigadistas' bitter mockery did not rule out affirmations of the importance and power of their communist convictions. In April 1938, after the Nationalist breakthrough in Aragon, Bessie recorded in his notebook that the Brigade was "practically annihilated." "But," he added, "for the benefit of folks at home" the Brigade "is 100% American and numbers about 1,000 to 2,000."[138] If he resented such communist propaganda, he nonetheless appreciated the fact that the party members in the Brigade continued to stand out as having "higher morale and more developed consciousness of responsibility."[139] He lauded precisely the linkage of sound politics and sound individual behavior that provided the satiric bite in the story of Minnie and her pups.

Stalinism as an international culture drew communists together with shared narratives, heroes, holidays, emblems, and enemies. But for all they shared, local communist political cultures remained distinct. In Spain, officers and commissars had a penchant for labeling all sorts of behaviors as "Trotskyite" and for threatening to arrest or shoot malingerers, deserters, and malcontents.[140] However, they rarely did – which is not to excuse or minimize the executions that occurred, such as the one Bessie matter of factly noted in March 1938: "One major (Spanish) and 2 Lts. and 1 Sgt. were shot yesterday for cowardice."[141] Rather, the point is that nothing like the Soviet terror existed in Spain. What was dangerous for Soviet advisors in Spain was

137 RGASPI, f. 545, op. 3, d. 473, ll. 161–3. See also "A lesson in dialectics," ibid., l. 159.

138 Bessie, *Civil War Notebooks*, 33.

139 Ibid., 34.

140 Merriman diary, vol. 2, pp. 32, 63, Merriman Papers, Box 1, Folder 3; Eby, *Between the Bullet*, 227–8; Szurek, *Shattered Dream*, 101.

141 Bessie, *Civil War Notebooks*, 17. On executions in spring 1938, see Petrou, *Renegades*, 131–3.

returning to the Soviet Union, where many were arrested and executed, among them Kol'tsov, Ćopić, military attaché Vladimir Gorev, Ambassador Marcel Rosenberg, the Soviet consul in Barcelona Vladimir Antonov-Ovseenko, head of military intelligence Yan Berzin, and economic advisor Artur Stashevskii.[142] Polish volunteers summoned to Moscow were likewise arrested and executed.[143] The lower level of political violence in Spain underscores the fact that in the Spanish context, it was possible to think – or threaten – like a Stalinist, but it was not always necessary or possible to act like one.[144] The story of "Minnie of Co. 1" was unlikely to be submitted for publication in the Soviet Union, yet it would not have been written without the powerful influence of Stalinist political culture.

Evaluating Communist Behavior

The willingness to label almost any sort of disruptive behavior "Trotskyite" drew on the longstanding communist convention of defining ostensibly private behaviors as politically meaningful.[145] This practice is particularly clear in the ratings of volunteers prepared by the Foreign Cadres Section of the Spanish Communist Party (Partido Comunista de España, PCE). In rating nonparty volunteers, the cadres section used a scale – "good," "fair," "drunk," "bad," or "very bad" – that made no distinction between personal behavior and military service. Thus Oscar Aho, a Finnish American from Minnesota was rated "Drunk," but with the notation "Brave at the front." Amos Archer, an African American from Ohio was rated "Bad. Stole rations from the kitchen to give to a woman." Alfred Litwin, a graduate of City College in New York, was also rated "Bad. Sexual pervert." Frank Lucas, a Croatian American who fought both at Brunete and the Ebro, was rated simply "Good."[146] There was a different scale for measuring party members: "cadre," "needs political instruction," "good," "fair," "weak," and "bad." Again, the ratings encompassed the military, political, and "moral sphere." The "bad" cadres were those who had

142 Radosh et al., *Spain Betrayed*, 93–4.Enrique Líster López, "¿Qué fue de ellos? El Destino de los militares soviéticos que participaron en la Guerra de España," in *Rusos en la guerra*, 116–20.

143 Fridrikh I. Firsov, "Dimitrov, the Comintern and Stalinist Repression," in Barry McLoughlin and Kevin McDermott, eds., *Stalin's Terror: High Politics and Mass Repression in the Soviet Union* (Basingstoke: Palgrave Macmillan, 2003), 72–3.

144 Radosh et al., *Spain Betrayed*, 176; Graham, *Spanish Republic*, 384–7.

145 Tim Rees, "Deviation and Discipline: Anti-Trotskyism, Bolshevisation and the Spanish Communist Party, 1924–34," *Historical Research* 82, no. 215 (February 2009): 152, 148. Brigitte Studer and Berthold Unfried, "Private Matters Become Public: Western European Exiles and Emigrants in Stalinist Russia in the 1930s," *International Review of Social History* 48, no. 2 (2003): 211–12.

146 "Primera lista alfabética de los voluntarios internacionales sin partido," 17 November 1938, RGASPI, f. 545, op. 6, d. 852, ll. 2–4. In the ALBA database, these volunteers are identified as party members, www.alba-valb.org.

"shown themselves to be largely useless or harmful to the antifascist cause in Spain." An explanation of the rating advised that "bad" comrades – there were 10 on the initial list of 207 – should not "be regarded as political enemies, but without exception their defects are serious ones such as constant drunkenness, cowardice coupled with indiscipline, disruptive tendencies, Trotzkyist [sic] tendencies, etc." and they should be "excluded from the Party without exception."[147]

These sorts of "characterizations" would have been familiar to most communists before they reached Spain. However, even having a formal party education provided no guarantee that a comrade would demonstrate behavior worthy of a communist. The Lenin School alumni who fought in Spain, for example, were not necessarily braver, better disciplined, or more politically correct than their peers. Some, such as Mack Coad who had spent two years at the Lenin School in the early 1930s at the time of the "white chauvinism" disputes, proved themselves exemplary communists and soldiers. Coad arrived in Spain in October 1937 and attended officer training school in early 1938. The instructors characterized him as having "plenty of intelligence politically" and as an "excellent student." Commissar John Gates judged him a "Very responsible and sincere comrade. Carries out party work well. Is even tempered."[148] In August 1938, he was wounded in his right eye at Gandesa; he was repatriated at the end of the year.[149]

By contrast, Sterling Rochester, who was among the Lenin students sent directly from Moscow to Spain, got into trouble in both places during his service. He, like many volunteers, was disciplined for drunkenness. When in custody he "attempted to start fights with several comrades," and the brigade's physician, Sidney Robbins, an Austrian communist, recommended the (unspecified) "usual procedure against uncontrolled drunkedness [sic]," perhaps a short stay in the guardhouse to dry out.[150] On the Soviet side, Rochester caused a disturbance by sending a letter from Spain to his girlfriend in Russia. The school immediately undertook an investigation of this breach of "conspiracy," which was especially egregious because he used his real name (not his school name, Stanley Taylor) in the correspondence. He seems, however, to have suffered no penalty in Spain.[151]

147 "To the Central Committee of the Communist Party," 20 December 1938, RGASPI, f. 545, op. 6, d. 852, l. 94ob; "Primera lista alfabética de los camaradas voluntarios de las Brigadas Internacionales – Militantes del Partido Comunista," 17 November 1938, ibid., l. 71.

148 "Coad, Mack," RGASPI, f. 545, op. 6, d. 874, l. 9.

149 Ibid., ll. 3–6.

150 S. S. Robbins to the Etat Major, XV Brigade, Judiciary Commission, nd, RGASPI, f. 545, op. 3, d. 451, l. 78. On punishments, see Petrou, *Renegades*, 128, 130. For a positive assessment of Rochester as a combatant, see John Tisa, *Recalling the Good Fight: An Autobiography of the Spanish Civil War* (South Hadley, MA: Bergin and Garvey, 1985), 50–1.

151 "Direktoru Leninskoi Shkoli tov. K. I. Kirsanovoi: Raport," 5 March 1937, RGASPI, f. 531, op. 1, d. 127, l. 2; Sterling Rochester to Nina [Strokova], 9 February 1937, ibid., l. 3.

FIGURE 7. Corporal Mack Coad, Company 2, MacKenzie-Papineau Battalion. Courtesy Tamiment Library, New York University. (ALBA Photo 11-0212 [Series B])

Two of the best-known American Lenin School alumni in Spain, Harry Haywood and Steve Nelson, served as political commissars, and both got into trouble, albeit of different sorts. They arrived in spring 1937 after the Lincoln battalion's disastrous losses at Jarama. Nelson (then thirty-four), who had no military experience, served as the Lincoln battalion's commissar; Haywood (thirty-nine), a veteran of World War I, became the Fifteenth Brigade's adjutant commissar. Both left Spain by the fall of 1937. In his 1978 autobiography, Haywood described his time in Spain as a "defeat, a setback which would affect my life in the Party for some years to come." Much to his surprise, on reaching the front Haywood recognized Ćopić as "Sanko" from their Lenin School days; however, the two took an almost immediate dislike to one another. As Haywood told the story, during the battle of Brunete, he was forced out of his position because Ćopić managed to turn the brigade staff against him.[152] Haywood's Comintern file tells a simpler story: "unworthy and non-party

[152] Harry Haywood, *Black Bolshevik: Autobiography of an Afro-American Communist* (Chicago: Liberator Press, 1978), 470, 475, 482, 487. Carroll, *Odyssey*, 134–5.

FIGURE 8. Sterling Rochester (right) with Slavonivitch, chief of information at Jarama and Brunete. Courtesy Tamiment Library, New York University. (ALBA Photo 177-178005)

behavior in Spain: drunkenness and cowardice in battle." In 1939, he was removed from the American party's central committee and politburo.[153]

Nelson, the battalion's best-loved and probably most effective commissar, had a much more positive experience in Spain. Unpretentious, a good listener, and pragmatic, he immediately won the men over and by all accounts contributed enormously to rebuilding morale in the battalion. Even the habitual complainers had a good word for Steve Nelson.[154] Wounded at Belchite in September 1937, Nelson returned to the United States, and it was there that he ran afoul of the International Brigade leadership. In a June 1938 letter to Gates, then the Lincoln battalion's commissar, Nelson, newly appointed to the American party's central committee, observed, "I hope by the time you get this letter that you will be on your way home along with dozens of other boys who have been there a long time already.... Naturally, I'm saying this because I feel that

[153] "Spravka," 27 December 1939, RGASPI, f. 495, op. 261 d. 6509, l. 9.
[154] Carroll, *Odyssey*, 131–2.

certain steps are being taken regarding our boys in Spain."[155] The letter arrived as the Internationals were preparing for the Ebro offensive, and the commissar was busy scotching rumors of repatriation. Jim Bourne, another Lenin School alumnus then serving as a PCE representative in the Fifteenth Brigade, sent word of the letter to André Marty, noting that "these views were held by the Central Committee of the American Party."[156] Marty in turn quoted Nelson in a letter to American party leader Earl Browder, in which he warned of "the bad effect of such letters on the moral [sic] of the fighters. And such letters are coming very numerous.... For that I inform you."[157] However, by September plans were being made to withdraw the Internationals, and no hint of this incident appears in Nelson's Comintern file. Instead, a later incident – his positive 1940 review of Ernest Hemingway's *For Whom the Bell Tolls* – brought criticism of his insufficient "political vigilance."[158] Whereas Haywood's alleged drunkenness and cowardice became a permanent political blot, Nelson's allegedly demoralizing letter and incorrect assessment of Hemingway scarcely affected his overall evaluation as a "loyal and steadfast comrade."[159]

Haywood's and Nelson's stories illustrate the ease with which in one case an ostensibly personal failing – fear at the front – could become a political marker and, in another, political missteps might be excused by loyalty and steadfastness. They also suggest that the most lasting result of the Lenin School experience was not necessarily behavior that was consistently worthy and party-minded. Rather the shared experience produced a web of personal ties that, although they did not always promote trust, as the case of Haywood and Ćopić demonstrates, did facilitate a sense of the reach of the Comintern network. In their memoirs, Haywood and Nelson emphasized both the presence of former schoolmates among the International Brigades and the acute pain of seeing a comrade whom they had met in Moscow die in Spain. When he arrived, Haywood learned that his "old friend and schoolmate" Dave Springhall had been wounded at Jarama. At Brunete, he "encountered the horrible sight of the bodies of women and children lying in the road, as well as members of the British Battalion," among whom he recognized someone he knew only as "Brown," "formerly of the Lenin School."[160] In telling the story of his years at the Lenin School, Nelson called attention to those, like Mack Coad who "also

155 Steve Nelson to Johnnie [Gates], 15 June 1938, RGASPI, f. 545, op. 6, d. 953, l. 33.

156 Jim Bourne to André Marty, 3 July 1938, RGASPI, f. 545, op. 6, d. 953, l. 34. *Hearings before the Committee on Un-American Activities, House of Representatives, Eighty-fourth Congress: Investigation of Communist Activities in the Seattle, Wash., Area* (Washington, DC: U.S. Government Printing Office, 1955), 357.

157 André Marty to Earl Browder, 13 July 1938, RGASPI, f. 545, op. 6, d. 953, l. 39. See also "Sección Anglo-Americano-Canadiense," 15 July 1938, ibid., op. 1, d. 3, l. 333.

158 "Tov. Raian [Eugene Dennis] II.IV.41 g kharkterizoval t. Stiv Nel'son," RGASPI, f. 495, op. 261, d. 108, l. 105.

159 "Spravka," 25 August 1941, RGASPI, f. 495, op. 261, d. 108, l. 105.

160 Haywood, *Black Bolshevik*, 474, 481–2.

FIGURE 9. Steve Nelson (left) with Douglas Roach. Courtesy Tamiment Library, New York University. (ALBA Photo 177-179075)

went to Spain" – Coad arrived in the fall of 1937 just as Nelson departed – and those he met "again on the battlefields of Spain." He remembered in particular George Brown, "a tall handsome Irishman from England" killed in July 1937 – perhaps the same Brown that Haywood knew. Nelson wrote, "The sight of his body stretched out on the road to Brunete is something I've never forgotten."[161]

The personal ties that linked international communists might also, as Rochester's case illustrates, cause unexpected political problems. Indeed the political and the personal were often entangled for individual communists. As Rochester wrote in his letter to Nina from Spain, "I can't forget the red capital of the world, or the sweetest girl there."[162] Recognizing the possibility of such entanglements, commissars and commanders in Spain closely monitored personal behavior for its political effects. Soviet advisor Karol Świerczewski argued against this practice in a report to Moscow, noting that efforts to control the private lives of Spanish troops were counterproductive. He quoted with disapproval the verdict in the case of a Spanish deserter who had abandoned the front to get married: "Marriage during war is a grave mistake, and the soldier who decides to take this step should not forget the responsibility that

[161] Nelson et al., *American Radical*, 126, 131.

[162] Sterling Rochester to Nina [Strokova], l. 3.

he must bear if his wife and child are orphaned." He derided such judgments as reflecting the "refined, sadistic-pharisaical virtue of impotent men who recommend celibacy to achieve victory over fascism."[163] That Świerczewski, who had a wife and children in Moscow, acquired a "wife" in Spain may account for some of the vehemence of his response.[164] Nonetheless, the objection highlighted a key feature of Stalinist culture and went to the heart of the contested and thorny question of how communist "virtue" – especially in the realm of sex, love, and family – ought to be defined.

[163] "Notes on the Situation," in *Spain Betrayed*, 455–6.
[164] Szurek, *Shattered Dream*, 182–3.

5

Best Comrades, Tough Guys, and Respectable Communists

Looking back on the Spanish civil war in 1996, Irene Falcón, Dolores Ibárruri's long-time secretary and friend, reflected that "when death is so close, love frequently comes and goes." In wartime, Falcón observed, men were forgiven when "new loves emerge in a flash, like bombs or gunfire," whereas in the case of women the "attitude of tolerance gave way to the oldest traditions and prejudices."[1] She remembered with particular bitterness the rumors that swirled around Ibárruri's affair with Francisco Antón, a political commissar some fifteen years her junior.[2] Underscoring the sexism involved, Falcón emphasized that it was usually men "who stir up this criticism."[3] Ibárruri never publicly acknowledged the affair, which ended in 1943.[4]

One of the men who stirred up criticism of Ibárruri's private life, Jesús Hernández, was himself involved in a wartime romance that highlights both the double standard identified by Falcón and the communist tendency to conflate the personally and politically scandalous. An evaluation of Hernández, who had served as the Republic's minister of education, which was based on

[1] Irene Falcón with Manuel Jiménez and Jesús Montero, *Asalto a los cielos: Mi vida junto a Pasionaria* (Madrid: Temas de Hoy, 1996), 215.

[2] Paul Preston, *¡Comrades! Portraits from the Spanish Civil War* (London: Harper Collins, 1999), 298; Carrie Hamilton, "Activism and Representations of Motherhood in the Autobiography of Dolores Ibárruri, *Pasionaria*," *Journal of Romance Studies* 1, no. 1 (2001): 22–3; Joan Estruch Tobella, *Historia oculta del PCE* (Madrid: Ediciones Temas de Hoy, 2000), 136–7. Sources disagree on exactly how many years younger Antón was; estimates range from fifteen to twenty years. Ivo Banac, ed., *The Diary of Gregory Dimitrov, 1933–1949* (New Haven: Yale University Press, 2003), 73.

[3] Falcón, *Asalto a los cielos*, 215.

[4] In her memoir, Ibárruri mentioned Antón only in passing, Dolores Ibárruri, *Memorias de Pasionaria, 1939–1977: Me faltaba España* (Barcelona: Planeta, 1984), 54, 126.

information provided by Spanish leaders and Comintern officials, emphasized concerns about his "relations with women," specifically "the way he took up with his current wife." Indeed the critique focused less on Hernández's own failings than on those of his wife, Pilar Boves, who had allegedly "lived with the fascist toreador Cagancho" [Joaquín Rodríguez Ortega], thereby arousing communist suspicions. When Boves left the secretary of the Madrid party organization Domingo Girón, her husband of only a few months, for Hernández their relationship precipitated "political discussions" (according to the Russian version of the report) and a "scandal" (according to an earlier evaluation by Palmiro Togliatti, the Comintern representative in Spain).[5] However, although the report questioned Hernández's judgment in the matter, Boves, whose behavior was described as sometimes inappropriately "petty-bourgeois," emerged as the primary culprit.[6] In this case, the affair was publicly acknowledged – Hernández and Boves wed – but it nonetheless underscored the contradictions of communist norms that at once embraced female emancipation and insisted on female virtue.

The promises and limits of the communist commitment to emancipation emerge even more clearly in the case of Salaria Kee's wartime romance. In Spain, Kee (or Kea), an African American nurse who apparently joined the communist party in 1935, fell in love with and married a wounded Irish volunteer, Patrick O'Reilly.[7] In a draft of her 1938 memoir she remembered their courtship as steeped in politics: O'Reilly recited poems and "We discussed North America, Ireland, and all groups and races who were victims of fascism and other injustices and how we two could help to abolish the enemies of the human race."[8] In December 1937, the marriage received celebratory coverage in the African American community's *Philadelphia Tribune*, which described it as "one of the most romantic interracial romances" and noted that in lieu of the wedding march "a chorus of young Spanish girls sang 'Joven Guardia,'" the Young Communist anthem.[9] At the same time, the interracial marriage posed a potential public relations problem for the party as it sought to attract broad support for the cause in Spain. When she returned to the United States in May 1938, the Medical Bureau and the North American Committee to Aid Spanish Democracy's press release mentioned the marriage and a planned fundraising

5 "Spravka," Rossiiskii gosudarstvennyi arkhiv sotsial'no-politicheskoi istorii (RGASPI), f. 495, op. 220, d. 44, ll. 41ob, 72; Gregorio Morán, *Miseria y grandeza del Partido Comunista de España, 1939–1985* (Barcelona: Planeta, 1986), 24.

6 "Spravka," ll. 41ob, 72; Morán, *Miseria*, 24.

7 Robert Stradling, *The Irish and the Spanish Civil War, 1936–1939* (Manchester: Manchester University Press, 1999), 197; Emily Robins Sharpe, "Salaria Kea's Spanish Memoirs," *Volunteer* 28, no. 4 (December 2011): 18, 19.

8 As quoted in Sharpe, "Salaria Kea's," 19.

9 "Interracial Romance Blooms, Blossoms in War-Torn Spain," *Philadelphia Tribune*, 2 December 1937.

tour.[10] However, just a month later, Pearl Levenstein at the Medical Bureau forwarded Kee a letter from organizers in Cincinnati, who believed it "unwise to publicize her marriage to a white man, this would prejudice her not only with the white people, but with the Negroes."[11] In response, Kee asked to be relieved of the obligation to speak in Cincinnati, because "I hate prejudice whether it comes from the Negroes or whites. I shall fight it unto death." For her, support for the cause simply ruled out such prejudice. "I really do not understand," she wrote, "how any people white or black who supposed to be interested in the loyal struggle in Spain can let my domestic affair excite them."[12] She clearly understood the political meanings of her marriage, but did not expect such prejudices among communists or even among the Popular Front left more generally.

These varied stories of communists in love open a view of the ambivalences, complexities, and contradictions in norms of communist comportment. Both the war itself, with its separations and anxieties, and earlier Soviet and socialist norms associated with the theories of Aleksandra Kollontai and August Bebel led communists like Falcón to advocate "personal freedom in matters of love."[13] However, they operated, as Falcón also noted, in an environment marked by a return of "rigor and puritanism" in communist gender norms, as exemplified by the 1936 Soviet legislation outlawing abortion and restricting divorce.[14] This chapter explores a number of intimate stories – of marital relations, homosocial bonding, and wartime romances – as a means of tracing the personal and political challenges of communists in love. As men and women crossed national, gender, and racial divides, they at once made good communism's promises of emancipation and exposed the degree to which traditional boundaries continued to operate within the international communist community.

"Thinking of My Best Comrade and Wife Back Home"

Many, if not most, of the international volunteers in Spain were single. As the historian Michael Petrou notes with regard to Canada, the "Communist Party preferred volunteers without families so that it would not be responsible

10 "For Immediate Release," 13 May 1938, Fredericka Martin Papers, ALBA 001, Box 9, Folder 84, Tamiment Library/Robert F. Wagner Labor Archives, New York University.

11 Pearl W. Levenstein to Salaria Kee, 18 June 1938, Martin Papers, Box 9, Folder 84.

12 Salaria Kee to Pearl Levenstein, 20 June 1938, Martin Papers, Box 9, Folder 84.

13 Falcón, *Asalto a los cielos*, 21; Richard Stites, *The Women's Liberation Movement in Russia: Feminism, Nihilism, and Bolshevism, 1860–1930* (Princeton: Princeton University Press, 1978), 354.

14 Falcón, *Asalto a los cielos*, 135; Wendy Z. Goldman, *Women, the State, and Revolution: Soviet Family Policy and Social Life, 1917–1936* (New York: Cambridge University Press, 1993), 296–336.

for widowed wives and orphans." He also suggests that choosing to fight and perhaps die for the cause was an "easier decision" for single men than their married comrades. In any case, Petrou finds that of the 611 Canadian volunteers for whom information is available, 103 (or about 17 percent) were married when they left for Spain.[15] Historian Peter Carroll similarly reports that "relatively few" of the American volunteers – about 15 percent – were married.[16] Adopting a somewhat broader measure, Rémi Skoutelsky finds that about 29 percent of the French volunteers, the largest single national group, were married or cohabitating, with communists more likely to be married than noncommunists.[17] Percentages similar to those in the American and Canadian contingents seem to have held across the Brigades.[18]

The prolific letter writers introduced in previous chapters are thus somewhat anomalous in that most were married. From his arrival in Spain in April 1937 through early 1938, Mito Kruth wrote faithfully to his wife Helen, often several times a week. In roughly the same period William Sennett sent frequent letters to Gussie Machen. Although the two married after his return from Spain in October 1938, as Sennett explained in an interview in the early 1980s, the couple "dated our wedding anniversary from September 1, 1934, the beginning of our nonlegal period of cohabitation."[19] From July 1937 to February 1939, Ben Gardner likewise wrote frequently to his wife Alice, who received and saved at least two letters per month. In his detailed letters to his wife Marion, Robert Merriman often included information about troop movements and military operations. Steve Nelson, by contrast, excused his less informative letters by reminding his wife Margaret, "You know why I can not go and talk about many things in letters under war conditions."[20]

That married communists, who constituted such a relatively small percentage of the volunteers, are well represented, even overrepresented, in the archival and published collections of letters from Spain may be a function of the fact that they felt a responsibility or desire to write home frequently or that they

15 Michael Petrou, *Renegades: Canadians in the Spanish Civil War* (Vancouver: University of British Columbia Press, 2008), 13.

16 Peter N. Carroll, *The Odyssey of the Abraham Lincoln Brigade: Americans in the Spanish Civil War* (Stanford: Stanford University Press, 1994), 16.

17 Rémi Skoutelsky, "L'engagement des volontaires français en Espagne républicaine," *Mouvement social*, no. 181 (October-December 1997): 12, 18.

18 Michael W. Jackson, *Fallen Sparrows: The International Brigades in the Spanish Civil War* (Philadelphia: American Philosophical Society, 1994), 47; Hywel Francis, *Miners Against Fascism: Wales and the Spanish Civil War* (London: Lawrence and Wishart, 1984), 92; Nir Arielli, "Induced to Volunteer? The Predicament of Jewish Communists in Palestine and the Spanish Civil War," *Journal of Contemporary History* 46, no. 4 (2011): 868.

19 William Sennett, "Communist Functionary and Corporate Executive," an oral history conducted 1981 and 1982 by Marshall Windmiller, Regional Oral History Office, The Bancroft Library, University of California, Berkeley, 1984, 42.

20 Steve Nelson to Margaret Nelson, 22 [June] 1937, Steve Nelson Papers, ALBA 008, Box 1, Folder 8.

wrote primarily to their spouses, who may have been particularly likely to save the letters. Leon Rosenthal, for instance, imagined his letters to his wife Lee as a means of having "a little chat" with her when he felt "lonesome for you."[21] Dave Gordon pledged to write his wife Lottie "daily," but was not always able to keep his word.[22] In 1989, Mary Rolfe, the wife of the poet Edwin Rolfe, had 350 pages of his civil war letters stashed in a closet.[23] By contrast, volunteers from countries with underground communist parties often hesitated to write to anyone back home.[24] Letters to the troops were often lost in what historian Hywel Francis calls "the normal ravages of war."[25] Thus, although letters from married American communists in Spain cannot be understood as typical, they nonetheless offer an interesting window into how committed communists understood the relationship between marriage and politics. How could one be at once married and married to the party?

In leaving spouses and, perhaps less commonly, children to risk their lives in Spain, the volunteers were in many ways stereotypical communists – selfless to the point of forgoing domestic comforts, serious to the point of humorlessness.[26] In two interviews published in the 1980s, Centa Herker-Beimler, the widow of Hans Beimler, a German communist killed in the defense of Madrid, depicted her husband in just such terms. She emphasized that Hans "subordinated everything to party work. The family too. I didn't always think that was a good thing." Her "I didn't *always* think" suggests that she shared – or tried to share – his principles to some degree. Still, there was little "time for each other" in a marriage that was "actually first and foremost illegal party work."[27]

[21] Leon Rosenthal to Lee [Rosenthal], 29 August 1937, in Cary Nelson and Jefferson Hendricks, eds., *Madrid 1937: Letters of the Abraham Lincoln Brigade from the Spanish Civil War* (New York: Routledge, 1996), 217. See also his letter of 29 September 1937, ibid., 114.

[22] Dave Gordon to Lottie [Gordon], 5 November 1938, in *Madrid 1937*, 442. See also his letter 19 November 1938, ibid., 415.

[23] Cary Nelson, "Introduction," *Madrid 1937*, 15. Marcel Acier, ed., *From Spanish Trenches: Recent Letters from Spain* (New York: Modern Age Books, 1937), does not always note the marital status of letter writers, but a number from the United States and Holland wrote to their wives.

[24] Jessie McLellan, "'I Wanted To Be a Little Lenin': Ideology and the German International Brigade Volunteers," *Journal of Contemporary History* 41, no. 2 (2006): 289.

[25] Hywel Francis, "'Say Nothing and Leave in the Middle of the Night': The Spanish Civil War Revisited," *History Workshop Journal*, no. 32 (Autumn 1991): 73. Few letters by Spanish combatants have survived; James Matthews, *Reluctant Warriors: Republican Popular Army and Nationalist Army Conscripts in the Spanish Civil War, 1936–1939* (Oxford: Oxford University Press, 2012), 138.

[26] Questionnaires distributed to the Internationals sometimes asked about marital status, but not about children. Letter writers often took special note of those who left children behind, suggesting that the situation was unusual. Elizabeth Roberts, "British and American Volunteers and the Politics of Dress and Demeanour in the Spanish Civil War," *Limina* 14 (2008): 64–5.

[27] Quoted in Josie McLellan, *Antifascism and Memory in East Germany: Remembering the International Brigades, 1945–1989* (New York: Oxford University Press, 2004), 125–6.

FIGURE 10. Soldiers writing letters home. Courtesy Tamiment Library, New York University. (ALBA Photo 11–1493 [Series E])

The volunteers who left for Spain without consulting or in some cases notifying their wives likewise appeared to put party or principles before family. In a letter to his cousin Gussie Moskowitz, Leo Gordon (born Mendelowitz) excused his abrupt departure for Spain as

> necessary. As a matter of fact, it was the only way. Some time ago I informed Agnes [his wife] that I wanted to go. She nearly passed out. She refused to discuss the question at all. Had I persisted it would have broken us up eventually.... I'm sorry I hurt her. It's the toughest part of being out here. But look at it this way. On all sides of me in camp, the same problem confronts hundreds of boys.... What's your solution? Stay home and fight fascism in the U.S. while the fascists take over Spain?[28]

Ben Gardner similarly emphasized the necessity of leaving, even without his wife Alice's consent. In August 1937, during a lull in the Brunete offensive, he wrote, "Alice dear, I want to repeat what I stated in previous letters. I was no doubt wrong by not consulting you, but I didn't do it willingly.... it is

[28] Leo Mendelowitz to Gus, 26 August 1937, as reproduced in Daniel Czitrom, "Volunteers for Liberty: Letters from Joe and Leo Gordon, Americans in Spain 1937–38," *Massachusetts Review* 25, no. 3 (Autumn 1984): 354.

unavoidable. Our lives are full of suffering & we are struggling to make it better."[29] Gardner returned home from Spain, only to be killed in 1944 in France, fighting his second war against fascism. Gordon was killed in Spain during the retreats of March 1938.[30]

In some cases, wives were consulted about the decision to fight in Spain and, however reluctantly or enthusiastically, apparently agreed with it. In a 1986 interview, Nelson emphasized that both he and his wife Margaret "had this complete commitment to the idea that the movement comes first. And we had no kids to worry about."[31] In contemporary letters, he simply assumed that Margaret would do whatever the movement required. Deeming it "a crime for the comrades back home not to write to every comrade here," he instructed her in a May 1937 letter to get the local comrades to send more letters to Spain.[32] William Sennett persuaded his partner Gussie to agree to his departure by emphasizing, as many volunteers did, that the war was likely to be short; he thought he would be home in three months.[33] As it turned out, he spent eighteen months in Spain, from February 1937 to October 1938. However, as in the cases of Alice Gardner and Agnes Gordon, the sources provide only the husbands' impressions of the wives' points of view.[34]

At least from the husbands' perspective, a defining feature of these communist unions – and what overcame even the pain of separation – was shared political commitments. Thus Leon Rosenthal assured Lee that "the hardship of being separated from each other is part of the sacrifice we must all make in this gigantic, decisive battle of the 'final conflict.'" He advised her to "Keep thinking of our victory, of what it will mean to everybody and continue your splendid work for Spain."[35] For him, at least, their marriage appeared to be a political and romantic union.

Husbands often emphasized that they followed their wives' political activities with real interest, and they offered touching, if sometimes condescending, advice. Robert Merriman wrote to Marion that "I am proud of you and the fine

[29] Ben Gardner to [Alice Gardner], 30 August 1937, Veterans of the Abraham Lincoln Brigade (VALB), Bay Area Post, BANC MSS 71/105 z, Container 1, Bancroft Library, University of California, Berkeley.

[30] "Gardner, Ben: Biographical Information," VALB, Container 1. Czitrom, "Volunteers," 352.

[31] Donald Miller and Steve Nelson, "Fighting in Spain: A Conversation with Steve Nelson," *Salmagundi*, no. 76/77 (Fall 1987–Winter 1988): 118.

[32] Steve Nelson to Margaret, 31 May 1937, Nelson Papers, Box 1, Folder 8.

[33] William Sennett to Gussie [Machen], 25 March 1937, VALB, Container 1. See also Marion Merriman and Warren Lerude, *American Commander in Spain: Robert Hale Merriman and the Abraham Lincoln Brigade* (Reno: University of Nevada Press, 1986), 72; Luigi Longo, *Las Brigadas Internacionales en España*, trans. Victor Flores Olea (Mexico City: Ediciones Era, 1966), 211.

[34] For the perspective of angry wives see Elizabeth Roberts, *"Freedom, Faction, Fame, and Blood": British Soldiers of Conscience in Greece, Spain, and Finland* (Portland, OR.: Sussex Academic Press, 2010), 93.

[35] Leon Rosenthal to Lee [Rosenthal], 2 September [1937], in *Madrid 1937*, 221.

work you are doing" – raising funds for Spain since her return to the United States – and concluded somewhat patronizingly that her work was "having the result I hoped for – to develop my Marion."[36] Emphasizing their shared commitments and also his superior knowledge, Bob offered specific advice on making speeches; in another letter he paraphrased Lenin, exhorting Marion to "Learn Learn Learn and be my sweet girl."[37]

Both Mito Kruth and William Sennett frequently encouraged their wives to assert themselves and to have greater confidence in their abilities. Mito concluded a letter to Helen with the request that she "Write more of what you are doing. If it helps I will try to express opinions from here."[38] Less than two months later, in August 1937, he wrote, "You certainly are developing fast and now that you work without my being there you will do very well."[39] In September 1937, he was "glad to hear in one of your letters that you were not afraid to assert yourself with the [party] section and speak up. That is about the only way to get recognized with some of them."[40] William Sennett offered similar assurance and encouragement to Gussie: "I know that in a short time you could be [a Young Communist League] section organizer – No kidding – Your main fault now is not enuf [sic] confidence and aggressiveness."[41] Three months later, in June 1937, he had nothing but praise for her, beginning his letter with these words: "While we're on this business of pride, I must say that with every letter you send I feel that the content is an expression of your development. It is a joy to be able to read that your own wife appreciates the upsurge in the labor movement and activizes [sic] herself accordingly."[42]

Such appreciations of their wives' progressive political engagement did not necessarily rule out expressions of their inability to look after themselves. Mito Kruth and Leon Rosenthal worried that their wives were working too hard. Leon warned Lee not to "wait for a nervous crisis" before taking a "week's vacation." He also admonished her to "don't lose any more weight, skinny!"[43] Mito likewise advised Helen, "Look out for dangerous signals of exhaustion" and to "put your foot down hard" if the comrades objected to her taking time off. "That is good communism."[44] With less apparent interest in his partner's

36 Robert Merriman to Marion [Merriman], 28 March 1938, Robert Merriman Papers, ALBA 191, Box 1, Folder 2.

37 Quotation in Robert Merriman to Marion, 29 August 1937, Merriman Papers, Box 1, Folder 2; on speeches see Robert to Marion, 28 March 1938, ibid.

38 Mito Kruth to Helen [Kruth], 25 June [1937], Mito Kruth Papers, ALBA 240, Box 1, Folder 10.

39 Mito Kruth to Helen, 17 August 1937, Kruth Papers, Box 1, Folder 11.

40 Mito Kruth to Helen, 11 September [1937], Kruth Papers, Box 1, Folder 11. See also Mito to Helen, 8 September 1937, ibid.

41 William Sennett to Gussie, 2 March 1937, VALB, Container 1.

42 William Sennett to Gussie, 12 June 1937, VALB, Container 1.

43 Leon Rosenthal to Lee, 2 August 1937, in *Madrid 1937*, 167, 168.

44 Mito Kruth to Helen, 5 August 1937, Kruth Papers, Box 1, Folder 11.

health than her looks, William Sennett berated Gussie for putting on weight, reminding her that she should not go over 130 pounds.[45]

The most pressing worries were often financial. Volunteers were relatively well paid, but in pesetas, and were thus unable to help support their wives, who struggled with unemployment and high rents. Leo Gordon tried to reassure his cousin Gussie and himself that "My staying at home wouldn't have altered [his wife Agnes'] financial status. On relief, one can live as cheaply as two."[46] He was nonetheless concerned when he finally received a letter from Agnes and learned "she's drifting around." "What's it all about?" he asked his cousin.[47] Ben Gardner was unhappy to discover that Alice was paying twenty-nine dollars a month in rent and was broke. He concluded in a January 1938 letter, "Yep, it looks like I have to control your budget as well."[48] A more sympathetic William Sennett wished that he could convert his extra pesetas to dollars to help Gussie out of debt.[49] Mito Kruth tried to remain optimistic, writing Helen that he felt things were looking up: "I am certainly glad you have a room and hope you will soon have a job."[50] A husband's decision to fight meant both greater loss of control and greater hardship for his wife than either may have anticipated.

These letters from men at war to their partners at home suggest the sometimes surprising and moving ways in which politics saturated communist marriages. Wanting to do something thoughtful for his wife, Sennett promised to send "Kerchiefs with Stalin's picture;" Ben Gardner sent Alice "a red hankey with a sickle & hammer & star."[51] Neither represented their gifts as mainly political: they were tokens of affection, apparently made more meaningful or sentimental because they included political symbols. In a rather less orthodox communist spirit, Robert Merriman proudly presented Marion with a gift "from a place [in Belchite] that I personally bombed (grenaded).... It is so beautiful that I decided to violate our rules about taking things and got this for you."[52] Here Merriman suggested that the unnamed object was special and beautiful because it flowed directly from his own (military) engagement in the cause. For Mito Kruth, the prospect of seeing the film *Chapaev* called to mind the time he and Helen "charged up to the Bronx in order to see it," and he wrote that he would be thinking of her while he watched it.[53] He connected the film both to a happy memory and their shared political commitment.

[45] William Sennett to Gussie, 3 July 1938, VALB, Container 1.
[46] Leo Mendelowitz to Gus [Moskowitz], 26 August 1937, in Ciztrom, "Volunteers," 354.
[47] Leo Mendelowitz to Gus, 18 February 1938, in Ciztrom, "Volunteers," 360.
[48] Ben Gardner to Alice [Gardner], 24 January 1938, VALB, Container 1.
[49] William Sennett to Gussie, 30 April 1937, VALB, Container 1.
[50] Mito Kruth to Helen, 9 November 1937, Kruth Papers, Box 1, Folder 12.
[51] William Sennett to Gussie, 14 September 1937, VALB, Container 1; Ben Gardner to [Alice Gardner], 24 October 1937, ibid.
[52] Robert Merriman to Marion, 8 [September] 1937, Merriman Papers, Box 1, Folder 2.
[53] Mito Kruth to Helen, 21 August 1937 (2nd letter), Kruth Papers, Box 1, Folder 11.

These communist men often noted that finding a personal space clear of politics posed a challenge. Gardner asserted, "Our correspondence must not and cannot be purely of a political nature, for our relations would be hollow, empty if we did not share our troubles, feelings, etc."[54] Nonetheless, he had "trouble in worrying about the sex problem.... After all, if we look at it from a Party point of view (& that is the only view we can hold) our life together has been rich."[55] William Sennett assured Gussie, "You need have no worries over other women occupying my attention. I am to [sic] occupied working and thinking of my best comrade and wife back home."[56] However, six months later, in November 1937, having not received a letter from her in a while, he began to worry that comradeship might not be enough for her: "I've been gone so long now that you've probably found some male friend."[57]

In an October 1937 letter, Mito Kruth confessed to Helen his ignorance of how to write about love. He reported that when a German comrade asked if he was writing a love letter, he had replied, "yes but then began to think how do you write one anyway. What a dope; here I am with a wonderful wife and don't even know how to write a love letter." He vowed to "try and make a study of them."[58] When in a February 1938 letter he imagined his homecoming, he relied on the most traditional, not to say bourgeois, clichés of marital bliss: when he returned home Helen "should tell me what to eat and what not to eat and you know how the song goes 'make a fuss over me.'" Apparently not entirely satisfied with this vision, he added, "Anyway I am sure you understand.... Be assured that I love you more than ever and hope we will be together again soon."[59]

Love and sex were plainly important components of these communists' marriages, but they often received less sustained attention than politics in letters home. As the editor of a collection of American letters notes, the knowledge that letters would be read by the censor "may well have made the Lincolns reluctant to be erotically explicit."[60] Indeed few letters suggested as much passion as the one Leon Rosenthal closed "With a last tight, hot, close fitting hug & wet, tonguey kiss & bite."[61] But censorship does not entirely explain these writers' tendency to present the excitement of shared political activism and the excitements of love and marriage as intimately related. Thinking of their wives as their "best comrades," these volunteers may have construed their decision to leave home and risk their lives less as a renunciation of personal

[54] Ben Gardner to Alice, 25 June 1938, VALB, Container 1.
[55] Ben Gardner to Alice, 25 February 1938, VALB, Container 1.
[56] William Sennett to Gussie, 29 May 1937, VALB, Container 1.
[57] William Sennett to Gussie, 24 November 1937, VALB, Container 1.
[58] Mito Kruth to Helen, 31 October 1937, Kruth Papers, Box 1, Folder 12.
[59] Mito Kruth to Helen, 22 February 1938, Kruth Papers, Box 1, Folder 13.
[60] Nelson, "Introduction," 15.
[61] Leon Rosenthal to Lee, 29 September 1937, in *Madrid 1937*, 114.

life than, as they themselves expressed it, a "necessary" and "unavoidable" – if also painful and difficult – consequence of being communists in love.

Real Men Drink, Real Communists Abstain

In a memoir written in 1996–7, Robert Gladnick recalled that, when the first group of American volunteers reached the fortress at Figueras that functioned as a collection point for those who had crossed the Pyrenees into Spain, their commissar Phil Bart made a "final appeal and threat" – "You are not to indulge in any alcoholic beverage!!" – and told them that anyone who drank would face a court martial. Following orders, the Americans refused the offered *porrones* (traditional long-necked decanters) of wine, even after the local anarchist militiamen demonstrated how to drink from them. According to Gladnick, the Catalans were at a loss; as far as they were concerned, only "maricones" – queers – "don't drink wine." Through an interpreter, the chief of the militia offered an alternative explanation: "You Americans come from a rich country & your wines are of a better quality than our Catalonian wine – I know you would prefer to drink the wine of Chicago – Washington or Scranton where my cousin lives but all we have is our poor Catalan wine." Not wanting the Americans to insult the Catalans – or to be thought homosexuals – the commissar relented, giving the volunteers the go ahead to drink, "but not too much."[62]

Gladnick's story illustrates how competing constructions of masculinity could complicate efforts to define and enforce appropriately communist behavior. The commissar's directive flowed from the premise that a politically engaged (male) worker abstained – from both too much alcohol and too much sex. He was aligning himself with what historian Paul Michel Taillon in his study of Railroad Brotherhoods in the United States calls "respectable" working-class manhood that prized temperance and self-discipline. By contrast, the Catalan anarchists viewed abstinence as effeminate and associated the consumption of alcohol with what Taillon characterizes as "rough" masculinity.[63] The decision to resolve the tension with a concession to "rough" behavior suggests that in practice these categories could be quite permeable. The commissar, committed to maintaining abstinent norms, could be moved to loosen if not abandon such strictures when drinking became a means of solidifying friendship and comradeship among soldiers. To drink

[62] Robert Gladnick memoirs, Hoover Institution Archives, chapter 5, pp. 6–7. Cecil Eby recounts a similar story, *Between the Bullet and the Lie: American Volunteers in the Spanish Civil War* (New York: Holt, Rinehart and Winston, 1969), 15.

[63] Paul Michel Taillon, "'What We Want Is Good, Sober Men': Masculinity, Respectability, and Temperance in the Railroad Brotherhoods, c. 1870–1910," *Journal of Social History* 36, no. 2 (Winter 2002): 319–38.

"for company" – to share wine with Catalan militiamen – might make for a less than respectable communist, but, particularly in wartime, might sometimes be necessary, even decent.[64]

By the end of the nineteenth century, trade unions, socialist parties, and workers' organizations in a wide range of contexts promoted some version of "respectable" working-class manhood as an alternative to a "rough" masculinity associated with whorehouses, saloons, and drinking on the job. Well before the October Revolution, Russian revolutionary discourse distinguished the "conscious" or "advanced" worker, who, according to historian Laura Phillips, "valued sobriety, clean language, neat dress, sexual restraint, political involvement, and educational improvement" from the "rank-and-file" or "backward" worker, who engaged in – even "esteemed" – "heavy drinking, brawling, womanizing, and cursing."[65] Here "advanced" and "backward" constituted alternative models of working-class masculinity. As Phillips's inclusion of "womanizing" on the list of characteristic behaviors suggests, the imagined "worker" in question was male. Moreover, as historian Kate Transchel points out, women were excluded "from taverns as well as from the drunken camaraderie of the shop floor."[66] Although "respectable" members of the Railroad Brotherhoods hardly shared the Russians' revolutionary aims, they emphasized many of the same behaviors: "self-control, self-improvement, and unflinching defense of one's rights against unjust oppression."[67]

In short, the construction of "advanced" or "respectable" working-class masculinity was neither uniquely Russian nor specifically communist. The German labor movement, which some Russian activists took as a model, "worked actively from the turn of the century to alter working class drinking behavior" and attitudes that equated alcohol consumption with "virility."[68] Similarly, historians have characterized the cultures of both Austrian and Swedish socialism as "puritanical."[69] Historian Andrew Thorpe emphasizes that British

[64] Laura L. Phillips, "Message in a Bottle: Working-Class Culture and the Struggle for Revolutionary Legitimacy, 1900–1929," *Russian Review* 56 (January 1997): 31.

[65] Ibid., 25, 26.

[66] Kate Transchel, *Under the Influence: Working-Class Drinking, Temperance, and Cultural Revolution in Russia, 1895–1932* (Pittsburgh: University of Pittsburgh Press, 2006), 10. On the tavern as a masculine space see Madelon Powers, "Women and Public Drinking, 1890–1920," *History Today* 45, no. 2 (February 1995): 46–52; Craig Heron, "The Boys and Their Booze: Masculinities and Public Drinking in Working-Class Hamilton, 1890–1946," *Canadian Historical Review* 86, no. 3 (September 2005): 446–50.

[67] Taillon, "'What We Want,'" 324.

[68] James S. Roberts, "Drink and Industrial Work Discipline in 19th Century Germany," *Journal of Social History* 15, no. 1 (Fall 1981): 32, 27; Phillips, "Message," 27.

[69] Barry McLoughlin, "Proletarian Cadres En-route: Austrian NKVD Agents in Britain, 1941–1943," *Labour History Review* 62, no. 3 (Winter 1997): 302; Madeleine Hurd, "Liberals, Socialists, and Sobriety: The Rhetoric of Citizenship in Turn-of-the-Century Sweden," *International Labor and Working-Class History* 45 (Spring 1994): 54, 55. See also Jacqueline Lalouette, "Alcoolisme et classe ouvrière en France aux alentours de 1900," *Cahiers d'histoire*

communists' much remarked "puritanism" not only "parallel[ed] developments in the Soviet Union" but also constituted an "organic growth" among activists who were "committed teetotalers long before the Comintern had even been thought of."[70]

However, after 1917 Bolshevik leaders were in the unique position of being able to muster state resources to promote the ideal of the "advanced" worker. Although officials encouraged Soviet workers to refrain from vodka, tobacco, cursing, and casual sex, less abstinent norms, particularly with regard to alcohol consumption, remained deeply embedded in the cultures of both workers and peasants.[71] Given the vital role that alcohol played in both "initiating and reinforcing comradely relations" and in shaping masculine identities, that failure is perhaps not so surprising.[72] Drinking, remained, as Phillips notes, a "'masculine' prerogative" – one that many working-class men perpetuated as they "invoked the language of revolution to affirm the legitimacy" of celebrating Soviet holidays with alcohol, visiting a workers' club while drunk, or drinking on the job.[73]

Even among the narrower and supposedly more politically conscious strata of party members, "rough" masculinity and the excessive drinking that went with it proved resilient. In the brutal and uncertain years of civil war that followed the Revolution (1917–21), the prototypical communist was a "crass commissar in a leather jacket, who swore, spat, drank heavily, and engaged in casual sex."[74] Worried that such communists represented a threat to both social order and socialist construction, Bolshevik leaders in the 1920s struggled to root out alcoholism and drunkenness among communists.[75] By 1928 "drinking

42, no. 1 (1997): 89–107; Renato Monteleone, "Socialisti o 'ciucialiter'? Il PSI e il destino delle osterie tra socialita e alcoolismo," *Movimento Operaio e Socialista* 8, no. 1 (1985): 3–22.

70 Andrew Thorpe, "The Communist International and the British Communist Party," in Tim Rees and Andrew Thorpe, eds., *International Communism and the Communist International, 1919–43* (Manchester: Manchester University Press, 1998), 79, 80.

71 Transchel, *Under the Influence*, 11. See also, O. I. Gorelov, "'P'iut partiitsy i komsomol' tsy, i vse, vse': Spavka Informatsionnogo otdela TsK VKP(b) I. V. Stalinu, 1925 g.," *Istoricheskii archiv* 2001, no. 1: 4–13. Mary Neuburger finds a similar inability to curb drinking and smoking among Bulgarian communists, *Balkan Smoke: Tobacco and the Making of Modern Bulgaria* (Ithaca: Cornell University Press, 2013), 80–1.

72 Phillips, "Message," 30; see also Heron, "The Boys," 411–12.

73 Laura L. Phillips, "In Defense of Their Families: Working-Class Women, Alcohol, and Politics in Revolutionary Russia," *Journal of Women's History* 11, no. 1 (Spring 1999): 98; Phillips, "Message," 33 (second quotation), 7.

74 David Hoffmann, *Stalinist Values: The Cultural Norms of Soviet Modernity, 1917–1941* (Ithaca: Cornell University Press, 2003), 60.

75 Igor' Grigor'evich Ivantsov, "Vnutripartiinyi kontrol' VKP(b) v bor'be s p'ianstvom v srede kommunistov (1920-e – nachalo 1930-kh godov)," *Prepodavanie istorii v shkole*, 2011, no. 2: 77–80; Matthias Braun, "Vremja Golovokruzenija – Zeit des Schwindels: Der Alkoholische Raush als Geste Kulturellen Beharrens in der Sowjetunion der 1920er – und 1930er-Jahr," *Zeitschrift für Geschichtswissenschaft* 51, no. 10 (2003): 896–911; Kate Transchel,

became the number one reason people lost their party membership."[76] But party members continued to imbibe – and the Soviet state continued to rely on revenues generated by the state vodka monopoly. In 1933, Stalin simply declared that "alcoholism had been overcome and encouraged workers to reward themselves for a job well done with a 'little glass of champagne.'"[77] Given that many ostensibly "advanced" workers often indulged in so-called backward behaviors, the imperative became less to eliminate such behaviors than to dress them in a veneer of *kul'turnost'*– literally "culturedness," a term that the literary historian Vera Dunham translates as a "fetish notion of how to be individually civilized."[78] Or, as critic Svetlana Boym notes, the "unwritten Soviet etiquette of *kul'turnost'*" mandated that "you drink a few shots of vodka accompanied by pickles and pleasantries, but you do not get drunk."[79] A "lavish" dinner with Soviet tankers recalled by Polish volunteer Alexander Szurek suggests how such norms operated in Spain. According to Szurek, vodka flowed freely, and the "atmosphere was cordial and good-humored, and, at the same time, disciplined."[80]

Although few international communists were likely to have been familiar with the Soviet concept of *kul'turnost'*, many internationals arrived with or quickly acquired an understanding of Bolshevik conceptions of appropriate (male) communist comportment. The Russian-born Gladnick recounted that only among the Russian tank crews in Spain did he learn that in the Soviet Union "old Russian words took on different meanings": a "cultured person" was no longer someone with "knowledge of the arts & literature" but rather "one who washed his hands & shaved his face."[81] He also emphasized that Russian communists often failed to meet even such rudimentary levels of "culture," as they "gorge & drink to a stupor."[82] By contrast, in his 1937 account of the war, British volunteer Esmond Romilly, a noncommunist who defended Madrid with the predominantly German Eleventh Brigade, identified restrained and respectable behavior as the mark of what he deemed a "Real Communist": "you had to be a serious person, a rigid disciplinarian, a member of the Communist Party, interested in all the technical aspects of warfare, and lacking in any such selfish motive as fear or reckless courage."[83] He included in this classification

"Staggering toward Socialism: The Soviet Anti-Alcohol Campaign, 1928–1932," *Soviet and Post-Soviet Review* 23, no. 2 (1996): 191–202.

76 Transchel, *Under the Influence*, 112.

77 Transchel, "Staggering," 202.

78 Vera S. Dunham, *In Stalin's Time: Middleclass Values in Soviet Fiction* (1976; reprint, Durham, NC: Duke University Press, 1990), 22.

79 Svetlana Boym, *Common Places: Mythologies of Everyday Life in Russia* (Cambridge, MA: Harvard University Press, 1994), 102.

80 Alexander Szurek, *The Shattered Dream*, trans. Jacques Grunblatt and Hilda Grunblatt (Boulder, CO: East European Monographs, 1989), 122.

81 Gladnick memoirs, "In the Tank Corps with Soviet Comrades," p. 13.

82 Ibid., p. 14.

83 Esmond Romilly, *Boadilla* (1937; reprint, London: Macdonald, 1971), 64.

men like Beimler, the British poet John Cornford, and his British comrade in the Eleventh Brigade Lorrimer Birch.[84] For these men – all of whom died in Spain – "communism was a thing which lasted seven days a week," a principled way of being more than a party card or a political creed.[85]

For many communists, discipline constituted a primary principle. Romilly found a straightforward articulation of norms of real communist behavior in notices tacked up at the Internationals' base in Albacete: "The Germans had printed a notice entitled 'Discipline.' 'We exalt discipline.' In French was an exhortation not to render ourselves unfit for service by getting diseases at brothels."[86] Kruth suggested that "discipline" could be defined largely in terms of abstaining from alcohol. Responding to the news that a friend had decided to volunteer, he noted in a May 1937 letter that "any tendencies to drink it will be held down here. They are getting very strict on discipline such as drunkenness."[87] Sennett had firsthand experience with strict discipline on the sexual front, because he had been in charge of keeping his cohort of volunteers in line while they waited in Paris for transport to Spain. In a February 1937 letter he described the French system of licensed prostitution and reported, "Among the boys here the penalty for seeing a prostitute is expulsion from the CP [Communist Party] and YCL [Young Communist League] and I as the leader of the Americans here have to deal with these people very sharply."[88] The primary concern was to check the spread of sexually transmitted disease – although Sennett did not emphasize this point in the letter to his wife.[89] Nor did he specify whether he ever imposed the maximum penalty.

The war in Spain brought out in particularly sharp relief the difficulties of realizing norms of "advanced" communist manhood. Drunkenness, although perhaps "backward," is hardly surprising among men at war for whom, as literary historian Paul Fussell notes in his study of behavior during World War II, "drinking far too much" constituted a "traditional comfort."[90] The ever-optimistic Kruth judged that sobriety "has not been a hard thing to enforce as we have plenty [of] good class-conscious material with whom self-discipline has almost become second nature."[91] However, disciplinary records from the Internationals' base at Albacete and the training center at Tarazona document that a regular stream of volunteers spent time in the guardhouse for engaging in behavior similar to that of new recruits Francis Daly and Wesley

84 Ibid., 64, 183.

85 Ibid., 42. Roberts makes a similar point in "Dress and Demeanor," 64.

86 Romilly, *Boadilla*, 46.

87 Mito Kruth to Helen, 23 May 1937, Kruth Papers, Box 1, Folder 9.

88 William Sennett to [Gussie Machen], 28 February 1937, VALB, Container 1.

89 John Tisa, *Recalling the Good Fight: An Autobiography of the Spanish Civil War* (South Hadley, MA: Bergin and Garvey, 1985), 18.

90 Paul Fussell, *Wartime: Understanding and Behavior in the Second World War* (New York: Oxford University Press, 1990), 105.

91 Mito Kruth to Helen, 23 May 1937, Kruth Papers, Box 1, Folder 9.

Mikalauskas – the latter a member of the Young Communist League – whom Merriman brought in on 20 July 1937, for "drunkedness [sic] and loitering in saloons on the square and failing to report for parade on pretense of being excused by the doctor."[92] The fact that, as noted in Chapter 4 in the case of Sterling Rochester, the Fifteenth Brigade's doctor had a "usual procedure against uncontrolled drunkedness [sic]"[93] suggests that such a procedure was necessary.

What Fussell defines as the soldier's other, but less readily available, comfort –"copulating" – left fewer traces in official brigade records. Where mentions of this behavior appeared, it was often presented as a failing of undisciplined women as much as undisciplined men. Thus the evaluation of Henny Peeks, a Dutch nurse, noted that she refused to do any work unrelated to nursing such as cleaning or working in the kitchen. Moreover, the evaluation continued, "this nurse, knowing that she was infected with a venereal disease, had sexual relations with comrades, now unable to return to the front until they are cured of this disease."[94] In early 1938, a report on the situation among the International Brigades noted that "due to the lack of leaves, there has been an increase in the cases of venereal diseases, which have also spread among the civilian population." The response – an increased number of instructional lectures and expanded distribution of prophylactics – suggests an effort to encourage abstinence along with a willingness to settle for safer sex.[95]

Veterans' accounts, both contemporary and retrospective, confirm the Spanish and International Brigades authorities' tendency to supply condoms and look the other way. In a May 1937 letter to Miriam Sigel, Harry Meloff emphasized the "heartbreaking" fact that the volunteers had no opportunity to use "the 'supplies' the doctor handed out when we first arrived" except as "tobacco pouches." Nonetheless, he concluded, "We still have hopes of going on leave in a big city like Valencia or Barcelona, and there find out if we are still men or not."[96] Driving the expectation that such hopes might be easily realized was the perception, noted by Alvah Bessie in his journal, that "Prostitution flourishes despite government discouragement."[97] In his 1998 memoir, William Herrick likewise recounted that although both "the Anarchists and the Party declaimed their opposition to prostitution" he "never discerned any attempt to prevent

92 "Guard Report," 20 July 1937, RGASPI, f. 545, op. 2, d. 265, l. 22. More generally: "Perepiska iuridicheskoi komissii shtaba XV brigady," 21 December 1937–January 1939, RGASPI, f. 545, op. 3, d. 451.

93 S. S. Robbins to Etat Major, XV Brigade, nd, RGASPI, f. 545, op. 3, d. 451, l. 78.

94 "Características de nuestro personal sanitario, Valencia," 13 May 1938, RGASPI, f. 545, op.1, d.1, l. 49.

95 "Informe sobre la situación de las brigadas internacionales," 1 January 1938, RGASPI, f. 545, op. 1 d. 3, l. 80.

96 Harry Meloff to Mim [Sigel], 6 May 1937, in *Madrid 1937*, 146.

97 Alvah Bessie, *Alvah Bessie's Civil War Notebooks*, ed. Dan Bessie (Lexington: University of Kentucky Press, 2002), 60.

it." Indeed Herrick claimed that one "magnificent bordello" in Barcelona was "inhabited by whores who belonged to the CNT [Confederación Nacional de Trabajo], the Anarchist union."[98] By contrast, in a July 1937 letter, Lee Royce suggested a more thorough crackdown, noting that in an effort to "prevent the spread of disease, the government closed most of the houses of prostitution." Nonetheless, the primary reason that the "sex problem is a difficult one for the men of the brigade" seemed to be that "the Spanish women – as far as I know – are amazingly virtuous."[99] Their parents and grandparents also had a reputation for being extremely protective. The constant presence of chaperones, Steve Nelson recalled, "cramped the style of the Americans, but they persevered."[100] In the realm of sex, apparently no one counted too much on the virtue of the volunteers.

Those, such as Kruth, who nonetheless considered the brigadistas fundamentally class conscious and self-disciplined, justified the occasional drink as a necessary escape or a concession to Spanish custom. Gladnick, for example, extolled the virtue of the well-timed drink, crediting a "slug of cognac at my baptism under fire" – supplied tellingly by a Belgian, not one of the excessively puritanical American comrades – of curing him once and for all of "the jitters."[101] In an October 1937 letter, American commissar Sandor Voros provided an informal transcript of a conversation with a Danish ambulance driver that offers understated evidence of the need to find some relief from the realities of war. The driver, "slightly drunk – former seamen – travelled in States," urged, "Have a drink. Have another one. I got another bottle. Have some more. I shouldn't. I haven't eaten all day. That's nothing. Will make you forget it."[102] Moreover, in Spain wine and cognac were staples, part of the troops' regular rations.[103] To abstain was impractical and ungracious, if not unmanly. In an August 1937 letter to his wife, Edwin Rolfe described a dinner with Spanish comrades in a small village during which, "All of us filled and refilled our glasses with excellent wine (and when I say glasses I do not mean the small wine glasses of America but the large glasses which *we* use for milk)."[104] Where wine flowed like milk, there perhaps seemed little harm in drinking.

98 William Herrick, *Jumping the Line: The Adventures and Misadventures of an American Radical* (Madison: University of Wisconsin Press, 1998), 185. See also Tisa, *Recalling*, 77–8, 113, 115; Szurek, *Shattered Dream*, 93; Michael Seidman, *Republic of Egos: A Social History of the Spanish Civil War* (Madison: University of Wisconsin Press, 2002), 74–5.

99 Lee Royce to Hy and Sal, 4 July 1937, in *Madrid 1937*, 107. See also Tisa, *Recalling*, 149.

100 Steve Nelson, James R. Barrett, and Rob Ruck, *Steve Nelson, American Radical* (Pittsburgh: University of Pittsburgh Press, 1981), 212. See also Sandor Voros to [Myrtle Hausrath Day], 30 July 1937, in *Madrid 1937*, 108.

101 Gladnick memoirs, chapter 2, pp. 13–14.

102 Sandor Voros to Sam [Handelman], 11 October 1937, in *Madrid 1937*,256.

103 Bessie, *Spanish Civil War Notebooks*, 20, 27. Gladnick memoirs, chapter 2, p. 13.

104 Emphasis in original. Edwin Rolfe to [Mary Rolfe], 17 August 1937, in *Madrid 1937*, 294.

The volunteers often blamed more serious infractions on the few reprobates and miscreants – probably French or Irish – among the otherwise upstanding Internationals. Thus in a July 1937 letter, Hank Rubin explained discipline problems as a result of the fact that "This is not a Communist army, but very much a general 'antifascist' army with many who are mainly adventurers. Some of these hit the 'vino front' and are put in the brig."[105] The Fifteenth Brigade's own documentary history emphasized that the Americans behaved in exemplary fashion, in sharp contrast to some of their less disciplined European comrades. According to this official account, when in January 1937 the first Americans arrived at their training base in Villanueva de la Jara, they "were greeted by closed shutters and a hostile atmosphere. Women, when they saw a comrade, dashed away from his presence." The Lincolns later learned that this hostility was a result of the "bad reputation made by a few undesirable elements among the French who preceded the Americans. These few among the French, it was alleged, became constantly drunk, caused nuisances, molested the townspeople, and even went so far as to attack the local women." Fortunately, concluded the report, "As a consequence of the excellent work performed by the Cuban comrades who naturally spoke the language of the villagers, a close attachment and comradeship gradually developed between the men of the Lincoln Battalion and the local people."[106] In a May 1937 letter, Alfred Amery told much the same story about the raucous French, despite the fact the he arrived in Villanueva de la Jara months after the group described in the brigade's history supposedly repaired relations with the locals. He concluded, "With only a handful of exceptions we have excellent self-discipline." Those exceptions included "a sailor of Irish descent, a 'tough guy'" who bought a bottle of rum, "got drunk, and after a bloody struggle with the guards was thrown in the guard house." His punishment included being "placed before the scornful eyes of the whole battalion and shamed to a condition lower than a dog's by the appropriate words of the battalion commander." Amery imagined that "His conscience must wrack him with indescribable tortures."[107]

This confidence in the power of communist shaming notwithstanding, at least some volunteers remembered embracing both drinking and the satisfaction of "strenuously heteroerotic" desire.[108] For these "tough guys," such behaviors served as markers of a rough masculinity that they deemed, at least in retrospect, appropriate to communists, and perhaps especially to communists at war. Some sixty years after he left for Spain, Gladnick represented himself as a tough seaman, recalling in his memoir that on board the ship to France he and the other "waterfront boys" among the volunteers "completely ignored the order"

105 Hank Rubin to Audrey, 27 July 1937, in *Madrid 1937*, 164.

106 "A Documentary History of the XV International Brigade," RGASPI, f. 545, op. 3, d. 471, l. 21; see also Eby, *Between the Bullet*, 23; Herrick, *Jumping the Line*, 147.

107 Alfred Amery to George & Lawrence, 24 May 1937, in *Madrid 1937*, 102, 103.

108 Fussell, *Wartime*, 109.

not to drink.[109] At a similar distance in time from the events he described, Herrick – like his friend Gladnick, a communist who later publicly broke with the party – confessed that his love for the girlfriend he left behind in New York "didn't stop me from wanting to have sex with a Folies Bergère dancer" on board the ship to France. According to Herrick, Gladnick, a stowaway, had discovered the troupe "as he perambulated freely about the boat;" Herrick speculated that Gladnick slept in one of their cabins.[110]

Bill Williamson, a Canadian communist, lumberjack, seaman, and self-taught photographer who made his own way to Spain and served in a Basque militia before joining the International Brigades in May 1937, similarly prized his tough guy status. In a 1990 interview, he expressed particular contempt for the "big percentage" of Americans "from City College in New York, a lot of them Jewish" who "allowed themselves to be shepherded around by keepers," who warned them "you mustn't get drunk."[111] As Williamson emphasized, many of the volunteers who had attended City College were in fact Jewish New Yorkers – although a fair number, like Kruth, were not.[112] However, his description of these New Yorkers as sheltered Jewish boys, who allowed themselves to be led around (by, perhaps, a Jewish communist like Sennett), tells us less about their activities in Paris than Williamson's own disdain for respectable communist masculinity, especially as practiced by (Jewish) intellectuals.[113]

Like many of the Canadian volunteers – predominantly miners, lumberjacks, and temporary or seasonal laborers, who, according to Edward Cecil-Smith, the top Canadian commander in Spain, had "been on the tramp since leaving school" – Williamson viewed the Americans as soft.[114] Jack Taylor, the Canadian party's representative in Spain, reported in a 1938 letter to the Central Committee of the Spanish Communist Party that he had heard one of the Canadian volunteers refer to the Americans as "New York ice cream boys."[115] Another allegedly complained that a "clique of New York [Young Communist League] Jews" ran the Fifteenth Brigade.[116] By contrast, the Canadians characterized themselves as uninterested in command, wanting only to be "one of the boys" – not disobedient, as volunteer John "Paddy" McElligott explained in a 1965 interview, but simply "Canadian; we're independent."[117] The

[109] Gladnick memoirs, chapter 5, p. 2.
[110] Herrick, *Jumping the Line*, 131, 133, 246.
[111] As quoted in Petrou, *Renegades*, 146.
[112] For profiles of volunteers who attended City College, see the Abraham Lincoln Brigade Archive database, www.alba-valb.org. Albert Prago, "Jews in the International Brigades," in Alvah Bessie and Albert Prago, eds., *Our Fight: Writings by Veterans of the Abraham Lincoln Brigade* (New York: Monthly Press, 1987), 97.
[113] Gladnick, who was Jewish, had similar disdain for "the New York City College (CCNY) and Brooklyn College boys," Gladnick memoirs, chapter 2, p. 11.
[114] As quoted in Petrou, *Renegades*, 17.
[115] As quoted in ibid., 111.
[116] Personnel file as quoted in ibid., 16.
[117] As quoted in ibid., 110.

emphasis on national identity is striking, because some 78 percent of the Canadian volunteers were foreign born and most of these were recent immigrants.[118] Here "Canadian" functioned as a surrogate for a certain kind of masculine identity, as the volunteers described themselves as proudly championing rough working-class norms that both the party and the more respectable, if no less working-class, New Yorkers judged uncultured and undisciplined.

Important as questions of drinking and sex may have been, in Spain many communists found the ultimate test of manhood in battle, where their civilian notions of manliness and toughness sometimes had to be revised. Ben Gardner, who had known Steve Nelson in Philadelphia, wrote that he gained new respect for Nelson after having seen him in combat:

> I'll never forget the day at Belchite when I carried about 15 canteens of water to the front line where my Co. was without a drop of it all day. On the road I met Steve, a little bent over looking sharply forward and stepping briskly to avoid fascist snipers.... I admired him in those moments & wondered why I haven't thought so much of him at home. The real man in him came to light in this war for freedom.

As Gardner's earlier letters to his wife made clear, he had long considered Nelson a good communist. Only in Spain, however, did he see him also as a "real man."[119]

In an August 1937 letter to his cousin, Leo Gordon offered a more ambivalent understanding of a real communist man in battle. Describing the profound transformation of a "guy from my neighborhood," Hy Stone, who had volunteered with his brothers Joe and Sam, Gordon wrote,"Back home," Hy "was sort of a quiet, retiring kind of egg. Out here he went thru hell and spat in the devil's eye." Near Brunete, after the entire command of his company was killed, Hy "ran the show." When Hy received the news "that both brothers had been killed," the company "watched him closely, fearing that he would break. Hy compressed his lips – and went into action." Emphasizing that Stone was "cited for bravery shortly after," Gordon was less clear about whether crossing the line between bravery and what Romilly described as "reckless courage" constituted conduct unbecoming a communist. Although Stone lectured Gordon on the importance of "ducking into cover & digging in at every available opportunity," he himself was known to have run "along a ridge once in order to draw enemy fire so that he could discover their positions." As Gordon clarified for his cousin's benefit, "That happens to be the closest substitute to suicide yet known to science." Although another friend of Hy's judged him a "damn

118 Ibid., 22.

119 Ben Gardner to [Alice Gardner], [31?] December 1937, VALB, Container 1. See also Ben Gardner to [Alice Gardner], 7 August 1937; Ben Gardner to [Alice Gardner], 23 November 1937, ibid.; Herbert Hutner to Mr. & Mrs. Wolman, 9 Dec. 1937, in *Madrid 1937*, 195; Steve Nelson to Maggie [Nelson], from Perpignan France, nd, Nelson Papers, Box 1, Folder 8; Bessie, *Civil War Notebooks*, 62; Tisa, *Recalling*, 143.

fool," Gordon's letter leaves the impression that there was something laudable and powerful in this reckless, suicidal bravery.[120]

At the same time, some soldiers described the transformation of communists into "real" men at the front in emotional, even loving terms. Kruth emphasized that communists safe at home failed to understand the experiences and attitudes of soldiers, and thus the compatibility of toughness and tenderness. Apparently responding to Helen's inquiry, he wrote that the troops had received the socks sent by the Finnish communists, but he regretted that they did not receive the "sentimental" notes written to accompany them: "War is a grim hard business and a little sentiment now and then goes a long way." There was no need, he concluded, to "try to toughen the boys that way. They don't need that."[121]

In September 1937, in the wake of the Brunete offensive, Sennett provided his wife a vivid picture of the rough and touching camaraderie of soldiers. "I'm in fine health," he assured her, "and never got to know real people, comrades so intimately as here.... We curse and swear as I've never heard cursing and swearing but its [sic] all in good stead. We lost one fellow who was hit by a bomb and another (confirmed now) was captured. It was like losing members of our family."[122] In a letter from the same period after Brunete, Sidney Kaufman, a New York merchant seaman, described an even more intense connection: "Vince & I have grown very close to each other here – read each other's mail – discuss our most intimate problems together, etc. We have a sort of mutual agreement that we won't go back to the States unless we can go together."[123]

For some, such sentiments were easily squared with a serious communist sense of purpose. Gardner, at the Internationals' base in Albacete, explained the pain of being separated from his comrades still at the front in terms at once deeply personal and politically correct. In an October 1937 letter to his wife, he wrote, "I miss them terribly, feel a great affection towards them... Never before did I feel such a deep regard for comrades, especially those who took the fight with a real antifascist and bolshevik stamina. I long for news of these comrades."[124]

Still, if drinking, whoring, and reckless daring raised fears of "excessive and uncontainable" masculinity, the intimate bonds among men forged at the front could generate anxiety about "insufficient" or "inadequate" masculinity.[125] However, such anxieties, linked to the communist equation of homosexuality and fascism (see Chapter 2), surfaced rarely in letters home or memoirs. In a May 1937 letter to Mim Sigel, Meloff adopted an irreverent tone that took

120 Leo Mendelowitz to Gus, 26 August 1937, in Czitrom, "Volunteers," 355.

121 Mito Kruth to Helen, 17 January 1938, Kruth Papers, Box 1, Folder 13.

122 William Sennett to Gussie, 7 September 1937, VALB, Container 1.

123 Sidney Kaufman to Eth, 8 September 1937, in *Madrid 1937*, 212.

124 Ben Gardner to [Alice Gardner], 24 October 1937, VALB, Container 1.

125 Iker González-Allende, "Masculinities in Conflict: Representations of the Other in Narrative during the Spanish Civil War," *Hispanic Research Journal* 11, no. 3 (June 2010): 194–5.

some of the edge off his worries about the possibility of "going 'fruit' altogether. Already the boys are beginning to ogle eyes at each other, and sometimes Ernie frightens me." He apparently feared both that close male friendships at the front might lead to what a psychoanalyst of the day called "emergency homosexuality"[126] and that soldiers' domestic activities might turn them into women: "You should see us washing our clothes, and yes, even sewing buttons on our underwear." However, Meloff described himself as unwilling to compromise his manhood to that extent, preferring to throw away his underwear and "go around without."[127]

In his memoir, Gladnick addressed communist anxiety about homosexuality more directly and more politically. Telling the story of "two German boys – no older than eighteen years – typically blonde & blue eyed," who were "caught by the guards – making oral sex to one another" and shot, he emphasized that communists understood homosexuality as a political failing. Gladnick claimed to have seen the "fallen bodies of the two German boys."[128] I have been unable to confirm the story in other sources; however, even if exaggerated, Gladnick's account suggests the persistence of communist anxieties about insufficient or effeminate masculinity as both a cause and symptom of fascism. He explained, "In Spain, as in most left wing circles in the 1930s homosexuals – because those known to be of that sexual persuasion – were from the upper classes – were regarded as Fascists."[129] Recognizing that in 1997 it was "politically correct to say the Nazis were Homophobes," Gladnick, by then an ardent anticommunist, argued that the communist view contained a "certain amount of truth," because the Nazis "had a great number of Homosexuals in their ranks & in the storm troops they dominated that organization."[130] From the vantage point of 1997, what horrified him was less the logic of the communist position than what might be termed "Bolshevik ruthlessness," the failure of the German and Bulgarian communists with whom the young men served to argue against the death penalty. Gladnick described himself as having "very little sympathy for homosexuals – but I certainly was not in favor of executing young men."[131]

The pervasive construction of homosexuality as incompatible with communist manhood encouraged both its official and informal erasure from the story of the brigades. This tendency was particularly clear in the German Democratic Republic, where state-approved editors removed "all references to

[126] German Marxist psychoanalysist Wilhelm Reich as quoted in Harry Oosterhuis, "The 'Jews' of the Antifascist Left: Homosexuality and Socialist Resistance to Nazism," *Journal of Homosexuality* 29, no. 2/3 (1995): 240.

[127] Harry Meloff to Mim [Miriam Sigel], 6 May 1937, in *Madrid 1937*, 146.

[128] Gladnick memoirs, chapter 8, pp. 2, 3.

[129] Ibid., p. 2; see also chapter 3, p. 2.

[130] Ibid., chapter 9, p. 2. On "the construction of homo-fascism," see Andrew Hewitt, *Political Inversions: Homosexuality, Fascism, and the Modernist Imaginary* (Stanford: Stanford University Press, 1996), 1–37.

[131] Gladnick memoirs, chapter 8, p. 3.

homosexuality" from the memoirs of Ludwig Renn and other volunteers.[132] However, discomfort with homosexuality was not limited to post–World War II people's democracies. The case of Finnish American communist Bill Aalto demonstrates that volunteers themselves might refuse to accept the possibility of a homosexual communist. A 1938 evaluation prepared by the Spanish party deemed Aalto, who had distinguished himself in a series of dangerous and dramatic guerrilla operations, as "Serious. Disciplined. Conscientious. The most outstanding American, militarily and politically, among the Americans in the Southern Zone."[133] During World War II, the Office of Strategic Services recruited Aalto along with a number of his fellow Soviet-trained guerrillas to undertake similar work in North Africa. However, after Aalto confessed to Irving Goff, one of his closest comrades from Spain, that he was gay, the other veterans asked that he be reassigned. In an interview, Goff recalled that he found the revelation simply unbelievable: "How could a big, athletic guy like that be one of those?"[134] Unable to square Aalto's wartime record with his "inappropriate masculinity,"[135] his comrades decided, however reluctantly, that he was no longer one of "us."

This exclusion of homosexuals from the community of real communist men marked a point of convergence in conceptions of communist masculinity. The Soviet party and many national parties – drawing on Soviet models as well as local traditions – promoted norms of disciplined, respectable working-class manhood, of proletarian "moral purity and chastity."[136] As communists never tired of reiterating, iron discipline constituted their defining characteristic and their principal asset in wartime.[137] Yet quite a few of the volunteers preferred to present themselves as exemplars of a rougher, less contained masculinity. Moreover, war often blurred the distinction between disciplined heroism and reckless courage, between laudable camaraderie and a drunken spree. According to his adjutant Szurek, General Karol Świerczewski, who "loved danger" and often exposed himself to enemy fire, was unable to conceal his approval when he saw a motorcyclist, who "nonchalantly stalled on the highway as bullets whistled around him and, elegantly and haughtily, pulled on a pair of

[132] McLellan, *Antifascism*, 119.

[133] "Primera lista de los comunistas norte-americanos de la zona del sur," 14 January 1938, RGASPI, f. 545, op. 6, d. 852, l. 175. See also the questionnaire dated 6–12–1938, RGASPI, f. 545, op. 6, d. 855, ll. 8–10ob; Carroll, *Odyssey*, 167–8.

[134] Undated interview as quoted in Carroll, *Odyssey*, 255. See also Helen Graham, *The Spanish Civil War: A Very Short Introduction* (New York: Oxford University Press, 2005), 53, 100–1, 148.

[135] González-Allende, "Masculinities," 195.

[136] George Mosse, *The Image of Man: The Creation of Modern Masculinity* (New York: Oxford University Press, 1996), 128.

[137] Burnett Bolloten, *The Spanish Civil War: Revolution and Counterrevolution* (Chapel Hill: University of North Carolina Press, 1991), 266–9; Helen Graham, *The Spanish Republic at War, 1936–1939* (New York: Cambridge University Press, 2002), 148, 173, 367; Longo, *Brigadas Internacionales*, 172; Szurek, *Shattered Dream*, 116.

white gloves."[138] Even Lorrimer Birch, Romilly's exemplary "Real Communist," visited a brothel – supposedly not to satisfy his own desires but as an act of solidarity with his comrades.[139] To cope with or forget fear and death, even the most respectable communist might, at least occasionally, indulge in "drinking far too much" and copulating. Like the tough guys, they worried that too much discipline – abstaining entirely from drinking, meekly sewing buttons on their own underwear – might mark them as "queer." Despite the fact that gay men served in the International Brigades, homosexuality remained for many communists presumptively fascist.[140] Imagined as at once savage and effeminate, homosexuals seemed to violate the norms of both respectable and rough communist masculinity.

Intimate Revolution

In October 1937, Milly Bennett, who had spent the better part of the previous decade producing propaganda for English-language communist newspapers in China and Moscow, applied to join the Communist Party of the United States. Bennett had arrived in Spain from Moscow in January 1937 to take up an assignment with the Foreign Press Bureau of the Republic's Press and Propaganda Service, under the direction of Constancia de la Mora; she also provided stories to the Associated Press.[141] Ten months later, she wrote from the Internationals' base at Albacete to Edward Bender, the head of the American Department of Cadres, in terms suggested by Steve Nelson:

> I have been in contact with the movement since 1917 when as a cub reporter on the S. F. News I worked on the [Tom] Mooney case.... In 1926–27 I worked with the Party in China as editor of the Peking "Chung Mei News Agency" until my arrest on the eve of the raid on the Soviet embassy in Peking... I worked on the organization of the Moscow News, remaining with that paper from 1931–1935.... I came to Spain on my own account... and am editor of an information bulletin in English issued by the prensa extranjera.... I am 37 years of age and have worked with the Party long enough so that I feel now that my period for "freelancing" is definitely at an end. I wish to join the Communist Party and accept Party discipline.[142]

138 Szurek, *Shattered Dream*, 104, 103. See also Nelson et al., *American Radical*, 223; James K. Hopkins, *Into the Heart of the Fire: The British in the Spanish Civil War* (Stanford: Stanford University Press, 1998), 177–8, 274.

139 Romilly, *Boadilla*, 185.

140 Many accounts mention in passing the service of gay men in Spain. For example, Eby, *Between the Bullet*, 136; Hopkins, *Into the Heart*, 180, 226, 269; Carroll, *Odyssey*, 256–7; Roberts, *"Freedom, Faction,"* 106.

141 "by milly bennett," [1937], Milly Bennett Papers, Box 9, Folder 5, Hoover Institution Archives; Safe conduct passes, ibid., Box 1, Folder 17; Milly Bennett to Hal [Harold Matson], 27 November 1940, ibid., Box 3, Folder 22.

142 Milly Bennett (Mitchell) to Edward Bender, 17 October 1937, RGASPI, f. 545, op. 6, d. 862, l. 96. Tom Mooney was a labor activist convicted in the 1916 Preparedness Day bombing in San Francisco.

Four days later she received a reply from Sol Rose in the personnel office, who advised her to "Get two comrades in good standing" to recommend her for membership. He was "sure that when you take this matter up with the comrades in Valencia who know you, that they will gladly take care of this."[143]

Although the brigades' archives provide no record of a previous application, in June 1937 letters to the geneticist Hermann Muller – with whom she had begun an affair in Moscow that briefly continued in Spain – Bennett described an earlier attempt to join the party. She explained her decision as the result of the recognition that only as a "party person" would the "good, loyal, but entirely inexperienced" people in the foreign press office take her journalistic advice.[144] She resolved that "if and when i go to the next revolution, it will be as a party member. then, at least you have a fighting chance."[145] At the time of her first application, probably in late May 1937, a representative of the American party advised her to apply when she returned to the United States. Nonetheless, she reapplied in October while still in Spain.[146]

What is striking about these efforts is not only Bennett's persistence but also her timing. Joining the party was something that she had long considered – not only as a means of being taken seriously by her comrades but also as an alternative to marriage. In an undated letter from Moscow, likely written between 1931 and 1933, Bennett confided, "I've more or less made up my mind to join the Party when I come home – that is, if I don't grab off a husband. I'm sick of dreams with obvious Freudian meanings. And if I don't get to mortify my flesh one way – I'll try the other."[147] However serious Bennett was at the time, in Spain a series of personal crises coincided with the long-delayed, doggedly pursued, and perhaps ultimately failed or abandoned effort to join the party. In a memoir that she tried to get published after she returned from Spain she wrote, "I never became a convert, although on one occasion, I escaped by the narrowest of squeaks."[148] She ended up leaving Spain with a (communist) husband, but apparently without a party card.

A few days before she left Moscow in December 1936, Bennett had begun an affair with the forty-six-year-old Muller. In a late April letter aimed at terminating their relationship, he recalled its beginnings. In Moscow, she had told him, "I've been trying to seduce you all year." He was surprised, he

143 Sol Rose to Comrade Milly Bennett, 21 October 1937, Bennett Papers, Box 4, Folder 23.

144 Bennett to Hermann [Muller], 9 June [1937], Bennett Papers, Box 9, Folder 6. The file holds multiple drafts of letters to Muller; it is not clear which, if any, Bennett actually sent.

145 Capitalization as in original. Bennett to Hermann [Muller], 2 June [1937], Bennett Papers, Box 9, Folder 6.

146 Bennett to Hermann [Muller], 9 June [1937], Bennett Papers, Box 9, Folder 6.

147 Bennett to Mary, nd, Bennett Papers, Box 1, Folder 21.

148 Milly Bennett, *On Her Own: Journalistic Adventures from San Francisco to the Chinese Revolution, 1917–1927*, ed. A. Tom Grunfeld (Armonk, NY: M. E. Sharpe, 1993), xix. On her efforts to publish the memoir, see Harold Matson to Milly Bennett, 3 November 1939, Bennett Papers, Box 3, Folder 22.

confessed in April 1937, to find out that she had "meant it in such a full and final way." When he arrived in Madrid in March, they resumed their affair because, he claimed, it seemed "obvious that we should be together like two shipwrecked people and at the same time two comrades with a common purpose on the same raft." But he had no interest in a long-term commitment, reminding, or perhaps informing her for the first time, "I have very free ideas & habits about these things, and thought you did, too; it has been a part of my 'philosophy,' hasn't it of yours?"[149]

However, the relationship did not end as cleanly as Muller might have hoped. Their liaison in Spain had been interrupted by what Muller, ever the rational biologist, called a "horrible irruption of the micro-invaders" and the possibility that he had infected Bennett with syphilis or gonorrhea. In mid-April, Bennett visited the American Hospital in Paris, where lab tests for sexually transmitted diseases came back negative.[150] Nonetheless, a month later, when Muller was already on his way back to the United States, she remained worried that the tests had been done too early to reveal the disease, particularly in light of the timing of Muller's encounter with "the frenchwoman," the suspected source of infection. Given that it was "not possible for me to go to the local doctors, after the last fiasco" – which she did not specify – she asked Muller to have himself tested in the United States "when the time falls due and cable me the results, so that i can take action, if it is needed."[151] I have found no evidence of further tests or treatment in Bennett's papers.

However, by early May it was clear that Bennett was pregnant. In their correspondence, she and Muller dubbed the fetus "medicine ball." Thus on 11 May 1937, Muller, then in Cambridge, England, wrote to advise her to "Come back if you continue to be sick – we must conserve the bird songs. And birds must take care of their medicine balls."[152] In a draft of a letter dated "2:40 27th," presumably of May, Bennett recounted an air raid that had begun at 2:30 a.m.: "I heard that steady drive of heavy bombing planes (many of them) . . . the hotel shook so violently as I ran down the hall, that I fell. . . . oh dear, I have tried to be so careful about medicineball – so much orange juice; and sleep; and sun baths on the beach – and eating properly and regularly." She planned to stay "flat on my back in this bed," but reported that she had a persistent temperature, and that the doctor was "pessimistic."[153]

In mid-June, Muller, then in Texas, received a letter dated 28 May 1937, with a version of these events. He again suggested that Bennett leave Spain "while you still can, before it is too late. Do not kill the goose that lays the

[149] Muller to Bennet, 25 April 1937, Bennett Papers, Box 4 Folder 6.

[150] "Bordet Wassermann," 16 April 1937, Bennett Papers, Box 1, Folder 17.

[151] All capitalization as in original. Bennett to Muller, 15 May [1937] (one of many drafts), Bennett Papers, Box 9, Folder 6.

[152] Muller to Bennett, 11 May 1937, Bennett Papers, Box 4, Folder 6.

[153] Bennett to Hermann [Muller], 27 [May 1937], Bennett Papers, Box 9, Folder 6.

golden medicine ball."[154] On 24 June, he cabled her regarding the possibility of an "operation" in Paris.[155] In mid-July, on his way back to Europe, he wrote to thank her "for taking hold of the situation and, in spite of all, thinking out just what had to be done, and offering to do it for me. You know I appreciate it, as I have appreciated all else you have done and sacrificed for me."[156] With its reference to "sacrifice" "for me," the letter may reference a decision to have an abortion. I have found no evidence to confirm an abortion or to suggest whether or not "medicine ball" survived the fall in May. However, it appears that Milly Bennett never had a child.

It was precisely in the midst of this crisis that Bennett made her first attempt to join the party. Working long hours (apparently despite her vow to stay in bed), earning less than her hotel bill, and living under threat of air attack seem to have clarified and solidified the nature of her commitment to the cause.[157] In the letter dated 9 June in which she described her own efforts to join the party, she also tried to understand Muller's decision to return briefly to Moscow to aid his former colleagues in their struggle against Lysenkoism. "It goes back strangely" she wrote, "to the cliché – what profit it a man that he gain the world if [he] loses his soul. I have felt that you saw the English job as somewhat of a 'retreat' from your revolutionary principles. Is that right?"[158] She may have seen her own situation in similar terms – although she seemed to have a difficult time articulating her perspective in an unsuccessful interview with a party representative, who "was audibly unsatisfied with the answers I gave to his questions.... and when he said 'why have you waited this long before applying?' – and I said 'because in America the Party discipline was distasteful to me' – and in Russia it isn't possible to join – he was clearly displeased."[159] She did not suggest what had made party discipline suddenly more palatable or even welcome. In the midst of high-stakes personal and political crises, she perhaps felt the time had come for a clear commitment. Or perhaps she hoped that joining the party would finally help her to achieve the "faith of my own conclusions" that, in an undated letter from Moscow, she imagined was the property of every "good communist."[160]

In July one further complication entered Milly Bennett's life: Wallace Burton, a brigadista with whom she had had an affair in the early 1930s in San

154 Muller to Bennett, 15 June 1937, Bennett Papers, Box 4, Folder 6.

155 "Telegram to Milly Bennett, care American consulate (Barcelona)," 24 June 1937, Bennett Papers, Box 4, Folder 6.

156 Muller to Bennett, 15 July 1937, Bennett Papers, Box 4, Folder 6.

157 Bennett to Wallace [Burton], 29 May [1937], Bennett Papers, Box 9, folder 6; Bennett to Jenny and Bob [Miller], 26 August [1937], ibid., Box 4, Folder 2.

158 Bennett to Muller, 9 June [1937], Bennett Papers, Box 9, Folder 6.On Muller's visit to Moscow see Peter J. Kuznick, *Beyond the Laboratory: Scientists as Political Activists in 1930s America* (Chicago: University of Chicago Press, 1987), 137.

159 Bennett to Muller, 9 June [1937], Bennett Papers, Box 9, Folder 6.

160 Bennett to Bessie, 30 November [1931?], Bennett Papers, Box 1, Folder 21.

Francisco – between her assignments in China and the Soviet Union. (She also had an affair with Wallace's twin brother Wilbur in the 1920s in China.[161]) Wallace Burton was a veteran of World War I, the French Foreign Legion, and the Gran Chaco War fought between Paraguay and Bolivia (1932–5). He was also a party member – Bennett hoped he would tell her "with or without a glass of beer, how you disciplined yourself into taking party discipline" – who in March 1937 enlisted in the International Brigades.[162] He earned several promotions during the battle at Brunete in July 1937. However, he was demoted to private when, bored with the sleepy village where his unit had been sent on leave after more than twenty days at the front, he led "his company," as Bennett described it, "in a flying raid on the [M]adrid whorehouse district."[163]

In draft letters to Jenny and Bob Miller, journalists and friends from Moscow, Bennett offered a romantic description of the early August morning when Burton arrived on her doorstep in Valencia. On 18 or 19 August, she was reading in bed when "the concierge slammed at the door and handed in a torn piece of paper with wallace f. burton written on it. i pull on my robe... and went down to the entrance and there he was, a deep reddish brown like an indian and big and greyeyed and dirty and sweaty and cognacy and with that funny, disarming smile of his – and i was in his arms and he was just where i left him some six years, eight months ago back in sanfranciso."[164] An hour or so later, she accompanied him back to the train station, where he introduced her as "my wife – this is my girl... she is going to marry me."[165] When they finally parted, "he said – this is five wars i've been to – and this is the only one i ever really cared about coming home from. we both cried, great, big, wringing tears."[166]

Two weeks later, Burton was killed on the Aragon front. Arriving at the front on 4 September to cover the capture of Belchite, Bennett spoke with a wounded man and "three sanitary squad men" who "had heard Wallace was killed." When she returned to Valencia, she found a note confirming that on 2 September he had been shot by a sniper. A few days later she confided to Jenny Miller, "In my whole life, I have never felt so entirely alone."[167]

161 Bennett to Mrs. [Barbara] Shaver, [1937], Bennett Papers, Box 5, Folder 5; Wilbur Burton to Mildred, 4 October 1937, Box 2, Folder 24.

162 Quotation from Bennett to Wallace [Burton], 29 May [1937], Bennett Papers, Box 9, Folder 6; "Reuters Special Service," 7 September 1937, ibid., Box 5, Folder 5; Eby, *Between the Bullet*, 133; Carroll, *Odyssey*, 74–5.

163 Bennett to Jenny and Bob [Miller], 26 August [1937], Bennett Papers, Box 4, Folder 2; see also Bennett to Jen and Bob, 12 September [1937], ibid.

164 All spelling and capitalization as in original. Bennett to Jen and Bob, 12 September [1937], Bennett Papers, Box 4, Folder 2.

165 Bennett to Jen and Bob, 12 September [1937], Bennett Papers, Box 4, Folder 2.

166 All capitalization as in original. Bennett to Jenny and Bob, 26 August [1937], Bennett Papers, Box 4, Folder 2.

167 Bennett to Jen and Bob, 12 September [1937], Bennett Papers, Box 4, Folder 2. For a slightly different account of Burton's death see "Interview with Emanuel Lanzer," 17 December 1937, RGASPI, f. 545, op. 3, d. 469, l.5.

On 17 October 1937, Bennett sent a formal letter seeking admission to the party. Once again, a personal tragedy seemed to make "accepting party discipline" attractive or possible. However, there is no evidence that she followed up with the advice that she find two members in good standing to sponsor her application. Rather, she sought out Burton's commander, Hans Amlie, in hopes of learning more details of her fiancé's death. Amlie had arrived in Spain as a socialist, but, disappointed with that party's weak show of support for the Republic, had joined the communist party.[168] Robert Merriman, Bennett's friend from Moscow and then the Fifteenth Brigade's chief of staff, judged Amlie an "ass;" in his diary he noted that Amlie was prone to "shooting off his mouth" and "encouraging the men to protest against saluting[,] for vacations etc. etc."[169] Bennett, however, formed a more favorable opinion. By the end of November, they had decided to wed and were married on 1 December. Amlie, who had been wounded and whose brother Thomas Amlie was a progressive member of the U.S. House of Representatives from Wisconsin, was scheduled to be repatriated, the party leadership having decided he was more valuable on the propaganda circuit at home than on the front in Spain.[170] On 1 January 1938, the couple arrived in New York.[171] Spain turned out to be Milly Bennett's last revolution.

Offering an unusually rich sense of the immediate circumstances surrounding a decision to apply for membership in the party, Bennett's story makes it possible trace the linkages between political commitment and an individual life. Indeed as she told her own story in letters to friends and lovers, the lines between personal and political life are difficult to discern. Her desire to "accept party discipline" flowed as much from her sense of the importance of the struggle in Spain as from a need to make sense of and cope with a series of personal shocks and losses. She seemed to understand her decision to stay in Spain, endangering herself and her pregnancy, as an unwillingness to "retreat" from "revolutionary principles." Her eventual decision to marry, be happy, and, as she told an interviewer in San Francisco, enjoy good coffee may have for her ruled out membership in the party.[172] Yet even this "personal" decision seems to have had connections to politics, specifically the party's sudden and dramatic change of line in the summer of 1939 from fighting fascism in Spain to embracing the Nazi-Soviet Pact.[173]

[168] Bennett to Jen and Bob, 12 September [1937]; Carroll, *Odyssey*, 72–3.

[169] Robert Merriman diary, vol. 2, pp. 2, 32, also 30, Merriman Papers, Box 1, Folder 3; Robert Merriman to [Marion Merriman], September [1937], ibid., Folder 2.

[170] "Averiguaciones sobre los cuadros," 28 October 1938, RGASPI, f. 545, op. 6, d. 857, l. 33.

[171] Milly Bennett, "Article Two," nd, p. 3, Bennett Papers, Box 9, Folder 5. "2 Americans in Spain Managed to Wed by a Ruse," clipping from *New York World Telegram*, 25 January 193[8], Bennett Papers, Box 1, Folder 13; "Millie Bennett Comes Home," clipping from *San Francisco Chronicle*, 9 March 1938, ibid.

[172] "Millie Bennett Comes Home."

[173] Milly Bennett, "Tom Wintringham Writes" [letter to the editor], *Nation*, 26 April 1941, 510.

Small-scale intimate stories of individual communists provide a unique and telling view of communist understandings of masculinity and femininity. In these idiosyncratic life histories, it is possible to see the difficulties of applying communist norms to the extraordinary circumstances of wartime. Did party discipline require abandoning wives and lovers to fight in Spain? Could homosexuals be good communists? How "tough" could a communist be without being undisciplined? As individuals acted as communists, they necessarily, if implicitly, made decisions about how communist principles should be enacted in everyday contexts that, even if disrupted by war, were not obviously political. For those who saw communism as a way of being, who aspired to be good communist men and women "seven days a week," the "private" sphere of family, lovers, husbands, and wives was always and intimately intertwined with the political. Political convictions shaped everyday behaviors, and, as became clear in the aftermath of the war, accommodating (or rejecting) shifts in the party line required both personal and political adjustments.

PART III

INTERNATIONAL COMMUNISTS AND THE MEMORY OF THE SPANISH CIVIL WAR, 1939–1953

6

From "Our War" to the Great Fatherland War

In 1939, the Spanish civil war ended with the fall of the Republic, and World War II began with the fall of Poland. For communists who understood the fight against fascism as the cause of "all advanced and progressive humanity," the announcement in August of the Nazi-Soviet Nonaggression Pact that hastened the invasion of Poland by both Germany and the Soviet Union came as a shock, and for some it was a betrayal. This was not the war they had expected. Even Comintern secretary-general Georgi Dimitrov was caught unawares. On the eve of the agreement, the secretariat had called on communist parties "to continue even more energetically the struggle against the aggressors, especially German fascism."[1] On 27 August, Dimitrov and Dmitrii Manuil'skii, a member of the Soviet party's central committee who also served on the Comintern's secretariat, asked Stalin's advice as to how "Communist parties of the capitalist countries," especially France and England, ought to respond to the pact. "We think," they ventured with regard to the party in France, "that the Communist Party must maintain its position of resistance to the aggression of fascist Germany." They received no answer.[2]

A clearer sense of how parties in "capitalist countries" should respond to the pact came with the German invasion of Poland on 1 September 1939. Having heard Foreign Minister Viachaslav Molotov's 31 August report on the pact, in which he affirmed that Germany and the Soviet Union were no longer

[1] Quoted in Monty Johnstone, "The CPGB, the Comintern, and the War, 1939–1941: Filling in the Blank Spots," *Science and Society* 61, no. 1 (Spring 1997): 28. Georgi Dimitrov, *The Diary of Georgi Dimitrov*, Ivo Banac, ed. (New Haven: Yale University Press, 2003), 112; Alexander Dallin and F. I. Firsov, eds., *Dimitrov and Stalin, 1934–1943: Letters from the Soviet Archives* (New Haven: Yale University Press, 2000), 112.

[2] Dimitrov and Manuil'skii to Stalin, 27 August 1939, in *Dimitrov*, 150; V. P. Smirnov, "Frantsuzkaia kommunisticheskaia partiia i Komintern v 1939–1940 gg.: Novyie arkhivy materialy," *Novaia i noveishaia istoriia*, 1994, no. 1: 33.

"enemies," Dimitrov now advised Maurice Thorez, the secretary-general of the French party, that he "ought not to announce your unqualified support" for the current French government, but rather should condemn its "betrayal" of Czechoslovakia and Spain and its support for the "policy of the English war-mongers against the USSR."[3] Still struggling to provide instructions to member parties, Dimitrov again asked for Stalin's advice. In a meeting at the Kremlin on 7 September, Stalin offered the explanation, according to Dimitrov's notes, that "*The division of capitalist states into fascist and democratic no longer makes sense.*"[4] Two days later, the Comintern sent a directive to member parties, informing them that "the bourgeoisie of all belligerent states bear equal responsibility" for the war. However, the French and British parties in particular were slow to respond to the new line, fully abandoning antifascism only in late September after the Soviets "liberated" eastern Poland in accordance with the pact's secret protocol.[5] A November 1939 article written by Dimitrov, revised by Stalin, and designed to provide guidance to national parties, moved beyond the claim of "equal responsibility" to identifying Britain and France as "the most zealous supporters of the continuation and further incitement of war."[6] The Popular Front against fascism was dead.

Communists, of course, had a long history of accommodating themselves to rapid and dramatic shifts in the party line. The key to weathering such changes in direction was the international communist's fundamental faith that Stalin and the Soviet party knew best. "Was it not," British communist Eric Hobsbawm asked in his 2002 memoir with regard to the Nazi-Soviet Pact, "the essence of 'democratic centralism' to stop arguing once a decision had been reached, whether or not you were personally in agreement? And the highest decision had obviously been taken."[7] Some version of the refrain "the great party line is correct," "Stalin is right," and "Stalin knows what he's

3 Dimitrov, *Diary*, 114; "Protokol," 1 September 1939, Rossiiskii gosudarstvennyi arkhiv sotsial'no-politicheskoi istorii (RGASPI), f. 495, op. 1, d. 1292, l. 8; Smirnov, "Frantsuzkaia," 33.

4 Emphasis in original. Dimitrov, *Diary*, 115.

5 Johnstone, "The CPGB," 29, 32; *About Turn: The British Communist Party and the Second World War: The Verbatim Record of the Central Committee Meetings of 25 September and 2–3 October 1939* (London: Lawrence and Wishart, 1990); Smirnov, "Frantsuzkaia," 33–5; Lynne Taylor, "The Parti Communiste Français and the French Resistance in the Second World War," in Tony Judt, ed., *Resistance and Revolution in Mediterranean Europe* (New York: Routledge, 1989), 53–79; Kevin McDermott and Jeremy Agnew, *The Comintern: A History of International Communism from Lenin to Stalin* (Basingstoke: Palgrave Macmillan, 1996), 195–7.

6 "Extracts from an Article by Dimitrov on the Tasks of the Working Class in the War," in Jane Degras, ed., *The Communist International 1919–1943: Documents*, vol. 3: *1939–1943* (London: Frank Cass, 1965), 451. See also Dallin and Firsov, *Dimitrov*, 153, 160, 164–5; N.S. Lebedeva and M.M. Narinskii, eds., *Komintern i vtoraia mirovaia voina: Chast' I: do 22 iunia 1941 g.* (Moscow: Pamiatniki istorichskoi mysli, 1994), 117.

7 Eric Hobsbawm, *Interesting Times: A Twentieth-Century Life* (New York: New Press, 2002), 153.

doing," shows up again and again in the reminiscences of communists and former communists attempting to explain their willingness to turn virtually overnight from condemning the British and French failure to aid Spain against Germany and Italy to celebrating Stalin's tactical brilliance in coming to terms with the Nazis.[8] As International Brigade veteran Steve Nelson noted in his 1981 memoir, "We treated the Soviet Union as the single pivot in the world around which everything else was centered. Nothing else mattered."[9] The note of regret was apparently retrospective. According to FBI surveillance, Nelson in 1939 enthusiastically supported the "imperialist war" line, arguing that in the event of war the American Communist Party's policy would be to "encourage the soldiers to turn their guns on their own leaders of capitalist countries and not upon the poor working men in the opposite trenches." The agent in charge of Nelson's case recommended that he "be considered for 'custodial detention' if the US entered a national emergency."[10]

The memory of the war in Spain potentially complicated such determination to follow the party line. After three years of war, the heroism, sacrifices, and struggles in Spain had become for many communists – particularly those who were there – a defining moment personally and politically. Although the communists' world continued to revolve around Moscow, the communist line as lived in Spain made strong claims on their emotions.[11] Just one month before the pact, in July 1939, the Spanish party leadership in the Soviet Union had drafted a resolution on "the lessons of the Spanish people's war for independence," reaffirming that it had been "*a struggle against international fascism, for democracy and for peace, liberty, and progress*." Spain's struggle was international and romantic: "the glorious International Brigades recall[ed] the best traditions of the last century's wars for independence, the traditions of the French Revolution's volunteers, of George Byron and of [Giuseppe] Garibaldi."[12] Such mythologized memories of the war provided compelling

[8] Wolfgang Leonhard, *Child of the Revolution*, trans. C. M. Woodhouse (1957; reprint, London: Ink Links, 1979), 81; Enrique Castro Delgado, *Mi fe se perdió en Moscú* (Barcelona: Luís de Caralt, 1964), 47; Ernst Fischer, *An Opposing Man*, trans. Peter Ross and Betty Ross (London: Allen Lane, 1974), 349; Santiago Carrillo, *Memorias: Testimonio polémico de un protagonista relevante de nuestra transición* (Barcelona: Planeta, 2008),383.

[9] Steve Nelson, James R. Barrett, Rob Ruck, *Steve Nelson, American Radical* (Pittsburgh: University of Pittsburgh Press, 1981), 249.

[10] Katherine A. S. Sibley, "Soviet Military-Industrial Espionage in the United States and the Emergence of an Espionage Paradigm in US-Soviet Relations, 1941–45," *American Communist History* 2, no. 1 (2003): 39 n.89, 40.

[11] Peter N. Carroll, Michael Nash, and Melvin Small, eds., *The Good Fight Continues: World War II Letters from the Abraham Lincoln Brigade* (New York: New York University Press, 2006), 3–4; Rémi Skoutelsky, "L'Espagne après l'Espagne: La mémoire des Brigades internationales," *Matériaux pour l'histoire de notre temps*, no. 7 (April-June 2003): 33.

[12] Emphasis in original. "Las enseñanzas de la guerra por la independencia del pueblo de España (Resolución del Comité Central del P.C. de España)," 14 July 1939, RGASPI, f. 495, op. 18., d. 1288, ll. 5, 21.

narratives of communist identity, narratives that were out of synch with the exigencies of the Nazi-Soviet pact, but not necessarily jettisoned entirely.

The 22 June 1941 invasion of the Soviet Union thus came for many as something of a relief. As Nelson noted, "The interests of the Soviet Union and the political principles for which we struggled throughout the thirties were no longer at odds."[13] However, the U.S. alliance with the Soviet Union did little to alleviate American officials' suspicions of veterans of the International Brigades. That American brigadistas maintained the connections they had forged during the Spanish civil war through a veterans organization and personal correspondence reinforced the impression that their primary loyalty was not to the United States, even though, during the war, they came together as Spanish civil war veterans (and, less explicitly, as communists) primarily to protest the U.S. military's tendency to deny them combat assignments and promotions. Still, evidence of espionage, such as Nelson's apparent efforts to gather, according to a 1943 FBI report, "some highly confidential data regarding the nuclear experiments then in progress" at the Berkeley Radiation Laboratory, suggests that suspicion of Spanish civil war veterans, although perhaps exaggerated, had some foundation.[14]

In the Soviet Union, Spanish exiles and veterans also faced a state suspicious of their identification with the Spanish cause. More than six hundred Spaniards fought for the Soviet Union, but they, too, were often denied the combat assignments they desired.[15] Maintaining links with one another, the exiles appealed to Spanish party leaders when the Soviet authorities rejected their petitions to serve at the front. Their difficulties were particularly ironic given the Soviet Union's appropriation of conventions developed during the Spanish civil war in its coverage of the Great Fatherland War. The stories of two of the most famous Spaniards to fall in the Great Fatherland War – Rubén Ruiz Ibárruri, the son of Spanish communist icon Dolores Ibárruri, and Santiago de Paúl Nelken, son of Margarita Nelken, who was expelled from the Spanish party during the world war – illustrate the complex linkages of the Spanish and Soviet wars in individual lives and communist propaganda.

Throughout the "strange interlude" of the Nazi-Soviet pact as well as the Soviet war against fascism, the Spanish civil war remained a vital element of the Stalinist cultural landscape.[16] The images central to the Soviet reporting (and mythologizing) of the war in Spain – civilians under siege, soldiers

[13] Nelson et al., *American Radical*, 253.

[14] Sibley, "Soviet Military-Industrial Espionage," 44. Nelson denied any involvement in espionage; Nelson et al., *American Radical*, 292–5.

[15] Immaculada Colomina Limonero, *Dos patrias, tres mil destinos: Vida y exilio de los niños de la Guerra de España refugiados en la Unión Soviética* (Madrid: Ediciones Cinca, 2010), 67; David Wingeate Pike, *In the Service of Stalin: The Spanish Communists in Exile, 1939–1945* (Oxford: Oxford University Press,1993), 152–3.

[16] Harold C. Deutsch, "Strange Interlude: The Soviet-Nazi Liaison of 1939–1941," *Historian* 9 (Spring 1947): 107–36.

standing against tanks, female combatants, mothers and the motherland – shaped representations and understandings of the Great Fatherland War. For those who fought it, "our war" in Spain remained a self-defining memory – one that could alternately reinvigorate, reconfigure, weaken, or subvert communist identities.[17]

Veterans of the Abraham Lincoln Brigade and the Politics of Memory

In January 1938, Milly Bennett and her new husband Hans Amlie, a former commander of the Abraham Lincoln battalion, returned to New York City. On February 13, they joined Lillian Hellman and "Hollywood magician and actor" Fred Keating on stage at the Belasco Theater in a celebration of the first anniversary of the "formation of the Abraham Lincoln Brigade"[18] Like many returning veterans, including Nelson, Amlie undertook a national fund- and consciousness-raising tour on behalf of the Americans in Spain. Starting on the West Coast at the end of March, he traveled throughout the Midwest giving speeches and attending events, arriving in Washington, DC, in late April.[19]

The Friends of the Abraham Lincoln Brigade organized fundraisers and speeches that reached an audience beyond party members, but nonetheless remained closely linked to party circles. In Los Angeles, Hellman "gave a little party" in Amlie's honor that, he wrote Bennett, included "movie people," most of whom "were writers and church people. Our kind of church of course."[20] In mid-April 1938, he regretfully informed Bennett that he would be returning to their home in Mill Valley, California, later than expected, because "the party thinks that I am the only man who can handle New England and the plans now call for a ten day extension in order to go there."[21] In Boston, he wanted to attribute the success of a fundraising dinner to "the work the party put behind it," but admitted that the presence of Robert Raven, a veteran who had been blinded in Spain "appeals to a certain group that otherwise would not be affected."[22] He was more enthusiastic about the Communist Party convention in New York City in May, describing a "packed audience 22,800 people"

[17] P. S. Blagov and J. A. Singer, "Four Dimensions of Self-Defining Memories (Specificity, Meaning, Content, and Affect) and Their Relationships to Self-restraint, Distress, and Repressive Defensiveness," *Journal of Personality* 72 (2004): 481–511; C. Lardi et al., "Further Characterisation of Self-Defining Memories in Young Adults: A Study of a Swiss Sample," *Memory* 18, no. 3 (April 2010): 293–309.

[18] Advertisement, Milly Bennett Papers, Box 1, Folder 4, Hoover Institution Archives.

[19] Bennett Papers, Box 2, Folder 9; Box 1, Folder 4; Nelson et al., *American Radical*, 233–5.

[20] Hans Amlie to [Milly Bennett] 24 [March 1938], Bennett Papers, Box 2, Folder 9.

[21] Hans Amlie to [Milly Bennett], 12 [April 1938], Bennett Papers, Box 2, Folder 9; see also Amlie to [Milly Bennett], 20 [May 1938], ibid.

[22] Hans Amlie to [Milly Bennett], 20 [May 1938]. On Raven see, Peter N. Carroll, *The Odyssey of the Abraham Lincoln Brigade: Americans in the Spanish Civil War* (Stanford: Stanford University Press, 1994), 105, 213.

at Madison Square Garden, where Bob Minor gave a "fiery" speech about Spain.[23]

Connected by their experiences in Spain and very often their communist convictions, veterans maintained a vital social and political network of formal organizations and personal contacts. During the Spanish civil war, the Friends of the Abraham Lincoln Brigade and the Veterans of the Abraham Lincoln Brigade (VALB), founded in late 1937 by Nelson among others, raised money for the Spanish Republic and for disabled veterans; it also organized protests against German and Italian intervention and in favor of lifting the American embargo on the Republic.[24] As the war wound down, the Friends honored the dead, raised money to bring Americans home, assisted foreign-born veterans detained at Ellis Island, and protested the polices of nonintervention in Spain and appeasement of Nazi Germany.[25]

The personal ties that sustained such networks emerge clearly in the case of efforts to locate Robert Merriman, who disappeared in April 1938 during the Great Retreats along the Ebro. Rumors circulated that he had been taken prisoner, and his wife Marion called on friends and acquaintances in the United States and Europe to put pressure on the Nationalists to provide information. She dispatched cables to Berkeley, where Merriman had been a graduate student, prompting a petition campaign, and to Hermann Muller, the renowned geneticist they had known in Moscow. Muller in turn organized a group of British and American scientists to send a telegram to General Francisco Franco expressing concern about Merriman.[26] Bennett contacted other friends from Moscow, including the journalist Bob Miller and his wife Jenny, then in Paris, where Bob worked for the Republic's information agency. The Millers followed up with their contacts in the press and the State Department, tracking the rumor that Merriman was being held in a Nationalist prison in Bilbao. Jenny wrote Bennett in September 1938, "Millichka darling, we are making real nuisances of ourselves, going around and asking people about

[23] Hans Amlie to [Milly Bennett], 27 May [1938], Bennett Papers, Box 2, Folder 9. "22,000 Communists Open Session Here," *New York Times* (*NYT*), 27 May 1938.

[24] Carroll, *Odyssey*, 219–23; "'Lift the Embargo' Cried in Times Sq.," *NYT*, 25 January 1939.

[25] Carroll, *Odyssey*, 215, 219; "Plan To Bring Back Americans in Spain," *NYT*, 1 October 1938; "Americans Who Died in Spain Honored," *NYT*, 23 February 1939; "Seek Funds to Aid Americans in Spain," *NYT*, 26 June 1938; "Czech Cause Urged in Belated Parade," *NYT*, 2 October 1938.

[26] Marion Merriman and Warren Lerude, *American Commander in Spain: Robert Hale Merriman and the Abraham Lincoln Brigade* (Reno: University of Nevada Press, 1986), 227; William P. Carney, "Writer Sees 80 Americans Held in Spanish Rebel Camp," *NYT*, 11 July 1938. "Telegram re: petition from Berkeley [22?] May 1938, Robert Brady to Henry F. Grady," National Archives College Park, Maryland (NACP), Record Group (RG) 59, 852.2221 Merriman, Robert H/7; Eugene Staley to Pierrepont Moffat,10 June 1938, ibid., 852.2221 Merriman, Robert H./20; "Telegram Received from Madrid (St Jean de Luz) dated June 29, 1938," ibid., 852.2221 Merriman, Robert H./37; Claude G. Bowers to Secretary of State, 1 July 1938, ibid., 852.2221 Merriman, Robert H/46.

Merriman," and asked Bennett to tell Marion that "nobody knows anything." They were willing to be nuisances because they had known the Merrimans in Moscow and sympathized with their politics; the Millers were then or would soon become party members. Moreover, in Paris they had a close view of "the whole Spanish business – these boys coming in armless and legless and having to go home and scratch for a living."[27] Shared experiences and commitments activated a transnational effort to learn Merriman's fate, although his body was never recovered.

The signing of the Nazi-Soviet Pact put pressure on such networks. The ostensibly nonparty VALB, which in December 1939 succeeded the Friends as the most visible organization of Lincoln veterans, ostentatiously embraced the new communist line, to some degree abandoning the antifascism that had been at the heart of the Spanish struggle.[28] At its December 1939 convention, the two hundred delegates adopted a resolution supporting the Soviet invasion of Finland and condemning "the people who prate about the rights of small nations." The veterans' organization adopted the slogan, "The Yanks Are Not Coming," an odd echo of the nonintervention policy they had opposed so recently and vehemently. Still, the veterans did not entirely forget the cause that had brought them together. Speakers at the December convention criticized the State Department for failing to assist the thousands of Spanish Loyalist refugees in France.[29] In early 1941, the VALB's newsletter, *The Volunteer for Liberty*, trumpeted the organization's "leading role" in demonstrations against the passage of the Lend-Lease bill, even as it saluted those who had died in Spain: "Salud! The fight still goes on. May we play such a part that we shall be entitled to the same high honor we give to you."[30] Where and how they expected the fight to continue remained (necessarily) obscure.

Drawing selectively on their memories of the Spanish civil war, some veterans reconciled themselves to the turn toward Nazi Germany by remembering their wartime anger at nonintervention. In the contemporary communist press and in interviews conducted decades later, many American veterans, as historian Peter Carroll notes, drew on "personal experience to rationalize" their support of the pact. Thus in his report to the VALB convention in December

[27] Jenny [Miller] to Milly [Bennett], 1 September 1938, Bennett Papers, Box 4, Folder 2; see also Bob [Miller] to Millichka [Milly Bennett], 5 September 1938; Jenny to Millichka, 10 July 1939, ibid. For the rumor that Merriman was alive, see William P. Carney, "Rebels Bar Talk with U.S. Captives," *NYT*, 29 May 1938. On the Millers' connections to the party and KGB see John Earl Haynes, Harvey Klehr, and Alexander Vassiliev, *Spies: The Rise and Fall of the KGB in America* (Ann Arbor: Sheridan Books, 2009), 253–6.

[28] "FBI Raids Spanish Loyalist Veterans Here," *NYT*, 10 February 1940.

[29] "Friends of Finns Condemned Here," *NYT*, 25 December 1939.

[30] "Vets Storm Capital," *Volunteer for Liberty* 3, no. 3 (March 1941): 1; see also, "Vets Act for Peace," *Volunteer for Liberty* 3, no. 1 (February 1941): 1; "Lincoln Veterans Condemn 'Lend-Lease,'" *Volunteer for Liberty* 3, no. 2 (February 1941): 1. "Our Victory Shall Be Your Vengeance," *Volunteer for Liberty* 3, no. 3 (March 1941): 2.

1939, David McKelvy White emphasized that veterans embraced the slogan, "The Yanks Are Not Coming," because "When the governments that stabbed Spain in the back claim they are fighting for democracy, we have good reason to call them hypocrites and liars."[31] Looking back from the vantage of 1988, Milton Wolff, a commander in Spain who in 1939 became the leader of VALB, recalled that during the period of the pact, "Everything I said was based on the Spanish experience – who had helped us; who had not helped us; who had been part of the sellout" of Spain.[32] In his 1981 memoir Nelson remembered a more emotional response: "Perhaps because I had been to Spain, I was more bitter than most people about British and French indifference to Hitler. When the Nazis attacked Poland in September 1939, and Britain and France were forced into war, my feelings were that 'the sons-of-bitches had it coming.'" The fate of Poland did not apparently concern him.[33]

The French government's internment of hundreds of thousands of retreating brigadistas and Spanish refugees in vast camps lacking adequate food, shelter, and sanitation also stoked the veterans' anger and their sense of international solidarity. The conditions in the "camps," beaches or other barren stretches of land ringed by barbed wire, were so appalling that in February and March 1939, about fifty thousand refugees voluntarily returned to Spain, where they faced prison or worse. (Ultimately, about 238,000 returned.[34]) American veterans supported the efforts of comrades in Uruguay and Mexico who were working to bring Spaniards, as well as International Brigade veterans unable to return to their countries of origin, to the Americas. *The Volunteer for Liberty*'s coverage of "Internationals in Other Lands" included a Canadian veteran's appeal to "remember our brothers in France" by sending letters to veterans – "American, German, Italian, Czechoslovakian, Polish, Rumanian" – held in French camps and prisons.[35] For communists, the shocking conditions in which the French government held Spanish Loyalists and their international

31 "The Main Report of the Veterans of the Abraham Lincoln Brigade's National Executive Committee, by David White, to the VALB Convention. December 23, 1939 in New York," in Carroll et al., *Good Fight*, 32.

32 Carroll, *Odyssey*, 226.

33 Nelson et al., *American Radical*, 248.

34 Michel Fabréguet, "Un groupe de réfugiés politiques: Les républicains espagnols des camps d'internement français aux camps de concentration nationaux-socialistes," *Revue d'histoire de la deuxième guerre mondiale et des conflits contemporains* 36, no. 144 (October 1986): 21–3. Juan B. Vilar, "El exilio español de 1939 en el Norte de Africa," in Abdón Mateos, ed., *¡Ay de los vencidos: El exilio y los paises de acogida* (Madrid: Ediciones Eneida, 2009), 71–2; Regina M. Delacor, "From Potential Friends to Potential Enemies: The Internment of 'Hostile Foreigners' in France at the Beginning of the Second World War," *Journal of Contemporary History* 35, no. 3 (2000): 361; Carroll et al., *Good Fight*, 3; Ave Buzzichesi to Dr. [Leo] Eleoesser, 31 January 1940 in ibid., 34–5; Skoutelsky, "L'Espagne," 28.

35 "Internationals in Other Lands," *Volunteer for Liberty* 3, no. 1 (February 1941): 3–4.

brothers-in-arms dramatized the hypocrisy of "democratic" states and the correctness of the Soviet line.[36]

Even for those who left the party, at least in part as a response to the pact, the Spanish civil war often remained a critical personal and political touchstone. Robert Gladnick had ceased to see himself as a communist during the war, a result, he claimed in his memoir, of exposure to Soviet personnel and especially Soviet antisemitism. In the wake of the pact, he and two other disillusioned Jewish communists, Morris Maken (aka Mickenberg) and William Herrick, expressed their dissatisfaction with the party by attempting to establish a rival to VALB, which they dubbed the Veterans of the International Brigades, Anti-Totalitarian. According to Gladnick, the "small vocal, well organized & well financed minority" of veterans who sided with Stalin "took over the Veterans of the Lincoln Brigade" and thwarted their efforts.[37] Although his assessment seems to underestimate the number of veterans who remained loyal to the party, the rival organization managed to attract only a handful of members before Gladnick left to join the Canadian army, where he was able to reactivate the antifascist principles that had led him to Spain.[38]

British veteran Tom Wintringham, who had been expelled from the party in 1938 because of his relationship with American journalist Kitty Bowler, an alleged Trotskyite spy, likewise continued to identify himself in terms of his experiences in Spain.[39] Moreover, despite his expulsion and the pact, the former British commander at Jarama continued to "see himself as a Communist," although in a mold currently rejected by the Comintern.[40] In July 1940, he took advantage of the British government's call to organize "local defense volunteers" to establish an unofficial Home Guard training school. Drawing explicitly on military and political lessons learned in Spain, Wintringham claimed that "in courses lasting only two days we gave a more coherent description of German tactics, and of the answer to these tactics, than was available elsewhere, in the Regular Army as well as the Home Guard;" the course also taught the "essential elements of guerrilla warfare."[41] Wintringham's second-in-command at the school, Hugh Slater, and at least one instructor were also

36 Antonio Mije, *Los refugiados republicanos españoles en Francia y la solidaridad americana* (Mexico City: Editorial Morales, 1940).
37 Robert Gladnick memoirs, "French Camp – Perpignan," p. 8, Hoover Institution Archives.
38 Carroll et al., *Good Fight*, 4; Carroll, *Odyssey*, 229–30; Gladnick memoirs, "French Camp," p. 18.
39 Hugh Purcell, "Kitty Bowler: The English Captain's Spy," *History Today* 62, no. 2 (February 2012): 16–17; Tom Buchanan, "Holding the Line: The Political Strategy of the International Brigade Association, 1939–1977," *Labour History Review* 66, no. 3 (Winter 2001): 294–312.
40 David Fernbach, "Tom Wintringham and Socialist Defense Strategy," *History Workshop*, no. 14 (Autumn 1982): 73, 78 (quotation). See also Hugh Purcell, "Tom Wintringham, Revolutionary Patriot," *History Today* 54, no. 10 (October 2004): 11–17.
41 Quoted in Fernbach, "Wintringham," 74–5.

International Brigade veterans. The staff included "three Spanish refugee miners teaching the use of explosives against tanks."[42] In an April 1941 letter to the editors of *The Nation*, Milly Bennett, who knew both Wintringham and his wife Kitty, quoted from a letter from him, emphasizing his status as someone who "fought with the Loyalists in Spain." Taking a stance not exactly at odds with the pact, Wintringham granted that "this war is not yet an anti-fascist war but can be made so if anti-fascists will show that they are better at all necessary jobs than the imperialists" – a position he deemed in line with "the real democracy we fought for in Spain."[43]

Bennett, too, seems to have struggled to reconcile allegiances to the communist and Spanish causes. In a February 1939 letter to her agent regarding an article about her experiences in the Soviet Union submitted to *American Mercury*, she described herself as "not anti-Soviet" and someone who "certainly could not afford, from the standpoint of my conscience, to be put in that position." Thus although she underscored that she and Amlie needed the hundred dollars and that she had no objection to the story being cut, she insisted on having "*a chance to check it in the form they are willing to buy it.*" The piece never appeared. In the meantime she was moving slowly on her book, because "*I had to give four or five days this week to Spain.*" She and Amlie "feel so goddam wretched about Spain and so terribly separated from it."[44] Fourteen months later, in the wake of the Nazi-Soviet Pact, she may have seen in Wintringham's letter a way to remain both "not anti-Soviet" and connected to Spain.

Indeed it was precisely the identification and self-identification of International Brigade veterans with "real democracy" that made Western governments hesitant to accept their expertise, even after the Nazi invasion turned the Soviet Union into their ally. Although the British War Office ultimately saw the value of the training offered by Wintringham's school, taking it over in late 1940, he himself became the victim of "security restrictions" that prohibited "instructors who had fought in Spain, or were regarded as left-wingers" from becoming commissioned officers.[45] Similarly, in 1942 the FBI investigated Hans Amlie, then in the far less sensitive position of camp manager at the Yuma Farm Labor Supply Center in Somerton, Arizona, to determine whether he ought to be dismissed from government service as "a person who is a member of an organization which advocates the overthrow of the Government of the United States."[46] From FBI director J. Edgar Hoover's perspective, veterans

[42] Fernbach, "Wintringham," 74. Purcell describes two Basque miners, "Wintringham," 15.

[43] Milly Bennett, "Tom Wintringham Writes," *Nation*, 26 April 1941, 510; Kitty [Bowler] to Millie [Bennett], 31 October (1937), Bennett Papers, Box 2, Folder 4.

[44] Emphases in original. Milly Bennett to Hal [Matson], 10 February 1939, Bennett Papers, Box 3, Folder 22. See also Milly Bennett, "More About José Robles" [letter to the editor], *New Republic*, 19 July 1939, 309–10.

[45] Fernbach, "Wintringham," 78; Purcell, "Wintringham," 15.

[46] T. Roy Reid to Hans Amlie, 16 December 1943, Bennett Papers, Box 5, Folder 20.

of the International Brigades were likely subversives. As he noted in a 1938 memo to President Franklin Roosevelt, the Communist Party had sent "men to Spain to fight in the ranks of the Loyalists" in order to train them "to lead the vanguard of the revolution in this country."[47] The FBI's investigation of Amlie turned up the fact that in 1936 he "was a registered Communist" in northern California.[48] Nonetheless, Amlie received notice in December 1943 that he had been cleared to work for the War Food Administration.[49] Indeed Bennett's FBI file suggests that her work for the Spanish Republic's Ministry of Press and Propaganda raised more suspicions than her husband's participation in the International Brigades. The American consul in Valencia reported that a "well-informed" source "described her as 'the Spanish government's best spy.'"[50]

The American military authorities likewise singled out those who fought in Spain, identifying them in their service dossiers as "Communist," "Red," "Subversive," or "Radical."[51] Because many of the more than four hundred American veterans of the International Brigades who served in World War II read *The Volunteer for Liberty* and corresponded with one another as well with Jack Bjoze, the executive secretary of VALB, they quickly perceived the discrimination. Their complaints – being passed up for promotions, thrown out of officer training programs, or relegated to clerical positions far from the front – had a numbing similarity.[52] In 1942, for example, John Gates, a commissar in Spain, wrote Wolff that he had been turned down for officers' training "only because, I must assume, of my political beliefs."[53] In 1943, he complained to Bjoze that a transfer out of a unit headed overseas had placed him in a headquarters company, writing reports and filling out forms – his two years' experience of "war against Nazis and Fascists in Spain," rendered

47 J. Edgar Hoover, "1938 Memorandum to Attorney General Homer Cummings and President Franklin Roosevelt on the Spanish Civil War and the New York Workers School," *Science and Society* 68, no. 3 (Fall 2004): 363; Carroll, *Odyssey*, 279–94; Phillip Deery, "'A Blot upon Liberty': McCarthyism, Dr. Barsky and the Joint Anti-Fascist Refugee Committee," *American Communist History* 8, no. 2 (December 2009): 167–96.

48 The investigation of Amlie is included in Bennett's FBI file; a Freedom of Information Act inquiry determined that he had no separate file. Report made by Eugene P. Greer, 8 January 1943, Mildred Bremler [Milly Bennett], Federal Bureau of Investigation File, HQ 100-124391/SF 100-12592 (FBI/Bennett).

49 T. Roy Reid to Hans Amlie.

50 Milton K. Wells, American Vice Consul, Valencia to Secretary of State, 7 November 1937, NACP, RG 59, 800.00B Mitchell, Mildred B./1; John Edgar Hoover to Special Agent in Charge, San Francisco, 22 July 1942, (FBI/Bennett); "Memorandum for Mr. Alden," 13 May 1943, ibid.

51 John Earl Haynes and Harvey Klehr, *In Denial: Historians, Communism, and Espionage* (San Francisco: Encounter Books, 2003), 123; Peter Carroll with assistance from Daniel Bertwell, "Premature Anti-Fascists, Again," *Volunteer* 25, no. 4 (December 2003): 5–6, 8.

52 Carroll, *Odyssey*, 252–4, 257–64; Carroll et al., *Good Fight*, 62–115.

53 John Gates to Milt [Wolff], 12 February 1942, Complaints of Discrimination during World War II, ALBA 069, Box 1, Folder 56, Tamiment Library/Robert F. Wagner Labor Archives, New York University.

"completely useless."[54] Wolff in turn complained to Bjoze that he had been assigned to a unit of Italians and Germans, who were considered, along with the communists, to be unreliable soldiers – a particularly unsavory fate for someone who had fought in Spain.[55] In 1943, Bjoze took the veterans' cause to the War Department and, more successfully, to the press, with the result that many who had been denied commissions or combat assignments now received them.[56]

The veterans themselves found such discrimination particularly galling because they understood the current war as a continuation of the war they had fought in Spain. If few affirmed as explicitly as Gates that the world war demonstrated that "our struggle was not in vain," their efforts to keep in touch with one another and their frequent evocations of Spain suggest the degree to which memories of Spain functioned as a point of personal and political reference.[57] Gates, sounding very much like the commissar he once was, attributed the Allied victory in North Africa to the toll taken on Franco's forces by the Republic's fierce resistance.[58] Ben Gardner's December 1943 letter to Bjoze suggested both a powerful connection to his fellow veterans – "our boys," whom he hated to see "getting it now, when they came thru Spain" – and an abiding interest in Spanish politics, as he noted with satisfaction Jesús Hernández's arrival in Mexico.[59] (Gardner himself died in France in October 1944.) Irving Goff, who served with the Office of Strategic Services in Italy, found that his status as a veteran of the International Brigades continued to connect him to an international antifascist network. After he was able to persuade communists in the Italian resistance that he had fought in Spain – he knew the street address of the Communist Party's offices in Madrid – they were willing to trust him.[60]

Often addressing one another as "camaradas" or "amigos" and signing their letters "Salud y Victoria," the veterans' World War II letters evoked the sound and spirit of Spain and suggested that both they and their political commitments remained deeply rooted in their Spanish experiences. Thus in a letter that alluded to pointed disagreements about the value of Ernest Hemingway's work on the Spanish civil war, the poet Edwin Rolfe addressed Wolff as

54 John Gates to Jack [Bjoze], 21 January 1943, ALBA 069, Box 1, Folder 56.

55 Milton Wolff to Jack [Bjoze], nd, ALBA 069, Box 3, Folder 70.

56 Carroll, *Odyssey*, 260, 263, 275; "Report: Summary of Discrimination Cases," nd, ALBA 069, Box 4, Folder 47; Drew Pearson, "Washington Merry-Go-Round: Heroes of Lincoln Brigade Complain of Discrimination," *Washington Post*, 14 April 1943; Milton Wolf to Lennie [Leonard Lamb], 10 January 1945, ALBA 069, Box 3, Folder 70; John Gates to Hal, 2 June 1944, ALBA 069, Box 1, Folder 56.

57 John Gates to Milt [Wolff], 12 February 1942, ALBA 069, Box 1, Folder 56.

58 John Gates to Jack [Bjoze], 26 February 1943, ALBA 069, Box 1, Folder 56.

59 Ben Gardner to Jack [Bjoze], 5 December 1943, ALBA 069, Box 1, Folder 54.

60 Carroll, *Odyssey*, 270.

"mi viejo amigo."[61] Political disagreements could not, he suggested, come between old friends from Spain. Bill Aalto called on his rather rough Spanish to send Rolfe and his wife Mary, whom he addressed as Maria, "Un saludo carinosa de ejercibo americano está vez" [an affectionate greeting from an American soldier, this time]. Apparently only the Spanish greeting could convey the necessary warmth and meaning.[62]

In contemporary letters and contributions to *The Volunteer for Liberty* as much as in memories recalled decades later, veterans of the International Brigades represented themselves as indelibly marked by their experiences in Spain. That their memories were deeply political – in the sense of being shaped by the moments in which they were remembered and by larger ideological considerations – was particularly clear during the months of the Nazi-Soviet Pact when what communists recalled about the war was British and French nonintervention, rather than the Nazi Condor Legion. At the same time, memories of the war were profoundly personal, grounded in comradeship and shared sacrifice and offering a means of endowing loss with meaning. The war, veterans suggested – and governments worried about subversives seemed to agree – had to some degree reforged them. Or, perhaps more accurately, it had reconfigured the networks that connected them to each other and to the wider world. Ever after, both those who left the party and those who remained in Moscow's orbit defined themselves and were identified by others as having fought with the Loyalists in Spain.

Fashioning Spanish Communist Identities in the Soviet Union

In the spring of 1939, many of the hundreds of thousands of civilians and soldiers who fled Spain as Franco's victorious Nationalists began a campaign of mass arrests and executions looked with hope to the Soviet Union.[63] The Soviet Union, after all, was the only major power to aid the Republic. In early 1939, the Soviet state contributed five million francs to aid Spanish refugees in France. However, after the fall of the Republic, it provided no additional humanitarian assistance to the refugees. Several hundred European communists who had traveled from Soviet exile to join the International Brigades and were now interned in France found themselves denied reentry. Despite Dimitrov and Manuil'skii's August 1939 appeal to Stalin, the Politburo also refused to admit some three thousand communists from throughout Europe – Poland,

[61] Edwin Rolfe to Milt [Wolff], 8 June 1943, ALBA 069, Box 3, Folder 9.

[62] Spelling as in original. William Aalto to Ed [Rolfe] and Maria [Mary Rolfe], 9 December 1941, in Carroll et al., *Good Fight*, 49. Numerous letter writers used Spanish, especially "Salud" or "Salud y Victoria." See for example, ibid., 25, 30, 39, 47, 48, 51, 53, 60, 66, 85, 88, 89, 94, 96, 97, 100, 101, 109, 111, 112, 113.

[63] Michael Richards, *A Time of Silence: Civil War and the Culture of Repression in Franco's Spain, 1936–1945* (New York: Cambridge University Press, 1998).

Yugoslavia, Germany, Austria, Italy, and Czechoslovakia – who were unable to return home or find asylum in the West.[64] Although about eighty thousand refugees ultimately found safe haven in Mexico or elsewhere in the Americas, more than one hundred thousand remained in France, soon engulfed by another war. After occupying France, the Nazis deported approximately nine thousand "Red" Spaniards to Mauthausen and other concentration camps; although exact figures are lacking, it seems likely that at least ten thousand refugees from Spain fought with the French resistance during the World War II.[65] Ultimately, only about two thousand refugees – mostly members of the Spanish Communist Party (Partido Comunista de España, PCE), including its most visible leader Dolores Ibárruri – were admitted to the Soviet Union.[66]

The Spaniards who sailed from Le Havre to Leningrad in April and May 1939 could imagine the passage into political exile as a homecoming. In many ways they were already insiders, who identified themselves with the Soviet project and were lionized by Soviet propaganda. At the same time, the Spaniards were also outsiders, communists who understood the "internationalist cause" in terms of their fight "to liberate Spain."[67] Their conceptions of the model communist filtered Soviet norms – encountered via travel or publications such as *USSR in Construction* – through the needs and possibilities of civil war Spain. Such conceptions did not necessarily correspond to those they found in a Soviet Union increasingly committed to Russian nationalism and, at least between August 1939 and the German invasion of June 1941, to peaceful relations with fascism.[68]

64 Daniel Kowalsky, "The Soviet Union and the International Brigades, 1936–1939," *Journal of Slavic Military Studies* 19 (2006): 698–702.

65 Friedrich Katz, "Mexico, Gilberto Bosques, and the Refugees," *The Americas* 57, no. 1 (July 2000): 4–12; Fabréguet, "Un groupe," 26, 34–7; Julio Martín Casas and Pedro Carvajal Urquijo, *El exilio español (1936–1978)* (Barcelona: Planeta, 2002), 118; John F. Sweets provides a figure of 300,000 refugees remaining in France, *Choices in Vichy France: The French under Nazi Occupation* (New York: Oxford University Press, 1986), 112–13; Secundino Serrano, *Maquis: Historia del la guerrilla antifranquista* (Madrid: Temas de Hoy, 2001), 123; Geneviève Dreyfus-Armand argues that a "significant percentage" of Spanish refugees participated in the French resistance, *L'exil des Républicains espagnols en France* (Paris: Albin Michel, 1999), 167.

66 Pike, *In the Service*, 17, 36. A. V. Elpat'evskii, *Ispanskaia emigratsiia v SSSR: Istoriografiia i istochniki, popytka interpretatsii* (Tver: GERS, 2002), 38–40. Alicia Alted Vigil, *La voz de los vencidos: El exilio republicano de 1939* (Madrid: Aguilar, 2005), 48, 162–3; RGASPI, f. 545, op. 6, d. 56, l. 11 (Statistics on volunteers); "Informe del camarada Checa," Archivo histórico del Partido Comunista de España (AHPCE), Dirigentes PCE, sig. 7/3.1.4, p. 18.

67 Xosé-Manoel Núñez and José M. Faraldo, "The First Great Patriotic War: Spanish Communists and Nationalism, 1936–1939," *Nationalities Papers* 37 (July 2009): 406.

68 Nicholas S. Timasheff, *The Great Retreat: The Growth and Decline of Communism in Russia* (New York: E. P. Dutton, 1946); David Brandenberger, *National Bolshevism: Stalinist Mass Culture and the Formation of Modern Russian National Identity, 1931–1956* (Cambridge, MA: Harvard University Press, 2002), 43–62; Jesús Hernández, *En el país de la gran mentira* (Madrid: G. del Toro, 1974), 22–3.

Ibárruri and the other PCE leaders in the Soviet Union often addressed the Spanish exiles as a community, which they assumed looked to the Spanish party for guidance in all aspects of their lives. On 20 August 1939, just four days before *Pravda* announced the signing of the Nazi-Soviet Nonaggression Pact, General-Secretary José Díaz sent a letter to his "dear comrades" in the Soviet Union. "In your new socialist life," he advised the new arrivals, "you can and must prepare for the future because the struggle in Spain has not ended and will not end until we liberate our people from fascist domination."[69] In these circumstances, their behavior had to be exemplary and revolutionary in both "public and private life." Combining an appeal to Spanish patriotism with deference to the Soviet fatherland, Díaz prescribed diligent work along with devotion to heroic Spain, the "grand Soviet people," and dear comrade Stalin, all in preparation for the great antifascist struggle ahead.

Díaz's letter took no account of the very different situations, both material and political, of Spaniards in the Soviet Union. The PCE leaders in Moscow, who were assigned posts in the Comintern apparatus, enjoyed the perks and privileges of the Soviet elite and were largely insulated from the day-to-day problems facing other émigrés.[70] Approximately thirty émigré military officers, including Juan Modesto and Enrique Líster, enrolled at the Frunze Military Academy, where, their shared privileges notwithstanding, relations between strong and weak students and between Spaniards and Catalans were apparently less than "cordial."[71] Another relatively privileged group of about 110 émigrés attended a newly organized "party school" under the auspices of the Comintern. Short biographies prepared before they were admitted indicate that all were members of the PCE or Catalan Communist Party (Partit Socialista Unificat de Catalunya), most (sixty-six) having joined between 1931 and 1935. All had ably undertaken "responsible" work during the war – as commanders, commissars, party organizers, or intelligence operatives; only thirteen were women.[72] The remaining émigrés, low-level party members or activists, were assigned to factories in and around Moscow, where about three hundred party members worked in December 1940, as well as further afield.[73] Often working in unfamiliar occupations and unable to keep up with the "shock" pace of Stalinist factories, many lived in impoverished conditions even before the

69 Díaz to Queridos camaradas, 20 August 1939, AHPCE, Dirigentes PCE, sig. 9/1.2.

70 RGASPI, f. 495, op. 18, d. 1317, ll. 111–35, 159, 178 (Comintern salaries and benefits).

71 AHPCE, Emigración política, caja 101/3 (Meeting at Frunze Academy, October 1939); ibid., caja 101/1 (Military academies). Alted, *La voz*, 166; Joan Estruch Tobella, *Historia oculta del PCE* (Madrid: Temas de Hoy, 2002), 147.

72 RGASPI, f. 495, op. 18, d. 1292, ll. 17–39 (Information on Party School); Alted, *La voz*, 166. Estruch, *Historia oculta*, 147. Head of the IKKI Cadres Department to Dimitrov, 2 September 1939, RGASPI, f. 495, op. 18, d. 1325, ll. 16–17.

73 RGASPI, f. 495, op. 18, d. 1325a, ll. 155–6 (Foreign workers in Moscow factories); Pike, *In the Service*, 35–6, 45.

German invasion substantially lowered living standards throughout the Soviet Union.[74]

These new arrivals joined several thousand Spaniards already in the Soviet Union. During the civil war, the Soviet Union had taken in approximately three thousand children of the more than thirty thousand Spanish children evacuated from the war zone. These children had been accompanied by more than one hundred teachers and caregivers.[75] When the war ended, there were also about 150 Spanish pilots training in the Soviet Union and about 200 sailors stranded in Soviet Black Sea ports.[76] Few nonparty people arrived from Spain in 1939, but many earlier arrivals – teachers, pilots, sailors, and of course the children – were not necessarily members. In many ways, the children were a special case and, at least initially, enjoyed something close to "celebrity status" in the Soviet Union.[77] In contrast, the nonparty adults, especially those who evinced a desire to leave, received little consideration; in 1940 and 1941, many were arrested, ending up in labor camps in Kazakhstan.[78]

As this brief sketch makes clear, the notion of a unified Spanish community in the Soviet Union was in many ways a fiction – even the small "community" of privileged officers was riven by national and educational differences. What potentially united the exiles was a tendency to understand their experiences in Spain, however they remembered and contested them, as significant personally and internationally. As Líster reminded his fellow students in the midst of their criticism and self-criticism, "we are Spanish combatants."[79] Their current situation, he suggested, could only be understood in relation to their war. It was to this sense of community – the community of those defined by their past and future struggle against fascism – that Díaz's letter appealed, even as it ignored the different paths that émigrés had taken to the Soviet Union and their differing experiences among the "grand Soviet people."

Imagining the exiles as a community bound by their memories of the Spanish civil war, the Spanish leadership explained the Nazi-Soviet Pact as a continuation of the spirit that had animated "our war." In a pamphlet addressed to Spanish exiles in the Soviet Union and the Americas, Díaz and Ibárruri justified the pact in the emotional language of memory, linking the current conflict to English and French perfidy during the civil war: "Tens of thousands

74 RGASPI, f. 495, op. 18, d. 1325a, ll. 154, 146 (Correspondence with Central Committee of VKP(b)).

75 Daniel Kowalsky, *Stalin and the Spanish Civil War* [electronic resource] (New York: Columbia University Press, 2004), chapter 5, http://www.gutenberg-e.org/kodo1/ (accessed 15 November 2014).

76 Elpat'evskii, *Ispanskaia emigratsiia*, 38–40. Alted, *La voz*, 48, 162–3.

77 Kowalsky, *Stalin and the Spanish Civil War*, chapter 5, paragraph 54. Pike, *In the Service*, 38.

78 Luiza Iordache, *Republicanos españoles en el Gulag (1939–1956)* (Barcelona: Institut de Ciències Polítiques i Socials, 2008), 13, 29–36.

79 AHPCE, Emigración política, caja 101/3. See also Manuel Tagüeña Lacorte, *Testimonio de dos guerras* (Barcelona: Planeta, 2005), 345.

of Spaniards who fell heroically on the field of battle, thousands of martyred women, and thousands of innocent children destroyed by shrapnel accuse the English and French bourgeoisie ... of having hands stained with the blood of antifascists."[80] They urged their compatriots to remember the tragic consequences of the democracies' refusal to supply the Republic with arms and implicitly to forget Nazi atrocities such as the bombing of Guernica.[81] Recognizing Stalin's decisive role, they also called on the exiles to maintain the distinctive "abnegation and heroism" forged in the Spanish civil war.[82]

A number of historians have taken such reconfigurations of the story of the Spanish struggle as evidence that Spanish communists, unlike their British and French comrades, suffered "no special problems of conscience" as a result of the pact and the subsequent partition of Poland.[83] The case of Santiago Carrillo, then a young communist who had publicly and vehemently accused his socialist father of treason, later a central figure in the elaboration of "Eurocommunism," seems to support such conclusions.[84] His retrospective accounts of this period – a 1948 article, a 1974 interview, and a 2006 memoir – emphasized that the pact harmonized with his own "anger" at years of British and French "cowardice."[85] Manuel Tagüeña Lacorte, who had commanded communist forces in the civil war and who, like Carrillo, was in France when the pact was announced, recalled the same "rancor" and the sense of vindication among the Spaniards, whose reactions, he emphasized, stood in sharp contrast to their "completely disconcerted" French comrades.[86]

Although anger of the sort emphasized by Carrillo and Tagüeña may have been deeply felt, it does not necessarily demonstrate that Spanish communists "found it easier to adapt to the consequences of the Nazi-Soviet pact than their British and French comrades."[87] After all, their public personas and very often their self-identifications were tightly linked to the sacrifices made in Spain. Líster's insistence on the community of "Spanish combatants" came in the course of an October 1939 meeting at the Frunze Military Academy in which the students affirmed the unabashed and now unorthodox antifascism of Díaz's August letter: "the struggle in Spain has not ended and will not end until we

80 José Díaz and Dolores Ibárruri, *España y la guerra imperialista* (Mexico City: Editorial Popular, 1939), 6.

81 Castro Delgado, *Mi fe*, 47.

82 Díaz and Ibárruri, *España y la guerra*, 9.

83 Juan Avilés Farré, *Pasionaria: La mujer y el mito* (Barcelona: Random House Mondadori, 2005), 151. See also Gregorio Morán, *Miseria y grandeza del Partido Comunista de España, 1939–1985* (Barcelona: Planeta, 1986), 30; McDermott and Agnew, *Comintern*, 197–8.

84 Victor Alba, *The Communist Party in Spain* (New Brunswick, NJ: Transaction, 1983), 302–6, 417.

85 Carrillo, *Memorias*, 383. For his earlier accounts see Pike, *In the Service*, 21, 22; Estruch, *Historia oculta*, 151; Santiago Carrillo, *Demain l'Espagne: Entretiens avec Régis Debray et Max Gallo* (Paris: Éditions du Seuil, 1974), 75.

86 Tagüeña, *Testimonio*, 364.

87 McDermott and Agnew, *Comintern*, 198.

liberate our people from fascist domination."[88] Despite the Nazi-Soviet pact, these officers understood the primary enemy as "fascism." Like the American veterans discussed earlier, they wanted to continue the fight.

This identification with antifascism was particularly powerful and public in the case of Ibárruri. Whatever claims about "imperialist war" she made in political pamphlets, she remained a vivid symbol of the Spanish struggle. The numerous letters, invitations, and gifts she received in this period from Soviet institutions and individuals suggest that the wartime press coverage of Spain in the Soviet Union made a lasting impression. The letter referenced in Chapter 4 from Nina Khor'uptenko, whose doctors had forbidden her to read about events in Spain because they agitated her so, dated to October 1939. In another letter dated September 1940, Khor'uptenko noted that she often looked into the eyes of the portrait of Ibárruri that "hangs on my wall with the portraits of the beloved leaders of our party and my beloved writers" and saw "all the pain, all the suffering of the Spanish people."[89] Ibárruri received dozens of less intimate letters, inviting her to speak in honor of International Women's Day or the seventieth anniversary of the Paris Commune, asking for permission to name a work collective in her honor, soliciting articles for the Soviet press, or requesting her presence at a meeting of a local branch of International Red Aid (MOPR). In early 1941, a seventh-grade student from the Donbas wrote to tell her about his progress studying Spanish – he included his grades – and to complain about his undisciplined classmates.[90] For these correspondents she remained Pasionaria, the "fiery Dolores, people's tribune of Spain."

In her contemporary correspondence with Spanish exiles, Soviet citizens, and international communists Ibárruri often played on her iconic status as the proletarian mother of Spain.[91] She seems to have left, however, no account of her "personal" reaction to the pact. Her silence, notably in her 1984 memoir, can be taken as a calculated cover-up, as well as an indication of the real difficulty for her of remembering this period; that is, of fitting it into a coherent picture of her life and her self. Ibárruri's account of her first months in Moscow consists of a catalog of the famous communists she met and an anecdote about studying Russian. Having learned the Cyrillic alphabet and realizing that "political terms are more or less alike in all languages," Ibárruri found that "with a little intuition and experience" she could decipher *Pravda* "– although," she admitted, "to tell the truth, at times I understood exactly the opposite of what they put in the newspaper."[92] The passage suggests not only

88 AHPCE, Emigración política, caja 101/3.

89 Nina Khor'uptenko to Dolores Ibárruri, 28 September 1940, Arxiu Nacional de Catalunya, El fons centro español de Moscú (ANC), sig. 202.

90 Letter from student dated 6 February 1941 and other examples in ANC, sig. 202.

91 Lisa A. Kirschenbaum, "Exile, Gender, and Communist Self-Fashioning: Dolores Ibárruri (La Pasionaria) in the Soviet Union," *Slavic Review* 71, no. 3 (Fall 2012): 577–89.

92 Dolores Ibárruri, *Memorias de Pasionaria, 1939–1977: Me faltaba España* (Barcelona: Planeta, 1984), 51–2.

a lack of facility in Russian but also the linguistic and emotional difficulties of understanding and internalizing the profound shift in communist rhetoric and policy.[93] In August and September 1939, communist "intuition," particularly intuition that drew on understandings shaped by the Spanish civil war, would have been a particularly poor guide to the contents of *Pravda*. The excision of the pact from her account of this period – she never specifies what she misunderstood – suggests that the experiences that "made" Ibárruri a communist served (temporarily) only to disorient her.

Spanish communists often made "our war" the center of their own self-understandings. Like American veterans of the International Brigades, Spanish communists rationalized the nonaggression pact with Germany as the bitter fruit of the democracies' abandonment of Loyalist Spain, emphasizing, even decades later, their anger at the British and French. Still, despite the fact that Spaniards in the Soviet Union had far less room for maneuver than communists in the West, as well as less incentive to voice even implicit criticism of the new line, some, such as the communist officers at the Frunze Academy, managed to express a continuing and fundamental identification with "our war" against fascism. Thus the "cause of all progressive humanity" in Spain remained part of the cultural memory of international communism, latent perhaps, but still emotionally powerful in the period of the Nazi-Soviet Pact.

"Our War" and the Great Fatherland War

On 22 June 1941, the day the Nazis and their allies invaded the Soviet Union, the "imperialist" war suddenly became a "people's war" against fascism.[94] The conventions developed in Soviet reporting of the Spanish civil war, notably the image, most strongly associated with Dolores Ibárruri, of the implacable and self-sacrificing mother, perfectly suited the Soviet media's emphasis on mothers and the motherland calling men to fight. Women like the sniper Liudmila Pavlichenko, "the girl who killed 300 fascists," followed in the footsteps of the Spanish militiawomen who had become emblems of the Spanish civil war. Stories of young women bravely standing watch on Leningrad's rooftops echoed stories of civilians under fire in Madrid.[95] Ibárruri's civil war slogan, "Better the widow of a hero than the wife of a coward," reappeared, without

93 Paul Preston, *¡Comrades!: Portraits from the Spanish Civil War* (London: HarperCollins, 1999), 304; Irene Falcón with Manuel Jiménez and Jesús Montero, *Asalto a los cielos: Mi vida junto a Pasionaria* (Madrid: Temas de Hoy, 1996), 187–8.

94 "Vystuplenie tov. Dimitrova G. M. na zasedanii sekretariata IKKI 22 iunia 1941 goda," RGASPI, f. 495, op. 18, d. 1335, l. 30b.

95 'Streliai, kak Liudmila Pavlichenko,"*Komsomol'skaia pravda* (*KP*), 2 June 1942; Ol'ga Chechetkina, "Leningradtsy," *KP*, 11 December 1943; Lisa A. Kirschenbaum and Nancy M. Wingfield, "Gender and the Construction of Wartime Heroism in Czechoslovakia and the Soviet Union," *European History Quarterly* 39, no. 3 (July 2009): 468–9.

attribution, in the Soviet press.[96] In September 1941, Dimitrov recorded in his diary that Ibárruri's "impassioned speech at a women's rally" impressed Stalin, who deemed it a "good speech" and Ibárruri a "good woman."[97] The new situation seemed to offer an opportunity for Spanish exiles to continue the struggle lost in Spain.

From the Soviet perspective, however, the current war – their war – was not simply the continuation of the war in Spain. Rather, it was a holy war, the Great Fatherland War – a conception that defined the Spaniards, their combat experience and impeccable antifascist credentials notwithstanding, as outsiders. Much to their chagrin, none of the Spanish officers then finishing their studies at the Frunze Academy received commands in the Red Army. A few days after the invasion, they were told that Stalin had denied their request to join the Red Army, "saying that our place was in Spain, and that we ought to be held in reserve to fight there."[98] At roughly the same time, 21 of the 200 Spanish pilots who had been training in the Soviet Union when the Spanish civil war ended and who had expressed a desire to leave were sent to the gulag.[99] About fifty of the Spanish sailors likewise stranded in the Soviet Union, who had hoped to leave for Spain or elsewhere, were also arrested in late June 1941 despite their offer to join the fight against the Nazis.[100]

Among those Spaniards most likely to gain entrance to the Red Army were the now teenaged refugee children, the *niños de la guerra*, who were, if not more Sovietized than the adult refugees, then more likely to speak Russian.[101] In total, more than six hundred Spaniards served in the Red Army and in partisan units, approximately two hundred of whom died defending the Soviet Union or went missing in action.[102] The most prominent Spaniards in the Red Army were not the officers who founded the Fifth Regiment, but Rubén Ruiz Ibárruri and Santiago de Paúl Nelken, the sons of two important Spanish communists; Santiago's mother, Margarita Nelken, had joined the Communist Party during the Spanish civil war.[103] Their connections may, as historian David Wingeate Pike asserts, have,won them the commissions denied so many of their

96 Lisa A. Kirschenbaum, "'Our City, Our Hearths, Our Families': Local Loyalties and Private Life in Soviet World War II Propaganda," *Slavic Review* 59 (Winter 2000): 833–4.

97 Dimitrov, *Diary*, 193.

98 Tagüeña, *Testimonio*, 416–17. See also Falcón, *Asalto a los cielos*, 217–18.

99 Iordache, *Republicanos*, 13.

100 Ibid., 56–7.

101 Glennys Young, "To Russia with 'Spain': Spanish Exiles in the Soviet Union and the *Longue Durée* of Soviet History," *Kritika* 15, no. 2 (Spring 2014): 406–11. I thank the author for sharing a draft of this article with me. Colomina Limonero, *Dos patrias*, 59–63; AHPCE, Emigración política, caja 100/64.2 (List of Spaniards mobilized, June 1941).

102 "Caídos en la defensa de la URSS en la Segunda Guerra Mundial," AHPCE, Emigración política, caja 99/3; ibid., caja 100/59 (List of Spanish guerrilleros); Pike, *In the Service*, 150–3; Colomina Lionera, *Dos patrias*, 67.

103 Paul Preston, *Doves of War: Four Women of Spain* (London: Harper Collins, 2002), 365–6.

compatriots.[104] However, it is also the case that as young teenagers before the Spanish civil war, both lived and studied in the Soviet Union, learning Russian and gaining an understanding of, and perhaps an attachment to, Soviet life. In 1936, both were too young to enlist – Santiago was fifteen, Rubén sixteen – but nonetheless they fought in Spain.[105] In 1939, the young veterans returned to the Soviet Union, Rubén joining his mother in Moscow and Santiago electing the Soviet Union over his mother's place of exile in Mexico and his father's home in the Netherlands.[106] Although Margarita Nelken's fame may have facilitated Santiago's emigration to the Soviet Union, she herself was expelled from the party in October 1942 as an enemy of the party and the "Spanish people," a year before her son completed artillery school; thus she may have hurt his chances of receiving a commission.[107] Both young men had deep ties both to Spain and the Soviet Union that, perhaps as much or more than their famous mothers, facilitated their Red Army service.

During the Great Fatherland War, Dolores Ibárruri constituted the most visible and most powerful embodiment of the link between "our war" and the Soviet cause, or so Spaniards in need of assistance hoped. A review of her copious correspondence with the émigrés provides a glimpse of her self-presentation and its reception, and it suggests that the role of Iberian mother was more than symbolic.[108] Ibárruri and her correspondents, both prominent and rank-and-file exiles, who wrote requesting everything from help securing a pension or housing to permission to join the party, took seriously her responsibility – as Pasionaria and, after Díaz's suicide in March 1942, as general-secretary – for their material and emotional well-being.[109] Those who, after the German invasion of June 1941, turned to Ibárruri in hopes of being allowed to fight with the Red Army trusted her to recognize their requests as grounded in their experiences in Spain. In November 1942, for example, a group of pilots who had petitioned unsuccessfully to go to the front appealed to Ibárruri as someone who "well understood the Spanish national character" and thus could appreciate the deep shame they suffered "doing nothing for the general

[104] Pike, *In the Service*, 153.

[105] Preston, *Doves*, 370; A. Ibarruri, "Moi brat Ruben," in V. R. Tomin, ed., *My budem borot'sia vmeste: Ocherki o boitsakh-internatsionalistakh* (Moscow: Izdatel'stvo politicheskoi literatury, 1985), 9, 11–12.

[106] Margarita Nelken, "Un héroe español del ejército rojo: Santiago de Paúl Nelken," Archivo Histórico Nacional, Archivo de Margarita Nelken (AMN), legajo 3245; Preston, *Doves*, 376.

[107] "Resolución sobre Margarita Nelken," 23 October 1942, AHPCE, Documentos PCE, carpeta 23; "Spravka," 17 September 1945, AMN, legajo 3235–150; Preston, *Doves*, 381.

[108] The fond of the Spanish Center of Moscow holds 170 letters written between 1939 and 1944, ANC, sig. 203. The PCE archive holds additional letters.

[109] Díaz had long suffered with stomach cancer. That the death was a suicide was not publicly acknowledged at the time. Daniel Arasa, *Los españoles de Stalin* (Barcelona:Editorial Vorágine, 1993), 28–30, 133–4.

cause of liquidating fascism."[110] Others relied on her apparent concern for the intimate details of the exiles' lives. In 1944 when comrade Pedro Felipe asked her to meet with his estranged wife Palmira on his behalf, Ibárruri agreed to try to effect a reconciliation. After the meeting, she sent a blunt update to the husband: "I have come to the conclusion that Palmira has separated from you because she has ceased to love you." Disregarding Stalinist efforts to impede divorce, she advised accepting "the situation and looking, dear Pedro, to your work and the fulfillment of your duty for some compensation for this lack of affection."[111]

Ibárruri also provided sterner advice, while still communicating both an intention to care for the exiles and respect for their contributions to the Spanish cause. Writing in 1943 to admonish Lupe Cantó for petitioning on behalf of a group of Spaniards evacuated to Uzbekistan who wished to return to Moscow, Ibárruri granted that "life is hard: but, comrade," she asked rhetorically, "don't the Soviet people suffer more than anyone?" She enjoined Cantó to remember that "cheering discord [and] collecting and spreading gossip" were activities unworthy of her militant past. (Cantó, who had been a local party secretary in Spain, had been recommended for the party school in 1939 as a comrade who was "politically well developed," "disciplined, and committed to the party."[112]) Despite the rather critical tone of the letter, Ibárruri signed herself, "Yours affectionately."[113]

The overlap of real and symbolic mothering and of commitments to the Spanish and Soviet causes emerged most powerfully when Ibárruri's son died at the Stalingrad front in September 1942. The *Komsoml'skaia pravda* story that ran under the headline "Our Rubén" began by quoting the telegram announcing his death. The words seem designed to call to mind the countless similar telegrams received across the Soviet Union.[114] Thus connected to the generalized experience of loss, Dolores Ibárruri appeared as a familiar Soviet mother in mourning. But she was also, the article quickly reminded its readers, "the heroine of the Spanish people, the fiery Dolores." Indeed in the newspaper's telling it was her exhortation, "Better to die on your feet than live on your knees," that appeared to have inspired Rubén, who began fighting against the "German-Italian fascists" on the "banks of the Ebro" and died defending Stalingrad. That the "son of the fiery Pasionaria died on his feet" lent credibility to her appeals to other mothers to send their men to war and perhaps brought some consolation to those whose sons, husbands, and brothers had fought and died.

[110] Elpat'evskii, *Ispanskaia emigratsiia*, 164. See also AHPCE, Emigración Política, caja 99/2.3; Manuel Tagüeña Lacorte to Ibárruri, 14 February 1944, ANC, sig. 203; Tagüeña, *Testimonio*, 416–17; Falcón, *Asalto a los cielos*, 217–18.

[111] Ibárruri to Pedro Felipe, [c. October 1944], ANC, sig. 203.

[112] RGASPI, f. 495, op. 18, d. 1292, l. 19.

[113] Ibárruri to Lupe Cantó, 29 October 1943, ANC, sig. 203.

[114] "Nash Ruben," *KP*, 24 October 1942.

Ibárruri's own public responses to Rubén's death emphasized the same connections between the battle lost in Spain and the war to be won in the Soviet Union that structured *Komsoml'skaia pravda*'s account. In letters she exchanged with Red Army soldiers in 1943, Ibárruri described Rubén as the embodiment of the linkage between Spain and Stalingrad. To Lieutenant Major P. Glukhov, who wrote to inform her of his unit's vow to avenge Rubén's death, Ibárruri replied, "Your letter was like a caress from my son, my Rubén, who sealed with his blood the battle brotherhood, born in the fields of Spain, of the Spanish people and the Soviet people, from whom we received generous aid in the difficult days of our war." As she may have expected, her letter was publicized by its recipients, who exulted in their reply to her, "Pasionaria wrote to us!"[115]

A hint of the personal pain that informed Ibárruri's efforts to understand Rubén's death in terms of the "fusion" of Spain and Stalingrad emerges in her 1984 memoir. Even at a distance of more than forty years, she had, she asserted, no adequate means of expressing the depth of her loss. "How," she asked, in one of the memoir's few reflective moments, "can I speak of my sorrow? It was the sorrow, the deepest of all sorrows, of a mother who lost her son. And he was my only son. Only Amaya was left to me of the six that I brought into the world."[116] Unable to represent her own pain, she told the story of "my Rubén" via an assemblage of public and semi-public texts by others that depicted her as at once a mother in pain and the symbolic mother of fighters in the international antifascist struggle. She quoted in full Dimitrov's emotional letter of condolence, which balanced the acknowledgment that the death of a "magnificent son" is the "most tragic personal blow that fate can deal" with the conviction that "you, dear Dolores, will know how to transform your great pain into a source of strength, energy, and ruthlessness toward the hated fascist."[117] A stanza from Chilean poet Pablo Neruda's "Canto a Stalingrado" echoed Ibárruri's evocation of childbirth and raised it to the level of allegory: "Spain shakes herself with your blood and your dead,/ Because you, Stalingrad, held out to her your soul/ when Spain gave birth to heroes like yours."[118] Such texts, Ibárruri suggested, embedded her son's death in a larger antifascist narrative that encompassed both the Soviet Union and Spain, endowing his sacrifice with world historical significance, but never really consoling his mother.

When Margarita Nelken's son was killed in action in January 1944, she, too, attempted to make sense of his death in "private" letters with a

[115] Dolores Ibárruri to Lieutenant Major P. Glukhov, nd, ANC, sig. 207. I have found no contemporary "personal" documents addressing her loss in the archives or referenced by her biographers.

[116] Ibárruri, *Memorias de Pasionaria*, 66. See also Falcón, *Asalto a los cielos*, 213, 212; Santiago Carrillo, "Dolores Ibárruri," in *Dolores Ibárruri* (Barcelona: Ediciones B, 2004), 152; A. Ibárruri, "Moi brat Ruben," 21.

[117] Ibárruri, *Memorias de Pasionaria*, 66.

[118] Ibid., 67.

potentially public readership that emphasized the fusion of the Spanish and Soviet causes.[119] In 1946, she wrote both to the director of the school in Moscow where her son had studied before the Spanish civil war and to the head of the local soviet in the town near which he died, proposing to establish memorial prizes in Santiago's honor. At the school, the prize would honor a fourteen-year-old – "the age of my son when he studied there" – and in Mitrofanovka a twenty-two-year-old, "the age of my son when he died there."[120] In both cases, Nelken proposed to award a gold watch engraved with the recipient's name, her son's name, and the date. In the letter to the school director, she prefaced her request with a long narrative establishing Santiago as a Spanish and Soviet hero. She emphasized that, in 1935, Santiago had quickly felt himself at home in the Soviet Union; nonetheless, in March 1936 he returned to Spain, where, after lying about his age, he spent the entire war in "the most dangerous posts." At seventeen, he was among the last to retreat from Catalonia; in France, he declined the safe haven of his grandmother's house, preferring to join the men under his command interned in the camp at Saint Cyprien. Omitting her own role in freeing both Santiago and Rubén Ruiz Ibárruri from the camp, Nelken emphasized that when the PCE leadership offered Santiago the opportunity to go the Soviet Union, he accepted "with enthusiasm." When the Nazis invaded, he immediately enlisted in the Red Army, and he became a hero in a second war against fascism.[121]

Alongside this heroic Spanish-Soviet narrative, Nelken also conveyed a sense of inconsolable loss. "As a mother," she pleaded with the president of the Mitrofanovka soviet to send her any information he could find about her son. She longed for "some information about his last days and his last moments.... how was he wounded; did he die immediately or in a hospital... did he have a girlfriend there." She asked also for details of her son's grave and perhaps a photograph. If it was an individual grave, she requested that it be marked with an inscription in Russian and Spanish reading "Santiago de Paúl Nelken, born in Madrid (Spain) 11 March 1921. Died in Mitrofanovka 5 January 1944, for the USSR, for Spain, and for the liberty of all peoples." She wished flowers to always be kept on the grave and offered to pay for them. Apologizing for "so much trouble," she explained, "you will understand the pain of a mother who has lost her only son."[122] Ensuring that her son's grave in the Soviet Union was

119 Rebecca Earle, "Introduction: Letters, Writers, and the Historian," in Rebecca Earle, ed. *Epistolary Selves: Letters and Letter-Writers, 1600–1945* (Aldershot: Ashgate, 1999), 2–4; Preston, *Doves*, 384; Yuri V. Daskevich (TASS) to Margarita Nelken, 13 June 1945, AMN, legajo 3235–142.

120 Margarita Nelken to the President of the Mitrofanovka Soviet, 1946, AMN, legajo 3240–109; Margarita Nelken to the Director of School 16 (Moscow), 23 February 1946, AMN, legajo 3235–159.

121 Margarita Nelken to the Director of School 16 (Moscow); Preston, *Doves*, 375.

122 Margarita Nelken to the President of the Mitrofanovka Soviet; A. E. Badalián to Margarita Nelken, 10 October 1949, AMN, legajo 3235–205 (confirming marker and flowers); Preston, *Doves*, 386–89.

well looked after became a means of preserving the sanctity of his death "for the liberty of all peoples," of convincing herself that he died in a just war, one that had begun in Spain.[123]

The emerging cold war complicated Nelken's efforts to sustain the fusion of the Soviet and Spanish causes that she believed gave meaning to her son's death. In 1948, she returned to Europe with "the hope of visiting the grave of my son;" however, the hostility in the West to those labeled communists rendered the visit impossible. She knew, as she wrote a friend, that "if I went there, no one would believe it was just for 'THAT,' and afterwards I wouldn't be allowed to teach courses in Mexico." The situation raised the "awful" thought that "those who fell, those who gave everything, have made their sacrifice in vain, for a world even more selfish and mean than the one they believed they were going to change."[124] Leaving open the question of whether she had in fact come to believe that her son died in vain, Nelken assigned no blame. Although expelled from the party in 1942, she never joined, as historian Paul Preston emphasizes, "the ranks of the ex-Communists who were shrilly denouncing the God that failed."[125] When in 1950, Jesús Hernández, who himself had been expelled from the party in 1944, asked her to sign a letter condemning communists' attacks on Yugoslav veterans of the International Brigades, she declined, explaining she did "not want those who look after" her son's "grave to see me as an enemy."[126] Remaining silent and outwardly loyal to the cause served in Nelken's case the deeply personal purpose of coping with, if not easing, persistent sorrow by keeping her son's memory alive in the Soviet Union.

In the cases of these two Spanish women whose sons died in the Soviet Union – as in the cases of so many communists who remembered and mythologized the Spanish civil war – antifascism was not merely or primarily a political line. Rather, it functioned as a marker of identity, a link to both the Soviet Union and to an international community defined by the struggle in Spain. The memory of "our war" was both powerful and malleable. For those who defended the Nazi-Soviet Pact, the British and French "betrayal" of Spain could provide an emotionally compelling justification of the Soviet about-face. Indeed the desire to remain connected to comrades from those heroic days encouraged continued loyalty to the cause. With the Nazi invasion of the Soviet Union in 1941, atrocities that communists had momentarily "forgotten" in 1939 might link the defense of the Soviet Union to the cause of all humanity. For the former communist Nelken as much as for the communist icon Ibárruri, the memory of Spain provided a means of making sense of their loss. In some cases, for

[123] Margarita Nelken, *Las torres del Kremlin* (Mexico City: Industrial y distribuidora, 1943), 245; Preston, *Doves*, 383.

[124] Margarita Nelken to Pablo Casals, 28 February 1948, as quoted in Preston, *Doves*, 395.

[125] Preston, *Doves*, 394.

[126] Margarita Nelken to Jesús [Hernández], 4 July 1950, AMN, legajo 3237–78; I have used the translation in Preston, *Doves*, 390–1. On Hernández's expulsion, see Kirschenbaum, "Gender, Exile."

example that of French veterans of the International Brigades who fought in the maquis, local victories in this wider antifascist war might eclipse memories of the war in Spain. But even among those who had such victories to celebrate, memories of Spanish solidarity and tragedy often remained self-defining.[127] Those who had been part of the struggle in Spain remained, whether they liked it or not, part of an international community and closely associated with Moscow.

127 Skoutelsky, "L'Espagne," 30–1.

7

The Early Cold War and the Fate of "Progressive Humanity"

As World War II ended, hopes ran high that victory over Nazi Germany and fascist Italy spelled the defeat of the regime in Spain that they had fought to create. In wartime radio broadcasts from Moscow, Dolores Ibárruri struck a remarkably optimistic note, encouraging Spaniards to understand Allied victory as a prelude to the inevitable destruction of fascism in Spain.[1] In late 1944, Josef Stalin approved the dispatch of Spanish communist officers from the Soviet Union to Yugoslavia, where they received training in guerrilla warfare, and from there to the south of France, with the aim of unifying Spanish partisan groups.[2] In February 1945, Ibárruri left the Soviet Union to join her comrades in France. They had, she remembered forty years later, Stalin's full support. "Comrade Dolores," he assured her before she left, "You can count on us. The Spanish antifascist fighters are our allies."[3] In France, where exiled Spaniards had played important roles in the underground, the resistance newspaper *Combat* promoted the Spanish cause, emphasizing that the war against fascism had begun in Spain "and thus had to end there as well."[4] In January 1945, International Brigade veteran Milton Wolff, then serving with the Office

[1] "El ejército ante el futuro de España," 13 October 1944, Dirigentes PCE, caja 16/2.4, Archivo Histórico del Partido Comunista de España (AHPCE); "De ventana a ventana," 8 June 1944, ibid., caja 16/1.2; "España no será una excepción," 11 January 1945, ibid., caja 17/3.1.

[2] A. A. Sagomonian, "Sovetskii soiuz i ispanskii vopros, 1944–1947 gody: Po novym arkhivnym materialam," *Novaia i noveishaia istoriia*, 2008, no. 2: 60.

[3] Dolores Ibárruri, *Memorias de Pasionaria, 1939–1977: Me faltaba España* (Barcelona: Planeta, 1984), 90.

[4] David A. Messenger, "A Real Break or Reluctant Parting? France, the United States, and the Spanish Question, 1946," *Journal of European Studies* 38, no. 2 (2008): 142. See also Tom Buchanan, "Holding the Line: The Political Strategy of the International Brigade Association, 1939–1977," *Labour History Review* 66, no. 3 (Winter 2001): 301.

of Strategic Services (OSS), met a group of Spanish maquis operating out of southern France who predicted victory in Spain within weeks.[5] In short, the end of fascism in Spain was widely understood as the necessary last act of World War II.[6]

Even those who doubted the imminence of regime change often framed the so-called Spanish question in terms of wartime politics and emotions. In 1945, President Franklin Roosevelt reminded Carleton Hayes, the former ambassador to Spain, who considered any effort to remove Francisco Franco "unrealistic," that "the present regime in Spain is one which is repugnant to American ideas of democracy and good government."[7] Harry Truman, who assumed the presidency when Roosevelt died in April 1945, shared his predecessor's distaste for Franco, whom he described as "no different" than Adolf Hitler and Benito Mussolini.[8] Responding to still powerful "resistance rhetoric and imagery," the French National Assembly's Foreign Affairs Commission unanimously approved resolutions in May 1945 and again in August to break diplomatic relations with Spain.[9] In June 1945, delegates at the founding conference of the United Nations (UN) in San Francisco approved by acclamation a Mexican proposal barring from membership any state established with the military aid of those who had fought against the Allies – that is, Spain. As the war ended, American public opinion was solidly against Franco.[10]

Although such attitudes could be quite resilient – Truman, for one, never abandoned the equation of Franco with Hitler and Mussolini – they were, from the American point of view, increasingly problematic as the Spanish question soon become an issue in the emerging cold war.[11] The tensions were visible by early 1946, when the French proposed that the UN Security Council consider imposing sanctions against Spain. The French government continued to view Spain through the lens of World War II: Franco was rumored to be sheltering Nazi atomic scientists working on a bomb designed to reverse the outcome of the war. When in February 1946 the Spanish government executed twelve Spanish guerrillas, including Cristino García, a hero of the French resistance, the French government – a coalition of Christian Democrats, Socialists, and

5 Milton Wolff to Lennie [Leonard Lamb], 10 January 1945, Complaints of Discrimination during World War II, ALBA 069, Box 3, Folder 70, Tamiment Library/Robert F. Wagner Labor Archives, New York University; Peter N. Carroll, *The Odyssey of the Abraham Lincoln Brigade: Americans in the Spanish Civil War* (Stanford: Stanford University Press, 1994), 275; Mark Byrnes, "Unfinished Business: The United States and Franco's Spain, 1944–47," *Diplomacy and Statecraft* 11, no. 1 (March 2000): 136.

6 Irene Falcón with Manuel Jiménez and Jesús Montero, *Asalto a los cielos: Mi vida junto a Pasionaria* (Madrid: Temas de hoy, 1996), 239.

7 Quoted in Byrnes, "Unfinished Business," 136. 137.

8 Quoted in ibid., 146.

9 Messenger, "Real Break," 141, 144.

10 August 1945 Gallup poll cited in Byrnes, "Unfinished Business," 142–3.

11 On Truman see ibid., 160 n.60; Jill Edwards, *Anglo-American Relations and the Franco Question, 1945–1955* (Oxford: Clarendon Press, 1999), 173–4.

Communists – closed the border with Spain and sought British and American support against Franco. Although the appearance of supporting Franco caused "severe embarrassment,"[12] both the British and Americans rejected the French bid to take the matter to the Security Council. Much to the French government's dismay, the Soviets offered their support for the French effort. The UN ultimately recommended only a withdrawal of ambassadors from Madrid.[13]

The French proposal came at a moment when the U.S. State Department increasingly saw the Spanish question through the lens of worsening relations with the Soviet Union. In a telegram sent to the U.S. secretary of state before the French closed the border, George Kennan, the American chargé in Moscow, provided a framework for understanding the French move as serving Soviet interests. The Soviets, Kennan argued, hoped to mobilize "western opinion against Franco" in hopes of pressuring Western governments to "make strong action to bring about downfall of Franco regime." In the ensuing chaos, he predicted, the Soviets would try by means of "superior discipline and revolutionary methods" to install a communist regime in Spain.[14] In a follow-up telegram sent 1 March 1946 – after both the French decision to close the border and his own "Long Telegram" of 22 February describing the Kremlin as "impervious to logic" but "highly sensitive to logic of force" – Kennan emphasized the importance of resisting "Soviet pressure groups everywhere beginning with the French Communists."[15] The 1943 dissolution of the Comintern had done little to challenge the conviction that national parties followed Moscow's orders.[16]

Growing suspicion of alleged "Soviet pressure groups" abroad coincided with and encouraged suspicion and persecution of such groups at home. The coincidence was not necessarily planned or welcomed by U.S. policy makers. Kennan closed his "Long Telegram" with the warning that "the greatest danger

[12] Edward Johnson, "Early Indications of a Freeze: Greece, Spain, and the United Nations, 1946–47," *Cold War History* 6, no. 1 (February 2006): 50, 51. See also Enrique Moradiellos, "The Potsdam Conference and the Spanish Problem," *Contemporary European History* 10, no. 1 (March 2001): 86.

[13] "The Ambassador in France ([Jefferson] Caffrey) to the Secretary of State," 27 February 1946 in *United States Department of State, Foreign Relations of the United States, 1946* (FRUS), vol. 5, *The British Commonwealth, Western and Central Europe* (Washington, DC: U.S. Government Printing Office, 1946), 1043–4 (http://digital.library.wisc.edu/1711.dl/FRUS.FRUS1946v05); David Wingeate Pike, "Franco et l'admission aux nations unies," *Guerres mondiales et conflits contemporains* 41, no.162 (April 1991): 107–11; Messenger, "Real Break," 148–51.

[14] *FRUS*, vol. 5, 1035, 1036; Messenger, "Real Break," 149–51; Sagomonian, "Sovetskii soiuz," 63.

[15] Telegram, George Kennan to George Marshall ["Long Telegram"], 22 February 1946, Harry S. Truman Administration File, Elsey Papers, (http://www.trumanlibrary.org/whistlestop/study_collections/coldwar/documents/pdf/6--6.pdf), p. 15."The Chargé in the Soviet Union (Kennan) to the Secretary of State," 1 March 1946, *FRUS*, vol. 5, 1045.

[16] Kevin McDermott and Jeremy Agnew, *The Comintern: A History of International Communism from Lenin to Stalin* (Basingstoke: Palgrave Macmillan, 1996), 210–11.

that can befall us in coping with this problem of Soviet Communism, is that we shall allow ourselves to become like those with whom we are coping."[17] Truman had little patience with people who insisted that the Spanish Republic had been "communistic," a charge that he dismissed as "the best retreat of every opponent of liberal policies."[18] Nonetheless, the premise that the Soviets were able to mobilize and even "control" Western public opinion legitimized, perhaps required, efforts to unmask purportedly idealistic or humanitarian organizations as communist fronts.[19] Kennan's warning that the Soviets managed to infiltrate trade unions, women's groups, and youth groups dovetailed with both anticommunist sentiments that predated the cold war and the "espionage paradigm" – the conviction that the "Soviet Union and its agents were a significant and growing threat to a vulnerable United States" – that emerged during World War II.[20] From this perspective, organizations advocating sanctions against Franco were particularly dangerous: Their appeals had emotional and political resonance, but they served Soviet interests, wittingly or not. Such convictions help explain why in early 1946 the first postwar subpoenas served by the House Un-American Activities Committee (HUAC) – and the first jail terms it imposed for contempt – went to board members of the innocuous-sounding Joint Anti-Fascist Refugee Committee, a nonprofit organization devoted to aiding Spanish refugees.[21]

In these same years, a wave of purges far deadlier than the American red hunts but with sometimes similar targets moved through the Soviet Union and its satellites.[22] In the Soviet sphere an "espionage paradigm" and fears of capitalist encirclement had long predated World War II. Masked enemies, Trotskyite spies, and foreign intelligence operatives had played central roles in the scripts of the great show trials of the late 1930s – and in Soviet representations of enemies in Spain. By the late 1940s, American intelligence operatives took over the parts formerly played by Gestapo agents or Japanese spies.

17 "Long Telegram," p. 17; X [George F. Kennan], "The Sources of Soviet Conduct," *Foreign Affairs* 25, no. 4 (July 1947): 582.

18 Harry Truman to Rep. William B. Barry, 8 January 1946, as quoted in Byrnes, "Unfinished Business," 146.

19 *FRUS*, vol. 5, 1033

20 Katherine A. S. Sibley, "Soviet Military-Industrial Espionage in the United States and the Emergence of an Espionage Paradigm in US-Soviet Relations, 1941–45," *American Communist History* 2, no. 1 (2003): 22, 21; Ellen Schrecker, *The Age of McCarthyism: A Brief History with Documents*, 2d ed. (New York: Palgrave, 2002), 20.

21 "War Fund Approves Refugee Committee," *New York Times* (*NYT*), 1 September 1944; Phillip Deery, "'A Blot upon Liberty': McCarthyism, Dr. Barsky and the Joint Anti-Fascist Refugee Committee," *American Communist History* 8, no. 2 (December 2009): 167, 172–3; Howard Fast, *Being Red: A Memoir* (New York: Laurel, 1990), 146–55, 173–7; Harvey Klehr, John Earl Haynes, and Fridrikh Igorevich Firsov, *The Secret World of American Communism* (New Haven: Yale University Press, 1995), 15–16.

22 Catherine Epstein, *The Last Revolutionaries: German Communists and Their Century* (Cambridge, MA: Harvard University Press, 2003), 130.

As the new threats of the atomic age added to Soviet insecurities, the Soviet state updated the old remedy of unmasking hidden enemies.[23] Defendants identified as "rootless cosmopolitans" were charged with "groveling before the West" and spying for the United States.[24]

Although many studies have noted the prominence of Spanish civil war veterans, the so-called Spaniards, among the victims of the postwar purges in Hungary, Czechoslovakia, Romania, and East Germany, the legacy of the Spanish civil war rarely figures in synthetic accounts of the early cold war.[25] Yet paying attention to the Spanish question illuminates the degree to which a desire not only to silence but also to discredit, even demonize, interwar and wartime internationalism shaped early cold war cultures on both sides of the iron curtain. In the United States, where Spain carried straightforward political significance – those who fought for the Republic were assumed to be communists or at best fellow travelers – the taint was nonetheless more than simply ideological.[26] The networks that linked veterans to their international comrades made them dangerously "un-American," and the ties fostered by the Veterans of the Abraham Lincoln Brigade (VALB), an alleged communist front organization, magnified their potential threat as conspirators and spies. On the Soviet side, fears of espionage that had long complicated Stalinist internationalism became paramount as Spain emerged as a key nexus in trials of alleged American spies throughout the eastern bloc. That the veterans, east and west, continued to define themselves in terms of their fight for "all progressive

[23] Vojtech Mastny, *The Cold War and Soviet Insecurity: The Stalin Years* (New York: Oxford University Press, 1998), 3–7, 23, 72; Kevin McDermott and Matthew Stibbe, "Stalinist Terror in Eastern Europe: Problems, Perspectives, Interpretations," in Kevin McDermott and Matthew Stibbe, eds., *Stalinist Terror in Eastern Europe: Elite Purges and Mass Repression* (Manchester: Manchester University Press, 2010), 5.

[24] Konstantin Azadovskii and Boris Egorov, "From Anti-Westernism to Anti-Semitism: Stalin and the Impact of the 'Anti-Cosmopolitan' Campaigns on Soviet Culture," *Journal of Cold War Studies* 4, no. 1 (Winter 2002): 68, 74; Epstein, *Last Revolutionaries*, 139–43; George H. Hodos, *Show Trials: Stalinist Purges in Eastern Europe, 1948–1954* (New York: Praeger, 1987), 35; Robert Levy, *Ana Pauker: The Rise and Fall of a Jewish Communist* (Berkeley: University of California Press, 2001), 210–13.

[25] Hodos, *Show Trials*, 35, 37, 73, 99; Levy, *Ana Pauker*, 153–62; Epstein, *Last Revolutionaries*, 130, 149–50; Mastny, *Cold War*, 67, 156; Josie McLellan, *Antifascism and Memory in East Germany: Remembering the International Brigades, 1945–1989* (New York: Oxford University Press, 2004), 57–61. An exception to the neglect of Spain is David Caute, *The Dancer Defects: The Struggle for Cultural Supremacy during the Cold War* (New York: Oxford University Press, 2003). Recent studies include Jonathan Haslam, *Russia's Cold War: From the October Revolution to the Fall of the Wall* (New Haven: Yale University Press, 2011); John Lewis Gaddis, *The Cold War: A New History* (New York: Penguin, 2006); Annette Vowinckel, Marcus M. Payk, and Thomas Lindenberger, eds., *Cold War Cultures: Perspectives on Eastern and Western European Societies* (New York: Berghahn, 2012); Douglas Field, ed., *American Cold War Culture* (Edinburgh: Edinburgh University Press, 2005).

[26] Reynold Humphries, *Hollywood's Blacklists: A Political and Cultural History* (Edinburgh: Edinburgh University Press, 2008), 18.

humanity" further stoked suspicions. As both sides worked to build impermeable barriers between opposing blocs, Spain became shorthand for the dangers of permeable borders and promiscuous, rootless international interaction.

By 1950, Spain itself was no longer a front in the cold war. Seeing little advantage in further antagonizing his former allies on the Spanish question, Stalin in 1948 recalled Ibárruri to Moscow. He counseled "patience," suggesting that the Spanish party abandon guerrilla warfare. Initially resistant, the Spaniards ultimately convinced themselves, as they had in 1939, that "Stalin was right."[27] The decision meant the abandonment of hopes for a speedy end to their Soviet exile and required a readjustment of their politics. In 1950, the year the United States dispatched an ambassador to Franco's regime and approved a $62.5 million loan, Ibárruri's correspondence with Spaniards in exile railed against "the Yankee colonization of Spain."[28] In 1953, the United States acquired naval and air bases in Spain in return for $226 million in military and economic aid. Two years later, the Soviets joined a unanimous UN vote in favor of Spanish membership: part of a "package deal" that brought sixteen states into the organization.[29] The cold war divide effectively quashed the Spanish exiles' and their supporters' optimism that the war against fascism would soon end where it had begun.[30] Nonetheless, the veterans of the Spanish civil war continued to offer a powerful and often unwanted reminder of both international solidarity and "the monsters we failed to destroy."[31]

Real and Imagined Spies: West

In the early years of the cold war, spy mania gripped states on both sides of the iron curtain. In both east and west, these concerns about espionage had a

[27] Ibárruri, *Memorias de Pasionaria*, 127; Sagomonian, "Sovetskii soiuz," 70–1. See also Haslam, *Russia's Cold War*, 94–8, 104.

[28] "Al congreso español de la paz," 30 October 1951, Arxiu Nacional de Catalunya, Fons centro español de Moscú (ANC), Sig. 207; "Los americanos buscan en España carne de canon," 12 September 1950, AHPCE, Dirigentes PCE, caja 17/3.2; Sonsoles Cabeza Sánchez-Albornoz, "Posición de la República española en el exilio ante el ingreso de España en la ONU," *Cuadernos de Historia Contemporánea*, no. 17 (1995): 164; Pike, "Franco," 13–14; Edwards, *Anglo-American Relations*, 168–74.

[29] Pike, "Franco," 114; Alberto José Lleonart Amsélem, "El ingreso de España en la ONU: Obstáculos e impulsos," *Cuadernos de Historia Contemporánea*, no. 17 (1995): 114–16; "United Nations Member States," http://www.un.org/News/Press/docs/2006/org1469.doc.htm (accessed 15 November 2014).

[30] Matilde Eiroa San Francisco, "Sobrevivir en el socialismo: Organización y medios de comunicación de los exilados comunistas en las democracias populares, "*Historia social* 69 (2011) : 82; Santiago Carrillo, *Memorias: El testimonio polémico de un protagonista relevante de nuestra transición* (Barcelona : Planeta, 2008), 542–52.

[31] Charlotte Delbo, *Auschwitz and After*, trans. Rosette C. Lamont (New Haven: Yale University Press, 1995), 260.

basis in reality. Soviet spies really acquired atomic secrets, although how vital they were to the Soviet bomb project remains an open question.[32] The U.S. government really organized covert operations to destabilize Soviet satellites, although none were successful.[33] The processes and the outcomes of Soviet and American espionage and counterespionage varied enormously, which is hardly surprising given their great differences in political culture.[34] Yet both sides can be described as often responding irrationally even to documented security threats and as frequently exaggerating or fabricating the dangers. The hysteria owed much to the tense and unstable world situation; ordinary people, if not the leaders, on both sides feared that conflicts in Berlin or Korea would spark World War III.[35] Still, such circumstances do not fully explain the depth of the shared anxiety. Focusing on the veterans of the Spanish civil war among the suspects on both sides opens a new perspective on the spy mania, suggesting that it was rooted not only in abiding fears of war, espionage, and sabotage but also in efforts to contain, discipline, and disgrace individuals whose (often celebrated) histories of crossing borders and hybrid identities challenged increasingly rigid global divisions.

During World War II, mounting evidence of Soviet military and industrial espionage in the United States had prompted "a vast expansion in the nation's security and counterintelligence apparatus."[36] By the late 1940s, that apparatus had exposed sometimes damaging acts of espionage. Historians long treated with skepticism the information that former Soviet spy Elizabeth Bentley provided to the FBI when she defected in 1945.[37] However, recently-opened American, Soviet, and Hungarian archives have confirmed many of her claims; the Alger Hiss case remains controversial, but even here much evidence

32 Christof Laucht, *Elemental Germans: Klaus Fuchs, Rudolf Peierls and the Making of British Nuclear Culture, 1939–59* (New York: Palgrave Macmillan, 2012), 90–3; Vladislav Zubok, "Atomic Espionage and its Soviet 'Witnesses,'" *Cold War International History Project Bulletin*, no. 4 (September 1994): 50, 52–3 (http://www.wilsoncenter.org/sites/default/files/CWIHPBulletin4_p2.pdf, accessed 15 November 2014); V. I. Lota, "Vklad voennykh razvedchikov v sozdanie otechestvennogo atomnogo oruzhiia, 1941–1945 gg.," *Voenno-istoricheskii zhurnal*, 2006, no. 11: 40–4.

33 Sarah-Jane Corke, *US Covert Operations and Cold War Strategy: Truman, Secret Warfare and the CIA, 1943–53* (New York: Routledge, 2008); Peter Grose, *Operation Rollback: America's Secret War behind the Iron Curtain* (Boston: Houghton Mifflin, 2000).

34 Kristie Macrakis, "Technophilic Hubris and Espionage Styles during the Cold War," *ISIS: Journal of the History of Science in Society* 101, no. 2 (June 2010): 378–85.

35 Fast, *Being Red*, 264; John Gates, *The Story of an American Communist* (New York: Thomas Nelson, 1958), 133–4; Scott Martelle, *The Fear Within: Spies, Commies, and American Democracy on Trial* (New Brunswick, NJ: Rutgers University Press, 2011), 94–5, 233–4; Elena Zubkova, *Russia after the War: Hopes, Illusions, and Disappointments, 1945–1957*, trans. Hugh Ragsdale (Armonk, NY: M. E. Sharpe, 1998), 82–3; Harrison E. Salisbury, *A Journey for Our Times* (New York: Carroll and Graf, 1983), 369–73.

36 Sibley, "Soviet Military-Industrial Espionage," 22, 21.

37 David Caute, *The Great Fear: The Anti-Communist Purge under Truman and Eisenhower* (New York: Simon and Schuster, 1978), 56.

supports her story that he was a Soviet agent.[38] Similarly, the atomic espionage case of Ethel and Julius Rosenberg, who were sentenced to death in 1951 and executed in 1953, remains contentious; however, available evidence suggests that Julius (but not Ethel) indeed engaged in extensive industrial and atomic espionage.[39]

As revelations such as Bentley's underscored the reach of Soviet wartime espionage, and as troubling events such as the Chinese revolution and the Soviet detonation of an atomic bomb provided further evidence of American vulnerability, the security apparatus constructed during World War II grew into an enormous, sometimes demagogic anticommunist contraption designed to ferret out all manner of communist activity. The U.S. government used legislative, judicial, and administrative means to locate and persecute communists: hearings before the House Un-American Activities Committee, criminal prosecutions under the Alien Registration Act of 1940 (the Smith Act) for advocating the overthrow of the U.S. government, and registration of front organizations by the Subversive Activities Control Board (SACB), respectively.[40] In these circumstances Bentley's testimony, which pointed to actual spies such as Julius Rosenberg, also set in motion the harassment of individuals "guilty" only of being or of having been communists. When Bentley revealed that Lee Fuhr (Lini De Vries) had recruited her into the party, the veteran nurse who had served in Spain became the target of FBI surveillance that forced her out of a number of jobs. Ultimately, she emigrated to Mexico.[41]

38 Eduard Mark, "*In Re* Alger Hiss: A Final Verdict from the Files of the KGB," *Journal of Cold War Studies* 11, no. 3 (Summer 2009): 26–67; John Earl Haynes and Harvey Klehr, *Venona: Decoding Soviet Espionage in America* (New Haven: Yale University Press, 1999), 167–72; Schrecker, *The Age*, 21–3, 31–42; Sibley, "Soviet Military-Industrial Espionage," 21–61; Mária Schmidt, "Noel Field – The American Communist at the Center of Stalin's East European Purge: From the Hungarian Archives," *American Communist History* 3, no. 2 (2004): 229–30, 242–3.

39 Steven T. Usdin, "The Rosenberg Ring Revealed: Industrial-Scale Nuclear and Conventional Espionage," *Journal of Cold War Studies* 11, no. 3 (Summer 2009): 91–143; John Earl Haynes and Harvey Klehr, *Early Cold War Spies: The Espionage Trials that Shaped American Politics* (New York: Cambridge University Press, 2006), 166, 176; for a more skeptical view, Bernice Schrank, "Reading the Rosenbergs after Venona," *Labour / Le Travail* 49 (Spring 2002): 189–210; Lori Clune, "Great Importance World-Wide: Presidential Decision-Making and the Executions of Julius and Ethel Rosenberg," *American Communist History* 10, no. 3 (December 2011): 266–7, 283.

40 Robert Lichtman and Ronald D. Cohen, "Harvey Matusow, the FBI, and the Justice Department: Becoming a Government Informer-Witness in the McCarthy Era," *American Communist History* 1, no. 1 (2002): 43–4, 46.

41 Elizabeth Bentley, *Out of Bondage* (New York: Devin-Adair, 1951); Kathryn Olmsted, *Red Spy Queen: A Biography of Elizabeth Bentley* (Chapel Hill: University of North Carolina Press, 2002), 8–10; Lauren Kessler, *Clever Girl: Elizabeth Bentley, the Spy Who Ushered in the Cold War* (New York: HarperCollins, 2003), 33–51; "Lini Moekerk De Vries," Fredericka Martin Papers, ALBA 001, Box 6, Folder 20, Tamiment Library/Robert F. Wagner Labor Archives, New York University; Fredericka Martin, report on interview with Lini Fuhr, 1980, Martin Papers, Box 6, Folder 23; Lini Fuhr, "Up from the Cellar" [typescript], Martin Papers,

Although the Smith Act prosecutions had "nothing to do with espionage," they reflected the assumption of the most zealous red hunters that every communist constituted a potential Soviet agent.[42] Essentially making it illegal to advocate communism, the Smith Act provided a means of pursing criminal charges against communists when the government lacked sufficient evidence for espionage prosecutions. The 1949 prosecution of eleven national leaders of the Communist Party of the United States directly followed the failed effort to obtain espionage indictments on the basis of Bentley's testimony, which could not be corroborated. Indeed the same grand jury that heard Bentley issued the indictments for the leaders of the Communist Party, who were charged not with spying or sabotage but with conspiring to "teach and advocate the overthrow and destruction of the Government of the United States by force and violence."[43] Similarly, Steve Nelson's 1948 appearance before the HUAC focused on FBI intelligence that seemed to establish his connection to efforts to pass atomic secrets to the Soviets; however, both his 1952 conviction under Pennsylvania's sedition statue and his 1953 conviction under the federal Smith Act relied not on evidence of espionage but rather, like the other Smith Act trials, on criminalizing speech. (In 1957, the U.S. Supreme Court found the Smith Act unconstitutional on First Amendment grounds.[44]) In some cases, Smith Act convictions rested on the perjury of "professional witnesses" paid by the government, a practice that suggests a desire – whether driven by fear or political ambition – for conviction by any means necessary.[45]

The lives of Milly Bennett and Hans Amlie illustrate how the presumed linkage of communism and subversion affected even obscure communists – perhaps by 1943, former communists – who posed no risk to national security. During the war, the FBI investigated both Bennett and Amlie, raising questions about her status as an alleged spy for the Spanish Republic and his communist past, including his service in Spain.[46] Bennett, if not Amlie, seemed to experience the surveillance as harassment. When an agent stopped by to

Box 6, Folder 27, pp. 112–17, 194; Cedric Belfrage, *The American Inquisition, 1945–1960* (Indianapolis: Bobbs-Merrill, 1973), 19, 45–7.

42 Schrank, "Reading the Rosenbergs," 193; Ellen Schrecker, "Before the Rosenbergs: Espionage Scenarios in the Early Cold War," in Marjorie Garber and Rebecca L. Walkowitz, eds., *Secret Agents: The Rosenberg Case, McCarthyism, and Fifties America* (New York: Routledge, 1995), 129.

43 Martelle, *Fear Within*, 19–23, 31, 40, 68–9; "Text of Indictment of 12 Communists," *NYT*, 17 January 1949; Schrecker, "Before the Rosenbergs," 135.

44 "Text of Report by House Committee on Un-American Activities Relating to Atomic Espionage," *NYT*, 28 September 1948; "Steve Nelson Guilty on 12 Sedition Counts," *NYT*, 1 February 1952; "Five Convicted as Reds in Long Trial at Pittsburgh," *NYT*, 21 August 1953; Julia M. Allen, "'That Accursed Aesopian Language': Prosecutorial Framing of Linguistic Evidence in *US v. Foster*, 1949," *Rhetoric and Public Affairs* 4, no. 1 (2001): 109–34; Martelle, *Fear Within*, 251–3.

45 Lichtman and Cohen, "Harvey Matusow," 45–6, 65–6.

46 See Chapter 6.

interview them in early 1943, Bennett took the opportunity "to berate the Federal Bureau of Investigation for conducting investigations of alleged members of the Communist Party." The agent, clearly annoyed, noted in his report that the "jurisdiction of the Bureau in such matters was explained to her." He did not note Bennett's response.[47] That confrontation notwithstanding, the investigation found "no evidence of Communist activity," and in July 1943 the Bureau cleared Amlie to continue as an employee of the federal government.[48]

As the cold war fed fears of Soviet espionage and sabotage, Amlie and Bennett found themselves once again under suspicion. In 1948, the FBI's Phoenix office recommended reopening the case and preparing a security index card identifying Amlie as a native-born communist.[49] Acknowledging that the earlier investigation had "failed to disclose present membership" in the Communist Party, the Phoenix agent emphasized that Amlie admitted that "he had fought with the Abraham Lincoln Battalion," an admission that warranted including him on the index of "dangerous" persons – this despite the fact that in 1943 Attorney General Francis Biddle had prohibited such a list as "unpractical, unwise, and dangerous."[50] In June 1948, FBI director J. Edgar Hoover confirmed that the "security index card has been prepared at the Bureau."[51] In January 1949, "in view of the tense international situation at the present time" – Hoover may have had in mind the progress of the Chinese Communists to Beijing – the director requested an updated report on Amlie. The Phoenix office thus interviewed at least a half-dozen of Amlie and Bennett's neighbors, but "developed" no evidence "of Communistic membership or activities."[52] In June 1949, the Bureau canceled its security index card on Amlie.[53] His death six months later, the result of a farm accident, did not, however, end the matter for his widow, who herself became the subject of a reinvestigation in 1950.[54]

Bennett's connections not only to Spain but also to China and the Soviet Union apparently established her as a potential threat. The FBI's renewed interest in her stemmed from the fact that her name appeared in the Shanghai Municipal Police records in relation to her work in the 1920s at the communist-affiliated Chung Mei News Agency.[55] Given the recent "loss" of China, the FBI saw such connections in a new and sinister light. Particularly suspicious were

47 "Report made by James T. Mullan," 1 March 1943, Mildred Bremler [Milly Bennett] Federal Bureau of Investigation File, HQ 100–124391/SF 100–12592 (FBI/Bennett).

48 "Report made by William John Hurley," 1 July 1943, FBI/Bennett.

49 Kenneth Logan to Director, FBI, 22 April 1948, FBI/Bennett.

50 SAC [Special Agent in Charge], Phoenix to Director, FBI, 3 May 1948, FBI/Bennett; attorney general quoted in Sibley, "Soviet Military-Industrial Espionage," 30.

51 John Edgar Hoover to Special Agent in Charge, Phoenix, 11 June 1948, FBI/Bennett.

52 "Report made by Robert C. Moody," 13 May 1949, FBI/Bennett.

53 SAC, Phoenix to Director, FBI, 15 June 1949, 19 December 1949, FBI/Bennett.

54 SAC, Phoenix, to Director, 12 October 1950; SAC Washington Field to Director, FBI, 22 June 1951, FBI/Bennett.

55 "Report made by Donald G. Hanning," 30 July 1951, FBI/Bennett.

her associations – more than twenty years previously– with William Prohme, a "notorious Communist," and Wilbur Burton, "said to be in the pay of the Soviet government," her then-lover and the twin brother of Wallace Burton to whom she was briefly engaged in Spain.[56] The FBI tried, without success, to uncover a connection between her and the Richard Sorge spy ring.[57] Bennett's long-term acquaintance in both China and the Soviet Union with Mikhail Borodin also attracted the FBI's attention, as it tried to determine whether one of his American-born sons was involved in Soviet espionage.[58]

Despite the scantiness of the evidence linking Bennett to the party, let alone to espionage, the FBI persisted in tracking her. Throughout 1952, its San Francisco office made repeated efforts to contact her, but was unable to do so because she was in Hawaii.[59] When Bennett finally returned to San Francisco in October 1952, the FBI's request for an interview was met by a phone call from Ernest Besig, the director of the American Civil Liberties Union of Northern California, who informed agents that "he would permit an interview" with Bennett "only in his office, at his convenience and in his presence." The memo to Hoover outlining the conditions was annotated with an emphatic "*No!*" in the margin and a directive to place a copy of "this serial" in Besig's file.[60] Whether or not Bennett had by then become an anticommunist, as Freda Utley, an old friend from Moscow, claimed in her 1970 memoir, she evidently retained the hostility to the FBI's investigations that she had displayed in 1943.[61]

Only in April 1953, after tracking her for the better part of a decade, did the FBI close Bennett's case. A handwritten note on the memo noting the decision summarized the reasons for ending the investigation: "No bona fide espionage or other complaint... Subject practically blind now – not considered to warrant S.I. [security index]."[62] Nonetheless, in late 1953, the San Francisco office once again attempted to "interrogate" Bennett without a third party

56 Ibid. The report references a State Department memorandum, 14 July 1933, National Archives College Park, Maryland (NACP), Record Group (RG) 59, 800.00B-Burton, Wilbur H/1.

57 SAC, San Francisco to Director FBI, 19 November 1951; Director, FBI to SAC, San Francisco, 13 December 1951, FBI/Bennett; A. G. Feslun, "Novye dokumenty po 'delu Zorge,'" *Novaia i noveishaia istoriia*, no. 2 (March 2000): 118–46.

58 SAC, San Francisco to Director, FBI, 23 May 1952; Director, FBI to SAC, New York, 9 April 1952, FBI/Bennett. Michael Gruzenberg [Borodin], Federal Bureau of Investigation 65-HQ-58053. On Norman Borodin, who was a Soviet agent, see http://www.hrono.ru/biograf/bio_b/borodin_nm.html (accessed 15 November 2014).

59 SAC, San Francisco to Director, FBI, 8 October 1952, FBI/Bennett. For earlier attempts to contact her, see SAC, San Francisco to Director, FBI, 3 January 1952, 22 March 1952, 23 May 1952, 8 July 1952, FBI/Bennett.

60 SAC, San Francisco to Director, FBI, 30 October 1952, FBI/Bennett. On Besig see Judy Kutulas, "In Quest of Autonomy: The Northern California Affiliate of the American Civil Liberties Union and World War II," *Pacific Historical Review* 67, no. 2 (May 1998): 201–31.

61 Freda Utley, *Odyssey of a Liberal: Memoirs* (Washington, DC: Washington National Press, 1970), 246.

62 SAC, San Francisco to Director, FBI, 6 April 1953; handwritten note dated 23 April 1953, FBI/Bennett.

present, in the hope that she might provide information on Anna Louise Strong or Owen Lattimore, a Far Eastern specialist at Johns Hopkins charged with perjury.[63] Indeed, in May 1959, in response to a request apparently from British intelligence, the FBI prepared yet another report on her activities.[64] Bennett died of cancer a year later, at age sixty-four.[65]

Although the FBI turned up no evidence to suggest that Bennett constituted a security risk, the decision to keep tabs on her for a decade was hardly surprising or unusual. A Jewish (former) communist (or fellow traveler) with ties to the Soviet Union, Spain, and China, she was the quintessential usual suspect. As the FBI's decision to reopen its file on Amlie illustrates, veterans of the International Brigades, not to mention reputed spies for the Republic, were presumed communist and dangerous. Association with the Abraham Lincoln battalion, deemed suspicious in its own right, also lent seeming credibility to charges that had little connection to Spain. Bennett's years in the Soviet Union and, especially after 1949, to China further marked her as dangerous. Her long-term connections with Borodin and Strong, both of whom had deep links to the Chinese revolution, reinforced suspicions. Antisemitism, a "barely disguised" subtext in many anticommunist investigations, is hard to discern in Bennett's FBI file, which only hints at her Jewish background, noting that she was born Mildred Bremler and that her father Max Bremler was born in "Posen, Germany, Poland."[66] Whether or not antisemitism was a factor in Bennett's case, Jews often found themselves under suspicion as communists – and communists were often assumed to be Jews. The ranks of the un-Americans included large number of minorities, including Jews, notably on the Hollywood blacklists, as well as homosexuals and African Americans – perhaps the only two "dangerous" categories into which Bennett did not fit.[67]

Such profiling was a central means of conflating membership in the Communist Party and subversive activity. A 1948 HUAC report on atomic espionage relied on such incriminating associations, describing Nelson as a known communist, who in 1934 had been "seen in Russia" where, under an alias, "he appeared to be engaged in taking various Communist courses of instruction,"

63 Director, FBI to SAC, San Francisco, 23 December 1953, FBI/Bennett; "Lattimore Moves to Kill Indictment," *NYT*, 17 February 1953; Robert P. Newman, *Owen Lattimore and the "Loss" of China* (Berkeley: University of California Press, 1992), 365–377.

64 Director, FBI to Legat, London, 5 May 1959, FBI/Bennett.

65 "Milly Bennett, 64, Former Reporter," *NYT*, 7 November 1960.

66 Paul Buhle, "The Hollywood Blacklist and the Jew," *Tikkun* 10, no. 5 (September/October 1995): 35; "Report made by William P. Jones," 20 November 1942, FBI/Bennett. After Germany's defeat in 1945, all of Posen/Poznań came under Polish control.

67 Humphries, *Hollywood's Blacklists*, 12–14, 41, 82; Morton J. Horwitz, "Jews and McCarthyism: A View from the Bronx," in *Secret Agents*, 257–64; David K. Johnson, *The Lavender Scare: The Cold War Persecution of Gays and Lesbians in the Federal Government* (Chicago: University of Chicago Press, 2004); Martin Halpern, "'I'm Fighting for Freedom': Coleman Young, HUAC, and the Detroit African American Community," *Journal of American Ethnic History* 17, no. 1 (Fall 1997): 19–38; Martelle, *Fear Within*, 196.

and in 1937 "was evidently fighting in the war in Spain."[68] Although not mentioned in the report, the FBI file on which the hearing relied described Nelson as having "Jewish" features, a detail the agent seemed to think relevant to the investigation.[69] In Nelson's case, unlike Bennett's, the FBI turned up evidence of espionage, but that evidence – not enough to support an indictment – was strengthened by the fact that he, like Bennett and so many others who found themselves before juries and congressional inquiries, neatly fit the profile of the world revolutionary connected to "dangerous" people and places. Such profiling made it easy to confuse real and imagined spies.

Real and Imagined Spies: East

Soviet spy mania, too, had grounding in reality. As early as 1949, Soviet agents infiltrated American and British guerrilla training camps in Europe and learned of the newly organized Central Intelligence Agency's (CIA) ambitious plans to destabilize Soviet-backed governments in Eastern Europe. The most infamous covert operation of this period, dubbed the "Albania tragedy" by a former CIA agent who helped plan it, was apparently undermined by double agent Kim Philby who, from his perch in British intelligence learned the details down to the drop sites for Albanian anticommunists parachuted in to lead the resistance, and turned them over to the Soviets. In similar operations attempted throughout Eastern Europe, "failure was the rule rather than the exception."[70] Of course even failed plans could inflame anxieties, especially when they were foiled by Soviet counterespionage.[71] The Soviets, like the Americans, uncovered enough evidence of covert activity to conclude that espionage posed a clear and present danger.[72] However, because American intelligence relied more on technology than human spies, the Americans never operated – and thus the Soviets never uncovered – anything like the far-reaching Rosenberg or Sorge spy networks.[73]

The most sensational Soviet bloc espionage cases in these years thus involved "spies" invented by the Soviet political police. In February 1949, the Soviet government expelled Anna Louise Strong as an American spy and arrested

[68] "Text of Report."

[69] Sibley, "Soviet Military-Industrial Espionage," 40.

[70] Quotations from John Limond Hart, *The CIA's Russians* (Annapolis, MD: Naval Institute Press, 2003), 6, 2; Corke, *US Covert*, 2–3; Grose, *Operation Rollback*.

[71] David Stafford, *Spies Beneath Berlin* (New York: Overlook Press, 2003); David E. Murphy, Sergei A. Kondrashev, and George Bailey, *Battleground Berlin: CIA vs. KGB in the Cold War* (New Haven: Yale University Press, 1997); George Feifer, "The Berlin Tunnel," *MHQ: Quarterly Journal of Military History* 10, no. 2 (Winter 1998): 62–71.

[72] Trevor Barnes, "The Secret Cold War: The CIA and American Foreign Policy in Europe, 1946–56, Part I," *Historical Journal* 24, no. 2 (June 1981): 399–415; Hart, *CIA's Russians*, 18; David E. Murphy, "Spies in Berlin: A Hidden Key to the Cold War," *Foreign Affairs* 77, no. 4 (July/August 1988): 171–8.

[73] Macrakis, "Technophilic Hubris," 380; P. P. Shchelchkov, "Brosok amerikanskogo diversanta na Sakhalin," *Voenno-istoricheskii zhurnal*, 2001, no. 10: 36–40.

most of the *Moscow News* staff, including Borodin. Strong was hardly an American agent. Skeptics suggested that the expulsion was a Soviet ruse to raise her prestige among anticommunists.[74] Strong, however, did little to win over anticommunists, because she blamed her arrest not on the Soviets, who held her at Lubianka for five days, prohibiting contact with the American embassy, but rather on the "war hysteria which the American Press has done so much to stir up."[75] The Soviets themselves seem to have been particularly concerned about Strong's pro-Chinese sentiments and apparently decided that charging her with being an American spy constituted a clever way of countering her enthusiastic promotion of Mao Zedong's brand of communism. The expulsion also rid them of a supporter who had turned into a nuisance, complaining to anyone who would listen that the Soviet government refused to grant her a transit visa to Manchuria.[76]

The lack of evidence notwithstanding, the Strong case served the broader Soviet purpose of ratcheting up the spy scare. Western journalists in Moscow, spooked by her expulsion and subject to a constant barrage of anti-American propaganda, immediately grasped the connection. Harrison Salisbury, who arrived as the *New York Times*'s Moscow correspondent shortly after Strong's expulsion, warned the newspaper's publisher Arthur Hays Sulzberger that anyone connected with the West was under suspicion. He worried that the "next 'case' will not be a mere eviction as in the instance of [NBC correspondent Bob] Magidoff and Anna Louise Strong but a public trial and a prison term." In May 1949, the Soviet journal *Ogonek* seemed to confirm Salisbury's admittedly "fantastic" fears, accusing American foreign correspondents of being "trained intelligence agents, spies, diversionists and devoted servants of capitalism."[77]

The unmasking of an alleged American agent was linked to the antiwestern and antisemitic purges then gearing up in the Soviet Union and its satellites. Although Borodin's connections to the "spy" Strong may have put him at risk, his arrest was also part of the so-called anticosmopolitan campaign. A secular Jew who had lived for more than a decade in the United States and who had since 1932 been the editor of the English-language *Moscow News*, Borodin

74 "Skepticism Voiced over Anna Strong," *NYT*, 16 February 1949; "Subpoenaed by U.S. Grand Jury," *NYT*, 24 February 1949; "Jury Hears Writer Moscow Expelled," *NYT*, 26 February 1949.

75 Tracy B. Strong and Helene Keyssar, *Right in Her Soul: The Life of Anna Louise Strong* (New York: Random House, 1983), 241–9, quotation from Associated Press report, 252; Bertram D. Hulen, "Soviet Bars Talk with Miss Strong," *NYT*, 18 February 1949; Philip Jaffe, "The Strange Case of Anna Louise Strong," *Survey*, no. 53 (1964): 131–9; "Miss Strong Arrives Here by Air," *NYT*, 24 February 1949.

76 Jaffe, "Strange Case," 137–8; Strong and Keyssar, *Right in Her Soul*, 243–4. On Soviet relations with Mao, see Haslam, *Russia's Cold War*, 112–16.

77 Harrison Salisbury to Arthur Hays Sulzberger, 15 April 1949, Harrison E. Salisbury Papers, Box 187, Folder 2, pp. 1, 2, Columbia University Rare Book and Manuscript Library; "Expelled Reporter Quits Russia," *NYT*, 19 April 1948; "US Correspondents 'Spies,' Says Russian," *NYT*, 9 May 1949.

could easily be fitted into the preferred categories of the postwar purges as a "rootless cosmopolitan," guilty of "groveling before the West." The *Moscow News* itself, whose staff a Kremlin official described in 1948 as consisting of "one Russian, one Armenian, twenty-three Jews and three others," was seen as a hotbed of cosmopolitanism and fell victim to the antisemitic crackdown.[78] Having worked during the war to document Nazi crimes against Soviet Jews, Borodin was also linked to the Jewish Antifascist Committee, itself a primary purge target.[79] Arrested in 1949, he died in 1951, probably shot in prison.[80]

In the Soviet satellites, real concerns about security likewise produced an urgent campaign against imagined spies, saboteurs, traitors, and a wide range of enemies, often defined by their ties to the West and increasingly identified as Jews.[81] The Soviet political police in coordination with local authorities concocted an elaborate espionage plot around Noel Field, the most notorious "spy" unmasked on the Soviet side during the early years of the cold war. Field, who knew a large number of East European communists as a result of his relief work in French internment camps following the Spanish civil war and in Switzerland during World War II, had at one time been a *Soviet* agent. During the war he had also worked to establish mutually beneficial relations between the OSS and underground communist resistance groups. By late 1948, as the case of his friend and former colleague in the State Department Hiss was breaking in the United States, Field decided to seek refuge in Eastern Europe. In May 1949, he was arrested in Prague and handed over to Hungarian security. Soviet agents supervised his interrogation in Budapest, extracting under torture the confessions subsequently used against communists throughout the Soviet bloc.[82] Later his wife, brother, and adopted daughter, the child of a German communist doctor who served in Spain, were arrested in Prague, Warsaw, and East Berlin, respectively; their coerced confessions further extended

78 G. V. Kostyrchenko, *Tainaia politika Stalina: Vlast' i antisemitzm* (Moscow: Mezhdunardnye otnosheniia, 2001), 329.

79 "Testimony by Isaac Fefer," in Joshua Rubenstein and Vladimir P. Naumov, eds., *Stalin's Secret Pogrom: The Postwar Inquisition of the Jewish Anti-Fascist Committee* (New Haven: Yale University Press, 2001), 103; Marina Sorokina, "People and Procedures: Toward a History of the Investigation of Nazi Crimes in the USSR," *Kritika* 6, no. 4 (Fall 2005): 816 n.59; Anna Arutunyan, "A Parallel Universe of Positive Soviet Facts," *Moscow News*, 30 May 2009 (http://rbth.ru/articles/2009/05/30/300509_universe.html, accessed 15 November 2014).

80 "Borodin (Gruzenberg) Mikhail Markovich," http://www.hrono.ru/biograf/bio_b/borodin_gizb.php (accessed 15 November 2014). Some sources claim he died in a Siberian labor camp. Theodore Shabad, "Soviet Rehabilitates Borodin, Aide in China in '20's," *NYT*, 1 July 1964; Dan N. Jacobs, *Borodin: Stalin's Man in China* (Cambridge, MA: Harvard University Press, 1981), 326.

81 McDermott and Stibbe, "Stalinist Terror," 5–10.

82 Schmidt, "Noel Field," 235–9, 224–5; Igor Lukes, "The Rudolf Slánský Affair: New Evidence," *Slavic Review* 58, no. 1 (Spring 1999): 168–71; Thomas Sakmyster, "Mátyás Rákosi, the Rajk Trial, and the American Communist Party," *Hungarian Studies Review* 38, no. 1–2 (Spring-Fall 2011): 45–6; Mark, "*In Re* Alger Hiss," 31–2.

and embroidered the plot.[83] With superhuman prescience, Field had allegedly masterminded a vast conspiracy, recruiting, as early as 1939, the future leaders of the postwar people's democracies as double agents ready to undermine states that did not yet exist. Field himself was never tried; he and his family were released in 1954 and 1955.

In the Soviet bloc, as in the Soviet Union (and indeed, the United States), particular profiles more than specific acts raised suspicions.Although local concerns and international events produced different patterns throughout the Soviet bloc, the usual suspects in the far-reaching conspiracy allegedly orchestrated by Field fell into a number of clear and often overlapping categories: those returning from exile or concentration camps in the West, many of whom had fought in the wartime resistance; the leaders of home underground movements; veterans of the International Brigades; and Jews.[84] The 1949 show trial in Hungary, which followed Stalin's decision to attack what he considered Josep Broz Tito's renegade communist regime in Yugoslavia, focused on a Titoist plot and implicated a number of Hungarian communists connected to the American party. The chief defendant, the former minister of the interior László Rajk, was charged with being the "agent of a European Trotskyist organization, which was in contact with the Americans" and later with the Yugoslavs, who allegedly took over the American spy network.[85] The primary "evidence" was Field's confession and Rajk's biography. In addition to being General-Secretary Mátyás Rákosi's primary political rival, Rajk fit three suspicious categories: A veteran of the Spanish civil war, he spent three years in a French internment camp before escaping and returning to Hungary in 1941, where he became a leader of the communist underground.[86]

In Czechoslovakia the proceedings took on an overtly antisemitic tone.[87] Eleven of the fourteen party leaders tried in 1952 were Jews, including the former general-secretary Rudolf Slánský. He fit no other "dangerous" categories; being neither a Spaniard nor a veteran of resistance movements in the West, Slánský fell into the usually safer category of "Muscovite," having remained in Czechoslovakia until 1938 when he fled to the Soviet Union.[88] Slánský's

83 Lukes, "Rudolf Slánský," 169–70; Schmidt, "Noel Field," 225–6; Hermann H. Field and Kate Field, *Trapped in the Cold War: The Ordeal of an American Family* (Stanford: Stanford University Press, 1999); Erica Glaser Wallach, *Light at Midnight* (Garden City, NY: Doubleday, 1967).

84 Hodos, *Show Trials*, 35; Karel Bartošek, "Central and Southeastern Europe," in Stéphane Courtois et al., eds., *The Black Book of Communism: Crimes, Terror, Repression*, trans. Jonathan Murphy and Mark Kramer (Cambridge, MA: Harvard University Press, 1999), 428–31; McDermott and Stibbe, "Stalinist Terror," 8–9.

85 Mihály Farkas quoted in Schmidt, "Noel Field," 216, 217; Sakmyster, "Mátyás Rákosi," 45–7.

86 Hodos, *Show Trials*, 36–7; Schmidt, "Noel Field," 216.

87 Hodos, *Show Trials*, 74.

88 Kevin McDermott, "A 'Polyphony of Voices'? Czech Popular Opinion and the Slánský Affair," *Slavic Review* 67, no. 4 (Winter 2008): 846–9.

right-hand man, Bedřich Geminder, who was accused of having contacts with Israeli diplomats and "agents of Western imperialism," had Jewish origins as well as personal ties to the West; not a Spanish civil war veteran, he was the former lover of Ibárruri's long-time secretary Irene Falcón.[89]

The targeting of these individuals rested on the assumption that people with transnational or "cosmopolitan" contacts, even within international communist circles, could be, and likely were, spies. Klement Gottwald, the communist president of Czechoslovakia, offered the explanation that International Brigade veterans in French internment camps had "lived in appalling conditions" and were "subjected to pressure and blackmail first from the French and American espionage services, and later by the Germans," who "managed to enlist a number of them as agents."[90] The biographies of many communists in Czechoslovakia could be understood as fitting this narrative. For example, Artur London's now suspicious behavior included fighting in both the International Brigades and French resistance, surviving Mauthausen, and recuperating in a Swiss hospital run by the Unitarian Service Committee, the employer of alleged American master spy Field.[91] Purges in Poland, Romania, and East Germany likewise played on suspicions of leaders, often with Jewish origins, who had international connections, notably Waclaw Komar (Mendel Kossoj), a veteran of both the International Brigades and the Polish Army in France, and Romanian International Brigade veterans Valter Roman (Ernö Neuländer) and Elisabeta Luca (née Birnbaum).[92] Purged German veterans included Franz Dahlem and Gerhart Eisler, who had spent the war years in the United States. Having been deemed a dangerous Soviet agent by the FBI and facing prison, Eisler fled the United States in 1949 as a stowaway. By 1953, the daring escape had come to be interpreted as part of an elaborate plot to infiltrate an American agent into East Germany.[93]

The selection of show trial defendants and purge targets was arbitrary in the sense that none had engaged in espionage or sabotage. Still, the particular categories from which they were chosen, as Kevin McDermott and Matthew Stibbe emphasize in their overview of "Stalinist terror in eastern Europe," highlight the degree to which purges aimed to create the "monolithic homogeneity" deemed essential – in Moscow as much as Prague or Budapest – to the construction of socialism.[94] The quest for homogeneity and purification of the body politic

[89] Karel Kaplan, *Report on the Murder of the General Secretary*, trans. Karel Kovanda (Columbus: Ohio State University Press, 1990), 194; Falcón, *Asalto a los cielos*,278–9.

[90] Quoted in Artur London, *The Confession*, trans. Alastair Hamilton (New York: William Morrow, 1970), 90.

[91] London, *Confession*, 83–114; Hodos, *Show Trials*, 78; Bartošek, "Central and Southeastern," 430–1.

[92] Teresa Toranska, *Them: Stalin's Political Puppets*, trans. Agnieszka Kolakowska (New York: Harper and Row, 1987), 331–2; Levy, *Ana Pauker*, 161, 198, 213.

[93] Epstein, *Last Revolutionaries*, 91–9, 140–1, 143–7.

[94] McDermott and Stibbe, "Stalinist Terror," 5.

had also been a factor in the Soviet terror of the late 1930s. However, that earlier terror had coexisted, however uneasily, with a pervasive and powerful internationalism symbolized above all by Soviet and international communist aid for the Spanish Republic. In the 1930s, international networks appeared at once threatening and galvanizing, offering both potentially dangerous conduits of hidden foreign enemies and a vital means of creating Moscow-centered solidarity if not homogeneity. The early cold war, by contrast, marked a victory of suspicion over solidarity. Ties to the West that had come in loyal service to the cause now worked to call loyalty into question. Indeed the trials of communists in the Soviet satellites attempted to rewrite the past and individual biographies, transforming the noblest of contacts with the West – in Spain, in resistance organizations, in Nazi camps – into evidence of treason.

Communists on Trial

Beginning in 1949, large numbers of prominent communists went on trial in the United States and in Eastern Europe, charged on both sides of the iron curtain with seeking the overthrow of their respective governments. The parallel trials constituted one of the stranger ironies of the cold war, although American communists convinced of the guilt of those accused in the Soviet satellites, and who, like their foreign comrades, saw their own arrests as evidence of nascent American fascism, were not inclined to see the situations as analogous.[95] Strong, seeking to portray her expulsion from the Soviet Union as the work of a few "stupid officials and bureaucrats" unable to distinguish good journalism from spying, was one of the few communist sympathizers who saw similarities.[96] To highlight her solidarity with the eleven American communists on trial in New York, she sent their defense fund a $1,000 donation check endorsed "For the American Communists who are getting as raw a deal from American justice as I got from the USSR. From a fellow victim of the cold war." The check was angrily returned.[97]

Indeed the trials operated quite differently. The 1949 Rajk trial in Hungary, as did the Slánský trial in Czechoslovakia a few years later, purported to uncover a vast and active conspiracy. The prosecution in both cases relied on coerced confessions and scripted courtroom exchanges. In Hungary, all the defendants were found guilty, with Rajk and two of his seven codefendants sentenced to death. In Czechoslovakia, all the defendants were likewise found guilty; Slánský, together with all but three of his thirteen codefendants, was executed.The leaders of the Communist Party in the United States, by contrast,

95 Sakmyster, "Mátyás Rákosi," 50–1; Martelle, *Fear Within*, 37–9; Fast, *Being Red*, 197–9; Steve Nelson, *The Thirteenth Juror* (Leipzig: Paul List Verlag, 1956), 266–8.

96 "Jury Hears Writer Moscow Expelled."

97 "Reds on Trial Refuse Aid of Anna Louise Strong," *NYT*, 30 March 1949; Strong and Keyssar, *Right in Her Soul*, 260.

stood accused of conspiring to advocate and teach – not actually undertake – the overthrow of the government. The prosecution relied on "literary evidence" such as *The Communist Manifesto* and the 1928 *Program of the Communist International.* Not only was much of this material "quite dated" but also the government, as legal scholar Michal Belknap emphasizes, "could offer no proof that American communists were about to translate into action any of the ideas it contained."[98] However, the Smith Act did not require such proof. All eleven defendants were found guilty, fined $10,000 each, and sentenced to jail terms of up to five years in federal prison. Additionally, the judge sent all five defense lawyers to jail for contempt, with terms ranging from thirty days to six months.[99]

For all their differences, the trials shared an interest in demonstrating that transnational networks were inherently conspiratorial and subversive. In the United States as much as in Eastern Europe, cold war divides made suspect those who had crossed borders under very different circumstances. Artur London's observation that in postwar Czechoslovakia "Everything we had done was judged in the light of the immediate international situation" effectively describes the situation on both sides of the iron curtain.[100] In both the East and West, prosecutors argued – albeit in distinctive ways and with far deadlier consequences in the East – that international connections once understood as idealistic had in fact been grounded in lies, conspiracy, and treason.

In the United States, the state's effort to establish the criminal, conspiratorial nature of the Communist Party as a whole produced trials focused on words rather than deeds, on abstractions rather than individuals. Much to the defendants' consternation, the judge presiding over the 1949 Smith Act trial severely limited opportunities for communists to present their individual biographies – especially any parts of their biographies, such as fighting for the Loyalist cause in Spain, that might cast them in an idealistic light. In May 1949, when defense attorney Harry Sacher asked John Gates, the first defense witness called five months into the trial, to recount his experiences fighting fascism in Spain, Judge Harold Medina cut him off, deeming such questioning a "waste of time."[101] Richard Gladstein, another member of the defense team, countered that biography was the best means of getting at "a man's past state of mind and intention," a critical issue in the case. Medina disagreed, ostensibly because such testimony would take too long: "It is obvious that if I permit these defendants to bring in everything they ever said, everything they ever wrote, all their conduct in all matters having to do with anti-Semitism, arguing matters

98 Michal R. Belknap, "Cold War in the Courtroom: The Foley Square Communist Trial," in Michal R. Belknap, ed., *American Political Trials*, revised ed. (Westport, CT: Greenwood Press, 1994), 215.
99 Ibid., 221; Martelle, *Fear Within*, 211–16.
100 London, *Confession*, 114.
101 Martelle, *Fear Within*, 170.

for the Negroes, being in support of the Republican government in Spain, being opposed to Chiang Kai-shek, and the Chinese government, and so on, we will be here for an indefinite period, and I have felt that I am drawing the line at the proper place. Now one of those places is that war in Spain is out."[102] Cutting off Gates's testimony may have saved time, although how much in a trial that lasted almost ten months is unclear. In any case, Medina's list of irrelevant topics included the actions and attitudes for which communists had suffered and of which they were most proud. Ruling that "Spain is out" meant denying communists the opportunity, as another defendant, Gilbert Green, wrote in a letter to his wife, "to defend everything that my life has meant to me, everything that communism stands for."[103] The trial thus reduced the meaning of communism, and the lives of individual communists, to the incendiary passages from communist tracts that the prosecution read into the record.

Only outside of the courtroom could American communists recount the actions that gave meaning to their lives. In a contemporary account of his trial and imprisonment for sedition in Pennsylvania, Nelson emphasized the formative importance of his fight against fascism in Spain. In 1952 the state of Pennsylvania sentenced Nelson to twenty years in prison and, denying him bail pending appeal, sent him to the Blawnox Workhouse to await trial under the federal Smith Act. Describing the prison as following "medieval practices in handling prisoners, who were treated as subhuman, beaten at will by the guards, thrown in the hole and kept on bread and water for nine days at a time," he recalled that a primary comfort was reading the letters sent by International Brigade veterans from many countries.[104] A small book published to build sympathy and defense funds for Nelson similarly emphasized that his actions in Spain revealed, as veteran Milton Wolff wrote, "the kind of guy Steve was."[105] Exiled Spanish poet Rafael Alberti contributed a poem underscoring that Nelson had been and remained a fighter for all humanity, who had given his "life for my people/ and for his people."[106] While prosecutors presented, as they did in Nelson's state sedition trial, "nearly all the works of Marx, Engels, Lenin, Stalin" as evidence against American communists, communists found ways to present their own life stories as the clearest and truest accounts of their political commitments.[107]

In Eastern Europe, by contrast, show trials and secret purges alike hinged on viciously, often brutally, rewritten life stories. The attacks on old

[102] Gladstein and Medina quoted in ibid., 171.

[103] Gilbert Green to Lil Green, 30 May 1949 as quoted in ibid., 180.

[104] Nelson, *Thirteenth Juror*, 61, 121. See also Steve Nelson, James R. Barrett, and Rob Ruck, *Steve Nelson, American Radical* (Pittsburgh: University of Pittsburgh Press, 1981), 341–71.

[105] Milton Wolff in *Steve Nelson: A Tribute by 14 Famous Authors* (no publication information, probably 1952), 14; available at University of Pennsylvania Rare Books and Manuscripts Library, Print Coll. 1, Box 130.

[106] Rafael Alberti, trans. Jose Yglesias in *Steve Nelson*, 10.

[107] Steve Nelson et al., *American Radical*, 330.

communists were everywhere "biography-based," drawing on and manipulating longstanding communist practices of autobiographical writing and self-criticism.[108] George Hodos, "one of the fortunate survivors of the Rajk trial," drew on his own experiences to describe the process in depersonalized but still chilling terms:

> The starting point was always the autobiography of the arrested person, his own account of his political life. Only then could the interrogators begin a political reinterpretation of that life, achieved with rubber truncheons, rifle butts, electric shocks, sleeplessness, hunger, and cold – a mixture of the most advanced and archaically barbaric methods of physical and psychological tortures. The interrogators suggested "reinterpretations" of previous arrests for underground communists' activities so they became informer services for the fascist police. Personal or professional contacts with the co-accused became plotting with and spying for the agents of imperialism. Step by step, each version was transformed by torture into a new and uglier one until every moment of the accused's life was reinterpreted into an abominable crime.[109]

This process of reinterpretation, Hodos emphasized, "destroyed not only... bodies but... entire lives."[110] London, too, recalled the pain of having his own biography – a past he was "proud" of – destroyed. He was shocked to find "political records," reports from Spain in which "we had been at pains to emphasize every shadow and error," in his interrogators' hands, transformed into "police records." Bolshevik self-criticism became evidence of treason: "And this was what became of our intransigence towards ourselves! Everything became petty and dirty. Everything was turned against us."[111]

The construction of often surreal biographies and their use as a disciplinary tool linked the East European show trials to earlier communist practices and purges, while clearly distinguishing them from their counterparts in the West. London's remembered surprise at finding self-criticism transformed into criminal accusation is itself somewhat surprising, given that he was in Moscow during the first of the show trials in 1936 and knew many who disappeared in the great terror.[112] In those earlier trials, too, accusations had "originated in the nightmarish world of omnipresent enemies and conformed to irrational and stereotype images."[113] Like the great terror in the Soviet Union, the postwar purges and show trials effectively sowed "terror in the party's ranks." As historian Catherine Epstein emphasizes in the case of East Germany, where planning for a show trial ended with Stalin's death in March 1953, the purges, for all

108 Epstein, *Last Revolutionaries*, 130.
109 Hodos, *Show Trials*, xiv, 46; see also Kaplan, *Report*, 110.
110 Hodos, *Show Trials*, 47.
111 London, *Confession*, 52, 53.
112 Ibid., 253–4.
113 Berthold Unfried, "Foreign Communists and the Mechanism of Soviet Cadre Formation in the USSR," in Barry McLoughlin and Kevin McDermott, eds., *Stalin's Terror: High Politics and Mass Repression in the Soviet Union* (Basingstoke: Palgrave Macmillan, 2003), 187.

their irrationality, had the "rational purpose" of disciplining even – and perhaps especially – the most distinguished communists by reminding them "that the party, the arbiter of revolutionary reputations, held sway over all that was most meaningful to them."[114] Signing a coerced confession, the accused became whatever the party dictated: a Titoist, Trotskyite, Zionist, bourgeois nationalist, agent of American imperialism, or spy.[115] Communists thus internalized a new understanding of the party if not of themselves. London remembered trying to reclaim his past in the hours between interrogations: "against the mud which [the interrogators] churned up day after day, I tried, when they left me alone, to reconstruct our Spain, the Spain which remained in my heart."[116] Nonetheless, he ultimately confessed and followed the required script at his trial.

The trials of communists in the United States and the far deadlier trials in the Soviet bloc were, for all their incommensurability, uncanny reflections of shared fears. States on both sides of the cold war divide responded, in however overblown and irrational a fashion, to deeply felt security concerns by constructing a remarkably similar gallery of suspicious types, enemies who carefully hid long-term ties with a foreign power and conspired to undermine an entire way of life. In the context of the early cold war, those who had connections to the other side were necessarily dangerous; the cause of Spain, which had united so many across national lines and had been mythologized so effectively, emerged as a particularly powerful source of anxiety. In transforming international solidarity into espionage, the American trials sought to equate communism and treason. In communist states, the same transformation served to discipline veterans, who nonetheless often maintained, as did their American comrades, a Spanish-centered understanding of the revolutionary movement.

International Networks and the Memory of the Spanish Civil War

In the spring of 1943, at Stalin's behest, the Comintern's executive committee recommended that the organization dissolve itself. Whether Stalin's chief motivation was a desire to improve relations with his British and American allies or, as he emphasized in a Politburo meeting in late May, to adjust to the fact that it had become "impossible to direct the working-class movement of all countries from a single international center," the news took both foreign communists and Soviet citizens by surprise.[117]

[114] Epstein, *Last Revolutionaries*, 130, 153, 154. McLellan makes a similar point, *Antifascism and Memory*, 10.

[115] London, *Confession*, 267, 272; Unfried, "Foreign," 190.

[116] London, *Confession*, 84; see also McLellan, *Antifascism*, 202–3; Epstein, *Last Revolutionaries*, 150; Kaplan, *Report*, 113.

[117] McDermott and Agnew, *Comintern*, 204–9; Georgi Dimitrov, *The Diary of Georgi Dimitrov, 1933–1949*, Ivo Banac, ed. (New Haven: Yale University Press, 2003), 275 (quotation); Enrique Castro Delgado, *Mi fe se perdió en Moscú* (Barcelona: Luís de Caralt, 1964), 248–50;

Ultimately, the dissolution entailed, as Kevin McDermott and Jeremy Agnew emphasize in their history of the Comintern, "no real weakening of Moscow's control of the international communist movement."[118] Georgi Dimitrov, the now former head of the Comintern, transferred his office to the Central Committee where he continued to direct international operations, retaining control of national radio broadcasting, the telegraph agency, and the Foreign Language Publishing House.[119] Three "special institutes," designated only by the numbers 99, 100, and 205, employed many former Comintern staffers in their previous capacities.[120] When in 1945 Stalin decided that American comrades had gone too far toward accommodating their noncommunist allies by dissolving the party and replacing it with a Communist Political Association, he got the message to American leaders via a letter that appeared under the byline of Jacques Duclos, the deputy head of the French party, in the journal *Cahiers du Communisme*. That the attack on Earl Browder came from Moscow was immediately obvious to American comrades. Steve Nelson recalled that he understood the letter "as a direct blast from Moscow" – a conclusion supported by documents in the archives of Institute 205, which suggest that the letter was drafted in Russian and then translated into French. The signal from Moscow proved effective. As Nelson remembered with a measure of retrospective regret, the American party's leaders, swayed by the "collective weight of international Communism," quickly set aside their shock and confusion in order to "return to the fold" and reconstitute the party.[121]

Important as such hierarchical links between center and periphery continued to be, they did not entirely displace more diffuse, informal personal networks among international communists. Ibárruri, residing in Moscow, stood at the heart of one such network. She maintained a far-flung circle of correspondents that included Spanish communists in Eastern Europe and Mexico, foreign veterans of the Spanish war, and a who's who of international communist leaders. Such networks persisted despite the campaign against "cosmopolitans" that

Wolfgang Leonhard, *Child of the Revolution*, trans. C. M. Woodhouse (1957; reprint London: Ink Links, 1979), 217–24; Timothy Johnston, *Being Soviet: Identity, Rumour, and Everyday Life under Stalin, 1939–1954* (Oxford: Oxford University Press, 2011), 73–4. "Protokol (B) No. 825: Zakrytogo zasedaniia prezidiuma IKKI," 17 May 1943, in N. S. Lebedeva and M.M. Narinskii, eds., *Komintern i vtoraia mirovaia voina: Chast' II: posle 22 iuniia 1941 g.* (Moscow: Pamiatniki istoricheskoi mysli, 1998), 359–65. The news appeared in *Pravda*, 22 May 1943.

118 McDermott and Agnew, *Comintern*, 209.

119 Dimitrov, *Diary*, 282.

120 McDermott and Agnew, *Comintern*, 210; N. S. Lebedeva and M. M. Narinskii, "Rospusk Kominterna i sozdanie Otdela mezhdunarodnoi informatsii TsK VKP (b). Mai 1943-mai 1945," in A. O. Chubar'ian, ed. *Istoriia Kommunisticheskogo Internatsionala, 1919–43: Dokumental'nye ocherki* (Moscow: Nauka, 2002), 231–4, 239–53.

121 Haslam, *Russia's Cold War*, 30–1; Harvey Klehr, John Earl Haynes, and Kyrill M. Anderson, *The Soviet World of American Communism* (New Haven: Yale University Press, 1998), 95–106; Nelson et al., *American Radical*, 273–4.

drove the postwar purges and show trials, the effects of which even Ibárruri, her international celebrity notwithstanding, could not entirely escape. As noted earlier, the 1952 show trial in Czechoslovakia touched her inner circle; her longtime companion Falcón suffered banishment from the party and loss of employment following the execution of her former lover.[122]

Ibárruri's correspondence in the years after the war can be understood as emphasizing and enacting the emotional and personal connections that underpinned communist internationalism and that were increasingly under attack on both sides of the iron curtain. On the occasion of International Women's Day in 1952, for example, Ibárruri sent more than a dozen telegrams to communist women in Europe, Mexico, and China. Each message was lightly tailored to the recipient. The note to Romanian communist Ana Pauker, whom Ibárruri had met when both were in Moscow during the war – and whom she allegedly did not much like – emphasized their personal acquaintance, concluding, "I remember you fondly, and send heartfelt greetings [te saludo con el alma] on International Women's Day."[123] At the same time, Stalin's growing suspicions worked against such international solidarity. Just over a month after Ibárruri warmly greeted Pauker, Stalin told visiting Romanian leader Gheorghe Gheorghiu-Dej to "get rid of Ana Pauker ... If I were in your place, I would have shot her in the head a long time ago."[124]

The continuing importance of international connections, despite the suspicions that such contacts engendered, emerges clearly in letters sent to Ibárruri. In 1951, American communist Elizabeth Gurley Flynn sent a telegram soliciting a "tribute to Mother Ella Reeve Bloor Great working class leader died August tenth." The appeal to an international communist then living in Moscow is particularly striking in the context of Flynn's June 1951 arrest for violating the Smith Act. (After a nine-month trial, she was convicted and served two years in a federal prison camp.) Ibárruri obliged the Americans with a formulaic but also seemingly heartfelt paean to Bloor's exemplary "strength and abnegation."[125] The request and Ibárruri's willingness to grant it suggest that communists valued such ritual expressions of sympathy and solidarity as a means of building and sustaining an international movement. A similar sense of the importance of such connections is visible in the letter that communists from a local party organization in Brno-Chrlice wrote to Ibárruri in 1951 to affirm that building socialism in Czechoslovakia constituted a means of "liberating the Spanish

122 Falcón, *Asalto a los cielos*, 278–87.

123 "Correspondencia de Dolores Ibárruri," 7 March 1952, ANC, Sig. 207; Castro Delgado, *Mi fe*, 78.

124 Levy, *Ana Pauker*, 203.

125 Elizabeth Gurley Flynn to Dolores Ibárruri; Ibárruri to Flynn, [1951], ANC, Sig. 207; Elizabeth Gurley Flynn, *The Alderson Story: My Life as a Political Prisoner* (New York: International Publishers, 1963).

and Yugoslav peoples from capitalist and fascist oppressors."[126] That Ibárruri herself remained an important "personal center" of international communism underscores the degree to which the memory of the Spanish civil war remained vital to communist imaginings of the international cause.[127]

In Ibárruri's correspondence with the Spanish exiles, the genre of the sentimental political letter that made little distinction between political goals and personal needs likewise provided a powerful means of maintaining a transnational network that conflated and solidified personal and party relationships. For example, her 1953 correspondence with Manuel Delicado, a central committee member then in Warsaw, focused on the positive effects that attending trade school in the Soviet Union had had on his son; thus it provided good news at once personal and political. For his part, Delicado, who apparently hoped to enlist Ibárruri's help with his medical problems, replied as both a father and a communist, readily endorsing her suggestion that his son's progress had been the result of the "grand Soviet school" and agreeing to let him visit Warsaw for a few weeks.[128] In the same period, Juan Modesto, a former Republican commander, petitioned Ibárruri to allow him a more active role in the Spanish struggle, emphasizing the personal impossibility of continuing his sedentary life in Prague. She responded in early March 1953, advising him that he should direct his eagerness to fight, which she deemed "a natural desire" for every communist, toward study and work. She reminded him of the example of the Bolshevik exiles, especially Lenin, who after the 1905 Revolution occupied themselves with "study and the formation of cadres to lead the fight at any time, in any circumstance."[129] Here, as in her correspondence with international communists, Ibárruri worked to build a web of relations, simultaneously personal and political, that linked communists to Spain, the Soviet Union, and one another.

How recipients read such letters is, of course, difficult to say. Nelson's recollection of receiving letters in prison underscores their potential emotional power: "Other veterans of the battles in Spain often wrote me – from Canada, Australia, England, South America, from various points in the United States – and their reminiscences of that struggle in which I shared, their pledges of support, and warm expressions of affection were wonderfully heartening."[130]

[126] Party organization, Brno region, Czechoslovakia to Dolores Ibárruri, 17 March 1951, ANC, Sig. 207.

[127] Kevin Morgan, "Parts of People and Communist Lives," in John McIlroy, Kevin Morgan, and Alan Campbell, eds., *Party People, Communist Lives: Explorations in Biography* (London: Lawrence & Wishart, 2001), 23.

[128] Dolores Ibárruri to Comrade Delicado, 26 January 1953, ANC, Sig. 207; Delicado to Ibárruri, 28 February 1953, ibid.

[129] Dolores Ibárruri to Comrade Modesto, 11 March 1953, ANC, Sig. 207; Modesto to Ibárruri, 27 March 1953, ibid.

[130] Nelson, *Thirteenth Juror*, 121.

Yet the letters, or at least the snippets he quotes, are not especially moving or personal. One Italian American communist deported after returning from Spain wrote "to let you know you are still remembered by an old *Camarada* of Spain."[131] Nonetheless, Nelson emphasized that the letters allowed him to transcend, at least briefly, the miseries and indignities of prison.[132] Indeed the physical fact of the letters appears to have been at least as important as their rather banal messages. Coming from all over the United States and the world, they offered evidence that he had not been forgotten, that he remained part of an international movement, still tied to his comrades from Spain.

Ironically, the lasting personal significance of such ties emerges with particular clarity in the statements of former communists who testified as government witnesses at the 1954 SACB hearing that deemed the Veterans of the Abraham Lincoln Brigade a communist front.[133] Three of the veterans who testified against VALB – William Herrick, Robert Gladnick, and Morris Maken (Mickenberg) – had known one another in Spain. Having returned disillusioned with communism, they became further disillusioned by VALB's decision to support the Nazi-Soviet Pact.[134] Thus their testimonies served the government's purpose of establishing a direct link between the party and the veterans. But for all their anticommunism, they remained proud of their service in Spain, distinguishing the "good," antifascist communism that brought them to Spain from the corrupt, Soviet-dominated communism that displaced it.

Maken in particular seemed to relish his opportunity to attack the communists who had expelled him from VALB. His testimony, as historian Peter Carroll notes, "emphasized the arrogance and incompetence of the Communist leadership running the brigade."[135] But it also struck a note of almost wistful nostalgia, a tone at odds with his self-described talent for composing "vicious" "ditties" about unpopular commissars.[136] Recalling the "romantic talk" among the volunteers on the ship to France, he noted that they had been "certain that we would be trained by and serve with and led by these legendary characters that we had been hearing about in our Communist world: German anti-Fascists, the underground fighters against Hitler, some of the Poles who had been living under grim semi-Fascist conditions in their country."[137] The closest the volunteers came to this romantic vision was apparently the train trip from Paris to the Spanish border, which Maken described in loving detail: "For

131 Ibid., 120.
132 Ibid., 121.
133 Carroll, *Odyssey*, 298–312.
134 Ellen Schrecker, ed., *Records of the Subversive Activities Control Board, 1950–1972: Microfilmed from the Holdings of the National Archives and Records Administration* (Frederick, MD: University Publication of America, 1988) (SACB microfilm), reel 32, 545, 881–8; reel 33, 1539–42.
135 Carroll, *Odyssey*, 304.
136 SACB microfilm, reel 32, 1079–80.
137 Ibid., 727.

whatever it is worth, it was just about the most wonderful experience a man could have in a lifetime, to see these many, many hundreds of men from all parts of the world, including one from Ethiopia, a Negro, and men from Latvia, men who looked laggard, sick, and frail. They had gone through hell to get to Paris. They were wonderful. So we had a joyous time of it, breaking the ice, getting acquainted, pioneers of the proletarian army."[138] As he completed his testimony, he reiterated, "Spain and the circumstances and events surrounding it will always be very important and precious to me, as the experiences of a lifetime."[139]

Even as they severed their connections with the party, Maken, Gladnick, and Herrick wanted to remain connected to the "experiences of a lifetime." Herrick testified that he had been slow to leave the party when he returned from Spain both because he relied on party-funded medical care and because "I knew too many people who were in Spain, too many people whom I respected and had great feeling for."[140] In the wake of VALB's endorsement of the Nazi-Soviet pact, Gladnick was heartened to learn that "quite a number of Veterans . . . were just as indignant as I was about the sacrilege committed in the name of men who had the guts and fortitude to fight for freedom, for democracy, for idealism in Spain."[141] Their contempt for the party, coupled with a desire to preserve the "precious" memory of Spain, ultimately led them to organize an alternative and short-lived "Anti-Totalitarian" veterans' organization.[142] Continuing to define themselves as antifascist, they remembered and desired an international solidarity untainted by association with Moscow.

However, it was, of course, the associations with Moscow – not fond memories of the "romantic" ideas that had brought the volunteers to Spain – that interested the Board. In May 1955, it handed down the "expected" conclusion that VALB "is substantially directed, dominated, and controlled by the Communist Party of the United States and is primarily operated for the purpose of giving aid and support to the Party and world Communist movement."[143] In December 1955, the SACB ordered the organization to register as a subversive organization. (VALB fought the order, which was finally overturned by the U.S. Supreme Court in 1965.[144])

More than a falling out of erstwhile allies against Hitler, the cold war represented an effort to impose global order by treating "cosmopolitan" identities and transnational dreams of "building a new egalitarian world"[145] as

138 Ibid., 736.

139 Ibid., reel 33, 1131–2.

140 Ibid., reel 32, 527, 671, 558 (quotation).

141 Ibid., reel 33, 1544.

142 Ibid., reel 32, 890–1; reel 33, 1670. See also Chapter 6.

143 Carroll, *Odyssey*, 309.

144 Ibid.,310.

145 Paul Preston, *The Spanish Civil War: Reaction, Revolution, and Revenge* (New York: Harper Perennial, 2006), 7.

dangerous and subversive – un-American on one side of the iron curtain, anti-patriotic on the other. The veterans of the Spanish civil war aroused suspicions as the embodiments of the border crossing and transnational interactions that both cold war powers attempted to limit and anathematize, if not eradicate. Labeled subversives and spies by authorities on both sides, they were harassed, tried, convicted, and, in the Soviet bloc, tortured and sometimes executed. In an undated letter to Nelson, Fredericka Martin, who had served as the chief nurse and administrator of the American medical personnel in Spain, worried that such pressures had perhaps undermined the international solidarity that was a core piece of the International Brigade members' identity. Reflecting on the American veterans' "feeble efforts" to "persuade Poland to cease her cruel treatment of Polish IB'ers of Jewish extraction," she felt it necessary to "ask ourselves– are we no longer internationalists?"[146]

The veterans' responses were political – defending the effort to remake the world across national boundaries for which they had sacrificed – and also deeply personal. Maintaining local and international networks, they perpetuated the story of the good fight in Spain as both a means of reasserting their political identity as internationalists and of protecting precious, self-defining memories. For many veterans, the memory of "the cause of all advanced and progressive humanity" remained an essential one, even as the fact that Stalin had coined the phrase became increasingly troubling – both personally and politically.

[146] Martin to Nelson, draft, nd, Martin Papers, Box 19, Folder 22.

Epilogue

Internationalism and the Spanish Civil War after Stalin

In the wake of Josef Stalin's death on 5 March 1953, his successors began – slowly, fitfully, partially – to repudiate his legacy. The first sign of a shift came in April, when *Pravda* reported that the conspirators in the so-called Doctors' Plot, the culmination of the anticosmopolitan campaign, had been falsely accused and that the investigators in the case had been arrested.[1] Beginning in 1955, a series of cultural exchanges brought Western art exhibitions, literature, films, music, theater, and tourists to the Soviet Union, dispelling the grim xenophobic mood that had gripped the country in Stalin's last years.[2] A more direct attack on Stalin's methods came in February 1956, when in a four-hour so-called secret speech at the Twentieth Party Congress Nikita Khrushchev offered a limited, but still stunning, disclosure of the former leader's crimes. Presented at a late-night session closed to foreign delegates, the speech did not remain secret for long, circulating among millions of activists within and beyond the Soviet Union.[3]

In contemporary and retrospective accounts of the speech, foreign and Soviet communists remembered their initial reaction as "bitter silence."[4] Some likened

[1] Jonathan Brent and Vladimir P. Naumov, *Stalin's Last Crime: The Plot against the Jewish Doctors, 1948–1953* (New York: Harper Collins, 2003), 324–5.

[2] Vladislav Zubok, *Zhivago's Children: The Last Russian Intelligentsia* (Cambridge, MA: Belknap Press of Harvard University Press, 2009), 88; Eleonory Gilburd, "The Revival of Soviet Internationalism in the Mid to Late 1950s," in Denis Kozlov and Eleonory Gilburd, eds., *The Thaw: Soviet Society and Culture during the 1950s and 1960s* (Toronto: University of Toronto Press, 2013), 364–5. I thank the author for sharing an advance copy of her work.

[3] William Taubman, *Khrushchev: The Man and His Era* (New York: W. W. Norton, 2003), 283–4; John Rettie, "How Khrushchev Leaked His Secret Speech to the World," *History Workshop Journal*, no. 62 (2006): 187; "Text of Speech on Stalin by Khrushchev as Released by the State Department," *New York Times* (*NYT*), 5 June 1956.

[4] Irene Falcón with Manuel Jiménez and Jesús Montero, *Asalto a los cielos: Mi vida junta a Pasionaria* (Madrid: Temas de Hoy, 1996), 305. See also Eleonory Gilburd, "Picasso in Thaw

their shock to a physical blow. Alexander Yakovlev, a thirty-two-year-old veteran of the Great Fatherland War (and later an architect of perestroika) recalled his faith "exploding in shrapnel like a grenade shell."[5] Steve Nelson, who chaired the meeting in late April 1956 at which the speech was read to about 120 activists in the American party, remembered that the "words of the speech were like bullets, and each found its place in the hearts of the veteran Communists. Tears streamed down the faces of men and women who had spent forty or more years, their whole adult lives, in the movement."[6] Nelson, who was himself among those who spent his entire adult life in the party, ultimately left it in late 1957.

Shocking as the revelations were, those who made and embraced them, first and foremost Khrushchev himself, emphasized that they were less a break than a return, a recovery of "Leninism" and of "lost revolutionary and internationalist values."[7] In his speech to the party congress, Khrushchev attempted to balance potentially risky disclosures of Stalin's crimes with legitimizing and optimistic tales of Lenin's revolutionary rectitude, of "Leninist" collective leadership and socialist legality, and of the "neo-Leninist future."[8] Moscow writers who assembled to discuss the speech in late March 1956 applauded the "return of Leninism" and "burst out singing 'The Internationale.'"[9] Spanish communist Santiago Carrillo recalled in his 2006 memoir that the speech itself came as less of a "shock" than listening to his old friend Artur London, recently released from a Czechoslovak prison, recount his torture and imprisonment. Although London's story "personalized" the "perversion of the police system" in a way that the speech had not and effectively disabused Carrillo of "the semireligious aspects of my communist convictions," it also offered a model for how to remain a communist in the shadow of the "darkest aspects of the Stalinist system." At least in retrospect, Carrillo concluded that the August

Culture," *Cahiers du monde russe* 47, no. 1–2 (January–June, 2006), 66; Steve Nelson, James R. Barrett, and Rob Ruck, *Steve Nelson, American Radical* (Pittsburgh: University of Pittsburgh Press, 1981), 387.

5 Zubok, *Zhivago's Children*, 61. See also Iurii Aksiutin, "Popular Responses to Khrushchev," in William Taubman, Sergei Khrushchev, and Abbott Gleason, eds., *Nikita Khrushchev* (New Haven: Yale University Press, 2000), 185.

6 Nelson et al., *American Radical*, 387. See also James R. Barrett, *William Z. Foster and the Tragedy of American Radicalism* (Urbana: University of Illinois Press, 1999), 253–62; Falcón, *Asalto a los cielos*, 302–7.

7 Zubok, *Zhivago's Children*, 72.

8 Polly Jones, "From the Secret Speech to the Burial of Stalin: Real and Ideal Responses to De-Stalinization," in Polly Jones, ed., *Dilemmas of De-Stalinization: Negotiating Social and Cultural Change in the Khrushchev Era* (London: Routledge, 2006), 42. The full text of the speech is available online, http://www.guardian.co.uk/theguardian/2007/apr/26/greatspeeches1 (accessed 15 November 2014).

9 Zubok, *Zhivago's Children*, 71.

1956 encounter with London at a holiday residence in Varna, Bulgaria, "filled me with great confidence" in communist "courage and honor."[10]

The potentially disconcerting and destabilizing opening to the West was also cast as a return to earlier revolutionary norms. In the fall of 1956, the first Soviet exhibition of Pablo Picasso's artwork upset long-settled notions of "socialist" art, and many viewers responded to it with hostility and suspicion.[11] But visitors to the exhibition and cultural authorities also linked the show to the purest of revolutionary values and the "most romantic period of Soviet history – the Spanish war."[12] The few sources of information on Picasso available to the Soviet public, including an article by Il'ia Ehrenburg, emphasized the artist's membership in the Communist Party and his monumental antifascist painting *Guernica*.[13] The 1957 Youth Festival that brought more than thirty thousand foreigners to Moscow likewise upset "the balance of social and moral order."[14] But it, too, could be understood as a part of a "revival of Soviet internationalism."[15]

However optimistic communists might be about the neo-Leninist future, making personal and political sense of de-Stalinization nonetheless required a reconsideration of the past. Focusing on Soviet reactions, historian Miriam Dobson observes that the condemnation of "Stalin and the terror compelled society to rethink the way it understood its own recent, and very bloody, past – and by extension how people were now to relate to their own life stories."[16] The same could be said for many foreign communists. In both cases, communists could validate lives spent in the party by narrating them as tales of communist idealism maintained in the face of Stalinist perversions. In the Soviet case, Khrushchev endorsed the recovery of the narrative of a people's war, emphasizing that the people (and the party) had defeated fascism despite, not because, of Stalin.[17] For foreign communists, Spain could serve a similar purpose. Indeed the Spanish civil war enjoyed a revival within the Soviet Union, where

[10] Carrillo uses the English word "shock;" Santiago Carrillo, *Memorias: El testimonio polémico de un protagonista relevante de nuestra transición* (Barcelona: Planeta, 2008), 563, 564.

[11] Gilburd, "Picasso in Thaw Culture," 83–5.

[12] Petr Vail' and Aleksandr Genis, "60-e: Mir sovetskaia cheloveka," in *Sobranie sochinenii v dvukh tomakh* (Ekaterinburg: U-Faktoriia, 2003), 1: 564; Zubok, *Zhivago's Children*, 119.

[13] Gilburd, "Picasso in Thaw Culture," 85; Il'ia Erenburg, "K risunkam Pablo Pikasso," *Inostrannaia literatura* 10 (1956): 243–53.

[14] Kristin Roth-Ey, "'Loose Girls' on the Loose: Sex, Propaganda, and the 1957 Youth Festival," in Susan E. Reid, Melanie Ilič, and Lynne Attwood, eds., *Women in the Khrushchev Era* (Basingstoke: Palgrave Macmillan, 2004), 90.

[15] Gilburd, "Revival of Soviet Internationalism," 390.

[16] Miriam Dobson, "The Post-Stalin Era: De-Stalinization, Daily Life, and Dissent," *Kritika* 12, no. 4 (Fall 2011): 908. Zubok makes a similar point, *Zhivago's Children*, 61.

[17] Lisa A. Kirschenbaum, *The Legacy of the Siege of Leningrad, 1941–1995: Myth, Memories, and Monuments* (New York: Cambridge University Press, 2006), 154–60.

enthusiasm for the Cuban revolution among "younger educated Russians" stirred up memories of the romance of Soviet support for Republican Spain.[18]

Remembering Spain provided veterans a means of coping with painful revelations and of insulating their own life stories as communists from the taint of Stalin's crimes. The importance of preserving Spain as a pivot for communist life stories emerges with particular clarity in the case of American veterans. The Subversive Activities Control Board's 1955 decision to list the Veterans of the Abraham Lincoln Brigade (VALB) as a communist front almost destroyed the organization. The drawn-out legal battle substantially depleted the organization's finances and membership. At a November 1956 meeting in New York, VALB's leaders, Milton Wolff and Moe Fishman, advocated disbanding. However, as historian Peter Carroll notes, "Most veterans disagreed."[19] Carroll attributes the subsequent resurgence of the organization to the emergence in 1958 of a galvanizing issue that resonated with the veterans' own experiences of "domestic persecution" – the "oppression of political prisoners in Spain."[20] But he offers little explanation of the 1956 decision to save the organization. I argue that the gathered veterans, mostly communists, were likely influenced by the Soviet invasion of Hungary that coincided with the meeting.

In voting to sustain their organization, the veterans sought a way to distance the memory of international solidarity in Spain from both Stalinism and the Soviet Union. The new executive secretary Maury Colow was a former communist expelled from the party in 1952.[21] His very presence suggested an effort to demonstrate that the organization was not a tool of the party. An article in the January 1957 issue of the *Volunteer for Liberty* emphasized that the VALB had "long lost whatever political character it formerly possessed," while also affirming the political truth for which the veterans had fought: "We the veterans of the fight for democracy in Spain, who, in effect, 20 years ago pledged the soul and heart of America to fight against Nazism and Francoism are a fact that no one and nothing can gainsay."[22] In February 1957, just as the national party conference convened to discuss reform, five hundred people, veterans and their supporters, gathered at a New York hotel to celebrate the twentieth anniversary of the founding of the Lincoln battalion and to pledge "Next year, in Madrid!"[23] At a time when the party was bitterly

[18] Zubok, *Zhivago's Children*, 118–19. See also, Gilburd, "Picasso and Thaw Culture," 100–1; Katerina Clark, *Moscow, the Fourth Rome: Stalinism, Cosmopolitanism, and the Evolution of Soviet Culture, 1931–1941* (Cambridge, MA: Harvard University Press, 2011), 348–9.

[19] Carroll, *Odyssey*, 311.

[20] Ibid., 360, 361.

[21] Ibid., 311.

[22] "We Are Going On!" *Volunteer for Liberty* 19, no. 1 (January 1957): 1, as quoted in Peter Glazer, *Radical Nostalgia: Spanish Civil War Commemoration in America* (Rochester: University of Rochester Press, 2005), 93.

[23] Carroll, *Odyssey*, 312.

split and losing members over the issue of how and whether Americans could interpret Marxism-Leninism for themselves, celebrating Spain made it possible to (re)define communism in terms of a glorious moment of international solidarity.[24]

For both the revisionists, who ultimately lost the battle to reform the party and dropped out, and for those who remained, VALB offered an alternative means of maintaining personal and political connections with comrades at home and abroad who shared a (perhaps romanticized) memory of communist antifascism in Spain. After Nelson left the party in 1957 and returned to New York, his chief "political and social activities... revolved around the Veterans of the Abraham Lincoln Brigade." In 1980, when he was working on his memoir, he described the veterans' organization as "my primary interest aside from my family."[25] The organization's new leaders focused on getting it removed from the attorney general's list of subversive organizations and on aiding Spanish political prisoners, a task that they coordinated with a prisoners' aid committee in Paris.[26] A few traveled to Berlin in the summer of 1961 to mark the twenty-fifth anniversary of the outbreak of the Spanish civil war.[27] By the twenty-fifth anniversary of the founding of the Lincoln battalion in 1962, the veterans' organization, still listed as a subversive organization, had rebounded. More than 1,100 veterans and their supporters met in New York to listen to a dramatic reading of Dolores Ibárruri's farewell to the International Brigades, to sing antifascist songs in German and Spanish, and to view enlarged photographs of scenes from the war. The gathering raised over two thousand dollars.[28] The veterans were thus part of an international network that circumvented (and largely ignored) Moscow; the Soviet Union, after all, had supported Francoist Spain's 1955 admission to the UN.

Separating the memory of the good fight in Spain from Stalinism relied on often nostalgic personal memories. In the 1960s, Fredericka Martin, who had served as the administrator of American medical personnel in Spain, began a massive project to collect information on international medical volunteers in Spain. She corresponded with hundreds of veterans from around the world, soliciting comprehensive accounts of their service in Spain. She compiled, for

[24] Barrett, *William Z. Foster*, 263–7; "Osnovanie: izlozhenie besedy s synom Polia Robsona," 26 February 1957, Rossiiskii gosudarstvennyi arkhiv sotsial'no-politicheskoi istorii (RGASPI), f. 495, op. 261, d. 108, l. 5.

[25] Nelson et al., *American Radical*, 409, 410.

[26] Ibid., 409; Miguel Sanchez-Mazas, *Spain in Chains: A Report on Political Repression in Franco Spain* (New York: Veterans of the Abraham Lincoln Brigade [1959?]).

[27] Alvah Bessie to Camarades Generales Wertrov y Smirnov and Camarada Marie Fartousse, 4 November 1966, Spanish Civil War Collection, correspondence, Box G1, Folder 005, University of Illinois Rare Book and Manuscript Library; Carroll, *Odyssey*, 359; Glazer, *Radical Nostalgia*, 94–6.

[28] "25th Year Marked by Lincoln Brigade," *NYT*, 26 February 1962; Glazer, *Radical Nostalgia*, 96–100.

example, everything from lists of medical personnel who married in Spain to information on the nurses and doctors from Czechoslovakia.[29] In a 1971 letter to Nelson, she emphasized the profound importance she attached to the project of recovering the volunteers' small, everyday stories: "All my life is focused now on writing a book that will move the hearts of readers and let them see us as we were."[30] In another letter to Nelson the following year, she suggested the political purposes of her project, explaining that she was trying "to show the unity of variety in such a way that it is convincing and contradicts without saying so the falsehoods told of Moscow control, etc."[31] Nelson supported her efforts, but suggested that she focus more on "the broad picture," asking her correspondents, for example, "Did you really think you could help stop Hitler?" Such questions, he emphasized would make the story of Spain relevant to the new left, especially activists involved in protesting the war in Vietnam who "don't care about if you were at Jarama or Teruel."[32] Still, he seemed to agree that personalized memories would best capture the true nature of the volunteers' commitments and their work in Spain. For those who fought in Spain, memories of the civil war performed essentially the same operation as Khrushchev's secret speech: They reclaimed what was good and true and revolutionary and even humanitarian about communism, while minimizing the impact and importance of Stalin.

Emphasizing the emotional and personal truth of international solidarity could thus require a large measure of forgetting. Nowhere was the forgetting clearer than in a 1977 interview that Ibárruri gave after returning to Spain. A question about the arrests of Spanish exiles and veterans in the Soviet Union drew an emphatic response from the eight-two-year-old Ibárruri: "If Spaniards were arrested I don't remember.... I don't remember, I don't remember, what more do you want?"[33] This is a startling lapse given the number of friends and acquaintances, both Spanish and Soviet, who disappeared in the purges.[34] It suggests the persistence of Ibárruri's Stalinism, the discipline or perhaps self-delusion that allowed her to recall in her 1984 memoir that she reconciled herself to Stalin's withdrawal of support for the Spanish guerrillas with the mantra, "Stalin is right."[35] At the same time, her unwillingness or inability to

29 "AMB personnel who married in Spain," Fredericka Martin Papers, ALBA 001, Box 5, Folder 6, Tamiment Library/Robert F. Wagner Labor Archives, New York University; "Czechoslovakia – Doctors, Nurses," ibid., Box 2, Folder 7.

30 Fredericka Martin to Steve Nelson, 6 February 1970, Martin Papers, Box 19, Folder 22.

31 Martin to Nelson, 3 March 1971, Martin Papers, Box 19, Folder 22.

32 Nelson to Martin, 13 March 1971, Martin Papers, Box 19, Folder 22.

33 Merle Wolin, "*La Pasionaria:* After Forty Years of Exile One of the Greatest Living Revolutionaries Speaks for the First Time from her Beloved Spain," *Viva,* September 1978, 87.

34 Luiza Iordache, *Republicanos españoles en el Gulag (1939–1956)* (Barcelona: Institut de Ciències Polítiques i Socials, 2008).

35 Dolores Ibárruri, *Memorias de Pasionaria, 1939–1977: Me faltaba España* (Barcelona: Planeta, 1984), 127. On self-delusion, see John McIlroy and Alan Campbell, "A Peripheral Vision: Communist Historiography in Britain," *American Communist History* 4, no. 2 (2005): 144.

remember arrests can be understood as the obverse of her powerful memory of the Spanish civil war. It is useful to contrast Ibárruri's vehement forgetting with her contemporary letter to Nelson on the occasion of his seventy-second birthday. Here she insisted that "the time and distance separating us notwithstanding, we have not for a moment forgotten the meaning of your [*vuestra*] participation in the struggle to liberate our people, and feel ourselves forever indebted to you."[36]

Of course, critics of Soviet intervention in Spain have long called attention to this sort of forgetting, dismissing as "myth" "illusion," or "fairy tale" the notion that the war was a "struggle to liberate our people."[37] On the other side, many historians have challenged this picture of the Soviets as matchless deceivers and the volunteers as utterly deceived, arguing that it is grounded in a misuse of historical evidence and a failure to attend to the "broader picture of Republican Spain at war."[38] What has received less attention is the postwar, post-Stalin context of many representations of the war as noble and selfless. This larger context suggests that veterans worked to preserve and perpetuate their memories of the good fight as a means of asserting that, whatever might be revealed about Stalin, their cause and their actions remained pure.

The persistence of such powerful and necessarily partial memories can help us see Stalinism itself in new ways, to see that it retained international dimensions even as the Stalinist state increasingly embraced Russian nationalism and xenophobia. Stalinism has often been understood in terms of the limitation, abandonment, or betrayal of the emancipatory promises of October as it criminalized abortion and homosexuality, sentimentalized motherhood and family, and promoted Russian nationalism. What is notable in the stories and memories of communists connected to Spain is that this sense of a return of traditional values and a turn away from individual emancipation, although visible, is not the whole story. For many communists, the communist community – international solidarity– mattered at least as much as individual emancipation. A large part of what attracted African Americans, emancipated women, and gay men to the party seems to have been its promise not only of liberation but also of a solidarity that transcended, but did not efface, difference – that, to borrow Fredericka Martin's phrase, fostered "the unity of variety." Communist

36 Dolores Ibárruri to Steve Nelson, 19 January 1975, Steve Nelson Papers, ALBA 008, Box 2, Folder 20.

37 Stanley G. Payne, *The Spanish Civil War, the Soviet Union, and Communism* (New Haven: Yale University Press, 2004), 290; Tony Judt, "Rehearsal for Evil," *New Republic* 225, no. 11 (10 September 2001): 34; Christopher Hitchens, "Who Lost Spain?" *Wilson Quarterly* 25, no. 3 (Summer 2001): 107.

38 Helen Graham, "Spain Betrayed? The New Historical McCarthyism," *Science and Society* 68, no. 3 (Fall 2004):367 (quotation); Peter Carroll, "The Myth of the Moscow Archives," *Science and Society* 68, no. 3 (Fall 2004): 337, 338; Chris Ealham, "'Myths' and the Spanish Civil War: Some Old, Some Exploded, Some Clearly Borrowed and Some Almost 'Blue,'" *Journal of Contemporary History* 42, no. 2 (2007): 372.

solidarity was not the solidarity of racial or national purity so prominent in many political movements of the interwar period, especially in Nazism, but rather a solidarity that crossed borders and that embraced border crossers, outsiders, heterogeneity, and hybrids of all kinds.

Through the late 1930s, this promiscuous solidarity of immigrants, exiles, and border crossers remained a communist ideal and to some extent a communist practice – nowhere more visibly and dramatically than among the International Brigades in Spain. It coexisted, however uneasily and precariously, with the contemporary show trials and purges that promoted a very different vision of communist solidarity, one that demanded vigilance and purity – first of all ideological purity, the absence of anything that smacked of "Trotskyism." Trotskyism, of course, could designate almost any sort of "enemy" and any sort of difference might arouse suspicions of it. By 1937 deepening anxieties about the threat of war brought hundreds of foreign communists under suspicion; any émigré might be a foreign agent in disguise.[39] And yet foreign communists were still bringing their children to the Soviet Union, appealing for help as participants in a vital international movement. Only in the aftermath of World War II did Stalinism decisively subordinate internationalism to anticosmopolitanism. However even then, the desire for and the memory of the hybrid solidarity of the interwar years remained a central element of the life stories of many communists especially, but not only, veterans of Spain. To stop being a communist, to stop wanting to be a communist – or to renounce the good that one had done as a communist – was to stop being oneself or one's imagined best self. By recovering the lives of individual communists and taking seriously their political and emotional ties to Moscow and one another, we can begin to understand the appeal of a cause that promised solidarity even as it practiced terror.

The personal dimension is particularly clear in the case of people like Nelson, who, as the extent of Stalin's crimes became clear, left the party, but "could not and would not renounce my past."[40] Among the "proud" moments he refused to abandon was participation in the war in Spain, a decision reinforced by "close kinship with the other vets."[41] Likewise, although Ibárruri's letters and Martin's memory project may have effectively whitewashed the Soviet role in Spain, they also worked to preserve international connections and personal memories from the corrosive influence of Khrushchev's revelations. For many veterans, the memory of "the cause of all advanced and progressive humanity" remained an essential one and therefore had to be uncoupled, consciously

39 William J. Chase, *Enemies within the Gates? The Comintern and Stalinist Repression, 1934–1939* (New Haven: Yale University Press, 2001), 226.

40 Nelson et al., *American Radical*, 399. Josie McLellan, "The Politics of Communist Biography: Alfred Kantorowicz and the Spanish Civil War," *German History* 22, no. 4 (November 2004): 541.

41 Nelson et al., *American Radical*, 409.

or not, from the knowledge that the phrase was Stalin's. Thus idealized, the cause offered a touchstone and a resource for others seeking to build a new egalitarian world without borders.[42] At VALB reunions, the veterans' literal and metaphorical grandchildren still raise their fists in antifascist salute and sing the *Internationale*, not in tribute to the Soviet Union or Stalin, but to remember a moment of palpable international solidarity when everyone knew the same song in dozens of languages.

[42] Glazer, *Radical Nostalgia*, 131–72.

Bibliography

Archives

Archivo Histórico del Partido Comunista de España (AHPCE), Madrid

Dirigentes PCE
Documentos PCE
Emigración Política

Archivo Histórico Nacional (AHN), Madrid

Archive of Margarita Nelken

Arxiu Nacional de Catalunya (ANC), Barcelona

Centro Español de Moscú

Bancroft Library, University of California, Berkeley

Veterans of the Abraham Lincoln Brigade, Bay Area Post (VALB) BANC MSS 71/105 z

Columbia University Rare Book and Manuscript Library

Harrison E. Salisbury Papers

Federal Bureau of Investigation (FBI) Files

Mildred Bremler [Milly Bennett], HQ 100-124391/SF 100-12592
Michael Gruzenburg [Mikhail Borodin], 65-HQ-58053

Hoover Institution Archives

Milly Bennett Papers
Robert Gladnick Papers

National Archives at College Park, Maryland (NACP)

Record Group 59 Department of State

Rossiiskii gosudarstvennyi arkhiv literatury i isskustva (RGALI), Moscow

Fond 2555 Kel'in, Fedor Viktorovich

Rossiiskii gosudarstvennyi arkhiv sotsial'no-politicheskoi istorii (RGASPI)

Fond 495 Executive Committee of the Comintern (Library of Congress, Washington, DC); Personal files (Moscow)
Fond 515 Communist Party of the USA (Tamiment Library, New York University)
Fond 531 International Lenin School (Library of Congress)
Fond 532 Communist University of the Toilers of the East (KUTV) (Moscow)
Fond 545 International Brigades of the Army of the Spanish Republic (Tamiment Library)

Tamiment Library/Robert F. Wagner Labor Archives, Elmer Holmes Bobst Library, New York University

Edward J. Falkowski Papers TAM 120 (Falkowski Papers)
Archive of the Abraham Lincoln Brigade
ALBA 001 Fredericka Martin Papers
ALBA 008 Steve Nelson Papers
ALBA 069 Veterans of the Abraham Lincoln Brigade: Complaints of Discrimination during WWII
ALBA 191 Robert Merriman Papers
ALBA 240 Mito Kruth Papers

University of Illinois Rare Book and Manuscript Library

Spanish Civil War Collection, correspondence

Published Primary Sources

Abbe, James E. *I Photograph Russia*. London: G. G. Harrap, 1935.
About Turn: The British Communist Party and the Second World War: The Verbatim Record of the Central Committee Meetings of 25 September and 2–3 October 1939. London: Lawrence and Wishart, 1990.
Abramson, Paulina and Adelina Abramson. *Mosaico Roto*. Madrid: Compañía Literaria, 1994.

Acier, Marcel, ed. *From Spanish Trenches: Recent Letters from Spain*. New York: Modern Age, 1937.

Beal, Fred E. *Proletarian Journey: New England, Gastonia, Moscow*. New York: Hillman-Curl, 1937.

Bennett, Milly. *On Her Own: Journalistic Adventures from San Francisco to the Chinese Revolution, 1917–1927*. Edited by A. Tom Grunfeld. Armonk, NY: M. E. Sharpe, 1993.

Bentley, Elizabeth. *Out of Bondage*. New York: Devin-Adair, 1951.

Bessie, Alvah. *Alvah Bessie's Civil War Notebooks*. Edited by Dan Bessie. Lexington: University of Kentucky Press, 2002.

Bessie, Alvah and Albert Prago, eds., *Our Fight: Writings by Veterans of the Abraham Lincoln Brigade*. New York: Monthly Press, 1987.

Canciones de las Brigadas Internacionales. 1938. Reprint. Seville: Renacimiento, 2007.

Carrillo, Santiago. *Demain l'Espagne: Entretiens avec Régis Debray et Max Gallo*. Paris: Éditions du Seuil, 1974.

——— *Memorias: Testimonio polémico de un protagonista relevante de nuestra transición*. Barcelona: Planeta, 2008.

Carroll, Peter N., Michael Nash, and Melvin Small, eds. *The Good Fight Continues: World War II Letters from the Abraham Lincoln Brigade*. New York: New York University Press, 2006.

Castro Delgado, Enrique. *Mi fe se perdió en Moscú*. Barcelona: Luís de Caralt, 1964.

Chen Leyda, Si-lan. *Footnote to History*. New York: Dance Horizons, 1984.

Chen, Percy. *China Called Me: My Life inside the Chinese Revolution*. Boston: Little Brown, 1979.

Communist International. *XIII Plenum IKKI: Stenograficheskii otchet*. Moscow: Partizdat, 1934.

Crome, Len. "Walter (1897–1947): A Soldier in Spain." *History Workshop Journal*, no. 9 (Spring 1980): 116–28.

Crossman, Richard, ed. *The God that Failed*. 1950. Reprint. New York: Bantam Books, 1965.

Czitrom, Daniel. "Volunteers for Liberty: Letters from Joe and Leo Gordon, Americans in Spain, 1937–38." *Massachusetts Review* 25 (Fall 1984): 348–54.

Dallin, Alexander and F. I. Firsov, eds. *Dimitrov and Stalin, 1934–1943: Letters from the Soviet Archives*. New Haven: Yale University Press, 2000.

Degras, Jane, ed. *The Communist International 1919–1943: Documents*. Vol. 3, *1929–1943*. London: Frank Cass, 1965.

Díaz, José and Dolores Ibárruri. *España y la guerra imperialista*. Mexico City: Editorial Popular, 1939.

Dimitrov, Georgi. *The Diary of Georgi Dimitrov, 1933–1939*. Edited by Ivo Banac. New Haven: Yale University Press, 2003.

Dollard, John. *Fear in Battle*. Washington, DC: Infantry Journal, 1944.

Edmonds, Lloyd. *Letters from Spain*. Edited by Amirah Inglis. Sydney: George Allen & Unwin, 1985.

Erenburg, Il'ia. *Memoirs: 1921–1941*. Translated by Tatania Shebunina in collaboration with Yvonne Kapp. Cleveland: World Publishing Co., 1963.

Falcón, Irene with Manuel Jiménez and Jesús Montero. *Asalto a los cielos: Mi vida junto a Pasionaria*. Madrid: Temas de Hoy, 1996.

Fast, Howard. *Being Red: A Memoir*. New York: Laurel, 1990.

Feslun, A. G. "Novye dokumenty po 'delu Zorge.'" *Novaia i noveishaia istoriia*, no. 2 (March 2000): 118–46.

Field, Hermann H. and Kate Field. *Trapped in the Cold War: The Ordeal of an American Family*. Stanford: Stanford University Press, 1999.

Fischer, Ernst. *An Opposing Man*. Translated by Peter Ross and Betty Ross. London: Allen Lane, 1974.

Fischer, Louis. *Men and Politics: An Autobiography*. 1941. Reprint. Westport, CT: Greenwood Press, 1970.

______ *Soviet Journey*. 1935. Reprint. Westport, CT: Greenwood Press, 1972.

Fitzpatrick, Sheila and Yuri Slezkine, eds. *In the Shadow of Revolution: Life Stories of Russian Women from 1917 to the Second World War*. Princeton: Princeton University Press, 2000.

Gates, John. *The Story of an American Communist*. New York: Thomas Nelson, 1958.

Glaser Wallach, Erica. *Light at Midnight*. Garden City, NY: Doubleday, 1967.

Gorelov, O. I. "'P'iut partiitsy i komsomol' tsy, i vse, vse': Spavka Informatsionnogo otdela TsK VKP(b) I. V. Stalinu, 1925 g." *Istoricheskii archiv*, 2001, no. 1: 4–13.

Haywood, Harry. *Black Bolshevik: Autobiography of an Afro-American Communist*. Chicago: Liberator, 1978.

Hearings before a Special Committee on Un-American Activities, House of Representatives, Seventy-fifth Congress, Third Session, vol. 2. Washington, DC: U.S. Government Printing Office, 1938.

Hearings before the Committee on Un-American Activities, House of Representatives, Eighty-fourth Congress: Investigation of Communist Activities in the Seattle, Wash., Area. Washington, DC: U.S. Government Printing Office, 1955.

Henderson, Loy W. *A Question of Trust: The Origins of US-Soviet Diplomatic Relations: The Memoirs of Loy W. Henderson*. Stanford: Hoover Institution Press, 1986.

Hernández, Jesús. *En el país de la gran mentira*. Madrid: G. del Toro, 1974.

Herrick, William. *Jumping the Line: Adventures and Misadventures of an American Radical*. Madison: University of Wisconsin Press, 1998.

Hobsbawm, Eric. *Interesting Times: A Twentieth-Century Life*. New York: New Press, 2002.

Hoover, J. Edgar. "1938 Memorandum to Attorney General Homer Cummings and President Franklin Roosevelt on the Spanish Civil War and the New York Workers School." *Science and Society* 68, no. 3 (Fall 2004): 361–3.

Ibarruri, A. "Moi brat Ruben." In *My budem borot'sia vmeste: Ocherki o boitsakh-internatsionalistakh*, edited by V. R. Tomin, 9–21. Moscow: Izdatel'stvo politicheskoi literatury, 1985.

Ibárruri, Dolores. *Memorias de Pasionaria, 1939–1977: Me faltaba España*. Barcelona: Planeta, 1984.

______ *They Shall Not Pass: The Autobiography of La Pasionaria*. New York: International Publishers, 1976.

Jaffe, Philip. "The Strange Case of Anna Louise Strong." *Survey*, no. 53 (1964): 129–39.

Kantorowicz, Alfred. *Chapaev – batal'on dvadtsati odnoi natsional'nosti*. Moscow: Khudozhestvennaia literatura, 1939.

Kennan, George F. [X, pseud.]. "The Sources of Soviet Conduct." *Foreign Affairs* 25, no. 4 (July 1947): 566–82.

Kennell, Ruth and Milly Bennett. "American Immigrants in Russia," *American Mercury* 25, no. 100 (April 1932): 463–72.

——— "They All Come to Moscow." *American Mercury* 24, no. 96 (December 1931): 394–401.

Kol'tsov, Mikhail. *Ispanskii dnevnik*. Moscow: Grifon, 2005.

Krymov, Afanasii G. *Istoriko-memuarnyie zapiski kitaiskogo revoliutsionera*. Moscow: Nauka, 1989.

Lebedeva, N. S. and M. M. Narinskii, eds. *Komintern i vtoraia mirovaia voina: Chast' I: do 22 iunia 1941 g*. Moscow: Pamiatniki istorichskoi mysli, 1994.

——— *Komintern i vtoraia mirovaia voina: Chast' II: posle 22 iuniia 1941 g*. Moscow: Pamiatniki istoricheskoi mysli, 1998.

Leder, Mary M. *My Life in Stalinist Russia: An American Woman Looks Back*. Edited by Laurie Bernstein. Bloomington: Indiana University Press, 2001.

Lee, Laurie. *Moment of War: A Memoir of the Spanish Civil War*. New York: New Press, 1991.

Leonhard, Wolfgang. *Child of the Revolution*. Translated by C. M. Woodhouse. 1957. Reprint. London: Ink Links, 1979.

London, Artur. *The Confession*. Translated by Alastair Hamilton. New York: William Morrow, 1970.

Longo, Luigi. *Las Brigadas Internacionales en España*. Translated by Victor Flores Olea. Mexico City: Ediciones Era, 1966.

Lyons, Eugene. *Assignment in Utopia*. New York: Harcourt Brace, 1937.

Merriman, Marion and Warren Lerude. *American Commander in Spain: Robert Hale Merriman and the Abraham Lincoln Brigade*. Reno: University of Nevada Press, 1986.

Mije, Antonio. *Los refugiados republicanos españoles en Francia y la solidaridad americana*. Mexico City: Editorial Morales, 1940.

Miller, Donald and Steve Nelson. "Fighting in Spain: A Conversation with Steve Nelson." *Salmagundi*, no. 76/77 (Fall 1987–Winter 1988): 113–32.

Murphy, J. T. "The First Year of the Lenin School." *Communist International*, 30 September1927: 267–9.

Nelken, Margarita. *Las torres del Kremlin*. Mexico City: Industrial y distribuidora, 1943.

Nelson, Cary and Jefferson Hendricks, eds. *Madrid 1937: Letters of the Abraham Lincoln Brigade from the Spanish Civil War*. New York: Routledge, 1996.

Nelson, Steve. *The Thirteenth Juror*. Leipzig: Paul List Verlag, 1956.

——— *The Volunteers*. New York: Masses and Mainstream, 1953.

Nelson, Steve, James R. Barrett, and Rob Ruck. *Steve Nelson, American Radical*. Pittsburgh: University of Pittsburgh Press, 1982.

Orwell, George. *Homage to Catalonia*. 1938. Reprint. San Diego: Harcourt Brace Jovanovich, 1980.

Paynter, Will. *My Generation*. London: George Allen & Unwin, 1972.

Regler, Gustav. *The Owl of Minerva*. Translated by Norman Denny. London: Rupert Hart-Davis, 1959.

Riddell, John, ed. *Workers of the World and Oppressed Peoples, Unite! Proceedings and Documents of the Second Congress, 1920*, vol. 2. New York: Pathfinder Press, 1991.

Riggio, Thomas P. and James L. W. West III, eds. *Dreiser's Russian Diary*. Philadelphia: University of Pennsylvania Press, 1996.

Romilly, Esmond. *Boadilla*. 1937. Reprint. London: Macdonald, 1971.

Rubin, Hank. *Spain's Cause Was Mine: A Memoir of an American Medic in the Spanish Civil War*. Carbondale: Southern Illinois University Press, 1997.

Rust, William. *Britons in Spain: The History of the XVth International Brigade*. London: Lawrence and Wishart, 1939.

Salisbury, Harrison E. *A Journey for Our Times*. New York: Carroll and Graf, 1983.

Schrecker, Ellen ed. *Records of the Subversive Activities Control Board, 1950–1972: Microfilmed from the Holdings of the National Archives and Records Administration*. Frederick, MD: University Publications of America, 1988.

Sennett, William. "Communist Functionary and Corporate Executive." An oral history conducted 1981 and 1982 by Marshall Windmiller, Regional Oral History Office, The Bancroft Library, University of California, Berkeley, 1984.

Strong, Anna Louise. *I Change Worlds: The Remaking of an American*. 1935. Reprint. Seattle: Seal Press, 1979.

Szurek, Alexander. *The Shattered Dream*. Translated by Jacques Grunblatt and Hilda Grunblatt. Boulder, CO: East European Monographs, 1989.

Tagüeña Lacorte, Manuel. *Testimonio de dos guerras*. 1978. Reprint. Barcelona: Planeta, 2005.

Tisa, John. *Recalling the Good Fight: An Autobiography of the Spanish Civil War*. South Hadley, MA: Bergin and Garvey, 1985.

Tuominen, Arvo. *The Bells of the Kremlin: An Experience in Communism*. Translated by Lily Leino. Hanover, NH: University Press of New England, 1983.

United States Department of State. *Foreign Relations of the United States, 1946* (FRUS), vol. 5, *The British Commonwealth, Western and Central Europe*. Washington, DC: U.S. Government Printing Office, 1946.

Utley, Freda. *Lost Illusion*. Philadelphia: Fireside Press, 1948.

______ *Odyssey of a Liberal: Memoirs*. Washington, DC: Washington National Press, 1970.

Wicks, Harry. *Keeping My Head: The Memoirs of a British Bolshevik*. London: Socialist Platform, 1992.

World Committee for the Victims of German Fascism. *The Brown Book of the Hitler Terror and the Burning of the Reichstag*. New York: A. A. Knopf, 1933.

Young, Glennys, ed. *The Communist Experience in the Twentieth Century: A Global History through Sources*. New York: Oxford University Press, 2012.

Zakharov, I. A., ed. "Pis'mo Germana Mellera – I. V. Stalinu." *Voprosy istorii estestvoznaniia tekhniki*, 1997, no. 1: 65–76.

Zhang, Guotao. *The Rise of the Chinese Communist Party, 1928–1938: Volume Two of the Autobiography of Chang Kuo-t'ao*. Lawrence: University Press of Kansas, 1972.

Selected Secondary Sources

Alba, Víctor and Stephen Schwartz. *Spanish Marxism versus Soviet Communism: A History of the POUM*. New Brunswick, NJ: Transaction Books, 1988.

Allen, David E. "The Soviet Union and the Spanish Civil War." PhD diss., Stanford University, 1952.

Allen, Julia M. "'That Accursed Aesopian Language': Prosecutorial Framing of Linguistic Evidence in *US v. Foster*, 1949." *Rhetoric and Public Affairs* 4, no. 1 (2001): 109–34.

Alpert, Michael. "The Clash of Spanish Armies: Contrasting Ways of War in Spain, 1936–1939." *War in History* 6, no. 3 (July 1999): 331–51.

——— *A New International History of the Spanish Civil War*. New York: St. Martin's Press, 1994.

Alted Vigil, Alicia. *La voz de los vencidos: El exilio republicano de 1939*. Madrid: Aguilar, 2005.

Arasa, Daniel. *Los españoles de Stalin*. Barcelona: Editorial Vorágine, 1993.

Avilés Farré, Juan. *Pasionaria: La Mujer y el mito*. Barcelona: Random House Mondadori, 2005.

Azadovskii, Konstantin and Boris Egorov. "From Anti-Westernism to Anti-Semitism: Stalin and the Impact of the 'Anti-Cosmopolitan' Campaigns on Soviet Culture." *Journal of Cold War Studies* 4, no. 1 (Winter 2002): 66–80.

Baldwin, Kate A. *Beyond the Color Line and the Iron Curtain: Reading Encounters between Black and Red, 1922–1963*. Durham, NC: Duke University Press, 2002.

Balfour, Sebastian. *Deadly Embrace: Morocco and the Road to the Spanish Civil War*. Oxford: Oxford University Press, 2002.

Barber, John. "Stalin's Letter to the Editors of *Proletarskaya Revoliutsiya*," *Soviet Studies* 28, no. 1 (January 1976): 21–41.

Bartošek, Karel. "Central and Southeastern Europe." In *The Black Book of Communism: Crimes, Terror, Repression*, edited by Stéphane Courtois et al., 394–456. Translated by Jonathan Murphy and Mark Kramer. Cambridge, MA: Harvard University Press, 1999.

Baxell, Richard. *British Volunteers in the Spanish Civil War: The British Battalion in the International Brigades, 1936–1939*. London: Routledge, 2004.

Beevor, Antony. *The Spanish Civil War, 1936–1939*. New York: Penguin, 1982.

Belfrage, Cedric. *The American Inquisition, 1945–1960*. Indianapolis: Bobbs-Merrill, 1973.

Belknap, Michal R. "Cold War in the Courtroom: The Foley Square Communist Trial." In *American Political Trials*, revised ed., edited by Michal R. Belknap, 207–32. Westport, CT: Greenwood Press, 1994.

Bolloten, Burnett. *The Spanish Civil War: Revolution and Counterrevolution*. Chapel Hill: University of North Carolina Press, 1991.

Bonnell, Victoria. *Iconography of Power: Soviet Political Posters under Lenin and Stalin*. Berkeley: University of California Press, 1999.

Boym, Svetlana. *Common Places: Mythologies of Everyday Life in Russia*. Cambridge, MA: Harvard University Press, 1994.

Brandenberger, David. *National Bolshevism: Stalinist Mass Culture and the Formation of Modern Russian National Identity, 1931–1956*. Cambridge, MA: Harvard University Press, 2002.

Braun, Matthias. "Vremja Golovokruzenija – Zeit des Schwindels: Der Alkoholische Raush als Geste Kulturellen Beharrens in der Sowjetunion der 1920er – und 1930er-Jahr." *Zeitschrift für Geschichtswissenschaft* 51, no. 10 (2003): 896–911.

Brome, Vincent. *The International Brigades: Spain, 1936–1939*. London: Heinemann, 1965.

Brooks, Jeffrey. *Thank You, Comrade Stalin: Soviet Public Culture from Revolution to Cold War*. Princeton: Princeton University Press, 2000.

Broué, Pierre. *Histoire de l'Internationale communiste: 1919–1943*. Paris: Fayard, 1997.

Buchanan, Tom. "The Death of Bob Smillie, the Spanish Civil War, and the Eclipse of the Independent Labour Party." *Historical Journal* 40, no. 2 (June 1997): 435–61.

_____ "The Death of Bob Smillie: A Reply." *Historical Journal* 43, no. 4 (December 2000): 1009–112.

_____ "Holding the Line: The Political Strategy of the International Brigade Association, 1939–1977." *Labour History Review* 66, no. 3 (Winter 2001): 294–312.

Buhle, Paul. "The Hollywood Blacklist and the Jew." *Tikkun* 10, no. 5 (September/October 1995): 35–40.

Byrnes, Mark. "Unfinished Business: The United States and Franco's Spain, 1944–47." *Diplomacy and Statecraft* 11, no. 1 (March 2000): 129–62.

Cabeza Sánchez-Albornoz, Sonsoles. "Posición de la República española en el exilio ante el ingreso de España en la ONU." *Cuadernos de Historia Contemporánea*, no. 17 (1995): 147–67.

Cabeza San Deogracias, José. "Buscando héroes: La historia de Antonio Col como ejemplo del uso de la narrativa como propaganda durante la Guerra Civil española." *Revista Historia y Comunicación Social* 10 (2005): 37–50.

_____ *El descanso del guerrero: El cine en Madrid durante la Guerra Civil española (1936–1939)*. Madrid: Ediciones Rialp, 2005.

Campbell, Alan, John McIlroy, Barry McLoughlin, and John Halstead. "The International Lenin School: A Response to Cohen and Morgan." *Twentieth Century British History* 15, no. 1 (2004): 51–76.

Cardona, Gabriel. "El Ejercito Popular y las Brigadas Internacionales ¿Cuál fue la importancia de las Brigadas? In *Las Brigadas Internacionales: El contexto internacional, los medidos de propaganda, literatura y memorias*, edited by Manuel Requena Gallego and Rosa María Sepúlveda Losa, 37–51. Cuenca: Ediciones de la Universidad de Castilla-La Mancha, 2003.

Carlson, Elof Axel. *Hermann Joseph Muller, 1890–1967*. Washington, DC: National Academy of Sciences, 2009.

Carr, E. H. *The Comintern and the Spanish Civil War*. New York: Pantheon, 1984.

Carroll, Peter N. *The Odyssey of the Abraham Lincoln Brigade: Americans in the Spanish Civil War*. Stanford: Stanford University Press, 1994.

Carroll, Peter with assistance from Daniel Bertwell. "Premature Anti-Fascists, Again." *The Volunteer* 25, no. 4 (December 2003): 5–6, 8.

Casas, Julio Martín and Pedro Carvajal Urquijo. *El exilio español (1936–1978)*. Barcelona: Planeta, 2002.

Cattell, David T. *Communism and the Spanish Civil War*. 1955. Reprint. New York: Russell & Russell, 1965.

_____ *Soviet Diplomacy and the Spanish Civil War*. Berkeley: University of California Press, 1957.

Caute, David. *The Great Fear: The Anti-Communist Purge under Truman and Eisenhower*. New York: Simon and Schuster, 1978.

_____ *The Dancer Defects: The Struggle for Cultural Supremacy during the Cold War*. New York: Oxford University Press, 2003.

Chase, William J. *Enemies within the Gates? The Comintern and the Stalinist Repression, 1934–1939*. New Haven: Yale University Press, 2001.

Chatterjee, Choi. "Soviet Heroines and the Language of Modernity, 1930–39." In *Women in the Stalin Era*, edited by Melanie Ilič, 49–68. Basingstoke: Palgrave, 2001.

Chubarin, A. O. ed. *Istoriia kommunisticheskogo internatsionala, 1919–1943: Dokumental'nye ocherki*. Moscow: Nauka, 2002.

Cierva, Ricardo de la. *Brigadas Internacionales, 1936–1996: La verdadera historia: Mentira histórica y error de Estado*. Madrid: Editorial Fénix, 1997.

Clark, Katerina. *Moscow, the Fourth Rome: Stalinism, Cosmopolitanism, and the Evolution of Soviet Culture, 1931–1941*. Cambridge, MA: Harvard University Press, 2011.

Claudín, Fernando. *The Communist Movement from Comintern to Cominform: Part One, The Crisis of the Communist International*. Translated by Brian Pearce. New York: Monthly Review Press, 1967.

Clune, Lori. "Great Importance World-Wide: Presidential Decision-Making and the Executions of Julius and Ethel Rosenberg." *American Communist History* 10, no. 3 (December 2011): 263–84.

Cohen, Gidon and Kevin Morgan. "Stalin's Sausage Machine: British Students at the International Lenin School, 1926–37." *Twentieth Century British History* 13, no. 4 (2002): 327–55.

——— "British Students at the International Lenin School, 1926–37: A Reaffirmation of Methods, Results, and Conclusions." *Twentieth Century British History* 15, no. 1 (2004): 77–107.

———"The International Lenin School: A Final Comment." *Twentieth Century British History* 18, no. 1 (2007): 129–33.

Cohen, Yves. "La co-construction de la personne et de la bureaucratie: Aspects de la subjectivé de Staline et des cadres soviétiques (années 30)." In *Stalinistische Subjekte: Individuum und System in der Sowjetunion und der Komintern, 1929–1953*, edited by Brigitte Studer and Heiko Haumann, 175–96. Zurich: Chronos, 2006.

Colodny, Robert G. *The Struggle for Madrid: The Central Epic of the Spanish Conflict, 1936–1937*. New York: Transaction Publishers, 2009.

Colomina Limonero, Immaculada. *Dos patrias, tres mil destinos: Vida y exilio de los niños de la guerra de España refugiados en la Unión Soviética*. Madrid: Ediciones Cinca, 2010.

Conquest, Robert. *The Great Terror: A Reassessment*. New York: Oxford University Press, 2008.

Corke, Sarah-Jane. *US Covert Operations and Cold War Strategy: Truman, Secret Warfare and the CIA, 1943–53*. New York: Routledge, 2008.

Corral, Pedro. *Desertores: La Guerra Civil que nadie quiere contar*. Barcelona: Random House Mondadori, 2006.

David-Fox, Michael. *Showcasing the Great Experiment: Cultural Diplomacy and Western Visitors to the Soviet Union*. New York: Oxford University Press, 2012.

Dawson, Graham. *Soldier Heroes: British Adventure, Empire and the Imagining of Masculinities*. London: Routledge, 1994.

Deery, Phillip. "'A Blot upon Liberty': McCarthyism, Dr. Barsky and the Joint Anti-Fascist Refugee Committee." *American Communist History* 8, no. 2 (December 2009): 167–96.

Delacor, Regina M. "From Potential Friends to Potential Enemies: The Internment of 'Hostile Foreigners' in France at the Beginning of the Second World War." *Journal of Contemporary History* 35, no. 3 (2000): 361–8.

Derrick, Jonathan. *Africa's "Agitators": Militant Anti-Colonialism in Africa and the West, 1918–1939*. New York: Columbia University Press, 2008.

Dillard, Angela D. *Faith in the City: Preaching Radical Social Change in Detroit*. Ann Arbor: University of Michigan Press, 2007.

Dreyfus-Armand, Geneviève. *L'exil des Républicains espagnols en France*. Paris: Albin Michel, 1999.

Dunham, Vera S. *In Stalin's Time: Middleclass Values in Soviet Fiction*. 1976. Reprint. Durham, NC: Duke University Press, 1990.

Ealham, Chris. "'Myths' and the Spanish Civil War: Some Old, Some Exploded, Some Clearly Borrowed and Some Almost 'Blue.'" *Journal of Contemporary History* 42, no. 2 (2007): 365–76.

Earle, Rebecca. "Introduction: Letters, Writers, and the Historian." In *Epistolary Selves: Letters and Letter-Writers, 1600–1945*, edited by Rebecca Earle, 1–12. Aldershot: Ashgate, 1999.

Eby, Cecil. *Between the Bullet and the Lie: American Volunteers in the Spanish Civil War*. New York: Holt, Rinehart and Winston, 1969.

Edwards, Jill. *Anglo-American Relations and the Franco Question, 1945–1955*. Oxford: Clarendon Press, 1999.

Eiroa San Francisco, Matilde. "Sobrevivir en el socialismo: Organización y medios de comunicación de los exilados comunistas en las democracias populares." *Historia social* 69 (2011): 71–90.

Elleman, Bruce. *Moscow and the Emergence of Communist Power in China: The Nanchang Rising and the Birth of the Red Army*. New York: Routledge, 2009.

Elorza, Antonio and Marta Bizcarrondo. *Queridos camaradas: La Internacional Comunista y España, 1919–1939*. Barcelona: Editorial Planeta, 1999.

Elpat'evskii, A. V. *Ispanskaia emigratsiia v SSSR: Istoriografiia i istochniki, popytka interpretatsii*. Tver: Izdatel'stvo "GERS," 2002.

Engerman, David C. "Modernization from the Other Shore: American Observers and the Cost of Soviet Economic Development." *American Historical Review* 105, no. 2 (April 2000): 383–415.

Epstein, Catherine. *The Last Revolutionaries: German Communists and Their Century*. Cambridge, MA: Harvard University Press, 2003.

Esenwein, George. "Freedom Fighters or Comintern Soldiers? Writing about the 'Good Fight' during the Spanish Civil War," *Civil Wars* 12, no. 1–2 (March–June 2010): 156–66.

Estruch Tobella, Joan. *Historia oculta del PCE*. Madrid: Ediciones Temas de Hoy, 2000.

Fabréguet, Michel. "Un groupe de réfugiés politiques: Les républicains espagnols des camps d'internement français aux camps de concentration nationaux-socialistes." *Revue d'histoire de la deuxième guerre mondiale et des conflits contemporains* 36, no. 144 (October 1986): 19–38.

Fernbach, David. "Tom Wintringham and Socialist Defense Strategy." *History Workshop*, no. 14 (Autumn 1982): 63–91.

Field, Douglas ed. *American Cold War Culture*. Edinburgh: Edinburgh University Press, 2005.

Filatova, Irina. "Indoctrination or Scholarship? Education of Africans at the Communist University of the Toilers of the East in the Soviet Union, 1923–1937." *Paedagogica historica* 35, no. 1 (February 1999): 41–66.

Firsov, Fridrikh I. "Dimitrov, the Comintern, and Stalinist Repression." In *Stalin's Terror: High Politics and Mass Repression in the Soviet Union*, edited by Barry McLoughlin and Kevin McDermott, 56–81. Basingstoke: Palgrave Macmillan, 2003.

Fowler, Josephine. *Japanese and Chinese Immigrant Activists: Organizing in American and International Communist Movements, 1919–1933*. New Brunswick, NJ: Rutgers University Press, 2007.

Fradkin, Viktor. *Delo Kol'tsova*. Moscow: Vagrius, 2002.

Francis, Hywel. *Miners against Fascism: Wales and the Spanish Civil War*. London: Lawrence and Wishart, 1984.

——— "'Say Nothing and Leave in the Middle of the Night': The Spanish Civil War Revisited." *History Workshop Journal*, no.32 (Autumn 1991): 69–76.

Fundación Pablo Iglesias. *Los rusos en la Guerra de España, 1936–1939*. (Madrid: Fundación Pablo Iglesias, 2009).

Fussell, Paul. *Wartime: Understanding and Behavior in the Second World War*. New York: Oxford University Press, 1990.

Gaddis, John Lewis. *The Cold War: A New History*. New York: Penguin, 2006.

Gerassi, John. *The Premature Anti-Fascists: North American Volunteers in the Spanish Civil War, 1936–1939*. New York: Praeger 1986.

Goldman, Wendy Z. *Women, the State, and Revolution: Soviet Family Policy and Social Life, 1917–1936*. New York: Cambridge University Press, 1993.

González-Allende, Iker. "Masculinities in Conflict: Representations of the Other in Narrative during the Spanish Civil War." *Hispanic Research Journal* 11, no. 3 (June 2010): 193–209.

Graffy, Julian. *Chapaev*. London: I.B. Tauris, 2009.

Graham, Helen. *Socialism and War: The Spanish Socialist Party in Power and Crisis, 1936–1939*. New York: Cambridge University Press, 1991.

——— "Spain Betrayed? The New Historical McCarthyism." *Science and Society* 68, no. 3 (Fall 2004): 364–69.

——— *The Spanish Civil War: A Very Short Introduction*. New York: Oxford University Press, 2005.

——— *The Spanish Republic at War, 1936–1939*. New York: Cambridge University Press, 2002.

Graziosi, Andrea. "Foreign Workers in Soviet Russia, 1920–40: Their Experience and Their Legacy." *International Labor and Working-Class History* 33 (Spring, 1988): 38–59.

——— "'Visitors from Other Times': Foreign Workers in the Prewar Piatletki." *Cahiers du monde russe et soviétique* 29, no. 2 (April–June 1988): 161–80.

Grose, Peter. *Operation Rollback: America's Secret War behind the Iron Curtain*. Boston: Houghton Mifflin, 2000.

Halpern, Martin. "'I'm Fighting for Freedom': Coleman Young, HUAC, and the Detroit African American Community." *Journal of American Ethnic History* 17, no. 1 (Fall 1997): 19–38.

Hamilton, Carrie. "Activism and Representations of Motherhood in the Autobiography of Dolores Ibárruri, Pasionaria." *Journal of Romance Studies*, 1, no. 1 (2001): 17–25.

Haslam, Jonathan. *Russia's Cold War: From the October Revolution to the Fall of the Wall*. New Haven: Yale University Press, 2011.

Haynes, John. *New Soviet Man: Gender and Masculinity in Stalinist Soviet Cinema*. Manchester: Manchester University Press, 2003.

Haynes, John Earl and Harvey Klehr. *Early Cold War Spies: The Espionage Trials that Shaped American Politics*. New York: Cambridge University Press, 2006.

______ *Venona: Decoding Soviet Espionage in America*. New Haven: Yale University Press, 1999.

Haynes, John Earl, Harvey Klehr, and Alexander Vassiliev. *Spies: The Rise and Fall of the KGB in America*. Ann Arbor, MI: Sheridan Books, 2009.

Healey, Dan. *Homosexual Desire in Revolutionary Russia: The Regulation of Sexual and Gender Dissent*. Chicago: University of Chicago Press, 2001.

Hellbeck, Jochen. *Revolution on My Mind: Writing a Diary under Stalin*. Cambridge, MA: Harvard University Press, 2006.

Hernández Sánchez, Fernando. "Jesús Hernández, pistolero, ministro, espía y renegado." *Historia 16*, no. 368 (2006): 78–89.

Heron, Craig. "The Boys and Their Booze: Masculinities and Public Drinking in Working-Class Hamilton, 1890–1946." *Canadian Historical Review* 86, no. 3 (September 2005): 411–52.

Herrmann, Gina. "The Hermetic Goddess: Dolores Ibárruri as Text." *Letras Peninsulares* 11 (Spring 1998): 181–206.

______ *Written in Red: The Communist Memoir in Spain*. Urbana: University of Illinois Press, 2010.

Hewitt, Andrew. *Political Inversions: Homosexuality, Fascism, and the Modernist Imaginary*. Stanford: Stanford University Press, 1996.

Hloušek, Vít and Lubomír Kopeček. *Origin, Ideology, and Transformation of Political Parties: East-Central and Western Europe Compared*. Burlington, VT: Ashgate, 2010.

Hodos, George H. *Show Trials: Stalinist Purges in Eastern Europe, 1948–1954*. New York: Praeger, 1987.

Holubnychy, Lydia. *Michael Borodin and the Chinese Revolution, 1923–1925*. Ann Arbor: University Microfilms for the East Asian Institute, Columbia University, 1979.

Hoffmann, David. *Stalinist Values: The Cultural Norms of Soviet Modernity, 1917–1941*. Ithaca: Cornell University Press, 2003.

______ "Was There a 'Great Retreat' from Soviet Socialism? Stalinist Culture Reconsidered." *Kritika* 5, no. 4 (Fall 2004): 651–74.

Hopkins, James K. *Into the Heart of the Fire: The British in the Spanish Civil War*. Stanford: Stanford University Press, 1998.

Horwitz, Morton J. "Jews and McCarthyism: A View from the Bronx." In *Secret Agents: The Rosenberg Case, McCarthyism, and Fifties America*, edited by Marjorie Garber and Rebecca L. Walkowitz, eds., 257–64. New York: Routledge, 1994.

Humphries, Reynold. *Hollywood's Blacklists: A Political and Cultural History*. Edinburgh: Edinburgh University Press, 2008.

Hurd, Madeleine. "Liberals, Socialists, and Sobriety: The Rhetoric of Citizenship in Turn-of-the-Century Sweden." *International Labor and Working-Class History* 45 (Spring 1994): 44–62.

Ilič, Melanie, ed. *Women in the Stalin Era*. Basingstoke: Palgrave, 2001.

Iordache, Luiza. *Republicanos españoles en el Gulag (1939–1956)*. Barcelona: Institut de Ciències Polítiques i Socials, 2008.

Ivantsov, Igor' Grigor'evich. "Vnutripartiinyi kontrol' VKP(b) v bor'be s p'ianstvom v srede kommunistov (1920-e – nachalo 1930-kh godov)." *Prepodavanie Istorii v Shkole*, 2011, no. 2: 77–80.

Jackson, Gabriel. *Juan Negrín: Spanish Republican War Leader*. Portland, OR: Sussex Academic Press, 2010.

Jackson, Michael W. *Fallen Sparrows: The International Brigades in the Spanish Civil War*. Philadelphia: American Philosophical Society, 1994.

Jacobs, Dan N. *Borodin: Stalin's Man in China*. Cambridge, MA: Harvard University Press, 1981.

Johnson, David K. *The Lavender Scare: The Cold War Persecution of Gays and Lesbians in the Federal Government*. Chicago: University of Chicago Press, 2004.

Johnston, Timothy. *Being Soviet: Identity, Rumour, and Everyday Life under Stalin, 1939–1954*. Oxford: Oxford University Press, 2011.

Johnston, Verle B. *Legions of Babel: The International Brigades in the Spanish Civil War*. University Park: Pennsylvania State University Press, 1969.

Johnstone, Monty. "The CPGB, the Comintern, and the War, 1939–1941: Filling in the Blank Spots." *Science and Society* 61, no. 1 (Spring 1997): 27–45.

Kaplan, Karel. *Report on the Murder of the General Secretary*. Translated by Karel Kovanda. Columbus: Ohio State University Press, 1990.

Katz, Friedrich. "Mexico, Gilberto Bosques, and the Refugees." *The Americas* 57, no. 1 (July 2000): 1–12

Kelley, Robin D. G. *Hammer and Hoe: Alabama Communists during the Great Depression*. Chapel Hill: University of North Carolina Press, 1990.

Kessler, Lauren. *Clever Girl: Elizabeth Bentley, the Spy Who Ushered in the Cold War*. New York: Harper Collins, 2003.

Khlevniuk, Oleg. "The Reasons for the 'Great Terror': The Foreign-Political Aspect." In *Russia in the Age of Wars, 1914–1945*, edited by Silvo Pons and Andrea Romano, 159–70. Milan: Feltrinelli, 2000.

Kirschenbaum, Lisa A. "Exile, Gender, and Communist Self-Fashioning: Dolores Ibárruri (La Pasionaria) in the Soviet Union," *Slavic Review* 71, no. 3 (Fall 2012): 566–89.

Klehr, Harvey. *Communist Cadre: The Social Background of the American Communist Party Elite*. Stanford: Hoover Institution Press, 1978.

Klehr, Harvey, John Earl Haynes, and Fridrikh Igorevich Firsov, eds. *The Secret World of American Communism*. New Haven: Yale University Press, 1995.

Kolb, Eberhard. *The Weimar Republic*, 2nd ed. New York: Routledge, 2005.

Kopstein Jeffrey S. and Jason Wittenberg. "Who Voted Communist? Reconsidering the Social Bases of Radicalism in Interwar Poland." *Slavic Review* 62, no. 1 (Spring 2003): 87–109.

Köstenberger, Julia. "Die Internationale Leninschule (1926–1936)." In *Biographisches Handbuch zu Geschichte der Kommunistischen Internationale: Ein deutsche-russisches Forschungsprojekt*, edited by Michael Buckmiller and Klaus Meschkat, 287–309. Berlin: Academie Verlag, 2007.

Kostyrchenko, G. V. *Tainaia politika Stalina: Vlast' i antisemitzm*. Moscow: Mezhdunardnye otnosheniia, 2001.

Kotkin, Stephen. *Magnetic Mountain: Stalinism as a Civilization*. Berkeley: University of California Press, 1995.

Kowalsky, Daniel. *Stalin and the Spanish Civil War* [electronic resource]. New York: Columbia University Press, 2004. (http://www.gutenberg-e.org/kodo1/index.html).

______ "The Soviet Union and the International Brigades, 1936–1939." *Journal of Slavic Military Studies* 19 (2006): 681–704.

______ "The Soviet Cinematic Offensive in the Spanish Civil War." *Film History: An International Journal* 19, no. 1 (2007): 7–19.

Krekola, Joni. "The Finnish Sector at the International Lenin School." In *Agents of the Revolution: New Biographical Approaches to the History of International Communism in the Age of Lenin and Stalin*, edited by Kevin Morgan, Gidon Cohen, and Andrew Flinn, 289–308. Bern: Peter Lang, 2005.

Krylova, Anna. *Soviet Women in Combat: A History of Violence on the Eastern Front*. New York: Cambridge University Press, 2010.

Kuromiya, Hiroaki. "Accounting for the Great Terror." *Jahrbücher für Geschichte Osteuropas*, Neue Folge, Bd. 53, H.1 (2005): 86–101.

Kuznick, Peter J. *Beyond the Laboratory: Scientists as Political Activists in 1930s America*. Chicago: University of Chicago Press, 1987.

Lannon, Frances. "Women and Images of Women in the Spanish Civil War." *Transactions of the Royal Historical Society*, 6th Ser., vol. 1. (1991): 213–28.

Laucht, Christof. *Elemental Germans: Klaus Fuchs, Rudolf Peierls and the Making of British Nuclear Culture, 1939–59*. New York: Palgrave Macmillan, 2012.

Lazitch, Branko. *Biographical Dictionary of the Comintern: New, Revised, and Expanded Edition*. Stanford: Hoover Institution Press, 1986.

Lenoe, Matthew. *Closer to the Masses: Stalinist Culture, Social Revolution, and Soviet Newspapers*. Cambridge, MA: Harvard University Press, 2004.

______ "In Defense of Timasheff's Great Retreat." *Kritika* 5, no. 4 (Fall 2004): 721–30.

______ *The Kirov Murder and Soviet History*. New Haven: Yale University Press, 2010.

Levy, Robert. *Ana Pauker: The Rise and Fall of a Jewish Communist*. Berkeley: University of California Press, 2001.

Lichtman, Robert and Ronald D. Cohen. "Harvey Matusow, the FBI, and the Justice Department: Becoming a Government Informer-Witness in the McCarthy Era." *American Communist History* 1, no. 1 (2002): 43–68.

Lleonart Amsélem, Alberto José. "El ingreso de España en la ONU: Obstáculos e impulsos." *Cuadernos de Historia Contemporánea*, no. 17 (1995): 101–19.

Lota, V. I. "Vklad voennykh razvedchikov v sozdanie otechestvennogo atomnogo oruzhiia, 1941–1945 gg." *Voenno-istoricheskii zhurnal*, 2006, no. 11: 40–4.

Lukes, Igor. "The Rudolf Slánský Affair: New Evidence." *Slavic Review* 58, no. 1 (Spring 1999): 160–87.

MacKay, Ruth. "History on the Line: The Good Fight and Good History in the Spanish Civil War." *History Workshop Journal*, no. 70 (2010): 199–206.

MacKinnon, Elaine. "Writing History for Stalin: Isaak Izrailevich Mints and the *Istoriia grazhdanskoi voiny*." *Kritika* 6, no. 1 (Winter 2005): 5–54.

Macrakis, Kristie. "Technophilic Hubris and Espionage Styles during the Cold War." *ISIS: Journal of the History of Science in Society* 101, no. 2 (June 2010): 378–85.

Mally, Lynn. "Performing the New Woman: The Komsomolka as Actress and Image in Soviet Youth Theater." *Journal of Social History* 30, no. 1 (Fall 1996): 79–95.

Manley, John. "Moscow Rules? 'Red' Unionism and 'Class against Class' in Britain, Canada, and the United States, 1928–1935." *Labour/Le Travail* 56 (Fall 2005): 9–49.
Mukhamatulin, Timur. "'Prisvoenie Ispanii': Ispaniia v sovetskom obshchestve v 1936–1939 godakh." *Bulletin des DHI Moskau* Band 6 (2012): 113–27 (Perspectivia.net).
Margulies, Sylvia R. *The Pilgrimage to Russia: The Soviet Union and the Treatment of Foreigners, 1924–1937*. Madison: University of Wisconsin Press, 1968.
Mark, Eduard. "*In Re* Alger Hiss: A Final Verdict from the Files of the KGB." *Journal of Cold War Studies* 11, no. 3 (Summer 2009): 26–67.
Martelle, Scott. *The Fear Within: Spies, Commies, and American Democracy on Trial*. New Brunswick, NJ: Rutgers University Press, 2011.
Mastny, Vojtech. *The Cold War and Soviet Insecurity: The Stalin Years*. New York: Oxford University Press, 1998.
Matthews, James. *Reluctant Warriors: Republican Popular Army and Nationalist Army Conscripts in the Spanish Civil War, 1936–1939*. Oxford: Oxford University Press, 2012.
McClellan, Woodford. "Africans and Black Americans in the Comintern Schools, 1925–1934." *International Journal of African Historical Studies* 26, no. 2 (1993): 371–90.
McDermott, Kevin. "A 'Polyphony of Voices'? Czech Popular Opinion and the Slánský Affair." *Slavic Review* 67, no. 4 (Winter 2008): 840–65.
McDermott, Kevin and Jeremy Agnew. *The Comintern: A History of International Communism from Lenin to Stalin*. Basingstoke: Palgrave Macmillan, 1996.
McDermott, Kevin and Matthew Stibbe, eds. *Stalinist Terror in Eastern Europe: Elite Purges and Mass Repression*. Manchester: Manchester University Press, 2010.
McIlroy, John, Barry McLoughlin, Alan Campbell, and John Halsted. "Forging the Faithful: The British at the Lenin School." *Labour History Review* 68, no. 1 (April 2003): 99–128.
McLellan, Josie. *Antifascism and Memory in East Germany: Remembering the International Brigades, 1945–1989*. New York: Oxford University Press, 2004.
______ "'The Politics of Communist Biography: Alfred Kantorowicz and the Spanish Civil War." *German History* 22, no. 4 (November 2004): 536–62.
______ "'I Wanted To Be a Little Lenin': Ideology and the German International Brigade Volunteers." *Journal of Contemporary History* 41, no. 2 (2006): 287–304.
McLoughlin, Barry. "Proletarian Academics or Party Functionaries? Irish Communists at the International Lenin School." *Saothar* 22 (1997): 63–79.
______ "Proletarian Cadres En-route: Austrian NKVD Agents in Britain, 1941–1943." *Labour History Review* 62, no. 3 (Winter 1997): 296–317.
Meaker, Gerald H. *The Revolutionary Left in Spain, 1914–1923*. Stanford: Stanford University Press, 1974.
Meshcheriakov, M.T. *Ispanskaia respublika i Komintern: Natsional'no-revoliutsionnaia voina ispanskogo naroda i politika kommunisticheskogo internatsionala, 1936–1939 gg*. Moscow: Mysl', 1981.
______ "Sud'ba interbrigad v Ispanii po novym dokumentom." *Novaia i noveiashaia istoriia*, 1993, no. 5: 18–41.
Messenger, David A. "A Real Break or Reluctant Parting? France, the United States, and the Spanish Question, 1946." *Journal of European Studies* 38, no. 2 (2008): 141–56.

Minina-Svetlanova, Mariia. "Two Motherlands Are Mine, and I Hold Both Dear in My Heart: Upbringing and Education in the Ivanovo Interdom." *Russian Studies in History* 48, no. 4 (Spring 2010): 74–96.

Momryk, Myron. "Ukrainian Volunteers from Canada in the International Brigades, Spain, 1936–1939." *Journal of Ukrainian Studies* 16 (June 1991): 181–94.

______ "Hungarian Volunteers from Canada in the Spanish Civil War, 1936–1939." *Hungarian Studies Review* 24 (Spring 1997): 3–14.

Moradiellos, Enrique. "The Allies and the Spanish Civil War." In *Spain and the Great Powers in the Twentieth Century*, edited by Sebastian Balfour and Paul Preston, 96–126. London: Routledge, 1999.

______ "The Potsdam Conference and the Spanish Problem," *Contemporary European History* 10, no. 1 (March 2001): 73–90.

Morán, Gregorio. *Miseria y grandeza del Partido Comunista de España, 1939–1985*. Barcelona: Planeta, 1986.

Morgan, Kevin. "Parts of People and Communist Lives." In *Party People, Communist Lives: Explorations in Biography*, edited by John McIlroy, Kevin Morgan, and Alan Campbell, 9–28. London: Lawrence & Wishart, 2001.

Mosse, George. *The Image of Man: The Creation of Modern Masculinity*. New York: Oxford University Press, 1996.

Naison, Mark. *Communists in Harlem during the Depression*. Urbana: University of Illinois Press, 1983.

Nash, Mary. *Defying Male Civilization: Women in the Spanish Civil War*. Denver: Arden Press, 1995.

Nelson, Cary and Jefferson Hendricks. *Edwin Rolfe: A Biographical Essay and Guide to the Rolfe Archive at the University of Illinois at Urbana-Champaign*. Urbana: University of Illinois Press, 1990.

Neuburger, Mary C. *Balkan Smoke: Tobacco and the Making of Modern Bulgaria*. Ithaca: Cornell University Press, 2013.

Newsinger, John and George Kopp. "The Death of Bob Smillie." *Historical Journal* 41, no. 2 (June 1998): 575–78.

Novikova, Olga. "Las visiones de España en la Unión Soviética durante la guerra civil española." *Historia del presente* no. 11 (2008): 9–44.

Núñez, Xosé-Manoel and José M. Faraldo. "The First Great Patriotic War: Spanish Communists and Nationalism, 1936–1939." *Nationalities Papers* 37 (July 2009): 401–24.

O'Keefe, Timothy. "The *Moscow News*: Russia's First English Language Newspaper," *Journalism Quarterly* 50, no. 3 (Autumn 1973): 463–8.

Olmsted, Kathryn. *Red Spy Queen: A Biography of Elizabeth Bentley*. Chapel Hill: University of North Carolina Press, 2002.

Oosterhuis, Harry. "The 'Jews' of the Antifascist Left: Homosexuality and Socialist Resistance to Nazism." *Journal of Homosexuality* 29, no. 2/3 (1995): 227–57.

Orttanelli, Fraser M. *The Communist Party of the United States from the Depression to World War II*. New Brunswick, NJ: Rutgers University Press, 1991.

Panin, E. V. "Kommunisticheskii Universitet Natsional'nykh Men'shinstv Zapada imeni Iu. Iu. Markhlevskogo." In *Platonovskie chteniia: XVI Vserossiiskaia konferentsiia molodykh istorikov*, 176–9. Samara: Izdatel'stvo "Samarskii universitet," 2010.

Pantsov, Alexander V. and Daria A. Spichak. "New Light from the Russian Archives: Chinese Stalinists and Trotskyists at the International Lenin School in Moscow, 1926–1938." *Twentieth Century China* 33, no. 2 (April 2008): 29–50.

Payne, Stanley G. *The Spanish Civil War, the Soviet Union, and Communism*. New Haven: Yale University Press, 2004.

Pennington, Reina. *Wings, Women, and War: Soviet Airwomen in World War II Combat*. Lawrence: University Press of Kansas, 2007.

Petrone, Karen. *Life Has Become More Joyous, Comrades: Celebrations in the Time of Stalin*. Bloomington: Indiana University Press, 2000.

Petrou, Michael. *Renegades: Canadians in the Spanish Civil War*. Vancouver: University of British Columbia Press, 2008.

Phillips, Laura L. "Message in a Bottle: Working-Class Culture and the Struggle for Revolutionary Legitimacy, 1900–1929." *Russian Review* 56 (January 1997): 25–43.

——— "In Defense of Their Families: Working-Class Women, Alcohol, and Politics in Revolutionary Russia." *Journal of Women's History* 11, no. 1 (Spring 1999): 97–120.

Pike, David Wingeate. "Franco et l'admission aux nations unies." *Guerres mondiales et conflits contemporains*, 41, no. 162 (April 1991): 105–14.

——— *In the Service of Stalin: The Spanish Communists in Exile, 1939–1945*. Oxford: Oxford University Press, 1993.

Powers, Madelon. "Women and Public Drinking, 1890–1920," *History Today* 45, no. 2 (February 1995): 46–52.

Preston, Paul. *¡Comrades! Portraits from the Spanish Civil War*. London: Harper Collins, 1999.

——— *Doves of War: Four Women of Spain*. London: Harper Collins, 2002.

Purcell, Hugh. "Kitty Bowler: The English Captain's Spy." *History Today* 62, no. 2 (February 2012): 16–17.

Radosh, Ronald, Mary R. Habek, and Grigory Sevostianov, eds. *Spain Betrayed: The Soviet Union in the Spanish Civil War*. New Haven: Yale University Press, 2001.

Rees, Tim and Andrew Thorpe, eds. *International Communism and the Communist International, 1919–43*. Manchester: Manchester University Press, 1998.

Rees, Tim. "The 'Good Bolsheviks': The Spanish Communist Party and the Third Period." In *In Search of Revolution: International Communist Parties in the Third Period*, edited by Matthew Worley, 174–202. New York: I. B. Tauris, 2004.

———"Deviation and Discipline: Anti-Trotskyism, Bolshevization, and the Spanish Communist Party, 1924–34." *Historical Research* 82, no. 215 (February 2009): 131–56.

——— "Living up to Lenin: Leadership Culture and the Spanish Communist Party, 1920–1939." *History* 97, no. 326 (April 2012): 230–55.

Reid, Susan E. "All Stalin's Women: Gender and Power in Soviet Art in the 1930s." *Slavic Review* 57, no. 1 (Spring 1998): 133–73.

Renshaw, Patrick. "The IWW and the Red Scare, 1917–24." *Journal of Contemporary History* 3, no. 4 (October 1968): 63–72.

Requena Gallego, Manuel ed. *Las Brigadas Internacionales*. Madrid: Marcial Pons, 2004.

Ribalkin, Iurii E. *Operatsiia "X": Sovetskaia voennaia pomoshch' respublikanskoi Ispanii (1936–1939)*. Moscow: AIRO-XX, 2000.

Richards, Michael. *A Time of Silence: Civil War and the Culture of Repression in Franco's Spain, 1936–1945*. New York: Cambridge University Press, 1998.

Richardson, Dan. *Comintern Army: The International Brigades and the Spanish Civil War*. Lexington: University of Kentucky Press, 1982.

Rittersporn, Gábor Tamás. "The Omnipresent Conspiracy: On Soviet Imagery of Politics and Social Relations in the 1930s." In *Stalinist Terror: New Perspectives*, edited by J. Arch Getty and Roberta Manning, 99–115. New York: Cambridge University Press, 1993.

Roberts, Elizabeth. "British and American Volunteers and the Politics of Dress and Demeanour in the Spanish Civil War." *Limina* 14 (2008): 59–70.

______ *"Freedom, Faction, Fame, and Blood": British Soldiers of Conscience in Greece, Spain, and Finland*. Portland, OR: Sussex Academic Press, 2010.

Roberts, Geoffrey. "Soviet Foreign Policy and the Spanish Civil War, 1936–1939." In *Spain in an International Context, 1936–1959*, edited by Christain Leitz and David J. Dunthorn, 81–103. New York: Berghahn, 1999.

Roberts, James S. "Drink and Industrial Work Discipline in 19th Century Germany." *Journal of Social History* 15, no. 1 (Fall 1981): 25–38.

Robins Sharpe, Emily. "Salaria Kea's Spanish Memoirs." *Volunteer* 28, no. 4 (December 2011): 17–19.

Rodríguez Jiménez, José Luis. "La 'Quinta Columna' en la Guerra Civil." *Historia y vida* 20, no. 226 (1987): 116–25.

Rosenstone, Robert A. *Crusade of the Left: The Lincoln Battalion in the Spanish Civil War*. New Brunswick, NJ: Transaction Publishers, 2009.

Rubenstein, Joshua and Vladimir P. Naumov, eds. *Stalin's Secret Pogrom: The Postwar Inquisition of the Jewish Anti-Fascist Committee*. New Haven: Yale University Press, 2001.

Ruiz Ayúcar, Ángel. *El partido comunista: Treinta y siete años de clandestinidad*. Madrid: Liberia Editorial San Martín, 1976.

Sagomonian, A. A. "Sovetskii soiuz i ispanskii vopros, 1944–1947 gody: Po novym arkhivnym materialam." *Novaia i noveishaia istoriia*, 2008, no. 2: 57–71.

Sakmyster, Thomas. *Red Conspirator: J. Peters and the American Communist Underground*. Urbana: University of Illinois Press, 2011.

______ "Mátyás Rákosi, the Rajk Trial, and the American Communist Party." *Hungarian Studies Review* 38, no. 1–2 (Spring-Fall 2011): 45–68.

Schlögel, Karl. *Moscow, 1937*. Translated by Rodney Livingstone. Malden, MA: Polity, 2012.

Schmidt, Mária. "Noel Field – The American Communist at the Center of Stalin's East European Purge: From the Hungarian Archives." *American Communist History* 3, no. 2 (2004): 215–45.

Schrank, Bernice. "Reading the Rosenbergs after Venona." *Labour / Le Travail* 49 (Spring 2002): 189–210.

Schrecker, Ellen. "Before the Rosenbergs: Espionage Scenarios in the Early Cold War." In *Secret Agents: The Rosenberg Case, McCarthyism, and Fifties America*, edited by Marjorie Garber and Rebecca L. Walkowitz, 127–42. New York: Routledge, 1995.

______ *The Age of McCarthyism: A Brief History with Documents*, 2d ed. New York: Palgrave, 2002.

Seidman, Michael. "Quiet Fronts in the Spanish Civil War." *Historian* 61, no. 4 (Summer 1999): 821–41.

——— *Republic of Egos: A Social History of the Spanish Civil War*. Madison: University of Wisconsin Press, 2002.

——— *Victorious Counterrevolution: The Nationalist Effort in the Spanish Civil War*. Madison: University of Wisconsin Press, 2011.

Serrano, Secundino. *Maquis: Historia de la guerrilla antifranquista*. Madrid: Temas de Hoy, 2001.

Shore, Marci. *Caviar and Ashes: A Warsaw Generation's Life and Death in Marxism, 1917–1968*. New Haven: Yale University Press, 2006.

Sibley, Katherine A. S. "Soviet Military-Industrial Espionage in the United States and the Emergence of an Espionage Paradigm in US-Soviet Relations, 1941–45." *American Communist History* 2, no. 1 (2003): 21–61.

Skoutelsky, Rémi. "L'engagement des volontaires français en Espagne républicaine." *Mouvement social*, no. 181 (October-December 1997): 7–29.

——— *L'espoir guidait leurs pas : les volontaires française dans les Brigades internationales, 1936–1939*. Paris: B. Grasset, 1998.

Smirnov, V. P. "Frantsuzkaia kommunisticheskaia partiia i Komintern v 1939–1940 gg.: Novyie arkhivy materialy." *Novaia i noveishaia istoriia*, 1994, no. 1: 30–46.

Smyth, Denis. "'We Are With You': Solidarity and Self-Interest in Soviet Policy toward Republican Spain." In *The Republic Besieged: Civil War in Spain, 1936–1939*, edited by Paul Preston and Ann L. Mackenzie, 87–106. Edinburgh: Edinburgh University Press, 1996.

Stern, Ludmila. *Western Intellectuals and the Soviet Union, 1920–1940*. New York: Routledge, 2007.

Stites, Richard. *The Women's Liberation Movement in Russia: Feminism, Nihilism, and Bolshevism, 1860–1930*. Princeton: Princeton University Press, 1978.

——— *Russian Popular Culture: Entertainment and Society since 1900*. New York: Cambridge University Press, 1992.

Storch, Randi. *Red Chicago: American Communism at its Grassroots, 1928–35*. Urbana: University of Illinois Press, 2007.

Stradling, Robert. *The Irish and the Spanish Civil War, 1936–1939*. Manchester: Manchester University Press, 1999.

Strong, Tracy B. and Helene Keyssar. *Right in Her Soul: The Life of Anna Louise Strong*. New York: Random House, 1983.

Studer, Brigette. *Un parti sous influence: Le Parti communiste suisse, une section du Komintern, 1931 à 1939*. Lausanne: L'Age d'Homme, 1994.

Studer, Brigitte and Heiko Haumann, eds. *Stalinistische Subjekete: Individuum und System in der Sowjetunion und der Komintern, 1929–1953*. Zurich: Chronos, 2006.

Studer, Brigitte and Berthold Unfried. "Private Matters Become Public: Western European Exiles and Emigrants in Stalinist Russia in the 1930s." *International Review of Social History* 48, no. 2 (2003): 203–23.

Sullivan, Brian R. "Fascist Italy's Military Involvement in the Spanish Civil War." *Journal of Military History* 59, no. 4 (October 1995): 697–727.

Sweets, John F. *Choices in Vichy France: The French under Nazi Occupation*. New York: Oxford University Press, 1986.

Taillon, Paul Michel. "'What We Want Is Good, Sober Men': Masculinity, Respectability, and Temperance in the Railroad Brotherhoods, c. 1870–1910." *Journal of Social History* 36, no. 2 (Winter 2002): 319–38.

Takayoshi, Ichiro. "The Wages of War: Liberal Gullibility, Soviet Intervention, and the End of the Popular Front." *Representations* 115, no. 1 (Summer 2011): 102–29.

Taylor, Lynne. "The Parti Communiste Français and the French Resistance in the Second World War." In *Resistance and Revolution in Mediterranean Europe*, edited by Tony Judt, 53–79. New York: Routledge, 1989.

Taylor, S. J. *Stalin's Apologist: Walter Duranty: The* New York Times's *Man in Moscow*. New York: Oxford University Press, 1990.

Thomas, Hugh. *The Spanish Civil War: Revised Edition*. New York: Modern Library, 2001.

Thorpe, Andrew. "The Communist International and the British Communist Party." In *International Communism and the Communist International, 1919–43*, edited by Tim Rees and Andrew Thorpe, 67–86. Manchester: Manchester University Press, 1998.

Thurston, Robert W. *Life and Terror in Stalin's Russia, 1934–1941*. New Haven: Yale University Press, 1996.

Timasheff, Nicholas S. *The Great Retreat: The Growth and Decline of Communism in Russia*. New York: E. P. Dutton, 1946.

Transchel, Kate. "Staggering toward Socialism: The Soviet Anti-Alcohol Campaign, 1928–1932." *Soviet and Post-Soviet Review* 23, no. 2 (1996): 191–202.

______ *Under the Influence: Working-Class Drinking, Temperance, and Cultural Revolution in Russia, 1895–1932*. Pittsburgh: University of Pittsburgh Press, 2006.

Tzouliadis, Tim. *The Forsaken: An American Tragedy in Stalin's Russia*. New York: Penguin, 2008.

Unfried, Berthold. "Foreign Communists and the Mechanisms of Soviet Cadre Formation in the USSR." In *Stalin's Terror: High Politics and Mass Repression in the Soviet Union*, edited by Barry McLoughlin and Kevin McDermott, 175–93. Basingstoke: Palgrave Macmillan, 2003.

Usdin, Steven T. "The Rosenberg Ring Revealed: Industrial-Scale Nuclear and Conventional Espionage." *Journal of Cold War Studies* 11, no. 3 (Summer 2009): 91–143.

Vásquez Montalbán, Manuel. *Pasionaria y los siete enanitos*. Barcelona: Random House Mondadori, 2005.

Vatlin, Aleksandr. *Komintern: Idei, resheniia, sud'by*. Moscow: Rosspen, 2009.

Vincent, Mary. "The Martyrs and the Saints: Masculinity and the Construction of the Francoist Crusade." *History Workshop Journal*, no. 47 (Spring 1999): 68–98.

Viñas, Ángel. *La soledad de la República : el abandono de las democracias y el viraje hacia la Unión Soviética*. Barcelona: Crítica, 2006.

______ *El escudo de la República : El oro de España, la apuesta soviética y los hechos de mayo de 1937*. Barcelona: Crítica, 2007.

Vowinckel, Annette, Marcus M. Payk, and Thomas Lindenberger, eds. *Cold War Cultures: Perspectives on Eastern and Western European Societies*. New York: Berghahn, 2012.

West, Nigel. "Dave Springhall." In *Mask: MI5's Penetration of the Communist Party of Great Britain*, 219–27. London: Routledge, 2005.

Whealey, Robert H. *Hitler and Spain: The Nazi Role in the Spanish Civil War*. Lexington: University of Kentucky Press, 1989.

Wixson, Douglas. *Worker-Writer in America: Jack Conroy and the Tradition of Midwestern Literary Radicalism, 1898–1990*. Urbana: University of Illinois Press, 1994.

Wood, Elizabeth. *The Baba and the Comrade: Gender and Politics in Revolutionary Russia*. Bloomington: Indiana University Press, 1997.

Wrigley, Chris. "Soldiers and Cigarettes: Smoking for King and Country." *History Today* 64, no. 4 (April 2014): 24–30.

Young, Glennys. "To Russia with 'Spain': Spanish Exiles in the Soviet Union and the *Longue Durée* of Soviet History," *Kritika* 15, no. 2 (Spring 2014): 395–419.

Youngblood, Denise. *Russian War Films: On the Cinema Front*. Lawrence: University of Kansas Press, 2010.

Zavala, José María. *En busca de Andreu Nin: Vida y muerte de un mito silenciado de la Guerra Civil*. Barcelona: Plaza & Janés, 2005.

Zhuravlev, Sergei. "Inostrannaia koloniia v Sovetskoi Rossii v 1920–1930-e gody (Postanovka problemy i metody issledovaniia)." *Otechestvennaia istoriia*, 1994, no. 1: 179–89.

——— *"Malenkie liudi" i "bol'shaia istoriia": Inostrantsy moskovskogo Elektrozavoda v sovetskom obshchestve 1920-kh–1930-kh gg*. Moscow: ROSSPEN, 2000.

——— "American Victims of the Stalin Purges, 1930s." In *Stalinistische Subjekte: Individuum und System in der Sowjetunion und der Komintern, 1929–1953*, edited by Brigitte Studer and Heiko Haumann, 397–414. Zurich: Chronos, 2006.

Zubkova, Elena. *Russia after the War: Hopes, Illusions, and Disappointments, 1945–1957*. Translated by Hugh Ragsdale. Armonk, NY: M. E. Sharpe, 1998.

Zubok, Vladislav. *Zhivago's Children: The Last Russian Intelligentsia*. Cambridge, MA: Belknap Press, 2009.

Index

For Jeff

Contents

Figure and tables

Acknowledgements

It is a great pleasure to acknowledge the many people who have contributed to the completion of this book.

I owe special thanks to those who read and provided detailed criticisms of the complete book in one of its various stages: Frans de Haas, Jim Hankinson, Jim Lennox, David Charles, Peter Stork, Sean Coughlin, and the readers for Cambridge University Press. Their comments have helped me to clarify and improve my arguments in countless places and have saved me from many errors. The errors that remain are solely my responsibility, and, of course, none of those mentioned above should be presumed to agree with the views expressed here. I also note my gratitude to Hilary Gaskin at Cambridge University Press for her patience and help on the manuscript.

My work has also benefited enormously from the comments I received on individual chapters and other parts of the manuscript. I particularly thank Bert van den Berg, Allan Bowen, Lesley Dean-Jones, Pieter Sjoerd Hasper, Devin Henry, Marije Martijn, Alex Mourelatos, Ineke Sluiter, David Sedley, Steve White, Christian Wildberg, my colleagues Anne Margaret Baxley, Eric Brown, Carl Craver, Dennis Des Chene, and John Doris, and all those who have participated in the discussion at the various conferences, colloquia, and classrooms where this material was presented.

The book was begun as a doctoral dissertation in the Faculty of Philosophy at Leiden University, and I am grateful for their support. Parts of the dissertation were completed while I was a visiting scholar in the Joint Program in Ancient Philosophy at the University of Texas at Austin, and I thank the Philosophy and Classics departments there for sponsoring my numerous visits, Jim Hankinson for being my advisor and friend at the same time, and the Leiden University Fund and OIKOS (the National Research School of Classical Studies in the Netherlands) for their financial support. The book has undergone its most substantial transformations since I joined the Philosophy Department at Washington University in

St. Louis. I thank my colleagues there for their encouragement, advice, and friendship.

Finally, I would like to thank my family and friends: my family whom I left behind in the Netherlands for their continuous support and encouragement; and my dearest old and new friends – in particular Carolien Trieschnigg, Maithe Hulskamp, Juliette Kars, Simone Vazire, and Emily Austin – for sharing all my laughs and tears, and for making me feel at home no matter where I am.

My deepest expression of gratitude goes to my husband, Jeff Laux, for his love, his invincible optimism, and for making everything worthwhile. You mean the world to me.

I should also like to thank Kelowna Publishers for their kind permission to reprint a slightly modified version of "Nature as a good Housekeeper: Secondary Teleology and Material Necessity in Aristotle's Biology" (forthcoming in *Apeiron*) as part of Chapter 3; Brill Publishers for their kind permission to reprint an expanded version of "Why Stars have no Feet: Teleological Explanations in Aristotle's Cosmology" (which appeared in A. C. Bowen and C. Wildberg (eds.), *New Perspectives on Aristotle's De Caelo*, Leiden, 2009, 245–271) as Chapter 5; and Oxford University Press for their kind permission to reprint an expanded version of "The Structure of Teleological Explanations in Aristotle: Theory and Practice" (which appeared in *Oxford Studies in Ancient Philosophy* 33, 2007, 145–178) as Chapter 6.

Abbreviations

ARISTOTLE'S WORKS

APo	*Analytica Posteriora* (*Posterior Analytics*)
APr	*Analytica Priora* (*Prior Analytics*)
Cael	*De Caelo* (*On the Heavens*)
DA	*De Anima* (*On the Soul*)
EE	*Ethica Eudemia* (*Eudemian Ethics*)
GA	*De Generatione Animalium* (*Generation of Animals*)
GC	*De Generatione et Corruptione* (*On Generation and Destruction*)
HA	*Historia Animalium* (*History of Animals*)
IA	*De Incessu Animalium* (*On Animal Progression*)
Juv	*De Juventute et Senectute* (*On Youth and Old Age*)
MA	*De Motu Animalium* (*On Animal Motion*)
Meta	*Metaphysica* (*Metaphysics*)
Meteor	*Meteorologica* (*Meteorology*)
NE	*Ethica Nicomachea* (*Nicomachean Ethics*)
PA	*De Partibus Animalium* (*On the Parts of Animals*)
Ph	*Physica* (*Physics*)
Pol	*Politica* (*Politics*)
Resp	*De Respiratione* (*On Respiration*)
Rh	*Rhetorica* (*Rhetoric*)
Sens	*De Sensu et Sensibilibus* (*On Sense and Sensibilia*)
Somn	*De Somno et Vigilia* (*On Sleep and Waking*)
Top	*Topica* (*Topics*)

WORKS BY OTHER GREEK AUTHORS

Euclid (Euc.)

El	*Elements*

Galenus (Gal.)
- *Meth Med* — *Methodus Medendi (On the Therapeutic Method)*

Philoponus (Phlp.)
- *In APo* — *In Aristotelis Analytica Posteriora commentaria*

Plato (Pl.)
- *R* — *Republic*
- *Smp* — *Symposium*
- *Ti* — *Timaeus*

Simplicius (Simp.)
- *In Cael* — *In Aristotelis de Caelo commentaria*
- *In Ph* — *In Aristotelis Physica commentaria*

Xenophon (X.)
- *An* — *Anabasis*
- *Cyr* — *Cyropaedia*

OTHER ABBREVIATIONS

DK H. Diels, rev. W. Kranz (1961), *Die Fragmente der Vorsokratiker*, 10th edn. Berlin.

Fr. Fragment

The texts cited in this book are all taken from the *Thesaurus Linguae Graecae Canon of Greek Authors and Works* (*TLG*), 3rd edn. (1990), Oxford. All translations are mine.

References to Plato follow the Stephanus pagination as found in the Oxford Classical Texts (OCT), J. Burnet (ed.) (1900–22), *Platonis Opera*, 5 vols., Oxford.

References to Greek Commentators are to H. Diels (ed.), *Commentaria in Aristotelem Graeca* (*CIAG*) (1892–1909), Berlin.

Introduction

Why do organisms reproduce? Why do birds have wings? Why do neither snakes nor stars have feet? And why do most of the hoofed life-bearing animals have horns (but not all of them)?

For Aristotle, questions such as these go to the heart of natural philosophy, which is the study of the coming to be and presence of beings that have their own internal principle of change and rest. Throughout his lifetime, Aristotle was deeply committed to investigating and explaining natural phenomena, which is reflected all through the surviving treatises on natural philosophy. Among these, Aristotle's *Physics* is most fundamental. In this treatise, Aristotle lays out the general theoretical framework for his natural philosophy, defining notions such as nature, motion, causation, place, and time. In the other treatises, Aristotle explores more specific problems related to the study of natural beings, such as coming to be and passing away (in *De Generatione et Corruptione*), the nature and motion of the elements (in *De Generatione et Corruptione* and the second part of the *De Caelo*), the motions and features of the heavenly bodies (in the first part of the *De Caelo*), atmospheric causes and changes (in the *Meteorologica*), the notion of soul and its dependence on natural bodies (in *De Anima*), and finally, the causes of the coming to be and presence of living beings and of their parts and motions (in the biological works).

What unites the questions explored in these natural treatises, exemplified by the questions above, is that they are predominantly questions asking for the purpose of things, or, as Aristotle puts it, questions asking for "that for the sake of which." By posing this specific kind of why question, Aristotle is inquiring after the *function* served by the presence, absence, or material and structural differentiation of a certain natural feature, or after the *goal* for the sake of which some natural process or animal motion takes place. According to Aristotle's understanding of scientific knowledge, the answers to these specific why questions constitute teleological explanations, because they pick out the final cause (in the form of a function or goal) for the sake

of which something has come to be or is present (or absent, etc.). These teleological explanations are a central feature of Aristotle's investigation of nature and reflect the importance he attributes to final causality in the coming to be and presence of regular natural phenomena. In Aristotle's view of the world, everything that exists or comes to be "by nature" comes to be or changes, unless prevented, for a purpose and towards an end, and is present for the sake of that purpose or end. This goal-directedness is an internal tendency possessed by all natural things, which means that teleology operates among all of nature, from the level of the inanimate elements, through that of living beings, and on to the eternal realm of the heavenly bodies.

Although the importance of teleology for Aristotle (and in the ancient world in general)[1] has been acknowledged widely,[2] its nature and scope have consistently been the focus of much debate.[3] These debates have progressively led to a better understanding of Aristotle's theory of natural teleology, and especially of its (meta-)physical underpinnings and its contrasts with Aristotle's notions of chance and necessity.[4] What is lacking in the literature, however, is a precise and comprehensive understanding of the role Aristotle attributes to teleology in *explaining* natural phenomena throughout Aristotle's natural scientific works. Setting aside the other issues that remain concerning the causal nature and scope of teleology, the question that this book sets out to resolve is how – granted that Aristotle has established final causality as a cause of natural phenomena – he then *uses* (e.g., refers to, draws inferences from, builds premises upon, rejects other possible explanations on the basis of) this theory of teleology in his explanations of such phenomena.

The present book, then, provides a new perspective on Aristotle's teleology by exploring and evaluating its *scientific role* in generating

1 Hankinson (1998, 6).

2 E.g., Caston (2006, 341); Gotthelf and Lennox (1987, 199); Gotthelf (1997b, 82); and Johnson (2005, 1–2).

3 Cf. Quarantotto (2005, 17). For a historical overview of the trends and circumstances that shaped the earlier interpretations of Aristotle, see Johnson (2005, 15–39). On the nature of Aristotle's teleology, see in particular Bradie and Miller (1999); Cameron (2002); Charles (1988); Cooper (1982; 1985; 1987); Gotthelf (1987); Irwin (1988); Johnson (2005); Lennox (2001a); Nussbaum (1978); Sauvé Meyer (1992); Scharle (2008); Sorabji (1980); and Wieland (1975). On the metaphysics of Aristotle's teleology, see in particular Charles (1994); Mirus (2004); Pavloupoulos (2003); and Witt (1998). On the scope of Aristotle's teleology, see in particular Cooper (1982); Furley (1985); Matthen (2001; 2009); Owens (1968); Sedley (1991); and Wardy (1993).

4 See especially Johnson (2005), who brings together many of the recent new insights concerning Aristotle's teleology in his monograph, and explicitly addresses and eliminates some of its most persistent "popular misconceptions." See also Cooper (1982, 1985; 1987) and Lennox (2001a, 225 and 251).

causal explanations of natural phenomena, both in the actual explanations recorded in Aristotle's natural treatises and more abstractly in his philosophy of science.

The core of my book, consisting of Chapters 1 to 5, investigates the function, structure, and explanatory power of Aristotle's actual teleological explanations of natural phenomena. This involves a close reading of selected texts in four of Aristotle's treatises on natural science, that is, in the *Physica* (book II), *De Anima, De Partibus Animalium* (including the practice in books II–IV), and *De Caelo* (book II). These are the treatises that are most relevant to the present investigation in that they cover the main areas of Aristotle's natural science,[5] and include texts that have often been ignored in previous studies of Aristotle's teleology.[6]

In the final chapter, which is Chapter 6, I juxtapose these findings concerning Aristotle's practice in the treatises on natural science with the theoretical picture of the structure of teleological explanations gained from Aristotle's theory of scientific demonstration.[7] For this purpose I present a new interpretation of *Analytica Posteriora* II.11, a notoriously difficult chapter in which Aristotle introduces his theory of four causes into the syllogistic framework of scientific demonstration. This study thereby contributes to recent scholarship on the interplay between Aristotle's philosophy of science and philosophy of nature,[8] while at the same time adding to our knowledge of Aristotle's theory of teleology in terms of its explanatory merits and limits.

[5] Note that although this book explores Aristotle's theory and practice of providing teleological explanations as comprehensively as possible, due to the limits of space and time I have narrowed down this study to Aristotle's *science of living nature*. On a few occasions, I have something to say about the (non-natural) teleology of deliberate action as well, but the ethical and political works of Aristotle mostly fall outside the scope of this book. My central hypothesis is that Aristotle developed his notion of "that for the sake of which" primarily in the context of his investigations of living nature and that this is where he applied the notion most successfully; a further study of the use of teleology in generating explanations in, among others, his ethics or politics, would have to start from and build upon the more "basic" uses in the natural treatises.

[6] Cf. Quarantotto (2005, 27). Quarantotto points to *Ph* II.8–9 and *PA* I.1 as the key texts on which most scholars have based their interpretation of Aristotle's notion of teleology; in her own work, she studies teleology from a more comprehensive perspective, including the whole of *Physica* book II, the whole of *De Partibus Animalium*, a few passages from *De Anima*, and *Meta* I.3–10.

[7] Although there have been quite a few studies on the nature of Aristotle's (teleological) explanations within the context of the first book of the *PA* and the second book of the *Physica*: see especially Balme (1987b); Bolton (1987; 1997); Charles (1997; 1999); Detel (1997; 1999); Gotthelf (1987; 1997a); Lennox (2001a) and Pellegrin (1986), with a few exceptions (i.e., Bolton 1997; Detel 1997; and Johnson 2005), Aristotle's theoretical remarks on the structure of teleological explanations in *APo* II.11 have been ignored.

[8] For this research program, see in particular Lennox (2001a, 1–6; 1997a; 2004a; 2006), and Lloyd (1990; 1996, 7–37).

In the course of these six chapters, I defend three main theses: first, that Aristotle postulates not one, but *two types of teleological causation* as underlying the coming into being and presence of regular beneficial outcomes in nature; second, that he uses teleological principles as *heuristic tools* for the discovery of causally relevant features to be picked out in causal explanations, where the causes that are being discovered, including the final causes, are real causes and not mere epistemic reasons why;[9] and, finally, that Aristotle never attributes *causal primacy* to final causes in his explanations (even though he believes they are "prior in nature"), but only *explanatory primacy*. This means, among other things, that his teleology resists the – in itself already anachronistic – charge of backward causation. Let me say more about these three theses in turn and indicate in which chapters I defend them.

First, I argue that a more thorough understanding of Aristotle's use of teleology in the explanation of natural phenomena requires that we distinguish between two types of teleological causation, a primary and a secondary type, which are both represented in Aristotle's explanations.

The primary type of teleology involves the realization of a preexisting, internal potential (or perhaps "potentials") for form[10] through stages shaped by conditional necessity. This is the "standard" form of teleology, according to which the form of the natural being specifies the functional features that are to be realized through the goal-directed actions of the formal nature; what is picked out as causally primary in the explanations of such features is the natural being's form. For instance, birds have wings for the sake of flying, but the need to perform this activity derives from the essential nature of birds, which is being a flyer. Wings, then, are exhibited to be the necessary prerequisites for the realization of the bird's form as flyer. Explanations of phenomena that have come to be and are present as the result of primary teleology (such as wings) thus typically include references both to the ends that constitute final causes (e.g., functions such as "flying") and to the definition of the substantial being of the organism in question (e.g., definitions such as "being a flyer"), which constitutes its formal cause.

The secondary type of teleology involves a formal nature of a natural being *using* materials that happen to be available (usually residues

9 Note that I take Aristotle to be a realist about (final) causation – it is only his *use* of teleological *principles* such as "nature does nothing in vain" that I argue serves heuristic purposes. I do not believe that his theory of teleology as a whole is heuristic.

10 My characterization of "primary teleology" builds on the understanding of teleological causation in the case of animal generation provided in Gotthelf (1987).

that have come to be of material necessity and that are not conditionally necessitated) for the production of parts that serve the animal's well-being. The presence of these parts is not a necessary prerequisite for the realization of the animal's form; instead, their presence is said to be "for the better." For instance, large land animals often have a surplus of earthen material, which – because of its hard potential – nature then uses for the production of horns in males, which serve the (non-necessary) function of defense. In these cases, functional features emerge as it were from the potentials of the materials that happen to be available, and the operation of the formal nature is secondary to the operation of material necessity that produced the materials. Explanations of phenomena that are the result of secondary teleology (such as horns) thus typically distinguish between the presence and the coming to be of those phenomena, where the presence is explained teleologically by reference to an end that constitutes the final cause (e.g., the function of "defense" served by the part) and the coming to be by reference to material necessity.[11]

Scholars usually try to reconstruct the causal nature of Aristotle's teleology by contrasting it to material necessity and chance, and therefore tend to reduce Aristotle's own references to material causation in teleological explanations to expressions of conditional necessity. By distinguishing primary from secondary teleology, however, it is possible to give an account of the role of necessity in teleological explanation that does not involve a reduction of material necessity to conditional necessity in all cases.[12] This interpretation also counteracts another unfortunate tendency among scholars, which is to treat all teleological explanations found in Aristotle's treatises as one homogeneous category, unified simply by the fact that the explanations all refer in some way or another to the goal-directedness of

[11] My distinction between primary and secondary teleology does not rely upon Aristotle's own distinction between two types of final causes, which are "that for the sake of which" and "that for the benefit of which" (he makes this distinction in, for instance, *Ph* II.2, 194a34–b1; *DA* II.4, 415b2–3; *DA* II.4, 415b20–21; *Meta* XII.7, 1072b1–3; and *EE* VII.15, 1249b15), and differs in that way from the interpretations of Kullmann, Bodnár, and Johnson. Kullmann (1985, 173) uses the term "secondary teleology" to indicate that an end is the beneficiary of something, but not a "that for the sake of which" in a strict sense. Bodnár (2005; 24–25) also builds upon Aristotle's own distinction: in "straightforward" teleology, the goals are not also the beneficiary of the teleological structure, while in inter-species teleology the goals are the beneficiary of the teleological structure. Finally, Johnson (2005) uses the distinction between the "that for the sake of which" and the beneficiary as one of his central tools for making sense of Aristotle's explanations. None differentiate between "primary" and "secondary" teleology in the way that I propose.

[12] My interpretation is aimed mostly against scholars who have either explained away the role of material necessity in teleological explanations (Balme, 1987c); reduced it to conditional necessity (Cooper, 1987; Johnson, 2005); or assigned to it primarily a "negative" role in constraining the realizations of function (Lennox, 2001a).

nature.[13] This tendency not only obscures the diversity and versatility of Aristotle's modes of explanation, but also leads to an impoverished understanding of the explanatory power of teleology.

I introduce the distinction between primary and secondary teleology in Chapters 1 and 2. More specifically, Chapter 1 shows how this distinction operates in Aristotle's defense of natural teleology in the famous rainfall example in *Physica* II.8. Chapter 2 demonstrates how it underlies Aristotle's conceptions of "living" versus "living well" in *De Anima*, which in their turn are used to ground the specific sets of capacities different kinds of living beings have. The causal patterns underlying the distinction between primary and secondary teleology are developed most fully in Chapter 3, which examines Aristotle's scientific theory of explanation in biology as introduced in *De Partibus Animalium* I.

My second thesis concerns the role of teleology in Aristotle's methods of discovery. There are a relatively small number of teleological explanations in Aristotle's natural treatises that do not refer directly to final causes, but that proceed through the use of teleological principles such as "nature does nothing in vain."[14] I argue that Aristotle uses these principles as *heuristic tools*. The principles are used to discover causal features, which then figure in teleological explanations, but the principles do not themselves play a causal role in the ultimate explanations of natural phenomena.

In the natural treatises, there are rare cases where the end that constitutes the final cause of some natural phenomenon is not immediately accessible for observation, or where the explanandum is otherwise particularly complicated. These are typically the contexts in which Aristotle posits a teleological principle and thereby generates the appropriate series of inferences that ultimately leads to the identification of the causally relevant

13 Sorabji (1980, 155–174) offers an account of how according to him the various kinds of teleological explanations work, but I believe his distinctions are not subtle enough to cover Aristotle's actual practice of explaining natural phenomena in a teleological way. Johnson (2005, 1 and 7) introduces his investigations into Aristotle's teleology as a study of "how ends are used by Aristotle as explanations in natural philosophy" (2005, 1). However, the core of his monograph contains a discussion of the sorts of things that according to Aristotle behave in a goal-directed way, and of the reasons why these things behave that way (and are thus explainable by reference to teleology). He does not produce any analysis of the different types of teleological explanation Aristotle uses, or any reflections upon why Aristotle uses the types of teleological explanation he does, or what he thinks these explanations amount to, which is the sort of reflection I offer in this book. Charles (1991), who recognizes that there is a plurality of teleological models at work in Aristotle's *Physica*, faults Aristotle for not presenting a unified model.

14 Although Lennox's work on the principle that nature does nothing in vain (2001a, 205–222) suggests that Aristotle uses teleological principles in very specific ways to explain their own set of explananda, some scholars still think that they are just "didactic mantras," to remind his students that he believes nature is goal-directed. See, for instance, Quarantotto (2005, 13).

feature, which is then picked out in the explanation of the phenomenon in question. An important part of the process of discovery in these cases is the identification of what type of teleology (i.e., primary or secondary teleology) is responsible for the presence of the natural phenomenon that needs to be explained; it is my contention that teleological principles help to make this identification, while they are not themselves part of the ultimate (syllogistic) explanation.

I argue for this thesis in Chapter 4, which examines Aristotle's heuristic strategies and actual (teleological) explanations as recorded in *De Partibus Animalium* II–IV, and trace its consequences for the possibility of understanding heavenly phenomena in Chapter 5.

My final thesis, which is perhaps the most important one from a contemporary perspective, is that for Aristotle the scientific value of final causes in natural science lies in their explanatory priority. Final causes, even though they certainly play a significant causal role in natural developments (they are, after all, one of the four types of causal factors Aristotle distinguishes in nature), nevertheless never receive causal priority *in the (syllogistic) explanation of those developments.*[15]

For Aristotle, scientific explanations or demonstrations ideally follow the pattern of a Barbara syllogism (i.e., AaB, BaC, ∴ AaC). In such demonstrations, some attribute (picked out by the major or predicative term) is demonstrated to hold always or for the most part of some subject (picked out by the minor or subject term) through some causally primary feature (picked out by the middle term). In addition, Aristotle argues that scientific demonstrations of natural phenomena – unlike those of mathematical states of affairs, which are timeless – ought to reflect the chronological order of causation in the world, moving from the start or origin of the natural development to its end. For the practice of demonstrating teleological natural processes, this means that final causes can never take the position of a middle term, which picks out the causally *primary* factor in a chain of development. For, although Aristotle repeatedly points out that final causes are prior in nature and in definition (and undeniably do have causal priority in those senses), in *generation* they are last, because the ends that constitute the final causes of natural phenomena are chronologically speaking the last to come about. Whereas the end that constitutes the final cause explains the *presence* of a given natural phenomenon, the *coming*

[15] This answers the question, addressed on a general level by Code (1997) and by Bolton (2004), why Aristotle assigns special explanatory power to explanations that pick out final causes and why he considers it to be the foremost (although not exclusive) task of natural philosophers to provide teleological explanations of the natural phenomena they investigate.

to be of that end must itself be explained further in terms of either the operation of formal-efficient causation or of material-efficient causation. These latter causes are *causally prior in generation* and they can therefore take the position of middle terms in scientific demonstrations of natural phenomena. In sum, because ends that constitute the final causes of natural phenomena can by definition never be prior in generation, and because it is priority in generation that is tracked by scientific demonstrations of natural phenomena, ends can never be identified as the causally primary fact in such demonstrations.

Thus I shall argue that the syllogistic patterns of teleological explanation that Aristotle employs in the biological practice and that he describes in his theory of science never pick out final causes as being explanatory of the conclusion, but rather include functions and ends as part of the conclusion that is being demonstrated. In other words, final causes are always picked out by the major term, in the predicative position, and never by the middle term. Under this scheme, teleological explanations are explanations in which a final cause is picked out as being responsible for the *presence* of some natural feature, where the end that constitutes that final cause is demonstrated to *come to hold* of that feature through the operation of some *other* type of cause (i.e., formal-efficient causes in the case of primary teleology; material-efficient causes in the case of secondary teleology).

Final causes thus exert no "mysterious causal pull" from the future and do not cause the coming to be of their own necessitating conditions, as some – anachronistically – have suggested. Final causes are prior in nature and in definition, and function quite literally as ends and limits of developments, which is why they function as the starting points of scientific demonstrations of natural phenomena. However, in the order of generation, final causes are last, and Aristotle does not conflate these different orders of priority.

This is the central thesis of Chapter 6, in which I present my interpretation of *Analytica Posteriora* II.11 and juxtapose this with my findings concerning Aristotle's practice of providing teleological explanations especially in the biological works.

My interpretation of Aristotle's teleology as (1) incorporating (at least in some cases) material necessity rather than opposing it, (2) allowing a heuristic use of teleological principles, and (3) resisting the charge of backward causation has important ramifications not only for the way we standardly depict the place of Aristotle in the history of science, but perhaps also for contemporary debates about the notion of biological function.

The Aristotelian worldview that came to be rejected in the sixteenth and seventeenth centuries in favor of mechanistic models of the world was in fact even less Aristotle's than is often assumed. For Aristotle, the theory of natural teleology is not an a priori assumption, but a scientific hypothesis, much like contemporary etiological or propensity theories of function are. A deeper understanding of the merits (and limits) of Aristotle's use of teleology in producing explanations might put us in a better position to reconsider notions of biological function that do not rely on the postulation of mystical forces or the existence of benevolent, intelligent gods, but rather on immanent, natural principles and laws.

CHAPTER 1

Aristotle's defense of natural teleology: setting the stage for teleological explanations in the Physica

1.0 INTRODUCTION

The *Physica* forms Aristotle's most fundamental treatise in his studies of natural science. In this treatise, Aristotle investigates the principles and causes of all things that have a nature – that is, of all things that have an internal principle of change and rest – with the purpose of generating knowledge of natural phenomena (*Ph* I.1, 184a10–16). In the course of doing so, Aristotle defines a large number of key notions of his natural philosophy, such as motion and change, space and time, matter and form, causal explanation, luck and spontaneity, teleology and necessity. The conceptual apparatus and framework laid out in the *Physica* are consequently applied and reshaped for the inquiries into the more specific and more complex segments of the natural world, written down in Aristotle's other natural treatises.[1]

Final causes and natural teleology figure especially prominently in the second book of the *Physica*, where Aristotle defines his concept of nature, introduces his theory of four types of cause or causal explanation,[2] and discusses the kinds of cause operative in art and nature. In this chapter, I shall focus on Aristotle's first argument in defense of natural teleology

[1] As Aristotle makes clear in his programmatic opening of the *Meteorologica* (I.1, 338a20–339a10), the whole investigation of nature will comprise the study of change and motion in the heavens (*De Caelo*), the elements and coming to be and perishing in general (*De Caelo, De Generatione et Corruptione*), atmospheric causes and changes (*Meteorologica*), and finally living beings (the biological works). On the importance of the *Meteorologica* passage for the systematic connection between Aristotle's works, see Burnyeat (2001, 118–119); Falcon (2005, 2–7); and Nussbaum (1978, 107–109).

[2] Aristotle is a realist concerning both causes and explanations, which means that the four types of causal explanations he distinguishes in *Ph* II.3 and *Ph* II.7 are grounded in four types of causal relations that obtain in the world: the four *aitiai* are the kinds of answers one gives to four different why questions, and these answers will only be explanatory and hence productive of scientific knowledge if they pick out real causes (and not merely epistemic reasons why) under their causally relevant description. Cf. Freeland (1991); Hankinson (1998, 132); Johnson (2005, 41); and Moravcsik (1991, 31). Pace Van Fraassen (1980). On Aristotle's erotetic concept of inquiry, see Hintikka (1989, 73) and Lennox (1994).

against his materialist predecessors (in *Ph* II.8, 198b16–199a8), which raises an important aporia about the role of teleology, necessity, and chance in the proper explanation of natural phenomena. The main purpose of this chapter is to provide an interpretation of this argument, which will build upon a distinction I draw between primary and secondary types of teleology. Since Aristotle's defense of natural teleology in the *Physica* is among the most disputed passages in the Aristotelian corpus, this chapter will also function as a modest *status quaestionis* of recent work on Aristotle's teleology, and as an introduction to some of the basic concepts necessary for the understanding of Aristotle's use of teleological explanations in the other natural treatises discussed in the remainder of this book.

In the sections below, I shall first, by way of background, discuss the role Aristotle assigns to final causes in teleological explanations of both art and nature, and define some of the key terms I use in this study. This is section 1.1. Next, I analyze Aristotle's first argument in defense of natural teleology in the *Physica*: section 1.2 provides a general outline of the interpretational problems pertaining to the nature and scope of Aristotle's theory of natural teleology, and section 1.3 presents my solution to these problems.

1.1 PRELIMINARY REMARKS ON FINAL CAUSES IN ART AND NATURE

The place of final causes in causal explanation

Aristotle conceives of scientific inquiry in book II of the *Physica* as a questioning procedure in which the answer to the question why provides the most fundamental knowledge, because it brings out the cause(s) of something. In *Ph* II.3,[3] Aristotle introduces four types of cause that may figure in such causal explanations: (1) the "that out of which" (*Ph* II.3, 194b24: τὸ ἐξ οὗ) or the material cause;[4] (2) the "what it is to be" (*Ph* II.3, 194b27: τὸ τί ἦν εἶναι) or the formal cause; (3) the "that from which the origin of motion or rest comes" (*Ph* II.3, 194b29–30: ὅθεν ἡ ἀρχὴ τῆς μεταβολῆς ἡ πρώτη ἢ τῆς ἠρεμήσεως) or the efficient cause; and (4) the "that for the sake of which" (*Ph* II.3, 194b33: τὸ οὗ ἕνεκα) or the final

[3] The four causes already figured implicitly in Aristotle's definition of nature in *Ph* II.1–2; note that *Ph* II.3 is virtually identical to the entry on *aition* in Aristotle's "philosophical dictionary" in *Meta* V.2, 1013a24–1014a25.

[4] The name "material cause" is somewhat misleading, since for Aristotle "matter" in the sense of physical stuff (*hulê*, literally, wood; the ancient Greeks did not have a term for matter in our modern sense) is just one sort of thing among many others that can be causative as a "that out of which" (as is evidenced by the examples Aristotle gives in *Ph* II.3, 195a16–20). Cf. Hankinson (1995a), 119n12.

cause. Below, I shall briefly discuss Aristotle's notion of the final cause as it appears in his discussions of art and nature in this book, and indicate how it is connected to the other three types of cause.

Broadly speaking, Aristotle introduces three kinds of final cause in the second book of the *Physica*:[5] these are (a) completed natural substances or artifacts as the end results of processes of generation; (b) functions performed by (parts of) natural substances, artifacts, or tools; and (c) objects of desire as the aims of (deliberative) actions. (For examples of category (a), see *Ph* II.8, 199a13–14; *Ph* II.8, 199b8; and *Ph* II.9, 200b3–4; for (b), see *Ph* II.8, 198b24–28 and *Ph* II.9, 200b4–8; for (c), see *Ph* II.3, 194b33–34.)

The first category of final causes, consisting of completed natural substances and artifacts, are the finished products of the realizations of a potential for form, where this form is being transmitted through a process of natural generation or artificial production. In natural generation,[6] the potential for form is transmitted by the father – who possesses that form in actuality and whose semen contains the initial efficient cause of the embryo in the form of vital heat – into the menstrual blood, which is the matter supplied by the mother (see, e.g., *GA* I.22, 730a32–b32). The menstrual blood is blood concocted up to a certain point: it has potentially the same species form as the mother has, and contains the source of the nutritive soul (which explains the phenomenon of parthenogenesis), but – because of its lack of heat – does not have the source of the sensitive soul (*GA* II.3–5). The source of the sensitive soul is transmitted through the motions contained in the male semen (*GA* I.21, 730a23–33): these motions have the capacity to shape and form the embryo, which – once its heart has been formed – takes over its own generation and then possesses its own internal principle of motion. Natural generation thus consists of the replication of form[7] by what possesses that form in actuality into what possesses that form in potentiality; the fully realized form constitutes the final cause of the process. Artificial production consists of a similar replication of form, but with the important distinction that here the efficient cause remains at all times *external* to the generative process (this is what ultimately differentiates art from nature: what makes something natural is that it has or develops its own *internal* source of change and rest). The art,[8] present in

[5] On the variety of final causes in the second book of the *Physica*, see Charles (1991, 102–103).

[6] For a detailed account of Aristotle's theory of natural reproduction, see Henry (2006).

[7] On this model of reproduction as "formal replication," see Gotthelf (1987); Lennox (2001a, 230–232); and Witt (1994b, 222–228).

[8] "Art" seems the most common translation of *technê*; but see Hankinson (1998, 128n.2) and Löbl (2003, 258–264), who point out that the notion of *technê* is in fact broader than that of the arts: it includes what we would call crafts, skills, and applied sciences. I use the translations "art" and "craft" interchangeably.

the soul of the craftsman and mediated through his mind, guides the hands and tools of the craftsman and thus realizes the appropriate form in a piece of material, which must have the right material potentials for receiving that form (*GA* II.1, 735a2–4; *GA* II.4, 740b25–29). As in natural generation, it is the form that guides the operation of efficient causation (note, however, that a craftsman does not reproduce his own form, but that of the art he possesses in his soul) and that – when fully realized – constitutes the final cause of the generative process.

Functions performed by natural beings, artifacts, and instruments constitute the second type of final cause invoked by Aristotle. They usually figure in the explanation of the material and structural features of their possessors. Just as completed natural beings and artifacts are the realizations of preexisting potentials for forms, so are these functions the actualizations of preexisting capacities for activities, which reside in the soul or in the material potentials of something. (For example, natural functions are the actualizations of capacities for the performance of the distinctive life functions of each kind of animal, grounded in and activated by the animal's soul.) Functions always play some contributory role to the system of which they are part, and they exist "on top of" the realized forms that constitute the first type of final cause. For instance, a completed house is the final cause and the fully realized form of the art of house-building, while "shelter" is the function and final cause of the realized house; providing shelter is thus a function that follows from and presupposes the existence of the house.

Objects of desire constitute a third category of final causes, which are picked out in the explanation of animal or human action. Actions differ from natural and artistic productions in that they do not involve a replication of form – actions are not generative processes (cf. *NE* VI.5, 1140b1–4). In addition, actions involve conscious intentionality: objects of desire operate as external unmoved movers that actualize the internal unmoved movers of self-moving agents, that is, their faculties of desire and imagination or thought (for human beings, deliberation plays a crucial role; cf. *NE* III.3, 1112b11–1113a2). Objects of desire guide our actions towards their achievement, but there is no formal identity or ontological connection between an end and the means towards that end, which explains why there is more room for mistakes in this kind of process (see, e.g., *EE* II.11, 1227b19–22).[9]

As may be clear from this brief overview, final causes *never operate in a vacuum*, but always in connection with at least one other kind of cause.

9 Pace Charles (1991, 118–119, 127), I do not believe that this model of action is important for Aristotle's defense of natural teleology.

First, Aristotle usually explains the relation between the function of something and its material constitution as one of conditional necessity (*Ph* II.9, 200a10–15):

> Thus on account of what is a saw like this? That this may exist and be for the sake of that. It is impossible, however, that this, which is that for the sake of which, comes to be, unless it is made of iron. *It is necessary, then, that it is of iron, if there is to be a saw and if there is to be its work.* The necessary, then, is necessary starting from some hypothesis (ἐξ ὑποθέσεως δὴ τὸ ἀναγκαῖον),[10] and not as an end: the necessary is in the matter, the "that for the sake of which" in the definition.

The function something needs to perform, which is given by its definition (e.g., a saw is a sawing tool, and sawing is a kind of dividing; cf. *Ph* II.9, 200b4–8), determines the kind of material that ought to be used for its production, because it is the potentials ("hard," "dry," etc.) the material has that allow for certain functions, but not for others. Thus, if there is to be a functioning (natural or artificial) part, then it will have to be made of a certain kind of material with *the appropriate kinds of material potentials*, which will have to be present first and undergo certain changes.[11] The potentials of the material that has been used for the production of some part in their turn explain why that part is able to perform the functions it performs.

Second, the relation between efficient and final causes in art, nature, and action is one of complementariness (*Ph* II.3, 195a8–11):[12] "And some are also causes of one another (ἔστιν δέ τινα καὶ ἀλλήλων αἴτια), as training is a cause of fine condition, and this [i.e., a fine condition] of training, though [they are] not [causes of one another] in the same way, but the one as end and the other as source of motion."

The continuous operation of efficient causes during both action and generation is limited by and directed towards the final cause (cf. *DA* II.4, 416a15–18: efficient causes that act independently of final causes are like a fire that spreads without direction, end, or limit), while the end that constitutes the final cause is the outcome and terminus of this efficient causal process. In the case of generative processes this means that there

10 On the expression *ex hypotheseôs* and the idea of conditionality, see Bobzien (2002, 363).

11 See also *PA* I.1, 642a8–13; for the inclusion of efficient causation into the notion of conditional necessity, see *PA* I.1, 639b25–30 and *GA* II.6, 743a21–26. Cf. Lewis (1988, 87n8).

12 Cf. *GA* II.6, 742a16-b18; 742a28–36; *EE* I.8, 1218b11–22; and *Meta* I.3, 983a31: "in a third way [we speak of a cause as] the source of the change, and in a fourth the cause opposed to this (τετάρτην δὲ τὴν ἀντικειμένην αἰτίαν ταύτῃ), that for the sake of which and the good – for this is the end of all generation and change."

cannot be an end that constitutes a final cause if it is not the outcome of some efficient causality that was directed towards producing this end.[13] In natural generation the efficient, final, and formal causes often "come to one" (*Ph* II.7, 198a24–27): "In many cases three [of these causes] come to one (ἔρχεται δὲ τὰ τρία εἰς [τὸ] ἓν πολλάκις); for that what something is and that for the sake of which it is are one, while that from which motion first originates is the same as them in kind: for man generates man."

The efficient cause of the father is not numerically the same as the efficient cause of the son, but formally they are identical, and they are directed towards the realization and maintenance of the same form,[14] which *in its fullest expression* (and only then) is identical with the final cause.

Third, the relation between formal and final causes is itself a teleological one. Aristotle conceptualizes generation as a process that is directed toward an ever fuller realization of a potential for form, which culminates in a state of full actuality, which then constitutes the final cause. The potential for form is for the sake of realizing that form in actuality (*Meta* IX.8, 1050a4–10),[15] which is ultimately for the sake of activity (see *Meta* IX.8, 1050a21–23; *PA* I.5, 645b14–20). It is in this sense that Aristotle claims formal and final causes are one or "almost one" (*GA* I.1, 715a6: ἕν τι σχεδόν): something's *realized* (but not its potential for) form is that thing's final cause. In generative processes, causal priority thus lies in the potential for form that is being realized (see, e.g., *PA* I.1, 639b13–19 and *PA* I.1, 640a17–20; cf. sections 3.2 and 4.3), whereas the end that constitutes the final cause, and which chronologically comes to be last, has priority in definition (see, e.g., *DA* II.4, 415a18–20, and 416b23–25; *Meteor* IV.12, 390a10–12 and *Pol* I.2, 1253a19–25). While we define what something is on the basis of the intrinsic[16] and non-accidental functions and activities it displays, we explain the presence of these functions and activities as being causally determined by what that thing is, "for generation is for the sake of being" (*PA* I.1, 640a17).

Finally, Aristotle sometimes groups together matter and form in the explanation of the *result* of a process of generation, i.e., of the static composition of things that are, and combines efficient and final causes in the explanation of the *dynamics* and the direction of generative processes. At

13 Cf. Broadie (1990, 391).

14 Moravcsik (1994, 236), calls this a "built-in schedule of development and maintenance."

15 See Witt (1998), for Aristotle's "metaphysical teleology."

16 I use "intrinsic" to refer to causes that are causes in virtue of themselves (*kath'hauto*), which are opposed to causes that are accidental (*kata sumbebêkos*); for the distinction, see, e.g., *Ph* II.5, 196b24–27.

other times, he joins the formal and final cause together as the basis of proper teleological explanation, while contrasting it with the pair of material and efficient causation as picking out the process of material necessity.[17] I shall say a little more about the way Aristotle pairs these different causes together in his explanations of natural phenomena in the remaining chapters of this book.

The analogy between art and nature in teleological explanations

At the very beginning of the second book of the *Physica*, Aristotle defines nature as an inner source of change and rest in that to which it belongs primarily of itself, and not accidentally (*Ph* II.1, 192b13–14; 192b20–23).[18] In this way, he distinguishes natural things from the class of artifacts, which require an external efficient cause – the art, hand, or tool of the artist – to become what they are (*Ph* II.1, 192b28–32), but are otherwise very similar to natural products. In the remaining chapters, and especially in his defense of natural teleology, Aristotle relies heavily on this assumed similarity between the causal processes that generate natural and artificial products. Even if it remains doubtful whether Aristotle's theory of natural teleology is in fact based on the etiology of artifacts,[19] the analogy between nature and art at least serves a clear didactic purpose:[20] art involves the operation of the same four causes that are operative in nature, but in a more conspicuous and differentiated way. The models of teleology involved in art and nature are similar, but not identical.

17 See, e.g., *GA* I.1, 715a4–9; *GA* II.1, 731b18–24; *GA* V.1, 778b1–10; *GA* V.1, 778b11–19; *GA* V.8, 789b19–22; and *DA* II.4, 415b10–12. Cf. Cooper (1982, 201), and Dudley (1997, 111).

18 Nature is also spoken of as (i) that which persists through change, i.e., the substrate or the primary underlying matter (*Ph* II.1, 193a29–30; this is presumably proximate matter: see *Meta* V.6, 1016a19–24; *Meta* VIII.4, 1044a15–25; *Meta* IX.7, 1049a24–7; and Bodnár and Pellegrin (2006, 274–275)), and as (ii) that which is generated in the change, i.e., the shape or form according to the definition (*Ph* II.1, 193a30–31), whereby the latter is *more* a nature than the former (*Ph* II.1, 193b6–12; *Ph* II.2, 194a12–27). Finally, nature is spoken of as (iii) that "towards which" processes take place (*Ph* II.1, 193b12–18; 193b17: εἶς ὅ) and as an "end" and "what something is for" (*Ph* II.2, 194a27–33; 194a28–29: ἡ δὲ φύσις τέλος καὶ οὗ ἕνεκα), where this end constitutes the culmination of a continuous change.

19 For the view that the model of art offered Aristotle the metaphysical schema for his theory of natural generation, see Granger (1993, 168) (Granger takes Aristotle's theory of action to be the model behind his natural teleology); Matthen (2009); and Broadie (1990, 393–396). I remain skeptical as to whether Aristotle needs the model of art to justify his theory of natural teleology, especially since in his view (as opposed to Plato's; see Johansen (2004, 83–86), and Lennox (2001a, 281)) the teleology of art is itself ontologically dependent on the teleology of nature (cf. Katayama, 1999, 79–80; 101–108).

20 Cf. Cooper (1982, 198n.2), and Wieland (1975, 151).

The analogy between art and nature usually exploits the following three aspects:[21] first, the way in which the end and the means to realize that end are complementary and adjusted to each other in art and nature, in a way that they are not in the model of animal and human action. Above, we saw that in nature, the efficient, formal, and final causes often coincide, such that the "formal nature" becomes its own internal goal-directed agent of the realization of its *own* form (and not of some other form). In the case of art, the knowledge the craftsman has acquired is the knowledge of how to produce the art-specific form in matter, and it is activated for the sake of producing precisely those art-specific products. Thus, the art of house-building is acquired for and guides the use of tools for the production of houses, and not for something else.

Second, it exploits the specialization of the arts, which resembles the ontological classification of natures: the arts are divided into different kinds of specializations, each of which aims at producing its own specific object. Things with a nature are similarly split into different kinds and species, each of which tends towards the realization of its own specific form or essence.

A third aspect exploited in the analogy is the reliability and regularity of efficient causation in both domains: because of the above-mentioned specialization of the arts, craftsmen will always or for the most part produce the objects that they are trained to produce, and they will do so almost "automatically" and usually without mistakes.[22] The experienced artist or craftsman will not have to deliberate about which object to produce (a shoemaker produces shoes, not houses), and presumably only rarely about the means to produce it: his art dictates both.[23] Nature as an internal efficient cause of change and generation operates in much the same way (*Ph* II.8, 199a20–30; *Ph* II.8, 199b26–33): it realizes on a regular basis its own form, without deliberating over the means to these ends, and realizes this form, unless something impedes it, without mistakes.

It is important to note that conscious intentionality plays no significant role in the analogy between art and nature in the second book of the *Physica*. Since art is the true efficient cause in artificial production, the psychological states of the artist only seem to matter in the sense that art cannot exercise itself and depends for its actualization on the "rational potentiality" of the artist, which is a separate psychological component.

21 Broadie (1990, 396–397), and Lennox (2001a, 287–290).

22 Pace Matthen (2009), Aristotle does not seem to recognize mistakes of conception or design, but only of production and of failing materials; see *Ph* II.8, 199a34–b5.

23 Broadie (1990, 398), and Lennox (2001a, 245n.9).

In Aristotle's depiction of art as an analogue of nature, human desires and intentions appear to play no crucial causal role,[24] nor do they figure in the operation of natural teleology, where the formal nature or soul is often characterized as an *internal* instantiation of an artist working through the natural body to which it belongs.[25]

Key concepts to be employed in this study

Above I explained that final causes never operate in a vacuum, but are always connected to the operation of at least one of the other kinds of cause. Based on Aristotle's analysis of natural teleological processes (for which I shall provide more evidence in Chapter 3), I shall henceforward distinguish between two causal patterns of teleology.

The first causal pattern represents what I call *primary teleology*. This process involves the realization of a preexisting potential for form through stages shaped by conditional necessity, where the fully realized form constitutes the final cause of the process. This is the "standard" form of teleology, according to which the form specifies the functional features that are to be realized through the goal-directed actions of the formal nature, and where those functional features are intrinsic to and necessary for the natural being that has them. The relevant causal connection here is thus between a potential for form and the realized potential, which constitutes the final cause. The formal nature of the animal in these cases acts as its own internal efficient cause for the realization of its own potential for form. Features that are the result of primary teleology can be exhibited to be the necessary prerequisites for natural beings such as animals to perform the functions specified in their form. Aristotle often refers to these features as being necessary, because they are of immediate vital or essential importance for the animal: hypothetically speaking, nature could not have "designed" the animal without these features, for without them it would not have been able to live or be the kind of animal it is. For instance, the definition of the

[24] Pace Bolotin (1998, 35); Broadie (1990, 401); and Owens (1981, 145). Additionally, I do not believe that this "de-psychologized" picture of art that Aristotle employs in his analogy misrepresents the ancients' conception of art; pace Broadie (1990, 400–401), and Charles (1991, 108). The emphasis on the proficiency and specialization of the arts is present in other sources (see, e.g., X. *Cyr* VIII.2, 5; I thank Peter Stork for bringing this text to my attention), and is part of the philosophical tradition (see, e.g., Pl. *R* II, 369e-370a). See also Johansen (2004, 69–91), who argues that in Plato's depiction of the Demiurge – the ultimate philosophical model of the artist – individual psychology plays no causal role.

[25] For the characterization of formal natures as craftsmen, see, e.g., *PA* I.5, 645a9 (*hê dêmiourgêsasa physis*); *PA* II.9, 654b27–655a4; *PA* II.1, 647b5–6; *PA* IV.10, 686a12; and *IA* 12, 711a18; cf. also *GA* I.22, 730b5–32; *GA* II.1, 734b20–735a4; and *GA* II.4, 740b25–741a4.

substantial being of birds exhibits these animals as flyers, and in order for birds to be able to fly, they will have to have wings (there is no other way in which nature could have realized the function of flying). Wings are present for the sake of flying, and there can be no bird without wings, because these are the parts through which the bird's form as flyer is realized (in other words, all birds must have wings, even if those wings do not actually allow the animal to fly). In the explanation of features that are the result of primary teleology, Aristotle tends to give one explanation that accounts for both the coming to be and the presence of that feature, and uses strong teleological language (e.g., a certain feature exists *for the sake of – heneka –* a certain function).

The second causal pattern represents what I call *secondary teleology*. This process involves a formal nature of an animal *using* materials for something good, where those materials "happen to be available" in the animal, usually as the result of material necessity, and are not strictly speaking the result of conditional necessity. The use that is made of the materials in these cases is one that is not already specified in the animal's form and/or is not immediately necessary for the animal's survival or its identity. In these cases, functional features emerge as it were from the potentials of the materials that happen to be available, which are then – secondarily – co-opted or adapted by the formal nature of the animal. Features that are the result of secondary teleology are never themselves the necessary prerequisites for the performance of a function that is specified in the definition of the substantial being of the animal. Rather, Aristotle explains their presence as being "for the better" or for "living well," because they help some other feature perform its function better (these are what I call "subsidiary parts") or because they give rise to a function the animal could – strictly speaking – do without (what I call "luxury parts").[26] For instance, the hair on our heads is presumably a "luxury" feature: Aristotle believes that these hairs come to be by material necessity, and that the formal natures of human beings then use or co-opt them for protection (the hard and earthy constitution of hair helps to protect human heads against excessive heat and cold) – a function that living beings in Aristotle's world may well do without.[27] In cases of secondary teleology, the relevant causal connection is thus that between the available material potentials and the function or use to which the materials with those potentials are put. The actions of the formal nature in these cases are guided by the potentials the available materials have, which determine

[26] For my categorization of animal parts, see section 3.2.

[27] This is a rather liberal interpretation of *PA* II.14, 658b2–10, which I offer here purely for the sake of explaining what I mean by secondary teleology; for actual examples, see Chapter 3.

the range of uses one can make of those materials, rather than by some preexisting potential for form that is to be realized. In the explanation of features that are the result of secondary teleology, Aristotle tends to give a separate explanation for the coming to be of that feature and for its presence, and prefers "weaker" teleological language (e.g., a certain feature comes to be of necessity, but exists *for* or *with a view to* – "*pros*," "*eis*," or "*charin*" – some good).

In both cases, the causal feature that is most salient to us is the function or final cause. When explaining the presence of either wings in birds or hair on human heads, we first point to their function: wings are present for the sake of flying, hair is present for protection. This is because final causes are often simply observable – we can infer what something is for by looking at what it typically does and by observing what contribution it makes to the life of the living being in question. For this reason, final causes tend to be the first causes to be picked out in a teleological explanation: they have what I call *explanatory priority*. Identifying something's final cause is the first and most important step in generating a teleological explanation.

However, as should also be clear given the distinction between two types of teleology, just identifying the final cause of some feature is not sufficient if we want to have a *complete* explanation of that feature (which is necessary if we want to have a full understanding of it). We also need to find out whether this end that constitutes the final cause is the realization of some preexisting potential for form, or rather a use that has been made of materials that were available of material necessity. In the remainder of this book, I shall refer to this issue as one of determining whether the coming to be and presence of some end that constitutes the final cause is primarily *driven by form* or primarily *driven by matter*. In the first case, it is the presence of a preexisting potential for form that guides the actions of the formal nature and that thereby directs the teleological process of its realization. In the second case, it is the presence of certain material potentials that allows for certain teleological uses (and not for others); the actions of the formal nature in making use of these materials are secondary to the operation of material necessity that produced the materials in the first place. Both processes thus involve the goal-directed actions of the formal nature – which is why *both processes qualify as being teleological*, but in the first case, the actions are primarily "driven by form" (e.g., the form of flyer requires the production of wings), in the second, they are primarily "driven by matter" (e.g., the availability of hard materials allows for the production of protective parts like horns and hair).

Both types of teleological process involve developments over time from some initial situation to the full realization of some functional feature. In primary teleology, the initial situation is the existence of a preexisting potential for form; in secondary teleology, the initial situation is the existence of "extra" material with certain material potentials. Thus, when it comes to *priority in generation* (as opposed to priority in nature or in definition, which is a kind of priority that belongs to final causes),[28] final causes are never *causally primary*. That is, final causes never initiate, so to speak, the teleological process that leads up to their realization (even if we do not interpret final causes anachronistically as acting as efficient causes, this would still be a case of backward causation). Final causes are not "active" or "productive" in that way (cf. *GC* I.7, 324b13–15; b14: τὸ δ' οὗ ἕνεκα οὐ ποιητικόν). Instead, the causally primary factors are always some combination of formal-efficient causes in the case of primary teleology, or material-efficient causes in the case of secondary teleology. Thus, the coming to be of an end that constitutes a final cause, and which (at least partially) explains the presence of the natural feature under investigation, needs itself to be further explained in terms of the operation of chronologically prior and necessitating causes. Note that I do not claim that final causes ought to be explained by (let alone reduced to) other types of cause, but rather that the *obtaining* of an end that constitutes a final cause in a certain subject ought to be further analyzed in terms of the underlying causes that necessitate its coming to be – that is, at least, if we want to have a full understanding of that subject.

The fact that final causes never have causal priority in the sense outlined above is important, because on Aristotle's account of scientific demonstration, demonstrative syllogisms ought to track the actual sequence and the timing of the various stages in the causal chain.[29] This is not a requirement Aristotle discusses in the early chapters of the *Posterior Analytics*, which focus rather narrowly on geometric-style demonstrations that are timeless and universal, and it is therefore easily overlooked. Instead, the requirement is introduced in the lesser-known chapters in book II (i.e., *APo* II.11–12), where Aristotle discusses the question of how one incorporates causes and change into the syllogistic framework of demonstrations. I shall discuss these chapters in more detail in Chapter 6, but for now it suffices to point out that in demonstrations of natural phenomena, because they involve

[28] For Aristotle's discussion of the distinction between "priority in generation" and "priority in nature/substantial being," see *PA* II.1, 646a24–646b2; cf. *PA* I.1, 640a10–b4.

[29] Cf. Charles (2000, 198–204).

changes over time, final causes can never take up the position of the middle term. The reason is that middle terms in such demonstrations ought to pick out the causally *primary* factor in the chain of development (i.e., the factor that cannot be explained any further), and in developments causal primacy and chronological primacy coincide. For the structure of teleological explanations this means that final causes will typically be picked out by the major terms, and as such will feature as part of the conclusion that is being demonstrated. Complete teleological explanations thus specify, first, the final cause which explains the *existence* of some natural feature, and second, the cause that is responsible for the end's (that constitutes the final cause) *coming to hold* of that natural feature.

With these preliminary distinctions set out, we can now turn to Aristotle's defense of natural teleology in Chapter 8 of the second book of the *Physica*.

1.2 ARISTOTLE'S FIRST ARGUMENT IN DEFENSE OF NATURAL TELEOLOGY

Causation in nature: the relation between teleology and necessity

Aristotle's defense of natural teleology takes place in the context of a larger exposition in the second book of the *Physica* on what nature is, what topics the student of nature should study, how nature relates to art, and what the causal role of luck and spontaneity is in nature. The problem Aristotle sets out to answer in the final two chapters of this book is the following (*Ph* II.8, 198b10–12): "We must first state the reason why nature is among the causes that are for the sake of something (ἡ φύσις τῶν ἕνεκά του αἰτίων), and next, about necessity, how it is present among natural things."

In the preceding chapters, Aristotle had defined nature in terms of each of the four kinds of cause, but first and foremost as an internal efficient cause.[30] The question Aristotle asks now is why nature, as an internal efficient cause, is among the causes that are for the sake of something, or, as I take it, why nature acts goal-directedly. The question is important, because, as Aristotle continues to explain (in *Ph* II.8, 198b12–16), his predecessors traced back all phenomena to necessity or material causation, and waved goodbye to

[30] This conception of nature as an internal efficient cause is itself characterized as a hypothesis that belongs to the first principles of the science of nature (*Ph* VIII.3, 253b2–6). It cannot be demonstrated through a syllogistic proof, and the same holds for the proposition that the world of natural changing things exists; cf. Bolton (1991, 19–21). The fact that there are natures or natural things Aristotle claims is evident – the attempt to demonstrate this would in fact be ridiculous (*Ph* II.1, 193a1–9).

any other kind of cause, thus leaving it unclear whether there is any causal role to be played by nature as a goal-directed efficient cause in addition to nature as a material-efficient cause.[31]

The way Aristotle introduces the issue here pertains directly to one of the most pressing problems in the scholarship on Aristotle's teleology: how exactly does Aristotle think teleology and necessity in nature are related to each other?[32] Recent scholarship has proposed the following four different interpretations for the way Aristotle perceives this relationship:

Based on the way Aristotle contrasts his own teleological view of nature with the views of his predecessors who explain everything in terms of material necessity, some scholars argue that Aristotle believes that the two views are incompatible with each other, and that he ultimately denies that there is such a thing as material necessity operative in nature that is independent of the operation of teleology.[33]

Others think that for Aristotle the two "forces of nature" are compatible, but that the operation of material necessity and the actualizations of element potentials as such are *not sufficient* to produce regular, good, or complex results. According to these scholars, natural phenomena could not come about without the operation of a final cause, and therefore explanations in terms of formal and final causation cannot be reduced to explanations in terms of efficient and material causation.[34]

Still others agree that necessity and teleology are compatible in Aristotle's worldview, but do so on the grounds that the theory of natural teleology has no ontological consequences. They claim that the theory of teleology is an explanatory framework that has the sole purpose of making things intelligible for us humans. Accordingly, these scholars believe that teleology is merely used by Aristotle as a heuristic device in his attempt to explain natural phenomena. It is argued that on the level of causation, material and efficient causes are all that is needed to bring about natural phenomena; on the level of explanation and understanding, however, we need the language of ends and functions in order to make sense of the natural phenomena.[35]

31 Cf. Sauvé Meyer (1992, 792–793).
32 I shall return to the question of the relation between teleology and necessity in section 3.3. For the present purposes, an outline of the problem and possible interpretations will suffice.
33 See, e.g., Balme (1965; 1987a).
34 Stronger and weaker versions of this so-called "irreducibility thesis" have been defended by amongst others Bradie and Miller (1999, 75); Charles (1988, 1–53); Cooper (1982, 197–222); Gotthelf (1987, 204–242); Irwin (1988, 109–112); Lennox (1982; 2001b); and Waterlow (1982, 69).
35 Stronger and weaker versions of this pragmatic viewpoint have been defended by Charles (1988); Irwin (1988); Nussbaum (1978); Sorabji (1980); and Wieland (1975).

All three views discussed above focus on the question of the compatibility and ontological reducibility of teleology and necessity. However, the position I adopt myself, and for which I shall offer further evidence in my discussion below, is the view first introduced by Sauvé Meyer (1992).[36] She argues that we should dismiss the question of whether or not teleology and necessity are mutually compatible or reducible to each other as not being the main point for Aristotle, and focuses, conversely, on the issue of intrinsic versus incidental causation.

Following this approach, I believe that the reason why Aristotle contrasts his own teleological worldview with that of his materialist predecessors is that the latter deny that high-order natural phenomena, such as animals and plants, have a privileged ontological status. According to the materialists, only the material elements are natures in a true sense, which means that the things that are constituted from them are mere accidental qualities or arrangements of these elements. The materialist view of nature eliminates those very things that Aristotle takes to be ontologically basic, and which in his view are in particular need of explanation, namely complex natural wholes such as living beings. In short, for Aristotle an animal is the primary example of a natural substance, whereas for the materialist an animal is merely a coincidental conglomeration of elements. The heart of the debate does not pertain (or at least not directly) to the question of reductionism, but rather to that of eliminativism: the mistake of the materialists is not just that they reduce plants and animals to their material elements, but more that, as a consequence of this reductionism, they deny that plants and animals are substances at all.[37]

Aristotle thus does not want to subsume all forms of material necessity under conditional necessity (he is not against all forms of reductionism),[38] nor does he require teleological explanations for all natural phenomena (he is also not a panglossian). He agrees that material necessity on its own may account for the coming to be of some low-level natural phenomena that have regular good outcomes (see, e.g., the production of eyebrows to be discussed in section 3.2), but denies that the presence of such outcomes

[36] Versions of this view are also defended by Bolton (1997, 122); Judson (2005); and Matthen (2009).

[37] Sauvé Meyer (1992, 794–795; 820–825); Johnson (2005, 98–99).

[38] Chapters that are traditionally read as endorsing an anti-reductionist view (e.g., *PA* I.1, *Ph* II.9, *GA* V.8) in fact make a more subtle point about what the appropriate modes of explanation are for what kind of natural phenomena: some natural phenomena cannot be explained in terms of material-efficient causes alone and require the *additional* assumption of formal-final causes. Aristotle's point is not that we should substitute conditional necessity for material necessity in all cases, but rather that we should *expand* the types of cause we invoke in our natural explanations.

on a regular basis[39] can be merely accidental. Instead, materially necessitated structures are "actively" co-opted or adapted in animals by their formal natures *because they are good for that animal*; their explanation thus requires references to teleology as well as to material necessity. High-level natural phenomena, such as the coming to be of complex natural wholes like (most) living organisms, are never due to an accidental combination of material elements, but are always the product of intrinsic causation involving teleology and conditional necessity.

In both low-level and high-level generations of natural products, Aristotle holds that these products can only be explained satisfactorily by reference to the goal-directed actions of nature as an internal efficient cause. Such a formal nature acts – always or for the most part – for the sake of something by either (i) realizing an internal, preexisting potential for form or (ii) by using materials produced by material necessity for the good of the natural being. The first causal pattern is what I characterized above as "primary teleology"; the second pattern is that of "secondary teleology." An important difference between the two types of teleology not mentioned above is that while primary teleology only pertains to the actions of *internal* formal natures working within the confines of the individual animal, the causal pattern underlying secondary teleology can also be extended to include what has been called "inter-species" teleology. In the latter case, it describes the causal pattern of any agent – internal or external – making use of things available by nature for its own good, such as living beings using each other as food.[40]

Bearing these distinctions in mind, I shall now resume my discussion of Aristotle's first argument in defense of natural teleology.

A first outline of the aporia and of Aristotle's solution

Aristotle's first answer to why nature is among the causes that are for the sake of something consists of a puzzle or aporia concerning the causal

39 See Nielsen (2008, 397–398), on the normative connotation of Aristotle's notion "for the most part": the notion need not always indicate actual frequency, but rather frequency *in ideal circumstances*.

40 In inter-species teleology the perspective of the user becomes important; see Judson (2005, 356–357). Things that are present for whatever reason can be used by a goal-directed agent, because of the material potentials these things have, either *within* natural beings (e.g., earthy material, because of its defensive potentials, can be used by the formal nature of deer for the production of horns), or *among* natural beings (e.g., the branches of a tree, because of their resistance against water, can be used by the shipbuilder for the production of ships). The outcomes of these processes of "using" have genuine functions or final causes (e.g., defense or floating), even though it would not be right to say that the constitutive materials that are used *came to be* for the sake of these functions or final causes.

relation between natural processes and the goodness or badness of their outcomes. In the hypothetical objection, raised by an imaginary materialist predecessor, Aristotle draws an analogy between the falling of rain and the growth or spoilage of crops on the one hand and the generation of animal parts and complete animals and their functions on the other hand (*Ph* II.8, 198b16–32). The base domain of the analogy runs as follows (*Ph* II.8, 198b16–23):

> There is a difficulty: what prevents nature not to act for the sake of something or because it is better, but in the way Zeus rains, not in order to make the crops grow, but of necessity (for it is necessary that that which has gone up cools down, and what cools down becomes water and falls down: when this has happened, it turns out that crops grow), and in the same way also that if someone's crops are ruined on the threshing floor, it does not rain for the sake of this, in order that they be spoiled, but that it happened to come about.[41]

Aristotle has his opponent suggest that instead of saying that a beneficial outcome, such as the growth of crops, is the result of nature acting for the sake of something (i.e., being the result of primary teleology) *or* of nature acting that way because it is better (i.e., the outcome being the result of secondary teleology),[42] we might as well say that the natural process took place of material necessity, in virtue of water elements acting according to their material natures, and that the outcome – whether good or bad – just happened to result in that way.

As Sedley points out,[43] the expression "Zeus rains" indicates that Aristotle portrays his opponent as a materialist who tries to provide a materialist explanation for something that is popularly viewed as an act of a providential god. This latter view, representing a naïve, religious, and anthropocentric assumption about the supposed providential teleology of the world, is ridiculed and rejected in favor of a naturalistic explanation in terms of the interactions of material elements. The materialist account interprets the relation between natural processes and their outcomes as an accidental one: the meteorological phenomenon of rainfall can be explained fully by reference to the mechanical cycle of evaporation, and the agricultural

41 ἔχει δ' ἀπορίαν τί κωλύει τὴν φύσιν μὴ ἕνεκά του ποιεῖν μηδ' ὅτι βέλτιον, ἀλλ' ὥσπερ ὕει ὁ Ζεὺς οὐχ ὅπως τὸν σῖτον αὐξήσῃ, ἀλλ' ἐξ ἀνάγκης (τὸ γὰρ ἀναχθὲν ψυχθῆναι δεῖ, καὶ τὸ ψυχθὲν ὕδωρ γενόμενον κατελθεῖν· τὸ δ' αὐξάνεσθαι τούτου γενομένου τὸν σῖτον συμβαίνει), ὁμοίως δὲ καὶ εἴ τῳ ἀπόλλυται ὁ σῖτος ἐν τῇ ἅλῳ, οὐ τούτου ἕνεκα ὕει ὅπως ἀπόληται, ἀλλὰ τοῦτο συμβέβηκεν.

42 Pace Scharle (2008, 169–170), who reads these two propositions conjunctively as exhibiting one and the same kind of natural teleology. For my reading of "because it is better" as a reference to secondary teleology, see sections 3.2 and 4.2.

43 Sedley (1991, 185).

outcomes – whether they are good or bad – are unrelated and coincidental to the event of rain itself. The end result does not explain the occurrence of rain (rather, material necessity does), nor does the occurrence of rain intrinsically necessitate a particular outcome (rather, as the use of the verb συμβαίνειν suggests, the outcomes are by chance and accidental).[44]

Next, the hypothetical opponent applies this causal scheme to the biological realm, starting with the generation of parts of animals and their functions. The first half of the target domain of the analogy runs as follows (*Ph* II.8, 198b23–29):

> So what prevents also parts in nature from being this way, for example that teeth shoot up of necessity, the ones in the front sharp, with the fitness for tearing, the molars broad and useful for grinding down the food – not because they came to be for the sake of this, but because they turned out that way. And similarly about the other parts, in as many as "that for the sake of something" seems to be present.[45]

The materialist again conceptualizes the causal relation between biological parts and their function as an accidental one: teeth grow of material necessity, and their functional differentiation is a matter of chance, resulting accidentally from the material potentials of teeth and from the structure in which they happened to grow, and not because of teleology. The same is said to hold of as many parts as seem to be for the sake of something: they all come to be due to material necessity, and their functional features are mere accidents.

The materialist then extends this causal scheme to the coming to be of complete living beings (*Ph* II.8, 198b29–34):

> Wherever then all [the parts] turned out in a way they would also [have done] if they had come to be for the sake of something, those survived, having been organized in a fitting way by spontaneity. As many as did not [turn out] in such a way perished and continue to perish, as Empedocles says about the man-faced ox progeny. This then is the argument, about which one might be puzzled, and there may be others just like it.[46]

44 I translate *hê tuchê* with "luck" and *to automaton* with "spontaneity"; I use "chance" as a general term covering both luck and spontaneity.

45 ὥστε τί κωλύει οὕτω καὶ τὰ μέρη ἔχειν ἐν τῇ φύσει, οἷον τοὺς ὀδόντας ἐξ ἀνάγκης ἀνατεῖλαι τοὺς μὲν ἐμπροσθίους ὀξεῖς, ἐπιτηδείους πρὸς τὸ διαιρεῖν, τοὺς δὲ γομφίους πλατεῖς καὶ χρησίμους πρὸς τὸ λεαίνειν τὴν τροφήν, ἐπεὶ οὐ τούτου ἕνεκα γενέσθαι, ἀλλὰ συμπεσεῖν· ὁμοίως δὲ καὶ περὶ τῶν ἄλλων μερῶν, ἐν ὅσοις δοκεῖ ὑπάρχειν τὸ ἕνεκά του.

46 ὅπου μὲν οὖν ἅπαντα συνέβη ὥσπερ κἂν εἰ ἕνεκά του ἐγίγνετο, ταῦτα μὲν ἐσώθη ἀπὸ τοῦ αὐτομάτου συστάντα ἐπιτηδείως· ὅσα δὲ μὴ οὕτως, ἀπώλετο καὶ ἀπόλλυται, καθάπερ Ἐμπεδοκλῆς λέγει τὰ βουγενῆ ἀνδρόπρῳρα. ὁ μὲν οὖν λόγος, ᾧ ἄν τις ἀπορήσειεν, οὗτος, καὶ εἴ τις ἄλλος τοιοῦτός ἐστιν·.

In a final move, the materialist claims that even the coming to be of entire natural beings can be explained by reference to the same causal model: the fact that some animal parts formed matching wholes is the result of spontaneity, not of nature acting for the sake of something. The view that is being ascribed to someone like Empedocles is thus that the present biodiversity is to be explained as the accidental result of a mix-and-match process of animal parts that is guided by chance and not by the goal-directed actions of nature.

Immediately following this aporia, Aristotle presents his own solution (*Ph* II.8, 198b34–199a8):

> It is impossible that things are that way. For those things, and all things that are by nature, come to be that way either always or for the most part, and none of them belongs to things that are due to luck or spontaneity. For it does not seem to be due to luck or spontaneity that it rains often in wintertime, but [it does] when [it rains] during the dog days. Nor do heat-waves [seem that way] during the dog days, but [they do] when they occur in winter. If, then, it seems that [these things] are either by accident or for the sake of something, [and] if it is not possible that these things are by accident or by spontaneity, they are for the sake of something. But that such things are by nature, even the people who make this argument would claim that. There is thus that for the sake of something among the things that come to be and are by nature.[47]

The structure of the counter-argument Aristotle provides is quite complex, so let me offer a brief paraphrase.[48] What is at stake in the argument is the nature of the causal relation between natural processes and their outcomes: the materialist presented three examples of natural cases in which this relation was one of chance. Aristotle's counter-position is that it is impossible that the outcomes of natural processes mentioned by the materialist are due to chance. It is impossible because natural processes produce such outcomes as described by the materialist either always or for the most part – their regularity excludes (by Aristotle's definition of chance as discussed in *Ph* II.4–6)[49] the possibility that they are due to chance.

47 ἀδύνατον δὲ τοῦτον ἔχειν τὸν τρόπον. ταῦτα μὲν γὰρ καὶ πάντα τὰ φύσει ἢ αἰεὶ οὕτω γίγνεται ἢ ὡς ἐπὶ τὸ πολύ, τῶν δ' ἀπὸ τύχης καὶ τοῦ αὐτομάτου οὐδέν. οὐ γὰρ ἀπὸ τύχης οὐδ' ἀπὸ συμπτώματος δοκεῖ ὕειν πολλάκις τοῦ χειμῶνος, ἀλλ' ἐὰν ὑπὸ κύνα· οὐδὲ καύματα ὑπὸ κύνα, ἀλλ' ἂν χειμῶνος. εἰ οὖν ἢ ἀπὸ συμπτώματος δοκεῖ ἢ ἕνεκά του εἶναι, εἰ μὴ οἷόν τε ταῦτ' εἶναι μήτε ἀπὸ συμπτώματος μήτ' ἀπὸ ταὐτομάτου, ἕνεκά του ἂν εἴη. ἀλλὰ μὴν φύσει γ' ἐστὶ τὰ τοιαῦτα πάντα, ὡς κἂν αὐτοὶ φαῖεν οἱ ταῦτα λέγοντες. ἔστιν ἄρα τὸ ἕνεκά του ἐν τοῖς φύσει γιγνομένοις καὶ οὖσιν.

48 For alternative reconstructions of the argument, see Quarantotto (2005, 90–95).

49 For Aristotle, luck and spontaneity indicate the causes of irregular and unexpected outcomes. These are outcomes that *typically* come to be due to thought, choice, or nature, but whose cause in this

This is clear from the following two examples (the use of δοκεῖ in *Ph* II.8, 199a1 indicates that Aristotle assumes that even his opponent would agree to this): nobody would say that frequent rain in the winter is due to chance (only rain in the summer is), nor would he say that frequent heat-waves in the summer are due to chance (only heat-waves in the winter are). If, then, these frequently occurring natural processes are either due to chance or for the sake of something (Aristotle again uses δοκεῖ in *Ph* II.8, 199a3 to suggest accordance),[50] they must be for the sake of something: the relation between natural processes and their outcomes must be teleological.

Although the general purport of the passage is clear enough (i.e., that nature is among the causes that act for the sake of something), there are three problems in Aristotle's response to the puzzle that I shall need to address in the next section.

First, Aristotle couches the dispute over which causes are operative in nature exclusively in terms of spontaneity and teleology; the notion of necessity is not mentioned in his response to the puzzle raised by the materialist.[51] This "disappearance" of the notion of necessity seems suspicious, for Aristotle usually counts material necessity among the causes of natural events that happen always or for the most part.[52] He often uses examples of meteorological phenomena such as the evaporation cycle that produces rain to illustrate the regularity of materially necessitated processes.[53] The mechanical explanation offered by the materialist for the

particular case is either: (i) an indeterminable cause; the event (e.g., "a falling stone that hits a person") *seems* to have been for a purpose (e.g., "someone throwing that stone with the purpose of hitting that person"), but the expected corresponding action that typically leads to this outcome did not take place (e.g., nobody actually threw the stone). The event must therefore be the result of some other action that from our perspective is indeterminable; the outcome is called a case of good or bad luck. Or (ii) a determinate cause (e.g., "going to the marketplace in order to litigate as a plaintiff") that has incidental and unforeseen results (e.g., "meeting his debtor and getting his money back"), possibly in addition to having a proper result and final cause (e.g., "litigating as a plaintiff"). The unforeseen result is also called a case of good or bad luck. Cf. Boeri (1995, 87–96), and Lennox (2001a, 250–258). For Aristotle's interpretation of the notion of luck in Empedocles, see *Ph* II.4, 196a17–24 and *GC* II.6, 334a1–9.

50 A materialist might well have disagreed with Aristotle's dichotomy: Waterlow (1982, 77).

51 Sauvé Meyer (1992; 797) suggests that Aristotle focuses solely on chance and teleology in order to frame the problem in terms of accidental causation on the one hand and intrinsic causation on the other: if the outcomes of natural processes are either accidents or the products of the goal-directed actions of nature, then on the basis of their regularity we should conclude that they are the result of teleology. This shift in terminology might also reflect the type of causation that the materialist claims is operative in the coming to be of complete living beings in the final part of the analogy: spontaneity is said to produce the same results one could expect from teleology.

52 Cf. Charlton (1970, 120).

53 The key passage is *GC* II.11, 338a14–b19, which will be discussed in more detail in section 3.3. See also *APo* II.12, 96a2–7 and *Meta* VI.2, 1026b27–35.

coming to be of rain matches Aristotle's own view:[54] rainfall is due to the circulation of material elements in the atmosphere, depending on the orbit of the sun and the change of seasons, and is therefore a regular natural phenomenon. Nowhere does Aristotle claim that rain is for the sake of something.

This brings us to the second problem in Aristotle's solution to the aporia: Aristotle seems to argue that if winter rain and summer heat are regular natural phenomena, they cannot be due to chance but must be for the sake of something. What, then, does Aristotle think winter rain is for? Traditionally, scholars have denied that Aristotle endorses the view that winter rain is for the sake of something.[55] However, more recently, other scholars have pointed out that the latter interpretation would make the solution to the aporia incomprehensible,[56] and I believe this is right. The text itself presents only one possible goal of winter rain: the growth of crops. Certainly, this need not be the only purpose served by winter rain, but if the argument is to be rhetorically effective, it seems that there must be some non-accidental way in which Aristotle thinks winter rain (even if not itself caused teleologically) serves the growth of crops and thus proves the materialist to be wrong.[57]

In the next section, I shall in fact argue that Aristotle believes that winter rain is for the sake of growing crops, where the type of teleology at stake is an external form of *secondary* teleology. The coming to be

54 For Aristotle's discussion of rain in terms of material and efficient causes, see *Meteor* I.9, 346b16–36; *Meteor* I.11, 347b12–33; and *GC* II.10, 337a1–7; in the biological works, Aristotle uses the mechanical explanation of rain as an analogy for physiological processes in the body: see *Somn* 3, 457b31–458a9 and *PA* II.7, 653a2–7.

55 See, e.g., Charlton (1970, 120–123); Gotthelf (1987); Irwin (1988, 102–107); Nussbaum (1978, 94), and, more recently, Pellegrin (2002, 309); Johnson (2005, 149–158); and Judson (2005, 345–348).

56 See Code (1997); Cooper (1982); Furley (1985); Sedley (1991; 2007); and Wardy (1993).

57 Most recently, Scharle (2008) has argued that winter rain is indeed teleological, but not for the sake of the growth of crops, since it is not *the nature* of winter rain to be for the sake of this, nor the nature of the cosmos to direct winter rain to this. She holds that winter rain is teleological because the motions of the water elements are fitted to the circular motions of the sun (which is the efficient cause of water motions) in a way that when they fall in the winter the rain is teleological, because it is properly due to the retraction of the sun and thus due to intrinsic causation, whereas when they fall in the summer, the rain is accidental, because it is not a proper result of the closeness of the sun. Although this presents an interesting and elegant alternative, I take it that the crux for Aristotle in *Ph* II.8 is to show that regular natural phenomena have regular beneficial outcomes due to the fact that *nature is an efficient cause that acts for the sake of something.* Under Scharle's interpretation, however, it is the retraction of the sun in the winter that is the efficient cause that makes the water return to its natural place, but this efficient cause itself never – neither in the winter, nor in the summer – acts for the sake of this outcome. In fact, the motions of the sun are an accidental cause of the entire water cycle, which Aristotle characterizes as a materially necessitated process, whereas the return of water elements to their natural place is always a case of primary teleology for Aristotle, regardless of what season it is. Cf. Sedley (1991, 184); Wardy (1993, 22), and Morison (2002, 26–28).

of crops is not a realization of an internal potential for form through the actions of winter rain (i.e., crops are not an outcome of primary natural teleology), nor is it an accidental outcome of winter rain (i.e., crops are not a spontaneous by-product of a materially necessitated natural process). Rather, the coming to be of crops is due to the goal-directed actions of human beings who make use of the natural material potentials of regular winter rain (and seeds) and impose the art of agriculture on what is naturally available, in order to secure the regular coming to be of beneficial outcomes (i.e., coming to be as crops is an extrinsic function of a certain kind of plant). It is thus an example of human beings using art to complete the goal-directedness present in nature in a way that resembles formal natures using extra materials for the production of subsidiary animal parts: both are cases of "using" what is naturally available, and in both the "goods" produced reveal the perspective of the user, rather than a feature intrinsic to the thing used. Of course, under this interpretation the causal connection between winter rain and the growth of crops is thus hardly a *natural* teleological one. However, it does illustrate the necessity of there being goal-directed efficient causes for the production of regular, beneficial outcomes, which is the main point Aristotle is making against his materialist opponent.

However, if we grant, then, that winter rain is for the sake of something, perhaps even for the growth of crops, we face a third problem, concerning the scope of Aristotle's natural teleology. The standard view is that Aristotle restricts the operation of natural teleology to the individual natures of substances,[58] but if rain comes to be to serve a function that is distinctly anthropocentric, then perhaps we ought to conclude that Aristotle's teleology itself is anthropocentric (i.e., that the goal-directedness of nature is *ultimately* for the benefit of man)[59] or even cosmic (i.e., that the goal-directedness of nature is *ultimately* for the sake of preserving the existing balance in the cosmos).[60] Below, I shall argue that these conclusions are not necessary if we interpret Aristotle to understand the coming to be of crops (just like the coming to be of teeth) as being a form of secondary, rather than of primary teleology. Serving an anthropocentric goal is something that is imposed on natural processes from the outside, not something that is intrinsic to their internal natures.

58 See especially Gotthelf (1987).

59 This controversial but thought-provoking interpretation is defended by Sedley (1991; 2007).

60 A cosmic view of Aristotle's teleology is assumed or defended by Cooper (1982); Furley (1985, 115–116); (1996, 75); Kahn (1985); Matthen (2001; 2009); Sedley (1991; 2007); and Wardy (1993, 19).

1.3 THE NATURE AND SCOPE OF NATURAL TELEOLOGY

Empedocles and Aristotle on the coming to be of teeth

The debate on Aristotle's first argument in defense of natural teleology traditionally focuses on the rainfall example, which is arguably the most problematic part of the argument, while much less attention is paid to the Empedoclean account of natural generation.[61] However, since the Empedoclean account forms the target domain in the analogy, we can use it for our interpretation of the rainfall example.

Let me start by briefly outlining Empedocles' zoogony as it can be reconstructed from the fragments that have been preserved.[62] According to the testimony by Aetius (*DK*31A72), Empedocles distinguishes four stages in the generation of animals and plants. The first two stages probably occur under the increasing influence of Love, in which animal generation is explained "bottom-up," as moving from parts to wholes (see in particular *DK*31B17; B57, B59, B60, B61, B96, and B98). First, the coincidental interactions amongst the four Empedoclean elements produce animal tissues such as flesh and bone. Next, similar interactions between these tissues produce separate animal parts, such as foreheads and arms. Finally, the random interactions between such isolated parts roaming the earth lead to the coming to be of different kinds of animals. Once Love's influence is strong enough, the parts will randomly stick together, forming all kinds of hybrids. Stages 3 and 4 probably occur under the increasing influence of Strife, in which complete plants, animals, and human beings come to be spontaneously from the earth (see *DK*31B62 and Strasbourg fragment d). They are said to rise up like shoots of plants, grow limbs, and then mature naturally to the point where they are able to reproduce themselves sexually (Strife pulls the uniform masses apart and thereby creates the extremities). Presumably, this is the world in which we live now. Ultimately, Strife will break up the organisms into their four elements again and soon Love's influence will make itself felt.

Empedocles' account of the biological past is thus cyclical,[63] and draws from two conceptually different models of the origin of species. The

[61] The passage is usually quoted to applaud Empedocles for offering a pre-Darwinian theory of natural selection; see, e.g., Bostock (2006, 50); Ross (1936, 78); Sedley (2003, 2, 11; 2007, 43).

[62] The exact details of Empedocles' zoogony have been the subject of much debate, especially after the publication of the Strasbourg papyrus by Martin and Primavesi (1999), which revealed some interesting new materials. I claim no originality or comprehensiveness in the overview I present here – my purpose is merely to put the *Physica* passage into context.

[63] On the nature of this cycle and the continuity between the phases of Love and Strife, see Sedley (2007, 39–40).

zoogony under Strife follows a mythological model according to which living beings come to be spontaneously from the earth. The first generation is explained as a transition from the stage of spontaneous generation of both males and females, growing out of the moisture due to fire, to a stage of sexual reproduction, thus resembling a botanical process of the growth and maturation of plants (without undergoing some kind of transformation of species). The zoogony under Love, on the other hand, seems to be an original invention by Empedocles and offers a fully naturalistic account of the growth of more complex organic compounds, resulting from random collisions of organic parts. The examples of creatures thus produced are rather fantastic hybrids, like the man-faced ox progeny mentioned by Aristotle, but the fragments do not rule out the possibility that these combinations also resulted in living beings like the ones that are alive now, such as, for example, ox-faced ox progenies. The reference to Empedocles we find in Aristotle's defense of natural teleology fits this second kind of zoogony.

Crucial for the understanding of the Empedoclean passage in *Ph* II.8, 198b23–34 is the distinction in the materialist account of generation between the two levels of "incidental fitness." The first level pertains to the "incidental fitness" of parts of animals: material necessity causes the coming to be of parts such as teeth that turn out to have the right potentials and structure for the performance of biological functions such as biting and grinding. The second level pertains to the "incidental fitness" of complete living beings: spontaneity causes animal parts to combine "in a fitting way," and the animals that result from these "matches" make up the present diversity of animal species (those combinations of parts that do not "fit" constitute the monsters that died and continue to die). For Aristotle, both causal accounts are mistaken, but as I shall expound below, they are not mistaken to the same degree.

Aristotle's biological treatises are full of references to teeth, so let me start by presenting his own explanation of the coming to be and presence of these parts (*PA* III.2, 663b22–35):

> We must say what the character of the necessary nature is, and how nature according to the account *has made use* of things present of necessity for the sake of something... For the residual surplus of this sort of [earthen] body, being present in the larger of the animals, is *used* by nature *for* protection and advantage, and [the surplus, which] flows of necessity to the upper region, it *distributes* in some animals to *teeth* and tusks, in others to horns.[64]

64 πῶς δὲ τῆς ἀναγκαίας φύσεως ἐχούσης τοῖς ὑπάρχουσιν ἐξ ἀνάγκης ἢ κατὰ τὸν λόγον φύσις ἕνεκά του κατακέχρηται, λέγωμεν... Τὴν γοῦν τοιούτου σώματος περισσωματικὴν

In this passage, Aristotle exhibits teeth to be paradigmatic products of secondary teleology. Just like his materialist opponent, Aristotle believes that the *coming to be* of teeth is primarily due to material necessity[65] and that the functionality of the teeth follows from the material potentials the constitutive materials of teeth happen to have. The terms "useful" (*chrêsimos*)[66] and "suitable for" (*epitêdeios*)[67] that are put in the mouth of the materialist to describe the incidental fitness of parts perfectly reflect Aristotle's own usage of these terms, indicating the "fitness" something has – not in virtue of being conditionally necessitated for that purpose, but in virtue of the material potentials a part or residue happens to have of material necessity. However, the *presence* and functionality of teeth must ultimately be explained by reference to the goal-directed actions of the formal nature of animals with teeth. The formal natures of these animals make use of these materials and "assign" a function to them in accordance with the potentials the materials have of necessity. Since in this case the materials are earthen and hard, which constitute the right potentials for the function of defense, the formal natures use them to make parts such as teeth, tusks, and horns (see *PA* II.9, 655b4–15). So even though the coming to be of teeth is not primarily driven by form (Aristotle never suggests that there is a preexisting potential for form that is being realized by the production of teeth; strictly speaking, he believes animals could nourish and defend themselves without teeth), Aristotle does not deny that natural, materially necessitated processes can have beneficial outcomes. He only denies that they can have such beneficial outcomes on a regular basis *without the intervention of goal-directed efficient causes*, which (actively)

ὑπερβολὴν ἐν τοῖς μείζοσι τῶν ζῴων ὑπάρχουσαν ἐπὶ βοήθειαν καὶ τὸ συμφέρον καταχρῆται ἡ φύσις, καὶ τὴν ῥέουσαν ἐξ ἀνάγκης εἰς τὸν ἄνω τόπον τοῖς μὲν εἰς ὀδόντας καὶ χαυλιόδοντας ἀπένειμε, τοῖς δ' εἰς κέρατα.

65 Other relevant passages are *GA* II.6, 745a18–745b9, in which Aristotle explains that teeth are made from the residues conducive to growth assigned to bones, and *GA* V.8, in which he explains the differentiations of teeth by reference to both material necessity and teleology. I discuss these passages in a separate paper, co-authored with Allan Gotthelf (2010).

66 *Chrêsimos* usually characterizes the potentials residues have for something; see, e.g., *GA* I.15, 720b34–35; *GA* I.18, 725a3–7; *GA* III.3, 754b6–7; *GA* III.10, 760b13–14; *GA* IV.8, 776a23–26; *GA* V.2, 781b26–28; *HA* II.1, 500a15; *HA* VI.22, 576a14–16; and *IA* 1, 704a4–5.

67 *Epitêdeios* is used to designate foodstuffs, natural places, and even thoughts that have certain "function-inducing" characteristics that these things just happen to have. For instance, Aristotle uses it with respect to certain areas in the sea that "are favorable for spawning"; see *HA* VIII.13, 589b3–6; cf. *HA* III.21, 522b22–23; *HA* III.21, 523a3–4; *HA* V.13, 544b8–9; *HA* X.5, 636b21–23; and *MA* 8, 702a17–19. Aristotle also uses the term to indicate the suitability of material mixtures for certain functions (*PA* IV.10, 686a8–11): "And nature placed some of the modes of perception on the outside of it [i.e., the head] as well, on account of the blend of the blood being well proportioned and *ensuring* both the warmth of the brain and the quietness and accuracy of perception." For this use of the term, cf. *Pol* VII.4, 1325b40–1326a4.

adapt or (passively) co-opt such features in order to support the animal's well-being.[68]

For Aristotle, it is the materialist account of the "fitness" of complete living beings that is most problematic. For Empedocles, animals that are "composed in a fitting way" and that therefore survive seem to be animals that are quite literally combinations of matching parts (i.e., of ox faces combined with ox bodies, etc.).[69] Aristotle, on the other hand, understands the well-adaptedness of each particular kind of animal primarily in terms of its being able to perform all its necessary vital and essential functions within its own specific natural environment. The regularity of animal species exhibiting this kind of fitness cannot be fully accounted for by reference to spontaneity or even to formal natures using what happens to be available for something good. The regular presence of functioning living beings requires, according to Aristotle, the assumption of a *stronger* form of teleology, i.e., of formal natures acting always or for the most part for the sake of realizing a preexisting potential for form (while thereby regulating the various necessary interactions of material-efficient causes), where this form is eternal in species in virtue of being continuously transmitted from father to offspring.

The failure of materialists such as Empedocles to recognize the operation of primary teleology is also highlighted in the following passage (*PA* I.1, 640a17–26):

> For generation is for the sake of being, but not being for the sake of generation. This is why Empedocles did not speak well when he said that many things belong to animals because they turned out that way during generation – for example that the backbone is such, because it happened to get broken when it was being twisted; he failed to see, first, that the seed previously constituted must already possess this sort of potentiality, and, next, that the producer was prior not only in definition but also in time; for it is a human being who generates a human being, such that it is because the one *is* such, that the other's coming to be happens in that way. (Cf. *GA* II.1, 735a3–4)

As Aristotle explains here, the core of his theory of primary teleology in natural generation is the fact that whatever organism comes to be already

68 See also Aristotle's criticism of Democritus in *GA* V.8, 789b2–15, where Democritus is rebuked for failing to acknowledge the operation of (secondary) teleology in the differentiation of teeth.

69 Empedocles' notion of fitness thus hardly foreshadows fitness in a Darwinian sense. For instance, in Empedocles there is no selection for the fittest, but only for the fit (where this selection procedure is a purely negative force eliminating the unfit); and "fitness" does not refer to a relation between the animal and its environment (pace, most recently, Nielsen 2008, 387), but only to an internal match of parts being mixed in the same ratio. Also, the concept of chance invoked by Empedocles is one of randomness, not one of statistical probability: all homogeneous hybrids survive, all heterogeneous hybrids die.

possesses its corresponding form in potentiality (where the process of generation is for the sake of realizing that form or the being of that animal), and receives it from something that possesses that form in actuality.[70] The process of primary teleology involves the eternal replication of form,[71] which can only be explained through the assumption of nature operating as an internal efficient cause that acts for the sake of realizing those forms. It is only at the level of the coming to be and presence of complete and functioning living beings that Aristotle claims that the goal-directed actions of nature as an efficient cause are always primarily driven by form (i.e., it is the potential for form that guides the actions of nature as an efficient cause): where Empedocles mistakenly believes that their presence can be explained bottom-up, as the coincidental outcomes of spontaneous combinations of material elements, Aristotle grounds his explanations of animals in their form and explains their necessary parts and material constitutions top-down.[72]

In sum, what Aristotle tries to establish in arguing against the puzzle raised by the materialist is not the priority of form as such (the notion of conditional necessity is not explained until the following chapter, i.e., *Ph* II.9), but the necessity of postulating goal-directed actions of natural efficient causes to account for regular beneficial outcomes *also* in those cases where material necessity is the primary cause in the coming to be of a part or structure. Aristotle is thus not trying to present a unified account of (natural) teleology here, but is rather making the more general claim that for the explanation of whatever level of "fitness" or functionality can be found in natural beings, one needs to assume the operation of an efficient cause acting for the sake of producing that functional feature, regardless of whether this goal-directedness is primarily driven by form or by matter.

The rainfall example and the scope of natural teleology

We now have a clearer picture of the analogy between the rainfall example and the Empedoclean theory of generation: according to the materialist, both kinds of "generations" are due to material necessity, where the beneficial (or detrimental) outcomes are spontaneous and incidental, rather than due to the actions of an intentional agent (such as Zeus) generating things for the sake of those outcomes. The materialist thus refutes the providential, external, and anthropocentric teleology of Zeus in favor of a purely material form of causation. Aristotle's own solution to the aporia

[70] Witt (1994b, 222–228). [71] Lennox (2001a, 231). [72] Cf. Furley (1996, 77).

must be sought to lie somewhere in the middle: material necessity may certainly play a role in the generation of some natural phenomena, but if the relation between natural processes and their good outcomes is to be explained in terms of intrinsic causation, we must – rather than assume divine providence – postulate immanent natural teleology. That is, we must postulate the existence of internal natures that operate as efficient causes for the sake of such good outcomes, where this teleology is primarily driven either by form or by matter. This much at least must be the implication of Aristotle's statement and subsequent argument that it is "impossible for things to be that way" (*Ph* II.8, 198b34). What remains is to explain how Aristotle's account of rain fits into this picture and what the implications are for the scope of natural teleology.

In the sections above, I have argued that for Aristotle's solution to the aporia to be effective we need to attribute to Aristotle a teleological explanation of winter rain, but that this teleology need not be of the primary, natural type. Aristotle's own explanations of teeth and living beings suggest that he has the materialist come up with examples that in his own view represent increasingly stronger cases of teleology. The examples move from secondary to primary teleology, with the most dubious teleological example of rainfall producing crops functioning as the base domain in the analogy. In order to reconstruct Aristotle's teleological account of winter rain, I thus propose to treat the rainfall example as a weaker analogue of his account of teeth, i.e., as a weaker version of what I have called secondary teleology.

I have already suggested that Aristotle would agree with the materialist explanation of the coming to be of rain as a materially necessitated process. He identifies the sun and the obliquity of its orbit as the overarching cause responsible for the circularity of the seasons and the regularity of winter rainfall: the simple elements imitate this circular motion, and this is what causes rain to fall regularly during the wintertime.[73] Following the pattern of secondary teleology, we now need to identify something for which the availability of winter rain can be used. In my discussions above, I already assumed the coming to be of crops to be a plausible final cause of rain. The anthropocentric character of this final cause (the materialist reference to the growth of crops, rather than to that of plants in general, reveals a strictly human agricultural perspective)[74] need not be a problem, since we do not have to postulate that according to Aristotle winter rain comes to be for the sake of producing crops in the strong sense, nor that by producing crops

[73] Cf. Matthen (2009). [74] Sedley (1991, 185–186).

rain is realizing some preexisting natural form that is anthropocentrically defined,[75] for neither of these conclusions hold for the example of teeth. Instead, what is needed for a teleological interpretation of winter rain is the identification of some overarching goal-directed natural efficient cause that guarantees the intrinsic causal connection between winter rain and some regular beneficial outcome of winter rain, such as the growth of crops.

In the case of teeth, the goal-directed efficient cause is represented by the animal's own internal formal nature, which uses what is available of material necessity for something that is good for that specific kind of animal, thus illustrating Aristotle's claim that "nature is among the causes that act for the sake of something." In the case of crops, however, the goal-directed efficient cause is represented by *external* agents, that is, by human performers of the art of agriculture. Crops come to be through the intervention of human beings who impart the art of agriculture on the water, which due to material necessity is regularly available in the winter for the irrigation of seeds: humans use what is naturally available for what is *good for them*.[76] Agriculture thus takes place in the winter because that is when it regularly rains; it does not rain regularly in the winter for the sake of agriculture.

The fact that human beings are the beneficiaries of the coming to be of crops does not imply that *all* goals in nature are anthropocentric. As Aristotle argues in the second part of his defense of natural teleology (see *Ph* II.8, 199a8–20), art is ontologically secondary to nature, which means that the ends of artistic production are subsidiary to what happens in nature. The ontological priority of nature forms the crux of the whole second argument: if art is limited to the imitation and completion (or "perfection") of natural goals, which it achieves through means congenial to nature, and if artistic processes are for the sake of something, then evidently (*Ph* II.8, 199a17: δῆλον) natural processes, too, are for the sake of something (cf. *PA* I.1, 639a19–21) – evidently, because the relations of priority and posteriority are the same in natural and artistic processes.[77]

75 There is no form or nature of winter rain; cf. Johnson (2005, 156), and Wardy (1993, 25), who draws an analogy with Aristotle's notion of the city: the city *is* by nature, but that does not entail that it also *has* a nature.

76 Cf. Matthen (2001, 183–184), who explains winter rain as an instance of "instrumental teleology." Note also that in this respect the example of winter rain is similar to the example of the light shining through a lantern in *APo* II.11, 94b27–37: light, consisting of relatively small particles, passes through larger pores of material necessity, but human beings make use of the potential of light by making lanterns, which will prevent them from stumbling in the dark. The use to which light is put is anthropocentric and secondary to the nature of light itself. Cf. Byrne (2002, 43).

77 The analogy between the processes of artistic production and natural generation for which Aristotle argues in this second argument is twofold: (i) if there is a sequence of which there is an end, the

However, it would be false to think that because the arts borrow their ends from nature and because artistic ends are (by definition) anthropocentric ends, therefore the ends in nature must be anthropocentric, too.[78] Instead, art imposes an anthropocentric outlook on natural entities that come to be and are present for the sake of realizing their own internal ends.

It is thus important to realize that *all art* is in some sense a form of secondary teleology (i.e., one that involves external, human agents), as we as goal-directed agents make use of what is present by nature for our own benefit (*Ph* II.2, 194a33–36):

> Indeed,[79] the arts too make their material: some [arts make it] without qualification, others [make it] good to work with, *and we use it as if everything exists for the sake of us* (καὶ χρώμεθα ὡς ἡμῶν ἕνεκα πάντων ὑπαρχόντων). For we, too, are in some sense ends: for that for the sake of which is double; this has been said in *On Philosophy*.[80]

In this passage, Aristotle indicates that the final cause in artistic productions (as opposed to final causes in natural generations) lies outside the performance of the art, and is always relative to what is beneficial to us: our desires and needs determine what will be the end results of art, building upon what is already available or happening in nature.[81] The structures and uses we impose upon natural things through the application of art are always – although the product of intrinsic causation – accidental to those things and secondary to their own proper natural ends.[82] Nature is not itself anthropocentric; we just *use* natural things to our own benefit.

previous motions leading up to this end must have been for the sake of this end; the sequence is organized and teleological (*Ph* II.8, 199a8–9); (ii) the temporal ordering of the various steps in the sequence leading up to the end is determined by this end (and is thus to be explained teleologically; *Ph* II.8, 199a18–20). See Charles (1991, 114–115).

78 Pace Sedley (1991, 187).

79 Ἐπεὶ picks up on the conditional sentence in *Ph* II.2, 194a21–22 "if art imitates nature."

80 Sedley (1991, 189; 2007, 203n.72) uses this text in support of his anthropocentric interpretation of Aristotle's natural teleology. He argues that the construction of *hôs* plus the participle of *huparcheô* should be read as "on the ground that everything exists" rather than as "as if everything exists"; however, according to Rijksbaron et al. (2000, 100), constructions like these indicate a "subjective reason" for which the narrator does not want to be held responsible (cf. X. *An* IV.2.5). Aristotle thus makes a concession to popular thought in claiming that we are *in some sense* (*pôs* should be read in a conciliatory way) an end, too.

81 Cf. Broadie (1990, 400–401).

82 Cf. Aristotle's discussion of Antiphon's example of a bed (*Ph* II.1, 193a11–17): "If someone planted a bed, and the decomposition acquired the ability to send up a shoot, what would come up would not be a bed but wood: this seems to show that the arrangement in accordance with habit and art belongs accidentally (τὸ μὲν κατὰ συμβεβηκὸς ὑπάρχον), while its substantial being is that which persists continuously while being affected in these ways (τὴν δ' οὐσίαν οὖσαν ἐκείνην ἣ καὶ διαμένει ταῦτο πάσχουσα συνεχῶς)." In the absence of external efficient causes and under the right conditions, artifacts behave according to the natures of their constitutive material and realize their natural, primary ends, such as wood growing into a tree.

In short, the three examples of natural products put forward by the materialist (i.e., crops, teeth, complete living beings) represent for Aristotle increasingly stronger versions of the operation of the goal-directedness of nature. The point Aristotle is trying to make in his solution to the puzzle is that none of these natural phenomena with their beneficial outcomes can be explained satisfactorily (i.e., in terms of intrinsic causation) without the postulation of efficient causes acting for the sake of something. The coming to be of crops exhibits a form of external, secondary, artificial teleology: the growth of crops involves the intervention of *human* agents who impose the art of agriculture on what is available by nature, and thus produce something that is good from a human perspective. The coming to be of teeth exhibits immanent, secondary, natural teleology: the growth of teeth involves the intervention of the *formal natures* of individual animals on materials and structures that come to be of material necessity; the formal natures thereby make use of what is available by nature for what is good for their own specific substantial being. Finally, the coming to be of complete animals exhibits immanent, primary, natural teleology: the generation of animals involves the formal natures of individual animals realizing a preexisting potential for form by conditionally necessitating all the required materials and by organizing them in the appropriate way.

Further reflections on the scope of natural teleology

The distinction between primary and secondary teleology also allows us to make sense of other passages in the Aristotelian corpus that reflect an anthropocentric perspective on teleology. All natural beings, while being primarily and intrinsically realizations of their own form and existing for their own sake, can be used as matter by other natural beings, either as food and constitutive material, or (exclusively by human beings) as the underlying matter in artistic production. This appropriation of other natural beings as food or underlying matter is to be understood as a form of secondary teleology. Both the internal form of secondary teleology and the external appropriation of other beings are characterized by the presence of goal-directed efficient causes that make use of what is naturally available. In both cases, the material (which is either internal or external to the living being) is used for what is good *from the perspective of the user*; and the potentials of the available materials are causally primary. In neither case is the end that constitutes the final cause a realization of a preexisting potential for form.

A crucial and notorious passage in this context is Aristotle's description of how nature provides food for all living beings as part of an attempt to establish the naturalness of the art of acquisition and warfare (*Pol* I.8, 1256a19–21; b7–22):

> But there are many kinds of food, and therefore also many ways of life, both of animals and of human beings . . . Such property seems to be given by nature herself to all, in the same way as it does immediately following their birth, so too when they are being completed. For some animals generate at the moment of childbirth at the same time also sufficient nutriment to last until the offspring can supply itself – for example as many animals as produce larvae or lay eggs. As many as bear live young have up to a certain time nutriment within themselves for their offspring, namely the stuff called milk. Hence it is equally clear that we should suppose that also for those that are coming to be, that plants are for the sake of animals and that the other animals [i.e. non-human animals] are for humans – domesticated animals *for both use and food* (διὰ τὴν χρῆσιν καὶ διὰ τὴν τροφήν), and if not all, at least most wild animals *for food and for other benefit* (τῆς τροφῆς καὶ ἄλλης βοηθείας ἕνεκεν), such that from them both clothes and other kinds of tools come to be. If, then, nature makes nothing incomplete or in vain, it is necessary that nature has made them all for the sake of human beings.

Aristotle explains that since there are many kinds of food and all living beings need food, there are many ways of life: nature has adapted each way of life (both of animals and of human beings) to the living being's preferences for food and to the ease with which it can acquire it (*Pol* I.8, 1256a26–28). However, the property of food itself is provided by nature to all things alive, both directly in the form of (for instance) milk or egg-white at the moment of birth, but also by extension during maturation, in the form of other natural beings. The passage ends with a hierarchical picture of the food chain, according to which nature has made plants to serve as food for animals, and animals as food for human beings; Aristotle claims that ultimately nature has made everything for the sake of human beings. The teleology Aristotle defends here is unmistakably anthropocentric.[83]

However, it is important to recognize that Aristotle's focus here is on the existence of natural beings *qua food*; plants and animals are for the sake of human beings *qua* being the foodstuffs without which humans would not be able to live. The teleology that accounts for the use human beings make of other living beings is therefore secondary: it reveals the perspective of the user, who makes use of what is provided by nature for his or her own

Bul: ST

[83] Sedley (1991, 181).

good.[84] This perspective is even more apparent in Aristotle's concluding remarks about the question of the naturalness of acquiring wealth (*Pol* I.10, 1258a19–24; 34–38):

> And the question about which we were puzzled in the beginning, [namely] whether it is the task of household management and of political science to acquire wealth or not, is also clear: it is necessary that [wealth] is present. For just as political science does not make men, but receives them from nature and uses them (ἀλλὰ λαβοῦσα παρὰ τῆς φύσεως χρῆται αὐτοῖς), so too is it necessary that that nature provides the earth or sea or whatever else for food . . . Most of all, as was said earlier, it is necessary that [wealth] is present by nature. For it is a task of nature to provide food to that which is born:[85] because for each living thing its food is what remains from that from which it comes into being. That is why the art of getting wealth out of crops and animals is natural for all people.

Just as nature produces human beings for politics to use, so too it is necessary that nature provides food for humans, in the form of other living beings, for humans to use.[86] The environment to which a living being naturally belongs is rich in other living beings that may serve as its food, but it is the predator that is adapted to use and digest the food that is available, not the food to the predator (cf. *Pol* I.8, 1256a19–22). As Pellegrin points out,[87] a camel (discussed in *PA* III.14, 674a28–674b18) has the kind of tongue and the number of stomachs it has to be able to digest the thorny bushes that are available in its habitat as a potential source of food. The thorny bushes are not the way they are (that is, bristly, woody, and fibrous), and do not grow when and where they do, because there are camels in their neighborhood that can only eat such food. Aristotle mentions no examples of plants or animals that are the way they are for the sake of becoming the right kind of food for some other being, and the fact that formal natures of animals – if possible – develop means for protection or defense indicates that natural teleology is restricted to the life and well-being of the individual animal.

84 Cf. Scharle (2008, 162): "plants are for the sake of animals in the sense that it is part of animal nature to make use of plants, and animals are for the sake of humans in the sense that it is part of human nature to make use of animals."

85 Cf. *GA* II.6, 744b17–25 where nature is compared to a good housekeeper who provides food to everyone, but according to a strict hierarchical pattern; for a discussion of this image, see section 3.2.

86 Cf. Lloyd (1996, 191–192).

87 Pellegrin (2002, 312); Scharle (2008, 164–165) makes the same point; pace Sedley (1991, 191; 2007, 202n.69). The direction of causality is important, because it shows that the formal nature of each kind of living being produces that living being *with a view to its own individual substantial being* (i.e., it adapts the camel in such a way that it can nourish itself from what is naturally available in its habitat), not with a view to the substantial being of other living animals (i.e., it does not adapt the bushes to the needs of camels).

So even though Aristotle seems to speak of a universal nature when he says that nature provides food for all, the *individual* formal natures of each kind of living being are what appropriate other kinds of (living) beings as their food and sustenance. In other words, the individual formal natures make sure that each individual kind of living being is able to benefit from the foods in its environment, which amounts – generally speaking – to "nature providing food for all."

Just as in the case of winter rain, plants and animals only have a potentiality for a secondary function *from a certain perspective*[88] or *relative to* other beings elsewhere in the food chain. The food chain imposes a hierarchy of conditional necessary relations between members of the present animal diversity, according to which the existence of the one is conditionally necessary for the coming to be and existence of the other.[89] Humans are on top of this food chain in virtue of having mastered a wide variety of arts and thus of being able to make the best use of what nature provides. Only humans move freely through different habitats and invent tools to increase their success in using things for their own advantage (and in protecting themselves against being eaten by others). Nature has made plants and animals for human beings to use as food or to benefit from them in other ways, but, I submit, the use human beings make of them is a secondary purpose (which is thus not part of the substantial being of plants and animals), and one that is imposed by human beings through the application of some kind of art.

In other words, the fact that human beings are often beneficiaries of natural processes does not reveal an essential characteristic of *natural* teleology (Aristotle's natural teleology is not in itself anthropocentric), but rather of *human art* that appropriates those natural processes to serve human ends.

A final passage that is relevant for the interpretation of the kind of teleology at stake in the natural food chain is Aristotle's discussion of the placement of the mouth in dolphins and selachians and the reason why they turn around while eating (*PA* IV.13, 696b25–34):

> In some [fish] the mouth is placed straight across, and towards the front, but in others on the underside, as for example in dolphins and selachians; and they grasp their nourishment after having turned belly up. And it appears that nature does this not only for the sake of the preservation of other animals (for during the turn the other animals escape, because of the delay; for all such creatures are carnivorous), but also in order that they do not follow their gluttonous ways regarding nourishment; for if they could grasp it easily, they would be destroyed

[88] See Judson (2005, 356–357). [89] Cf. Simpson (1998, 49).

owing to being quickly sated. And in addition, being curved and narrow the nature of the snout is unable to open widely.[90]

The explanandum in this passage is not the existence of the mouth as such in a particular group of fish (which is presumably the result of primary teleology: a mouth is a necessary part for the intake of food in all animals), but rather its peculiar placement, which appears to be the result of secondary teleology.[91] Aristotle gives three – related – explanations for the peculiar positioning of the mouth and eating habits of dolphins and selachians. The final two explanations resemble a common pattern of explanation in Aristotle's biology (see sections 4.2–3) in which a feature is explained both by reference to the better (i.e., to how the feature contributes to the well-being of the animal) and to material necessity. Not being able to eat *easily* – obviously, dolphins and selachians still need to be able to catch some food – prevents these animals from eating themselves to death, but is also a necessary consequence of the structure of the snout they have, which is unable to open widely. However, the intrinsic function that is being served by the position of the snout and the turning around – i.e., the preservation of such animals as dolphins and selachians – is closely connected to a second, extrinsic function, which Aristotle mentions first (perhaps because this explanation is immediately accessible to observation, or because it is popular among the people of his time): the only way in which nature can prevent these animals from overeating is by allowing their food to escape. Since all dolphins and selachians eat fish, their peculiar eating habits serve *as a corollary* also to preserve the life of (some of) these fish (cf. *HA* VIII.2, 591b23–30). The direction of the hierarchy in the food chain is the reverse from the one outlined in the *Politics*: here the "lower" animals benefit from the eating habits of "higher" animals. This indicates that there is no absolute subordination of the good of one living being to that of another.[92]

Even if there is no need for an anthropocentric interpretation of Aristotle's natural teleology, the passages discussed above still leave room for a *cosmic* interpretation of this teleology. The examples of an eternal cycle of rainfall without which no plant could grow (let alone crops) and of formal

[90] Τὰ μὲν γὰρ κατ' ἀντικρὺ ἔχει τὸ στόμα καὶ εἰς τὸ πρόσθεν, τὰ δ' ἐν τοῖς ὑπτίοις, οἷον οἵ τε δελφῖνες καὶ τὰ σελαχώδη· καὶ ὕπτια στρεφόμενα λαμβάνει τὴν τροφήν. Φαίνεται δ' ἡ φύσις οὐ μόνον σωτηρίας ἕνεκεν ποιῆσαι τοῦτο τῶν ἄλλων ζῴων (ἐν γὰρ τῇ στρέψει σῴζεται τἆλλα βραδυνόντων· πάντα γὰρ τὰ τοιαῦτα ζῳοφάγα ἐστίν), ἀλλὰ καὶ πρὸς τὸ μὴ ἀκολουθεῖν τῇ λαιμαργίᾳ τῇ περὶ τὴν τροφήν· ῥᾷον γὰρ λαμβάνοντα διεφθείρετ' ἂν διὰ τὴν πλήρωσιν ταχέως. Πρὸς δὲ τούτοις περιφερῆ καὶ λεπτὴν ἔχοντα τὴν τοῦ ῥύγχους φύσιν οὐχ οἷόν τ' εὐδιαίρετον ἔχειν.

[91] The correct interpretation of this passage is highly contested: see Balme (1980, 9; 1987b, 279); Johnson (2005, 209); and Lennox (2001b, 341–342).

[92] Pace Bodnár (2005, 23–4).

natures of dolphins constructing their eating habits such that their prey may escape suggest that there exists a natural tendency in all individual things towards the regularity and goodness of the cosmos as a whole. Some suppose that this regularity exists over and above the one inherent in the individual natures of living beings and that it ensures the preservation of the cosmos as it is. Under a cosmic interpretation of Aristotle's natural teleology, the harmony, interaction, and well-adaptedness between individual natural entities is derived from or is an expression of an overall nature, i.e., the nature of the cosmos, which has its own form.[93]

There is no doubt that Aristotle on occasion conceptualizes the cosmos as a unity in which beings contribute to the existence and well-being of other beings,[94] and we should certainly expect him to provide a teleological explanation of this order (see *PA* I.1, 641b10–23[95] and section 5.4). The crucial question is thus not whether there is *a* form of cosmic teleology in Aristotle, but whether he explains the cosmic order in terms of a *separate* teleology in which everything is a realization of one underlying cosmic form, or rather in terms of *natural* teleology in which the actions of the individual formal natures of everything natural also account for order on a cosmic or global level. The key passage quoted in support of the cosmic reading is *Meta* XII.10, 1075a11–25:[96]

We must also consider in which way the nature of the whole (ἡ τοῦ ὅλου φύσις) contains the good and the best – whether as something separated and by itself, or as its arrangement. Or [is it] in both ways, as an army does? For the good [of an army] is in its order and is also the general; but it is mostly the latter: for he is not due to the order but the order is due to him. All things are ordered together in some way, but not in the same way – even swimming animals and flying animals and plants. And it [i.e., the order] is not such that there is no relation between one thing and another – there is one: for all things are ordered together towards one (πρὸς μὲν γὰρ ἓν ἅπαντα συντέτακται), but it is as in a household, where for the free people it is least possible to act at random, but all or most [of their actions] are arranged, while it is possible for slaves and animals – their contribution to what is communal being little – much to act as they chance: for that is the kind of principle that nature is of each of them (τοιαύτη γὰρ ἑκάστου ἀρχὴ αὐτῶν ἡ φύσις ἐστίν). I mean, for example, that it is necessary for everything to come to

93 See Sedley (1991, 192). 94 Furley (2004, 83); Hankinson (1998, 147); Matthen (2009).

95 In this passage, I take Aristotle to make the a fortiori argument that if sublunary natural beings are the product of natural teleology, then the more so should we consider the heavenly order to be the product of such teleology (even if the heavens did not come to be in a chronological sense). The fact that nature is for the sake of something is picked out as the cause for *both* sublunary and heavenly order; I see no evidence for Sedley's claim (2007, 195–196) that Aristotle here prioritizes cosmic teleology over that of individual natural processes.

96 See Sedley (1991, 192–194; 2007, 198–200); Cooper (1982, 213). Cf. also Matthen (2001), who argues for the existence of a cosmic nature on the basis of *De Caelo* book I; however, Bodnár (2005, 10–17) offers convincing arguments that undermine such a reading.

be dissolved, and that there are likewise other things in which everything shares in the whole.

This passage forms the opening of a chapter in which Aristotle discusses the place of the good in "the whole." He first presents his own view and then continues with a discussion of the *endoxa* of his predecessors. Aristotle's own account – which I shall discuss only in outline – makes use of two analogies. First, comparing the "nature of the whole" to an army, he indicates that the good of the cosmos is exhibited most by the Unmoved Mover (who is analogous to the general), because he is the cause of the good of the order of the cosmos (which is analogous to the order of the army). Next, he compares the order of the whole to a household, thus illustrating what seems to be the necessity involved in the movement of the stars and planets on the one hand, and the passing or deconstruction of bodies in the sublunary world on the other hand.[97] The "one," towards which everything else is ordered, is again the Unmoved Mover, who – as Aristotle explained in *Meta* XII.7–9 – is the final cause that drives all motion in the cosmos.

Defenders of the cosmic reading interpret Aristotle's expression "the nature of the whole" (perhaps picked up in 1075a22–23: "for that is the kind of principle that nature is of each of them") as a reference to a separate cosmic nature with its own form that underlies the order of everything. However, the fact that Aristotle picks out the Unmoved Mover as the cause of the good of the order and of the joint arrangement of the constitutive parts in both the images speaks against this interpretation:[98] the goodness and interrelations of things in the cosmos are not an expression of the nature of the cosmos itself,[99] but rather of all individual natures trying to approximate as much as possible the *same* ultimate final cause (cf. *Cael* II.12,

97 Cf. Balme (1987b, 278) and *Cael* II.12, which I discuss in section 5.3.

98 See Bodnár (2005, 17–21) for a discussion of the philological and interpretational problems of this cosmic reading of the expression.

99 The nature of the city does not provide a good parallel for a universal nature here: the city comes to be by nature for the sake of living and *is* in that sense a nature (since it is the endpoint of a process, just as a house is: *Pol* I.2, 1252b27–1253a4), but it does not *have* a nature that is being realized by this natural development. Rather, the city *receives* a form through an act of lawgiving, where the lawgiver is similar to a craftsman who makes use of what is naturally available to create a social structure for the sake of living well (see, e.g., *Pol* I.2, 1253a29–31; I.10, 1258a21–22; II.12, 1273b30–33; VII.4, 1325b39–1326a4). The natural priority of the city to the household and individual human beings pertains to the fact that separated from the city nobody is able to achieve the *good life* (see, e.g., *Pol* I.2, 1253a18–22; III.6, 1278b15–30; III.9, 1280b29–1281a4). I believe that the "ethical" city, as opposed to the "natural" city, is a product of secondary teleology, and that there is therefore no natural form of the city. For my interpretation of Aristotle's account of the city, see Leunissen (in progress).

292b20–25). That is, the goodness, order, and joint arrangement of the cosmos as a whole *emerge* from the goal-directed actions of the individual parts of the cosmos towards the same end, the Unmoved Mover.[100] This goal-directedness is *usually* explained as being steered by the *individual* natures acting as efficient causes for the sake of something (see *DA* II.4, 415a25–b7; *GA* II.1, 731b24–732a1 and *GC* II.11, 338b6–19), and presumably this is also the cause identified in the expression "for such is the kind of principle that nature is of each of them." I do not see what explanatory work would be left to do for a cosmic nature.[101] The expression "the nature of the whole" may simply be periphrastic for the universe.[102]

In short, I believe that cosmic teleology is ultimately grounded in natural teleology, and that natural teleology in its primary form is limited to individual natures that act as efficient causes for the sake of something.

1.4 CONCLUSION

Aristotle's defense of natural teleology in *Ph* II.8 lays the foundations for the use of teleological explanations in the other natural treatises. His theory of natural teleology is presented as the better alternative to the materialist mode of explanation of nature, which explains beneficial outcomes in nature as the accidental results of materially necessitated processes and therefore cannot explain the regularity of such outcomes in terms of intrinsic causation. Aristotle proposes instead that natural efficient causes act – either always or for the most part – for the sake of something, which means that natural processes and their outcomes are intrinsically connected, and that we thus should explain the beneficial outcomes of natural processes teleologically.

At the level of complete natural beings, this teleology is always primarily driven by form: natural generation of complete organisms consists in the realization of a potential for form, transmitted by something that possesses that form already in actuality. The teleology exhibited is primary teleology. At the level of natural parts, this teleology may primarily be driven by either form or matter (and thus be a form of either primary or secondary teleology): whereas form is the primary cause for the development of necessary parts, the availability of extra matter – often due to material necessity – is the primary cause for the development of subsidiary parts, such as teeth. (Aristotle thus does not replace material necessity by natural teleology: for

100 Cf. Bodnár (2005, 10, 21) and Scharle (2008, 158–161); pace Kahn (1985, 203).
101 Cf. Johnson (2005, 276n.44) and Scharle (2008, 167).
102 Bodnár (2005, 18); Sedley (2000, 329).

Aristotle, material necessity is a genuine cause in nature, but the incorporation of the results of material necessity in complex natural beings can only be accounted for by reference to the goal-directed actions of the formal nature of those beings.) At the inter-species level, the teleology at stake is always secondary: the formal nature of one natural being appropriates the potentials available in another natural being in order to use it for its own benefit. The systematic appropriation of natural materials by human beings is called art: artists act as the external efficient causes in "informing" materials for the sake of completing natural goals (such as the growth of crops) or of producing artifacts, both of which serve some human good. The perspective of artistic production (but not that of natural teleology) is inherently anthropocentric. Finally, the harmony, interaction and well-adaptedness among natural beings seem to follow from the internal and individual striving of these natural beings towards immortality and the First Unmoved Mover: cosmic teleology can thus be explained in terms of natural teleology, without the postulation of a cosmic form that is being realized.

According to Aristotle's defense of natural teleology, its operation is restricted to the actions of the individual formal natures of natural beings, but its scope ranges from the generation of low-level biological parts such as teeth to high-level cosmological phenomena such as the motions of the heavenly bodies. In the next chapters, I shall pursue Aristotle's actual use of teleological explanations in these domains.

CHAPTER 2

Aristotle's bio-functional account of the soul: establishing the starting points of teleological explanation in the De Anima

2.0 INTRODUCTION

Aristotle introduces his investigation of the soul in *De Anima* as being among the primary kinds of knowledge, on account of both its accuracy and its dealing with better and more wonderful things (*DA* I.1, 402a1–5). Knowledge of the soul contributes especially to natural philosophy (*DA* I.1, 402a6–7; cf. *DA* I.1, 403a27–28), because the soul is "a sort of[1] principle of living beings" (*DA* I.1, 402a8: ἔστι γὰρ οἷον ἀρχὴ τῶν ζῴων) and living nature represents Aristotle's concept of nature in the fullest sense.[2] For Aristotle, then, the study of the soul and its embodiment is the starting point of biology,[3] and as such forms an important part of his broader investigation into nature.

The issues Aristotle sets out to address in *De Anima* are, first, the nature and essence of the soul and, second, the soul's attributes – both the ones proper to the soul and the ones living beings have in virtue of having a soul (*DA* I.1, 402a8–11). This program leads Aristotle, among others, into investigations of the ontological status of the soul and its parts, of the relation between the body and the soul, and of the various capacities of the soul that living beings share. In this chapter, sidestepping many of the difficulties in the interpretation of this treatise, I shall focus rather narrowly on Aristotle's bio-functional analysis of the soul, i.e., on his study of the soul as a non-aggregative unity[4] of teleologically organized

1 Aristotle's qualification of the soul as "a sort of principle of living beings" might indicate that it remains to be seen in what sense the soul is a principle, i.e., that there are some senses in which the soul is a principle of living beings (i.e., in the sense of formal, efficient, and final cause), but that in others it is not (i.e., not in the sense of material cause); cf. *DA* II.4, 415b8–10; Ross (1961, 176). Lennox (2006, 308) proposes that the qualification foreshadows Aristotle's thesis that the soul is also a principle of *plant* life, a view that is perhaps not immediately shared with his contemporary readership.

2 Lennox (2006, 294).

3 Cf. Cohen (1992, 58); Lloyd (1992, 148–149); Sorabji (1974, 65–66); and Van der Eijk (1997, 231–232).

4 On the unity of the soul, see *DA* II.3, 414b28–32 and *DA* III.9, 432a22–b6.

functions that make the natural body in which they are realized alive.[5] Of particular interest in this context is Aristotle's distinction between the concepts of "living" and "living well" in his teleological explanations for why different kinds of living beings have the kind of soul functions they have. I shall first, in section 2.1, by way of background, outline Aristotle's use of teleological notions in his account of the soul as a principle of life (in particular in *DA* I.1–3 and *DA* II.1–4), and then, in section 2.2, turn to his teleological explanations for why different living beings possess the specific soul functions they do (in *DA* III.9–13). These latter explanations show, I believe, some interesting resemblances to and deviations from the patterns of explanation to be found in the – methodologically later – biological works.

My purpose in this chapter is to show how Aristotle, in establishing a bio-functional conception of the soul, provides the starting points and the foundations for explanations in the biological works. Since for Aristotle the soul is the first actuality and the final cause of a natural body that potentially has life, the various parts and features living beings have will be explainable in terms of the kind of soul (or combination of capacities for the performance of life functions) they possess;[6] and part of what Aristotle does in *De Anima* is to define and teleologically ground the different kinds of soul.

2.1 TELEOLOGY IN THE ANALYSIS OF THE NATURE OF THE SOUL

Teleological notions in the preliminary characterizations of the soul in DA *I.1*

Aristotle presents two accounts of the nature of the soul as a principle of life in *De Anima*: one (in *DA* II.1) that defines the soul as the first actuality of a natural body that is instrumental; and one (in *DA* II.4) that identifies the soul as the formal, efficient, and final cause of a living being. As I shall indicate below, teleological notions play an important role in both these characterizations of the nature of the soul.[7]

However, the framework for both these approaches to the study of the soul, one in terms of definition, the other in terms of a causal analysis, is laid down in *DA* I.1. In this opening chapter of the treatise, Aristotle

[5] Rorty (1992, 7), calls this Aristotle's "philosophical bio-psychology." [6] Lloyd (1992, 149).
[7] Pace Code and Moravscik (1992, 132, 134–135, and 138).

tries to determine the appropriate method for the study of the soul,[8] while taking three assumptions about the soul as starting points.

The first of these assumptions is that the soul is a principle of life – not only of human beings, but of *all* living beings, including animals and divine beings (*DA* I.1, 402b7; plants are included among things that have souls in *DA* II.2, 413a25–b1). In this way, the soul operates for Aristotle also as a principle of individuation: different kinds of living are coextensive with different kinds of soul, which makes living beings be what they are in virtue of having the specific kind of soul they have.[9]

Second, Aristotle assumes that the soul is a combination of "parts" that perform different kinds of life functions and that have their own objects (*DA* I.1, 402b9–14). For instance, the faculty of the soul that perceives (τὸ αἰσθητικόν) performs the function of perception (τὸ αἰσθάνεσθαι), and has as its object the perceptible (τὸ αἰσθητὸν). This conception of the soul is teleological, for it defines and explains the existence of each aspect of the soul in terms of the specific work it performs: souls are essentially capacities that exist for the sake of the performance of a wide variety of life functions, which are explored more fully in *DA* II–III.[10]

Third, Aristotle claims that the affections[11] of the soul are "enmattered structures" (*DA* I.1, 403a25: δῆλον ὅτι τὰ πάθη λόγοι ἔνυλοί εἰσιν).[12]

8 The methodological questions Aristotle raises pertain to: (i) the genus of the soul (is the soul a *tode ti* and *ousia* or one of the other categories?); (ii) the ontological status of the soul (is it in potentiality or is it rather a kind of actuality?); (iii) the structure of the soul (does the soul have parts or not?; is every soul *homoeidês* or not?; if it is *homoeidês*, is the difference one of genus or species?); (iv) the definition of the soul (is there one definition only, or is there a definition for the soul of each separate kind of ensouled being?). On the programmatic importance of *DA* I.1, see Menn (2002, 102–103) and Rorty (1992, 7–8).

9 *DA* II.2, 413b32–414a1: "Moreover, some animals have all of these [functions of the soul], others have only some of them, and still others have only one – and this causes a differentiation between living beings (τοῦτο δὲ ποιεῖ διαφορὰν τῶν ζῴων)." Cf. Everson (1997, 3–4) and Sorabji (1993, 163–165).

10 The terminology Aristotle uses in his discussions might require some brief clarification. Aristotle speaks of the *dunameis* of the soul (e.g., *DA* II.2, 413a22), which I translate as the capacities of the soul. Sometimes Aristotle calls them *môria* (parts) of the soul, but this should not be taken too literally (perhaps "aspects" would be a better translation). The *energeia* or *praxis* (activity) of these *dunameis* (a *dunamis* is a capacity or potentiality for an activity) is what Aristotle equates with the performance of *erga* (functions). The individual functions are usually rendered by the use of the substantive form of the infinitive (*to -ein*; e.g., *to noein*), or with an action noun (*-sis*; e.g., *noêsis*), while the *adjectivum verbale* (*to –ikon*; e.g., *to noêtikon*) refers to either the capacities of the soul or to that which has these capacities. The *supinum* (*to –on*; e.g., *to noêton*) refers to the objects of the capacity.

11 In the first book of *De Anima* Aristotle uses the term *pathê* rather loosely to refer to emotions, pleasures and pain, and functions (see, e.g., *DA* I.5, 409b14–19).

12 The expression is obscure; on the problems involved, see Everson (1997, 234–236). My translation follows Caston (2006, 318).

Concerning the relation between the soul and its affections (this problem is raised in *DA* I.1, 403a3–b19), Aristotle believes that he has evidence (*DA* I.1, 403a19: μηνύει; *DA* I.1, 403a22–23: ἔτι δὲ μᾶλλον τοῦτο φανερόν) that the affections of the soul – with the exception perhaps of the function of thinking – are always "with body," and that they are therefore ontologically inseparable from the body. The affections of the soul are not just realized in matter, but the matter itself is also a constitutive part of what the affections are (*DA* I.1, 403a25–27): "[Affections are enmattered structures] such that their definitions are such as, for instance, 'being angry' is a certain change, belonging to a distinct kind of body or bodily part or capacity, originating from this, for the sake of that."

As the example of anger makes clear, a proper definition of an affection of the soul must include references to all four Aristotelian causes, including the *specific* kind of body to which the change belongs as the material cause. The fact that the affections of the soul involve body makes the study of the soul "immediately" part of the field of the natural philosopher (*DA* I.1, 403a27–28; but see *PA* I.1, 641a29–b10 for the exclusion of the rational part of the soul from the field of natural philosophy). And, as Aristotle's subsequent discussion of the task of the natural philosopher makes clear (*DA* I.1, 403a27–403b16), the relation between body and soul is ultimately one of conditional necessity. Form and matter cannot be separated in a definition of the affections of the soul, because if the affection is to be what it is, it needs to be realized in a particular kind of body (*DA* I.1, 403b2–3): "For the one is an account of the thing, but it is necessary for that [i.e., craving for revenge] to be in a particular kind of body, if it is to be."

The affections of the soul are inseparable from the body, because being realized in an appropriate material constitution is itself a necessary condition[13] for the existence of these affections. Aristotle concludes the chapter by pointing out that the true natural philosopher needs to study

[13] For the implicit reliance on the notion of conditional necessity, see also Aristotle's criticism of his predecessors for not further specifying the body that receives the soul in *DA* I.3, 407b20–26: "But people put their effort into saying what sort of thing the soul is, while they determine nothing further (προσδιορίζουσιν) about the body that receives it, just as though, in the manner of the Pythagorean myths, any random soul were to be clothed *in any random body* (τὴν τυχοῦσαν ψυχὴν εἰς τὸ τυχὸν ἐνδύεσθαι σῶμα). For while each body seems to have its own proper (ἴδιον) shape and form, they talk as if one were to say that carpentry is to be clothed in flutes; but the art has to use tools and the soul has to use the body." Aristotle believes that just as each art needs its *own proper and befitting* instruments, so the soul needs its *own proper and befitting* body – proper and befitting, that is, for the functions it is to perform; cf. Hett (1936, 43); *DA* II.2, 414a22–25 and *DA* II.2, 414a27.

the functions and affections of the soul as the products of both matter and form, and not as abstractions (*DA* I.1, 403b16–19).[14]

In sum, the implicit assumption in this chapter seems to be that the relation between soul and body is a teleological one: living beings have the kind of bodies and bodily parts they have for the sake of performing all their characteristic life functions.

The definition of the soul as the first actuality of a natural instrumental body in DA *II.1*

Aristotle's discussion of the soul in *DA* II.1 builds mainly upon the first and the third of these assumptions. His purpose in this section is to provide a definition of the soul that is as comprehensive as possible (*DA* II.1, 412a3–6): "But let us go back and, as though from the beginning, try to distinguish what the soul is and what would be its most common definition."

Aristotle carries out this program in different stages. He offers two intermediate definitions before stating – cautiously – his final common definition, which characterizes the soul as "the first actuality of a natural body that is *organikon*" (*DA* II.1, 412b4–6). The first definition, characterizing the soul as "a substantial being in the sense of the form of a natural body which potentially has life" (*DA* II.1, 412a19–21), follows from an analysis of the genus of substantial being and the identification of living beings as composite substances: the soul is form and the natural body is matter that has life in potentiality. The second definition gives a specification of the kind of substantial being the soul is as being a "first actuality"[15] (*DA* II.1, 412a27–28), which means that the soul is like a *hexis* or disposition for life functions, rather than the *energeia* or exercise of them (which would be the "second actuality"). For a natural body to be properly called alive, then, it needs to possess all the relevant life functions by way of a fully developed disposition, such that they can be exercised or activated at any given time. The third and final definition follows from a specification of what it means for a natural body to have life potentially as being "instrumental"[16]

14 Hamlyn (2001, 80) and Ross (1961, 200). Although I cannot defend my position in full here, I believe that passages such as these give reason to doubt functionalist readings of Aristotle's theory of the soul; for an overview of the functionalism debate, see Caston (2006, 320–322).

15 The term *entelecheia* was coined by Aristotle, and designates a completed state resulting from an internal movement towards this state; see Ritter (1932; 1934) and Johnson (2005, 88–90).

16 The traditional reading of *organikon* as "having organs" or "being composed of organs" (see, e.g., Ross 1961, 51, 313; Hamlyn 2001, 85) must certainly be wrong: elsewhere in the Aristotelian corpus the term *organikon* (coined by Aristotle; see Byl 1971, 132) always means "instrumental" and there is no reason to assume it means something different here. The new reading is defended most notably

(*DA* II.1, 412a28–b1: τοιοῦτον δὲ ὃ ἂν ᾖ ὀργανικόν). In this way, Aristotle characterizes the natural body living beings have as the instrument of the soul,[17] presumably in the sense that the whole body – including all its constitutive parts (cf. *DA* II.1, 412b1–4) – is present for the sake of the performance of all the characteristic life functions that make up that being's life,[18] making the unity of body and soul explicitly a teleological one (see *DA* II.1, 412b6–9).

Aristotle illustrates his general definition of the soul with the following analogy (*DA* II.1, 412b12–17):

> Just as if one of the instruments, for example an ax, were a natural body: for being an ax would be its substantial being, and that would be its soul. If this were separated from it, it would no longer be an ax, except in name, but in fact it is an ax. For the soul is not what it is to be and the structure of *such* a body, but of *a particular kind of natural body* – one that has a principle of movement and rest within itself.

Just as what it is for an ax to be an ax is determined by the function it performs (i.e., cutting), which would be its soul, so too for natural bodies their being is determined by the kind(s) of functions they perform, which in fact is their soul. Take away something's capacity to perform its characteristic function, and it will no longer be what it is, except homonymously, that is, the name will be used inappropriately to refer to something that is no longer what it is.[19] Because for Aristotle what something is is determined by the function(s) it performs, the soul constitutes the essence of the living beings that have it (instruments do not have souls, because they lack an internal principle of movement and rest, and always require an external source of movement). The same holds for the parts of living beings

by Bos (2001, 187, 190–192; 2003, *passim*; 2008, 12, 177), but see also Everson (1997, 64–65); Kosman (1987, 376–377, 381–382); and Menn (2002, 108–117).

17 Cf. *PA* I.1, 642a11–13: "So too, since the body is an instrument (ἐπεὶ τὸ σῶμα ὄργανον) – for each of the parts is for the sake of something, and likewise also the whole – it is therefore a necessity that it be of such a character and constituted from such things, if that is to be." On this passage, see Lennox (2001b, 149–150). See also *DA* I.3, 407b25–26, quoted above in n.13.

18 This is how, e.g., Kosman (1987, 376) and Lennox (2001b, 142) interpret it. However, this is not the only possible interpretation: Bos (2001, 188–190), argues that "the natural body that potentially has life" and that is "instrumental to the soul" must be one of the elemental bodies, namely pneuma (for animals and human beings; the instrumental body for plants is vital heat); Everson (1997, 63–69) argues that the natural body to which Aristotle refers is not the whole animal body, but rather a part of it, so that the animal would not have one soul, but as many souls as it has instrumental parts – a view that is strongly criticized by Barnes (1999, 121).

19 For Aristotle's use of the principle of homonymy for things that have lost their capacity to perform their characteristic function, either in virtue of having died or in virtue of being constituted from the wrong kind of material (in e.g., *PA* I.1, 640b33–641a5; *Meteor* IV.12, 389b28–390a13; and *GA* II.1, 734b24–25), see Furth (1987, 37) and Shields (1999, 131–154). It is possible that death also involves a material change of the body: see *PA* I.1, 641a17–21 and Lennox (2001b, 138).

(*DA* II.1, 412b17–22): the substantial being or soul of, for example, an eye would be sight, which is its function. On this account, living beings are a unity of a natural body that has life potentially (and not that has lost it) and of the soul as first actuality, which is the capacity for the performance of that living being's characteristic life functions, in which the body exists for the sake of the soul (*DA* II.1, 412b27–413a4).

Aristotle's "common" definition of the soul (cf. *DA* II.1, 412b10: καθόλου), then, exemplifies both in what way the soul is a principle of life and how it is related to the natural body: having life is the possession of life functions (i.e., a soul) by a natural instrumental body, which is able to exercise those functions through its instrumental parts. For Aristotle's explanatory program in biology this means that at least the majority of bodily features a living being possesses will be explainable by reference to the life functions for which these features are instrumental (and hence conditionally necessary) and the possession of which constitutes the living being's substantial being. However, as Aristotle repeatedly indicates, this "rough" definition will only be helpful to a certain extent (*DA* II.1, 413a9–10):[20] since the soul is an essence, rather than being something that has an essence, it would be "ridiculous" to define the soul properly in abstraction from the living beings that have soul (*DA* II.3, 414b20–28; 414b25: γελοῖον). Therefore the natural philosopher must try to establish what the soul of *each kind of living being* is (*DA* II.3, 414b32–33; *DA* II.3, 415a12–13): he must determine what the particular set of life functions is that defines each kind of living being (this is where Aristotle's second assumption of the soul as a set of life functions comes in), and these functions will provide the most appropriate starting points for explanations of biological phenomena.

Aristotle's conception of the soul as a final cause of natural bodies in DA *II.4*

In defining the soul as the first actuality of a natural body that is instrumental, Aristotle characterizes the soul as the form of a living being, where its instrumental body is its matter (cf. *DA* II.2, 414a14–19). In a later discussion of the nutritive and generative faculty of the soul, Aristotle claims that as the cause and principle of the living body (*DA* II.4, 415b8), the soul – in addition to being that body's formal cause – is also an efficient and final cause (*DA* II.4, 415b8–12). Aristotle then explains why the soul is also a "that for the sake of which" (*DA* II.4, 415b15–21):

[20] Cf. Everson (1997, 174–175).

> It is apparent that the soul is a cause also as that for the sake of which. For just as the intellect acts for the sake of something, in the same way, too, does nature, and that is its end. Such is among living beings the soul according to nature: for all natural bodies are instruments of the soul, just as the bodies of living beings, so too also the bodies of plants, because they are for the sake of the soul. And that for the sake of which is double, there is the "of which" and the "for which" (διττῶς δὲ τὸ οὗ ἕνεκα, τό τε οὗ καὶ τὸ ᾧ).

Nature – just like intellect – acts for the sake of something, and among living beings "that for the sake of which" is the soul (cf. *PA* I.1, 641a19–21). Aristotle explicitly restates the teleological relationship between natural bodies and soul: natural bodies are instruments of and exist for the sake of the soul. This means both that the soul *operates* through the natural body and that the natural body with (at least most of) its features is the *conditionally necessary prerequisite* for the realization of the capacities for the performance of a living being's life functions that constitute its soul. Aristotle adds, however, that there exists an ambiguity concerning the kind of end the soul is, since there are two kinds of ends: there is the "that for the sake of which" or the final cause properly speaking, and there is the "for which" or "beneficiary of which," which plays no causal role.[21] He does not make clear whether he conceives of the soul as an end in the sense of a final cause or of the beneficiary of a natural body, or of both, but his explicit characterization of the soul as a "that for the sake of which" in *DA* II.4, 415b15 seems to indicate that Aristotle only mentions the two possibilities in order to limit his conception of the soul to an end in the proper, causal sense.[22]

[21] Cf. Kullmann (1985, 172) and Judson (2005, 358). Johnson (2005, 65–69), for whom the distinction between the two senses of *to hou heneka* is central to resolving "the problems of Aristotelian teleology," offers an alternative interpretation, characterizing the distinction as "a difference between the aim of something and the beneficiary of the achievement of that aim," using for the latter the formula "for the sake of which for which beneficiary." He takes *to hou heneka – hou* to refer to the end proper and *to hou heneka – hôi* to refer to the beneficiary of (the realization of) the end, and believes that sometimes both senses are simultaneously operative. Applying this distinction to the characterization of the soul as a final cause, Johnson explains that "The body exists for the aim of the soul's functioning, and the soul's functioning exists for the benefit of the individual organism that lives through the soul and with the body." Despite the interesting parallels Johnson offers to illustrate his reading of *to hou heneka hôi* (2005, 67n.8), I am not convinced that this is the most natural reading of the expression. See also *Ph* II.2, 194a34–b1: when Aristotle states that "we also are in a sense an end" he means that we benefit from what is naturally available without being the proper end of natural processes.

[22] Cf. *Meta* XII.7, 1072b2–3, *EE* VII.15, 1249b15, and *DA* II.4, 415b2–3, where Aristotle first introduced the distinction in the *De Anima* only to indicate that becoming as divine as possible through reproduction is something living beings do for their own sake, not for some god's benefit. See also Gotthelf (1987, 210) and Polansky (2007, 205–207).

In short, although Aristotle does not define the soul itself teleologically (the soul is not itself characterized as being for the sake of something, although, taken as the combination of capacities, the soul can be understood as being for the sake of the actualization of those capacities), by identifying it as a final cause, he establishes that the characteristic activities living beings for the most part perform are in fact their natural functions in a technical sense. For the activities living beings perform are the exercise of the capacities they have in virtue of the kind of soul they possess, and their bodies are thus to be exhibited as the conditionally necessary instruments for the performance of these capacities.

2.2 TELEOLOGY IN THE ANALYSIS OF THE CAPACITIES OF THE SOUL

The hierarchy of the capacities of the soul: living versus living well

Since for Aristotle soul is coextensive with life, and since life is one of those things that are "spoken of in many ways," one of the main purposes of *De Anima* is to demarcate both living from non-living and each particular form of living from the other forms. As is to be expected from our introductory remarks above on the nature of the soul, Aristotle carries out this program of demarcation by identifying those functions that are characteristic for life in general and for the different forms of life in particular.

In *DA* II.2–4, Aristotle distinguishes the living from the non-living broadly in terms of the presence of at least one capacity for a life function (*DA* II.2, 413a20–25):

> So we say, taking this as a starting point for the inquiry [i.e., that definitions should not only state the fact but also reveal the reason why], that what is ensouled is distinguished from what is soulless by living. But living is said in more than one way, and if any one alone of the following is present in something, we say that it is alive, such as for example intellect, perception, motion and rest with respect to place, and in addition motion with respect to nutrition and decay and growth.[23]

The one capacity for a function in virtue of which all living things are alive (at least in the sublunary realm: Aristotle's general characterization of life as the presence of at least one life function leaves open the possibility for the existence of a divine form of life, characterized by the function

[23] Sometimes Aristotle also adds appetite (ὄρεξις) and imagination (φαντασία) to the list of characteristic life functions. On this list of life functions for Aristotle's conception of life, see also Matthews (1992, 185–193).

of thinking only) is the capacity of nutrition, which involves both self-nutrition (τὸ θρεπτικὸν) and reproduction (γεννήσις).[24] The particular combination of life functions that each sublunary kind of living being is able to perform (cf. *DA* II.3, 414a29–32) presupposes the presence of this most basic function of life (it is the only function – except for maybe thinking – that is ontologically independent[25] from the other functions, whereas all other functions depend on it: *DA* II.2, 413a31–32) and builds up from there to more complex forms of life.

The most basic form of sublunary life is exhibited by plants, which have no other capacity of the soul except the capacity of nutrition (which demonstrates that this capacity can exist independently of the other capacities for life functions).[26] For this reason, the ability to perform the function of nutrition is both what demarcates something as a living being (it constitutes both a necessary and a sufficient condition for life) and what – if found alone – constitutes the defining or essential function of plants (*DA* II.2, 413a25–b1; *DA* II.3, 414a32–33). The essential function of animals, which represent a more complex form of life, is the perceptive function of touch (ἁφή; *DA* II.2, 413b2–10; cf. *DA* II.3, 414b1–4). Aristotle uses perception as a collective term encompassing a number of perceptive functions for which an animal may or may not have the capacity (i.e., touch, smell, hearing, and vision). Touch is the first and most basic one among them, for it is the only perceptive capacity that can exist independently of the other perceptive capacities, whereas they cannot exist without it (*DA* II.2, 413b5–7; *DA* II.3, 415a4–5). For human beings, who represent the most complex form of life, the essential capacity that marks off their specific kind – although it is possibly also shared by "more honorable beings" – is thinking (*DA* II.3, 414b18–19), the highest capacity of all.[27]

Each form of life is thus characterized by its own specific combination of capacities for life functions, but none of these combinations is random. Each particular set of life functions that different kinds of animals and human beings have represents a strict hierarchy of higher functions that are ontologically nested in lower ones. Aristotle explains this relation between different life functions through an analogy with complex rectilinear figures (*DA* II.3, 414b28–415a5):

[24] See, e.g., *DA* II.2, 413b2–3 (nutrition is the principle of life) and *DA* II.4, 415a22–25 (nutrition is the first and most commonly possessed capacity of the soul); cf. also *GA* I.23, 731b5–7.

[25] Aristotle uses the verb χωρίζεσθαι to describe the "ontological separability" of one life function from another; see Broadie (1996, 163–164) and Polansky (2007, 169–170, 197).

[26] See *DA* II.2, 413a33–b1; *DA* II.3, 414a33–b1; *DA* II.3, 415a2–3; and *DA* II.4, 415a23–26.

[27] In human beings, this function seems to be dependent on the capacity of imagination (*DA* III.8, 432a8–9), but presumably it exists independently in divine beings.

> What applies to the soul is almost the same as what applies to geometrical figures. For in both figures and things that are ensouled, that which is prior always exists potentially in that which follows in order, for instance, the triangle in the quadrilateral, and the nutritive capacity in the perceptive. Such that we must investigate concerning each kind what the soul is of each, for instance what [the soul is] of plant and what of human being and what of animal. What the explanation is for why they are in such state of arrangement, we must investigate. For without the nutritive capacity there is no perceptive capacity, but the nutritive capacity is present in separation of the perceptive capacity in plants. Again, without the sense of touch none of the other perceptive capacities is present, but touch is present without the others.[28]

Aristotle claims that what is prior in complexity is present in potentiality in what is more complex: just as more complex rectilinear figures contain in themselves the more basic ones in potentiality (four-sided figures divide into three-sided figures, etc.), so do more complex capacities of the soul contain in themselves the more basic ones in potentiality. The unity between the capacities of the soul is one of order (*taxis*),[29] which is here rendered as being ontological in nature: whereas the lower capacity can exist separately and does not need the higher capacities, the higher cannot exist without the lower ones (the existence of the "basic" capacities is a necessary condition for the existence of the more complex ones).[30]

Aristotle investigates the question (announced in *DA* II.2, 413b9–10; 413b32–414a1; and *DA* II.3, 414b33–415a1) of why living beings possess the precise sequence of nested capacities they have in *DA* III.9–13. As we shall see in more detail below, the ontological hierarchy of nested capacities is there shown to be in fact a "taxonomical" hierarchy[31] in which the more basic capacities constitute a necessary prerequisite for the existence of the higher and in which the realization of the more complex capacities contributes to the goals pursued by the basic ones.[32]

28 παραπλησίως δ' ἔχει τῷ περὶ τῶν σχημάτων καὶ τὰ κατὰ ψυχήν· ἀεὶ γὰρ ἐν τῷ ἐφεξῆς ὑπάρχει δυνάμει τὸ πρότερον ἐπί τε τῶν σχημάτων καὶ ἐπὶ τῶν ἐμψύχων, οἷον ἐν τετραγώνῳ μὲν τρίγωνον, ἐν αἰσθητικῷ δὲ τὸ θρεπτικόν. ὥστε καθ' ἕκαστον ζητητέον, τίς ἑκάστου ψυχή, οἷον τίς φυτοῦ καὶ τίς ἀνθρώπου ἢ θηρίου. διὰ τίνα δ' αἰτίαν τῷ ἐφεξῆς οὕτως ἔχουσι, σκεπτέον. ἄνευ μὲν γὰρ τοῦ θρεπτικοῦ τὸ αἰσθητικὸν οὐκ ἔστιν· τοῦ δ' αἰσθητικοῦ χωρίζεται τὸ θρεπτικὸν ἐν τοῖς φυτοῖς. πάλιν δ' ἄνευ μὲν τοῦ ἁπτικοῦ τῶν ἄλλων αἰσθήσεων οὐδεμία ὑπάρχει, ἁφὴ δ' ἄνευ τῶν ἄλλων ὑπάρχει·

29 See *Meta* V.11, 1018b26–29; 1019a2–4.

30 For the ontological interdependency among the various capacities of the soul, see *DA* II.2, 413b23–25 and *DA* II.3, 414a32–b19.

31 Cf. Caston (1996, 184–186) on the conception of *chôristos* as "taxonomical separability."

32 *Pace* Johnson (2005, 9), who thinks that the simpler functions exist for the sake of the more complex ones.

The crucial distinction Aristotle draws within this hierarchy is between capacities whose realization is necessary to make possible a specific way of *living* itself and capacities whose realization is rather for the sake of *living well*. In the first case, the realization of a certain capacity is of *immediate* vital or essential importance for all the subspecies within the same widest form of life as considered in *De Anima*, i.e., plants, non-human animals, and human beings. Without the possession of and the means to realize that capacity, the living being could not have existed at all or would not have been able to be the specific kind of being it is. For instance, having the capacity of touch is both a necessary and sufficient condition for being an animal, and *all* animals therefore will have touch; without it, no animal can exist or could have been an animal. In the second case, which pertains only to non-human and human animals, the possession of and means to realize a certain capacity is not of immediate vital or essential importance for all subspecies (and therefore not necessary in a strict sense), but it does serve the well-being of *some* of them: the capacity seems to be present for the sake of *optimizing* the living being's performance of the essential and vital life functions, rather than for the sake of the basic performance of such life functions. For instance, having the capacity of voice is not necessary for all animals: hypothetically speaking, nature *could* have "designed" animals that are currently able to produce sounds in such a way as to be able to function without this ability. For Aristotle, this is evidenced by the observation that there are in fact animals that lack this capacity and that are nevertheless perfectly able to live and reproduce. The capacity is present only in those animals that take in air, and its function is to express pain and pleasure (see *Pol* I.2, 1253a8–18), which as Aristotle indicates contributes to the well-being of these animals (I return to this example below). Of course, this does not mean that taking away this capacity from *actual* animals that are "designed" to have the capacity for voice would not harm or kill them; the idea is just that *in other possible worlds* these animals too could have existed without the capacity for voice.

The strategies Aristotle uses to determine whether a capacity is necessary for living or rather for the sake of living well are remarkably similar to the ones he uses in the biological works to determine the ontological status of parts. In the biological works (which I shall discuss in Chapters 3 and 4), we shall see that Aristotle often makes use of the "rule" that if a part can be observed to be present in all members of a particular kind, it must be a necessary prerequisite for the performance of a vital or essential

function of that kind.[33] If a certain part is present only in some members of a particular kind, whereas the whole kind can be observed to be able to perform the function that is associated with that part, Aristotle infers that its possession cannot be necessary for all the members of that kind, but that the part must rather have a contributory or subsidiary function serving the well-being of some subspecies. (In Chapter 3, I shall submit that the first category of "necessary parts" is the result of primary teleology, whereas the second category of "subsidiary parts" is the result of secondary teleology.) In using this kind of reasoning, Aristotle seems to build on the same pattern of investigation as he applies here in *De Anima* with regard to the two categories of capacities: if the capacity is present in all members of a widest kind it must be conditionally necessary for that kind; the kind could not have existed or be the kind it is without it. The capacity must be a basic one, shared by all members of that kind. If it is present only in some members of that widest kind, it must be for the sake of the well-being of those members of the kind only and the capacity must be a more complex one.

It is important to note here that these distinctions are not supposed to work as *descriptive* accounts of actual, realized living beings: as I suggested earlier, it is usually not the case that we can simply remove a capacity or part that contributes to the animal's well-being without also severely harming or even killing that animal, and so de facto many if not most parts or capacities turn out to be necessary (in this immediate sense) for the living beings that have them. Rather, I believe that these distinctions operate at a more theoretical level – in "design space," so to speak, where nature is still metaphorically speaking "deciding" what parts and capacities a certain kind of animal can and should have, how many of those parts it should have, and where the parts should be placed, etc.[34] (Cf. Aristotle's explanation of the footlessness of snakes in *IA* 8, 708a9–20: here it appears that the "initial design" of snakes includes the possession of four feet, but nature then "takes away" those feet in the actual realization of snakes, because their presence would inhibit their swift motion; I discuss this example in more detail in sections 4.2 and 5.4.) At this level, the relevant question is not whether a particular, actual species can continue to live on when we remove its

33 See, e.g., *GA* I.4, 717a12–31; I discuss this example and Aristotle's use of teleological principles in section 4.2.

34 Even though species are eternal for Aristotle, he sometimes appears to offer quasi-genetic accounts for why a particular species "turned out" the way it is; I say more about these personifications of nature and the thought experiments Aristotle employs in Chapters 3–5.

subsidiary capacities or parts, but whether nature hypothetically speaking *could have* "created" a certain kind of living being without a certain part or capacity. If the answer is "yes" – for instance, because we observe among the present biodiversity that there are in fact members of the same kind that do not possess the part or capacity in question – then that feature must be for the sake of living well, rather than a necessary prerequisite for the life of that kind. Accordingly, it is not "among the natural possibilities" for nature to design *any* kind of animal without the sense of touch – for such beings would simply not qualify as being an animal. However, nature could have – and has, based on the empirical evidence Aristotle is using – created animals without voice, which means that this capacity cannot be a necessary one for all animals. The "thought experiment" about whether or not nature could have "created" a certain living being without a certain part or capacity helps to determine the status of that feature as either being necessary for a specific widest kind ("nature has to include this feature in the design of the animal") or rather being subsidiary for a specific subspecies within that widest kind (the feature is an optional feature at the design level – nature implements it where possible and where the possession of this feature would be for the better).

The distinction between living and living well can therefore be used by Aristotle to determine the position of a certain capacity in the hierarchy of soul capacities. The more kinds of living beings have a certain capacity, the more basic that capacity must be to life; "necessity" thus refers here to the extent to which a capacity is required for the basic survival or being of the living being and is thus conditionally necessary for it. Capacities that are less widespread (among and within kinds) must be less basic to that form of life and must therefore predominantly contribute to living well, where the "well" indicates a more complex performance of the being's life functions. The *scala naturae* that Aristotle sketches here and in the biological works (see *HA* VIII.1, 588b4–22; *PA* IV.5, 681a10–15 and *PA* II.10, 656a3–13; 656a5–6: "And there is still greater variety among those whose nature partakes not only of living but, in addition, of living well") is thus functionally defined: he calls those forms of life "higher" or "more honorable" that display greater organic and functional complexity on top of their basic survival activities.[35]

In short, living beings have the capacities of the soul they have for the sake of living and living well, where the capacities that serve living are first in order in the hierarchy and most basic, and the capacities that serve living

[35] Cf. Lennox (1999, 6–7) and Polansky (2007, 541–542).

well are later in order and are more complex, with the capacity of thinking serving the ultimate, highest purpose of living well in an ethical sense (see, e.g., *NE* X.7, 1178a5–8 and *NE* X.8, 1178b21–23). Ultimately, Aristotle explains the ontological hierarchy and the specific sequence of nested soul functions found in living beings in terms of teleology and conditional necessity,[36] while building upon the functional analyses of each capacity.[37]

In the next sections, I shall provide an analysis of the specific explanations Aristotle provides for the capacities of nutrition, perception, and – more indirectly – locomotion; the capacity of thinking – perhaps because it is not necessary for life as such and therefore not strictly speaking a biological capacity – is left undiscussed.

Teleological explanations for why living beings have the capacities of nutrition and perception

The nutritive capacity is, as we saw above, the ultimate principle of life and the one capacity that is common to all living beings (*DA* II.4, 415a23–25). Aristotle defines it as the capacity for both reproducing and using food (*DA* II.4, 415a25–26), which are the "most natural functions" among living beings (*DA* II.4, 415a27: φυσικώτατον γὰρ τῶν ἔργων τοῖς ζῶσιν; cf. *Pol* I.2, 1252a28–30). The capacity for reproduction has as its final cause "the production of another just like itself" (*DA* II.4, 415a28: τὸ ποιῆσαι ἕτερον οἷον αὐτό; cf. *GA* I.4, 717a21–22), such that sublunary living beings – which as individuals are perishable – can participate in the eternal and the divine by eternally replicating themselves in form (*DA* II.4, 415a29–b7). Participation in the divine is, according to Aristotle, the ultimate goal of all actions, for being is better than not being, and living is better than not living (*GA* II.1, 731b24–732a1; *GC* II.11, 338b6–19; cf. Pl. *Smp* 207c–208b), and formal replication is the only way for sublunary living beings to achieve this. Note that individual living beings are not themselves concerned with the preservation of their species; rather it is the individual's striving for participation in the divine for its own individual good that is the true final cause of reproduction.[38]

36 Cf. Hankinson (1998, 154).

37 Note that each capacity is defined by reference to the function of the activity it is the capacity for (where this function constitutes the proper final cause of that activity), but that the teleological explanation for why certain living beings have this capacity will refer to the (necessary) contribution this function makes to the life of that living being as a whole. For instance, the capacity for perception is for sight, where the function of sight is for the sake of the detection of food, sexual mates, and potential predators.

38 Balme (1987c, 279–80) and Lennox (2001a, 133–137).

The use of food, on the other hand, is ultimately for the sake of self-preservation of the living being: by nourishing itself, the living being "saves its substantial being, and exists as long as it also feeds itself" (*DA* II.4, 416b14–15: σώζει γὰρ τὴν οὐσίαν, καὶ μέχρι τούτου ἔστιν ἕως ἂν τρέφηται). The nutritive capacity also prepares food for activity – without food, a living being is not able to exist (*DA* II.4, 416b17–20) or reach sexual maturity and reproduce itself. When – in a later chapter – Aristotle explains why living beings have the nutritive capacity and why it is most basic to life, he refers primarily to the role of the use of food in living beings (*DA* III.12, 434a22–26):[39]

It is necessary for everything that lives and has a soul to possess the nutritive soul (τὴν μὲν οὖν θρεπτικὴν ψυχὴν ἀνάγκη πᾶν ἔχειν ὅτι περ ἂν ζῇ καὶ ψυχὴν ἔχῃ), from birth until death; for it is necessary that what comes to be has growth, maturity, and decline, and these things are impossible without nourishment. It is thus necessary that the capacity for nutrition is present in all growing and declining things.

Aristotle stresses the necessity of metabolism as a basic principle of life: the ability to use food and to regulate the flow of matter is a first prerequisite if living beings are to complete a life cycle of coming into being, growing, thriving, and perishing (cf. *PA* II.10, 655b30–2: "it is not possible to be or to grow without food"). The presence of the nutritive capacity is thus a conditional necessity for living. There is no justification for why the nutritive and generative capacities are considered to be one and the same "part" of the soul; however, both serve the preservation of life, the one of the individual animal itself through the process of metabolism, the other – indirectly – of the whole animal kind through the process of formal reproduction. Self-preservation of a particular kind of life is the most basic end Aristotle picks out in teleological explanations of biological phenomena.[40]

The perceptive capacity, to which Aristotle turns next, is defined as a form of alteration or as a kind of being moved and affected (*DA* II.5, 416b32–417a2). Aristotle explains that it is not necessary for all living beings, but that it is necessary for all animals (*DA* III.12, 434a30–32):

For an animal it is necessary to have perception, <for without that it would not be able to be an animal>, if nature does nothing in vain. For all things that are

[39] I treat the accounts in *DA* II.4–5 and *DA* III.12–13 as thematically continuous. For the hypothesis that *DA* III.12–13 was in fact originally placed in between *DA* II.4 and *DA* II.5, see Hutchinson (1987, 373–381) and its critique by Burnyeat (2002, 30n6).

[40] Cf. Johnson (2005, 171–178).

according to nature are for the sake of something, or are accidents of those things that are for the sake of something.[41]

Sense perception, in the sense of touch, is not only an essential or defining capacity of animals (cf. *DA* III.13, 435b16–17); Aristotle also wants to argue that it is a *vital* capacity. He explains, first, that a full range of sense perception is necessary for all *locomotive* animals and, second, that the capacity of touch by itself is of vital necessity for all animals.

Aristotle's explanation that the capacity of sense-perception is present in the locomotive animals that have it, because it is necessary for living, starts from the principle that nature does nothing in vain. In the biological works, Aristotle often invokes this principle to explain "paradoxical" absences of parts (see my discussion of this principle in section 4.2): by imagining the part in question to be present it is possible to detect what other feature the animal has that would have interfered with the functionality of the now missing part, and the presence of this (typically more necessary) feature explains why the part is absent in the actual animal. The part's presence would have been in vain, and nature – so it is posited – does nothing in vain. It thus seems that in the biological works Aristotle uses the reversed form of the same heuristic strategy he uses in *De Anima*: for here we are to imagine the *absence* of a capacity that is in fact present in order to detect the cause for its presence.

Specifically, Aristotle proposes that we imagine the existence of locomotive animals without the capacity of sense perception and then "observe" what the consequences of this absence would be: clearly, the animal "would be destroyed and would not reach the end which is the function of its nature" (*DA* III.12, 434a33–b1: φθείροιτο ἂν καὶ εἰς τέλος οὐκ ἂν ἔλθοι, ὅ ἐστι φύσεως ἔργον; cf. *Ph* II.6, 197b22–29). The reason why the animal would die is that it would not be able to find its food (*DA* III.12, 434b1–8):

> (For how would it be nourished? For in those living beings that are stationary that [i.e., food] is available from that out of which they have been born, and it is not possible for a body to have a soul and an intellect that can distinguish things, but not to have perception, if it is not stationary and has been generated – and even if it were not generated – for why would it not have it [i.e., perception]? For it is either better for the soul or for the body; but now neither is the case (ἢ γὰρ τῇ ψυχῇ βέλτιον ἢ τῷ σώματι, νῦν δ' οὐδέτερον): the soul will not think better, nor will the body exist more because of it.) Therefore no body that is not stationary has a soul without sense perception.

[41] τὸ δὲ ζῷον ἀναγκαῖον αἴσθησιν ἔχειν, <οὐδὲ ἄνευ ταύτης οἷόν τε οὐθὲν εἶναι ζῷον,> εἰ μηθὲν μάτην ποιεῖ ἡ φύσις. ἕνεκά του γὰρ πάντα ὑπάρχει τὰ φύσει, ἢ συμπτώματα ἔσται τῶν ἕνεκά του.

Sense perception (although Aristotle does not state this explicitly, he clearly has the full range of capacities for sense perception in mind here)[42] is thus ultimately present for the sake of enabling locomotive animals to gather food after birth: without this capacity, they would die and would certainly not be better off in any way (apparently, the absence of a capacity is justified if and only if the animal's functioning benefits from this absence). Since nature never produces living beings that are not sufficiently equipped to achieve their natural ends (such beings would be in vain), it does not produce locomotive animals without the capacity of sense perception.

The presence of the capacity of touch is equally explained teleologically as being ultimately necessary for the sake of the self-preservation of *each* kind of animal, including the stationary ones (*DA* III.12, 434b10–14): "And it is necessary that it has it [i.e., the capacity for touch]. This is clear from the following. Because, since an animal is an ensouled body and every body is tangible, it is necessary that the body of an animal is able to touch, if the animal is to survive" (εἰ μέλλει σώζεσθαι τὸ ζῷον).

Aristotle believes that touch is necessary for survival, because anything that touches something else without sensing or registering it (i.e., undergoing some kind of change by being affected by the object), will not be able to flee from some things (e.g., predators) or catch others (e.g., food or possible mates); and "in that case, it will be impossible for the animal to survive" (*DA* III.12, 434b16–18: εἰ δὲ τοῦτο, ἀδύνατον ἔσται σώζεσθαι τὸ ζῷον).[43] This ultimate function of the capacity of touch to preserve the animal through enabling it to seize (or to flee from) things when sensing their presence also leads Aristotle to the conclusion that taste is a kind of touch (*DA* III.12, 434b18). Taste is the touching – or the perceiving – of what is tangible and nutritive, i.e., food, without which the animal cannot be (*DA* III.12, 434b22–24): "So these [i.e., touch and taste] are necessary for an animal, and it is manifest that without touch it is impossible for an animal to be."[44]

The capacity of touch, then, and its subcapacity of taste, both presuppose and contribute to the performance of the nutritive capacity, and as such are present for the sake of the preservation of the animal (cf. *DA* III.13, 435b17–18). However, in terms of hierarchy, touch is more necessary and therefore more universal than the other perceptive capacities (*DA* III.12, 434b24–27):

[42] Cf. Polanski (2007, 536–537).

[43] Note that by connecting touch to the appetitive capacities, Aristotle is able to explain the basic "flee and chase" behavior of animals. See Freeland (1992, 236–237).

[44] αὗται μὲν οὖν ἀναγκαῖαι τῷ ζῴῳ, καὶ φανερὸν ὅτι οὐχ οἷόν τε ἄνευ ἁφῆς εἶναι ζῷον.

> The others [i.e., smell, hearing, and sight] are for the sake of the good and come to be not in whichever of the animals; but in some, such as in the locomotive kind, their presence is necessary. For if it is to be preserved, it needs to perceive not only what it touches but also what is far away.[45]

Whereas touch is necessary for the existence of *all animals*, without qualification (cf. *Sens* 1, 436b12–15), the other perceptive faculties are necessary *only for those animals that are capable of locomotion.* In stationary animals, the other perceptive faculties, if present (and there are stationary animals without these additional perceptive faculties), are "not for the sake of their existence but for the sake of the good" (*DA* III.13, 435b19–21: οὐ τοῦ εἶναι ἕνεκα ἀλλὰ τοῦ εὖ).[46] The higher sense perceptions thus constitute a hybrid category: they are necessary and for the sake of living for all locomotive animals, but subsidiary and for the sake of living well if present in stationary animals.

This is, in the first place, because Aristotle believes that touch is the only capacity for sense perception that, if destroyed, destroys the animal with it, whereas excesses in color, sound, flavor, or smell only destroy the organ of perception, but not the animal itself (*DA* III.13, 435b4–19): this shows that touch is more basic to life than the other perceptive capacities are. Second, touch is more basic because the other senses are subsidiary to the achievement of *its* goal (i.e., detection of food and predators, and ultimately the preservation of the animal; cf. *DA* II.3, 414b6–9). For an animal has sight in order to see changes or effects in the transparent medium, be it air or water; taste (or perhaps rather smell)[47] to experience what is pleasant and painful in food and to adjust its desires accordingly; and hearing and voice for the sake of communication (*DA* III.13, 435b19–25) – which are all for the sake of enabling animals to detect objects at a distance.

The presence of the higher perceptive capacities expands in a way the capacity for touch and thereby allows even stationary animals to live a more complex life in terms of their activities, i.e., to live well in addition to living at all. As Aristotle explains in the introductory chapter of *De Sensu*, the higher senses (and especially hearing) contribute to the growth of intelligence and what has intelligence has the capacity to achieve higher

45 αἱ δὲ ἄλλαι τοῦ τε εὖ ἕνεκα καὶ γένει ζῴων ἤδη οὐ τῷ τυχόντι· ἀλλὰ τισίν, οἷον τῷ πορευτικῷ, ἀνάγκη ὑπάρχειν· εἰ γὰρ μέλλει σώζεσθαι, οὐ μόνον δεῖ ἁπτόμενον αἰσθάνεσθαι ἀλλὰ καὶ ἄποθεν.

46 Cf. Polanski (2007, 540–541).

47 It is odd that Aristotle here lists taste among the capacities for sense perception that are for the sake of living well, rather than as being necessary, while leaving out smell: Hutchinson (1987, 377n.2) suggests that instead of γεῦσιν we should read ὄσφρησιν at *DA* III.13, 435b22, which would conveniently solve both problems.

perfection beyond mere self-preservation and reproduction (*Sens* 1 436b10–437a16; cf. *EE* I.7, 1217a21–29). Here he reiterates that for animals that are capable of locomotion, the higher senses are necessary for their preservation (*Sens* 1, 436b20: σωτηρίας ἕνεκεν), but adds that for those that also have intelligence, the higher senses serve their well-being (*Sens* 1, 437a1: τοῖς δὲ καὶ φρονήσεως τυγχάνουσι τοῦ εὖ ἕνεκα).

Voice, which is mentioned as one of the higher capacities that are for the sake of living well (in *DA* III.13, 435b24–25), is a special form of producing sound that belongs uniquely to animals (*DA* II.8, 420b5–6). Aristotle gives a more elaborate teleological explanation of why animals have this capacity in the following text (*DA* II.8, 420b13–22):

> Voice is sound made by an animal not with any chance part [of his body]. But since everything that makes a sound does so because something strikes something else in something else again, and this is air, it is reasonable that the only creatures to have voice should be those which take in air. For nature then uses the air already breathed in for two functions; just as it uses the tongue for both tasting and articulation, and of these tasting is necessary (and so is found in a greater number [of living beings]), while expression is for the sake of well-being, so also nature uses breath both for the inner warmth, as something necessary (the reason will be stated elsewhere) and also for voice so that there may be well-being.[48]

In explicating the purpose of voice, Aristotle again draws a distinction between two types of ends: some capacities are necessary for life, but others serve the animal's well-being. The first are present because they are conditionally necessary for the animals that have them (i.e., they are the product of primary teleology); the second are present because *nature uses* what is already present – here: what is already present for the sake of performing a necessary function – for the performance of a second function that serves the animal's well-being (i.e., they are the product of secondary teleology; see sections 4.2–3). As Aristotle makes clear, voice performs a secondary function: just as tongues are present because they are a necessary prerequisite for the realization of the function of taste, and nature makes use of tongues for articulation (that is, if the tongues that are already present

[48] φωνὴ δ' ἐστὶ ζῴου ψόφος οὐ τῷ τυχόντι μορίῳ. ἀλλ' ἐπεὶ πᾶν ψοφεῖ τύπτοντός τινος καί τι καὶ ἔν τινι, τοῦτο δ' ἐστὶν ἀήρ, εὐλόγως ἂν φωνοίη ταῦτα μόνα ὅσα δέχεται τὸν ἀέρα. τῷ γὰρ ἤδη ἀναπνεομένῳ καταχρῆται ἡ φύσις ἐπὶ δύο ἔργα – καθάπερ τῇ γλώττῃ ἐπί τε τὴν γεῦσιν καὶ τὴν διάλεκτον, ὧν ἡ μὲν γεῦσις ἀναγκαῖον (διὸ καὶ πλείοσιν ὑπάρχει), ἡ δ' ἑρμηνεία ἕνεκα τοῦ εὖ, οὕτω καὶ τῷ πνεύματι πρός τε τὴν θερμότητα τὴν ἐντὸς ὡς ἀναγκαῖον <ὄν> (τὸ δ' αἴτιον ἐν ἑτέροις εἰρήσεται) καὶ πρὸς τὴν φωνὴν ὅπως ὑπάρχῃ τὸ εὖ.

have the right material potentials),[49] in the same way air is present in those animals that have it because it is a necessary prerequisite for the realization of the function of cooling, which preserves the vital heat within an animal, and nature makes use of air for the sake of voice. This explains both why only animals that cool themselves through air have voice (only they possess air that nature can use for voice), and why those animals have voice: its presence serves the animal's well-being.

In other words, if an animal does not require the possession of the primary function to stay alive or to be the kind of animal it is, and therefore lacks the parts that are the necessary prerequisites for the performance of that function, it will also lack the secondary, non-necessary function. This is why, for instance, fish have no voice (*DA* II.8, 421a3–6): "It is manifest, too, why fish have no voice; for they have no larynx.[50] They do not have this part because they do not take in air or breathe in."

As Aristotle explained earlier, throats are organs for breathing, and they exist for the sake of the lung (i.e., throats are subsidiary parts; *DA* II.8, 420b21–24), which implies that only animals that breathe air have throats. The primary function of throats is to contribute to the function of cooling which is primarily and properly performed by the lungs; the secondary function of the throat is communication. Now, fish do not breathe air (they cool themselves through water), and therefore do not have lungs; animals without lungs lack throats, and without a throat, the materially necessary condition for the production of voice is lacking, too. Fish lack the necessary physiological requirements to produce voice, because their primary essential and vital functions do not require the presence of those organs (and, of course, the presence of air itself), which nature then can use (and needs) for the realization of a function that serves the well-being of the animal. As we shall see in Chapters 3 and 4, Aristotle provides many more teleological explanations in his biological works that are similar to this one in building upon the fundamental distinction between something being necessary for living or being subsidiary to the animal's well-being.

49 Secondary functions may not obtain if a part lacks the right material potentials: for instance, human beings have tongues that are "the most detached, softest, and broadest, so that it may be useful for both its activities – the soft and broad tongue being useful both for the perception of flavors (for man is the most keenly perceptive of animals, and his tongue is soft, for it is most tactile, and taste is a sort of touch); and for the articulation of words and speech" (*PA* II.17, 660a17–22), whereas four-footed animals that are blooded and live-bearing are hardly capable of vocal articulation because "they have a tongue that is hard, undetached, and thick" (*PA* II.17, 660a34–5).

50 For the complexities involved in translating the word *pharunx*, see Lennox (2001b, 252).

Finally, Aristotle also provides a teleological explanation for why there are several capacities for perception, rather than just one (*DA* III.1, 425b4–11):

> One might ask for the sake of what we have several senses and not just one. Is it perhaps in order that the common objects which accompany [the special objects], e.g., motion, size, and number, may less escape our notice? For if there were only sight, and this [sight] was of white, they would escape our notice more and they would all seem to be the same, on account of color and size invariably accompanying each other. Now, since the common objects are present in another perceived thing too, this makes it clear that each of them is something distinct.

The five senses combined are for the sake of enabling animals to detect the common objects of perception, which would otherwise escape our notice. If we were only able to see a white ball, it would be difficult to distinguish the whiteness in color from the magnitude in shape, because the two necessarily come together. Once we are also able to touch the ball, and feel a hard shape, we are able to recognize that the magnitude is something different from the color and from the hardness of the ball, and thereby get a clearer perception of its magnitude and of the nature of magnitude in general.

In sum, the presence of all five perceptive capacities in locomotive animals is for the sake of perceiving common objects and thus for the perception of everything that Aristotle believes is possible to be perceived.[51]

A teleological explanation for why animals have the capacity for locomotion

Aristotle's discussion of what locomotion is for and why it is present in the animals that have it is intimately connected to his discussion in *DA* III.9–11 of the nature of locomotion, the capacity of the soul that is responsible for it, and its physiological realization. I shall therefore closely follow Aristotle's analysis in these chapters.

Since locomotion appears to be different from such "automatic" motions as growth and decay (which all living beings have on account of their nutritive soul), respiration and expiration, and sleeping and waking, Aristotle first sets out to determine what capacity of the soul moves animals in respect of place and whether this is a separate capacity (*DA* III.9, 432a19–20; *DA* III.9, 432b7–8). His method is one of elimination.

First, Aristotle rules out the nutritive capacity, which is responsible for movement with respect to growth and decay, as being responsible for

[51] Polansky (2007, 378–379).

locomotion. Aristotle takes it as a given that locomotion is always for the sake of something (as a progressive motion it is itself an intrinsically teleological activity) and that it can only be voluntary and according to nature if it involves imagination and desire (*DA* III.9, 432b14–16). Since the nutritive capacity does not involve imagination or desire, it cannot be the cause of locomotion. Besides, Aristotle adds, if the nutritive capacity were responsible for locomotion, plants would also have had the capacity for locomotion and hence the parts instrumental for this kind of movement, which is not the case (*DA* III.9, 432b18–19). The underlying teleological principle at play here is that no living being lacks the instruments that are the necessary prerequisites for the realization of a necessary function. If a particular kind of living being lacks the instruments that are typically used for the performance of such a function, then it is reasonable to assume that it also lacks that function (presumably, because that function is not vital or essential to it).

Next, Aristotle eliminates the perceptive capacity as a candidate for producing locomotion: since there are many perceptive animals that are stationary and motionless (*DA* III.9, 432b20–21) – which indicates that perception and locomotion do not correlate universally – perception cannot be responsible for locomotion either. Aristotle refers again to the absence of locomotive parts as evidence for the absence of the capacity for locomotion, this time while positing the teleological principle that nature does nothing in vain (*DA* III.9, 432b22–26):

> If nature does nothing in vain and never leaves out any of the necessary [parts], except in those beings that are maimed and incomplete, while such living beings are complete and not maimed (and a sign of this is that they are able to reproduce themselves and they have maturity and decline [of life]) – then they too would have instruments for locomotion.[52]

If nature indeed never produces living beings that lack the means to realize their capacities, the only plausible explanation for why stationary animals – that are otherwise complete – lack instruments for locomotion is that these parts are not the necessary prerequisites for the realization of perception and that thus the presence of the capacity for perception is not the (sufficient) cause of locomotion.

[52] εἰ οὖν ἡ φύσις μήτε ποιεῖ μάτην μηθὲν μήτε ἀπολείπει τι τῶν ἀναγκαίων, πλὴν ἐν τοῖς πηρώμασι καὶ ἐν τοῖς ἀτελέσιν τὰ δὲ τοιαῦτα τῶν ζῴων τέλεια καὶ οὐ πηρώματά ἐστιν (σημεῖον δ' ὅτι ἐστὶ γεννητικὰ καὶ ἀκμὴν ἔχει καὶ φθίσιν) – ὥστ' εἶχεν ἂν καὶ τὰ ὀργανικὰ μέρη τῆς πορείας.

Finally, Aristotle considers the intellective or calculative capacity, which he defined earlier as "that by which the soul both knows and understands" (*DA* III.4, 429a9–10). However, this capacity cannot be the mover either (*DA* III.9, 432b27–28): "For the intellective capacity thinks of nothing practical and it says nothing about what is to be avoided and pursued." Since the intellect is concerned with abstractions and not with the avoidance or pursuit of something, it cannot as such be the source of locomotion.[53] Merely thinking about something that is to be avoided or pursued does not bring about the emotional state necessary for the initiation of locomotion. Even if the intellect were to tell the animal to avoid or pursue something, the animal would not be moved; instead, the animal acts in accordance with desire (*DA* III.9, 433a1–3). Aristotle uses an analogy with the art of healing to point out that the intellective capacity is not sufficient as a cause of locomotion, because there is a difference between having knowledge and acting according to that knowledge. On the other hand, desire on its own is also not sufficient to cause locomotion: the case of continent people shows that although they may have the cravings and the desire for things, "they do not do those things for which they have a desire, but follow reason" (*DA* III.9, 433a7–8). Both intellect and desire seem to be involved in locomotion, but on their own they are insufficient.

From these considerations Aristotle draws the preliminary conclusion that desire and imagination *together* produce locomotion, given that imagination is some kind of thinking and that it is the only intellectual capacity that human beings and animals have in common (*DA* III.10, 433a9–13). He indicates that the capacities of the practical intellect and desire are equally goal-directed (*DA* III.10, 433a15–17): in contrast with the theoretical intellect that (typically) finds its end in its own activity, the *practical* intellect and desire are both directed towards an (external) end. The practical intellect starts from the object of desire, which is the end of the capacity of desire, and the endpoint of reasoning is what initiates locomotion towards that object.[54] The *primary* cause of locomotion is desire and ultimately the object of desire (*DA* III.10, 433b10–13).[55]

[53] Cf. *PA* I.1, 641a29-b10, where Aristotle argues that the natural philosopher need not speak about all parts of the soul, but only about those parts that are a source of movement; because intellect is not a source of movement (at least not on its own), that part of the soul does not belong to the domain of the natural philosopher. See Lennox (2001b, 143–145).

[54] See Charles (1984, 89–96) for the view that the conclusion of the practical syllogism is not an action, but *becomes* an action; the conclusion is a proposition, which – when accepted – by the activity of desire explains the action as an efficient cause. On the purpose of practical syllogisms, see Natali (2001, 61–67); cf. Charles (1984); Cooper (1975); Corcilius (2008a–c); Hardie (1968); Nussbaum (1978); and Santas (1969).

[55] This object of desire may be either the good or the apparent good (where good means the practical good, which is capable of being otherwise); *DA* III.10, 433a28–31.

Within this framework, Aristotle distinguishes three constituents of locomotion (*DA* III.10, 433b13–31). The first constituent is the mover or the moving cause (*DA* III.10, 433b13: ἓν μὲν τὸ κινοῦν), which is "double": there is a moving cause that is itself unmoved and one that both moves and is moved (*DA* III.10, 433b14–15). The unmoved moving cause is the practical good, which is the object of desire, external to the animal that is capable of locomotion. The moved moving cause is the capacity of desire, a part of the soul internal to the locomotive animal. Thus, the practical good, without being moved itself, initiates movement towards it in the capacity of desire; the capacity of desire is thereby itself moved, and in its turn moves the animal. The second constituent is that with which the moving cause produces movement (*DA* III.10, 433b14: δεύτερον δ' ᾧ κινεῖ). These are the "bodily instruments" that are conditionally necessary for animals to effect movement, such as feet, wings, and fins, which are to be "investigated among the functions common to body and soul" (*DA* III.10, 433b19–21: διὸ ἐν τοῖς κοινοῖς σώματος καὶ ψυχῆς ἔργοις θεωρητέον περὶ αὐτοῦ). The third and last constituent involved in locomotion is that which is moved (*DA* III.10, 433b14: ἔτι τρίτον τὸ κινούμενον), which is the animal or human being that is moved towards an end.

This, then, implicitly yields the teleological explanation of why some living beings are capable of locomotion: locomotion is progression towards (or away from) an object of desire (or of dislike) initiated by imagination for the sake of pursuing (or avoiding) that object of desire (or of dislike) perceived at a distance. The goal-directedness of locomotion itself is crucial for why animals have this capacity: locomotion would be of no use if it were merely progression in just any direction – the actualization of the capacity for locomotion is progression *towards* or *away from some (non-)desired object*. This may also explain why the locomotive capacity is not a separate part of the soul that is realized by its own object, in the way that the capacity of hearing is actualized by some object producing sound. Rather, the capacity for locomotion is concomitant to the capacity of desire that is present in an animal that also has imagination (*DA* III.10, 433b27–29): "In general then, as we have said, insofar as the animal is capable of desire, to that extent it is capable of moving itself; and it is not capable of desire without imagination."

The capacity for locomotion emerges, as it were, from the capacities of desire and of imagination, and is therefore present only in those animals that have these two capacities. The reason why animals that only possess the most basic capacity for perception, i.e., touch, are incapable of locomotion follows from this: these animals also only have imagination and appetite in

a very rudimentary form,[56] and are therefore unable to identify objects of desire or to focus on such objects – which would be necessary while moving towards them (*DA* III.11, 433b31–434a10).[57] This makes their motions "indeterminate" (*DA* III.11, 434a4–5: κινεῖται ἀορίστως) and random – they will eat only when they happen to touch upon something edible.

In sum, Aristotle does not explain the presence of locomotion in animals that have desire and imagination by reference to the contribution the function of locomotion makes to either living or living well; rather, he seems to treat the level of desire and imagination present in an animal as explanatorily basic, and uses this to explain why some animals have locomotion and why others do not, and then explains the number of perceptive capacities these animals have by reference to whether or not they have locomotion. Roughly, there are thus two main kinds of animals. Some animals have (nutrition and) touch and a rudimentary form of desire and imagination. They are not capable of locomotion and therefore do not need any of the higher perceptive capacities (if they do possess some of these, they are for the sake of living well). Other animals have (nutrition and) touch, desire and imagination, and therefore also locomotion. They possess the higher perceptive capacities for the sake of this latter capacity. The more capacities a living being has, the more complex its life and the more it partakes in well-being (cf. *Cael* II.12, 292b1–19 and my analysis of this passage in section 5.3). Plants, which only possess the capacity for nutrition, only partake in living; and human beings, who possess – in addition to all the other capacities that are present in the most complex animals – the capacity of thinking, have the highest share in living well.

2.3 CONCLUSION

Following the methodological order of the natural treatises of Aristotle, we have shifted from Aristotle's defense of the teleology of nature as an internal principle of motion and rest in the *Physica* to his teleological analysis of *living* nature in *De Anima*, where living is identified with the realization of soul capacities in a natural, instrumental body.

The teleological framework that Aristotle sets out in the *Physica* seems to be presupposed in the explanatory strategies of *De Anima*. For instance, in order to gain knowledge about the nature of the soul, Aristotle invokes his theory of four causes, and subsequently defines the soul as the efficient, formal, and final cause of the living being, and its natural body as the

[56] Cf. Schofield (1992, 272n.55). [57] Frede (1992, 290); Richardson (1992, 384).

material cause. In order to gain better understanding of the soul's operation on and interaction with the natural body, he uses his analogy between nature and art, and thereby establishes a functional conception of the soul and the instrumental and conditionally necessary character of the body. In order to explain why certain kinds of living beings have the soul capacities they have, he frequently posits the teleological principle that nature does nothing in vain, and then shows how the capacities they have are necessary for their living or rather contribute to their living well.

From the very outset, Aristotle's analysis of the soul is teleological in nature: the soul is that for the sake of which the bodily aspects of the living being are as its instruments. The soul constitutes a hierarchical and non-aggregative unity of capacities for the performance of functions in virtue of which a natural, instrumental body has life – and, in some cases, also well-being. The complete body with its main parts and features is conditionally necessitated by or subsidiary to (and therefore explainable by reference to) these life functions. Because of this, the characteristic activities and physical realization of each form of life – whether of a widest kind or of an individual subspecies – becomes explainable by reference to the particular combination of interdependent soul capacities that specific form of life has as its final cause.

The different capacities of the soul are themselves teleologically grounded as well: their presence in the living beings that have them is either necessary for those beings in terms of their basic survival and/or identity, or is rather for the sake of the living being's well-being. Not all capacities are thus equally necessary for life as such: the most basic capacities such as nutrition and reproduction are those that are most common among all living beings because they are most necessary for life; the higher capacities – which, except perhaps for the capacity of thinking, all presuppose the presence of the basic ones – are less prevalent, because they are less necessary for staying alive and reproducing, but rather serve the living being's well-being by allowing it to live a more complex life.

We shall see in the next two chapters that the teleological explanations for why animals have the parts they have in the biological works reflect this gradual scale of necessity and thus build upon the foundations laid down in *De Anima*.

CHAPTER 3

Introducing biology as a demonstrative science: the theory of teleological explanation in the De Partibus Animalium *I*

3.0 INTRODUCTION

Aristotle's theory of natural teleology applies in particular to living natural substances: their coming to be and existence, their change and development, and many of their differentiations are the result of the goal-directed actions of their formal natures. In the following two chapters, I discuss the role of teleology in the explanations Aristotle provides of the presence, absence, and differentiations of animal parts in *De Partibus Animalium*.

In Chapter 4, I shall present an analysis of the structure, role, and explanatory of force of the actual explanations recorded in *De Partibus Animalium* books II–IV; here, in Chapter 3, I shall first outline Aristotle's theory of explanation in biology as introduced in *De Partibus Animalium* book I. In section 3.1, I sketch the demonstrative character of the science of biology; this will provide some background to the larger scientific context within which Aristotle's use of teleological explanations takes place. In section 3.2, I discuss the notions of teleology that Aristotle employs in his discussion of the standards for explanation in the natural sciences in *De Partibus Animalium* book I. My aim here is to show that there are *two types* of teleology underlying these explanations: a primary kind that involves formal natures realizing a preexisting potential for form through conditional necessity, and a secondary kind that involves formal natures using materials that have come to be of material necessity for something good. Finally, in section 3.3, I define the different notions of necessity that appear in Aristotle's natural treatises and explain what role each plays in explanations of biological phenomena. In particular, I shall counter a possible objection to the positive role my notion of secondary teleology ascribes to material necessity in natural generation, i.e., the view that Aristotle's own discussions of the relation between teleology and

necessity – notably in *PA* I.1 – deny such a positive role.[1] I argue that this objection is grounded in a failure to distinguish between the causal and modal[2] ways in which Aristotle uses the concept of necessity.

The two arguments, which are developed independently of each other, together demonstrate that the material constraints and the influence of material necessity on the goal-directed actions of formal natures are relatively strong. Animals are the way they are not just because they have kind-specific potentials for form that are being realized, but also because of the material and the material potentials that are available to the formal nature during embryogenesis and the animal's subsequent development. This is not a negative claim: the goal-directed actions of the formal nature of an animal often (although not always) turn to a good use those materials that have come to be as a result of material necessity, and thereby equip living beings with features that are perhaps not strictly necessary for their survival or identity, but that contribute significantly to their well-being.

3.1 BIOLOGY AS A DEMONSTRATIVE SCIENCE

The relation between Aristotle's theory of scientific demonstration and inquiry as outlined in the *Analytica* and his practice in the physical and biological works has been the subject of much discussion in recent years among scholars of Aristotle,[3] and I do not wish to elaborate too much on this issue yet (I shall return to this question in Chapter 6). Instead, let me present as a working hypothesis for this chapter the thesis that Aristotle intended his biology to be a proper demonstrative science that approximates and builds upon the "guidelines" of his *Analytica Posteriora*.[4] This thesis is informed by the following two observations from the biological works: first, Aristotle shows genuine concern for identifying and following the appropriate scientific method in natural inquiry, and second, he repeatedly indicates that the materials presented in the biological treatises contain

1 Consequently, scholars have explained away all material necessity in biology (Balme, 1987c); subsumed it under the operation of conditional necessity (Cooper, 1987; Johnson, 2005); or assigned a mostly constraining role to it in the realizations of function: see Gill (1997); Lennox (2001a, b) and especially (2001a, 187, 195–196) on "pre-conditional necessity"; and Pavlopoulos (2003, 164–166). The positive role I assign to material necessity is foreshadowed in Lennox's discussion of the omentum; see Lennox (2001b, 290–292).

2 My account of necessity in Aristotle is much indebted to the analysis of modal and causal uses of necessity by Kupreeva (forthcoming).

3 See Barnes (1981); Gotthelf (1987); Kullmann (1990); Lennox (2001a); and Lloyd (1990; 1996).

4 For a defense of this thesis, see Gotthelf (1987), Lennox (*passim*), and Leunissen (2010).

the necessary ingredients for generating demonstrations of the natural kind.

Aristotle sets out the principles and standards for biological investigations in the first book of *De Partibus Animalium*.[5] His aim there is to provide standards from which one will be able to assess the "manner of the things demonstrated" (*PA* I.1, 639a12–15; 13–14: τὸν τρόπον τῶν δεικνυμένων) in the natural sciences, of which the study of animals is a part. Aristotle proceeds mainly through a discussion of methodological dilemmas, dealing with varied questions such as which causes the natural scientist should pick out and what their priority relations are (Aristotle argues for the priority of teleology over necessity, but without denying explanatory force to the latter); what the relation is between form and matter in animals (Aristotle explains that the two are complementary, and that therefore the natural scientist needs to study both); and whether the natural scientist should study the whole soul or only a part of the soul (Aristotle states that the capacity for thinking does not belong to the study of nature). Aristotle also offers a revision of the Platonic method of division and definition. This latter critique of dichotomous division leads, among other things, to the establishment of what exactly constitutes an animal kind: kinds share "a single common nature and forms in it that are not too distant" (*PA* I.4, 644b3–4: ἔχει τε μίαν φύσιν κοινὴν καὶ εἴδη ἐν αὐτῷ μὴ πολὺ διεστῶτα). Animals that belong to the same kind differ only in degree ("by the more and less" or "by bodily affections"), while animals that differ in kind are similar to each other only by analogy (*PA* I.4, 644a16–22; 644b12).[6]

The most striking feature of *De Partibus Animalium* book I is perhaps that in it Aristotle not only follows but also enriches the *Analytica*'s conception of science in order to make it applicable to the special and distinct study of living beings. For instance, the *Analytica* lacks a clear distinction between matter and form and seems devoid of the causal concept of conditional necessity.[7] Both are crucial to the study of (living) nature, and are therefore introduced and further refined in Aristotle's methodological discussion in *De Partibus Animalium* book I. This, I believe, gives evidence for the thesis that Aristotle self-consciously attempts to integrate his newly

[5] For an outline of *PA* I and its connections with the method presented in the *Analytica Posteriora*, see Lennox (2001a, 100–104).

[6] For what it means for animals within one genus to have a common nature, see Charles (2000, 316–326).

[7] See Lennox (2001a, xxii, 102, and *passim*).

developed science of biology into the scientific framework supplied by the *Analytica*.

Aristotle's conviction that his investigations contain what is needed to provide demonstrations of biological phenomena is visible in a few (but very well-known) methodological statements in the biological works. The clearest and least controversial text concerning the demonstrative nature of biology is the following (*HA* I.6, 491a7–13):

> These things, then, have been put forward in outline, to provide a foretaste of what things we have to investigate and what it is about them [that we have to investigate]. Later we shall discuss them in greater detail, in order that we may first gain understanding of the differences and the attributes belonging to all. After this, we must try to discover the causal explanations of these things. For it is the natural method to do this after having started with the investigation of the details concerning each thing; for from these it becomes apparent both about which things the *demonstration* must be, and from what things it must proceed (περὶ ὧν τε γὰρ καὶ ἐξ ὧν εἶναι δεῖ τὴν ἀπόδειξιν, ἐκ τούτων γίνεται φανερόν) (cf. *PA* I.1, 639a12–15; 640a1–9; *GA* II.6, 742b23–36).

The zoological research program sketched in this passage recommends the natural scientist to start with a collection of the basic facts to be explained (i.e., of the *hoti* in the language of the *Analytica*), and is mainly carried out in the *Historia Animalium* through (Aristotelian) divisions of the differences between animals. In this collection, Aristotle records the attributes and *differentiae* of animals (the *differentiae* are the differences with respect to the animals' modes of life, their activities, their characters, and their parts), with the purpose of establishing their correlations.[8] For example, Aristotle discusses similarities and differences between animals concerning the possession of hair as follows (*HA* II.1, 498b16–18):

> All animals, as many as are four-footed and live-bearing (πάντα δ' ὅσα τετράποδα καὶ ζῳοτόκα), are hair-covered, so to speak, and they are not like man who is sparsely haired and short-haired except on the head; with regard to the head he is the hairiest among animals.

Note that in this example Aristotle records both correlating features ("being a four-footed live-bearing animal" and "being hair-covered") and their precise extension ("all . . . as many as are . . ."), in addition to indicating how this correlation is different in another genus ("being a human" correlates

[8] I borrow these points, and the example below, from Lennox (2001a, 7–38); cf. also Lennox (1990, 175–182).

with "having the most hairy head of all animals"). Following the demonstrative model of the *Analytica* (see, e.g., *APr* I.30, *APo* I.13 and *APo* II.1), according to which the investigation of the facts is separate from and precedes the investigation of the reasons why, Aristotle thus collects in *Historia Animalium* the biological facts that always or for the most part go together, and therefore form possible candidates for being picked out as terms in syllogistic demonstrations in either the predicate or the subject position. These correlating pairs of facts constitute the "about which" of demonstrations. In this case, one of the explananda is why "having the most hairy head" (picked out by the predicate term) correlates always or for the most part with "being a human" (picked out by the subject term).

Ultimately, Aristotle also hopes that because of this collection we will be in a better position to single out those features and *differentiae* that are causally basic (i.e., factors that themselves cannot be explained any further through other factors) from the ones that are explained through these factors (see, e.g., *PA* II.14, 658b2–10). The *Historia Animalium* is thus also supposed to help us discover those causal features "from which" demonstrations (or the *dioti*) come about, and forms in that way a preliminary to the next, demonstrative stage in which Aristotle proceeds to *identify* these causes, which is recorded predominantly in *De Partibus Animalium* and *De Generatione Animalium*. The exceptional hairiness of human heads, for instance, is explained in *De Partibus Animalium* (see *PA* II.14, 658b2–10) by reference to both teleology and material necessity: due to the presence of the brain in the human head, this place is moistest, which makes it both very weak and most conducive to the growth of hair. At the same time, hair is what provides protection, and nature provides protection to the place that needs it most. The causally basic factors which are to be picked out as middle terms are "moistness" and "need of protection," both of which belong *most* to the human head (I shall explain the causal mechanism underlying this type of "double" explanation below).

Demonstrations in the natural sciences are, of course, as Aristotle explains in *De Partibus Animalium* book I (see especially *PA* I.1, 640a1–9; *PA* I.1, 640a33–b3; *PA* I.1, 642a32–b2), different from demonstrations in the mathematical sciences that form the main model of demonstrative science in *Analytica Posteriora*, even though both are a kind of theoretical science (*Meta* VI.1, 1026a6–8). Unlike the latter, the conclusions of biological demonstrations do not hold always and without exception, but merely "for the most part," and the necessity that governs the deduction is conditional, rather than unqualified (see below in sections 3.3 and 6.4).

However, already within the *Analytica Posteriora*, Aristotle indicates that there are also demonstrations of things that hold for the most part (see especially *APo* I.8, I.30, and II.12) and occasionally uses examples (e.g., thunder, lunar eclipses, and the shedding of leaves) that are drawn from the natural sciences. It thus seems safe to conclude that Aristotle attempts to build his science of biology on the model set out in his *Analytica Posteriora*, and that the differences we will find between the theory of the *Analytica Posteriora* and that of *De Partibus Animalium* book I do not affect the status of biology as a demonstrative science.

3.2 PRIMARY AND SECONDARY TELEOLOGY

The image of nature as a good housekeeper

In order to get a better grasp of Aristotle's theory of explanation in *De Partibus Animalium* book I, and perhaps of his explanatory project in the *De Partibus Animalium* as a whole, we need to make a distinction between what I call "primary" and "secondary" teleology. I shall illustrate this distinction by offering an elaborate interpretation of an image Aristotle draws of nature acting as a good housekeeper in *De Generatione Animalium*, and use my findings to shed light on Aristotle's standards for how to construe demonstrations of biological phenomena provided in the first book of *De Partibus Animalium*.

The image of nature that I believe is most helpful for understanding the double nature of Aristotle's teleology (even though one has to realize that Aristotle is not himself concerned with presenting a two-fold theory of teleology in this image) is part of an investigation into the natural order of generation of the various animal parts within the embryo in *De Generatione Animalium* book II (see *GA* II.1, 733a32; 734a16–34; and *GA* II.4, 740a2–16). Before quoting the image in full, I shall first sketch its context.

One of the issues Aristotle tries to settle in the second book of *De Generatione Animalium* is the order in which animal parts come to be. In *GA* II.4, he argues that, within the embryo, which "possesses all parts potentially in a way" (*GA* II.4, 740a2–4: καὶ ἐν τῷ κυήματι τρόπον τινὰ πάντων ἐνόντων τῶν μορίων δυνάμει), the heart is the first to take shape because it is the source of movement for the developing animal (*GA* II.4, 740b2–4; cf. *PA* III.4, 666a18–21). In *GA* II.6, he lays out a detailed method for how to determine the order in which the parts of an animal develop further, starting from the heart. As Aristotle points

out, this is something that cannot always simply be observed (bigger parts often appear earlier, even though they start developing later: *GA* II.6, 741b26–27) and is therefore "not easy" to make out (*GA* II.6, 742b6–7; cf. *GA* II.6, 742b9–10). According to the method Aristotle proposes, parts that generate other parts must come to be before all other parts, and parts that serve as an instrument must come to be after those parts that are "that for the sake of which" and that make use of the former (*GA* II.6, 742a16–b18). The underlying teleological principle in this threefold division in the chronology of the coming to be of parts is that nature does not produce parts before the animal is actually able to use them (otherwise, these parts would be in vain; see the analogy with the flute player in *GA* II.6, 742a26–28), conjoined with the fact that parts that are of the nature of an origin necessarily come to be first.

Aristotle accordingly explains that the generation of the heart is followed first by the blood vessels, out of which then all the other parts are formed – first the internal, then the external parts; first the upper, then the lower parts (*GA* II.6, 742a36–742b18). Within this sequence of generation, Aristotle notes that the time of the formation of the eyes presents a difficulty: although their formation starts – as one would expect based on their location in the animal body – early on in the formation of the embryo, they are the last organs to reach their completion (*GA* II.6, 743b32–744b11). Aristotle explains this peculiarity by reference to the principle that nature does not create parts too early or too late for an animal to be able to use them (see *GA* II.6, 744a35–b1; cf. *GA* V.8, 788b20–789a2 concerning teeth). With the image of nature as a good housekeeper Aristotle returns to his discussion of the *normal* sequence of the generation of animal parts (*GA* II.6, 744b11–27):

> Each of the other parts [i.e., all the parts of an animal with the exception of the eye and the heart discussed before] is formed out of the nutriment, (A) the parts that are the noblest and that partake in the most important principle [i.e., the essential parts: cf. *GA* II.6, 742a34–35 and V.1, 778b12–13] are formed from the nutriment which is concocted first and is purest; (B) the parts that are necessary, that is to say that are for the sake of the former parts, are formed from the inferior nutriment and the residues and leftovers. For just like a good housekeeper, so also nature is not in the habit of throwing away anything from which it is possible to make anything useful. Now in a household the best part of the food that comes in is set apart for (A) the free people, the inferior and the residue [of the best food] for (B1) the slaves, and the worst is given to (B2) the animals that live with them. Just as the intellect from the outside does those things with a view to growth, so nature in the things coming to be forms from the purest material (A) the flesh and the body of the other sense organs, and from the residues thereof (B1) bones

and sinews and (B2) hair, and also nails and hoofs and all similar parts; for this reason these are the last to assume their formation, for they have to wait till the time when nature has some residue to spare.[9]

This image is representative for the way Aristotle commonly picks out nature in his explanations of biological phenomena: nature is always personified as an agent, and portrayed as acting for the sake of something, while following a certain *logos* or formula (cf. *PA* I.1, 641b23–37). Aristotle calls this the "formal nature" of an animal, which incorporates the efficient, final, and formal cause of an animal, and is to be identified with its soul (see, e.g., *PA* I.1, 641a23–28; *DA* II.1, 412a19–21 and *GA* IV.4, 770b17).[10] Contrasted with this formal nature is the animal's "material nature": this is its body, its basic elemental make-up, and the kinds and amounts of food it can process. The material nature is a source of the constitutive matter for the formation of parts and is thus in constant interaction with the formal nature of the animal.

What is particularly important for our understanding of Aristotle's teleology in this image is the hierarchy of different types of animal parts that Aristotle develops in it, linking the ontological status of a part to the quality of its constitutive material and its place in the sequence of coming into being. According to the image drawn, nature uses the best materials to make the most important parts of the body, and makes those first, just as in a household, the housekeeper gives the best food to the most important members of the household, who are fed first.

Specifically, I take the image to suggest that not all biological parts are "created equally" (the first group of parts receive some kind of priority treatment, whereas others have to wait for their formation until nature has some residue to spare), which indicates that the underlying teleological processes that account for their coming to be and presence must be different. The most important parts in the image (A) are those that partake in the essence of an animal: they are made of the best nutriment, and come to be first.

9 Τῶν δ' ἄλλων γίγνεται μορίων ἕκαστον ἐκ τῆς τροφῆς, τὰ μὲν τιμιώτατα καὶ μετειληφότα τῆς κυριωτάτης ἀρχῆς ἐκ τῆς πεπεμμένης καὶ καθαρωτάτης καὶ πρωτης τροφῆς, τὰ δ' ἀναγκαῖα μόρια καὶ τούτων ἕνεκεν ἐκ τῆς χείρονος καὶ τῶν ὑπολειμμάτων καὶ περιττωμάτων. ὥσπερ γὰρ οἰκονόμος ἀγαθὸς καὶ ἡ φύσις οὐθὲν ἀποβάλλειν εἴωθεν ἐξ ὧν ἔστι ποιῆσαί τι χρηστόν. ἐν δὲ ταῖς οἰκονομίαις τῆς γιγνομένης τροφῆς ἡ μὲν βελτίστη τέτακται τοῖς ἐλευθέροις, ἡ δὲ χείρων καὶ τὸ περίττωμα ταύτης <τοῖς> οἰκέταις, τὰ δὲ χείριστα καὶ τοῖς συντρεφομένοις διδόασι ζῴοις. καθάπερ οὖν εἰς τὴν αὔξησιν ὁ †θύραθεν ταῦτα ποιεῖ νοῦς οὕτως ἐν τοῖς γιγνομένοις αὐτοῖς ἡ φύσις ἐκ μὲν τῆς καθαρωτάτης ὕλης σάρκας καὶ τῶν ἄλλων αἰσθητηρίων τὰ σώματα συνίστησιν, ἐκ δὲ τῶν περιττωμάτων ὀστᾶ καὶ νεῦρα καὶ τρίχας, ἔτι δ' ὄνυχας καὶ ὁπλὰς καὶ πάντα τὰ τοιαῦτα· διὸ τελευταῖα ταῦτα λαμβάνει τὴν σύστασιν ὅταν ἤδη γίγνηται περίττωμα τῆς φύσεως.

10 On formal natures, see also Lennox (2001a, 182–194).

Elsewhere Aristotle refers to these parts as being necessary (without further qualification) for the animal, as they are conditionally necessary for the performance of vital and essential functions. This presumably means that these parts are the result of the standard form of teleology, or of what I here call primary teleology. I shall explain this further below. The other parts in the image (B) are also necessary, but *in a more restricted and qualified way.*[11] These parts are said to exist for the sake of the first category (which is why I prefer to refer to them as "subsidiary" parts), and are made of inferior nutriment, and only come to be if nature has enough leftovers to spare. In *De Partibus Animalium*, Aristotle somewhat paradoxically refers to these parts as being "not necessary" (presumably, because they are not necessary without qualification, but rather necessary for the sake of other parts) and as being "for the better," because their presence improves the functioning and well-being of the animal in question. Even though the accounts in *De Generatione Animalium* and *De Partibus Animalium* are thus not overtly consistent in their ascriptions of "necessity" to these two types of parts, they do provide the same causal descriptions of the actions of the formal natures in the production of subsidiary parts: in both treatises, they are described as the product of nature *using* leftovers to make some useful feature for the animal in question. This, I believe, illustrates a different – secondary – kind of teleological causation.

In the next subsections, I shall work out this hierarchical picture of animal parts in more detail, mostly by drawing from material from the *De Partibus Animalium* (for a schematic outline, see Table 3.1).

Vital and essential parts

I submit that the first category of parts – represented by the "free people" in the image – consists of those parts that are the necessary prerequisites for the performance of the vital[12] and essential[13] functions specified by

[11] I translate the second *kai* in *GA* II.6, 744b14 epexegetically as "that is to say," which is arguably not the most natural reading of the text. However, I believe that I can justify this reading based on how Aristotle treats this group of parts in *other* contexts, most notably in *De Partibus Animalium*. See my discussion below.

[12] For examples of vital functions with their respective necessary parts, see *PA* II.3, 650a6–8; *PA* II.7, 652b15; *PA* II.10, 655b28–31; *PA* III.4, 665b10–15; *PA* III.4, 666a22–24; *PA* III.14, 674a13–19; *PA* IV.5, 681b13–16; *PA* IV.10, 686a5–7 and *GA* I.2, 716a18-I.8, 718b28.

[13] For examples of essential functions with their respective necessary parts, see *PA* II.2, 647a20–23; *PA* II.8, 653b19–23; *PA* III.6, 669b8–12; *PA* IV.5, 681b13–16; *PA* IV.12, 693b2–13; *PA* IV.13, 695b17–25 and *GA* V.1, 778a32–34. Note that flying is not an essential function of insects: some insects have wings by way of compensation for a lack of feet (*PA* IV.6, 682b5–6). For species being demarcated by the specific combination of necessary parts, see *Pol* IV.4, 1290b25–37.

Table 3.1 *The hierarchy of parts in the image of nature as a good housekeeper*

	Biological part	Timing in growth	Material used	Example
A	Vital and essential parts ↔ Free people *Perform necessary functions*	Made first	Best nutriment	Fins *Necessary for swimming*
B1	Subsidiary parts ↔ Slaves *Contribute to necessary functions*	Made second	Inferior nutriment	Kidneys *Help collection of residue*
B2	"Luxury" parts ↔ Animals *Perform non-necessary functions*	Made third	Residues	Horns *Provide protection*

the definition of the substantial being of that animal (this is what it is to partake in the "most important principle" or essence of the animal).[14] Elsewhere Aristotle claims that their presence is *necessary* for the animal: through these parts the animal's form is realized, and without them the animal would not be able to survive, or it would not be able to be the specific kind of animal it is.

Outside the *De Generatione Animalium*,[15] Aristotle employs a very strict notion of necessity in his characterizations of such vital and essential parts. He calls a part necessary for an animal when he believes that nature could not have "designed" that animal without the part in question; without the part, the animal *immediately* fails to reach its natural ends (cf. *GA* IV.4, 771a11–14). This is clear from, for example, his description of the liver, which he considers to be a vital part of all blooded animals (*PA* IV.2, 677a36–b5):

> For it is reasonable that, since the nature of the liver is vital (ἐπίκαιρον) and necessary (ἀναγκαίαν) to all the blooded animals, its being of a certain character is a cause of living a shorter or longer time . . . and none of the other viscera is necessary to these animals, but only the liver (τῶν δ' ἄλλων οὐδὲν σπλάγχνων ἀναγκαῖόν ἐστι τοῖς ζῴοις, τὸ δ' ἧπαρ μόνον).

According to Aristotle, the presence of the liver is so basic to the life and survival of blooded animals that it is the only visceral organ they absolutely

14 For examples of parts whose function is specified by the definition of the substantial being, see Code (1997, 139–140) and Gotthelf (1985, 27–54; 1987, 190–191).

15 For evidence within the *De Generatione Animalium*, see especially *GA* I.4, 717a11–21, which I discuss in section 4.2.

cannot be without; that is, of course, in addition to the heart, which Aristotle had already established as being the *origin* of blood (cf. *PA* II.1, 647a35–b8 and III.4, 665b10–15). Because only the heart and the liver are necessary in this strict way for blooded animals, these are the only viscera present in *all* blooded animals (cf. *PA* III.4, 665a28–30; 665b10; 666a24–25; and III.7, 670a23–28). The other visceral parts, such as, for instance, the kidneys and the spleen, are not in the same way necessary for all blooded animals (Aristotle even calls them "non-necessary"; see my discussion of the kidneys below), which is why they are also not present in all blooded animals (cf. *PA* III.7, 670a30; III.9, 671a26–30; and III.12, 673b12–14). In other words, nature cannot produce blooded animals without a heart and liver, but it is among the natural possibilities to produce blooded animals lacking some of the other visceral parts.

The explanations Aristotle offers for the necessary vital and essential parts in *De Partibus Animalium* provide textbook examples of what I call primary teleology. For example, Aristotle explains the presence of fins in fish by reference to the definition of their substantial being (*PA* IV.13, 695b17–26):

> Fish do not have distinct limbs [such as arms or feet], owing to the fact that their nature according to the definition of their substantial being is to be able to swim (διὰ τὸ νευστικὴν εἶναι τὴν φύσιν αὐτῶν κατὰ τὸν τῆς οὐσίας λόγον), and since nature makes nothing either superfluous or pointless. And since they are blooded in virtue of their substantial being, it is on account of being swimmers (διὰ μὲν τὸ νευστικὰ εἶναι) that they have fins.

Fish are essentially swimmers: that is, being able to swim is part of the nature or substantial being of fish, and having fins is a necessary condition for fish being able to swim; hence fins are *kath'hauta* features of fish.[16] (It is important to note here that Aristotle treats the absence of fins in a small number of fish not as a refutation of his observation that fins are essential parts of the genus fish, but as an exception that deserves special explanation. I shall discuss such exceptional cases in section 4.2.) The coming to be and presence of these parts is thus explained by reference to

[16] Cf. *PA* III.6, 669b8–12; *PA* IV.5, 678a31–35; and *PA* IV.13, 697b1–13. Note that this type of explanation also holds for those parts whose presence can be deduced directly from the presence of necessary parts or can be "traced" to the definition of the substantial being of an animal (cf. *GA*. V.1, 778a34–35: ἐπ' ἐνίων πρὸς τὸν λόγον συντείνει τὸν τῆς οὐσίας): for example, while wings and being blooded are necessary parts of birds (i.e., they are *kath'hauta* features of birds; see *PA* IV.12, 693b10–14), being two-footed is a *kath'hauta sumbebêkos* feature of birds; see *PA* IV.12, 693b5.

their necessary function,[17] and that function in its turn is grounded in the substantial being of the animal. Teleological explanations of this primary kind exhibit parts to be the necessary prerequisites for the performance of vital or essential functions.

Aristotle introduces this type of teleological explanation as the primary kind of explanation in his methodological introduction to biology in *PA* I.1 (*PA* I.1, 639b13–19):

> Now it is apparent that the primary [kind of explanation] is the one we describe as being for the sake of something (φαίνεται δὲ πρώτη, ἣν λέγομεν ἕνεκά τινος). For that is an account, and an account is a starting point alike in things that are composed according to art and in those composed by nature. For after having defined by thought or perception – the physician [having defined] health, and the house-builder [having defined] the house – they [i.e., the physician and the house-builder] provide the accounts and the explanations (ἀποδιδόασι τοὺς λόγους καὶ τὰς αἰτίας) of that which each of them produces, and the reason why they have to be produced in that way.

These lines are usually taken as a defense of the priority of final causality over efficient causality,[18] but I believe that they rather pertain to the priority of teleological explanation over efficient explanation: the explanans is not a function, but a form that specifies the functions to be realized.[19] Just as in art the artifact that is produced and the way in which it is produced are explained by reference to the definition of the end product (i.e., "house") that specifies the function of that product (i.e., "shelter"), so too in nature the coming to be of an animal and its parts is explained by reference to the definition of the substantial being of that animal, which specifies – among other things – the functions to be realized (cf. *Meta* VII.7, 1032b5–22). This also explains why Aristotle believes his predecessors failed to provide explanations in terms of forms and functions for biological phenomena (*PA* I.1, 642a25–26: "because there was no 'what it is to be' and no 'defining of the substantial being'"). They lacked a proper starting point from which to determine functional parts and a means to connect them with the essential being of an animal – they were not able to recognize functional features

17 Cf. *PA* I.5, 645b18–20. That fins are for the sake of swimming is not stated explicitly here, perhaps because this is obvious and/or has already been suggested previously: see *PA* IV.8, 684a14–15; *PA* IV.9, 685b16–23; and *PA* IV.12, 694b10–12.

18 E.g., Lennox (2001b, 124–126).

19 Cf. Bostock (2006, 62). Aristotle sometimes suggests that in natural science form and function are "almost one" (*GA* I.1, 715a4–6; 715a6: ὡς ἕν τι σχεδὸν ὑπολαβεῖν δεῖ), but I believe that a full identity between form and function only obtains in the case of fully realized forms (see section 1.1). What guides the process of generation is the potential for form that is being realized, whereas functions constitute the limits and end points of development.

as the realization of a preexisting potential for form that specifies the functions in need of realization. Aristotle's argument is that because definitions are primary, so too are explanations that proceed through such definitions.

He later explains that in nature, just as in house-building, generation is for the sake of being, and not being for the sake of generation, and that therefore the coming to be of parts should be explained by reference to the form that is being realized (*PA* I.1, 640a10–19).[20] From this he concludes that explanations in the natural sciences should be given in the following form (*PA* I.1, 640a33–35): "Therefore one should state in particular that since this is what it is to be a human being, on account of that it has these things (ἐπειδὴ τοῦτ' ἦν τὸ ἀνθρώπῳ εἶναι, διὰ τοῦτο ταῦτ' ἔχει): for it is not possible to be without those parts." Here, the definition of the substantial being of humans is implied to specify the functions a human being needs to perform for him to be the kind of being he is (i.e., what it is for a human being to be human is to be able to perform certain functions). And it is because these functions need to be realized, that he has certain parts – he has those parts that are necessary for the performance of the functions that are involved in making a human human.

Aristotle's statement that "it is not possible for a human being to be without those parts" indicates that the process responsible for the coming to be of such vital or essential parts is conditional necessity:[21] *given* that a living being has to be able to perform the functions specified in its form, it has to have such and such parts, and such and such differentiations of parts (which Aristotle defines as differences of "the more and the less" in *PA* I.4, 644b7–15), made of such and such constitutive materials, put in such and such a structure or configuration. In the context of *De Generatione Animalium*, Aristotle describes the actions of the formal nature of an animal in these cases as first using the spermatic residue that is present,[22] but then as "*making*" the required materials by processing (i.e., concocting)

[20] Empedocles evidently got this priority relation wrong, and is criticized by Aristotle for explaining "being" in terms of what happened to happen during generation (*PA* I.1, 640a19–24).

[21] See *PA* I.1, 642a7–12: "For we say nourishment is something necessary according to neither of those two modes of necessity, but because it is not possible to be without it. And this is as in the conditional type (τοῦτο δ' ἐστὶν ὥσπερ ἐξ ὑποθέσεως). For just as – since the ax must split – it is necessary for it to be hard, and if hard, then made of bronze or iron, so too since the body is an instrument (for each of the parts is for the sake of something, and likewise also the whole), it is therefore a necessity that it be of such a character and constituted from such things, if that is to be (ἀνάγκη ἄρα τοιονδὶ εἶναι καὶ ἐκ τοιωνδί, εἰ ἐκεῖνο ἔσται)." Cf. *GA* V.1, 778b15–19 and *PA* IV.10, 689a20–21.

[22] A crucial text in this context is *GA* II.6, 743a36-b8: here Aristotle explains that the formal nature makes use of heating and cooling (i.e., of material necessity) for the production of parts, which I take it describes the process of primary teleology involved in embryogenesis, in which the formal nature of an animal uses material potentials to conditionally necessitate the organs required for

the incoming food,[23] and shaping them into parts. The formal nature of an animal thus conditionally necessitates the materials it needs for the formation of parts that are necessary for the performance of necessary functions (cf. *GA* II.6, 743a36–b5).

In sum, the primary mode of explanation in biology exhibits parts to be the necessary prerequisites for the realization of functions specified by the definition of the substantial being of the animal that has those parts. The teleology operative in the coming to be and presence of such parts is primary; the necessity is conditional.

Subsidiary parts

The second category of parts – represented by the slaves in the image – consists of parts, I submit, that are not themselves necessary for the performance of vital or essential functions specified in the definition of the substantial being of a particular kind of animal. Instead, they are necessary in the sense that they *exist for the sake of* the "noblest" parts. The function of this second category of parts is thus to *contribute* to the performance of necessary vital or essential functions (without having a proper function of their own) and thereby to contribute to the well-being or living well of the animal, rather than to its living.[24] The distinction is similar to the one Aristotle makes with regard to the capacities of the soul, where the most basic capacities are said to be necessary for living, whereas the higher ones are depicted as being necessary for the sake of the good or living well (see, e.g., *DA* III.13, 435b20–21, discussed in section 2.2). Since the coming to be of these parts is said to be dependent upon and later in generation than that of the first category of vital and essential parts, I propose calling these parts "subsidiary."

In addition, I shall follow Aristotle's practice in the *De Partibus Animalium* of referring to these parts as being "non-necessary" for the widest

the realization of a potential for form. The operations of material necessity in these cases are thus entirely subsumed under the goal-directed actions of the formal nature of the animal (which makes it a form of conditional necessity) and only influence the coming to be of parts by materially constraining it.

23 In *GA* II.6, 744b27–36, Aristotle distinguishes between the spermatic residue (*GA* II.6, 744b27: ἐκ τῆς σπερματικῆς περιττώσεως) already available for the development of the embryo and the "natural food" (*GA* II.6, 744b30: ἐκ τῆς φυσικῆς τροφῆς), coming in later through the process of nutrition of the mother and later of the animal itself. There are two kinds of natural foods: the first is "nutritious" and is used for the formation of complete parts; the second is "conducive to growth" and is used for the quantitative increase of existing parts (*GA* II.6, 744b34–36). Within the animal there may be residues of both types of food (*GA* II.6, 745a1–4).

24 Cf. Aristotle's characterization of actual slaves in *Pol* I.4 as instruments of actions – not of their own, but of their masters. I thank Sean Coughlin for bringing this parallel to my attention.

kind of animals that needs to perform the function related to this part (because these parts are not immediately necessary for the performance of the particular vital or essential function in question) and as being "for the better" for the subclass of animals that do possess these extra features (because they serve the well-being or living well of the animals that have them).

Consider Aristotle's explanation of the presence of kidneys (*PA* III.7, 670b23–27):

> The kidneys are present in those that have them *not of necessity*, but *for the sake of the good and doing well.* That is, they are present, in accordance with their distinctive nature, for the residue which collects in the bladder in those animals in which a greater amount of such excrement comes about, in order that the bladder may better perform its own function.[25]

Kidneys are viscera, but unlike a heart or a liver, they are not present in all blooded animals. They are present only in those that have blooded lungs, because *they help the bladder perform its function better* by providing extra storage room for residue. Kidneys do not possess a function of their own. Apparently, Aristotle thinks that the kidneys are not themselves strictly necessary[26] for the collection of residue (only the bladder is), even though animals that have a bladder usually also have kidneys (see *PA* III.9, 671a26–671b3 and *GA* IV.4, 771a2–6, where Aristotle claims that while no animal can live without a heart or a liver or any other of the necessary parts, it can live "without a spleen or with two spleens or with one kidney"). The suggestion is thus that animals with blooded lungs could have been designed in a way that would not require the presence of kidneys; the presence of kidneys is not conditionally necessitated in the way that the presence of a bladder is. Instead, Aristotle believes that kidneys are present for the better: they assist the bladder in the collection of residues in those animals that produce larger amounts of residues and thereby contribute to their well-being.

According to the image, the matter nature uses to make subsidiary parts is second-best: presumably, it is the nutritious residue left over from the

[25] Οἱ δὲ νεφροὶ τοῖς ἔχουσιν οὐκ ἐξ ἀνάγκης, ἀλλὰ τοῦ εὖ καὶ καλῶς ἕνεκεν ὑπάρχουσιν· τῆς γὰρ περιττώσεως χάριν τῆς εἰς τὴν κύστιν ἀθροιζομένης εἰσὶ κατὰ τὴν ἰδίαν φύσιν, ἐν ὅσοις πλεῖον ὑπόστημα γίνεται τὸ τοιοῦτον, ὅπως βέλτιον ἀποδιδῷ ἡ κύστις τὸ αὑτῆς ἔργον.

[26] Similarly, Aristotle describes the presence of limbs as being "*not* among the necessities of life" (*PA* III.4, 665b21–27; 25–26: οὐκ ἔστι τῶν πρὸς τὸ ζῆν ἀναγκαίων), on account of the fact that animals continue to live after a limb is taken away or has been added; technically speaking, limbs are not part of "the necessary body" (*PA* III.4, 665b23: τοῦ ἀναγκαίου σώματος).

foodstuffs concocted for the formation of the vital and essential parts (cf. *GA* II.6, 744b26–745a1). However, since these parts are not themselves a necessary prerequisite for the performance of a necessary function, it seems that their coming to be cannot be conditionally necessitated by an internal potential for form, and is therefore not a case of primary teleology. Instead, Aristotle suggests (in *GA* II.6, 744b16–17) that it is the presence of residues that allows nature to *use* these extra materials to make parts that are serviceable to the animal's well-being.

This causal pattern of nature "using" as opposed to "making" features is especially clear in Aristotle's (otherwise puzzling) discussion of the female menses, which are said to come to be of material necessity and are then used by nature "for the better" (*GA* II.4, 738a33–b5):

> Thus the coming to be of this residue [i.e., the menses] among females is the result of necessity (ἐξ ἀνάγκης) because of the causes mentioned. Because her nature is not capable of concoction, it is necessary that residue must come to be, not only from the useless nourishment, but also in the blood vessels, and that they must overflow, when there is a full complement of [this residue, i.e., the menses] in those very fine blood vessels. And nature uses it for the sake of the better and the end for this place, for generation (ἕνεκα δὲ τοῦ βελτίονος καὶ τοῦ τέλους ἡ φύσις καταχρῆται πρὸς τὸν τόπον τοῦτον τῆς γενέσεως χάριν), in order that it may become another creature of the same kind as it would have become. For, even as it is, it is in potentiality the same in character as the body of which it is the secretion. In all females, then, residue necessarily comes to be.

Even though the presence of female menses is necessary for reproduction, Aristotle treats these menses as subsidiary parts, perhaps because they play no *active* role in reproduction and only play a role in reproduction *on occasion*.[27] The menses are not conditionally necessitated for this purpose, but come to be of material necessity. Only because they have the right material potentials (i.e., they are potentially the body from which they are secreted), nature uses them for reproduction at those times when there is also male sperma available in the womb. I shall return to this mode

27 I borrow this argument from Lennox (2001b, 186–187), who uses it to explain why Aristotle insists on calling the menses residues. The following considerations may also have played a role in Aristotle's depiction of menses as subsidiary rather than as vital or essential parts: (i) menses, as does male sperma, come to be later in life during puberty, and are thus not formed in the first generation of parts; (ii) the coming to be of the menses correlates strongly with the availability of food and the amount of exercise one performs, which suggests that they are "leftovers," rather than structural features of the body; and (iii) even though the menses are necessary for reproduction, their presence is not required all the time (as, for instance, the presence of the heart is) and they are not always used for this purpose; in fact, for the most part, they are not used for reproduction but are secreted from the female body.

of explanation, and Aristotle's comments on it in *De Partibus Animalium* book I, after my discussion of the luxury parts and secondary teleology.

"Luxury parts"

The presence of animals in the image of nature as a good housekeeper, which receive the worst of food (presumably the residues from the growth-conducive food as described in *GA* II.6, 745a1–4), suggests that there exists a second kind of subsidiary part. I believe that these parts are neither immediately necessary nor contribute to the performance of necessary vital or essential functions. Their presence rather contributes to the well-being of animals in some other way. For lack of a better term, I shall refer to these parts as "luxury parts."[28]

This distinction between two kinds of subsidiary parts is not explicit in the final section of the image (*GA* II.6, 744b24–27). There Aristotle mentions bones, sinews, hair, nails, hoofs, "and all similar parts" as all being examples of parts that are made from residues. However, in the discussion that follows Aristotle separates this group into two: while bones and sinews are formed from the same material, namely the spermatic and nutritious residue, parts like nails, hairs, hoofs, horns, beaks, the spurs of birds, etc. are made from "the nutriment that is taken in later and that is concerned with growth, which is acquired from the mother and from the outer world" (*GA* II.6, 745a3: ἐκ τῆς ἐπικτήτου τροφῆς καὶ τῆς αὐξητικῆς, ἥν τε παρὰ τοῦ θήλεος ἐπικτᾶται καὶ [τῆς] θύραθεν). From this I conclude that the "luxury parts" are made from the residue of nutriment concocted for the sake of the sustenance of parts performing necessary functions, which have already fully developed before the animal's birth (i.e., they are fully developed in the sense of being complete; they may still grow in size).[29] Since there will be a continuous supply of this kind of nutriment and hence of residues thereof throughout the animal's life (their coming to be strongly correlates with the changes in supply due to aging), it is a distinctive feature of these parts that they can come into being *after the birth* of the animal, and often can keep on growing (*GA* II.6, 745a4–19).

[28] Note that Sorabji (1980, 157–158) uses the term "luxurious" with regard to all non-necessary parts, while I use it in a more restricted manner to refer only to those parts that are not immediately necessary for the performance of functions that are specified in the definition of the substantial being of the animal, and that do not contribute to their performance.

[29] Cf. *PA* II.2, 647b27–28; *PA* II.7, 653b10–18; *PA* II.9, 655a23–27; *PA* III.2, 663b28–35; *PA* III.8, 671a1–6; *PA* IV.10, 690a6–9; *GA* I.18, 724b22–725a5; *GA* II.6, 744b12–27; and *GA* II.7, 757a21–6.

From Aristotle's discussion of these parts in *De Partibus Animalium*[30] we learn that they share two more distinctive features. First, since all these parts are earthy and uniform, Aristotle calls them "tool-like": they have to be moved "from the outside" and are therefore only produced in animals that are able (and strong enough) to use them, which is why parts such as stings, spurs, horns, and tusks are often present in males, but absent in females.[31] Their earthy and uniform nature also explains why these parts can only perform simple functions (*PA* II.1, 646b10–25) and why there is no sensation in them (*DA* III.13, 435a11–435b4). Second, most of these parts serve the function of protection, defense, or coverage: a function that is not listed among the typical functions of the soul in Aristotle's *De Anima*. Perhaps, given that for Aristotle species are eternal, and that nature, as a good housekeeper, provides food for each kind of animal, protection and defense are not strictly necessary functions to be performed by the animal in order to survive or to reproduce. Presumably, then, there is no internal potential for form that is realized through the coming to be of these defensive parts. Luxury parts are parts *actual* animals can – at least temporarily – do without.

The causal pattern underlying the production of luxury parts, which is identical to that of the subsidiary parts, is outlined in the image: Aristotle explains that nature is not in the habit of throwing away residues if it is possible to make something useful from them (*GA* II.6, 744b16–17) – an image that is reflected in the actual explanations provided in *De Partibus Animalium*. Take the example of horns. After having explained that horns

30 *PA* III.2, 663b31–35: teeth, tusks, and horns in the four-footed animals; *PA* IV.10, 687b22–24 and *PA* IV.10, 690a4–9: nails and hoofs; *PA* IV.12, 694a22–27: hard and large beaks, and spurs or claws in birds; *PA* II.14, 658b3–5: hair in human beings; *PA* IV.5, 679a28–30: ink in sepia. Cf. also *GA* V.1, 778a29–35. Aristotle's inclusion of beaks (ῥύγχη) in his second list of subsidiary parts is puzzling, since one would expect beaks to be essential parts of birds. In *PA* IV.12, 694a22–27, Aristotle suggests that it is the *differentiation* of beaks that is the result of nature using extra materials, rather than the presence of beaks themselves, which might be a more accurate characterization. In *HA* IX.32, 619a16–18, he mentions a kind of eagle whose beak keeps growing, ultimately causing the bird to die of starvation, which might imply that in their growing potential and earthy constitution, (some) beaks are similar to hair, nails, teeth, etc.

31 *PA* III.1, 661b28–662a2:

> Of the tool-like parts that are for strength and protection, nature provides each of them only or more to those animals that are able to use them, and especially to the animals able to use them most – parts such as sting, spur, horns, tusks, and any other such part there may be. And since the male is stronger and more spirited, in some cases he alone has such parts, in other cases he has them more [than the female]. For as many parts for which it is necessary that the females have them as well (ὅσα μὲν γὰρ ἀναγκαῖον καὶ τοῖς θήλεσιν ἔχειν), e.g., parts related to nourishment, they have, but they have them less; while *those related to none of the necessities* (ὅσα δὲ πρὸς μηδὲν τῶν ἀναγκαίων), they do not have. It is also on account of this that among deer, males have horns, while the females do not.

are *present* for the sake of self-defense and attack, Aristotle explains their *coming to be* as a case of the formal nature using what is present of necessity (*PA* III.2, 663b21–22): "We must say what the character of the necessary nature is, and how nature according to the account has made use of things present of necessity for the sake of something."[32] Horns are made in larger animals from the surplus of earthen material that has come to be of necessity, which is then used by the formal nature (i.e., "the nature according to the account") of those animals to make defensive parts, *because* of the kind of material potentials the available material has (*PA* III.2, 663b25–35). Aristotle does not refer to a potential for form that would have been realized by the coming to be of horns, but instead points to the kind of potentials the residues happen to have that are used for the production of horns: because those materials are hard they have a potential for defense, and this makes them suitable for the production of defensive parts.[33]

In many cases, the materials that have come to be "of necessity" will be the result of material processes (see, e.g., *PA* III.10, 673a32–b1; *PA* IV.3, 677b22–29; and *PA* IV.4, 678a3–10), which themselves take place in an animal body of conditional necessity for the sake of sustaining the parts performing necessary functions. However, these material processes lead *incidentally* to the generation of residues (which are thus technically speaking not conditionally necessitated for the sake of realizing some preexisting internal form), some of which[34] are then used by nature for (*pros* or *charin*) something – a purpose which is usually picked out in the second half of the explanation of the presence of parts such as these.

In a few cases, the materials – and sometimes even complete functional parts – are the result of material elements acting entirely of their own

[32] πῶς δὲ τῆς ἀναγκαίας φύσεως ἐχούσης τοῖς ὑπάρχουσιν ἐξ ἀνάγκης ἡ κατὰ τὸν λόγον φύσις ἕνεκά του κατακέχρηται, λέγωμεν.

[33] I take this to be the meaning of *PA* II.9, 655b2–12:

> Close to bone according to the sense of touch are also such parts as claws, solid hoofs, split hoofs, horns, and the beaks of birds. All these [parts] animals have for protection; for the whole [parts] constituted from these [uniform parts] and the ones synonymous with those parts, for instance the whole hoof and whole horn, have been constructed with a view to the safety of each of these animals . . . Of necessity all of these parts have an earthen and hard nature; *for this potential is of the defensive kind* (ὅπλου γὰρ αὕτη δύναμις).

[34] Cf. *PA* IV.2, 677a15–18:

> Sometimes nature makes use even of residues for some benefit (κατάχρηται μὲν οὖν ἐνίοτε ἡ φύσις εἰς τὸ ὠφέλιμον καὶ τοῖς περιττώμασιν), yet one should not on this account search for what something is for in every case; on the contrary, when certain things are such as they are, many other such things happen from necessity because of these (ἀλλὰ τινων ὄντων τοιούτων ἕτερα ἐξ ἀνάγκης συμβαίνει διὰ ταῦτα πολλά).

accord. This is, for instance, how eyebrows and eyelashes come to be (*PA* II.15, 658b14–25):

> The eyebrows and eyelashes are both for protection . . . The eyelids are at the ends of small blood vessels; for where the skin terminates, the small blood vessels also reach their limit. So because the moist secretions oozing are bodily, it is necessary that – unless some function of nature stops it with a view to another use – even owing to a cause such as this, hair from necessity comes to be in these locations.[35]

Eyebrows and eyelashes come to be of material necessity and because the formal nature did not *stop*[36] the flow of materials in order to use it for something else. Their presence is for (*charin*) protection – a function they seem to be able to perform due to the material potentials and the structure they have of necessity (cf. also Aristotle's account of the omentum, a fatty membrane covering the stomach and the intestines, in *PA* IV.3, 677b22–32 and my discussion of this example in section 4.3).

In short, both subsidiary and luxury parts *come to be* of material necessity, but are *present* for a function. The formal natures of animals make use of the extra materials, and it is this use that determines the function of these parts and that explains why the materials are still present. The process is teleological, because the goal-directed actions of the formal nature determine the ultimate use that is being made of the residues, but these uses are not realizations of a preexisting potential for form; rather, they "emerge" from the kind of potentials the available materials happen to have. In addition, these subsidiary and luxury parts are not strictly speaking necessary for the execution of necessary functions, but they may contribute to their performance, or allow the animal to perform a non-necessary function. In either case, the parts contribute to the well-being or the living well of the animal, rather than to its mere existence or living.

35 Αἱ δ' ὀφρύες καὶ αἱ βλεφαρίδες ἀμφότεραι βοηθείας χάριν εἰσίν . . . αἱ δὲ βλεφαρίδες ἐπὶ πέρατι φλεβίων· ᾗ γὰρ τὸ δέρμα περαίνει, καὶ τὰ φλέβια πέρας ἔχει τοῦ μήκους. Ὥστ' ἀναγκαῖον διὰ τὴν ἀπιοῦσαν ἰκμάδα σωματικὴν οὖσαν, ἂν μή τι τῆς φύσεως ἔργον ἐμποδίσῃ πρὸς ἄλλην χρῆσιν, καὶ διὰ τὴν τοιαύτην αἰτίαν ἐξ ἀνάγκης ἐν τοῖς τόποις τούτοις γίνεσθαι τρίχας.

36 Lennox (2001a, 192; 2001b, 42) translates this section as "unless some function of nature *redirects* it to another use" (emphasis is mine) and concludes (in 2001a, 192) that the necessity involved must be conditional. However, nature is not doing anything yet, but may *stop* the flow with a view to another use; this suggests that the operation of necessity cannot simply be a case of conditional necessity and primary teleology. For similar examples of the formal nature of an animal refraining from taking action in the formation of parts that seems to take place of material necessity, see *GA* I.8, 718b16–28 and *GA* I.11, 719a14–15.

Secondary teleology

Summing up, the causal processes responsible for the coming to be and presence of both kinds of subsidiary parts are teleological in Aristotle's view – since all parts are *present* for the function they perform, but they are not so without qualification. The formal nature of the animal assigns a function to (1) a flow of materials or (2) a part, but only *after* this material or even the whole part has already come into being as a result of material necessity. In the first case, nature actively *uses* materials that have come to be of material necessity for the formation of parts by redirecting, distributing, or organizing these materials, instead of throwing them away (see, e.g., *PA* II.9, 655a26–28; *PA* III.2, 664a1–3; *PA* IV.12, 694a28–694b1; *GA* III.1, 749b27–750a4). In the second case, nature passively "co-opts" entire parts that have come to be solely of material necessity. It does so simply by not intervening in the materially necessitated process, because their coming to be will be useful for the animal (see, e.g., *PA* II.15, 658b14–25 and *PA* IV.3, 677b22–32).[37] In neither case does the function the part ends up performing conditionally necessitate its coming into being, even though that function does explain why it is present (for it explains why the formal nature of the animal retained the materials) and is thus a necessary part of our knowledge of it (see *PA* II.9, 655b15–20).

Additionally, Aristotle oftentimes seems reluctant to say that these parts are *for the sake of something* (*heneka tinos*) in the more technical sense, and rather speaks in terms of something being "for" (*pros*, *charin*, *eis* or *epi*) some function.[38] Both Aristotle's cautious use of teleological language and his references to material necessity as a cause of coming to be suggest that the teleology involved is "secondary," rather than primary. While primary

[37] Devin Henry argues (in personal correspondence) that the second case, in which formal natures passively co-opt materially necessitated parts, constitutes in fact a tertiary kind of teleology, where both the matter and the actual formation of the part occur through material necessity alone and where there is therefore no sense in which that part can be said to have come to be for the sake of an end. However, Aristotle's explanations do not reflect this extra distinction. The primary distinction Aristotle draws is between (1) parts that both come to be and are present for the sake of something and (2) parts that come to be of material necessity but are present for something. The latter category also includes parts such as eyebrows and the omentum (see *PA* IV.3, 677b22–32), in which there appears to be no active role at all for formal natures in the coming to be. Even though their coming to be is thus not for the sake of something, Aristotle believes that their presence still is, for it is the goal-directed formal nature that has "allowed" the materially necessary processes to take place in the first place. Additionally, even where a formal nature actively uses materials that have come to be of material necessity, Aristotle will not say that those parts have *come to be* for the sake of something, but only that they are *present* for something. The distinction between the two types of explanation thus indicates whether a part is conditionally necessitated for the performance of a vital or essential function, or whether it is the result of nature using extra materials for a good purpose.

[38] Cf. Lennox (2001b, 291).

teleology only pertains to individual formal natures and the realization of their own form, I suggested in Chapter 1 that secondary teleology applies both to the interaction within an animal between its formal and material natures (in which the former "uses" what has been produced by the latter for something good), and to the so-called "inter-species" teleology, where living beings use what is available to them for their own benefit.

If my interpretation is right, then the material nature of an animal has a much larger and more positive influence on the generation of animals and their parts than is usually attributed to it: the material nature does not merely constrain the realizations of parts necessary for the animal's life or being;[39] it also creates possibilities for the formal nature of the animal to make additional, "non-necessary," subsidiary and luxury parts that will contribute to the animal's well-being or even produces parts independently of the actions of the formal nature, which allows these parts to grow. While primary teleological processes thus guarantee life and identity to a living being, I believe that secondary teleology is responsible for the living being's quality of life and its well-being.

In *PA* I.1, Aristotle refers to the modes of teleological explanation that pick out secondary teleology right after his example of the primary mode of explanation that picks out primary teleology discussed above (*PA* I.1, 640a33–35). If it is not possible to explain the parts an animal has as the necessary conditions of some animal being the kind of animal it is, then Aristotle believes we should rely on an alternative mode of explanation (*PA* I.1, 640a35–b4):

> If one cannot [say this], [one should say] the nearest thing, namely that it is thus either in general (because it cannot be otherwise), or that it is in a good way thus. And these things follow. And since it is such, its generation necessarily happens in this way and is such as it is. This is why this one of the parts comes to be first, then that one. And similarly in this way with regard to all things that are constituted by nature.[40]

I take this elliptical passage to mean that in cases where it is not possible to say that a particular animal cannot be without certain parts because either (i) the function that part performs is not part of the definition of the substantial being of the animal; or (ii) the part is not necessary for

39 On this "constraining" role of material necessity in the generation of animals, see Lennox (2001a, 182–204).

40 Εἰ δὲ μή, ὅτι ἐγγύτατα τούτου, καὶ ἢ ὅλως (ὅτι ἀδύνατον ἄλλως) ἢ καλῶς γε οὕτως. Ταῦτα δ' ἕπεται. Ἐπεὶ δ' ἐστὶ τοιοῦτον, τὴν γένεσιν ὡδὶ καὶ τοιαύτην συμβαίνειν ἀναγκαῖον. Διὸ γίνεται πρῶτον τῶν μορίων τόδε, εἶτα τόδε. Καὶ τοῦτον δὴ τὸν τρόπον ὁμοίως ἐπὶ πάντων τῶν φύσει συνισταμένων.

the performance of a necessary function, the explanations (as presented in *PA* I.1, 640a35–b1) will have to refer to material necessity and/or the good. The "good" indicates that the feature contributes to the well-being of the animal and hence refers to a subsidiary or luxury function.[41] As Aristotle points out next, the alternative type of explanation applies to parts that are formed at later stages in the development of the animal. The parts that are necessary for the performance of necessary functions are first in the order of generation (the phrase starting with "since it is such . . ." in *PA* I.1, 640b1–2 refers back to parts that are necessary for an animal on account of its essence; the parts that come to be first are these necessary parts). The parts that contribute to the performance of necessary functions, or whose functions are not necessary but do contribute to the well-being of the animal (and are therefore good) come to be next.

The expression "and these things follow" could refer to a third mode of explanation in which references to teleology are completely absent.[42] This type of explanation pertains to parts such as the spleen, residues, and some of the animal's affections (such as possibly eye color or pitch of voice in some kinds of animals; see *GA* V.1, 778a18–21) which do not perform any function of their own, or contribute to the function of any other part, and come to be entirely as a result of materially necessitated processes that take place during generation (see, e.g., *PA* III.7, 669b27–670a32 and *PA* IV.2, 677a15–18). The coming to be of this third type of part "follows" from the animal's material nature.

In sum, Aristotle introduces three general modes of explanation in *De Partibus Animalium* book I: explanations that pick out primary teleology; explanations that pick out secondary teleology; and, finally, explanations that pick out purely material necessity. I shall return to these three modes of

[41] I take the necessity and the good mentioned here to refer to the causes of why an animal has certain parts (i.e., as referring back to "on account of that it has these parts" in *PA* I.1, 640a34), and not to the relation between the part and the animal as such, as Code (1997, 139–142) believes. Code distinguishes three types of parts: (i) those that follow from the definition of the animal; (ii) those that are necessary, but do not follow from the definition; (iii) those that are not necessary, but are present in the animal because it is good. Under this scheme, the second category only comprises parts such as the spleen (in fact, it is the only part Code mentions as an example), which seems unlikely. The spleen is an exceptional case in Aristotle's biology (see *PA* III.6, 669b25–31 and *PA* III.7, 670a31–32): it does not have a proper function; it is present for the sake of symmetry; it comes to be of material necessity; and the relation between the spleen and the animals that have it is accidental. I also disagree with Gotthelf (1987, 189), who takes the second category to refer to those parts that are "necessary given an essential function because it makes some necessary contribution to the performance of that function." For Aristotle contributory parts are never necessary (cf. *PA* III.7, 670b23–27); if they were, such parts could never be absent, and observation shows that they sometimes are (*GA* I.4, 717a11–21).

[42] See Lennox (2001b, 135) for an overview of possible interpretations.

explanation and their application in *De Partibus Animalium* books II–IV in section 4.2.

3.3 "NECESSITY IS SPOKEN OF IN MANY WAYS"

The problem of necessity

The positive role I have attributed to material necessity in natural generation needs further argumentation, since many scholars believe that Aristotle's own discussions of the relation between teleology and necessity (in *APo* II.11, 94b27–95a3; *Ph* II.8, 198b10–199a7; *Ph* II.9, 199b34–200b11; *GC* II.11, 337a35–338b19; *PA* I.1, 639a1–642b4, and *Meta* I.3, 983a24–984b22) deny such an independent role of material necessity in the sublunary natural realm. These scholars argue that, because Aristotle denies that there is any *unqualified* necessity in the sublunary natural realm, ultimately references to *material* necessity in biological explanations need to be subsumed under, if not reduced to, the operation of *conditional* necessity.[43] Building instead on Kupreeva's analysis of necessity in Aristotle,[44] I shall here argue that this view rests upon confusions about the ways in which Aristotle uses the different concepts of necessity.

In particular, I believe that scholars have mistakenly taken Aristotle to be talking uniformly about the nature of *causality* that governs natural processes in his discussions of teleology and necessity, while in fact (or at least so I shall argue) he is often rather concerned with the nature of *causal inferences* and with the necessity that obtains between cause and effect in causal sequences (i.e., with whether cause and effect follow each other always and necessarily, or rather for the most part and contingently). In addition, it appears that in some cases they have wrongly identified Aristotle's notion of material necessity with his notion of unqualified necessity.[45]

The crux for a better understanding of Aristotle's use of the different notions of necessity lies in what Kupreeva calls a difference between a "causal use" and a "modal use" of necessity.[46] Usually, and especially when

43 Cooper (1987, 255–259); Lennox (2001a, 36n.38); Lennox (2001b, 233): "A single explanandum is explained both as necessary and for the sake of protection. The necessity is presumably conditional, but Aristotle does not make this obvious." My account is most congenial to that of Gill (1997, 146–147).

44 Kupreeva (forthcoming).

45 For the identification of material necessity with unqualified necessity, see for instance Cooper (1987, 259–60 (also 260n.20), 266); Gill (1997, 147 (also 147n.6)); and Johnson (2005, 154–155, 191).

46 A third use of necessity – which will not be discussed further in this chapter – refers to the notion of logical implication or consequence, characterizing the conclusion of an account; see, e.g., *PA* III.4, 666a16–19; 31–33.

discussing the types of cause that are operative in nature, Aristotle refers to necessity to indicate a particular type of causality. This is the causal use of necessity: it refers to the necessity of materials acting according to their own material nature in a way that is either dependent on or independent of some preexisting internal potential for form that needs to be realized (i.e., conditional versus material necessity). For instance, in *Ph* II.9, 199b34–200a15, Aristotle explicates how necessity operates in natural things[47] that are for the sake of something and concludes, without rejecting the necessity of material natures altogether, that in natural generation the necessity that is operative is not unqualified material necessity as his predecessors had thought, but rather conditional necessity (*Ph* II.9, 200a13: ἐξ ὑποθέσεως δὴ τὸ ἀναγκαῖον).

In other contexts, however, and in particular when discussing the type of demonstration required in the natural sciences as opposed to that required in the other theoretical sciences dealing with eternal objects (such as in *PA* I.1, 639b29–640a9, *Ph* II.9, 200a15–22, and *GC* II.11, 337b14–25), Aristotle uses necessity to refer to a particular type of modal relationship that holds between two either consecutive or simultaneous states of affairs in a continuous causal sequence. This is what Kupreeva calls the modal use of necessity:[48] it pertains to the question of whether a cause necessitates its effect always, or only for the most part (i.e., unqualified necessity versus material or conditional necessity). For instance, suppose that ice is the solidification of water due to a complete cessation of heat (for the example, see *APo* II.12, 95a16–21). In order to provide the appropriate form of demonstration, Aristotle wonders whether, whenever there is a complete cessation of heat, we can be sure that there will always be, without exception, the solidification of water (for Aristotle, the complete cessation of heat and the solidification of water are simultaneous processes). In other words: is the relation between "complete cessation of heat" and "solidification of water" necessary in an unqualified or in a qualified way? If the relation is one of unqualified necessity, we can infer the presence of the effect from the current presence of the cause (for the cause will always, without exception, necessitate its effect). If the relation is one of necessity *in a qualified way* (i.e., either material or conditional), then we cannot

47 Cf. *Ph* II.8, 198b11–12: ἔπειτα περὶ τοῦ ἀναγκαίου, πῶς ἔχει ἐν τοῖς φυσικοῖς. See Cooper (1987, 262).

48 Note that Kupreeva's observation that Aristotle sometimes *uses* (his familiar notions of) necessity in a *modal way* (i.e., in order to identify the type of necessity that obtains between cause and effect in causal sequences) does not require us to attribute a (contemporary) notion of "modal necessity" to Aristotle, which is a move I would resist.

draw any causal inferences from cause to effect (for it is not absolutely necessary that when the cause occurs, the effect occurs as well), but only from effect to cause (given that the effect has occurred, it is absolutely necessary that the cause has occurred as well). Aristotle is interested in the nature of the relation between cause and effect, because it determines what kind of causal inferences we can draw about different causal sequences, and these inferences play a role in his theory of scientific demonstration (see especially *APo* II.11–12, discussed in Chapter 6).

What Aristotle denies, then, when he claims in *PA* I.1 or *GC* II.11 that there is no unqualified necessity in the sublunary natural realm, is that causes in this realm are ever sufficient for their effects. This means that we can never draw any causal inferences from cause to effect about non-cyclical sublunary natural phenomena, and that our demonstrations will have to start from effects, rather than from causes.

Let me further clarify these distinctions between causal and modal uses of necessity below.

Three types of necessity: material, conditional, and unqualified

Since it is not possible to present a discussion of all the relevant texts here, I shall instead offer an overview of the three main types of necessity that Aristotle distinguishes in his natural treatises and apply this analysis to key passages in *PA* I.1, the text that is most relevant for the understanding of Aristotle's theory of explanation in biology.

First, Aristotle uses "necessity" *simpliciter* (or more specifically, the expression "of necessity," *ex anagkês*) for the most part to refer to the causal process of coming to be in which some outcomes are necessary, given the *material natures* of the things involved in that process. This is the type of necessity that is known in the scholarly literature as "material necessity." Aristotle uses this expression to refer either to a certain type of causality (in opposition, for instance, to final causality) or to a certain type of causal chain. That is, within a materially necessitated causal sequence in which the cause (e.g., a complete cessation of heat in water) is responsible for the (here, simultaneous) coming to be of the effect (e.g., the formation of ice), the expression "of necessity" signifies that it is the material nature of the subject (e.g., water), that – in the sublunary realm, for the most part – necessitates the coming to be of the effect (e.g., given the material nature of water, a body of water will solidify due to complete cessation of heat). Because material necessity does not always necessitate its effects in the sublunary realm, the inference we can draw on the basis of the presence

of the cause in such rectilinear materially necessitated processes is that the effect will only come to be as well *for the most part*, but not that it always does.

Second, "conditional necessity" usually refers to the kind of causal necessitation involved in primary teleology, in which the things that come to be do so because they are necessary for the realization of an end, which is itself specified by the definition of the substantial being of something. When used in reference to a causal chain, it indicates that the coming to be of the prior event in that causal chain is conditional upon the necessity of the posterior, i.e., the effect and final cause, to come to be. The direction of necessity here works from the (prior) necessitating causes to the effect (i.e., from the possession of a form in potentiality to the realization of that form), although what chronologically comes to be last (i.e., the end that constitutes the final cause) is prior in explanation. In those cases where conditional necessity obtains, the coming to be or presence of the prior (e.g., a foundation) is necessary *only on the condition* that the posterior (e.g., a house) is to be realized. Inferences in these cases are one-directional: the coming to be or presence of the prior does not always necessitate the coming to be or presence of the posterior, and hence one can only draw the inference that if the posterior has come to be or is present, then necessarily the prior has also come to be or is present. In other words, the chronological end point of the causal chain provides the starting point for the inference to be used in a demonstration or explanation.

Finally, Aristotle mostly uses the expression "unqualified necessity" to refer to the "absolutely" necessary relation between the prior and the posterior in a consecutive causal sequence, in which the prior always, without exception, necessitates the posterior, because the occurrence of the posterior is necessary without qualification – the process of necessitation cannot be stopped by the interference of other factors. This allows for inferences from the prior to the posterior in those cases where unqualified necessity obtains (for instance, in mathematics, or in cyclical natural processes): if the prior (e.g., clouds) comes to be, then necessarily and without exception the posterior (e.g., rain) will come to be too. As we would say, the prior in these cases is both necessary and sufficient for the coming to be and presence of the posterior. In cyclical processes, the inference works in both directions, because the causal nexus is reciprocal.[49]

In some cases, Aristotle also uses the expression "unqualified" to indicate that the necessity responsible for some outcome does not presuppose and is

[49] Cf. Charles (1988, 14–17).

Table 3.2 *Causal and modal uses of necessity*

Necessity	Causal use	Modal use
Material	Outcomes are necessary, *given the material natures* of the things involved in that process; materials act according to their own natures.	Necessity between two items in a materially necessitated causal chain is qualified, because the cause necessitates its effect *for the most part.*
Conditional	The coming to be of antecedents is necessary, *given that the end is to come to be*; formal natures use materials acting according to their own natures for the realization of a preexisting internal potential for form.	Necessity between two items in a teleologically caused chain is qualified, because the antecedents necessitate the end that constitutes the final cause for the most part.
Unqualified	Equals material ("unconditional") necessity; materials act according to their own natures independently of ends that are to be realized.	Necessity between two items in an eternal/cyclical causal chain is unqualified, because the cause necessitates its effect always and without exception.

not dependent on the presence of a potential for form that is to be realized, and that in that sense the necessity involved is "simple" or "unconditional," as opposed to "conditional" (see for instance *Ph* II.9, 199b34–200a15). This use, however, is less prevalent than the modal one. Unqualified necessity, understood as a means of qualifying the necessity between two events in a causal chain, cannot as easily be identified with material necessity, which indicates primarily a type of causality. This is even more so, because most materially necessitated processes in the sublunary realm are rectilinear and allow for exceptions (the effect need not always come about), while unqualified necessity indicates that effect follows cause necessarily and always.

A fourth type of necessity, which I shall just mention here for the sake of completeness, is what Aristotle calls "enforced necessity," which causes things to behave against nature and inclination. Aristotle mentions it in *APo* II.11, 95a1–2 (ἡ δὲ βίᾳ ἡ παρὰ τὴν ὁρμήν), but the notion does not seem to play a major role in Aristotle's natural treatises. For a schematic outline of the three main uses of necessity,[50] see Table 3.2.

[50] It is unclear how exactly Aristotle's list of five types of necessity in *Meta* V.5 is supposed to map on to his treatment of necessity in the natural treatises; for suggestions, see Cooper (1987, 260n.20) and Gill (1997, 147n.6).

These distinctions between "causal" and "modal" uses of necessity, and between material and unqualified necessity, are important, for it is only unqualified necessity in a modal sense that Aristotle explicitly denies applies to rectilinear natural processes in the sublunary realm. Aristotle explains the difference between a conditionally necessary causal chain and an absolutely necessary causal chain in the following text (*GC* II.11, 337b14–25):

> If it is the case that the coming to be of something earlier is necessary if a later thing is to be, e.g., if a house, then foundations, and if that [i.e., foundations], then clay, does it follow that if there have come to be foundations, a house too must necessarily come to be? Or can we not yet say this, unless it is necessary without qualification that the latter itself come to be? If that is the case, then it is necessary that the house also comes to be when the foundation has come to be: for such was the relation of the earlier to the later, namely that if that one is to be, necessarily the other one will be first. If, accordingly, it is necessary for the later one to come to be, it is necessary also for the earlier one; and if the earlier one comes to be, it is accordingly necessary for the later one [to come to be too] – but not because of the earlier one, but because it was assumed that it was necessary that it would exist. So in those cases where it is necessary for the later one to exist, there is conversion, and it is always necessary, if the earlier has come to be, that the later should also come to be.[51]

The distinction is this: in the case of conditionally necessitated processes, of which house-building is a standard example (see *Meta* VII.17, 1041a23–30, *APo* II.12, 95b32–38, and *DA* I.1, 403b3–7), the coming to be of the prior (i.e., the foundations) is necessary *if* the posterior (i.e., the house) is to be, but it is not the case that once the prior has come to be, the posterior necessarily will come to be as well (i.e., the presence of foundations does not guarantee the presence of the house). Only if a process of coming to be is absolutely necessary – for instance, when we posit that the relationship between foundations and a house is necessary "without qualification" – would the causal inference "if there are foundations, the house will be as well" be valid. Aristotle explains that this kind of unqualified necessity only holds for things that are eternal and/or are subjected to eternal cyclical processes (such as the movement of the heavens, the evaporation cycle, and

[51] Εἰ δὴ τὸ πρότερον ἀνάγκη γενέσθαι, εἰ τὸ ὕστερον ἔσται, οἷον εἰ οἰκία, θεμέλιον, εἰ δὲ τοῦτο, πηλόν, ἆρ᾽ οὖν καὶ εἰ θεμέλιος γέγονεν, ἀνάγκη οἰκίαν γενέσθαι; ἢ οὐκέτι, εἰ μὴ κἀκεῖνο ἀνάγκη γενέσθαι ἁπλῶς· εἰ δὲ τοῦτο, ἀνάγκη καὶ θεμελίου γενομένου γενέσθαι οἰκίαν· οὕτω γὰρ ἦν τὸ πρότερον ἔχον πρὸς τὸ ὕστερον, ὥστ᾽ εἰ ἐκεῖνο ἔσται, ἀνάγκη ἐκεῖνο πρότερον. Εἰ τοίνυν ἀνάγκη γενέσθαι τὸ ὕστερον, καὶ τὸ πρότερον ἀνάγκη· καὶ εἰ τὸ πρότερον, καὶ τὸ ὕστερον τοίνυν ἀνάγκη, ἀλλ᾽ οὐ δι᾽ ἐκεῖνο, ἀλλ᾽ ὅτι ὑπέκειτο ἐξ ἀνάγκης ἐσόμενον. Ἐν οἷς ἄρα τὸ ὕστερον ἀνάγκη εἶναι, ἐν τούτοις ἀντιστρέφει, καὶ ἀεὶ τοῦ προτέρου γενομένου ἀνάγκη γενέσθαι τὸ ὕστερον.

the cycle of air; see *GC* II.11, 337b30–338a18). In contrast, conditional necessity holds for the generation of animals, which is a sublunary natural process that is rectilinear and that concerns beings whose substances are perishable (*GC* II.11, 338b6–11; 338b9–11: "For it is not necessary if your father came to be, that you come to be, but if you came to be, then he came to be").

In short, in the sublunary realm, Aristotle says that we cannot simply draw inferences from the existence of the prior to the existence of the posterior – especially not if those inferences are to play a role in scientific demonstration. The difference between the two domains is that in the realm of the heavenly bodies, where all causal chains are eternal and cyclical, the prior always necessitates the posterior (i.e., sequences are necessary without qualification); while in the changing, sublunary realm the prior necessitates the posterior only for the most part (either by material or by conditional necessity). Aristotle needs to clarify these distinctions, because the validity of demonstrations – especially in the natural sciences – depends on the correct representation of the necessary relation between items in a causal sequence in those demonstrations.[52] The problem of the structure of demonstration in the natural sciences is central to Aristotle's discussion of teleology and necessity in *PA* I.1, to which I shall now turn.

Teleology, necessity, and demonstration in PA *I.1*

The discussion of demonstration in the natural sciences in *PA* I.1, and how it is different from demonstration in the other theoretical sciences (that deal with non-perishable substances), is itself part of a critique of the modes of explanation employed by Aristotle's predecessors, who attempted to trace back all their explanations to necessity (*PA* I.1, 639b21). The problem Aristotle finds with the materialist explanations of his predecessors, however, is not so much that this type of explanation is wrong, or that the type of causality picked out in these explanations has no independent role to play in the sublunary natural world, but rather that they had not made the right distinctions between the ways in which necessity in nature is spoken of (*PA* I.1, 639b22: οὐ διελόμενοι ποσαχῶς λέγεται τὸ ἀναγκαῖον).[53] Aristotle puts

[52] See Charles (1988, 7–8) and Leunissen (2010). For the idea that demonstrations of natural processes are to reflect the actual order of causation in the world, see *APo* II.11, 94b23–26; *APo* II.12 and *APo* II.16.

[53] Cf. Aristotle's criticism of Democritus and the natural philosophers in *PA* I.1, 641a5–8: "He spoke way too simply . . . So is also the way in which the natural philosophers speak of the generations and causes of configuration". According to Aristotle, Democritus thought that things are what they

forward two types of necessity that both pertain to natural beings: "unqualified necessity" and "conditional necessity" (*PA* I.1, 639b22–29):

The [necessity] that is unqualified belongs to the eternal things, and the one that is conditional also belongs to all things that come to be (ὑπάρχει δὲ τὸ μὲν ἁπλῶς τοῖς ἀϊδίοις, τὸ δ' ἐξ ὑποθέσεως καὶ τοῖς ἐν γενέσει πᾶσιν), as well as to things produced, such as to a house and to any other such thing. For it is necessary that such material is present if there is to be a house or any other end: and it is necessary that first this comes to be and is changed, and next [that] that [comes to be and is changed], and so step by step up to the end and that for the sake of which each thing comes to be and is. It is the same way too for things that come to be by nature.

In this passage, Aristotle differentiates the domains of the natural world[54] according to the type of necessity that pertains to them, and thereby introduces a special type of necessity into the domain of generated natural beings. While unqualified necessity holds of the eternal, natural realm of the heavenly bodies, among the *generated* natural beings there is *also* a kind of necessity present, namely conditional necessity (this is what I take to be the most natural reading of the particle *kai* in *PA* I.1, 639b23). Aristotle then gives a characterization of conditional necessity in terms of the material that has to be present first, and the changes that have to take place, if some (natural or artificial) end is to be realized.

The aim of this passage is not to deny the existence of material necessity in the sublunary realm, but to introduce a special kind of necessity in that realm, which is conditional, and which involves a special form of causal inference. The same holds for Aristotle's claim in *PA* I.1, 642a1–7 that there is a *third* type of necessity present in things that partake of generation, thereby adding conditional necessity to the two types of

are in virtue of their configuration and color. Against this theory, Aristotle claims that although, for instance, a corpse has the same shape as a human being, we would not call a corpse a human being, except homonymously, because it cannot perform the functions that belongs to a human. The same holds for bronze or wooden hands, a drawing of a physician, or a flute made of stone: we do not call them a hand, a physician, or a flute, because they cannot perform their proper functions (*PA* I.1, 640b29–641a5). Aristotle thus stresses that what something is, is ultimately determined by the function(s) it performs. In Aristotle's view, Democritus' theory is not specific enough or is stated "too simply," because he failed to connect the notion of form to characteristic functions. The deficiency in the account of the natural philosophers is that they answer the question "By what powers is something crafted?" only in terms of the nature of the elements, but neglect to explain for the sake of what the elements move the way they do (*PA* I.1, 641a8–13). This is why Aristotle concludes that these natural philosophers "did not speak correctly" (*PA* I.1, 641a14).

54 Pace Gotthelf (1987, 170–171), I believe that the contrast between the eternal and the generated is a contrast *within* the realm of the natural, and not between mathematics and the science of nature; this is clear from the introduction of the issue (*PA* I.1, 639b20: Τὸ δ' ἐξ ἀνάγκης οὐ πᾶσιν ὑπάρχει τοῖς κατὰ φύσιν ὁμοίως).

necessity introduced in *APo* II.11. 94b37–95a2,[55] which are "natural" or material necessity (*APo* II.11, 94b37–95a1: ἡ μὲν γὰρ κατὰ φύσιν καὶ τὴν ὁρμήν) and "enforced" necessity (*APo* II.11, 95a1–2: ἡ δὲ βίᾳ ἡ παρὰ τὴν ὁρμήν).[56] He does not exclude the presence of these other two types of necessity in nature,[57] nor does he reduce all necessity in nature to conditional necessity.[58] All Aristotle says here is that it must be this third type of necessity that is meant by "those who speak of 'from necessity.'"

Aristotle's explication of conditional necessity in *PA* I.1, 639b26–29, is important in this context, because it shifts the focus from causality to causal inferences: it specifies the causal sequence and the type of inference that belongs to (non-cyclical) generations of sublunary natural things. The "mistake" Aristotle's predecessors made is to have neglected the conditionality of necessity pertaining to all generated things, both natural and artificial. Thus, when giving explanations in terms of necessity with regard to (non-cyclical) *generated* natural things, one should not make the mistake of thinking that the necessity of the causal sequence is absolute (as is the case in eternal natural processes). That is, one should not think that the prior *necessitates without exception* the coming to be of the posterior, but rather acknowledge the fact that the prior is merely a necessary precondition of the posterior.

The distinction between the necessity involved in different kinds of causal sequences is relevant for the discussion of demonstration proper, to which Aristotle turns next (*PA* I.1, 639b29–640a9):

However, the mode of demonstration and of necessity is different in the natural and the theoretical sciences. These have been discussed elsewhere. For the starting

55 Rather than the five different meanings of necessity discussed in *Meta* V.5, pace Charles (1988, 8–10) and Cooper (1987, 259n.19).

56 Interestingly, Aristotle connects these two types of necessity with teleology in *APo* II.11, but without introducing his notion of conditional necessity yet. Aristotle provides two examples, illustrating how "it is possible for the same thing to be both for the sake of something and from necessity" (*APo* II.11, 94b27–28). Both examples concern phenomena (i.e., light shining through lanterns in *APo* II.11, 94b28–31, and thunder in *APo* II.11, 94b31–32) in which the necessity involved is material necessity (which is not conditional upon the end for the sake of which the phenomenon is said to occur), and in which the proclaimed purposes of the phenomena do not seem to be the *proper* ends or final causes of these phenomena. (I believe that these examples illustrate secondary teleology, in which a function or use is imposed by an external goal-directed agent on things that happen of material necessity.) At least in this context, Aristotle allows material necessity to operate independently and at the same time to serve some (secondary) purpose.

57 Lennox's translations of this passage (2001b, 7: "but it is especially in things that . . ." and 2001a, 186: "but the third sort *is* present in those things which come to be") are misleading, as they suggest that the two types of necessity mentioned first do not exist in things that partake of generation. The Greek, on the other hand, does not exclude this possibility, but rather emphasizes that in things that partake of generation there is a *third* type of necessity.

58 As Balme (1972, 76–84, 100; 1987c, 283–5) holds.

point is in some [i.e., the theoretical sciences] what is, but in others [i.e., the natural sciences] what will be. For: "since health or man is such, it is necessary that this is or comes to be," but not "since this is or has come to be, that of necessity is or will be." Nor is it possible to connect the necessity in such a demonstration to eternity, so as to say, "since this is, therefore that is." These matters too have been determined elsewhere, namely in what sorts of things [this kind of necessity] is present, what kind of processes convert, and for what cause.[59]

Demonstrations have to pick out the right kind of necessity: for most generated natural beings, causal sequences from the prior to the posterior can be interrupted (for the necessity is not connected to eternity), which is why one can only draw inferences from what has already come to be to its antecedent causes. The starting point for demonstrations in the natural sciences[60] is thus the posterior, or the realized end, from which its necessary antecedents can be deduced. The inference in natural demonstrations is one-directional from the end to the preconditions of the end, and the necessity to be picked out is thus conditional. For the objects of the theoretical sciences, where the necessity can be connected to eternity and where the sequences of causes convert, the inferences work also in the other direction: if this is, then that too will be.[61] For a demonstration to be valid, it has to capture the "direction" of the inference in the right way.

At the end of *PA* I.1, Aristotle offers an example of what such a demonstration in the natural sciences should look like (*PA* I.1, 642a32–642b2):

59 Ἀλλ' ὁ τρόπος τῆς ἀποδείξεως καὶ τῆς ἀνάγκης ἕτερος ἐπί τε τῆς φυσικῆς καὶ τῶν θεωρητικῶν ἐπιστημῶν. Εἴρηται δ' ἐν ἑτέροις περὶ τούτων. Ἡ γὰρ ἀρχὴ τοῖς μὲν τὸ ὄν, τοῖς δὲ τὸ ἐσόμενον· ἐπεὶ γὰρ τοιόνδε ἐστὶν ἡ ὑγίεια ἢ ὁ ἄνθρωπος, ἀνάγκη τόδ' εἶναι ἢ γενέσθαι, ἀλλ' οὐκ ἐπεὶ τόδ' ἐστὶν ἢ γέγονεν, ἐκεῖνο ἐξ ἀνάγκης ἐστὶν ἢ ἔσται. Οὐδ' ἔστιν εἰς ἀΐδιον συναρτῆσαι τῆς τοιαύτης ἀποδείξεως τὴν ἀνάγκην, ὥστε εἰπεῖν, ἐπεὶ τόδε ἐστίν, ὅτι τόδε ἐστίν. Διώρισται δὲ καὶ περὶ τούτων ἐν ἑτέροις, καὶ ποίοις ὑπάρχει καὶ ποῖα ἀντιστρέφει καὶ διὰ τίν' αἰτίαν.

60 Normally, Aristotle depicts natural science as being itself one of the theoretical sciences (see Lennox 2001b, 129; *Meta* VI.1, 1025b18–1026a23 and *PA* I.1, 641b11), and distinguishes the theoretical sciences from the practical and productive ones. In this passage, however, Aristotle singles out that part of the science of being that is concerned with *generated* things from that which is concerned with *eternal* things. I believe that this reading is most consistent with the preceding distinctions between the natural generated beings on the one hand and the eternal (natural) beings on the other. Natural science thus has to be understood in the narrow sense of the science that deals with natural beings whose substances are perishable. For alternative interpretations, see Lloyd (1996, 29), and Johnson (2005, 162–163).

61 Cf. *Ph* II.9, 200a15–22, where Aristotle discusses the validity of inferences from the prior to the posterior (and the other way around) in causal sequences dealing with mathematical objects on the one hand, and natural, generated objects on the other hand. In some sense, inferences pertaining to mathematical objects are *similar* to inferences pertaining to natural, generated things: for in both cases, the causal sequence and the necessitation are linear and one-directional, and hence the inference works in one direction only. What is *different* in the two cases is that the starting point and the end point of the inference are reversed (this is also what the different uses in tense in this passage point to): in mathematics, the inference is from the prior to the posterior, while in natural generation the inference is from the posterior to the prior. See also Gotthelf (1987, 197–198).

One should give demonstrations in the following way: for example, breathing *exists* for the sake of this [i.e., cooling], while it [i.e., cooling] *comes to be* from necessity because of these. But "necessity" sometimes means that if this is to be "that for the sake of which" then these must be so [i.e., by conditional necessity]; but at other times it means that things are so in respect of their character and nature [i.e., by material necessity]. For it is necessary for the hot to go out and come in again upon meeting resistance, and for the air to flow in – that is already necessary. But because the heat meets internally with resistance, the reason for the entrance of the air from outside is in [for this use of ἐν compare *Ph* IV.3, 210a21] the cooling.[62]

In this example, Aristotle illustrates the structure of demonstrations in the natural sciences, but also, and perhaps more importantly, acknowledges explicitly the explanatory power of references to both conditional necessity and the type of necessity rooted in the material nature of elements. Breathing is for the sake of something, namely cooling, and an animal will have to be able to cool itself if it is to live (cf. *PA* III.6, 669a11–13); hence the organs for cooling come to be by conditional necessity. However, the circulation of air itself does not occur for the sake of something, nor is it conditional upon some end: it happens in accordance with and due to the element's natures and powers. As Aristotle puts it: the circulation of air is *already* (i.e., not conditionally, but materially) necessary (*PA* I.1, 642a36: ἤδη ἀναγκαῖόν), and can subsequently be used by the formal nature of an animal for a secondary purpose (such as voice: see *DA* II.8, 420b13–20). In sum, if Aristotle's own example[63] of an explanation of a natural phenomenon refers to both conditional and material necessity, we should expect his actual explanations to include references to material necessity as well.[64]

62 Δεικτέον δ' οὕτως, οἷον ὅτι ἔστι μὲν ἡ ἀναπνοὴ τουδὶ χάριν, τοῦτο δὲ γίγνεται διὰ τάδε ἐξ ἀνάγκης. Ἡ δ' ἀνάγκη ὁτὲ μὲν σημαίνει ὅτι εἰ ἐκεῖνο ἔσται τὸ οὗ ἕνεκα, ταῦτα ἀνάγκη ἐστὶν ἔχειν, ὁτὲ δ' ὅτι ἔστιν οὕτως ἔχοντα καὶ πεφυκότα. Τὸ θερμὸν γὰρ ἀναγκαῖον ἐξιέναι καὶ πάλιν εἰσιέναι ἀντικροῦον, τὸν δ' ἀέρα εἰσρεῖν. Τοῦτο δ' ἤδη ἀναγκαῖόν ἐστιν. Τοῦ ἐντὸς δὲ θερμοῦ ἀντικόπτοντος, ἐν τῇ ψύξει τοῦ θύραθεν ἀέρος ἡ εἴσοδος. Cf. *PA* I.1, 642a13–15.

63 However, as Lennox (2001b, 151) points out, this example does not exactly represent Aristotle's own account of the mechanics of breathing as he describes it in *Juv* 27, 480a25-b4. Of course, it is not uncommon for Aristotle to use examples that draw from common beliefs, rather than from his own theories (cf. Balme 1972, 101), but this does not mean that Aristotle is not committed to the general pattern of explanation – especially since he is giving an example of good practice. Bos and Ferwerda (2008, 189–196) suggest that the main subtext for Aristotle's example is Plato's account of respiration in *Ti* 78d and 79d: under this interpretation, Aristotle acknowledges the causal influence of material necessity in the process of respiration as described by Plato, but corrects him for having neglected teleology: ultimately, it is the function of cooling that explains why breathing takes place in animals.

64 Cf. Cooper (1987, 257–258).

3.4 CONCLUSION

Building upon key passages in Aristotle's natural treatises, this chapter has outlined an interpretation of Aristotle's theory of teleological explanation in *De Partibus Animalium* book I that integrates both conditional and material necessity, and that lays out three basic modes of explanation for biological phenomena.

I have argued that in his explanations Aristotle picks out (roughly speaking) two types of teleology that go together with two types of necessity: primary teleology with conditional necessity, and secondary teleology with material necessity. Parts are always *present* in the animals that have them because of the function they perform, but their *coming to be* is due to either one of two different kinds of necessity in interaction with different kinds of actions performed by the formal nature of an animal. Sometimes nature conditionally necessitates the coming to be of the part's constitutive materials and generates that part; at other times it uses materials that are already available due to material necessity for something good, or simply lets materially necessitated processes take their own course in the formation of structures, because they are beneficial for that animal. All these processes are teleological, but not in the same way, and accordingly, explanations of biological phenomena will have to pick out either primary or secondary teleology. In a small number of cases, material necessity will cause the generation of non-functional features that are not discarded by the formal nature of an animal; explanations of these cases will therefore only pick out material necessity, constituting the third and final mode of explanation.

The integration of material necessity in secondary teleological explanations lends support to the view that Aristotle's theory of teleology was not developed for the sake of replacing the materialist explanations of his predecessors.[65] For Aristotle, material natures usually operate under the constraints of teleology, but not always, and not every feature of an animal is a realization of a preexisting internal potential for form. When Aristotle restricts unqualified necessity to the eternal realm of the heavenly bodies he does not thereby deny the existence of material necessity in the sublunary realm. He rather points out that in causal sequences that take place in the heavenly realm the prior always necessitates the coming to be of the posterior, because the coming to be of the posterior is necessary "without qualification." In the sublunary realm the posterior in a causal sequence is (unless the sequence is circular) never necessary "without qualification,"

[65] First put forward by Sauvé Meyer (1992, 794–795; 820–825).

whether it is necessitated by conditional necessity or by material necessity – a fact that has repercussions for the structure of demonstrations to be offered in the natural sciences.

The role of material necessity in the sublunary realm is therefore not confined to the negative part of constraining the realizations of ends in natural beings. It also has a more positive role to play, in that it provides extra possibilities – "extra" in the sense that the possibilities are not already given with the soul a certain kind of animal possesses – for the realization of features that may contribute to the animal's well-being. Nature does more than just provide the means for living – if possible, it also provides the means for living well.

CHAPTER 4

Explaining parts of animals: the practice of teleological explanation in the De Partibus Animalium *II–IV*

4.0 INTRODUCTION

This chapter investigates Aristotle's application of his theory of natural teleology in the actual explanations he provides in the biological treatises. My discussion draws mainly on the heuristics and explanations Aristotle displays in *De Partibus Animalium* II–IV, but I complement this account where appropriate or necessary with examples from the other biological treatises.

I shall first, in section 4.1, provide some introductory remarks about the organization of *De Partibus Animalium* books II–IV and Aristotle's basic heuristic strategies for the formulation of predominantly teleological explanations. In section 4.2, I turn to those cases in books II–IV where Aristotle's usual heuristic strategies prove insufficient and where he engages in a series of inferences building upon the postulation of a teleological principle, such as "nature does nothing in vain," before or while formulating the actual explanation. I argue that these principles are part of Aristotle's method of discovery and that they function predominantly as heuristic tools for the identification of causally relevant features when these are not immediately discernible. Note that I am *not* making the claim here that Aristotle's entire theory of natural teleology serves a heuristic function;[1] instead I suggest that his *use of teleological principles* is best characterized as serving such a function. I take it that the (final) causes these principles help discover are all non-eliminable features of the biological world, which are realized through the goal-directed actions of the formal natures of animals. Finally, in section 4.3, I present an overview of the basic patterns of explanation Aristotle uses in books II–IV to account for the presence, absence, and differentiations of animal parts and specify the causal and explanatory role of final causes therein.

[1] For this view, see Wieland (1975), Nussbaum (1978), and Sorabji (1980); for my realist interpretation of Aristotle's theory of natural teleology, see also Chapter 1.

Together these sections provide a comprehensive account of the structure, use, and explanatory force of teleological explanations in Aristotle's biology, both those that involve the application of teleological principles and those that refer immediately to final causes.

4.1 THE ORGANIZATION AND HEURISTIC METHODS OF *DE PARTIBUS ANIMALIUM* BOOKS II–IV

The project and organization of De Partibus Animalium *books II–IV*

The focus in *De Partibus Animalium* is, as the title of the treatise indicates, not on individual animal kinds, but rather on the distribution and configuration of their parts.[2] There are no entries on specific animal kinds, and instead of naming all the individual animal kinds with which a certain presence, absence, or differentiation of a part correlates, Aristotle refers to the cluster of *differentiae* that characterize the entire group of animals or to the name[3] of the widest class of animals that have the part. The precise extension of the correlation between features and the animals that have them is usually left open.[4] Species are only singled out when they exhibit unique differentiations or otherwise anomalous features (note that there are relatively few animal species that are mentioned by name in *De Partibus Animalium*).[5]

This focus on parts guides both the overall organization of *De Partibus Animalium* and the organization of the explanations themselves. Aristotle seems to follow two principles of exposition. First, following the teleological hierarchy between parts, he discusses – part by part – first the uniform parts, then the non-uniform parts. Second, the discussion of the non-uniform, external parts takes human physiology as a starting point (*PA* II.10, 656a9–14; cf. *HA* I.6, 491a19–26; for the internal parts Aristotle is forced to rely on analogies with animals close to human beings; see *HA* I.16, 494b19–24), and works from top to bottom: separating the blooded animals from the

[2] This does not mean that the animals to which the parts belong are unimportant: parts are only truly (and not merely homonymously) parts when they belong to a living being and are able to function for the sake of its life and well-being. Parts and their differentiations are explained first and foremost in terms of the functional contribution they make to the animal as a whole.

[3] Sometimes this class has no preexisting name, as is the case with "lung-possessors": *PA* III.6, 669b10–13 (669b10: ἀλλ' ἀνώνυμον τὸ κοινὸν ἐπ' αὐτῶν).

[4] Cf. Lennox (2001a, 70n.31).

[5] For instance, the Indian ass and the oryx are singled out for having only one horn, while the majority of animals with horns have two (*PA* III.2, 663a21–23). Cf. Balme (1987b, 88) on the famous case of the mole.

bloodless, Aristotle first covers all the parts located on or around the head, then the parts located around the heart, and finally the limbs.

The organization of *De Partibus Animalium* books II–IV runs as follows. Aristotle opens book II with an elaborate and general discussion of the *uniform* parts (*PA* II.1–9), focusing on their teleological relationships to other parts, their distinctions (based on whether they have soft, moist, dry or solid material potentials), their role in the animal's body, and their influence on the animal's character. He then moves on to a discussion of the *external, non-uniform* parts. First (in *PA* II.10-III.2), Aristotle discusses the non-uniform parts that are located on the *head* of blooded animals, such as the organs of sense perception, kinds of eye protection (eyelids, eyelashes, and eyebrows), and the mouth. Next (in *PA* III.3–VI.4), moving down from the neck, Aristotle turns to a discussion of all the *internal, non-uniform* parts located around the *heart,* such as the heart and blood vessels, lungs, liver, and other viscera. At this point, Aristotle moves to a discussion of the *external and internal non-uniform* parts of *bloodless* animals (mainly the crustaceans and insects; *PA* VI.5–9), limiting his discussion to the features that are different in the bloodless animals from the blooded ones. Having discussed the bloodless animals, Aristotle returns to his exposition of the *remaining external, non-uniform parts* of blooded animals (*PA* VI.9–13). Here Aristotle's organization of his discussion of parts is more intrinsically connected to the kinds of animals that have those parts: he first discusses the parts left unexplained in the live-bearing animals, then in the egg-laying animals, and finally in birds and fish. Aristotle ends his explanation of parts by a brief discussion of animals that dualize between two natures, such as dolphins, whales, seals, bats, and the Libyan ostrich (*PA* IV.13–14). At the end of his treatise, Aristotle sums up the general aims of his investigation in *De Partibus Animalium* and refers forward to the project recorded in *De Generatione Animalium* (*PA* IV.14, 697b26–29): "About the parts, then, the cause owing to which each is present in the animals has been stated, of each of the animals in turn; these things having been determined, the next step is to go through the facts about their generation."

Within this larger organizational structure, the actual explanations provided observe the following format:[6]

1. Identification of part P;
2. Identification of the widest kind of animals (A_{1-n}) to which P belongs;

[6] For explicit statements about Aristotle's explanatory project, see the references in Lennox (2001a, 5) and *PA* II.7, 653b9–18; *PA* III.4, 667b12–14; and *PA* IV.14, 697b27–30.

3. Explanation of why P belongs to each A that has P, by identifying the cause(s) of the coming to be and presence of P in A;
4. Explanation of why P is absent in those animals in which the presence of P could have been expected;
5. Identification of the differentiations of P (ΔP);
6. Identification of the widest kind of animals (B_{1-n}) to which ΔP belongs;
7. Explanation of why P is differentiated the way it is in each kind of animal that has P, by identifying the cause(s) of the differentiation of P (ΔP).

The investigation of why a certain part is absent (mentioned in the list above as item 4) is usually prompted by some form of comparative observation or analogical reasoning.[7] The question why snakes have no feet, for instance, is prompted by comparative observation: all blooded land-dwellers possess feet, except for snakes (which belong to this wider kind of blooded land-dwellers), and hence this absence needs to be explained. The investigation into the absence of outer ears in birds is prompted by analogical reasoning: all human beings and four-footed live-bearing and egg-laying animals have outer ears, and are blooded, just like birds. And given that birds do have auditory channels, it is reasonable to expect birds to have outer ears as well. In short, when an animal lacks a part that has been observed to be present among all the other kinds of animals that belong to the same wider class, or when an animal only possesses one of the two parts that are usually observed to be present together, this immediately leads to the question of why this particular animal lacks the part in question.

I shall discuss Aristotle's heuristics for the discovery of the causes of such "significant" absences in section 4.3; for the present purposes it will suffice to outline Aristotle's basic strategies for the formulation of explanations of the presence and differentiation of parts.

Aristotle's basic heuristic strategies

Aristotle is not usually very explicit about his methods for the discovery of the causally relevant features that are to be picked out in his explanations, but his remarks indicate that for the most part he relies on the following two strategies.

First, causally relevant features, and in particular functions, can usually be detected by visual inspection of the part in question.[8] This is because

7 Cf. Lennox (2001a, 214).
8 See also Bolton (1997, 118) on final causes being "better known to us."

a function is often simply the (regular and good or beneficial) "work" performed by a part when used. Aristotle frequently refers to observations in the presentation of his findings in the biological works: external parts are available for immediate perceptual scrutiny (see, e.g., *PA* II.8, 653b30–31; *PA* III.14, 674a12–13; *PA* IV.10, 689a20–21; cf. *HA* I.6, 491a23 and *GA* II.4, 740a5–6), whereas the causal features of internal parts can be revealed through dissections (see, e.g., *PA* IV.5, 679b35–680a3; *PA* II.7, 652b3–6; *PA* III.4, 667b10–13; *PA* III.5, 668b27–30; and *HA* I.17, 497a30–35).

Second, there are cases where the explanation of the presence of a part involves nothing more than to link it to one of the functions already specified in the definition of the animal's substantial being, and then exhibit it as a necessary prerequisite for the realization of that function. Once the full and real (as opposed to the nominal) definition of an animal has been established through division, the per se functions and the parts that are necessary for their realization follow from that definition. For instance, "animal" is defined by its perceptive capacity, and from this, Aristotle claims, it follows that it necessarily has a heart, the primary perceiver (*PA* III.4, 666a34–5), and flesh, the organ of touch, which is the primary mode of perception (*PA* II.8, 653b22–23). The causally relevant features in these cases (i.e., the form of the animal and the functions it specifies) are already known, and Aristotle only needs to identify which part performs the function in question.

The use of observations and definitions is complemented by either one of the following two "search strategies": Aristotle either specifies the widest class of animals to which a particular part belongs (thereby subsuming "lower" species under a "higher," more extensive kind; cf. *APo* II.13, 96a20–38), or attempts to identify the particular combination of *differentiae* that correlates with the presence of a part within a particular species.

(Note that these two patterns largely coincide with what Lennox labels A-type and B-type explanations.[9] Although I grant that my distinction is somewhat artificial, I prefer to treat these strategies primarily as heuristics and only secondarily as explanations, because in most cases they present an *intermediate* stage between the identification of explananda and the exposition of the ultimate and complete explanation. I do not wish to deny that this intermediate stage also carries some explanatory power and even constitutes an explanation – of the preliminary sort – in itself, but I believe that there is a deeper level of explanation possible that Aristotle is ultimately

[9] See Lennox (2001a, 7–38).

searching for and which cannot always be immediately identified with the application of these strategies as such.[10])

The first strategy, the identification of the widest class of animals that has a particular part, allows Aristotle to *unify* animals with a particular feature under the same form (or definition of their substantial being) or under the same material nature. The identification of the widest class thus helps to demarcate what formal or material features are shared by all the animals within this wider kind, and which are thus most likely to be the causally primary facts to be picked out in the full explanation. The class to be identified can consist of one of the "major genera" (i.e., live-bearing four-footers, egg-bearing four-footers, birds, fish, cetaceans, cephalopods, crustaceans, testaceans and insects; sometimes human beings also count as a separate genus), but also of one of the other classes (e.g., blooded or bloodless; terrestrial, aquatic, flying or stationary; or even "lunged" or "horn-bearing" animals).

Take, for instance, Aristotle's discussion of the viscera (in *PA* III.4, 665a27–31). From the outset Aristotle indicates that having viscera is distinctive of blooded animals (ἴδια τῶν ἐναίμων), while none of the bloodless animals have them (τῶν δ' ἀναίμων οὐδὲν ἔχει σπλάγχνον); the widest class to which viscera belong primitively is thus identified as the class of blooded animals. The presence of viscera in all the animals that have them correlates with the availability of the constitutive material of viscera, i.e., blood, in these animals (cf. *PA* II.1, 647a34–b9). Animals with viscera thus share the same material nature, which in turn is determined by the definition of the substantial being these animals have (*PA* IV.5, 678a31–35). It is this commonality in their form that ultimately explains why all and only those animals have viscera.

In the case of animals that "dualize,"[11] the identification of the two wider kinds to which these animals tend not only helps to find the causally primary fact that accounts for the presence of a part (e.g., in *PA* III.6, 668b32–669a14 the identification of dolphins and whales as breathers of air helps to explain the presence of lungs in these animals, which seems paradoxical for animals that do not dwell on land), but also reveals absences of parts that require explanation. In the latter case, Aristotle takes the two

[10] Cf. also Lennox (2001a, 67–8n.16) and Gotthelf (1997a, 94n.23).

[11] The expression in Greek is ἐπαμφοτερίζει τὴν φύσιν. Balme (1987b, 85–86) defines "dualizers" as animals that "tend to both sides of a division" and therefore escape precise grouping; they partake at the same time in both forms and in none of them (*PA* IV.13, 697b1–5): "because of tending towards both sides . . . on this account they partake of both and neither" (διὰ τὸ ἐπαμφοτερίζειν . . . διὰ τοῦτο ἀμφοτέρων τε μετέχουσι, καὶ οὐδετέρων).

widest classes to which an animal tends as a starting point, deduces what parts should be present if the animal were in fact a full member of both classes, and finally matches his "thought experiment" with the parts actually found in the animal under discussion. Without this search strategy, some explananda (such as the absences of both tails and buttocks in apes; see *PA* IV.10, 689b31–34)[12] would have escaped Aristotle's notice.

The second strategy is employed when a feature seems to belong to a particular animal kind in virtue of being the specific kind of animal it is. Aristotle then searches among the animal's *differentiae* in order to detect the one *differentia* or combination of *differentiae* that correlates with and therefore possibly accounts for this feature's presence. Note again that here the boundaries between "heuristic strategy" and "explanation" become somewhat fuzzy, because in many cases the identification of the correlating *differentia(e)* is the full explanation of the feature in question; in some cases, however, and especially when there are several *differentiae* involved, the explanation may not be complete until the causal hierarchy of the relevant *differentiae* has been established as well.

It is hard to find examples of the application of this strategy where the identification of the causally relevant *differentia* also immediately yields the explanation of the *presence* of a part;[13] the strategy seems mainly successful in discovering the causes of the *differentiations* of parts. Since differentiations for the most part serve the functional optimization of a part in the particular kind of animal that has it, these differentiations will be intimately connected to the animal's specific material or formal nature (see *PA* II.2, 648a13–19 and my discussion of this text in section 4.3 below), rather than to its generic nature.[14] For instance, whereas an elephant has a nose in virtue of being a breather of air (i.e., in virtue of being part of a wider kind that universally possesses noses as a necessary prerequisite for the performance of a necessary function), it has the *specific* nose it has in virtue of possessing a unique combination of *differentiae*, several of which turn out to be causally primary (namely being a land-dweller, a swamp-dweller, blooded, and having a large size; see *PA* II.16, 658b32–659a35).[15]

12 For this example, see Lennox (1987a, 108). Cf. the case of seals and bats in *PA* IV.13, 697b1–13 and of the river crocodile in *PA* IV.11, 690b19–24.

13 For an example of a "*mediated*" explanation of a presence of a part, see *PA* IV.10, 689b1–31: the discovery that having a tail correlates universally with being four-footed *points to* the causally basic fact that four-footers are dwarf-like and are hence in need of protection of their residual outlet, which is provided by the presence of tails.

14 Lennox (2001b, 331) aptly speaks of "adaptation explanations" in this context.

15 Elephants have *long* trunks because they need an organ that allows them to breathe air while being in the water looking for nourishment (being both swamp-dwellers and land-dwellers, elephants get their nourishment from the water, but because of their large size they can only move very slowly, and need an instrument to breathe while in the water). The special use that elephants make of

Being the specific kind of animal it is, the elephant needs to realize its vital function of breathing air in a specific way, and by making the nose long, nature enables the elephant to do this (i.e., the formal differentiation of this particular breather requires a functional differentiation of the nose, which is realized by adding length).

For the most part, these two strategies suffice for the generation of explanations. When they do not, Aristotle applies a third and alternative heuristic strategy: the use of teleological principles.

4.2 ARISTOTLE'S USE OF TELEOLOGICAL PRINCIPLES AS HEURISTIC TOOLS

The status of teleological principles as hypotheses in the natural sciences

Teleological principles, such as "nature does nothing in vain," consist of generalizations over the goal-directed actions of the formal nature (or soul) of an animal while engaged in animal generation. The principles stand out from other sentences describing the actions of the formal natures of animals by their appeal to the universality of the actions described: it is posited that in generating the animal and its parts, the formal nature (for instance) *always* does what is better or best, or *never* does what is in vain, and that these actions take place in contrast or in addition to what happens "of necessity."[16] The principles are thus causal characterizations of the actions of formal natures at the most general level possible. I take it that the different kinds of actions ascribed to these formal natures reflect the operations of different kinds of causality that typically obtain in the production of animals and their parts. Teleological principles are thus no mere metaphors; they all carry ontological force.

Although Aristotle does not tell us much about how he conceptualizes their role in the natural sciences, we are reasonably well informed about their scientific status.[17] There are two important passages in which Aristotle refers to these principles as "hypotheses" (or "suppositions"), while offering some additional insight into their scope and nature. The first passage

this trunk (i.e., they use it for grasping) is a case of secondary teleology, in which nature makes use of the trunk's softness and flexibility (which are conditionally necessary for the trunk to be long) for a second purpose (*PA* II.16, 659a20–23): "Since the trunk is such [i.e., has the right material potentials], nature, as usual, uses the same parts for several things, [here using] it in place of the use of front feet (ὑπάρξαντος οὖν τοιούτου τοῦ μυκτῆρος, ἡ φύσις παρακαταχρῆται, καθάπερ εἴωθεν, ἐπὶ πλείονα τοῖς αὐτοῖς μορίοις, ἀντὶ τῆς τῶν προσθίων ποδῶν χρείας)." On the elephant's trunk, see also Gotthelf (1997a).

16 For Aristotle's use of value terms in these principles, see Gotthelf (1988).

17 On the nature and scientific status of teleological principles, see Lennox (2001a, 182–204). My account here draws heavily on his analysis.

indicates that the scope of such principles is *the whole science of nature* (*IA* 2, 704b12–705a2):

> The starting point of our investigation is achieved by positing [principles] that we are accustomed constantly to use for our science of nature, assuming that this is the way in which things are in all the works of nature (ἀρχὴ δὲ τῆς σκέψεως ὑποθεμένοις οἷς εἰώθαμεν χρῆσθαι πολλάκις πρὸς τὴν μέθοδον τὴν φυσικήν, λαβόντες τὰ τοῦτον ἔχοντα τὸν τρόπον ἐν πᾶσι τοῖς τῆς φύσεως ἔργοις). One of these is that nature does nothing in vain, but always, given the possibilities, does what is best for the substantial being of each kind of animal; therefore, if it is better in a certain way, that is also how it is by nature. Next, we must posit [as principles] the dimensions of magnitude as many and of whatever kind belong to whichever kind of animal . . . Further, [we must posit] that the sources of movements in place are thrusts and pulls.

Each of the principles mentioned in this passage posits "that something is the case or is not the case," which according to the distinctions made in the *Posterior Analytics* indicates that these posits are hypotheses rather than definitions (*APo* I.2, 72a19–21): "A posit that assumes either of the parts of a contradictory pair, I mean that something is the case or is not the case, is a hypothesis" (cf. also *APo* I.10, 76a31–37 and 76b3–23).

Whereas definitions demarcate the subject domain of a particular investigation at hand, hypotheses are propositional assertions about this domain. The hypotheses are used in the context of the *De Incessu Animalium*, because they are assumed to apply to "*all* the works of nature":[18] they pertain to everything that has a formal nature, which includes both the sublunary animals and the heavenly bodies.

In the second passage that is relevant for our discussion, Aristotle uses a teleological principle to explain why teeth come to be at the precise moment they do, and indicates that the source of these principles lies in *empirical evidence* (*GA* V.8, 788b20–24):

> But since we suppose – making suppositions based on the things we observe (ἐπεὶ δὲ τὴν φύσιν ὑποτιθέμεθα, ἐξ ὧν ὁρῶμεν ὑποτιθέμενοι) – that nature neither falls short, nor produces anything pointless among the possibilities in each case, it is necessary for animals that are to take in nourishment after suckling to have instruments for the chewing of food.

For Aristotle, the ability to lay down hypotheses correlates with the amount of experience one has with the domain of investigation, and in the natural

[18] The *De Incessu Animalium* passage suggests that the three principles mentioned are only a subset of all the principles we should already be familiar with (perhaps from having worked through other biological treatises); Aristotle singles out these three in order to provide the appropriate framework for the explanation of animal progression.

sciences this experience is the result of the accumulation of observations, preserved by memory (see *GC* I.2, 316a5–10 and *APr* I.30, 46a17–27).[19] In other contexts, Aristotle points out that domain-specific principles concerning perceptible phenomena (such as the teleological principles under discussion) are empirical in a double sense (see especially *Cael* III.7, 306a5–17). Not only do they need to be derived from perceptible phenomena, they also always need to be checked and judged against what is actually perceived.[20] The implication is that if the principles cannot successfully account for the observations as they stand, they must have been assumed wrongly, and should be rejected (cf. *GA* III.5, 756a2–5; *GA* III.10, 760b28–33; and *NE* I.8, 1098b11–12). The teleological principles are empirical in nature, just as the theory of teleology itself is empirical.[21]

The role of teleological principles in explanation

As for their role in the natural sciences, Lennox has made it clear that these principles are no mere slogans, written down by Aristotle to remind his readers of his commitment to the teleology of nature; nor are they expressions of Aristotle's supposed demiurgic or cosmic conception of nature.[22] Rather, as is evidenced by the two passages discussed above, we should consider these teleological principles to play an important *explanatory* role in Aristotle's science of nature. In fact, so Lennox argues, these principles are explicitly used as premises in the explanations recorded in *De Partibus Animalium*.[23]

This may well be the case for the way Aristotle uses teleological principles in some pre-scientific contexts, but I believe that their role in *De Partibus Animalium* (and perhaps also in the other biological works) is better described as that of a heuristic tool that *points towards* the ultimate explanation of some phenomenon, where this ultimate explanation is to be reconstructed without the teleological principle figuring as one of its premises. As I shall argue in the sections below, Aristotle invokes teleological principles in those cases where simple, immediate observation and the use of definitions do not yield the required (final) causes. These principles are then used to generate a set of inferences that will lead to the identification of the causally relevant features, and these features are then to be picked out in the ultimate, syllogistic explanation.

19 Cf. Kullmann (1990, 338–340). 20 Matthen and Hankinson (1993, 421).

21 Gotthelf (1987, 214, 229). Cf. *Resp* 10, 476a13: "[S]ince we *see* (ὁρῶμεν) that nature does nothing in vain."

22 Lennox (2001a, 182–204). 23 Lennox (2001a, 211–218).

Of course, this set of inferences, which includes the postulation of a teleological principle, is part of the larger explanatory account of some feature, and the teleological principles themselves are certainly not devoid of explanatory content (they are, after all, as I indicated above, causal characterizations of the actions of the formal nature at the most general level). My claim is merely that these principles are not part of the demonstrative explanation *properly speaking*, but function rather as intermediate steps towards it. My considerations for proposing this refined explanatory role for teleological principles in the production of Aristotelian explanations are threefold.

First, I believe that, consistent with Aristotle's theory of science as set out in the *Posterior Analytics* and with his recommendations for how to provide explanations in the science of nature in *PA* I.1, the implicit structure of many of the explanations Aristotle provides in *De Partibus Animalium* is that of a demonstrative syllogism, which is of the form AaB, BaC, ∴ AaC.[24] This pattern, of course, does not exhaust all the possible forms of explanation that can be used in biology, but given Aristotle's discussion of it in *PA* I.1 (see especially *PA* I.1, 640a3–6 and my discussion of this text in Chapter 6), it might well be the most "scientific" one. However, since the teleological principles are propositional in form (the principles are hypotheses that posit that something is or is not the case, and hypotheses are "among the propositions": see *APo* I.2, 72a20 and *APo* I.10, 76b35–37),[25] they do not fit well into the formal structure of a demonstrative syllogism, which requires premises to have a universal predicative structure.[26] Even if the principles are part of the partial or informal explanation of some phenomenon,[27] the formal requirement of the demonstrative syllogism

[24] See Lennox (2001a, 5–6; 2001b, 206); see also Chapter 6.

[25] Pace Charles (2000, 72n.20) and Lennox (2001a, 209) who take *APo* I.10, 76b36 (ἀλλ' ἐν ταῖς προτάσεσιν αἱ ὑποθέσεις; "the hypotheses are among the propositions") to mean that the hypotheses are among the *premises* of demonstrations, and Gotthelf (1987b, 185–194), who uses the terms "principle" and "premise" interchangeably for all three types of principle he distinguishes in Aristotle. Goldin (1996, 54, 54n.26), on the other hand, argues that in *APo* I.10, 76b36 "hypotheses" means "premises," and that accordingly the claim is that "premises belong to the propositions." I believe that Aristotle's use of technical terms in *APo* I.10 is consistent with his introduction of these terms in *APo* I.2, and in the latter context "*protasis*" means proposition; cf. Barnes (1993, 97–8). In short, Aristotle says here that the hypotheses are among the propositions, which does not imply that they are also among the premises.

[26] This is especially clear in the case of disjunctive principles: "doing everything because it is necessary *or* for the better" is not the kind of predication that Aristotle typically uses in the *Analytica Posteriora*. On this issue, see also Detel (2006, 255–256).

[27] As Lennox (2001a, 6, 36n.37) points out, such informal explanations often contain important content that will be lost in the ultimate, syllogistic demonstration, and I acknowledge that they play a crucial role in our process of learning about biological phenomena; however, at the level of strict demonstration, they no longer play a role.

(to which I believe Aristotle adheres at least to some extent in *De Partibus Animalium*) thus makes it unlikely that they can be part of the explanation properly speaking.[28]

Second, since these principles are *generalizations* of the actions of formal natures, they cannot (because of their universal nature) exhibit *the most basic* or *primary* causal fact of each particular biological phenomenon – and the latter is what is picked out in the ultimate explanation of that phenomenon. Reconstructions of the demonstrative syllogism in which "what is best" or "what is in vain" function as middle terms would in the theory of the *Posterior Analytics* resemble explanations that "are stated extravagantly" in that the middle terms are too far away to carry much explanatory force (see *APo* I.13, 78b28–31; cf. *Ph* II.3, 195b21–25 and *GA* II.8, 747b27–748a15). They would provide explanations only of a very unspecific and weak kind. It would also make Aristotle's explanations vulnerable to objections of being ad hoc and circular, since by using a predicate such as "what is best" as a middle term one can demonstrate an animal to have *any* feature it has because it is best, whereas the real issue for Aristotle is to get to know *whether* a certain feature is actually "what is best" for a particular kind of animal and if it is, *why* it is so.

Third, the twofold nature of teleology itself (as discussed in Chapter 3) implies that teleological explanations in *De Partibus Animalium* need to do more than merely identify some feature's final cause: a complete explanation will also reveal whether it is a formal or a material factor that is primarily driving the realizations of functions (i.e., whether the underlying causality is that of primary or of secondary teleology), and whether that feature is immediately necessary or rather subsidiary to the animal that has it. The complex causal relations between animals, parts, and functions demand heuristic strategies that go beyond immediate observation and division.

In other words, while I believe that teleological principles in *De Partibus Animalium* provide the framework within which the causally relevant facts can be detected, and as such are certainly part of the larger explanatory context, they do not specify these facts themselves. Their function in *De Partibus Animalium* books II–IV is therefore mainly *heuristic*. I shall argue for this interpretation in the section below through an analysis of Aristotle's actual use of teleological principles in the biological works.

[28] Cf. Gotthelf (1997a, 89), who – in drawing a diagram of Aristotle's explanation of the elephant's nose in *PA* II.16 – places the teleological principles "in a horizontal box at the bottom, to indicate their role in underwriting the explanations, without indication as to how exactly they do."

Examples of the heuristic use of principles of "optimal production"

There are at least three different kinds of teleological principles operative in Aristotle's *De Partibus Animalium*, which are all used in specific explanatory contexts and ascribe different kinds of goal-directed actions to formal natures.

One type of principle concerns the *distribution* of parts over the animal's body, and posits that nature – if nothing prevents it – always places parts at the most valuable[29] location possible, while at the same time safeguarding the balance or symmetry between the two halves of the body (along the three dimensions: up and down, left and right, front and back), such that each part has a counterpart. Aristotle uses this type of principle to generate teleological explanations of why parts are *located* where they are: the principles help to identify what aspect of the animal's material or formal nature explains why the part's location is the best possible for this kind of animal.[30]

A second type of principle concerns the number of parts an animal has, and posits that nature always *assigns* or *gives* as many parts to an animal as are both necessary and sufficient for it to function. Nature's actions in giving parts to animals are always economical: if possible, animals have one part for the performance of each function (and never more than one), but if necessary, nature will use the same part for multiple functions. Aristotle uses this principle to generate teleological explanations of why animals have the *number* of parts they have by relating this number to some aspect of the animal's material or formal nature.[31]

Ultimately, these two types of principle are variations of the principle that "nature does nothing in vain, but always, given the possibilities, does what is best for the substantial being of each kind of animal."[32] This

29 For the notion of the most honorable as linked to biological functions, see *PA* II.10, 656b22–25; *PA* III.3, 665a13–15; and *PA* IV.7, 683b19–24; see also *IA* 4, 705a29–b5, *IA* 4, 706a21–25, *IA* 5, 706b12–16. Cf. Lennox (2001a, 266–272).

30 I call these principles "principles of balanced distribution." They are used in, e.g., *PA* II.7, 652a30–33; *PA* II.10, 656b27–657a12; *PA* II.14, 658a18–24; *PA* III.3, 665a23–26; *PA* III.4, 665b18–21; *PA* III.6, 669b18–26; *PA* III.10, 672b19–24; *PA* IV.11, 691a28-b4; and *PA* IV.12, 695a9–13; cf. also *GA* I.8, 718b25-b29; *GA* I.11, 719a13–15; *GA* II.1, 732a3–8; *IA* 2, 704b18–22; *Cael* II.2, 284b10; *Cael* II.2, 285a11; *Cael* III.4, 303b2.

31 I call these principles "principles of economical assignment." They are used in, e.g., *PA* II.16, 659a20–22; *PA* III.1, 661b28–31; *PA* III.1, 662a18–24; *PA* III.2, 663a17–18; *PA* IV.6, 683a19–25; *PA* IV.7, 683b5–7; *PA* IV.10, 689a4–15; *PA* IV.8, 684a27–30; and *PA* IV.10, 687a10–15; cf. also *GA* I.1, 716a24–27. Note that parts that come in pairs, such as eyes, ears, lungs, and kidneys, are no exception to the "economical" workings of nature: these parts are one in form, but double in structure because of the doubleness of the body: see *PA* II.10, 656b32–657a10 and *PA* III.7, 670a4–7; Lennox (2001b, 227).

32 Cf. Lennox (2001b, 188).

principle operates at the most basic level in the context of determining the causal processes governing the *production* of parts and of establishing why an animal has or lacks a part to start with. Since this is the primary level at which teleology operates, I shall focus in my discussion below on Aristotle's use of those two principles that posit that nature always "makes" or "produces" features because it is necessary, better, or best to do so.

The first principle of what I call "optimal production" posits that nature always does everything either because it is necessary or because it is better. Aristotle rarely quotes the principle in full, but his *De Partibus Animalium* is full of references to features being either necessary or for the better, and I take it that those references provide equal evidence for Aristotle's use of this principle (see, e.g., *PA* III.7, 670a23–29; *PA* III.7, 670b23–27; and *PA* IV.11, 691b32–692a8). For the most informative text on how Aristotle uses the principle, however, we need to turn to Aristotle's *De Generatione Animalium* (*GA* I.4, 717a11–21; 26–31):

> With regard to the differences of spermatic organs in males, if one is to search for the explanations of why they are there, one must first grasp for the sake of what the structure of testes exists. Now if nature does everything either because it is necessary or because it is better, then this part too must be because of one or the other (εἰ δὴ πᾶν ἡ φύσις ἢ διὰ τὸ ἀναγκαῖον ποιεῖ ἢ διὰ τὸ βέλτιον, κἂν τοῦτο τὸ μόριον εἴη διὰ τούτων θάτερον). That it is not necessary for generation is evident (ὅτι μὲν τοίνυν οὐκ ἀναγκαῖον πρὸς τὴν γένεσιν φανερόν): for it would be present in all that generate, but as it is neither the snake nor the fish have testes (for they have been seen coupling and with the channels full of semen). It remains then that they are for the better in some way (λείπεται τοίνυν βελτίονός τινος χάριν) . . . Those who need to be more temperate have in the one case [of nutriment] intestines that are not straight, and in the other case [of sexual reproduction] their ducts twisted to prevent their desire being too violent and hasty. The testes are contrived for this (οἱ δ᾽ ὄρχεις εἰσὶ πρὸς τοῦτο μεμηχανημένοι); for they make the movement of the spermatic secretion steadier.

The phenomenon Aristotle seeks to explain here is why there is a differentiation of spermatic organs *in all males that reproduce sexually*, that is, why some of these male animals have ducts for semen, testes, and a penis, whereas others only have ducts. As he points out, the first step towards formulating an explanation is identifying the function of testes. From the outset it is clear that testes must have something to do with sexual reproduction (and not just with any form of reproduction). What needs to be determined is what their *specific* function is, and then relate this to their presence in some animals, and their absence in others. This is where the use of teleological principles comes in: if parts such as testes are either necessary

(where "necessary" indicates "conditionally necessary" for the performance of some function) or for the better (where "for the better" indicates that the feature is subsidiary to the animal that has it), and cross-species observation reveals that not all animals that reproduce sexually have testes, then the only option that remains is that testes are "for the better."

It is important to note here that for Aristotle the two options are mutually exclusive (if a part is not necessary, then it *must* be for the better), and that he uses these qualifications for parts in an absolute manner, without regard for the level of specificity of animal kinds in which these parts are realized. For instance, Aristotle keeps referring to testes as being "for the better" for the animals that have them (i.e., their status as subsidiary parts is a fixed one), even though they seem necessary for reproduction in those animals. This points out that the permanent qualification of a part as being necessary or for the better is not meant to be *descriptive* of a part's status in actual, realized living beings (take away some actual animal's testes, and it will not be able to reproduce anymore – in the current realization of many animals, testes are certainly necessary). I take it that these qualifications rather pertain to the *hypothetical "design"* of animals, where nature is, metaphorically speaking, still figuring out how to best realize the potential(s) for form for each individual kind of animal. Definitions of the substantial being of animals, which are themselves fixed and eternal, only determine what functions ought to be realized in animals of what size, not what parts ought to be made, how many of them there should be, or where they should be placed. Thus, if a male animal is to reproduce sexually, nature cannot make it without having ducts for semen, because without these ducts, sexual reproduction would be entirely impossible. Ducts for semen are thus conditionally necessary for sexual reproduction (they are the primary "realizers" of this function). However, nature could make – and in fact has made, as observation of the current biodiversity shows – male animals without testes, because testes are, strictly speaking, not necessary for sexual reproduction, but rather *enhance* this function in those which are already able to sexually reproduce in virtue of their possession of ducts for semen. A complete explanation of the presence of testes will thus also have to specify their exact contribution to the function of sexual reproduction. This also implies that having the potential(s) for form of a sexually producing male animal does not conditionally necessitate the coming to be of testes (otherwise they would have been present in all that sexually reproduce). The manner of causation that underlies the coming to be and presence of testes will therefore be different from that of ducts for semen. I submit that necessary parts such as ducts for semen are the

result of the operation of primary teleology, whereas subsidiary parts such as testes are the result of the operation of secondary teleology.

Aristotle continues his investigation into why animals that all perform the same function of sexual reproduction do not all have the same set of parts associated with that function by relating the presence of testes to the structure of the ducts and to the character of the animals that have their ducts twisted rather than straight. In this way, Aristotle discovers that the contribution testes make to sexual reproduction is that they make the emission of seed steadier, thus slowing down copulation in animals that are hot-tempered in character and that need to be more temperate in reproduction. This, then, ultimately provides the answer to why only some animals have testes in addition to ducts for semen: testes are present only in those animals which are too passionate and for which it is better to generate in a more temperate manner. Testes are thus present not for sexual reproduction, but for *slower* reproduction in those animals that without them would copulate too quickly. The causally primary factor of the presence of testes is the passionate character of some animals: it is this formal feature that requires a functional differentiation, which nature – if possible – realizes by adding an extra part in these animals.[33]

Aristotle relies on the same principle to find the causally primary facts explaining material differentiations of parts (*PA* II.2, 648a13–19):

> And similarly with the other parts, both parts such as these and the non-uniform parts should be assumed to possess a differentiation, in some cases with a view to what is better or worse, in other cases with a view to each animal's functions and substantial being. For instance, two kinds of animals may both have eyes, but in one these eyes are hard, while in the other they are of fluid consistency; and while the one does not have eyelids, the other has them – both are with a view to a greater accuracy of vision.[34]

According to this passage, material differentiations of parts are present either "with a view to what is better or worse," or "with a view to each

[33] Reconstructing the explanation using the principle as one of the premises (e.g., premise 1: nature does everything either because it is necessary, or because it is better; premise 2: testes are not necessary but for the better; conclusion: nature makes testes) would obscure both the relevant causal features: the function of testes being to make the emission of seed steadier, and the formal feature of "being too passionate" that explains why the presence of testes is helpful only to some of the male animals that reproduce sexually.

[34] Ὁμοίως δὲ καὶ περὶ τῶν ἄλλων καὶ τῶν τοιούτων μορίων καὶ τῶν ἀνομοιομερῶν ὑποληπτέον ἔχειν τὴν διαφοράν, τὰ μὲν πρὸς τὸ βέλτιον ἢ χεῖρον, τὸ δὲ πρὸς τὰ ἔργα καὶ τὴν οὐσίαν ἑκάστῳ τῶν ζῴων, οἷον ἐχόντων ὀφθαλμοὺς ἀμφοτέρων τὰ μέν ἐστι σκληρόφθαλμα τὰ δ' ὑγρόφθαλμα, καὶ τὰ μὲν οὐκ ἔχει βλέφαρα τὰ δ' ἔχει πρὸς τὸ τὴν ὄψιν ἀκριβεστέραν εἶναι.

animal's functions and substantial being." Although Aristotle does not refer to a complete teleological principle here, I believe that the two options that are mentioned match the distinctions referred to in the principle that "nature does everything either because it is necessary or because it is better." Differentiations of parts are usually for the functional optimization of that part in the specific animal that has it, but whereas some of these functional optimizations are immediately necessary for the animal to survive as the kind of animal it is (nature could not have made these animals without these differentiations), others rather contribute to their well-being (nature makes these differentiations, not because they are necessary, but because they are for the better).

Differentiations of parts that are "with a view to what is better or worse" are primarily the result of material necessity, the outcomes of which may or may not be used for the better by the formal nature of the animal for the functional optimization of a part (only in the latter cases does Aristotle qualify these differentiations as teleological). Differentiations that are for the better are not strictly necessary for the animal – i.e., the differentiation is not of immediate vital or essential importance to it – but they do serve its well-being. For instance, whether an animal has relatively hard or fluid eyes depends largely on its material constitution (cf. *GA* V.1): if the eyes are hard, this is for the worse in terms of vision, but for the better in terms of protection; if the eyes are fluid, this is for the better in terms of vision, but for the worse in terms of protection. Similarly, Aristotle explains the presence of webbed feet in water birds by identifying why such feet are *for the better* in these animals (*PA* IV.12, 694a22–b11):

> It is of necessity that this comes about during generation (ἐξ ἀνάγκης δὲ τοῦτο περὶ τὴν γένεσιν συμβέβηκεν). For the earthen and warm material in the body becomes parts useful for protection . . . In some [nature] constructs length for the legs, in others – instead of this – it fills the gaps in their feet . . . Of necessity, then, these things happen owing to these causes (ἐξ ἀνάγκης μὲν οὖν ταῦτα συμβαίνει διὰ ταύτας τὰς αἰτίας); but it is for the better that they have such feet, for their way of life (ὡς δὲ διὰ τὸ βέλτιον ἔχουσι τοιούτους τοὺς πόδας τοῦ βίου χάριν), in order that, since they live in water where wings are useless, they have feet useful for swimming. For they become oars for sailing just like the fins of fish. Therefore, when of the first group the fins fail, or of the second group the material between their feet, they no longer swim.

Nature uses the residues that have come to be of material necessity in birds that live in water to fill in the gaps between their toes, so that they can paddle while being in the water: having webbed feet is subsidiary to their aquatic way of life.

Differentiations of parts that are "with a view to each animal's functions and substantial being" are the result of primary teleology: these differentiations are strictly necessary for the animals that have them. Without this functional optimization of the part, the animal would not at all have been able to live or be able to be the kind of animal it is. For instance, animals with moist eyes that need to see sharply have eyelids by way of protection for their eyes, whereas animals with hard eyes do not need any eye protection (see *PA* II.13). Similarly, Aristotle explains the presence of strong wings in some birds by identifying that feature of their substantial being that makes it *necessary* for them to have such wings (*PA* IV.12, 693b28–694a9):

> Further, some of the birds are able to fly and have large, strong wings, e.g., those with talons, and the flesh-eaters; it is a necessity for them to be able to fly on account of their way of life (ἀνάγκη γὰρ πτητικοῖς εἶναι διὰ τὸν βίον), so for the sake of this they have both many feathers and large wings . . . But some birds are not able to fly, but are heavy – those whose way of life is earthbound and that are fruit-eaters or are swimmers and spend their life around water.

Only birds whose way of life requires them to be good flyers have strong wings: this differentiation is conditionally necessary for their survival (cf. *PA* II.13, 657b22–29 on why terrestrial birds do not have sharp vision: "for nothing related to their way of life requires them to have it").

In all the examples discussed above, the principle that "nature does everything either because it is necessary or because it is better" helps to determine the ontological status of some feature (i.e., whether it is necessary and the product of primary teleology or subsidiary and the product of secondary teleology) and thereby to discover the causally primary fact responsible for its coming to be and presence. Necessary features are to be explained by reference to some formal aspect of the substantial being of the animal that *requires* (and therefore conditionally necessitates) the presence of a part or its differentiation. Subsidiary (including luxury) features are to be explained by reference to some material aspect of the animal that makes the coming to be of a part or its differentiation possible, in addition to some formal aspect of the substantial being of the animal that reveals why the animal *benefits* from this feature's presence. The presence of both features is thus ultimately due to the goal-directed actions of the formal nature of the animals involved, either by realizing a preexisting potential for form that requires certain differentiations of parts to be present, or by using available materials to make differentiations that are for the better.

The second principle that is concerned with the production of parts posits that "nature does nothing in vain, but always, given the possibilities,

does what is best for the substantial being of each kind of animal." The principle is never stated in full in *De Partibus Animalium*, but there are many partial references (for formulations of the complete principle, see *IA* 2, 704b12–18; *IA* 8, 708a9–12; and *IA* 12, 711a18–29).

In accordance with the line of interpretation proposed by Lennox,[35] I believe that Aristotle employs the "nature does nothing in vain" part of the principle *for the most part* in cases where he needs to provide an explanation of "paradoxical" *absences* of parts, and I focus on these cases in my analysis below. Note, however, that in a minority of cases Aristotle also uses this part of the principle in order to discover the cause of the *presence* of biological phenomena, such as capacities without which a living being would not be able to achieve its natural ends (see, e.g., *DA* III.12, 434a30–b8 and my discussion of this example in section 2.2), or the presence of the male in the process of reproduction in animals whose sexes are separate (see *GA* II.5). The underlying heuristic mechanism, I believe, is the same in both cases: imagine the opposite scenario where the phenomenon that is *now* present (or absent) is absent (or present), and the "observable" consequences of the reversed condition for the living being in question will point towards the causally primary facts related to its substantial being.

When dealing with "paradoxical" absences of parts, observations as such are of no help in finding the relevant causal factors for why these parts are absent. Aristotle suggests that instead of using immediate observation, we should theorize about why nature (hypothetically speaking) would have designed the animal the way it is. We do this by assuming that nature does nothing in vain, and from there reason counterfactually that *if* the formal nature of a particular animal had equipped that animal with the part that is now absent, the presence of that part would have been in vain, *because of* some other feature of that animal that is more necessary (or "basic") to the animal's substantial being.[36] What this feature is can only be discovered through this kind of thought experiment: if the absence of a part is to be explained teleologically, then it is necessary to exhibit some other, more

35 See Lennox (2001a, 205–223).

36 There are several reasons why Aristotle concludes that the presence of a part would have been in vain: (i) the animal is not able to use the part, either at all or to use it properly (see, e.g., *PA* IV.12, 694a13–20: heavy birds have talons and not spurs because they cannot use the latter); (ii) the animal already possesses a part that performs a similar function (see, e.g., *Resp* 10, 476a11–15: no animal needs both gills and lungs); (iii) the animal does not need the function for the sake of which the part would come to be (see, e.g., *PA* II.13, 658a6–10: fish do not need eyelids since their eyes do not need any protection in the water); and, finally, (iv) the presence of the part would have been harmful to the animal (see, e.g., *PA* IV.12, 694a16–18: the presence of crooked claws would harm heavy birds; *GA* V.2, 781b22–28: the presence of outer ears in seals would lessen their hearing ability instead of improving it).

basic feature of the animal as interfering with the functionality of the part that is now missing.

The use of the teleological principle thus reveals a design problem, which nature has solved by "removing"[37] the part which is the least crucial or necessary to the animal's substantial being. If the thought experiment does not reveal any design problems it means that there is no teleological explanation to be provided for the absence of the part. Instead, the explanation is likely to be material: the part is missing because the suitable constitutive material is missing in this animal kind (for examples, see below in section 4.3). Once one identifies the feature that would have made the presence of the other part in vain, the principle allows the inference that that is in fact why the part is absent: nature never produces parts that are in vain.[38]

Aristotle's explanation of why snakes have no feet illustrates this use of the principle that nature does nothing in vain (*IA* 8, 708a9–20):

> In snakes the cause of why they are footless is both that nature does nothing in vain, but always from among the possibilities, [does] what is best for each thing, preserving the proper substantial being of each and its essence; and, in addition, that which we stated before, namely that no blooded animal can move itself at more than four points. For from these [two principles] it is evident that of the blooded animals *whose length is out of proportion to the rest of the nature of their body*, such as snakes, none of them can possibly have limbs. For they cannot have more than four feet (since in that case they would be bloodless), and if they had two feet or four they would be almost completely immobile: so slow and useless would their movement necessarily be.[39]

Observation shows that all blooded animals that live on land have feet; blooded land-dwellers share to a certain extent the same formal nature, which explains the occurrence of certain co-extensive features such as the possession of a maximum of four feet. The snake, however, also possesses all the properties that belong to blooded land-dwellers, except for feet. This

37 For nature "taking away" parts if their presence would have been in vain, see *PA* IV.11, 691b1–5 and *Cael* II.8, 290a29–35 (and my discussion of this passage in section 5.4); cf. *PA* III.2, 663a32–33; 664a1–3; *PA* IV.9, 685a25–27; and *GA* III.10, 760a30–33; b25–27.

38 This type of reasoning reflects what Aristotle elsewhere calls a "syllogism from a hypothesis." See Bobzien (2002, 365).

39 τοῖς δ' ὄφεσιν αἴτιον τῆς ἀποδίας τό τε τὴν φύσιν μηθὲν ποιεῖν μάτην, ἀλλὰ πάντα πρὸς τὸ ἄριστον ἀποβλέπουσαν ἑκάστῳ <ἐκ> τῶν ἐνδεχομένων, διασῴζουσαν ἑκάστου τὴν ἰδίαν οὐσίαν καὶ τὸ τί ἦν αὐτῷ εἶναι· ἔτι δὲ καὶ τὸ πρότερον ἡμῖν εἰρημένον, τὸ τῶν ἐναίμων μηθὲν οἷόν τ' εἶναι πλείοσι κινεῖσθαι σημείοις ἢ τέτταρσιν. ἐκ τούτων γὰρ φανερὸν ὅτι τῶν ἐναίμων ὅσα κατὰ τὸ μῆκος ἀσύμμετρά ἐστι πρὸς τὴν ἄλλην τοῦ σώματος φύσιν, καθάπερ οἱ ὄφεις, οὐθὲν αὐτῶν οἷόν θ' ὑπόπουν εἶναι. πλείους μὲν γὰρ τεττάρων οὐχ οἷόν τε αὐτὰ πόδας ἔχειν (ἄναιμα γὰρ ἂν ἦν), ἔχοντα δὲ δύο πόδας ἢ τέτταρας σχεδὸν ἦν ἂν ἀκίνητα πάμπαν· οὕτω βραδεῖαν ἀναγκαῖον εἶναι καὶ ἀνωφελῆ τὴν κίνησιν. Cf. *IA* 2, 704b12–18; *IA* 4, 705b25–29 and *PA* IV.11, 690b14–18.

absence is explained by showing counterfactually how the presence of four feet would have been in vain: given that a snake – being blooded as it is – can only possess a maximum of four feet (this is a non-teleological principle of nature; giving the snake more than four feet would damage its substantial being and is therefore not a natural possibility), those four feet if present would not enable it to move swiftly at all. The reason why becomes apparent when one imagines the four feet to be present: the length of the snake is out of proportion to the rest of its body, and with only four feet it would rub its belly against the ground. It is thus the snake's disproportionate dimensions that render the presence of a maximum of four feet non-functional: no blooded animal whose length is out of proportion to the rest of its body can move with a maximum of four feet, and snakes are such animals. It is for this reason that nature did not equip snakes with feet (cf. *PA* IV.13, 696a10–15). Notice again that the level of reasoning pertains to the hypothetical design of snakes: even though the "original design" of snakes – as being blooded land-dwellers – may have required the possession of four feet, such animals were never actually realized. The thought experiment is supposed to reveal what other feature of the animal made nature adjust the design of snakes and "take away" their feet in realizing them. Once we have identified that feature, we can formulate an explanation that works without having to attribute any actual conscious intentionality to nature.[40]

Aristotle invokes the second part of the principle to generate explanations of the presence of parts[41] and their differentiations almost always in those cases where observation of the wider kind shows that there are *several* possible ways in which nature could have fulfilled a certain functional need. Aristotle uses this principle as a means to find the causally primary feature connected to the animal's substantial being that reveals why the one part, rather than the other one, is the best fit for this kind of animal to perform a particular function. The "possibilities" from among which nature – in the hypothetical setting – determines which kind of part to produce in each kind of animal are *natural* possibilities:[42] the range of what is *possible* for a

40 Using the format of the *Posterior Analytics*, the explanation of the footlessness of snakes can be reconstructed as follows: premise 1: having (a maximum of) four feet holds of no blooded animal whose length is out of proportion to the rest of its body; premise 2: having the length out of proportion to the rest of their body holds of all snakes (which are blooded animals); conclusion: having (a maximum of) four feet holds of no snakes.

41 Lennox (2001a, 215–218; 220–221n.4) proposes a similar interpretation, but the examples he provides (*PA* IV.13, 695b17–27 and *IA* 8, 708a9–20) in fact illustrate the use of this principle in explaining the *absence* of parts. Note that the same principle can also be applied to explain the timing of a part's coming to be: see *GA* II.6, 744a35-b1 and *GA* V.8, 788b20–789a2.

42 Lennox (2001a, 207): "the range of possibilities is represented by the generic features of the more extensive kind to which an animal belongs."

certain kind of animal to have is in fact what can be observed to be *realized* in actual, similar animals (at whatever level of generality is appropriate). The possibilities are thus established inductively through observation.

Aristotle uses this principle, for example, to explain why human beings have hands instead of forelimbs (*PA* IV.10, 687a15–18):

> And being upright in nature, mankind has no use (οὐδεμία χρεία) for forelimbs, and instead of these, nature provides arms and hands . . . So if it is better thus, and nature does, among the possibilities, what is best (εἰ οὖν οὕτως βέλτιον, ἡ δὲ φύσις ἐκ τῶν ἐνδεχομένων ποιεῖ τὸ βέλτιστον), it is not because they have hands that human beings are most intelligent, but because they are the most intelligent of animals that they have hands.

All blooded live-bearing and land-dwelling animals have forelimbs, except for human beings, who have hands – and it is this distribution that needs to be explained. The causally relevant facts that explain this distribution are found by applying the principle that nature does what is best among the possibilities: between the two options, hands and forelimbs, hands are the best option available for human beings given their particular substantial being. This is so for two reasons: first, since human beings walk upright (this is an essential feature of humans: see *PA* IV.10, 686a25–31), they do not need forelimbs for walking, and – as we saw above – nature does not produce non-functional features. This, however, explains only why humans do not have forelimbs. Second, and more importantly, nature has given hands to human beings because they of all animals are the most able to use them *on account of* their being the most intelligent. Being most intelligent is what distinguishes human beings from the other blooded live-bearing and land-dwelling animals, and it is this feature of their substantial being that is picked out as the explanatory middle term in the explanation for why human beings have hands (cf. *PA* IV.10, 687a9–10: "it is reasonable that *because of their being most intelligent*, they received hands"; *PA* II.14, 658a21–24 and *PA* IV.10, 690b3–4).

Whereas "for the better" in the first principle discussed above refers to the ontological status of the part (it indicates that the part is a product of secondary teleology and that it serves the animal's well-being), "what is best" referred to in this second principle rather refers to what realization of a certain function constitutes the optimal fit for an animal *given the kind of animal it is*.[43] If observation shows that there are multiple natural

[43] It is because of this that the principles of balanced distribution and economical assignment can be subsumed under the principle that nature does what is best, given the possibilities, for the substantial being of each kind of animal. See in particular Aristotle's explanation of the differences

possibilities (i.e., that there are multiple parts an animal potentially could have had as the realization of a certain potential for form), Aristotle needs to explain why this, rather than another possibility is realized in this particular animal. As is clear from the example discussed above, this involves not just giving a specification of the function for the sake of which the part is present, but also, and even more so, identifying that element in the definition of the substantial being of the animal that reveals *why this part is in fact the best fit for the animal that has it.* These causally primary features are what the teleological principle helps to identify. If there is no such feature to be found, then there is no teleological explanation for the particular differentiation between parts and animals that have them. Compare in this context also *PA* IV.9, 685b12–16, where Aristotle states that the presence of one row of suckers in one kind of octopus is not because it is best, but because it is necessary: observation shows that octopuses can have either one or two rows of suckers, but there is no teleological explanation for this variation in the distribution of parts. Rather, the differentiation is conditionally necessary given the differences in dimensions between different kinds of octopuses.

In sum, the examples discussed above all involve phenomena that cannot simply be explained by the identification of (observable) functions.

In the first examples discussed, the function of a part or its differentiation is known, but it needs to be established whether the coming to be and presence of this function is primarily driven by matter or by form. That is, it still needs to be determined whether the part is a necessary prerequisite for the performance of the function in question and is the result of formal natures realizing a preexisting potential for form, or whether the part contributes to the performance of the function in question and is the result of formal natures using materials that have come to be of material necessity for the betterment of the animal.

The second series of examples concerned parts that can be observed to be present in one group of animals, but that are found to be absent in another group that is otherwise very similar or related to the first group. In both cases, it is some aspect of the definition of the substantial being of each particular kind of animal that explains why the part is present or absent in that group.

of the location of hair in different kinds of animals in *PA* II.14, 658a16–24; 658a22–24: "Therefore nature adds this protection to the more valuable parts, because it is always a cause of the better among the possibilities (τοῖς τιμιωτέροις ὑπέγραψεν ἡ φύσις τὴν βοήθειαν· ἀεὶ γὰρ ἐκ τῶν ἐνδεχομένων αἰτία τοῦ βελτίονός ἐστιν)."

The causally relevant features are in both cases discovered through the use of teleological principles: they provide the heuristic framework within which the exact causal relation between part, function, and specific kind of animal can and needs to be found. It is this use to which Aristotle alludes in the following passage (*Resp* 3, 471b24–29):

> The main cause of why [investigators] do not speak well about these things is on the one hand that they lack experience of the internal parts, and on the other hand do not make the assumption that nature in every case acts for the sake of something (καὶ τὸ μὴ λαμβάνειν ἕνεκά τινος τὴν φύσιν πάντα ποιεῖν); had they inquired for the sake of what respiration belongs to animals, and had they investigated this question in the presence of the parts involved, that is, the gills and lungs, they would quickly have found the explanation (εὗρον ἂν θᾶττον τὴν αἰτίαν).

In this passage, Aristotle seems to imply that the importance of the assumption that nature acts in every case for the sake of something lies in its power to guide our investigations towards the discovery of explanations. If this passage is representative of Aristotle's general views about teleological principles in all of his natural treatises,[44] it would seem that their use is indeed (also) heuristic.

4.3 EXPLANATIONS IN BIOLOGY: REFERENCES TO FORM, MATTER, AND FUNCTION

Classifying patterns of explanation in De Partibus Animalium

In this final section, I shall provide an appendix-style overview of the most important patterns of explanation that can be found in Aristotle's *De Partibus Animalium* (note, however, that this overview is not meant to be exhaustive and that my discussion of representative examples necessarily has to remain brief). The patterns discussed can be consulted independently.

My purpose in presenting this listing of patterns of explanation is both to demonstrate the richness and flexibility of Aristotle's explanatory project in this biological treatise, and to illustrate the different roles played by the four Aristotelian causes and especially by the final cause in his explanations. It is my contention that whereas the importance of final causes lies in their explanatory priority (they are easily identified through observation and often form the starting points of explanations), material or formal features constitute the causally primary factor in the explanations. That is,

44 Pace Lennox (2001a, 219–220), I believe that this passage illustrates the main use of teleological principles.

the coming to be and presence of ends that constitute the final causes are themselves – depending on whether the teleology is primary or secondary – primarily driven by either material factors (i.e., by the availability of extra materials that formal natures may or may not use for the betterment of the animal) or formal factors (i.e., by the presence of a potential for form that needs to be realized), which have causal priority. In Chapter 6 I shall provide a tentative explanation for why teleological explanations have this particular structure; for now it will suffice to lay out the basic patterns of explanation.

Since my focus lies on the identification of the roles and interrelations of the four causes in Aristotle's explanations, I have organized my overview accordingly. I shall first discuss patterns of explanation in which Aristotle refers first to formal(-efficient) causes, next the ones in which he refers first to material(-efficient) causes, and finally those patterns in which he refers first to final causes. In those cases where Aristotle refers to more than one cause in the same explanation, my analysis will make clear which factor has explanatory priority and which has causal priority. Also, following the order in which Aristotle presents his explanations, my exposition will start with the explanations of the presence of parts, proceed with those of the absence of parts, and end with the explanations of their differentiations.

Explanation by reference to formal causes

Pattern I: Explanation of the presence of vital and essential parts by reference to (functional) features included in the definition of the substantial being of an animal

As we saw in section 3.2, Aristotle usually explains the presence of vital and essential features by reference to the definition of the substantial being of the animal. These features are exhibited as the necessary prerequisites for the performance of vital or essential functions. In these cases, the animal's essence or form is picked out as the causally primary factor in the explanation of the feature's presence.

For instance, Aristotle explains the presence of fins in fish by reference to fish being essentially swimmers: fins can be exhibited to be (the usual) necessary prerequisites for an animal to be able to swim (*PA* IV.13, 695b17–26; see section 3.2). Another important example is his explanation of why some animals have blood (*PA* IV.5, 678a31–35): "For that some animals are blooded while some are bloodless will belong in the account defining their substantial being (ἐν τῷ λόγῳ ἐνυπάρξει τῷ ὁρίζοντι τὴν οὐσίαν αὐτῶν)" (Cf. *PA* IV.12, 693b2–13; *PA* IV.13, 695b17–25 and *PA* II.2,

648a20). Being blooded is a feature that is specified by the definition of the substantial being of these animals: it is a *kath'hauta* feature. Besides blood (or its analogue), there are a few other parts that are explained to be present in *all* animals in virtue of what it is to be an animal. The definition of the substantial being of "animal" specifies the necessary functions of perception and nutrition, and all animals will therefore have a heart or its analogue (as the primary seat of perception) and at least flesh, and a mouth and stomach, because these parts are the necessary prerequisites for the realization of these necessary functions (see *PA* II.8, 653b19–29, *PA* III.4, 666a34–5, and *PA* IV.5, 678b1–6). Note, however, that definitions of substantial beings do not only specify the necessary functions an animal needs to perform, but also its dimensions and other non-functional features, and presumably (as evidenced by the example of being blooded) also the basic material make-up of an animal.[45]

The same pattern of explanation applies also to those features that are not themselves specified by the definition of the substantial being, but that immediately follow from it (i.e., features that belong to the animal *kath'hauta sumbebêkos*). For instance, having a heart (here: as an origin and container of blood) and liver is explained as being a necessary consequence of being a blooded animal (*PA* III.7, 670a23–27): "Now the heart and liver are necessary to all animals . . . All blooded animals must have both of these (πάντα δὲ δεῖται τὰ ἔναιμα δυοῖν τούτοιν), which is why these two viscera alone are possessed by all blooded animals, while those that breathe have a third, the lung." The causally primary feature that explains the presence of the heart and the liver is the fact that the animal is blooded, which is part of its essence or form.

Sometimes, especially in the case of dualizers, Aristotle explains the presence of a part in a particular kind of animal by reference to the definition of the substantial being of the wider class of animals to which that animal kind belongs. For example, Aristotle explains the two-footedness of the ostrich by identifying it as being *in this respect* a bird (*PA* IV.14, 697b13–27): "The same mode [i.e., that of being a dualizer] also pertains to the Libyan ostrich; for it has some parts of a bird, others of a four-footed animal . . . and while it is two-footed like a bird, it is hoofed, as though four-footed."

[45] E.g., the length and thinness of a certain kind of octopus (*PA* IV.9, 685b12–15; cf. *IA* 8, 708a9–20); "being segmented into parts" in insects (*PA* IV.6, 682b27–29); "having claws" in lobsters (*PA* IV.8, 684a32-b1); and "being divine" in humans (*PA* IV.10, 686a25–31); dimensions of some insects (*PA* IV.6, 683a18–19); and dimensions of animals in general (*DA* II.4, 416a15–18; *GA* II.6, 745a5–6; and perhaps also *Pol* V.9, 1309b18–35). See also Code (1997, 139–140); Gotthelf (1985, 41, 44–45, 53n.22); and Gotthelf (1987, 189–192).

Since two-footedness is a *kath'hauta sumbebêkos* feature of birds (see *PA* IV.12, 693b5),[46] and since ostriches share to some extent the features of birds, ostriches are also two-footed.

In these examples, the causally primary fact is constituted by the definition of the substantial being of the widest class of animals to which the part to be explained belongs. Functions play a role in these explanations only by being subsumed in this definition (i.e., even though fins are for the sake of swimming, their presence is explained by reference to fish being swimmers).

Note that Aristotle never refers to formal causes as the ultimate causes of absences of parts: "bloodlessness" (see *PA* IV.5, 678a31–35 quoted above) is not really an exception to this rule, since it indicates, not that an animal lacks blood altogether, but that it lacks *red* blood. Bloodless animals possess a part analogous to red blood, with similar material potentials (see *PA* I.5, 645b9–10).

In the case of dualizers, Aristotle sometimes explains the absence of a part that is a necessary realization of one of the two forms at stake by stating that in this case the animal tends towards the *other* form. Aristotle then continues by identifying features that are more basic to the dualizer's substantial being, and indicates how the presence of the missing part would have been in vain given the presence of these other features. Ultimately, it seems, Aristotle is reluctant to say that an animal lacks a part because it lacks the form of which the part is a necessary realization, but rather explains the absence in terms of formal features the animal does have, and with which the presence of the now missing part would have functionally interfered (for an example, see Aristotle's discussion of the lack of tails and a rump in bats in *PA* IV.13, 697b1–13).

Pattern II: Explanation of the necessary differentiations of parts by reference to differentiae *and dimensions included in the definition of the substantial being of an animal*

Aristotle explains differentiations of parts that are necessary for an animal by reference to the *differentia* – specified in the definition of the animal's substantial being – for which this differentiation is a necessary requirement. In other words, Aristotle identifies the formal differentiation of this particular animal relative to the form of other animals that are part of the same wider kind, and then points to this formal differentiation as what conditionally necessitates the differentiation of the part relative to its realization in other related animals.

[46] Cf. Bayer (1998, 501–502).

We have already discussed some examples in which a *differentia* explains the presence of a differentiation of a part: birds that hunt for food need *strong* wings (*PA* IV.12, 693b28–694a9) and elephants, who search for food in swamps, need *long* noses for the sake of breathing air (*PA* II.16, 658b32–659a35). Whereas the definition of the substantial being of the wider kind of animals to which a particular kind of animal belongs explains the presence of its necessary parts (e.g., wings in birds and noses in breathers of air), it is a *differentia* of that animal that accounts for (many, but not all) the differentiations of those parts (e.g., strong wings in hunting birds and long, flexible noses in elephants) and that defines it as a subspecies.

In addition to *differentiae* in character, lifestyle, and activities, Aristotle also refers to differences in dimensions between animals as the formal cause of a part's differentiation (*PA* IV.9, 685b12–16):

> Now while the other octopuses have two rows of suckers, one kind of octopus has a single row. This is because of the length and thinness of their nature; for it is necessary that the narrow tentacle should have a single row of suckers. It is not, then, because it is best that they have this feature, but because it is necessary owing to the distinctive account of their substantial being (οὐκ οὖν ὡς βέλτιστον ἔχουσιν, ἀλλ' ὡς ἀναγκαῖον διὰ τὸν ἴδιον λόγον τῆς οὐσίας).

The differentiation between one or two rows of suckers is not due to one row being a better fit for one kind of octopus, given its particular substantial being, and two rows being a better fit for the other kind. Rather the differentiation is a necessary consequence of the essential differences in the dimensions of these two kinds of octopuses. The kind of octopus that is longer and thinner than the other kind has, necessarily, in virtue of lack of space, only one row of suckers.

In these examples, the causally primary fact of a part's differentiation is a particular *differentia* specified in the definition of the substantial being of the animal in question. And again, even though most necessary differentiations are for the sake of a functional optimization of a part (e.g., stronger wings are for the sake of better flying), it is the animal's essence that is causally primary (e.g., some birds are hunters in their way of life).

Explanation by reference to material causes

Pattern III: Explanation of the coming to be of subsidiary and luxury parts by reference to material necessity

As I argued in section 3.2, Aristotle explains the coming to be of subsidiary and luxury parts in the first place by reference to material necessity. Parts are subsidiary or luxury items if they are not the necessary prerequisites

for the performance of vital or essential functions and are therefore not realizations of preexisting internal potentials for form as specified in the definition of the animal's substantial being. In these cases, the availability of residual material or even of entire structures that have come to be of material necessity is what "allows" the formal nature of an animal to make use of them. Formal natures can only produce parts that contribute to the animal's well-being when there are extra materials available to do so. The functions such parts serve or contribute to are usually picked out in the second half of these "double-barreled" explanations. However, the material potentials of the available materials constitute the causally primary facts: the potentials both constrain and guide the uses to which nature can put them, which are either to make a part that contributes to the performance of a necessary function, or to make a part that performs a "luxury function," such as defense or coverage.

Let me analyze one more example to clarify the interrelations of the causally relevant factors involved (*PA* IV.3, 677b22–32):

> The generation of this part [i.e., the omentum] occurs of necessity in the following way; when a mixture of dry and moist is heated, the surface always becomes skin-like and membranous, and this location is full of such nutrient . . . The generation of the omentum, then, occurs according to this account, and nature makes use of it for a good concoction of the nutrient, in order that the animals may concoct their nutrient easier and faster; for what is hot is able to concoct, and what is fat is hot, and the omentum is fat.[47]

The *coming to be* of the omentum is explained entirely in terms of material necessity: the presence of dry and moist materials that make up the stomach and intestines, combined with the presence of heat, results in the solidification of the materials on the outside of the stomach. It is this "sheet" or membrane that constitutes the omentum. The formal nature of the animal plays no role in this part's coming into being. However, once the membrane is in place, the formal nature co-opts it as a subsidiary part. Since the membrane is fat, and fat is hot, and since what is hot is able to concoct, the membrane contributes to the concoction of food, by making the process easier and faster. The membrane's contribution to the function of food concoction thus explains why it is *present*: because the part is useful,

[47] Ἡ μὲν οὖν γένεσις ἐξ ἀνάγκης συμβαίνει τοιαύτη τοῦ μορίου τούτου· ξηροῦ γὰρ καὶ ὑγροῦ μίγματος θερμαινομένου τὸ ἔσχατον ἀεὶ δερματῶδες γίνεται καὶ ὑμενῶδες, ὁ δὲ τόπος οὗτος τοιαύτης πλήρης ἐστὶ τροφῆς . . . Ἡ μὲν οὖν γένεσις τοῦ ἐπιπλόου συμβαίνει κατὰ τὸν λόγον τοῦτον, καταχρῆται δ' ἡ φύσις αὐτῷ πρὸς τὴν εὐπεψίαν τῆς τροφῆς, ὅπως ῥᾷον πέττῃ καὶ θᾶττον τὰ ζῷα τὴν τροφήν· τὸ μὲν γὰρ θερμὸν πεπτικόν, τὸ δὲ πῖον θερμόν, τὸ δ' ἐπίπλοον πῖον.

the formal nature of the animal retains the part and does not prevent its growth. The material potentials of the omentum give rise to the function it performs in the animals that have it, and are as such causally primary.

In a small number of cases, Aristotle refers solely to material necessity to explain both the coming to be and the presence of a part. Examples of such parts are the spleen[48] and many of the differentiations in the affections (such as hair color, eye color, and pitch of voice) that Aristotle discusses in *GA* V.1–7. These parts and differentiations are not strictly necessary for the animal to have, nor do they make any significant contribution to the well-being of the animal; but they are also not too harmful for the animal. In these cases, the formal nature of the animal has neither co-opted the part for a good purpose, nor excreted it from the animal's body. Such parts are solely the result of the interactions of materials during the generation of the animal (cf. *GA* V.1, 778a29–b1), and the potentials of the materials involved are causally primary in the explanations of both their coming to be and their presence.

In both cases, material necessity has causal primacy in the development of the part.

Pattern IV: Explanation of the absence of parts by reference to the lack of constitutive material

Aristotle often explains the absence of a part by reference to the lack of constitutive materials for that part in a particular animal. What is causally prior in these cases is the material nature of an animal, which puts up insurmountable constraints on the actions of the formal nature: since the animal lacks the appropriate kind of materials necessary for the production of a certain part, that animal therefore also lacks that part.[49]

For instance, this is how Aristotle explains the absence of outer ears in birds and egg-laying four-footers (*PA* II.12, 657a17–22):

[48] Reconstructing the precise causal explanation of the spleen is difficult. The spleen comes to be as a necessary consequence (*PA* III.7, 670a29–30: Ὁ δὲ σπλὴν κατὰ συμβεβηκὸς ἐξ ἀνάγκης ὑπάρχει τοῖς ἔχουσιν) of the availability of residues around the gut and bladder. Its presence is accounted for by reference to the principle of optimal balance (*PA* III.7, 669b27–670a2): "And it is on account of the liver being positioned more on the right that the nature of the spleen has developed; so that while in a way it is necessary, it is not exceedingly necessary [on this reading, see Lennox (2001b, 326)] in all the animals." The spleen is thus necessary for the bilateral symmetry of the body, and even though it does not perform any proper function, it is also not entirely useless (*PA* III.7, 670b4–6): "For the spleen draws off the residual fluids from the stomach and because it is blood-like it can assist in the concoction (δύναται συμπέττειν) of them." Another part that does not perform a proper function and that might just be a necessary consequence is the esophagus; see *PA* III.3, 664a24–31.

[49] On this pattern of material explanation, see Lennox (2001b, 228).

> Birds only have [auditory] channels because of the hardness of their skin, and because they do not have hairs but are feathered: they do not have the sort of matter from which ears may be formed (οὐκ οὖν ἔχει τοιαύτην ὕλην ἐξ ἧς ἂν ἔπλασε τὰ ὦτα). And the same holds of those among the four-footed animals who lay eggs and have scales: for the same account also applies to these.

The material nature of birds and of some of the four-footers simply does not contain materials suited for the formation of outer ears, which is why they are absent (cf. *PA* II.5, 651a26–27; *PA* II.13, 657b13–15; b36; *PA* III.3, 664b20–665a9 and *PA* IV.5, 678a27–34).

A variation on this kind of explanation is the one in which the absence of a part is explained by reference to there *not being enough* constitutive material for the production of this part and another part, where the presence of this second part is either better for this particular animal or takes away the usefulness of the presence of the first part.[50]

Examples of the first pattern can be found in Aristotle's explanation of the lack of a complete set of upper teeth in horned animals (*PA* III.2, 664a1–3: nature takes from the nourishment assigned to the upper teeth for the growth of horns) and of the absence of tails in long-legged birds (*PA* IV.12, 694b18–20: the matter that is used in other birds to make tails is used up in these birds for the growth of legs). In each case, nature diverts the flow of materials designated or available to produce one part for the production of a different part, which explains why the first part remains incomplete or is entirely absent. The hierarchy according to which nature assigns priority to the production of the second rather than to that of the first is presumably a functional one:[51] necessary parts are realized first and completely, whereas subsidiary or luxury parts are realized later and are either missing or realized in incomplete form.

An example of the second pattern can be found in Aristotle's explanation of the absence of tails in human beings (*PA* IV.10, 689b21–25):

> Mankind, then, has both haunches and fleshy legs because of the explanation just stated, and because of this it is tailless – for the nourishment which is being driven there is used up on these, and because it has haunches the necessity of the use

50 Another variation of this type of explanation is used in *GA* I.5, 717b14–19 (cf. *GA* I.7, 718a18):

> Further, whereas the four-footed animals have the organ for coition, since it is possible for them to have it, birds and footless animals cannot have it because the former have their legs up by the middle of the belly and the latter have no legs at all, while the nature of the penis is connected with the legs and its position is there (καὶ τῇ θέσει κεῖσθαι ἐνταῦθα).

Here the absence of a part is explained by reference to the absence of the "proper location" of that part.

51 On this "principle of functional priority", see Lennox (2001a, 192–193).

of tails is taken away (ἥ τε γὰρ ἐκεῖ τροφὴ πορευομένη εἰς ταῦτα ἀναλίσκεται, καὶ διὰ τὸ ἔχειν ἰσχία ἀφῄρηται ἡ τῆς οὐρᾶς ἀναγκαία χρῆσις) – but for four-footers and the other animals it is the opposite.

Human beings, in order to be able to walk upright, need to have upper bodies that are lighter than their lower ones (which is why nature takes the bodily parts from the upper body and adds them to the lower one: *PA* IV.10, 689b11–13). However, by making the lower body heavier, nature has used up all the fleshy parts, which means that it cannot produce tails in human beings. In addition, the fleshiness of the haunches provides in itself sufficient protection for the residual outlet (cf. *PA* IV.10, 689b28–30), so that there is no more use for the presence of a tail (i.e., the presence of a tail would have been in vain). The absence of tails thus receives a complex explanation: tails are absent because their constitutive material has been used up for the production of a second part, whose presence makes the presence of tails superfluous.

In all the examples discussed above, what has causal priority is the material nature of the animal (cf. *PA* IV.12, 694b18: "all [birds] are from the same matter" and, perhaps, *PA* III.2, 664a5–6: "the cause of this is that both are of the same [material] nature, namely that of horn-bearers"). It is this factor that determines whether or not the materials necessary for the production of particular parts are available, either at all or in a sufficient supply.

Pattern V: Explanation of the coming to be of differentiations of parts that are "for the better" by reference to material necessity

In line with his explanations of the coming to be of subsidiary and luxury parts, Aristotle explains the coming to be of differentiations that are "for the better" primarily by reference to material necessity. It is the availability of residual materials that "allows" the formal nature of an animal to make use of them for the functional optimization of a part, which, although not strictly necessary for the animal, serves the animal's well-being. The potentials of the available materials are again the causally primary facts that give rise to the function to which the material is ultimately put by the animal's formal nature.

Earlier I discussed why human beings have the hairiest heads of all animals with hair (*PA* II.14, 658b2–10; see section 3.1) and why the feet of ducks are webbed (*PA* IV.12, 694a22–694b10; see section 4.2). Let me here present a slightly different example in which Aristotle explains why kidneys are the fattest of all viscera (*PA* III.9, 672a1–21):

> The kidneys have the most fat of all the viscera: on the one hand, this is out of necessity, because the residue is filtered through the kidneys . . . So of necessity [they] come to be fatty because of this cause, as a result of what happens of necessity in animals with kidneys; on the other hand, they are also [fatty] for the sake of the preservation of the hot nature of the kidneys.[52]

The explanandum at stake is a differentiation between the realizations of parts within the same class of parts, namely viscera. For the kidneys are the fattest of all viscera, and according to Aristotle, this is due primarily to processes that take place of material necessity in the kidneys themselves.[53] By filtering fatty residue, the kidneys become more and more fatty themselves. But because what is fat is also very hot (see *PA* IV.3, 677b31–32), the formal nature of animals that have kidneys can make use of this material potential to preserve the heat of the kidneys, which contributes to the well-being of these animals.

The material causes picked out in explanations such as these are all materials that come to be of material necessity; due to the material potentials they have, nature can use or co-opt them for the functional optimization of parts.

Explanation by reference to final causes

Pattern VI: Explanation of the presence of parts by reference to the function these parts perform

In the patterns of explanation discussed above, final causes are picked out either indirectly (through the definitions of the substantial beings of animals), or directly, but in combination with material causes which are primarily responsible for the coming to be of functional features (the functions to which the materials are put account for their presence). Here I shall turn to the pattern of explanation in which Aristotle explains the presence of parts by first identifying their function.

In many cases, especially when explaining the presence of necessary parts, the reference to the function the part performs in the animal that has it completes the full explanation of the part's presence. This, for instance,

52 Ἔχουσι δ' οἱ νεφροὶ μάλιστα τῶν σπλάγχνων πιμελήν, ἐξ ἀνάγκης μὲν διὰ τὸ διηθεῖσθαι τὸ περίττωμα διὰ τῶν νεφρῶν· . . . Ἐξ ἀνάγκης μὲν οὖν πιμελώδεις γίνονται διὰ ταύτην τὴν αἰτίαν ἐκ τῶν συμβαινόντων ἐξ ἀνάγκης τοῖς ἔχουσι νεφρούς, ἕνεκα δὲ σωτηρίας καὶ τοῦ θερμὴν εἶναι τὴν φύσιν τὴν τῶν νεφρῶν.

53 Here I disagree with Lennox (2001a, 106–108), who argues (2001a, 107) that "we are told that kidney fat arises for the sake of the contribution it makes to preserving the (hot) nature of the kidneys."

is how Aristotle explains the presence of the larynx (*PA* III.3, 664a17–20): "The larynx is naturally present for the sake of breath (Ὁ μὲν οὖν φάρυγξ τοῦ πνεύματος ἕνεκεν πέφυκεν); for through this part animals draw in and expel breath when they inhale and exhale." The larynx is a necessary prerequisite for the function of breathing, and it is with a view to allowing the larynx to perform this function (together with the part's second function in humans of speech) that nature has made it from cartilaginous material (*PA* III.3, 664a35–b2; the reference to necessity in this passage is clearly conditional necessity). Aristotle does not always explicitly relate necessary functions such as breathing to the definition of the substantial being of those animals as breathers, but on occasion he does, as in the explanation of the presence of lungs (*PA* III.6, 669b8–13):

> In general then the lung is for breathing, and it is bloodless and of such a kind for the sake of living beings. But what is common to these animals is nameless, and no name has been given such as "bird" [has been given] to a certain kind. For this reason, just as being for a bird is from something, so too having a lung belongs to the substantial being of these animals (καὶ ἐκείνων ἐν τῇ οὐσίᾳ ὑπάρχει τὸ πλεύμονα ἔχειν).

Summarizing his discussion of lungs, Aristotle first gives the function for the sake of which lungs are present (i.e., breathing), and then connects this function to what is common in the substantial being of the animals that have lungs. This suggests that it is ultimately a shared formal feature (i.e., being a breather of air) that is the causally primary factor in the explanation of why all "lunged animals" have lungs.

In the explanations of the presence of subsidiary and luxury parts, Aristotle also often starts his explanation by identifying the specific function a part serves. In section 3.2 we discussed Aristotle's explanation of the presence of kidneys: kidneys are present for the contribution they make to the collection of residue – a function that is primarily performed by the bladder in all animals with blooded lungs (*PA* III.7, 670b23–27). Kidneys are not necessary for this function (nature could have made these animals without kidneys, and they would still have been able to collect their residue in virtue of the fact that they possess a bladder), but their presence optimizes the functional performance of the bladder and they are therefore good for the animal to have (had nature made these animals without kidneys, they would not have been able to collect their residues as well as they can now that they do have kidneys). However, since kidneys are not the necessary prerequisites for the animal to perform this function of collecting residue (for otherwise, they would have been present in all blooded animals), it

seems that the coming to be of kidneys cannot be explained by reference to conditional necessity and primary teleology. The function subsidiary parts such as kidneys end up performing is instead primarily caused by material necessity: it is because material necessity produced extra materials with certain potentials that formal natures can use those materials for the production of parts that serve the animal's well-being. Even though the goal-directed actions of the formal natures are responsible for the structure, retainment, and presence of such parts, these parts would never have come to be if it were not for the prior operation of material necessity.

This pattern of what I have called secondary teleology is much clearer in the case of luxury parts: again, Aristotle starts by identifying the function for which the luxury part is present, but then often continues to discuss the causal role played by materially necessitated processes in the coming to be of that part. For example, this is how Aristotle starts his discussion of horns (*PA* III.2, 662b23–30):

> We must speak about horns. For those, too, grow naturally in those that have them on the head. No animal that is not live-bearing has them. In virtue of similarity and extension "having horns" is also attributed to some other animals, but the function of horns belongs to none of them (ἀλλ' οὐδενὶ αὐτῶν τὸ ἔργον τοῦ κέρατος ὑπάρχει). For live-bearing animals have them for protection and strength (βοηθείας γὰρ καὶ ἀλκῆς χάριν), which turns out to be the case for none of the other animals said to have horns. For none of them use their horns either while defending themselves or for overpowering, which are the functions of strength.

However, as we saw in section 3.2, in the second half of his discussion of horns, Aristotle turns to the question of how "nature according to the account has made use of things present of necessity for the sake of something" (*PA* III.2, 663b21–22) and states that it is the defensive potentials of the residual material available in these animals that allowed nature to use it for the production of horns (*PA* III.2, 663b22–35). What is causally primary in the full explanation of the presence of horns is thus the potentials the materials have of necessity; the function of defense is imposed on the available materials only secondarily.

In all these examples the presence of parts is explained first and foremost by reference to the function they serve, but this function is not necessarily also the causally primary fact in the full explanation. The primary cause of the coming to be and presence of vital and essential parts is form;[54] the

[54] Cf. Charles (1997, 30): "The favoured mode of explanation applicable to biological natural kinds is teleological, and the Form of the kind is the explanatorily basic feature."

primary cause of the coming to be and presence of subsidiary and luxury parts is matter.[55]

Pattern VII: Explanation of the differentiation of parts by reference to a second function a part needs to perform

Sometimes Aristotle refers to two or even more functions in the explanation of the presence of parts. An example of this is Aristotle's account of teeth (*PA* III.1, 661a36–b6):

> In other animals [i.e., other than human beings], the nature of the teeth is present in common [cf. *PA* III.1, 661b7: *koinê chrêsis*] for the preparation of nutrition, yet distinctively according to kinds in some for strength, which in turn has been divided into the performance of strength and the avoidance of it – for some have it for the sake of both, namely both the avoidance of it and the performance of strength, such as for example as many among the wild animals as are of the nature of flesh-eaters; others have them for protection, such as many of the wild and tame animals do.

According to this passage, the *common* function of teeth is the preparation of nutrition, which presumably means that in all animals that have teeth, their presence is to be explained by reference to this function (teeth are presumably subsidiary parts for the function of nutrition; cf. Aristotle's discussion of teeth in *GA* V.8). In addition to producing and differentiating the part for the performance of this primary function, nature may also adapt or co-opt it for a secondary function, which is distinctive for different kinds of animals (*PA* I.5, 645b20–28; *PA* III.1, 662a22–24): "But nature has collected all these uses together in one, producing a differentiation of this part for the differences of its operation."[56] This second function is in many cases a luxury function, or a function that is already realized by some other part that is the necessary prerequisite for the realization of that function. So, although this second function is not part of the causal account of the part's coming to be as such, it may play a role in causing its material or structural differentiation(s).

What guides the actions of the formal nature in producing one part for the sake of one function or in uniting several functions in one and the same part are the principles of "economical distribution" (see above, section 4.2), illustrated by Aristotle in the following analogy (*PA* IV.6, 683a19–25):

[55] Note that Aristotle never refers directly to functions to explain absences of parts; instead he invokes the principle that nature does nothing in vain; see my discussion of this principle above, in section 4.2.

[56] Ἡ δὲ φύσις ἅπαντα συνήγαγεν εἰς ἕν, ποιοῦσα διαφορὰν αὐτοῦ τοῦ μορίου πρὸς τὰς τῆς ἐργασίας διαφοράς.

> And it is better, where possible, not to have the same instrument for dissimilar uses, but the one that is defensive [i.e., the sting] most sharp, and the one that is to be a tongue spongy and able to draw in nourishment. For where it is possible for two things to be used for two functions without impeding each other, nature is unaccustomed to making things as does the coppersmith who, to economize, makes a spit-and-lampstand; but where this is not possible, nature makes use of the same thing for multiple functions.[57]

Nature prefers to produce one part for the performance of one function (here, stings for protection and tongues for nourishment), but where this is not possible, for instance because the animal is too small to carry more parts, nature uses – (παρα)καταχρῆται[58] – one part for several functions (here, in small two-winged insects, the tongues serve for both nourishment and protection).

In all these examples, the part's primary function explains its presence as such; the animal's *differentiae* explain the part's primary differentiations; and the secondary function explains the part's secondary differentiations.[59]

Pattern VIII: Explanation of differentiations of parts by reference to the functional optimization they serve

Aristotle explains differentiations of parts by reference to the functional optimization they serve in the animals that have those differentiations, both when they are necessary for the animal to survive or to be the kind of animal it is, and when they are "for the better" and serve the animal's well-being. We have already seen several examples of both necessary and subsidiary functional optimizations of parts; here I present one more example of each kind of explanation.

As Aristotle points out, not only are the differentiations of wings in birds necessary for their distinctive ways of life (*PA* IV.12, 693b28–694a9), but so are those in insects (*PA* IV.6, 682b7–11):

57 Βέλτιον δ' ἐνδεχομένου μὴ ταὐτὸ ὄργανον ἐπὶ ἀνομοίας ἔχειν χρήσεις, ἀλλὰ τὸ μὲν ἀμυντικὸν ὀξύτατον, τὸ δὲ γλωττικὸν σομφὸν καὶ σπαστικὸν τῆς τροφῆς. Ὅπου γὰρ ἐνδέχεται χρῆσθαι δυσὶν ἐπὶ δύ' ἔργα καὶ μὴ ἐμποδίζειν πρὸς ἕτερον, οὐδὲν ἡ φύσις εἴωθε ποιεῖν ὥσπερ ἡ χαλκευτικὴ πρὸς εὐτέλειαν ὀβελισκολύχνιον. Ἀλλ' ὅπου μὴ ἐνδέχεται, καταχρῆται τῷ αὐτῷ ἐπὶ πλείω ἔργα.

58 See, e.g., *PA* II.16, 659a20–23: "Since it [i.e., the trunk] is such, nature, as usual, uses the same parts for several things (ἡ φύσις παρακαταχρῆται, καθάπερ εἴωθεν, ἐπὶ πλείονα τοῖς αὐτοῖς μορίοις), here using the trunk in place of the front feet." Cf. *PA* II.16, 659a34–36 (again about the elephant's trunk); *PA* II.16, 659b34–660a2 (tongue; lips); *PA* III.9, 671a35-b2 (kidneys); *PA* IV.10, 689a5–7 (outlets for residues and semen); *PA* IV.10, 688a19–25 (mammae); and *PA* IV.10, 689b34–690a4 (tails).

59 Cf. Lennox (2001b, 245).

> Among those [i.e., insects] that are flyers – the ones whose life is nomadic and for whom it is necessary to range widely for nutrition (διὰ τὴν τροφὴν ἀναγκαῖον ἐκτοπίζειν), are both four-winged and have a light body mass, such as for instance the bees and the animals related to them: for they have two wings on each side of the body.

Those insects that are flyers do not all have the same number of wings (and the same body mass): bees, for instance, have four wings (rather than two or none) because their nomadic way of life and expansive search for food *require* a specific functional optimization of their ability to fly. Note that Aristotle only identifies the *differentiae* in virtue of which bees have the number of wings they have, without specifying the exact function that is being served by this differentiation. Even though the differentiation of wings is present for a functional optimization of those parts, the *differentiae* are causally primary in this explanation.

Another example of a differentiation that is not necessary, but better for the animal to have (again, because nature could have designed the animal without this differentiation), is the distinctive ability of snakes to turn their head to the rear while the rest of their body remains at rest (*PA* IV.11, 692a2–8):

> A cause of this is that, like insects, they are capable of coiling, such that they have their vertebrae flexible and cartilaginous. This thus happens to them from necessity (ἐξ ἀνάγκης), because of this cause, but it is also for the better (πρὸς δὲ τὸ βέλτιον), for the sake of protection against being hurt from behind.

The function the differentiation of backbones serves in snakes is that of protection: it allows them to turn their head and watch out for dangers, and this is beneficial to them. This benefit, however, is not what conditionally necessitated the differentiation; the special ability is rather a necessary consequence of material potentials that are present for the sake of allowing the snake the capacity for locomotion. Again, the material potentials are causally primary in this explanation; they give rise to the function of coiling of necessity, which is then co-opted by the formal nature of snakes for their protection.

In sum, whereas material or structural differentiations of parts typically serve a functional optimization of that part in the animal that has it, these functional differentiations themselves are either given with the substantial being of the particular kind of animal, or follow from the available material potentials.

4.4 CONCLUSION

In the sections above, we have seen that Aristotle uses a wide variety of heuristic and explanatory strategies in order to explain the presence, absence, and differentiations of biological features in *De Partibus Animalium* books II–IV.

When the explananda are so complex that both mere observation of the animals in question and the use of their definitions fail to reveal the causes sought for, Aristotle relies on a third strategy. It involves the use of teleological principles, which generate thought experiments that help to discover the relevant causal factors to be picked out in explanations. There are many different kinds of principles at play in Aristotle's biology (as is evidenced by the wealth of examples from his *De Partibus Animalium*), but each seems to have its own specific use. The verbs of agency ascribed to the formal natures in these principles are more than mere metaphors, or reflections of the analogy between art and nature: rather, they reflect different causal patterns underlying the generation of animals and their parts. This also holds of the uses of "better" and "best" in these principles: the terms are not univocal, but whereas "for the better" picks out the operation of secondary teleology, "the best" identifies some feature as being the best solution in the "design" of a particular kind of animal relative to its specific substantial being.

In addition, I have argued that Aristotle uses teleological principles predominantly as heuristic tools in *De Partibus Animalium*, which help to determine the exact causal relationship between a part, the function it performs, and the animal to which it belongs in those cases where this relationship is not immediately discernible. The principles are not a priori postulates that cannot be refuted: they are established inductively through observation and are used – each in its own context – to help set up a framework within which inferences to the best explanation can be drawn, and thereby help Aristotle to yield the phenomena in the most plausible, coherent way.

The three basic patterns of explanation in *De Partibus Animalium* books II–IV reflect the causal differences between the operation of primary and secondary teleology. Functions are often picked out first in explanations, but references to final causes alone only rarely constitute the complete explanation provided by Aristotle, and they are never causally primary. The presence and differentiations of parts that are necessary for the animal to have are explained by reference to the functions (or functional optimizations) they perform, but these functions are ultimately referred

back to the definition of the substantial being of either the animal itself or of its wider kind. Vital and essential parts and differentiations are exhibited to be the necessary prerequisites for the realization of the animal's form. The presence of features that are "for the better" and that are not strictly necessary for the design of the animal (although the actual animal might not be able to function without it) is also explained by reference to the functions or functional optimizations served. However, what ultimately gives rise to these functions is the availability of materials with certain kinds of material potentials. Subsidiary and luxury features are exhibited to be the result of the formal nature using or co-opting materials that are already available and have often come to be by material necessity. In both cases, functions are most salient in the explanations of biological phenomena – they have explanatory priority, but the material or formal causes are to be picked out as middle terms in those explanations, because they are prior in causation.

CHAPTER 5

Making sense of the heavens: the limits of teleological explanation in the De Caelo

5.0 INTRODUCTION

In his programmatic opening to the *Meteorologica* (*Meteor* I.1, 338a20–339a10), Aristotle puts the issues discussed in *De Caelo* at the center of his science of nature. The study of "the stars ordered according to their upper motion" (*Meteor* I.1, 338a21–22), and of "the bodily elements, their number and nature, and their change into each other" (*Meteor* I.1, 338a22–24) is said to follow his examination of the first principles of nature and of natural change in general, but to precede his investigations of sublunary living nature.[1] In accordance with this outline, Aristotle first – in *De Caelo* book I – argues for the existence of a fifth, heavenly element (i.e., aether) in addition to the familiar four sublunary, changeable ones (i.e., air, water, fire, and earth), and discusses the nature and characteristics of the universe in its entirety (i.e., its size, uniqueness, and eternity). Then, in book II, Aristotle turns to the motions and features of the heavens as a whole, of the individual planets and stars, and lastly of the Earth. Next, in book III, he focuses on the nature and motions of the four sublunary elements, saving his definitions of "weight" and "lightness" associated with these elements for book IV. By engaging with the heavenly phenomena in the first two books and only then turning to the sublunary elements, Aristotle mimics the order of exposition of Plato's *Timaeus*.[2] It is this latter treatise, and the theory of cosmology presented in it, that also forms the main target of philosophical and scientific debate in the *De Caelo*.

In this chapter, my main concern will be with Aristotle's methods of discovery and the explanations he provides of the features and motions of

[1] The order outlined in the *Meteorologica* passage is presumably didactical rather than chronological. On this issue, and on the place of the *De Caelo* in Aristotle's science of nature, see Burnyeat (2004, 13–16) and Falcon (2005, 2–13).

[2] Cf. Burnyeat (2004, 15); on Aristotle's critical response to the *Timaeus* in *De Caelo*, see Johansen (2009, 1–23).

the heavenly bodies in the second book of the *De Caelo*.[3] Within this book, traces of Aristotle's teleological worldview are not hard to find. In book I, Aristotle had already argued that the nature of the sublunary elements is such that it provides these elements with an immanent capacity to exercise their specific motions to reach their natural places.[4] In book II he adds that teleology also permeates the heavenly domain of the stars and planets, as all celestial motions are said to be trying to reach "the most divine principle" as a final cause (*Cael* II.12, 292b20–25).

Although teleology as a natural tendency is thus without doubt an important part of the make-up of Aristotle's cosmology and celestial physics, his general reliance on teleology to *explain* the different motions and features of the heavenly bodies seems to be limited in comparison with the other physical and biological treatises I discussed in the previous chapters. For the whole of the *De Caelo* contains only seven instances of explicit teleological explanation, six of which pertain to the heavenly phenomena in the second book (there is only one instance of teleological explanation in book I, pertaining to circular motion in general, and there are none in books III and IV, which deal exclusively with the sublunary elements). For an overview of the explananda and the teleological principles used, see Table 5.1.

Moreover, with one exception (in *Cael* II.3, 286a8–9), none of these explanations refer directly to final causes. Instead, they all proceed through the application of teleological principles, such as "nature does nothing in vain," which – as we saw in section 4.2 – in biology are only applied in very specific explanatory contexts, namely, in those cases where the discovery of final causes by means of mere observation or use of definitions is relatively difficult. This suggests that teleology is not readily discernible in the case of the heavens.

Aristotle's use of teleological principles in the *De Caelo* is all the more remarkable because the teleological explanations are the only fully fledged physical explanations Aristotle offers in this treatise. By this I mean that the teleological explanations are the only explanations in the *De Caelo* that

[3] In *De Caelo* book II, Aristotle first discusses the features, motions, and shape of the heaven as a whole (*Cael* II.1–6: the heaven is eternal; possesses the dimensions left and right, above and below; moves forward in circular, regular motions; and is spherical in shape); then turns to the composition, shape, and motions of the heavenly bodies (*Cael* II.7–12: the heavenly bodies are made of aether; are spherical in shape; move in virtue of the spheres in which they are fixed; differ in relative speeds by which they move and in complexity of motions); and ends with an exposition of the position, motion, and shape of the Earth (*Cael* II.13–14: the Earth rests at the center of the universe and is therefore motionless; its shape is spherical).

[4] Left to their own devices, the four sublunary elements would naturally move to their natural places and thus constitute four separate, concentrically arranged spheres. See also Bodnár and Pellegrin (2006, 282).

Table 5.1 *The seven teleological explanations and principles used in the* De Caelo

No.	Text passage	Explananda and teleological principle used
1.	*Cael* I.4, 271a22–33	Why is there no motion contrary to that in a circle? *Teleological principle:* nature does nothing in vain.
2.	*Cael* II.3, 286a7–9	Why is there a plurality of motions of the heavens? *Teleological principle*: everything that has a function is for the sake of that function.
3.	*Cael* II.5, 288a2–12	Why do the heavens move in the direction they do? *Teleological principle:* nature always does what is best among the possibilities.
4.	*Cael* II.8, 290a29–35	Why do stars not move on their own (or, why do stars not have any organs for motion)? *Teleological principle:* nature does nothing in vain.
5.	*Cael* II.9, 291a23–25	Why do stars not move on their own (or, why is there no harmony of the spheres)? *Teleological principle:* nature does nothing in vain.
6.	*Cael* II.11, 291b10–15	Why do stars not move on their own (or, why do stars not have a shape fit for locomotion)? *Teleological principle:* nature does nothing in vain.
7.	*Cael* II.12, 292a15–b25	Why is there a difference in the complexity of the motions of the different heavenly bodies? *Teleological principle*: actions are for the sake of something.

address the nature and causes of natural phenomena and that build upon some evidence from observation. For the most part, Aristotle's cosmological treatise consists of statements of fact and of dialectical arguments building upon mathematical or numerological principles, which mainly address the number, shape, and possible motions of the heavenly bodies.[5]

The purpose of the present chapter is to shed light on the specific nature of the teleological explanations in Aristotle's cosmology and on the problems related to their application within this particular branch of the science of nature.[6] In particular, I shall argue that the way in which Aristotle uses

5 On this type of "dialectical" argument in *De Caelo*, see Bolton (2009).

6 The issues that I should like to discuss in this chapter have received relatively little attention in the scholarly literature on Aristotle. Scholars who have studied teleology in Aristotle's cosmology have focused almost exclusively on the role of the Prime Mover as a final cause in Aristotle's *Physica* and *Metaphysica*. See, in particular, Kahn (1985). Other studies on cosmology have either left out the question of teleology completely (Falcon 2005), or have subsumed it under the "normal" use of teleology (Johnson 2005). On the other hand, Leggatt, in his commentary on the *De Caelo*, claims that Aristotle consciously played down the role of teleology in his cosmological treatise, because

teleological principles to generate explanations of heavenly phenomena is proper to the natural sciences and builds upon their – very successful – heuristic usage in biology.[7] This chapter thus traces Aristotle's heuristic use of teleological principles outside the immediate context of biology and shows how these principles are operative throughout Aristotle's natural treatises. The fact that the heavenly domain – as opposed to the biological realm (see, e.g., *PA* I.5, 644b23–645a4) – is empirically underdetermined, limits the explanatory force of these explanations (hence Aristotle's "warning" that the explanations he will offer are at most reasonable), but this does not mean that the explanations themselves are not *phusikôs* or scientific: they generate the best causal accounts of the features and motions of the heavenly bodies Aristotle can offer.

In section 5.1 I shall say more about the scientific status of cosmology. In sections 5.2–5.4, I shall discuss three representative examples of Aristotle's use of teleological principles to generate explanations in the second book of the *De Caelo*.

5.1 COSMOLOGY AS SCIENCE OF NATURE

The approach to the study of the heavens taken by Aristotle's predecessors and contemporaries had often been mathematical in nature. (In the *De Caelo*, Aristotle refers to them as "mathematicians concerned with ἀστρολογία" – where ἀστρολογία is best rendered by "astronomy" – or simply as "mathematicians.")[8] The theory reportedly put forward by Eudoxus and revised by Callippus represented the apparent motions of the stars and planets as outcomes of systems of concentric rotating spheres. This theory as reported did not explain the physical mechanics and causes underlying those motions, perhaps because neither Eudoxus nor Callippus was concerned with those issues. In *Ph* II.2, 193b22–194a12, Aristotle distinguishes this theoretical manner of studying the heavens

of his alleged dissatisfaction with the type of intentional and psychological teleological explanation deployed by Plato in the *Timaeus*; see Leggatt (1995, 18, 36–37, 207). Hence, Leggatt offers little analysis of the teleological explanations actually provided in this treatise, because he believes them to be of little importance.

7 The possible relative chronology of Aristotle's works (according to which the *De Caelo* is an early work and the biological works are late) does not affect my claim: since none of these treatises were published during Aristotle's lifetime, he may well have adjusted and revised them continuously in the light of new discoveries or conceptual distinctions made. For a defense of this view (based on a pedagogical interpretation of the cross-references in Aristotle), see Burnyeat (2004, 21–22).

8 See *Cael* II.14, 297a2–4 (Μαρτυρεῖ δὲ τούτοις καὶ τὰ παρὰ τῶν μαθηματικῶν λεγόμενα περὶ τὴν ἀστρολογίαν, "what the mathematicians say in *astrologia* also testifies to this"); *Cael* II.10, 291a29–b9; and *Cael* II.14, 298a15.

from the proper study of nature by pointing out that astronomers – like mathematicians – study the properties of bodies not *qua* properties of those bodies, but *qua* separable from them.[9]

For Aristotle, however, just as for Plato in the *Timaeus*[10] and for some of the Presocratics before him, the study of the heavens is *also* part of the investigation of nature,[11] and thus the heavenly bodies and their features will have to be studied not only *qua* spheres but also in a manner that takes their nature fully into account – nature in the sense of both form and matter. Aristotle intends his *De Caelo* to be a treatise in natural science, not in mathematics or mathematical astronomy. This physical approach to the study of the heavens is evidenced, for instance, in Aristotle's claim that each of the spheres in his system is corporeal, and thus not simply a mathematical construct (*Cael* II.12, 293a7–8): "For each sphere is some kind of body (σῶμά τι τυγχάνει ὄν)."

Therefore, if for Aristotle cosmology is part of the science of nature, and if cosmological phenomena are – at least for the most part – teleological in nature, as Aristotle seems to believe,[12] then scientific knowledge of these phenomena will involve knowledge of all four causes.[13] A merely

9 See also *APo* I.13, 78b39; *Meta* I.8, 989b33–990a15; *Meta* III.2, 997b16–998a1; and *Meta* XIII.2, 1076b39–1077a4, where Aristotle describes astronomy as not dealing with perceptible magnitudes or with the heavens above. Cf. Simplicius *In Ph.* 293, 7–10 and 290, 20–24 on the Greek conception of astronomy as being part of mathematics, not physics; Mueller (2006, 179–181).

10 Cf. also Pl. *R* 529a–530e.

11 Aristotle emphatically introduces his study of the heavens as a part of the study of nature: see for instance *Cael* I.1, 268a1: Ἡ περὶ φύσεως ἐπιστήμη; *Cael* III.1, 298b2–3: τῆς περὶ φύσεως ἱστορίας; and *Meteor* I.1, 338a20–5.

12 Aristotle repeatedly offers the a fortiori argument that if one agrees that animals and plants neither come to be nor exist by spontaneity (but for the sake of something), then the claim that spontaneity is the cause of the heavens – which are most divine and exhibit the greatest order – must be absurd, and that one has to conclude that final causality pertains to the heavenly realm as well. See *Ph* II.4, 196a24–b5; *Ph* II.6, 198a1–13, and *PA* I.1, 641b10–23:

> In addition, natural science can pertain to nothing abstract, because nature makes everything for the sake of something. For it seems, just as in artifacts art is present, so too in things themselves there is some other principle and such cause, which like the hot and the cold we have from the universe (ἐκ τοῦ παντός). This is why it is more likely that the heavens have been brought into being by such a cause – if they have come to be – and are due to such a cause, than that the mortal animals have been. Certainly the ordered and definite are far more apparent in the heavens than around us, while the fluctuating and random are more apparent in the mortal sphere. Yet some people say that each of the animals is and comes to be by nature, while the heavens, in which there is not the slightest appearance of chance and disorder, were constituted in that way by chance and the spontaneous.

13 Note that Aristotle does not believe *all* heavenly phenomena to be teleological, but only those that involve natural substances: knowledge of phenomena such as eclipses will therefore only involve knowledge of material-efficient causes. For scientific knowledge involving knowledge of all four (or at least of all possible) causes, see, e.g., *APo* I.2, 71b9–13; *APo* II.11, 94a20–27; *Ph* I.1, 184a10–16; *Ph* II.3, 194b17–23; and *Meta* VIII.4, 1044a33–b20; cf. also Falcon (2005, 15).

mathematical approach – such as that favored by the astronomers and by Aristotle himself in many of the arguments in the *De Caelo* – will not be sufficient to generate complete knowledge concerning the heavens. For instance, by its very nature, mathematical reasoning cannot yield understanding of final causes (there are no final causes in mathematics, because there is no change or good in that domain; see *Meta* II.2, 996a21–b1). Astronomy therefore only yields understanding of the shape and size of the heavenly bodies, and of their distances from each other and from the Earth. This gives important information about the quantitative properties of the heavenly bodies and their motions, especially if combined with arguments drawing from principles of physics. However, as a natural philosopher, Aristotle is also interested in the nature of the heavenly bodies, in their material composition, and in the causes of their motions. The opening words of the *De Caelo* are significant (*Cael* I.1, 268a1–4): "The science of nature (ἡ περὶ φύσεως ἐπιστήμη) is patently concerned for the most part with bodies and magnitudes, the affections and motions of these, and further, with all the principles that belong to this kind of substance."

Because the natural sciences are typically concerned with identifying all four types of cause, and since for teleological phenomena such as the heavenly features and motions the understanding of final causes is especially crucial, Aristotle needs an additional strategy to extend scientific knowledge as he understands it to the domain of the heavens. This strategy involves the application of teleological principles of the sort he employs in his biology precisely as a heuristic means for finding final causes when they are not immediately observable. Since these teleological principles are generalizations – based on observations of actual natural phenomena – over the goal-directed actions of formal natures (or souls) of living beings, Aristotle can use these principles as a possible means of discovering the underlying causal mechanisms in cases where the causally relevant factors are *not* open to visual inspection: this, of course, on the assumption that nature acts in a similar goal-directed way in all cases. However, whether the explananda at hand are actually similar enough to the phenomena that have known, observable causes, and thus whether the application of the teleological principle will be successful, is an open question: there will be cases where a teleological principle is applied but no final cause is found (cf. the question of why some octopuses have one row of suckers whereas others have two; see *PA* IV.9, 685b12–16 and sections 4.2–4.3 above). In short, Aristotle uses teleological principles in the *De Caelo* to discover purposes and functions among the heavenly

phenomena, and thereby tries to turn his study of the heavens into a proper natural science.[14]

As outlined in section 3.1, scientific research comprises for Aristotle two stages of enquiry: the first stage consists in the systematic collection of observations of the phenomena, and the second one in the attempt to detect correlations and to give causal explanations of those phenomena. However, as Aristotle makes clear several times in the *De Caelo* (see his introductions to teleological explanations discussed below in section 5.2), it is not at all an easy undertaking to give such explanations of cosmological phenomena. The central problem is the limitedness – or even lack – of empirical evidence: the observations of the heavens we have are too few, and the objects of observation are too far away to offer any certain evidence (cf. *Meteor* I.7 and *APr* I.30). The only observation that seems to be rock solid is that of the rotation of the heavens (*Cael* I.5, 272a5–6: "we see the heavens turning about in a circle"). Notwithstanding the many methodological caveats we find in *De Caelo*, Aristotle remains confident that it is still possible to give explanations of cosmological phenomena that go beyond the mere fact that the heavens rotate, and also beyond the conclusions mathematical or numerological reasoning yields about numbers, sizes, shapes, and distances, for instance.

My contention is that Aristotle's use of teleological principles, by analogy with their use in the biological domain,[15] forms an important part of his strategy to increase the possibility of gaining scientific knowledge of the heavens. Thus, when Aristotle does proceed to give "physical" or

[14] Aristotle's treatment of cosmology as part of the study of nature also explains why the teleological explanations are mainly found in the second book of the *De Caelo*. For it is this book that deals most specifically with the heavenly bodies *qua* subjects of motion, that is, with the plurality, direction, and complexity of their motions, the physical mechanisms underlying those motions, and the shape of the heavenly bodies required to perform those motions. On the other hand, we find no teleological accounts regarding Aristotle's views on the nature of the heavens as a whole (discussed primarily in book I), or regarding the motions and features of the four terrestrial elements (dealt with in books III and IV), which are not part of cosmology properly speaking. Aristotle's use of causal language in the *De Caelo* also reveals that the second book is more concerned with Aristotle's *own* attempts to provide physical explanations than any of the other books: of the twenty-eight occurrences of the term *aition* in the whole of the *De Caelo*, ten can be found in the second book (as opposed to four in the first book; three in the third, and eleven in the fourth book), and of the twenty-eight occurrences of the term *aitia*, twenty-one can be found in the second book (as opposed to none in the first and the third book, and seven in the fourth), while the references to causes and explanations in the fourth book are often (i.e., in *Cael* IV.1, 308a25; *Cael* IV.2, 309a5; *Cael* IV.2, 309a10; *Cael* IV.2, 309a28; *Cael* IV.2, 310a2; *Cael* IV.6, 313a22) – although not exclusively – used in descriptions of views entertained by Aristotle's predecessors.

[15] Pace Falcon (2005, 101), who argues that "Aristotle is reluctant to extend the results achieved in the study of plants and animals to the imperishable creatures populating the celestial world."

"scientific" explanations in the *De Caelo*, he is unremittingly teleological in his approach. The explanations thus presented will not qualify as demonstrations in a strict sense (i.e., not as demonstrations approaching the model as described in the *Analytica Posteriora* or in the first book of the *De Partibus Animalium*),[16] since they do not attempt to demonstrate necessary truths; they rather attempt to show the reasonableness of supposing certain causal scenarios. However, they go a long way towards taking away some of the puzzlement pertaining to the heavenly realm and thus in making sense of the heavenly phenomena. And, as Aristotle has indicated elsewhere,[17] "making sense" in such difficult circumstances entails giving an account of the heavens that is free of impossibilities.

Let us finally turn to some examples of the actual teleological explanations Aristotle provides in the *De Caelo*. Broadly speaking, Aristotle gives two kinds of teleological explanations. The first kind consists of explanations that stand on their own (that is, they do not form part of an interrelated sequence of arguments), and that set out to explain the *presence* of certain features and motions of the heavens. In these cases (i.e., *Cael* II.3, 286a7–9; *Cael* II.5, 288a2–12; and *Cael* II.12, 292a15–b25), Aristotle explains the presence of some observed fact by reference to the function it serves within the heavens as a whole. The basic teleological assumption is that whatever can be seen to be present must be there because it has a function or is good or better that way.

The second kind consists of those teleological explanations that explain the *absence* of heavenly features (this kind is used in *Cael* I.4, 271a22–33; *Cael* II.8, 290a29–35; *Cael* II.9, 291a23–25; and *Cael* II.11, 291b10–15). They usually follow a series of mathematical or numerological arguments following the style of the astronomers. While the latter point out that it is, for instance, mathematically impossible for some motion or feature to be present, the teleological explanation is set up to provide a counterfactual argument claiming that those motions or features in reality could not exist in the heavenly realm, because if they did, they would be in vain. The teleological principle invoked in all of these cases is that nature does nothing in vain.

In the next three sections, I shall discuss two examples from the first group and one example from the second group.

16 Cf. Lloyd (1996, 182).

17 *Meteor* I.7, 344a5–7: "We consider a satisfactory explanation of phenomena inaccessible to observation to have been given when we reduce them to what is possible."

5.2 Explaining Why There Is a Plurality of Motions of the Heavens (Example 1)

A first example of a teleological explanation in the *De Caelo* pertains to the plurality of the heavenly motions: different heavenly bodies are observed to move in different directions – why is it that they do not all move in the same direction? Aristotle introduces his explanation as follows (*Cael* II.3, 286a3–7):

> Since there is no motion in a circle contrary to motion in a circle, we must examine why there are several locomotions, though we must try to conduct the inquiry from far off – far off not so much in their location, but rather by virtue of the fact that we have perception of very few of the attributes that belong to them [i.e., the motions]. Nonetheless, let us speak of the matter. The explanation concerning these things must be grasped from the following [considerations].[18]

This text shows that Aristotle is very well aware of the fact that it is problematic and difficult to offer explanations of what is present in the heavens, given the lack of empirical evidence. We are simply too far removed from the objects of inquiry in distance.[19]

It is significant that Aristotle nevertheless is confident that there is a way of answering this particular question, and that this answer follows from a *teleological* consideration. As we will see shortly, the consideration "from which the explanation must be grasped" is the supposition of the teleological principle that everything that has a function must exist for the sake of that function. By positing a teleological principle, and hence by setting a framework within which one can search for the possible functions of those very features that have been observed, one might be able to find the explanation of why those features are present. On the other hand, the implication also seems to be that this kind of knowledge cannot be gained by other means: observation is certainly ruled out (observation in this case will only yield knowledge of the fact that there are several motions, not

[18] Ἐπεὶ δ' οὐκ ἔστιν ἐναντία κίνησις ἡ κύκλῳ τῇ κύκλῳ, σκεπτέον διὰ τί πλείους εἰσὶ φοραί, καίπερ πόρρωθεν πειρωμένοις ποιεῖσθαι τὴν ζήτησιν, πόρρω δ' οὐχ οὕτω τῷ τόπῳ, πολὺ δὲ μᾶλλον τῷ τῶν συμβεβηκότων αὐτοῖς περὶ πάμπαν ὀλίγων ἔχειν αἴσθησιν. Ὅμως δὲ λέγωμεν. Ἡ δ' αἰτία περὶ αὐτῶν ἐνθένδε ληπτέα.

[19] Cf. Burnyeat (2004; 15–16) who observes that "*De Caelo* I contains an unusually high number of occurrences of words like εἰκότως and εὔλογον which express epistemic modesty: this or that is a *reasonable* thing to believe." I should like to add to this observation that words of "epistemic modesty" are even more abundant in book II where the explanation of the presence and absence of heavenly features properly speaking is at stake (I counted only two occurrences of the word εὔλογον and none of the word εἰκότως in book I; in book II, I counted fifteen occurrences of the word εὔλογον and two of the word εἰκότως).

of the reason why), but also mathematical arguments will not do, again because they cannot yield the reason why there are several motions.

Interestingly, the other two teleological explanations that stand on their own and that explain the presence of heavenly phenomena are also immediately preceded by a discussion of the methodological problems related to this very enterprise of providing explanations in the strong sense for phenomena at such a remove (see *Cael* II.5, 287b29–288a2, II.12, 291b24–28 and II.12, 292a14–18). In all these methodological introductions, Aristotle expresses his conviction that, even though the empirical evidence is scanty, it is still possible to state the phenomena; and given all the limitations, the explanations offered are the best ones possible.[20] For that reason, he says, one should not criticize the person conducting the investigation for being overly ambitious or for not providing more accurate and necessary truths (*Cael* II.5, 287b29–288a2); rather one should be content with "small solutions in things in which we have the greatest difficulties" (*Cael* II.12, 291b28). The explanations that follow these introductions are all teleological in nature, which shows that Aristotle also has great confidence in the explanatory force of teleology in these difficult cases.[21]

Returning to our example from *Cael* II.3, the teleological principle from which "the explanation of why there are several locomotions of the heavens must be grasped," is that "each thing that has a function is for the sake of that function" (*Cael* II.3, 286a8: Ἕκαστόν ἐστιν, ὧν ἐστιν ἔργον, ἕνεκα τοῦ ἔργου). This is a common principle in Aristotle's biology (see, e.g., *PA* I.5, 645b15–18), where it is claimed that each part of the body is for the sake of the performance of some function. By stating it here, Aristotle makes explicit that, in his view, teleology extends to the heavenly domain, and that hence some of the puzzling cosmological phenomena can be explained by reference to teleology. Aristotle also *must* refer to teleology here, since material causes alone cannot account for the differences in

20 Pace Guthrie (1939, 165).

21 This point is also made by Lloyd (1996, 171) with regard to the explanations in *Cael* II.5 and II.12: "Thus it is surely significant that both on the problem of why the heavens revolve in one direction rather than in the other – in II 5 – and on the difficulty of the complexities of the motions of the non-fixed stars – in II 12 – his positive speculations invoke teleology." I disagree, however, with Lloyd's interpretation of the significance of this connection between Aristotle's methodological disclaimers on the one hand and his use of teleology on the other. According to Lloyd (1996, 161, 173, 175, 180), Aristotle's main interest in cosmology follows from his concern to establish his teleology, and especially the orderliness of the heavens. However, I do not believe that Aristotle's epistemological hesitations are not genuine here, or that Aristotle's concern for the establishment of teleology is all that prominent in the *De Caelo*. On the contrary, I believe that Aristotle uses his teleology, already firmly established on the basis of the abundance of empirical evidence discussed in the biological works, to extend – where possible – his knowledge of the heavens.

locomotion in the heavens (for all spheres appear to be made of the same material, which is aether),[22] and there are no other kinds of explanation available. The assumption that everything that has a function is present for the sake of that function allows a series of inferences that ultimately yield the explanation of why there are several motions of the heavens: if this principle applies, then each of the motions must serve its own function.

Aristotle continues his explanation by identifying the function of the first motion in the following way (*Cael* II.3, 286a8–11):

> The activity of god is immortality, and that is everlasting life. In consequence it is necessary that an eternal motion belongs to the divine (ὥστ' ἀνάγκη τῷ θειῷ[23] κίνησιν ἀΐδιον ὑπάρχειν). Since the celestial sphere is such (for its body is a divine thing), for that reason it has a circular body, with which it naturally moves in a circle for eternity.

The reasoning is that, if the function of the divine is immortality, and if the heavens are divine, then the function of heaven is immortality. Furthermore, if being immortal is the defining function of heaven, then it is a necessary prerequisite for it to possess an eternal motion. That is, for heaven as a whole to be able to perform its defining function or its activity of being immortal, it has to perform at least one kind of eternal motion. And the only kind of motion capable of uniform eternal continuity is motion in a circle.

This explanation, curious as it may sound, resembles a particular type of explanation that Aristotle frequently offers in his biological works (see sections 3.2 and 4.3). Consider the following example taken from *De Partibus Animalium*, where Aristotle provides an explanation of why birds have wings (*PA* IV.12, 693b6–14): "For the substantial being of the bird is that of the blooded animals, but at the same time it is also a winged animal . . . and the ability to fly is in the substantial being of the bird."[24] Aristotle takes the essence, or the substantial being of the animal, as a starting point, and derives from this essence the necessary prerequisites for the animal to have in order to be able to perform its defining function. Just as birds must have wings because they are essentially flyers (and the only way for birds

22 Cf. Simplicius, quoting Alexander, *In Cael* 396, 6–9: "it is not possible to make either natural or material necessity responsible for these things, since both spheres have the same matter, but it is necessary to give an account of the difference in terms of some divine governance or ordering." For an analysis and defense of Aristotle's arguments for the existence of aether, see Hankinson (2009).

23 Here I follow Leggatt in reading θειῷ instead of θεῷ with most manuscripts; see Leggatt (1995, 227). I believe Aristotle's argument to be that the celestial sphere is *like* a divine being in the sense that both partake in eternal motion, not that it itself is a god.

24 τῶν γὰρ ἐναίμων ἡ τοῦ ὄρνιθος οὐσία, ἅμα δὲ καὶ πτερυγωτός . . . τῷ δ' ὄρνιθι ἐν τῇ οὐσίᾳ τὸ πτητικόν ἐστιν. Cf. *PA* IV.13, 697b1–13 and *PA* III.6, 669b8–12.

to perform their defining function is by having and using their wings), so too the heavens must have a spherical body and move eternally in a circle because they are essentially immortal. According to this argumentation, eternal motion in a circle is the proper attribute of an immortal body such as the heavens.

However, Aristotle has not yet explained why there are *several* motions of the heavenly bodies. The second part of the explanation of why there are several motions consists of a complicated chain of arguments, based on a total of six assumptions. The starting point of this chain is the conclusion of the first part of the explanation, which is the necessity of there being an eternal motion of the outer sphere in order for the heaven to be immortal. The reasoning Aristotle employs is deductive, but the type of necessity to which Aristotle refers is sometimes that of a necessary consequence, while at other times it is the necessity of something having to be present first if something else is to be present (the latter is what Aristotle calls conditional necessity).[25] Let me give a summary of the chain of arguments (*Cael* II.3, 286a13–286b2):

(a) If there is to be a body that moves in a circle eternally, it must have a center that remains at rest.
(b) For there to be a fixed center, the existence of the element earth is a necessary condition (i.e., since whatever is made of aether cannot remain at rest, there must be a second element next to aether, the natural motion of which is to move towards the center and then to remain at rest in the center).
(c) If there is to be earth, then it is a necessary consequence that there is also fire (for earth and fire are contraries, and if one exists, so does the other).
(d) If there is to be fire and earth, then it is a necessary consequence that the two other elements exist (for water and air are in a relation of contrariety to each of the other two elements).
(e) From the existence of the four elements, it necessarily follows that there must be generation (for none of the four sublunary elements can be everlasting).
(f) If there must be generation, then it is necessary that there exists some other motion.

[25] The formula "ἀνάγκη . . . εἶναι" is repeated six times: in *Cael* II.3, 286a13; II.3, 286a20; and II.3, 286b2 (see (a), (b), and (f) in the following summary) the necessity is conditional; in *Cael* II.3, 286a22; II.3, 286a28; and II.3, 286a32 (see (c), (d), and (e) in the summary) the necessity indicates a necessary consequence.

According to this account, generation is a necessary consequence of there being sublunary elements, whose existence is a necessary condition for there to be an eternal, cyclical motion of the outermost sphere of the heavens carrying the fixed stars. However, having established that it is necessary for there to be generation (as a consequence of there being four sublunary elements), Aristotle turns the argument around, and reasons that if there is to be generation, then it is conditionally necessary for there to be other motions, because the motions of the outermost sphere alone cannot cause generation. Accordingly, generation is that for the sake of which all the other motions (namely, the motions of the planets) take place. This is how Aristotle summarizes his explanation (*Cael* II.3, 286b6–9):

> For the moment so much is clear, for what reason there are several bodies moving in circles, namely because it is necessary that there is generation (ὅτι ἀνάγκη γένεσιν εἶναι), and generation [is necessary], if there also has to be fire, and that one and the others [are necessary] if there also has to be earth, and that one because it is necessary that something always remains at rest, if there has to be something that is for ever in motion.

The complete explanation of why there are several motions of the heavens is thus that there are different functions that require the presence of different motions. There is one eternal motion in a circle (performed by the outer sphere carrying the fixed stars) that is required for the sake of realizing the immortality of the heavens, and there are other motions (performed by the inner spheres carrying the planets) that must take place, if there is to be generation.

Here, the use of the teleological principle allows Aristotle to draw an organic picture of the cosmological system in which all the observed motions can be explained by the purpose they serve.[26] Arguably, this picture and the type of reasoning behind it are not without problems,[27] but at least Aristotle is able to give some rationale for some phenomena the astronomers did not explain. The plurality of the motions of the heavenly bodies makes sense in the light of the need for the heavens as a whole to perform an eternal motion, if they are to be truly immortal, and – as a corollary – of the need for there to be generation, if this eternal motion is to be at all.

[26] Cf. Aristotle's – perhaps even less satisfactory – analogy of the cosmos with a household in *Meta* XII.10, 1075a19–22, which equally depicts the sublunary realm (the slaves and animals in the analogy) as a necessary condition for the heavenly realm (the freemen in the analogy).

[27] For instance, it does not establish an explanation for *each* of the individual motions of the planets, or for the need for there to be generation; this latter point is well brought out by Hankinson (2002–2003, 31–32); see ibid. for further criticisms of the argument.

5.3 EXPLAINING WHY THE HEAVENLY BODIES MOVE WITH DIFFERENT COMPLEXITIES (EXAMPLE 2)

Let me now turn to a second example from the first group of teleological explanations, which is part of Aristotle's solution to the first problem under scrutiny in *Cael* II.12, and pertains to the number of movements each of the heavenly bodies undergoes. The example is particularly representative for Aristotle's "tentative" explanatory strategy in the *De Caelo* in that it relies heavily on analogical reasoning and employs a thought experiment.[28]

Aristotle states that among the many cosmological problems "the one that is most amazing" (*Cael* II.12, 291b29) is that, while one would expect the heavenly bodies that are nearer to the outer sphere to undergo fewer motions than the ones further away, observations[29] and old sources both give evidence that there is in fact no correlation between the distance of a heavenly body to the outer sphere and the complexity of its motions. For the Sun and the Moon, although further away from the outer sphere, perform fewer motions than some[30] of the other planets that are closer to it. Aristotle introduces his solution as follows (*Cael* II.12, 292a17–22):

About these things it is well to seek more understanding, even though we have very few resources to start from and are at such a great distance from their attributes. Nonetheless, by beginning our study from the following [sort of consideration], the present difficulty will not appear as anything absurd. We think about them as if they are bodies only, and units with a certain order, but being altogether without soul; but it is necessary to suppose that they partake in action and life: for in that way the outcome will seem to be nothing unreasonable.[31]

28 Aristotle frequently relies on thought experiments (usually in the form of counterfactuals) in the *De Caelo*. The most interesting one is perhaps in *Cael* II.2, 285b1–7, where he asks us to think of the body of the heavens as a thing (i) in which left and right are functionally differentiated (even though this is not obvious to perception, as it is covered by a sphere) and (ii) as having an origin of motion from where it would have started to move (even though, since the heavens are eternal, there is no actual chronological beginning or end of motion). On this thought experiment, and on the teleological explanation of the direction in which the heavens move in *Cael* II.5, see Lennox (2009). For a general discussion of thought experiments in antiquity, see Ierodiakonou (2005).

29 *Cael* II.12, 292a2: "it is clear also to observation (τῇ ὄψει) that that happens with some of them."

30 Modern commentators point out that Aristotle's claim in *Cael* II.12, 291b34–292a1 that "the Sun and the Moon undergo fewer movements than some (ἔνια) of the planets" is problematic, since whatever version of the theory of concentric spheres one accepts, the Sun and the Moon undergo fewer movements than *all* of the other planets. See Leggatt (1995, 246) for an outline of and a possible solution to this problem.

31 Περὶ δὴ τούτων ζητεῖν μὲν καλῶς ἔχει καὶ τὴν ἐπὶ πλεῖον σύνεσιν, καίπερ μικρὰς ἔχοντας ἀφορμὰς καὶ τοσαύτην ἀπόστασιν ἀπέχοντας τῶν περὶ αὐτὰ συμβαινόντων· ὅμως δ' ἐκ τῶν τοιούτων θεωροῦσιν οὐδὲν ἄλογον ἂν δόξειεν εἶναι τὸ νῦν ἀπορούμενον. Ἀλλ' ἡμεῖς ὡς περὶ σωμάτων αὐτῶν μόνον, καὶ μονάδων τάξιν μὲν ἐχόντων, ἀψύχων δὲ πάμπαν, διανοούμεθα· δεῖ δ' ὡς μετεχόντων ὑπολαμβάνειν πράξεως καὶ ζωῆς· οὕτω γὰρ οὐθὲν δόξει παράλογον εἶναι τὸ συμβαῖνον.

As in example 1 discussed above, the methodological caveat is followed by the proposition to think about the motions of the heavenly bodies within a teleological framework (as we saw in section 4.2, ὑπολαμβάνειν is the technical verb for positing principles). If we think of the heavenly bodies as living beings, which act and move for the sake of ends and do so in virtue of possessing an internal principle of movement (i.e., their soul), the observed phenomena will make sense.

Before applying the notion of goal-directed action to the motions of the heavenly bodies, Aristotle first explicates two "rules" that govern this type of action. The first pertains to the number of actions needed to achieve the good (*Cael* II.12, 292a22–24): what is in the best state possesses the good without action; what is close achieves it by few motions or even by one; and what is further away achieves it by many motions. Aristotle uses an analogy of the number of exercises a body needs to undergo in order to acquire a healthy condition: a person who is already in good condition does not need to exercise; those who are not in such good condition need to perform one or more kinds of exercises to achieve a good condition; and some can never achieve a healthy condition at all, but only some substitute for it. The second "rule" states that the higher the number of intermediate goals that need to be achieved, the more difficult it is to achieve the ultimate end; Aristotle illustrates this with an analogy drawn from the game of knucklebones (*Cael* II.12, 292a28–b1). Because these are the correlations that exist between the number of actions needed to reach the good and the initial distance of the agent from this good, this is how we should think (δεῖ νομίζειν)[32] of the actions of the stars and planets (*Cael* II.12, 292b1–2): "This is why it is necessary that we consider also the action of the stars as being of the exact same sort as the action of living beings and plants."

Subsequently, Aristotle fills in the details of this analogy between the actions of sublunary living beings on the one hand and the motions of heavenly bodies on the other hand (*Cael* II.12, 292b2–19; see Table 5.2 for an overview). In the world around us (*Cael* II.12, 292b2: ἐνταῦθα), different kinds of beings perform a different number of motions and have different levels of access to the good. And just as in the case where health is the ultimate good, different people require a different number of actions to achieve the good, or, if they cannot achieve it, try to get as close to their goal as possible, since "a thing is better the nearer it is to the best" (*Cael* II.12, 292b18–19). Thus we get the following base domain of the analogy: a person in the best state performs no actions, because he already

[32] For the terminology, see Bogen and McGuire (1986–7, 424–425).

Table 5.2 *The analogy between the actions of sublunary beings and the motions of the heavenly bodies*

Kinds of sublunary living beings	Number of actions needed to achieve the good	Kinds of heavenly bodies	Number of motions needed to achieve the good
Humans	Need many actions, but are able to achieve the good	Other planets	Need many motions, but are able to achieve the good
Person in the best state	Needs no actions, already possesses the good	Outer sphere	Needs one motion, but is able to achieve the good
Animals	Need few actions, but only have limited access to the good	Sun and moon	Need few motions, but only achieve the good to a certain degree
Plants	Need few actions, but are only able to achieve intermediate goods	Earth	Performs no motion, and is unable to achieve the good.

possesses the good. Humans who are not already in the best state perform many motions, and have full access to the good. Animals perform few actions, which allows them to achieve only an intermediate good (performing more actions would serve no purpose, since animals will never achieve the highest good). And, finally, plants perform few actions, but they are completely unable to achieve the ultimate good.

Next, Aristotle is in a position to apply these general patterns to the target domain of the analogy, i.e., to the motions of the heavenly bodies (*Cael* II.12, 292b19–25):

> And because of this the Earth does not move at all, and the ones that are close [i.e., the Sun and the Moon] have only few movements: for they do not reach the end, but they are able to reach the most divine principle only to a certain point. The first heaven attains it immediately through one movement. The ones in between the first and the last [i.e., the other planets] reach it, but they reach it through several movements.

In other words, Aristotle urges us to think of the Earth as plants: the Earth is like plants in that it is unable to achieve the good, and therefore does not move at all. The Sun and the Moon are like animals, in that they have only limited access to the good, which is supposed to explain why they perform few motions – it is no use performing more motions, as they will

never achieve the highest principle. The outer sphere is like a person who is already in the best condition; but unlike the person in the best state who does not need to perform any actions, the outer sphere performs one motion, which allows it to reach the highest principle. And finally, the intermediate planets are like humans: they are able to achieve the highest principle, but need many motions to do this.

Aristotle seems to believe that this reasoning suffices to make the differentiation regarding the complexity of the motions of the heavenly bodies less perplexing, as he moves on in the next lines to deal with the second problem introduced at the beginning of the chapter.

If my reconstruction is correct, however, Aristotle must have meant this analogy to work quite loosely.[33] As is clear from my summary above, the Earth is not really like plants, because the Earth does not move at all, and the outer sphere is not really like the person who is in the best state, because the outer sphere performs one (eternal) movement. The thought experiment cannot fully explain the differentiation (the causal model of the different motions of the heavenly bodies is not literally that of goal-directed actions, nor are there any functional differences between the heavenly bodies),[34] but it does reduce the puzzlement, and that is all Aristotle set out to achieve. As was the case in example 1, lack of empirical evidence makes it hard to provide fully fledged physical explanations in cases like these, but through the use of teleological principles Aristotle at least succeeds in mitigating some of the perplexities pertaining to the heavenly motions.

5.4 EXPLAINING WHY STARS HAVE NO FEET (EXAMPLE 3)

I shall now turn to an example of the second type of teleological explanations, where Aristotle uses some form of the teleological principle that nature does nothing in vain in order to explain the *absence* of heavenly features, usually after a series of mathematical arguments or discussions of the available empirical evidence.

The explanandum to be discussed concerns the question whether or not the stars and planets possess a motion independently of the motion of the spheres. One explanation is given in chapter II.8, where Aristotle tries to show that the heavenly bodies most likely do not possess a motion of their own, but are carried around fixed in concentric spheres. The basic idea is

33 Pace Johnson (2005, 139) who interprets the analogy in a strong causal sense, arguing that its point is "that the motion of the heavens is purposeful activity."

34 For the distinction between a "strong" and a "weak" use of analogy, see Hankinson (1998, 22).

that if the stars possessed their own motion, they would be self-movers, and this would make them in principle capable of stopping their motions, which would threaten the eternity of the heavens and life as we know it. First, Aristotle sketches three possible scenarios of the motions of the heavenly bodies and their spheres (*Cael* II.8, 289b1–3). As both are observed to move as a whole, it is necessary that the change of position takes place with both the heavens and the stars being at rest, or with both moving, or with the one moving and the other at rest. Aristotle then refers to empirical evidence (*Cael* II.8, 289b5 and b10) and gives mathematical arguments (*Cael* II.8, 289b27–28) in order to show that the scenario in which the spheres move while the heavenly bodies are at rest is "the least absurd" (*Cael* II.8, 289b34–35: μόνως γὰρ οὕτως οὐθὲν ἄλογον συμβαίνει). In addition to this, Aristotle offers a final teleological argument in favor of this theory, arguing for the unlikelihood of the stars and planets possessing a motion on their own. The argument runs as follows (*Cael* II.8, 290a29–35):

> In addition to these arguments, it would be absurd that nature gave them no organ for motion (since nature does nothing as a matter of chance), and that she should care for animals, but disregard such honorable beings; rather, it seems that nature, as though deliberately, has taken away everything by means of which they might possibly in themselves have effected forward motion, and that she set them at the greatest distance from those things that possess organs for motion.[35]

In a way, Aristotle's explanation here parallels that of Plato in the *Timaeus.* In this dialogue, Timaeus explains that the divine craftsman did not think it to be necessary to equip the heaven – self-sufficient and perfect as it is – with hands or feet for walking (*Ti* 33d–34a):

> For he thought that a being which is self-sufficient would be much better than one which is in need of other things. And he did not think it was necessary to attach hands to it to no purpose – hands for which there would be no need either to grasp or to defend itself against anything; nor had it any need of feet, nor of the whole apparatus of walking (χειρῶν δέ, αἷς οὔτε λαβεῖν οὔτε αὖ τινα ἀμύνασθαι χρεία τις ἦν, μάτην οὐκ ᾤετο δεῖν αὐτῷ προσάπτειν, οὐδὲ ποδῶν οὐδὲ ὅλως τῆς περὶ τὴν βάσιν ὑπηρεσίας). For he assigned to it the motion that is most suited to its body, [the motion] which, of the seven, is the most appropriate to mind and to thinking. And therefore he caused it to move in the same manner and on the same spot and revolving in a circle within its own limits. All other six [motions] he took away (τὰς δὲ ἓξ ἁπάσας κινήσεις ἀφεῖλεν) and it was made not to partake

[35] Πρὸς δὲ τούτοις ἄλογον τὸ μηθὲν ὄργανον αὐτοῖς ἀποδοῦναι την φύσιν πρὸς τὴν κίνησιν (οὐθὲν γὰρ ὡς ἔτυχε ποιεῖ ἡ φύσις), οὐδὲ τῶν μὲν ζῴων φροντίσαι, τῶν δ᾿ οὕτω τιμίων ὑπεριδεῖν, ἀλλ᾿ ἔcικεν ὥσπερ ἐπίτηδες ἀφελεῖν πάντα δι᾿ ὧν ἐνεδέχετο προϊέναι καθ᾿ αὑτά, καὶ ὅτι πλεῖστον ἀποστῆσαι τῶν ἐχόντων ὄργανα πρὸς κίνησιν.

in their deviations. And as this circular motion required no feet, the universe was created without legs and without feet.

In this passage, Plato describes how the heaven was created and was given its circular motion, which is most appropriate for its spherical shape. The other types of motion – forwards/backwards, to the left/to the right, and up/down – were taken away from it. However, instead of this mythological account for why the stars have no feet, Aristotle opts for a naturalistic explanation.

The structure of Aristotle's argument is quite complex. In short, it consists of a *reductio ad absurdum* followed by an alternative account proclaiming the purposiveness, or perhaps even the providence, of nature. The first part of the argument builds upon the implicit counterfactual assumption that if the stars "were intended by nature" to be moving on their own, it would be absurd for nature not to have given them organs for motion, given the fact that nature did provide such organs to "lesser" beings. I take the expression that "nature does nothing as a matter of chance" to be equivalent to the principle that nature does nothing in vain: living beings always have the parts that they need, and if the heavenly bodies lack organs for motion, that lack must be for the sake of something. Or, to put it the other way around, if the organs for motion are absent in heavenly bodies it must be because their presence would have been in vain (they would have had no function to fulfill in this particular kind of being). The reference to the honorable status of heavenly beings implies that Aristotle takes the teleology of nature to apply even *more* to them than to the sublunary beings.

The *implicit* underlying teleological principle here is that each capacity (in this case the capacity for locomotion) requires an organ (cf. *GA* I.2, 716a24–25) and that thus locomotion of the stars is possible if and only if they have organs for locomotion. The absurdity lies in the fact that nature *did* provide less honorable beings with organs for motion, and that we would have to conclude, were we to accept this account as true, that nature purposely neglected more honorable beings such as the stars. Since this account is of course unacceptable within Aristotle's view of the way nature operates, the opposite scenario, set out in the second part of the argument, must be the case: nature has *taken away* every means of locomotion, and thereby set a distance between the heavenly bodies and the sublunary beings equipped with organs for motion.[36] As Aristotle explains, spherical

[36] Aristotle considers it to be better for the superior to be separated from the inferior; cf. *GA* II.1, 732a6–8.

bodies are least fit to effect forward motion on their own, because they lack "points of motion" (*Cael* II.8, 290b5–8): "[F]or forward motion it is least fit, since it is least like to those things that produce motion on their own; for it does not have any appendage or projection, as does a rectilinear figure, but stands most apart in shape from those bodies equipped for locomotion."

The core of this teleological argument for why the heavenly bodies do not have a motion of their own, and hence must be fixed in spheres, is thus the assumption (presented as a fact) that heavenly bodies do not have feet or any other organs for locomotion. For, if nature – for the most part – does nothing in vain and the heavenly bodies have no feet, then the conclusion is reasonable that nature must have "designed" the heavenly bodies not to be able to move on their own.

The teleological argument Aristotle offers here is again in many ways similar to explanations we find in the biological works. In biology, Aristotle holds that all animals that are capable of locomotion must have organs for motion and that animals without organs for motion are not capable of locomotion.[37] These two "laws" are exhaustive with regard to all blooded land-walkers. The one and only exception to this rule is formed by the footless snake, which obviously does not have organs specifically designed for locomotion, but moves forward by bending itself. Just as in our example concerning the heavenly bodies, we saw that Aristotle explains the absence of feet in snakes by invoking the principle that nature does nothing in vain (*IA* 8, 708a9–20; quoted above in section 4.2).

In section 4.2, I argued that in the case of the footless snake, Aristotle invokes the principle that nature does nothing in vain in order to set up the counterfactual argument that if nature had equipped snakes with feet, snakes would move very badly and the feet would have been next to useless. The cause of the uselessness of the feet is the extraordinary body-length of the snake: no kind of animal whose length is out of proportion to the rest of its body can have four feet, because having four feet makes such animals completely immobile; and snakes are animals that have such a body size. Given the principle that nature does nothing in vain (*and* that

[37] *PA* IV.10, 686a35–b1: "all (animals) that walk must have two hind feet" and *IA* 3, 705a19–25: "That which moves always makes its change of place by the employment of at least two organic parts, one as it were compressing and the other being compressed. And so nothing that is without parts can move in this manner; for it does not contain in itself the distinction between what is to be passive and what is to be active." Cf. *GA* II.3, 736b22–24: "for it is clear that the principles of which the activity is bodily cannot exist without a body, such as walking [cannot exist] without feet" (οἷον βαδίζειν ἄνευ ποδῶν).

nature cannot give snakes more than four feet, since, in that case, the snake would not be blooded), snakes do not have feet.[38]

There is, however, an important difference between the explanatory force of the use of this principle in biology as opposed to its use in cosmology, and this difference derives directly from the lack of observational evidence in the latter domain.[39] For in the biological domain *observation* determines the possibilities of what nature does and does not produce.[40] The design possibilities that Aristotle allows to enter into thought experiments are thus also strictly limited by the range of features that can actually be observed to be available in nature. In the case of the footless snake, observation shows that all other blooded animals that live on land have feet; blooded land-dwellers share to a certain extent the same formal nature, which explains the occurrence of certain co-extensive features like the possession of a maximum of four feet. The snake also possesses all the properties that belong to blooded land-dwellers, except for one. It is therefore rational to ask why this particular property is absent in snakes, and, in the thought experiment, to imagine feet to be present. It is not rational to ask why snakes lack wings, telescopic eyes, or any other part that cannot be observed to belong to the wider class to which snakes belong, or to imagine these features to be present in snakes. As there is a virtual infinity of properties that any animal does not have, it only makes sense for a natural scientist to explain the absence (by means of imagining the presence) of those properties that belong to the "natural possibilities" of that animal; and what those natural possibilities are can be established inductively, on the basis of observation and through comparison with related beings.

In the cosmological domain, on the other hand, the range of possible ways in which a certain feature or motion could be present is only partly determined by observation. What cannot be observed might still be present, and what can be observed might be the result of a visual illusion. Aristotle often struggles with this question of how much credence we must attribute to our observations of the heavens, and of which observations we should

[38] However, the fact that snakes do not have organs for motion does not mean that they are not capable of locomotion: they move forwards by bending themselves (see *IA* 7, 707b6–31; *IA* 8, 709a25–b4; and *IA* 10, 709b27–28). This may point to a problem for Aristotle's argument concerning the heavenly bodies: for the absence of *organs* for locomotion as such does not provide conclusive evidence that the stars in fact are not capable of locomotion. Of course, as the remainder of *Cael* II.8 points out, Aristotle is actually committed to the stronger claim that spherical bodies do not only lack organs for motion, but also "points of motion," which (at least given Aristotle's laws of sublunary mechanics) rules out any possible way of locomotion.

[39] For the question whether or not principles from biology can be applied legitimately in cosmology, see *Cael* II.2, 284b6–24 and its discussion in Lennox (2009).

[40] Lennox (2001a, 214–215).

explain and which we should explain away. His general strategy is to explain the phenomena and hence to save them, but on occasion, especially where there are contradictory observations, the observations that conflict with the theory of the stars moving around fixed in concentric spheres are rather explained away. This is exactly what happens in the paragraphs leading up to the explanation of why stars have no feet in *Cael* II.8, 290a12–29. Before giving his teleological argument demonstrating the likelihood of the absence of feet in stars, Aristotle argued that if the heavenly bodies were to move on their own, they would either roll or rotate, but that neither of these motions is observed to take place. The impression that the Sun rotates in rising and setting[41] is then explained away: according to Aristotle, the rotation is merely a visual illusion, caused by the weakness and unsteadiness of our vision.

What this makes clear is, first of all, that while in biology observations clearly show that snakes lack feet, observational evidence of the heavens gives much less certainty about the absence of feet in the heavenly bodies. For all we can tell, the heavenly bodies might be too far away for us to see their organs of motion. Second, observations of the heavens will not tell us whether there are any *natural* limitations to the possible ways in which nature could have "designed" stars in order to make them able to move on their own. The absence of feet in the heavenly bodies in itself seems hardly enough to establish the reasonableness of the alternative theory that they do not effect any forward motion at all.

This difference between the reliability and applicability of observational evidence in biology and cosmology is important, because Aristotle's explanation in the case of the heavenly bodies is not *prompted* by the observation that they do not have organs for motion, as it is in the case of snakes.[42] There are no observations of the heavens that would reasonably lead to the expectation of heavenly bodies having feet in the first place. (One might object, however, that in this case the philosophical tradition within which Aristotle is working prompts this question.[43]) Rather, Aristotle works the other way around: because he wants to make the theory that the stars do

41 Xenophanes might have observed the same phenomenon, and gives it a similar explanation; see *DK*21A41a: δοκεῖν δὲ κυκλεῖσθαι διὰ τὴν ἀπόστασιν; "[the sun] seems to turn in a circle due to its distance."

42 As I argued in section 4.2, Aristotle uses the principle in *De Partibus Animalium* typically when he discovers that an animal lacks a part that is present in all other members of its wider class. For examples, see *PA* IV.12, 694a13–20; *PA* IV.12, 694a16–18; *PA* IV.13, 696a10–15 and *PA* IV.13, 696a12.

43 On this tradition, see Cornford (1975, 55–56); besides Plato, Empedocles also seems to have argued for the footlessness of the celestial sphere (*DK*31B29: οὐ γὰρ ἀπὸ νώτοιο δύο κλάδοι ἀίσσονται, οὐ πόδες, οὐ θοὰ γοῦν(α), οὐ μήδεα γεννήεντα, ἀλλὰ σφαῖρος ἔην καὶ <πάντοθεν> ἶσος ἑαυτῶι).

not move on their own as reasonable as possible, he uses the teleological principle that nature does nothing in vain to argue for the likelihood of the absence of the organs of motion in the heavenly bodies (cf. *Cael* II.11, 291b11–17, where Aristotle repeats the argument in a slightly modified way).

In sum, it seems that in this example Aristotle goes out of his way to establish the reasonableness of the assumption that the heavenly bodies do not have a motion of their own, and hence must be carried around while being fixed in concentric spheres. In the biological realm, the observation of what happens always or for the most part in nature is what allows us to draw inferences about cases in which the goal-directedness is less evident. In a domain such as cosmology, which is empirically underdetermined, such inferences are necessarily of a conjectural nature. However, if teleology extends to the heavenly realm, and Aristotle assumes that it does, then the use of teleological principles allows Aristotle to make the most sense of the phenomena, and to provide explanations appropriate to the science of nature, rather than merely astrological or mathematical ones.

5.5 CONCLUSION

In the ears of a modern audience, Aristotle's teleological explanations of heavenly phenomena may sound rather unusual, but what I hope to have made clear in this chapter is that they make perfect sense within Aristotle's conception of natural science. If the heavens are part of nature, then we need at least to attempt to state all possible causes for their motions and features, even if the investigation has been made difficult because of the scarcity of empirical data. Aristotle's use of teleological principles thus follows from his treatment of the study of the heavens as part of the study of nature, and we have seen that this approach is especially prominent in the second book of the *De Caelo*, where Aristotle searches for explanations of the features and motions of the heavens as a whole and of the heavenly bodies. The scientific investigation of an empirically undetermined domain such as the heavens is difficult, and as his methodological reflections show, Aristotle is mostly well aware of all the problems involved. However, if one wants to gain knowledge of the heavens and its bodies, one has to try and give explanations that at least make the phenomena – both in terms of what can and of what cannot be observed – seem as reasonable as possible.[44]

The strategy that Aristotle employs to generate these plausible accounts is to posit teleological principles as a means of finding causal factors in

[44] Cf. Irwin (1988, 34).

difficult cases. As I argued in Chapter 4, the principles used are not a priori postulates, but suppositions derived from empirical evidence. They are generalizations over the actions of the formal nature of beings, based on numerous observations made in the biological domain. Just as the use of these principles helped Aristotle to find final causes in cases where these were not immediately observable in biology, in the same way Aristotle hopes to find explanations for natural phenomena in the cosmological realm. This gives a very central role to Aristotle's scientific practice in biology: one could say that where Aristotle's philosophy of science as described in the *Analytica Posteriora* offers the student of nature his scientific toolbox, the accessible and rich domain of biology is the student's main workplace. The experience and knowledge acquired in studying the biological phenomena may then – of course with suitable adaptations and refinements – be applied to other, less accessible domains of nature, such as the heavens.

The application of teleological principles to the cosmological domain is itself based on the assumption that the heavens are no less teleological – and perhaps even more teleological – than the sublunary realm is. However, as I have pointed out above, the lack of empirical evidence in the cosmological realm also weakens to some extent the inferences Aristotle draws within this teleological framework:[45] the explanations are plausible, but not as "conclusive" as the ones we can find in the biological works.

For the *De Caelo* this means that Aristotle argues as much from as towards teleology: starting from the assumption that the heavens as a whole are goal-directed, Aristotle tries to give a coherent, plausible, and reasonable picture of the heavens in which things are present or absent for a reason. This is Aristotle's main goal in the *De Caelo*: even if it is not possible to give deductions that demonstrate why the heavens and the heavenly bodies have the features they have, one can still offer plausible physical accounts that take away some of the puzzlement concerning the heavens.

[45] Cf. Falcon (2005, ix): "there are features of the celestial world that outrun the explanatory resources developed by Aristotle for the study of the sublunary world."

CHAPTER 6

Aristotle's model of science: formalizing teleological explanations in the Analytica Posteriora

6.0 INTRODUCTION

In the *Analytica Posteriora*, Aristotle defines scientific knowledge as knowledge of the reason why. Knowing why something is the case amounts to being able to provide a scientific demonstration (*apodeixis*), which consists in a valid syllogistic argument in the mode Barbara (i.e., AaB, BaC, ∴ AaC). Such demonstrations typically deduce the necessity of an attribute belonging per se to a certain subject through a middle term that picks out the cause of that necessary relationship. Thus, if formalized in accordance with the recommendations of the *Analytica Posteriora*, causal explanations (i.e., linguistic expressions that identify the cause of some phenomenon) will constitute scientific demonstrations. However, despite the long tradition of Aristotelian scholarship on this treatise, many details concerning the precise nature and syllogistic structure of demonstration remain enigmatic, and are subject of much controversy.[1]

In this chapter, I aim to shed light on Aristotle's pivotal discussion of the integration of the four types of causal explanation into the syllogistic framework of demonstration in *APo* II.11, and specifically on his suggestions on how to formalize teleological explanations. In the first part of this chapter (sections 6.1–6.3), I shall clarify the examples Aristotle provides to illustrate his theoretical remarks about how to formalize causal explanations into the syllogistic structure of scientific demonstration. In particular, I hope to make sense of the teleological example of walking after dinner for the sake of health. In the second part (section 6.4) of the chapter, I shall juxtapose these findings with conclusions from the previous five chapters concerning Aristotle's practice. In particular, I shall focus on the structure of three of the most common types of actual teleological

[1] For present purposes, I leave aside the question of whether the *Analytica Posteriora* is supposed to present a theory of scientific methodology and investigation or a theory of the organization and presentation of the finished scientific system. On this matter, see among others Barnes (1993, xi–xix).

explanations provided in Aristotle's *De Partibus Animalium*. This will show that Aristotle's theory and practice of teleological explanation are in agreement with each other, and that both are more flexible and comprehensive than has been acknowledged so far.

6.1 CAUSES, EXPLANATIONS, AND MIDDLE TERMS

The problem: the middle terms of the examples in APo *II.11 do not pick out all four causes*

In *APo* I.2, Aristotle explains that demonstrations are syllogistic in form and causal in content. A demonstration is a special kind of deductive argument that produces scientific knowledge (*APo* I.2, 71b17–19), where scientific knowledge is defined as knowledge of why things are the case (*APo* I.2, 71b9–13):

> We think we have <scientific> knowledge (ἐπίστασθαι) of each thing without qualification (and not in the sophistic way, incidentally), when we think we know the explanation because of which the state of affairs is the case (ὅταν τήν τ' αἰτίαν οἰώμεθα γινώσκειν δι' ἣν τὸ πρᾶγμά ἐστιν), that it is its explanation, and also that it is not possible for this [state of affairs] to be otherwise. It is clear that something of this kind is what it is to have <scientific> knowledge.

At the beginning of *APo* II.11, Aristotle specifies – and, from our perspective, complicates – this assertion by introducing his "doctrine" of four *aitiai* or causal explanations, which, he claims, are all to be demonstrated[2] through the middle term (*APo* II.11, 94a20–27):

> Since we think we have <scientific> knowledge when we know the explanation, and there are four types of explanation: one, what it is to be a thing, and another, given what things being the case it is necessary for that to hold; another, what first initiated the motion; and fourth, the for the sake of what – all of them are demonstrated through the middle term.[3]

After this short introduction to the topic of this chapter, Aristotle moves on to give syllogistic examples of how each of the four explanations (*aitiai*) is indeed demonstrated through the middle term.

[2] I follow Barnes (1993, 282) in translating both forms of *apodeiknunai* and *deiknunai* with the verb "to demonstrate," and forms of *epideiknunai* and *dêloun* with the verb "to show."

[3] Ἐπεὶ δὲ ἐπίστασθαι οἰόμεθα ὅταν εἰδῶμεν τὴν αἰτίαν, αἰτίαι δὲ τέτταρες, μία μὲν τὸ τί ἦν εἶναι, μία δὲ τὸ τίνων ὄντων ἀνάγκη τοῦτ' εἶναι, ἑτέρα δὲ ἡ τί πρῶτον ἐκίνησε, τετάρτη δὲ τὸ τίνος ἕνεκα, πᾶσαι αὗται διὰ τοῦ μέσου δείκνυνται. See the appendix for a complete translation of *APo* II.11, 94a20–94b26.

In contrast to the apparent clarity of structure and argument in this chapter, its content has raised many interpretative problems for modern scholars, most of which pertain to the general purpose of the chapter and to the nature of the individual syllogistic examples. The sentence stating that "all the *aitiai* are demonstrated through the middle term" has traditionally been interpreted as meaning that all four Aristotelian causes can or even must be picked out by the middle term in scientific demonstrations.[4] However, under this interpretation the syllogistic examples Aristotle gives to illustrate his introductory sentence present us with two major difficulties. In the first place, contrary to the expectations of many interpreters, the syllogisms posited in no way constitute typical Barbara demonstrations where the predicates hold universally and necessarily of the subjects.[5] In the second place, it is not immediately clear how the middle terms in the given examples refer to the causes in question. In particular the section that shows how final causes are demonstrated through the middle term is notorious, because the final cause is not picked out by the middle term, but by the major or predicate term.[6] Some scholars have taken up Aristotle's own suggestion that things will become clearer if we "change the *logoi*" (94b21–22: *metalambanein tous logous*), taking it to mean that we as readers are supposed to rearrange the syllogism so that the middle term picks out the final cause after all.[7] However, it is not an easy undertaking to construct such a syllogism, let alone to do so while remaining close to the Aristotelian

4 This interpretation ultimately goes back to Philoponus, who criticizes this chapter in his commentary on the *Analytica Posteriora* (*In APo* 376, 12–14; 376, 16–18; 376, 31–2; 377, 21–22 and 377, 26–27). He thinks that the examples are wrong and rebukes Aristotle for having set out the syllogisms in a confused way (*In APo* 378, 16–19; 379, 4–9; 379, 33–380, 3). In order to correct Aristotle, Philoponus rearranges the examples and thereby maneuvers the causes into the preferred position of the middle term (*In APo* 378, 19–22; 379, 33–380, 3; 381, 35–36).

5 Cf. Barnes (1993, xvi) ("In chapters B11–12 the syllogism is, alas, a positive embarrassment and a bar to understanding") and (1993, 228) and Ross (1949, 647) (Ross calls Aristotle's examples "quasi-syllogisms").

6 For the difficulties modern commentators encounter in this section, see Barnes (1993, 225, 229); Detel (1993, 695, 707); and Ross (1949, 642). The problem is expressed most emphatically in Detel (1997, 65–66):

> The syllogistic reconstruction of the first of these [two teleological] examples Aristotle seems to offer in the subsequent passage (94b12–20) turns out to be, at first sight, extremely problematic, though, since he represents the aim of being healthy, not by the middle term, B, but by the major term, A. This is *clearly incompatible* with his general claim, expressed in 94a20–24, that the aim too must be proved through the middle term (the italics are mine).

7 See in particular Detel (1993, 684–716; 1997, 65–67). Recently, Johnson (2005, 52–55) argued that "changing the terms" should be read as entailing that "health" and "good digestion" are convertible in this explanation. This, however, is only possible if the terms were coextensive, which seems unlikely in this case. Bolton (1997, 115), saves the example, but suggests that ultimately what is picked out by the major term (the final cause) is "in its primitive definition" equal to what is picked out by the middle term (the material cause).

original. On the whole, the verdict of interpreters on this chapter has been very negative.[8]

The hypothesis: the causality of the explanation and of the explanatory middle term can be different

The hypothesis that I put forward in order to solve the problem outlined above is a fairly simple one. I submit that it is not the examples that are wrong, but rather our interpretation of what Aristotle means by saying that "all the *aitiai* are demonstrated through the middle term." What is crucial for the understanding of this chapter is that within an Aristotelian demonstration there can be a difference between the type of causality expressed in the *explanation* of a phenomenon (i.e. the type of causality expressed by the whole demonstrative syllogism), and the type of causality expressed in the middle term that picks out the explanans or cause of this phenomenon. In the case of demonstrations of teleological phenomena, I shall even argue for the stronger case that the type of causality expressed by the middle term *must be* different from that expressed in the explanation that is being formalized into a demonstration. The upshot of this distinction for Aristotle's theory of demonstration is that all the four types of explanation will be demonstrated through the middle term (because it is through the middle term that a demonstrative syllogism is construed), but that the middle term itself will *not* have to refer to the corresponding cause in all four cases.

I shall give an example to illustrate this distinction. Consider the *dia ti* question of what is ice. Aristotle takes this question (as presented in *APo* II.12, 95a16–21; cf. *Meta* VIII.2, 1043a9–10) to be about the essence of ice – about what ice *is*. An adequate explanation thus needs to be a formal one. By assuming (the nominal definition) that ice is solidified water Aristotle makes a first move towards such a formal explanation. However, this preliminary answer does not qualify as a demonstration yet, because we do not know why it is that "solidified" belongs per se to "water", or why there is ice. This is where the explanatory middle term comes in: the middle term picks out the explanans of why solidified belongs to water. The explanatory middle term that Aristotle proposes for this particular example is a complete cessation (*ekleipsis*) of heat: ice comes about when there is a complete cessation of heat. The middle term, which picks out

[8] This might explain why the chapter has largely been ignored by some recent studies on the *Analytica Posteriora*, including those of Byrne (1997); Goldin (1996) and McKirahan (1992).

the efficient cause[9] of the solidification of water, reveals the essence of ice: ice is solidified water resulting from a complete cessation of heat in water. While the explanation that is being formalized is thus a formal explanation (because it answers the question "what is ice?"), the middle term bringing out this explanation picks out an efficient cause.

In sum, Aristotle's claim that "all the *aitiai* are demonstrated through the middle term" means under this scheme that all the four types of explanations are demonstrated through the middle term, but that these demonstrations may proceed through middle terms that pick out causes of a different type.

The semantic distinction between hê aitia *and* to aition

Within the context of the *Analytica Posteriora* this philosophical distinction is supported by a semantic distinction between the term *hê aitia* (fem.; pl. *aitiai*) and the term *to aition* (neut.; pl. *aitia*). Frede has argued that the two terms were used differently in the original legal context in which they arose: *to aition* (which is the neuter noun formed from the adjective *aitios*, originally meaning "culpable" or "responsible") designated the agent responsible for a state of affairs, while *hê aitia* designated the accusation – i.e., a propositional item expressing the charges.[10] This distinction between *aition* as the thing responsible or cause and *aitia* as causal account or explanation seems to be preserved in Plato's *Phaedo*, and perhaps also in Chrysippus and in Diocles.[11]

Outside the *Analytica Posteriora*, there is little or no evidence that Aristotle also endorsed this distinction,[12] but within the *Analytica Posteriora* I believe there is. The semantic distinction is not crucial for the philosophical distinction, but a short sketch of the semantic distinction might help to get a clearer view of the theory Aristotle is setting out in *APo* II.11.

First *to aition*: usually, *to aition* is characterized as a condition for knowledge.[13] More specifically, in "demonstrations of the reason why"

9 I here follow Charles (1999, 233–235), who identifies *ekleipsis* as a process (the suffix *–sis* indicates a *nomen actionis*) and as an efficient cause.

10 Frede (1980, 222–223).

11 Diocles, fr. 176 (Van der Eijk, 2001 edn).

12 In other treatises the distinction may only be preserved in "technical discussions" of demonstrations such as *DA* II.2, 413a11–21; this, however, requires further research. Interpreters of the *Analytica Posteriora* usually take the terms to be semantically equivalent, and translate them more or less randomly as cause, reason, or explanation.

13 Knowing why is to know *by means* of *to aition* (*APo* I.6, 75a35); this knowledge proceeds *from aitia* (*APo* I.9, 76a19–20) that are primitive (*APo* I.13, 78a25–26). See also *APo* II.8, 93a4–8; *APo* II.8, 93b19; *APo* II.9, 93b21–26; *APo* II.12, 95a10–12; *APo* II.12, 95a22–25; and *APo* II.12, 95b14.

the middle term must always refer to an *aition*.[14] This is what Aristotle points out at the end of the following passage (*APo* II.2, 89b37–90a9):

When we seek the fact or if something is without qualification, we are seeking whether or not there is a middle term for it. And when, having come to know either the fact or if it is – either partially or without qualification – we again seek the reason why or what it is, we are then seeking what the middle term is . . . Thus it results that in all our searches we seek either if there is a middle term or what the middle term is. For the middle term is the *aition* (τὸ μὲν γὰρ αἴτιον τὸ μέσον), and in all cases it is this which is being sought.

The middle term must pick out whatever is responsible for the connection between the two terms it mediates. In this way, the middle term clarifies the causal relation between the two terms by providing the real cause (and not merely the epistemic reason) of why the one extreme term holds of the other. I therefore translate the noun *to aition* as "cause."[15]

The term *hê aitia* is used less frequently in the *Analytica Posteriora*, and is usually part of the definition of scientific knowledge. Scientific knowledge is always knowledge of *hai aitiai*.[16] For instance, in *APo* I.2, 71b20–33 Aristotle first picks up on his definition of scientific knowledge as being knowledge of *hê aitia* of something, and then continues by stating that this knowledge can be reached through things that are, among other things, *aitios* of the conclusion (αἰτίων τοῦ συμπεράσματος). Other passages (especially *APo* I.13, 78b28–31) point out that Aristotle conceives of these *aitiai* as being larger linguistic or syllogistic formulas that state the reason why in answer to the question "why" (*to dioti* or *to dia ti*).[17] At least within the *Analytica Posteriora* it is thus implied that *hê aitia* itself is a kind of *syllogismos* containing an explanatory middle term, where *to aition* is a subordinated element of *hê aitia*.[18] I therefore translate the noun *hê aitia* as

14 The middle term in demonstrations of the reason why always picks out the *aition* that is immediate and primitive (*APo* I.34, 89b15; *APo* II.2, 90a7–9; *APo* II.8, 93a4–8; *APo* II.12, 95a10–12; *APo* II.12, 95a17; *passim* in *APo* II.16–18). If the deduction does *not* proceed through the *aition*, but through the more familiar of the (non-explanatory) converting terms, then the demonstration that follows is not a demonstration of the reason why, but of the fact (*APo* I.13).

15 See, for example, *APo* I.13, 78b17; *APo* I.24, 85b22; *APo* II.12, 94b8; *APo* II.12, 94b18; *APo* II.12, 95b20; *APo* II.12, 95b28; *passim* in *APo* II.16–18.

16 See *APo* I.2, 71b9–13; *APo* I.2, 71b30–31; *APo* I.31, 87b40; and *APo* II.11, 94a21–4.

17 These are explanations of the reason why, picking out *to aition* through the middle term (cf. *APo* I.13, 78b12–34; *APo* I.24, 85b23–27 and 85b35–36). In *APo* II.10, 93b33, *hê aitia* indicates a non-syllogistic causal account.

18 One might object that in *APo* I.24, 85b24–27 Aristotle uses the expressions "of the *aitia* and of the *dia ti*" and "of the *aition* and of the *dia ti*" interchangeably. However, the first expression applies to the nature of the demonstrative syllogism (what is demonstrated is the explanation and the reason why), while the second applies to the nature of the universal premise, which is more explanatory in the sense that it shows the *aition* more clearly (cf. *APo* I.31, 88a5–6).

"explanation," and the adjective *aitios* as either "causative" or "explanatory," depending on the context.

Assuming that this semantic distinction between *aition* and *aitia* illustrates a philosophical distinction between the type of causal explanation that is demonstrated through the middle term and the type of causality picked out by the middle term, I shall now present a new reading of *APo* II.11.

6.2 TOWARDS A NEW READING OF *APO* II.11

Making sense of the opening statement and the examples in APo *II.11*

In his opening statement of the chapter, Aristotle first recapitulates his definition of scientific knowledge. That is, we know something when we know its explanation, which is the syllogistic formula stating the *aition* of the state of affairs to be explained. He then specifies four kinds of explanations, which are formulated as four different questions as to the reason why: formal explanation is an explanation of *what* it is to be a thing. Material explanation – if we can indeed speak of *material* explanation in this case[19] – is an explanation of *given what* things being the case it is necessary for that to hold. Efficient explanation is an explanation of *what* initiated the movement. And teleological explanation is an explanation of the for the sake of *what*. As the "since" (Ἐπεὶ) indicates, this should all be common knowledge.

The new information is that all of these explanations are demonstrated through the middle term. This is the process of demonstration: the explanations of the reason why are demonstrated through middle terms that explain why the predicate holds of the subject in the conclusion. The middle term thus reveals a causal connection underlying the per se relation between these two terms (on the causal notion of per se, see *APo* I.4, 73a10–17). The point is that it is only by setting out the whole syllogism and thereby expressing explicitly the cause of why the predicate holds of

[19] The expression Aristotle uses to refer to material causation in *APo* II.11 (i.e., τὸ τίνων ὄντων ἀνάγκη τοῦτ' εἶναι) is puzzling, but cf. perhaps *GA* V.3, 782a22–23 (τίνων δ' ὑπαρχόντων καὶ διὰ τίνας ἀνάγκας συμβαίνει); *PA* I.5, 645b32–33 (ὧν ὄντων ἀναγκαῖον ὑπάρχειν); and *PA* IV.2, 677a17–18 (ἀλλά τινων ὄντων τοιούτων ἕτερα ἐξ ἀνάγκης συμβαίνει διὰ ταῦτα πολλά). I believe Aristotle to imply that material causes for the most part necessitate their results, or at least do so in the case of phenomena that are the subject of demonstrations. Here I treat the expression and the example discussed below as "canonical" examples of material explanation, taken in the broad sense as an explanation stating "that out of which." For the problems involved (which do not affect the interpretation presented here), see Barnes (1993, 226–227); Detel (1993, 685 and 690–694); and Ross (1949, 638–642).

the phenomenon picked out by the subject term that we come to reach true understanding of something.

Aristotle then works out three examples of explanations (material, efficient, and final) that are demonstrated through the middle term. He gives no separate example of formal explanation, supposedly because this "has already been demonstrated" (*APo* II.11, 94a35–36) in earlier chapters.[20] For the sake of completeness, I shall supply a formal cause explanation from an earlier chapter in my discussion below.

My reconstruction of the four examples and their formalizations into syllogisms is as follows:

Example 1: Material explanation (*APo* II.11, 94a27–35; cf. Euc. *El* III.31)

Explanandum:	i. [Why (*dia ti*) is there a right angle?]	[Why A?]
	ii. Why is the angle in a semicircle a right angle?	[Why A of C?]
A = right; B = half of two rights (*aition* = *material cause*); C = angle in a semicircle		
AaC because of B: right holds of the angle in a semicircle because of being half of two rights.		

Example 2: Formal explanation (*APo* II.8, 93b8–13; *APo* II.11, 94b34–36)

Explanandum:	i. What is thunder?	[What is A?]
	ii. Why (*dia ti*) is there noise in the clouds?	[Why A of C?]
A = thunder (a sort of noise); B = extinction of fire (*aition* = *efficient cause*); C = cloud		
AaC because of B: thunder is noise in the clouds because of fire being extinguished.		

Example 3: Efficient explanation (*APo* II.11, 94a36–b8)

Explanandum:	i. [Why (*dia ti*) is there a Persian war?]	[Why A?]
	ii. Why did the Persian war come upon the Athenians?	[Why A of C?]
A = war; B = being the first to attack (*aition* = *efficient cause*); C = Athenians		
AaC because of B: being warred upon holds of the Athenians because of being the first to attack.		

20 I take Aristotle to refer to *APo* II.8, which is part of his larger investigation into the relation of definition and causal explanations in *APo* II.8–10.

Example 4: Teleological explanation (*APo* II.11, 94b8–26)

Explanandum:	i. Why (*dia ti*) does he walk?	[Why C?]
	ii. [Why does healthy hold of walking?]	[Why A of C?]
A = being healthy; B = food not floating (*aition* = *material cause*); C = walking after dinner		
AaC because of B: being healthy holds of walking after dinner because of the food not floating.		

Before turning to an analysis of these examples, let me state from the outset that contrary to the traditional interpretation I see no decisive indications in the text as to why Aristotle should only be concerned with syllogisms in the mode Barbara. I submit that the introduction of the four types of explanations in *APo* II.11 rather shows that Aristotle is concerned with laying out a general syllogistic structure in which *every* causal relation can be fitted. Reading the chapter in this way, the contingency and singularity of the examples noted by critics of Aristotle need no longer constitute a lingering problem. They can be accounted for within the larger framework of causal relations Aristotle is interested in, and so can the other examples Aristotle mentions in the remainder of the chapter (*APo* II.11, 94b27–34).[21]

The example of material explanation

The first example of material explanation is developed in the context of a discussion of the necessary nature of demonstrative syllogisms (*APo* II.11, 94a24–27).[22] The example can be analyzed as follows (for the proof see Figure 6.1). The *dia ti* question Aristotle poses is "because of what is the angle in a semicircle a right angle." An adequate explanation should thus state the geometrical proof showing "that out of which" it follows that the angle in a semicircle is right. This example of material explanation is in

21 These latter examples are rather more fanciful than serious, such as the Pythagorean belief that it thunders in order to frighten the inhabitants of Tartarus, or they report scientific views that Aristotle rejects elsewhere, such as the explanation of thunder as being the extinction of fire in the clouds (this explanation is explicitly rejected in *Meteor* II.9, 369b12–24). For a discussion of these examples, see Wians (1996, 137).

22 Here Aristotle states that, given a middle term shared by two propositions, it is necessary for the conclusion of the syllogism to hold. The middle term, or the two premises taken as one, literally bring about the conclusion, and are therefore in a sense the material causes of the conclusion (cf. *Ph* II.3, 195a18–19).

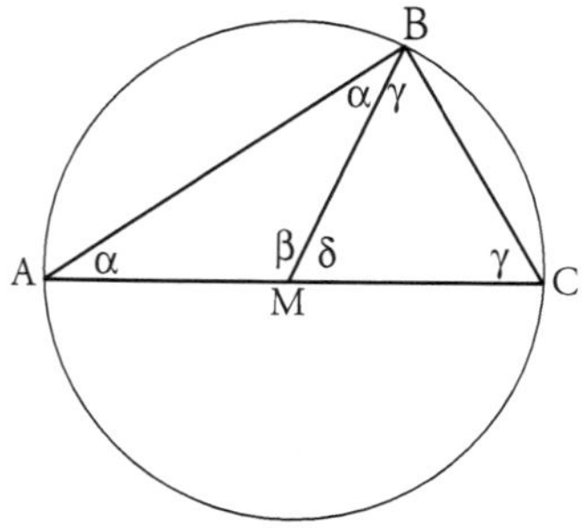

Demonstration: ∠AEC = 90°

∠MAB = ∠MBA (α)

∠MCB = ∠MBC (γ)

(i) $\beta + \delta = 180°$

(ii) $2\alpha + \beta = 180°$; $2\gamma + \delta = 180°$

(iii) $2(\alpha + \gamma) + \beta + \delta = 360°$

(iv) $2(\alpha + \gamma) = 180°$

(v) $\alpha + \gamma$ ("the angle in a semicircle") = 180° ("two rights") divided by 2 ('half") = 90° ("right")

Figure 6.1 Material explanation in *APo* II.11, 94a27–35

fact reflected in a theorem from Euclid (*El.* III.31), and the proof might be so as well.

Here Aristotle induces the search for the middle term by rephrasing the question explicitly in terms of material necessity: "given what being the case is it a right angle?" What we are looking for is a condition that necessitates the rightness of the angle in a semicircle – a condition, incidentally, that will be immediately evident once the right mathematical figure has been discovered (cf. *Meta* IX.9, 1051a21–29). Aristotle then formalizes the explanation, while introducing "half of two rights" as the middle term (B) that explains why "right" (A) holds of "angle in a semicircle" (C).

The rationale Aristotle offers in this section is somewhat obscure, but is not too problematic once we presuppose the familiarity of Aristotle's readership with the relevant mathematical figure and the proof of the proposition as we know it from Euclidean geometry (Aristotle hints at both of them in the above mentioned passage in *Meta* IX.9). Important in this proof is that the geometrical relations between "right angle" and "angle in a semicircle" are discovered by *division*.[23] It is this division that Aristotle refers to when claiming that "[the term B] is equal to A, and C to B, because it [C] is of two rights – half."[24] It is this "being half" that necessitates the angle in a semicircle being a right angle. In sum, the angle in a semicircle is a right angle because it is half of two rights; "being half of two rights" is the material cause of "right" holding of "the angle in a

23 Cf. *Meta* IX.9, 1051a22–23: "mathematical figures, too, are discovered by actualization; for they find them by dividing [the figures] (διαιροῦντες)."

24 Note the word order in the Greek: while B is defined as ½-2R (*APo* II.11, 94a29: ἡμίσεια δυοῖν ὀρθαῖν; 94a32–33: ὄντος ἡμίσεος δύο ὀρθῶν, C is explained as 2R-½ (*APo* II.11, 94a32: δύο γὰρ ὀρθῶν ἡμίσεια).

semicircle." The angle in a semicircle is by necessity a right angle *given that it is two rights – divided in half.*

In this case, both the causation expressed by the explanation and the explanatory middle term that brings out this explanation are of the material type.

The example of formal explanation

The second example of formal explanation (taken from *APo* II.8, 93b8–13) can be analyzed as follows. The *dia ti* question Aristotle poses is why there is thunder. This is a reformulation of the question "what is thunder," which is a question for the definition of thunder (Aristotle answers the "what is" question by stating that it is the extinction of fire in cloud, which is not a demonstration of the essence of thunder yet). For Aristotle, the question why there is thunder is equivalent to the question what thunder is, except that the first is a question for a demonstration and the latter for a definition (see *APo* II.10, 94a1–8). An adequate explanation of why there is thunder thus needs to be a formal explanation expressing the essence of thunder through a middle term that brings out this essence.

However, as Aristotle indicates in another text where he discusses the same example (*Meta* VII.17, 1041a24–32),[25] the only way to get a demonstration is by converting the explanandum into a predicative relation.[26] This can be done, first, by taking the nominal definition of thunder (as being "a sort of noise in the cloud"; *APo* II.8, 93a22–23). Second, one can do this by turning the request for a definition into a *dia ti* question for a demonstration, in which the object of inquiry is "a something of something else" (i.e. why is there thunder in the clouds). Because the explanation in this case is already known (i.e. thunder comes about through the extinction of fire in the cloud), Aristotle sets out immediately to formalize the example: the subject term (C) is "cloud"; the middle term (B) is "extinction of fire"; and the predicate term (A) is "thunder." Now, B holds of C, because the extinction of fire takes place *in* the cloud (the cloud is the locus in which the phenomenon typically resides), and A – "thunder" (i.e. a sort of noise) – holds of B, because B is a definition of A.

In this case, the explanatory middle term picks out an efficient cause of why there is thunder or noise in the clouds: the origin of motion of the noise lies in the extinction of fire. It is through this efficient cause that

[25] For the thunder examples in the *Analytica Posteriora* and the *Metaphysica*, see Charles (1999, 233–239).
[26] Lennox (2004, 90n2).

the essence of thunder, and thereby the formal explanation of why there is thunder, is revealed: thunder is noise in the clouds caused by fire being extinguished.[27]

The example of efficient explanation

The third example of efficient explanation (*APo* II.11, 94a36–b8) is fairly straightforward. Here Aristotle picks a historical example in asking why it is that the Persian war came upon the Athenians, rephrased as what the explanation is for the Athenians being warred upon. As in the other examples, it is not clear from the outset which type of explanation will be demonstrated.[28] However, the short explanation Aristotle offers first ("because the Athenians attacked Sardis with the Eretrians") shows that he is looking for some state of affairs that initiated the movement, which is an efficient cause (and not for that for the sake of which, such as the desire of the Persians to gain an empire). Aristotle then formalizes the example in the following way: "War, A; being the first to attack, B; Athenians C." It is significant that Aristotle here adds the notion of "first" to the attack: it is being the *first* to do wrong that is explanatory for being wronged, and this is the origin of motion.

In this case, the middle term picks out the efficient cause of why war came upon the Athenians: for "people make war on those who first began," which is why being warred upon holds of those who first began. The Athenians were the ones who first began (they fall under this formal description), and this explains the origin of the Persian war.[29]

The example of teleological explanation

Aristotle introduces the section on teleological explanation (*APo* II.11, 94b8–26) with a somewhat puzzling clause: Ὅσων δ' αἴτιον τὸ ἕνεκα τίνος. From what follows it is clear that the explanations that are at stake

[27] Charles (1999, 239); Lennox (2001b, 141).

[28] A similar example in *Ph* II.7, 198a18–19 ("[for the why ultimately leads back either] to the first source of motion, e.g., why did they go to war? Because they were plundered, or to that for the sake of which, e.g., in order to rule") points out that the question why there is war can be answered in different ways.

[29] Note that in all three examples the primary explanandum is the occurrence of a certain phenomenon (i.e. "rightness," "thunder," and "war") that can be expressed in a predicative relation with a subject in which the phenomenon typically and for the most part inheres (i.e. "angle in a semicircle," "cloud," and "Athenians"). The demonstration that follows reveals that there is some aspect of this subject that explains the holding of its attributes.

are teleological ones: Aristotle gives two parallel examples ("For what reason does he walk? In order to be healthy. For what reason is there a house? In order to protect possessions"), and identifies the final cause or the purpose in each example ("In the one case it is in order to be healthy, in the other in order to protect"). He also explains that in these cases there is no difference between a "because of what" question and a "for the sake of what" question. However, it is not immediately clear whether or not Aristotle means that the final cause has to be picked out by the middle term.

The introductory clause (*APo* II.11, 94b8) has often been read as implying just that (i.e., that in these cases the cause is that for the sake of which),[30] but it does not have to be read in this way. The Greek has τὸ ἕνεκά τίνος, which means something different from τὸ οὗ ἕνεκα. The latter (i.e., *to hou heneka*) is the more common expression and is used more or less as a stock phrase designating the end (literally, "that for the sake of which," in which οὗ is a relative pronoun).[31] In contrast, the first expression (i.e., *to heneka tinos/tou*) designates the teleological relation of one item being for the sake of something else (literally, "that which is for the sake of something," where τινος is an indefinite pronoun). Here, the τό is not used as a definite article to substantivate the prepositional phrase, but is used to identify either the item that is for the sake of something, or the teleological relation that exists between two items.[32]

Under this interpretation, the point Aristotle makes here is not that the explanatory middle term in this case is the final cause, but that the causal relation involved is teleological, and that the middle term must pick out the causal factor that explains how one item is for the sake of something else. The teleological explanation is demonstrated through a middle term that need not itself be a final cause, but that rather shows how an end can hold of some subject. This causal relation is then illustrated by the two examples: walking is for the sake of health, and a house is for the sake of protection. The middle term that we are looking for needs to pick out a state of affairs that shows why this teleological relation between walking and being healthy obtains.

30 E.g., Apostle (1981, 59): "Lastly, there is a final cause [or, that for the sake of which]," and Barnes (1993, 60): "suppose it is the purpose which is explanatory."

31 Cf. *Ph* II.2, 194a27–30 "Further, that for the sake of which (τὸ οὗ ἕνεκα), or the end, as well as whatever is for the sake of these (ὅσα τούτων ἕνεκα), belong to the same study. But nature is an end and a 'that for the sake of which' (τὸ οὗ ἕνεκα)." *Cael* II.12, 292b6–7: "for action always consists in two factors, when there is that for the sake of which (οὗ ἕνεκα) and that which is for the sake of something (τὸ τούτου ἕνεκα)."

32 Cf. *Ph* II.5, 196b17 and b20–22; *DA* III.12, 434a32; *GA* I.1, 715a4; *GA* V.1, 778b13; *MA* VI, 700b26–27; and *Meta* XI.8, 1065a31.

In a simplified version of the demonstrative syllogism, the predicate term (A) is being healthy, the middle term (B) is the food not floating, and the subject term (C) is walking after dinner. In this case, the middle term picks out the material cause of why being healthy holds of walking after dinner, because it identifies the physiological condition that is healthy – a condition that itself is initiated by walking that brings about health as an efficient cause.[33] For the identification of "the food not floating" as a material cause, compare Aristotle's qualification of the boiling of the blood surrounding the heart as a material cause of anger in *DA* I.1, 403a25–b1.

In all four examples, the different explanations that are at stake are revealed through the middle term, which picks out a cause for the holding of the predicate term of the subject term. However, in my analysis of the example of teleological explanation, I have left two important questions unanswered. First, if Aristotle did not intend the final cause to be picked out by the middle term, what does he mean by "changing the *logoi*"? Second, one might wonder what it is about this example – or about teleological explanations in general – that makes it so hard to rewrite the demonstrations in such a way that the final cause is actually picked out by the middle term. The following sections address these questions.

6.3 THE FORMALIZATION OF THE EXAMPLE OF TELEOLOGICAL EXPLANATION

Why walking is for the sake of health

The argument of the section on final causes is fairly long compared to the illustration of the other types of explanation, and it proceeds in quite a complicated way. Here I shall first separate the different steps in the argument and give a detailed interpretation of each; next, I shall propose two possible interpretations of "changing the *logoi*". Let me start by introducing the way Aristotle originally formulates the terms of the explanation (Table 6.1). For the sake of clarity, I also add the alternative formulations of the terms that Aristotle uses during the argument (Table 6.2).[34]

The argument itself proceeds roughly in the following four steps. First Aristotle asks us to suppose that to make the food not floating (B_2), holds of C, walking after dinner, and that this is healthy (A_2). Note that Aristotle changes the formulations of the terms A and B, presumably to show that

[33] As Bolton (1997, 113–15) suggested.

[34] I shall retain the numbering in my discussion of the example of teleological explanation; where it is not clear which formulation Aristotle has in mind the term is not numbered.

Table 6.1 *The original formulations of the terms in* APo *II.11, 94b8–26*

A_1	Being healthy	τὸ ὑγιαίνειν	Condition	Final cause
B_1	The food not floating	τὸ μὴ ἐπιπολάζειν τὰ σιτία	Condition	*Aition*
C	Walking after dinner	περίπατος ἀπὸ δείπνου	Activity	Explanandum

Table 6.2 *The alternative formulations of the terms in* APo *II.11, 94b8–26*

A_2	Healthy	ὑγιεινός	Productive of condition
B_2	To make the food not floating	τὸ ποιεῖν μὴ ἐπιπολάζειν τὰ σιτία	Activity productive of condition

walking (which is an activity) holds of another activity that produces the condition of the non-floating of food. It is this latter activity that Aristotle calls healthy, for healthy is just that which produces (or is useful to) the condition of being healthy. This is in fact the way Aristotle characterizes "healthy" in the *Ethica Eudemia* (*EE* I.8, 1218b16–22):

And that the end stands in a causal relation to the means subordinate to it is shown by teaching. For, having defined the end they show, regarding other things, that each of them is a good, because "that for the sake of which" is the cause (αἴτιον γὰρ τὸ οὗ ἕνεκα). [Note that Aristotle uses "*to hou heneka*" here, and not "*to tou heneka*"]. For example, since "being healthy" is such and such a thing, then necessarily this other thing will be what is useful for it. And what is healthy will be the efficient cause of health (τὸ δ' ὑγιεινὸν τῆς ὑγιείας αἴτιον ὡς κινῆσαν), though only the cause of its being, but not of health being a good.

By characterizing walking as an activity that is productive of the food not floating, and the latter as being productive of health, Aristotle implies that C is an efficient cause of A_1, being healthy: walking is productive of a healthy condition (cf. *Rh* I.6, 1362a31–34). Walking and health are thus causes of each other: while walking is the efficient cause of health, health is the final cause of walking (cf. *Ph* II.3, 195a8–11). Now, if walking is a health-producing activity, it remains for the teleological demonstration to exhibit why it is that walking effects a change that is directed towards health. Health, as the final cause of walking, explains why there is walking after dinner, but apparently, this is not sufficient for a complete demonstration of this phenomenon: we also need to know why this teleological relationship between walking and health obtains (for, as we saw in section 1.1, final causes never operate in a vacuum). Accordingly, Aristotle continues the

argument – and this is step 2 – by explaining that it is thought that B_1, the material condition where the food is not floating on the surface, holds of C, walking, and healthy (A_2) holds of B (B_1). This opinion points towards the causal role of the phenomenon picked out by B_1.

Indeed, Aristotle now (third) poses the question of what the *aition* is that causally connects C, walking, and A, which picks out the "that for the sake of which."[35] The answer is B_1, the not floating. Aristotle adds that "this is like a definition of that" (*APo* II.11, 94b19–20). Probably the first "this" refers to B_1, the not floating, while "that" refers to A_1, being healthy, "for," Aristotle explains, "in that way the A will be explained." The not floating of the food is like a definition of being healthy in the sense that it shows how being healthy in this context (i.e. in the context of a person who just had dinner) is to be understood. Part of what it means to be healthy in this case is to be in a condition where the food is not floating on the surface of the stomach.[36]

Finally, Aristotle turns to an account of the minor premise: "For what reason does B hold of C?" He answers that the reason is "because that is what being healthy is: to be in such a condition." The formulation of this response suggests that we have touched upon a premise that is not further analyzable but is immediately evident (i.e. the premise is immediate). At this point, Aristotle ends his discussion of this particular example of teleological explanation.

Two possible interpretations of "changing the logoi*"*

The section is completed by the enigmatic statement (Barnes called it the "Delphic injunction")[37] that one needs to "change the *logoi*", and that "in that way each of them will become clearer" (*APo* II.11, 94b21–22). The traditional interpretation reads this sentence in an apologetic way: Aristotle realizes that his example of the final cause is ill-chosen and messy, and that by mistake the middle term does not pick out the final cause. In order to make sense of this example, we should therefore (stipulate that the terms are coextensive and) rearrange the order of the terms or of the premises in such a way that the middle term will pick out health as the final cause. However, I see two problems with this reading that strongly suggest that we should look for a different interpretation.

35 The apposition "the for the sake of which" in *APo* II.11, 94b18 belongs to A, not to the *aition*.

36 Other definitions of health are "having one's body in a uniform state" (*Meta* VII.7, 1032b6–8), or "having fasted for a while" (*Ph* II.3, 194b36).

37 Barnes (1993, 229).

First, Aristotle spends quite some time expounding the example of teleological explanation, and it seems not very charitable to assume that this is not the example he actually would have liked to present to his readers. In fact, the explanation that walking is for the sake of health is a stock example in the Aristotelian corpus, and the rationale Aristotle provides for health holding of walking in this chapter is perhaps not entirely transparent, but very much in line with other accounts of the example. If my interpretation holds, then we might say that Aristotle succeeds quite well in demonstrating how the middle term, i.e. the food not floating, exhibits the teleological relation between walking and health (and does so without using the psychological language of desires or wants, which Aristotle evades in this example as well). There is thus no need to rearrange the example.

Second, Aristotle uses the verb μεταλαμβάνειν as a technical term in the *Prior Analytics* and in the *Topics*, where it means without exception "to substitute for."[38] This suggests that we should expect μεταλαμβάνειν τοὺς λόγους to mean something like "substituting the *logoi* (for something else)." In fact, the use of μεταλαμβάνειν as some kind of technical procedure of substitution in these texts presents two options for how to interpret the expression in the context of the *Analytica Posteriora*, neither of which implies a rearrangement of the example.

One possible interpretation[39] is that the substitution concerns the formulations (*logoi*) of the terms. This reading is based on Aristotle's use of μεταλαμβάνειν in the following passage of the *Analytica Priora* (*APr* I.34, 48a1–27):

> Mistakes frequently will happen because the terms in the premise have not been well set out . . . The reason for this is that the terms are not set out well with regard to formulation, since if the terms for being in the conditions are substituted [for the terms for the conditions themselves], there will not be a deduction; for example, if instead of "health" "healthy" is posited, and instead of "disease" "diseased." For it is not true to say that being healthy cannot hold of someone diseased. But if this is not assumed, there is no deduction, except in respect of possibility: and that is not impossible. For it is possible that health holds of no man . . . It is evident then that in all these cases the fallacy results from the setting out of the terms; for if the terms for being in the conditions are substituted, there is no fallacy. Thus, it

[38] Smith (1989, 137, 261). See *APr* I.17, 37b15; *APr* I.20, 39a27; *APr* I.22, 40a34–35; *APr* I.23, 41a39; *APr* I.29, 45b12–20; *APr* I.34, 48a1–27; *APr* I.38, 49b1–2; *APr* I.39, 49b3–6; *APr* II.4, 56b7–8; *APr* II.8, 59b1–11; *Top* II.2, 110a4–9; *Top* V.2, 130a29–b10; *Top* VI.4, 142b3; *Top* VI.9, 147b12–14; and *Top* VI.11, 148b24–149a7 (*passim*).

[39] Already suggested by Fortenbaugh (1966, 192).

is clear that in such premises the term for being in the condition always needs to be substituted and posited instead of that of the condition itself.[40]

In this passage, Aristotle deals with fallacies that occur when the terms of the syllogisms have not been set out well with regard to formulation (48a9: κατὰ τὴν λέξιν).[41] The problem is solved by substituting terms "for being in the conditions," that is, adjectives such as "healthy" (ὑγιαῖνον) and "diseased," instead of the terms for the conditions themselves, that is, nouns such as "health" (ὑγίεια) and "disease." We might postulate that a similar kind of substitution of the formulation of the terms has taken place in *APo* II.11: the terms indicating the conditions are substituted by terms indicating what is in the condition, or rather, by terms indicating what is productive of the condition. We have seen that Aristotle substituted "healthy" (A_2) for "being healthy" (A_1), and "to make the food not floating" (B_2) for "the food not floating" (B_1). Through these substitutions A and B could be predicated of C (a term indicating an activity), and also the causal relations (in this case, both material causal and efficient causal ones) between the three terms would become more evident.

Another possible interpretation[42] is that the substitution concerns the replacement of words by their definitions. This is the stock use of the expression in the context of the *Topica*, and, accordingly, we should supply ἀντὶ τῶν ὀνομάτων in the passage in *APo* II.11. One context in which the expression "to substitute the definitions for the words" is used in the *Topics* is in that of the fallacy of repeating the word that is being defined or predicated in the definition or predication. The failure pertains to not having used the prior or better-known term in the definition or predication. The procedure of substituting definitions for words is one of the recommended ways to detect the fallacy (*Top* VI.9, 147b12–14; VI.4, 142a34–b6):

40 πολλάκις δὲ διαψεύδεσθαι συμπεσεῖται παρὰ τὸ μὴ καλῶς ἐκτίθεσθαι τοὺς κατὰ τὴν πρότασιν ὅρους . . . τούτου δ' αἴτιον τὸ μὴ καλῶς ἐκκεῖσθαι τοὺς ὅρους κατὰ τὴν λέξιν, ἐπεὶ μεταληφθέντων τῶν κατὰ τὰς ἕξεις οὐκ ἔσται συλλογισμός, οἷον ἀντὶ μὲν τῆς ὑγιείας εἰ τεθείη τὸ ὑγιαῖνον, ἀντὶ δὲ τῆς νόσου τὸ νοσοῦν. οὐ γὰρ ἀληθὲς εἰπεῖν ὡς οὐκ ἐνδέχεται τῷ νοσοῦντι τὸ ὑγιαίνειν ὑπάρξαι. τούτου δὲ μὴ ληφθέντος οὐ γίνεται συλλογισμός, εἰ μὴ τοῦ ἐνδέχεσθαι· τοῦτο δ' οὐκ ἀδύνατον· ἐνδέχεται γὰρ μηδενὶ ἀνθρώπῳ ὑπάρχειν ὑγίειαν . . . Φανερὸν οὖν ὅτι ἐν ἅπασι τούτοις ἡ ἀπάτη γίνεται παρὰ τὴν τῶν ὅρων ἔκθεσιν· μεταληφθέντων γὰρ τῶν κατὰ τὰς ἕξεις οὐδὲν γίνεται ψεῦδος. δῆλον οὖν ὅτι κατὰ τὰς τοιαύτας προτάσεις ἀεὶ τὸ κατὰ τὴν ἕξιν ἀντὶ τῆς ἕξεως μεταληπτέον καὶ θετέον ὅρον.

41 For parallels for this method of *metalêpsis* in the ancient grammar tradition, see Sluiter (1990, 111ff).

42 Suggested by Pieter Sjoerd Hasper (in personal correspondence).

> Another [failure] is, if one has used the term that is itself being defined. This passes unnoticed when the actual name of the object being defined is not used, e.g., supposing anyone had defined the Sun as a star that appears by day. For in bringing in day he brings in the Sun. To detect errors of this sort, substitute the definition for the word (μεταλαμβάνειν ἀντὶ τοῦ ὀνόματος τὸν λόγον), e.g., the definition of day as the passage of the Sun above the Earth.

The expression is also used in the context of examining the correctness of definitions rendered of a complex term. For the definition to be correct, the words of the complex term have to be replaced by the definitions of the words (*Top* VI.11, 149a1–3). The substitution of definitions of words used in definitions also helps to clear up whether or not the predications hold non-accidentally (*Top* II.2, 110a4–9):

> One should substitute definitions also for the words contained in the definitions (λαμβάνειν δὲ καὶ ἀντὶ τῶν ἐν τοῖς λόγοις ὀνομάτων λόγους), and not stop until one comes to something familiar; for often when the definition is given as a whole, the thing looked for is not cleared up, (οὔπω δῆλον) whereas if for one of the words used in the definition a definition be stated, it becomes obvious (κατάδηλον).

Under this interpretation, we need to replace the words set out in the syllogism – such as "walking," or "being healthy" – by their definitions (perhaps just as Aristotle did himself), until we find the more familiar terms,[43] and in that way the predications will become clearer. A striking parallel is provided by Galen, who – plainly following Aristotle – uses μεταλαμβάνειν in this exact same way while discussing scientific demonstrations.[44]

The expression μεταλαμβάνειν τοὺς λόγους may be too elliptical to help us decide which of the two possible interpretations we should favor, but this problem need not concern us too much. Both uses seem to be at play in the *Analytica Posteriora* context: Aristotle probably meant some technical procedure of substitution that he applied himself in discussing the example, and through which the causal relations between the terms and the predications became clearer.

43 This type of substitution might be connected to the one Charles observes in the *Analytica Posteriora* concerning the example of thunder: the predicative term "thunder" is replaced by its nominal definition "noise in the clouds," which both gives us more familiar terms and indicates how thunder is to be understood in the relevant syllogism. See Charles (1999, 240).

44 See Galen, *Meth Med* X.39, 5–10: "that with regard to every inquiry one needs to substitute the definition for the word" (ὡς ἐπὶ πάντων τῶν ζητουμένων εἰς λόγον χρὴ μεταλαμβάνεσθαι τοὔνομα). I am grateful to Jim Hankinson for bringing this parallel to my attention.

Ends cannot be picked out by middle terms

If my interpretation is right, then Aristotle has offered us an example of teleological explanation where the middle term picks out a material cause, while the final cause is picked out by the predicate term. This leaves us with the question why Aristotle did not simply provide us with an example of teleological explanation where the middle term picks out a final cause.

I believe that Aristotle indirectly addresses this question in the passage where he brings up the order of causation in different types of demonstrations (*APo* II.11, 94b23–26):

> Here the events occur in the opposite order from the cases where the causes are according to motion. For in the latter the middle term must occur first, while here C, the ultimate term, [must occur first] and last the for the sake of which.[45]

In this passage, Aristotle contrasts the order of causation in demonstrations of efficient causal explanations with that of teleological explanations. As we saw earlier, the middle term in the example of efficient explanation (i.e. being the first to attack) picked out an event that *later* initiated the war against the Athenians. The efficient cause picked out by the middle term thus precedes the explanandum in time. However, in the example of teleological explanation, we saw that the action picked out by the subject term (i.e. walking) occurred first. The final cause, health, came about last. It seems that in demonstrations of teleological explanations the final causes are literally, in a temporal sense, the *telos* or the end (and culmination) of the events to be explained.

Aristotle returns to this issue in the next chapter (*APo* II.12), where he discusses the syllogistic features of demonstrations of processes, i.e., of attributes *coming to hold* of certain subjects.[46] Unlike demonstrations of being, which are typically illustrated by mathematical examples in which the attributes hold always and necessarily of their subjects, the premises of demonstrations of processes do not pick out relations between universals that are timeless and necessary without qualification. Instead, they track causal developments over time and pick out relations between attributes and subjects that hold only for the most part. For the syllogistic structure of such demonstrations this means, first, that the terms get tensed: the

[45] αἱ δὲ γενέσεις ἀνάπαλιν ἐνταῦθα καὶ ἐπὶ τῶν κατὰ κίνησιν αἰτίων· ἐκεῖ μὲν γὰρ τὸ μέσον δεῖ γενέσθαι πρῶτον, ἐνταῦθα δὲ τὸ Γ, τὸ ἔσχατον, τελευταῖον δὲ τὸ οὗ ἕνεκα.

[46] I discuss the models of demonstration outlined in this chapter and their possible influences on Aristotle's methods in his biological works in Leunissen (2010). On demonstrations of processes, see also *APo* I.8, *APo* I.30, and *APo* II.16.

processes picked out by the major and middle terms have to be characterized as either past, present, or future happenings. This is, for instance, how Aristotle formalizes the example of the *coming to be* of an eclipse (*APo* II.12, 95a14–16):

> For instance, because of what did an eclipse come about? Because the Earth came in the middle; and it is coming about because [the Earth] is coming [in the middle], and it will come about because [the Earth] will come in the middle, and there is [an eclipse] because [the Earth] is [in the middle].[47]

Second, Aristotle explains that the state of affairs picked out by the middle term has to be either *simultaneous* with the states of affairs it explains in the case of "simultaneous processes" (*APo* II.12, 95a10–24), or *precede* it in the case of "consecutive processes" (*APo* II.12, 95a24–95b1 and *APo* II.12, 95b13–b37). Simultaneous processes are processes in which attributes come to hold of their subjects simultaneously with the operation of the cause picked out by the middle term, i.e., A comes to hold of C at the same time as B comes to hold of C. For instance, the eclipse comes to hold of the Moon at the same time as the Earth moves in between the Moon and the Sun. Consecutive processes are processes in which attributes come to hold of their subjects some time after the (start of the) operation of the cause picked out by the middle term, i.e., A comes to hold of C sometime after B has come to hold of C. As an example of the latter, Aristotle states that the coming to be of a house is demonstrated through a middle term that picks out a state of affairs that is chronologically prior to the explanandum: i.e., the earlier coming to be of a foundation (*APo* II.12, 95b38: ἔσται γὰρ θεμέλιος πρότερον).[48] Demonstrations such as these are thus to reflect the – chronological – order of causation in the real world,[49] which means that the relevant type of causal priority pertaining to the middle terms picked out in demonstrations of processes is "priority in generation," not "priority in nature."

Now, from Aristotle's earlier treatment of the walking-for-the-sake-of-health example, we can infer that teleological processes are consecutive processes (health comes about some time *after* walking has made our food no longer float on the surface of the stomach), whose demonstrations

47 οἷον διὰ τί γέγονεν ἔκλειψις; διότι ἐν μέσῳ γέγονεν ἡ γῆ· γίνεται δὲ διότι γίνεται, ἔσται δὲ διότι ἔσται ἐν μέσῳ, καὶ ἔστι διότι ἔστιν.

48 Note that Aristotle typically depicts the causal sequence involved in house-building as a proper and paradigmatic case of an (artificial) teleological causal chain. See, e.g., *Ph* II.9, 200a24–29; *PA* II.1, 646a27–28; and *PA* III.5, 668a13–24.

49 Cf. Charles (2000, 198–204) on the dependence of the practice of definition on the order of causation.

should satisfy the formal requirements outlined in *APo* II.12. The upshot of this is that, unlike material, formal, and efficient causes (which can all be prior in generation), final causes of processes cannot be picked out by the middle terms in demonstrations (ends that constitute final causes are never prior in generation, but come about when the necessary prerequisites have been fulfilled), but must always be part of the conclusion that is being demonstrated.[50] A teleological explanation explains that some feature is present or comes to be for the sake of some end, where that end is the final cause of that feature; demonstrations of teleological phenomena show that this end in fact comes to hold of that subject through the operation of some other type of cause. That is, demonstrations of teleological phenomena show that there is a genuine and intrinsic teleological relationship between the end and the feature of which it is the end. This is exactly what Aristotle has shown us, namely that the action of walking in fact leads to health, because walking is what makes the food not floating, and being in a condition of having the food not floating is what being healthy is (i.e., health comes to hold of walking once – after some walking around – walking has made the food not floating). On this account, ends are part of the conclusion that needs to be demonstrated, and cannot be picked out by the middle term through which the conclusion is demonstrated.

The question I shall focus on below is how this picture of the structure of demonstrations of teleological phenomena as described in the *Analytica Posteriora* relates to the structure of the actual teleological explanations offered by Aristotle in his *De Partibus Animalium*. I shall first return briefly to his discussion of demonstration in the natural sciences, and then analyze three predominant types of explanation in biology that involve final causality. Without going into too much detail, I shall show that the structure of the actual teleological explanations illustrates our findings about the theory of explanation rather well.[51]

50 This might explain why in the case of the teleological explanation in *APo* II.11 the explanandum is picked out by the subject term ("why does walking after dinner occur?"), rather than by the predicate term as in the other three types of explanation.

51 This question touches upon the important debate on the relation between the ideal of scientific investigation and demonstration set out in the *Analytica Posteriora* (the "theory") and the methodological reflections and actual explanations Aristotle offers in his treatises on natural science (the "practice"). Although I cannot defend my position here, I am more sympathetic to the approach defended *passim* in the works of Lennox and Gotthelf, who hold that Aristotle builds upon and elaborates his scientific standards for the different sciences, than to the approach defended by Lloyd (1996), who argues that Aristotle is a methodological pluralist, and that theory and practice cannot be reconciled with each other.

6.4 THE STRUCTURE OF ACTUAL TELEOLOGICAL EXPLANATIONS: EVIDENCE FROM *DE PARTIBUS ANIMALIUM*

The structure of demonstration in the natural sciences according to PA *I.1*

Aristotle brings up the issue of demonstration in the natural sciences in the first book of *De Partibus Animalium*. As we saw in more detail in Chapter 3, Aristotle argues there that the modes of demonstration in the theoretical sciences and in the natural sciences are different, because the modes of necessity and the direction of the causal inference are different (*PA* I.1, 640a3–6):

> For the starting point is in some [i.e. the theoretical sciences] what is, but in others [i.e. the natural sciences] what will be. For, "since health or man is such, it is necessary that this is or comes to be," but not "since this is or has come about, that from necessity is or will be."[52]

The causal mode of necessity operative among sublunary (non-circular) natural phenomena is identified as conditional necessity, which Aristotle explains as the necessity of certain things being present first, if the end is to come to be (*PA* I.1, 639b26–30). Demonstrations in the natural sciences thus pertain to linear, causal – typically, teleological – sequences in which the causally relevant items are separated in time (and not to timeless or eternal phenomena, which are the objects of demonstration in the other theoretical sciences), and they will thus have to track the order of causality in the natural, sublunary world. However, since those causally relevant items never necessitate their outcomes without exception, but only for the most part,[53] the direction of the inferences that pertain to them can never be from the prior to the posterior. Rather, the necessity that governs the deduction in the natural science kind of demonstration has to be conditional too, and move – one-directionally – from the posterior (which is the end that already has come to be) to the prior (which are the antecedent causes of the coming to be of that end). In other words, the proper mode of reasoning has to be that, if the end has come to be or is (such and such), then its necessary prerequisites have had to come to be or be present

[52] Ἡ γὰρ ἀρχὴ τοῖς μὲν τὸ ὄν, τοῖς δὲ τὸ ἐσόμενον· ἐπεὶ γὰρ τοιόνδε ἐστὶν ἡ ὑγίεια ἢ ὁ ἄνθρωπος, ἀνάγκη τόδ' εἶναι ἢ γενέσθαι, ἀλλ' οὐκ ἐπεὶ τόδ' ἐστὶν ἢ γέγονεν, ἐκεῖνο ἐξ ἀνάγκης ἐστὶν ἢ ἔσται.

[53] This is because, as Aristotle explains (in *PA* I.1, 640a6–9 and *GC* II.11), the relation between the cause and effect in the natural, sublunary world is never one of unqualified necessity and the necessity involved in these cases does not convert.

first (its necessary prerequisites cannot not be; cf. *Ph* II.9, 200a19–22). The deduction is not of the consequences of a certain starting point, but of the antecedents of the end.[54]

These remarks about the nature and structure of demonstrations in the natural sciences present the following picture of what these demonstrations in practice would look like. First, it is clear that the predominant form of demonstration in the natural sciences will be teleological in nature. The main project of the *De Partibus Animalium* is, as we saw, to explain why particular parts and their differentiations belong to the animals that have them, and Aristotle's first move in answering these questions is usually to identify the function the part performs. It is the function that constitutes the part's final cause and that explains its presence.

Second, we ought to expect the explanations Aristotle provides (which are potentially transformable into demonstrations of the natural science kind) to do more than just identify the final causes of natural phenomena. Aristotle's discussion of demonstration in *PA* I.1 puts the ends that constitute the final causes of natural phenomena in the position of (observational) starting points for demonstration in the natural sciences. It is from knowing the realized end that we can then deduce its necessary antecedents, which the realization of this end demands. This inference scheme implies, I submit, that the ends that constitute the final causes will be picked out by the major terms in the demonstration, and that they are part of the conclusion that is being demonstrated, whereas the necessary antecedents will figure as middle terms in the demonstration. In other words: a certain animal part is present in the animal that has it for sake of the function it performs, but it is through specifying the necessary antecedents that Aristotle demonstrates the teleological relationship between the animal, the part, and its function. Indeed, *De Partibus Animalium* is not a treatise that simply lists parts of animals and their respective functions. Aristotle also specifies why, for instance, this particular animal needs to perform this function (or at least benefits from being able to perform it), why it performs this function with only one kind of part rather than with two kinds (as some of its related species do), why the part can perform the function it performs, etc.

I take it that this picture is largely consistent with the example of why one walks after dinner in *APo* II.11. The question why one walks after dinner parallels the biological question why a certain part is present in a certain

[54] Lloyd (1996, 32); as Lloyd rightly points out, the antecedents that are deduced are antecedents of the final cause in a chronological or ontological sense, not in a logical one.

animal. The question is answered by identifying the final cause: in the case of walking, health; in the case of biological parts, the function of the part. In both cases, the middle term will have to pick out the conditionally necessary antecedents that for the most part will bring about the end that constitutes the final cause.

I shall strengthen this general picture by an analysis of the three most common types of teleological explanation that Aristotle uses in his *De Partibus Animalium*.[55]

The place of final causes in actual teleological explanations

(1) The explanation of the presence of vital and essential parts: functions are subsumed under the formal cause

The most common question in *De Partibus Animalium* is why a certain part belongs to a certain animal, and Aristotle typically answers this question by pointing to the function that part plays within the particular animal kind that has that part. The presence of parts is thus explained teleologically through reference to their function (which is the part's final cause), but usually the need to perform these functions is explained by reference to the definition of the substantial being of the animal. It is the definition of the substantial being of the animal that specifies, among others, the functional features that are to be realized and that is thus causally primary in the explanation of the presence of those features.

Let me explain this by returning to a by now familiar example. The question why birds have wings is answered by reference to the function of flying as a part of the definition of the substantial being of birds (*PA* IV.12, 693b6–14, quoted above in section 5.2): birds are essentially flyers, and flyers necessarily have wings. In a formalization of this example, the middle term would be "flyers" (which picks out a functionally defined form), not "flying," which would pick out the function or final cause. That "being a flyer" is causally prior to "flying" in the explanation of the presence of wings in birds is evidenced by the fact that there are also kinds of birds that have wings but are not actually able to fly: these birds, too, have wings in virtue of being flyers, even though those wings cannot be said to be present for the sake of flying.[56] It is thus the definition of the substantial being of birds that is causally primary, and which is picked out to explain why such necessary parts as wings with certain functions hold of

[55] These three types of teleological explanation coincide with patterns I, III, and VIII discussed in section 4.3.

[56] See, e.g., *PA* IV.12, 694a6–13. Cf. Aristotle's discussion of sedentary insects in *PA* IV.6, 682b12–17.

all birds. Note that from the definition of birds as blooded flyers not only can the presence of wings be demonstrated, but also many of the bird's other features, such as the possession of two feet (rather than four, or six).

Additionally, Aristotle sometimes explains the presence of parts in subspecies by reference to the functions that are part of the definition of the substantial being of the wider kind. The fact that birds are essentially flyers explains according to Aristotle why ducks have wings for the sake of flying. Here, the functions tend to be subsumed under the definition of the substantial being (or the formal cause) of the animal's wider kind. Wings belong to ducks because ducks are essentially birds, and all birds necessarily have wings (even if those wings do not actually enable the bird to fly).

In these cases, functions are picked out by the predicate term and only "indirectly" through the middle term as being part of the definition of the substantial being of something – that is, as being included in the formal cause.[57] Final causes of parts are demonstrated to belong to parts through the functionally defined substantial being of an animal (i.e., the ends that constitute the final causes are exhibited as being the realization of a preexisting potential for form), and it is this formal cause that has causal primacy.

(2) The explanation of the coming to be and presence of subsidiary and luxury parts: secondary teleology

A second type of explanation that is fairly common in Aristotle's *De Partibus Animalium* is the so-called "double-barreled" explanation. In these cases, Aristotle explains the *presence* of a part or its differentiation by reference to the function it performs (he sometimes merely states that the part or its differentiation is "for the better"), whereas he explains their *coming to be* by reference to material necessity. This type of explanation usually pertains to features that are not of vital or essential importance to the animal, either because the functions these features perform are already performed by some other part (where this other part can be exhibited to be the necessary prerequisite for the performance of that function), or because the functions themselves are not strictly necessary for the animal's life or identity. In both cases, nature theoretically *could* have designed the animal without the possession of these features. Instead, Aristotle indicates that these features are present because they contribute to the well-being of the animal.

[57] *PA* I.1, 640a33–35: "hence we must in particular say that since this is what it is to be a human being, on account of this it has these things; for it cannot be without these parts." Cf. *Ph* II.9, 200a14 and *PA* I.1, 639b13–14.

One category of such parts consists of horns, spurs, hoofs, nails, teeth, hair, and eyebrows; these parts all serve the luxury function of defense or protection. The doubleness of the explanation indicates that these parts are due to what I have called "secondary teleology." That is, the *coming to be* of the materials out of which the luxurious parts are constituted is entirely due to material necessity (see, e.g., *PA* IV.3, 677b22–29 and *PA* IV.4, 678a3–10). The *presence* of these parts, on the other hand, and their organization and distribution in an animal's body are due to the goal-directed actions of the formal nature of the animal. Aristotle describes the action of the formal nature of the animal in these cases as *using* materials that are present of necessity for a good purpose, rather than as *producing* those materials for the sake of the realization of some function.

Let us return to the example of horns (*PA* III.2; see also sections 3.2 and 4.3). First, Aristotle summarizes his account that horns are present in the animals that have them for self-defence and attack (*PA* III.2, 663b21–22). Next, he poses the following question (*PA* III.2, 663b22–24): "We must say what the character of the necessary nature is, and how nature according to the account has made use of things present of necessity for the sake of something."[58] The necessary nature of the animal indicates, as I argued above in Chapter 3, the amount and kind of materials that come to be as a result of material necessity, as a by-product or surplus of conditionally necessitated processes (without being themselves conditionally necessary). As Aristotle explains, large animals seem to produce more earthen material than is conditionally necessary (and necessitated) for the production of their bones, and it is this residue which is then "used by nature for protection and advantage" (*PA* III.2, 663b25–35). There is no potential for form that directly necessitated the coming to be of extra materials, and, had there not been a surplus of material available, the formal nature of the animal would not have been able to use it for the production of horns.

In cases like this, the function to which the formal nature of the animal puts the part is highly *determined* by the potentials the available material has. The earthen residue is used by the formal nature of an animal to produce parts like horns, *because* this kind of material has a defensive

[58] πῶς δὲ τῆς ἀναγκαίας φύσεως ἐχούσης τοῖς ὑπάρχουσιν ἐξ ἀνάγκης ἡ κατὰ τὸν λόγον φύσις ἕνεκά του κατακέχρηται, λέγωμεν. Here Ogle's translation (1912; "Let us now consider the character of the material nature whose necessary results have been employed by rational nature for a final cause") is grammatically closer to the Greek than Lennox's translation is (2001b; "Since there is a necessary nature, we must say how the nature according to the account makes use of things present of necessity for the sake of something"). *Pôs* should be taken with *echousês* in the genitive absolute, *and* with *katakechrêtai*: as soon as we know what kind of thing the necessary nature is, we can explain how nature makes use of the things that are present on account of this necessary nature.

potential.[59] Formalizations of examples like these are not easy, but for our purposes, it suffices to notice that again a function is demonstrated to belong to some feature through another more basic feature, in this case the availability of materials with certain material potentials due to material necessity.

(3) The explanation of differentiations of parts: differentiae *or residues are causally primary*

A third common question in Aristotle's *De Partibus Animalium* is why a part has the structural and material properties it has in the particular kind of animal that has it. Or, in other words, Aristotle seeks to explain why the part is differentiated in the way it is in this particular animal, relative to the realization of other parts with the same name and approximately the same function in other animals.

Take the example of eyes: both birds and insects have eyes for the sake of vision, but birds have eyes made of fluid eye jelly, while insects have hard eyes. This material differentiation of eyes cannot be explained by reference to the function of vision as such, which only requires eyes to be made of some transparent stuff (the generic function only explains the presence of parts, not their differentiations). Aristotle explains these differentiations by claiming that they are either for the better or necessary for the animal's way of life (or some other *differentia* that is part of their specific substantial being). In both cases, they are present for the sake of the functional optimization of that part within the particular animal kind. Thus, in *PA* II.2, 648a13–19 (quoted above in section 4.2), Aristotle explains the (relative) fluidity of the eyes of birds as being for the sake of *better* vision in birds: birds have fluid eyes to be better able to see.

However, Aristotle explains the need for functional optimizations like these by reference to the specific nature, habitat, and needs of the animal in question, for which he believes they are either necessary or subsidiary. That is, in the case of necessary differentiations, the causally primary feature in these explanations will be one of the four kinds of *differentia* of the animal kind, which are the other parts (and functions) the animal has, the animal's *bios* (lifestyle and habitat), its activities, and its disposition. These four *differentiae* immediately necessitate the variation among parts through conditional necessity. The *differentiae* demand a functional fine-tuning of the part, and this will in its turn conditionally necessitate

[59] Pace Lennox (2001a, 194–195), who holds that "such material is present for the sake of constituting parts which must have a material propensity suitable for defense."

material-structural changes or a relocation of the part. This is clear in the following example (*PA* II.13, 657b22–29):

> The four-footed, egg-laying animals do not blink in the same way [as the birds], because it is unnecessary for them to have moist and accurate vision since they are terrestrial (ὅτι οὐδ' ὑγρὰν αὐτοῖς ἀναγκαῖον ἔχειν καὶ ἀκριβῆ τὴν ὄψιν ἐπιγείοις οὖσιν). But for the birds it is necessary (τοῖς δ' ὄρνισιν ἀναγκαῖον): they use vision to see from a great distance. Accordingly, crook-taloned birds have sharp vision (for they search for their food from above, which is also why these most of all birds soar to the heights), while those which are terrestrial and incapable of flight, such as domestic fowl and the like, do not have sharp vision. For nothing related to their way of life requires them to have it (οὐδὲν γὰρ αὐτὰ κατεπείγει πρὸς τὸν βίον).

A reconstruction of the premises involved in this example shows that the fact that crooked-taloned birds search for their food from above explains why they need accurate vision, and it is this need for accurate vision that conditionally necessitates the moistness of the eyes of these birds (crooked-taloned birds have moist eyes for the sake of better vision, because better vision is required for their way of life).[60]

However, in the case of differentiations that are for the better, Aristotle indicates that what primarily caused their coming into being is the availability of extra materials, usually due to material necessity. The potentials of this material then determine for what purpose the formal nature of the animal *can* use the material, where the ultimate function is determined relative to the animal's specific substantial being. Water-birds have webbed feet, for instance, because by using the available earthy residues in this way, nature improves the animal's way of life and thereby improves its well-being (*PA* IV.12, 694a22–b11); had the residues not been earthy, nature would have to have used them for some other purpose or would have had to discard the residues. The function for which nature can use the available materials is guided and limited by the material potentials that material has, which indicates that these potentials are causally primary. In both cases, the final cause is part of the conclusion of the demonstration, while the middle term refers to formal or material-efficient causes.

Let me end this exposition of common types of teleological explanation in the *De Partibus Animalium* by pointing out that although the actual explanations are more complicated than the example of walking after dinner in the *Analytica Posteriora*, the basic structure and the role of final causes

[60] For the identification of habitat as a causally basic feature, see Gotthelf (1997a, 85–89) and Charles (1999, 249–250).

seem to be the same. In biology, Aristotle attributes functions to (differentiations of) parts in order to explain the presence of the latter. However, the holding of these functions follows from other, more basic features, such as the animal's essence (which comprises functions), its lifestyle, or the availability of certain material potentials. It thus seems that in practice too Aristotle picks out final causes as part of the explanation, but not as the causally primary feature in the complete explanation.

6.5 CONCLUSION

In the preceding sections, I have argued that *APo* II.11 shows how each of the four types of explanation is demonstrated through an explanatory middle term, which need not express the same type of causality as the explanation does.

This interpretation, supported by the lexical difference between *aitia* and *aition*, takes away the need to rearrange Aristotle's syllogistic example of walking after dinner for the sake of health. Nothing in the text of the *Analytica Posteriora* suggests that final causes *must* be picked out by the middle term in a teleological demonstration. A comparison with the use of μεταλαμβάνειν in the *Prior Analytics* and the *Topics* shows that the expression μεταλαμβάνειν τοὺς λόγους should be taken as referring to some kind of procedure of substitution that Aristotle has applied himself while setting out his example, rather than as an admonition to us to change the order of the terms or premises. The fact that ends that constitute the final causes of natural phenomena are chronologically speaking the last to come to be, together with Aristotle's requirement that demonstrations of processes have to reflect actual causal sequences and track priority in generation, explains why it is impossible to construct a syllogism in which the middle term picks out this end as a final cause.

A short analysis of Aristotle's methodological remarks about demonstration in the natural sciences and of his actual practice of teleological explanation in *De Partibus Animalium* confirms the general picture found in the *Analytica Posteriora* with regard to the structure of teleological explanations. Functions explain the presence (or differentiations) of parts in the animals that have those parts, but the coming to be of these functional parts is itself explained further by reference to either the definition of the substantial being of the animal (which specifies the potentials for form that conditionally necessitate the coming to be of the vital and essential parts), or the availability of extra materials (which are used by the formal nature of the animal for the production of subsidiary or luxury parts). Final causes

are the starting points from which the conditionally necessary antecedents are to be traced back, but it is the presence of these prerequisites that necessitates – for the most part, and if nothing interferes – the coming to be of ends.

In sum, final causes form important and necessary ingredients of teleological explanations, but the ends that constitute the final causes are themselves demonstrated to come to be because of other causally prior facts, and these need to be picked out in the complete explanation as well.

APPENDIX

Translation of Aristotle's Analytica Posteriora II.11, 94a20–94b26

Since we think we have <scientific> knowledge when we know the explanation, and there are four explanations – one, what it is to be a thing, and another, given what things being the case it is necessary for that to hold; another, what first initiated the motion; and fourth, the for the sake of what – all of them are demonstrated through the middle term. For, "given what thing being the case it is necessary for this to hold" does not occur when one proposition is assumed, but when at least two are. This is the case when they have one middle term. Thus when this one is assumed, it is necessary for the conclusion to hold. It is clear too in the following way. Because of what is the angle in a semicircle a right angle? Given what thing being the case is it a right angle? Suppose then that right is A, half of two rights B, the angle in a semicircle C. Thus of A's – right – holding of C – the angle in a semicircle B is the cause. For this [B] is equal to A and C to B, because it [C] is of two rights – half. Thus given B, half of two rights, being the case, A holds of C (for that was it that [necessitates] the angle in a semicircle being a right angle). And that [B] is the same as what it is to be it, since the definition signifies this [i.e. what it is to be it].

Now it has also been shown that the middle term is explanatory of the essence.

For what reason did the Persian war come upon the Athenians? What is an explanation of the Athenians' being warred upon? Because they attacked Sardis with the Eretrians. For that initiated the movement. War, A; being the first to attack, B; Athenians C. B holds of C, the Athenians being the first to attack, and A holds of B, because people make war on those who have wronged them first. Therefore A holds of B, being warred upon to those who first began, and this, B, holds of the Athenians – for they first

began. And in this case, too, the cause, that what initiated the movement, is the middle term.

Regarding the cases in which the causal relation is that something is for the sake of something – for example, for what reason does he walk? In order to be healthy. For what reason is there a house? In order to protect the possessions. In the one case it is in order to be healthy, in the other in order to protect. There is no difference between for what reason it is necessary to walk after dinner and for the sake of what it is necessary. Call "walking after dinner" C, "the food not floating on the surface" B, and "being healthy" A. Suppose then that to make the food not floating on the surface at the mouth of the stomach holds of walking after dinner, and suppose the first is healthy. For it is thought that B, the food not floating on the surface, holds of to walk, of C, and that thereof (of B) A, healthy, holds. What then is the causal factor for C of A's – the for the sake of which – holding of it? B, the not floating. This is like a definition of it <of A>; for A will here be explained in this way. And for what reason does B hold of C? Because that is what being healthy is: being in such a state. Surely one must substitute the definitions, and in that way each of them will become clearer. Here the events occur in the opposite order from the cases where the causes are according to motion. For in the latter the middle term must occur first, while here C, the ultimate term, [must occur first] and last the for the sake of which.

CHAPTER 7

Conclusion

Aristotle appeals in a variety of ways to his theory of natural teleology in order to generate explanations of biological phenomena. At the most basic level, living beings are explained to have the capacities of the soul they have in virtue of those capacities being necessary for the sake of *living*, and in the case of the more complex and less widespread capacities, in virtue of being necessary for *living well*. At the more complex level, Aristotle explains that living beings – and also the heavenly bodies – have the bodily parts and features they have for the sake of exercising their vital and essential capacities, or for contributing to the performance of those vital and essential capacities, or because they serve their well-being in some other way.[1]

What unifies these teleological explanations is that they all pick out a function or beneficial end as that for the sake of which some feature is present. In addition, the presence of this function or end is identified as the outcome of the operation of a goal-directed efficient cause (i.e., as being due to the goal-directed actions of the formal nature or soul of a natural being), where this process of coming to be either consists in the realization of a potential for form, or in nature making good use of excess materials.

Aristotle characterizes the first process of coming to be as being due to teleology and conditional necessity. This kind of causation, which I call

[1] As for the token questions I raised in the introduction, we have found the following teleological explanations: organisms reproduce for the sake of preserving their own kind such that they can participate in the eternal and the divine. Birds have wings because they are essentially flyers (being a flyer is part of the substantial being of birds), and wings are a necessary prerequisite for being a flyer. Neither snakes nor stars have feet, because in these beings the presence of feet would have been in vain, and nature does nothing in vain. Most of the hoofed life-bearing animals have horns, because there is an excess of earthen material present in their bodies, and because of the defensive potentials this material has, nature uses it for the better to make horns in all the males. In the females, however, the excess of material is excreted, because females are not strong enough to be able to use the horns, and nature never includes any features in the actual design of an animal that it would not be able to use.

"primary teleology," is responsible for the coming to be and presence of those features that can be exhibited to be the necessary prerequisites for the performance of vital and essential functions. The end that constitutes the final cause in these cases is prior "in nature" and "in definition," and is causative in virtue of being formally one with the formal and efficient causes of the living being in question, such that the realization of the form is the end state towards which the efficient cause is intrinsically directed and by which its operation is confined.

Aristotle characterizes the second process of coming to be as "the nature according to the account making use of what is present of necessity." This kind of causation, which I call "secondary teleology," is responsible for the presence and sometimes also for the shaping of subsidiary and luxury features that increase the well-being of living beings; the coming to be of their constitutive materials, and sometimes even of entire structures, is due to material necessity. Both causal patterns are teleological for Aristotle, since in either case it is the operation of a goal-directed efficient cause that ensures the intrinsic and regular connection between natural processes and their beneficial outcomes.

In the sections below, I conclude my account of the merits and limits of Aristotle's use of teleology to generate explanations by specifying (1) the priority Aristotle attributes to teleological explanations, (2) their syllogistic structure, (3) the way they integrate references to final causes and necessity, and finally (4) their explanatory power.

7.1 THE PRIORITY OF TELEOLOGICAL EXPLANATIONS

Aristotle considers it the foremost task of natural philosophers to state teleological explanations such as the ones cited above, because he is convinced that these explanations are the most effective at serving the function of providing scientific knowledge.

For Aristotle, who is a realist concerning causal explanation, the discovery of explanations supplies scientific knowledge. We know something when we know its causal explanation, and there are four types of this: i.e., formal, material, efficient, and teleological explanation. In natural philosophy, we have seen that Aristotle stresses the importance of teleological explanations. Apparently, the most important way of explaining the presence, absence, or differentiation of natural phenomena is by picking out the final causes of these phenomena under their causally relevant and appropriate description, and then (and this step is crucial) to show how the ends that constitute the final causes come to hold of the phenomena under explanation.

The importance Aristotle attributes to teleological explanations does not derive from a denial of the causal force of the material and efficient causes in natural phenomena. Aristotle argues that the operation and interaction of *all* four causes are necessary for teleological natural phenomena to come about, and acknowledges that there are some natural phenomena (such as the coming to be of eclipses, ice, and perhaps the spleen) that only involve the operation of material and efficient causes. However, the fact that most natural (and especially, biological) processes occur regularly and have regular beneficial outcomes indicates, according to Aristotle, that there exist such things as natures and that those processes are intrinsically directed towards the realization of such outcomes. The regular coming into being and presence of natural beneficial outcomes cannot be accidental and a matter of chance. Thus, Aristotle argues, in addition to material and efficient causes operating from the "bottom up," there must be overarching formal and final causes at work that from the "top down" guarantee the regularity of those outcomes by ordering, timing, and limiting the complex sequence of natural events in general and of the stages in biological development in particular. Aristotle repudiates his materialist predecessors for treating the results of such processes as being incidental to chance interactions between material elements. They were not able to account for those results in terms of intrinsic causation. Aristotle holds that the explanation of such phenomena requires the assumption of final and formal causes *in addition to* material and efficient causes.

The importance of teleological explanations also does not lie in the fact that they pick out final causes as being the causally primary factors in the sequence of development, for final causes never are. The implicit model for explanation that Aristotle employs here is that of *demonstrations of (non-cyclical) processes*, and not that of geometric-type demonstrations of timeless and/or eternal states of affairs. This former model, as described in *APo* II.12, requires the scientist to lay bare the order and timing of events or stages of development within a causal sequence. In simultaneous processes, the item picked out by the middle term ought to be simultaneous with (and therefore have the same tense as) the process to be explained. However, in consecutive processes – such as teleological ones – the item picked out by the middle term has to *precede* the process to be explained. As Aristotle points out, the middle terms in such demonstrations have to pick out the immediately necessary prerequisite for the effect (i.e., the coming to hold of an attribute of a subject) that has come about. For demonstrations of natural phenomena of the teleological type, this means the following. First, since such demonstrations track the chronological ordering of items

involved in the processes under explanation, the middle terms of these demonstrations have to pick out that which is causally prior *in generation*. Second, since the ends that constitute final causes are – although causally prior in nature – last in generation, they cannot figure as the causally primary factors in demonstrations of teleological phenomena. Instead, ends and functions figure in the predicative position in the demonstration of natural phenomena and are therefore part of the conclusion that is being demonstrated. (Note that this is *not* to say that final causes have no causal force or ought not to be picked out in teleological explanations; I merely claim that final causes have no causal *primacy* in teleological explanations in the sense outlined above.)

The importance of final causes, then, and hence of teleological explanations that pick out those final causes, lies in their *explanatory* priority. The reason for this is that the functions and ends that constitute final causes are in most cases easy to identify: they are immediately apparent to observation. Once these functions and ends have been established, one can then proceed to determine the conditionally necessary antecedents, which will be part of the complete causal explanation. Because final causes are "closer to us," they provide the best starting points for the discovery of the other causally relevant features and developments related to the explanandum. Since all properties and developments are equally significant or insignificant from a material-efficient point of view, the boundary between essential and incidental properties can only be determined by studying natural beings as teleologically organized wholes. For Aristotle not every terminus of a continuous process is a final cause, but only that in which this process – if nothing prevents it – would typically and for the most part culminate. The end that constitutes a final cause is a "good," that is, something that contributes to the existence, essence, or well-being of the whole of which it is part. Through the investigation of natural phenomena from a teleological viewpoint, one is able to distinguish the causally relevant features of those phenomena, and thereby to discover the features that are to be included in the complete explanation of them. The identification of final causes thus helps to frame the search for material, formal and efficient causes of some phenomenon and thereby to find its complete causal explanation.

7.2 THE (SYLLOGISTIC) STRUCTURE OF TELEOLOGICAL EXPLANATIONS

The general structures underlying Aristotle's actual teleological explanations provided in the natural treatises are largely consistent with the theory

of demonstration as described in *APo* II.11. Both practice and theory, however, prove to be more complex and flexible than has traditionally been acknowledged.

Aristotle's actual teleological explanations consist for the most part of explanations that refer directly to final causes, but also of explanations that follow the use of teleological principles. In those cases where the final causes are immediately discernible, Aristotle starts by identifying that final cause and then proceeds to show why it is that this function or goal is necessary or beneficial for the natural being in question. In the case of living beings, the functions for the sake of which the parts of living beings are present are typically the realizations of the capacities of the soul, which are themselves teleologically grounded as being necessary for or otherwise contributory to the preservation of life and the reproduction of the living being in question. The "classification" of the various soul functions that living beings have and Aristotle's teleological account of their nested hierarchy in *De Anima* form the reference points for explanations of biological phenomena.

The strategy Aristotle employs to connect the function with the bearer of that function in each of these cases depends first and foremost on the type of question that needs to be answered (i.e., on whether one needs to explain the presence, absence, or differentiation of some part or feature) and, second, on the status of the part or feature in question. Parts or features that are immediately necessary for the living being that has them (and without which formal natures – hypothetically speaking – could not have designed these living beings) are shown to belong to the living being through reference to their essence, picked out by the definition of their substantial being, which includes (among other features) the necessary vital and essential functions to be realized.

Parts or features that Aristotle characterizes as non-necessary (because, again, hypothetically speaking, formal natures could have designed the animal without them), and which are "for the better" or "for the sake of well-being," are shown to belong to living beings by reference to their possession of extra materials, which are then said to have been used by their formal nature for something good. I have called such features subsidiary or luxury parts, depending on whether they contribute to the performance of a vital or essential function, or rather perform a non-necessary, "luxury" function such as defense.

Similarly, vital or essential differentiations of parts are usually shown to belong to the living beings that have them by reference to one of their specific *differentiae* (i.e., the being's way of life, its activities, character, and

the other parts it possesses), which are then shown to require a functional optimalization of the part or feature in question. Subsidiary and luxury differentiations of parts, on the other hand, are shown to be present on account of the availability of extra material that has come to be by material necessity, and which is then used by the animal's formal nature for the better.

The absence of parts or features is explained either by reference to their lack of function within this particular kind of animal (often because the animal has some other, more necessary feature that interferes with the functionality of the now missing part), or non-teleologically by reference to the absence of the constitutive material (or natural place) in this animal.

In explaining the actions of animals or human beings, Aristotle first picks out the goal of that action. He then shows how this action comes about by reference to the intermediate efficient causes, which usually take the form of the desire for an object and of the perception of that object as something good.

Teleological principles, such as "nature does nothing in vain," are generalizations over (or "causal abstractions" of) the observed outcomes of the goal-directed actions of formal natures, explicating what they "always" or "never" do or make when they are said to produce living beings and their parts. The principles, which are suppositions of Aristotle's natural science, function predominantly as heuristic tools for the identification of the causally relevant facts to be picked out in explanations, but are not part of the ultimate explanation itself. The principles provide a framework, established inductively through observation, of what is (and what is not) among the natural possibilities by which the actions of formal natures are constrained, and thereby set the natural boundaries within which the explanation of a particularly difficult phenomenon must take place, if it is to be explained teleologically.

Teleological principles are used in the following way. First, the presence of parts is explained through the use of the principle that nature does everything either because it is necessary or because it is for the better. The principle helps to determine the type of teleology responsible for the coming to be and presence of that part, and thereby makes it easier to identify the part's specific function. If the part can be observed to be present in all animals that are able to perform the function associated with that part, then the part must be necessary (i.e. be a necessary prerequisite for the performance of that function); it will be a product of primary teleology; and there will be some commonality in the form of all the animals that have that part that explains the part's presence. If the part is present only

in some animals that are able to perform the function associated with that part, then the part must be for the better; it will be a product of secondary teleology; and there will be a *differentia* in combination with the availability of extra materials that explains the part's presence in the subspecies.

The absence of parts is explained through the use of the principle that nature does nothing in vain. Aristotle constructs a counterfactual argument of the following form: if the formal nature of this particular being had designed the animal with this part, the part's presence in that animal would have been in vain, because some other, more necessary feature that being has would have interfered with its functionality. The part is absent, then, because nature does nothing in vain (and because nature could not tinker with the other, more necessary feature).

Finally, the principle that nature does what is best is mostly used for explanations of the presence of parts or of their differentiations in cases where observation shows that there are several possible natural means for nature to fulfill a certain functional need. Aristotle shows how the features an animal has are the best for it, given its specific substantial being, relative to the other natural possibilities.

In short, in all the actual teleological explanations provided in the natural treatises it is either a formal cause (e.g., an essential property specified by the definition of the substantial being of a living being, a *differentia*), an efficient cause (e.g., a desire, an action of a formal nature), or a material cause (e.g., a flow of earthen material with certain potentials) that turns out to be causally prior in generation. Ends and functions, on the other hand, which are prior in nature, are picked out as what explains the presence of features and as what guides and limits the processes of coming into being of those features. This picture is largely consistent with the *theory* of the structure of teleological explanations Aristotle provides in *APo* II.11, where he integrates his theory of four causes with the syllogistic pattern of scientific demonstrations. In this chapter Aristotle shows how there *may be* a difference between the type of causality expressed in the explanation of some feature and the type of causality expressed in the middle term that picks out the explanans of that feature. In teleological explanations, there *must be* a difference between the two. In addition, Aristotle argues that it is through the explanans that a certain type of causal relation is shown to obtain. In contrast with the traditional interpretation of *APo* II.11, I have argued that in teleological explanations final causes are never to be picked out by the middle term as being explanatory of the conclusion, but rather are themselves part of the conclusion that is being demonstrated. Walking

after dinner is for the sake of health, because walking brings about the physiological condition of having the food not floating on the surface of the stomach, which is exactly what being healthy is in the context of a person who has just had dinner. The middle term that picks out the condition of having the food not floating brings out the *teleological relation* that obtains between walking and health. Under this scheme, demonstrations of the teleological type are demonstrations in which an end that constitutes the final cause is demonstrated to come to hold of some state of affairs through the operation of other types of cause picked out by the middle term.

This scheme is consistent with the idea (mentioned earlier) that for Aristotle the structure of scientific demonstrations in the natural sciences, which pertain to processes, is to reflect the order of causation in the real world. Additionally, if the necessity that obtains in the world of change and development is conditional, then the necessity that governs deductions of natural phenomena has to be conditional as well: if the end is to come to be, then its necessary prerequisites have to come to be first. In the natural treatises, Aristotle never produces actual syllogisms, but the underlying pattern is largely the same. Phenomena are explained to be present for the sake of some end that constitutes the final cause. This end, then, needs to be demonstrated to come to hold of those phenomena through other prior necessitating factors.

This schematic picture of the structure of teleological explanations points also to the wider ramifications of this book: both the incorporation of conditional necessity into the demonstrative framework, and the room for variability between the type of explanation that is being demonstrated and the type of causation picked out by the middle term allow for a very flexible and comprehensive model of scientific demonstration, going far beyond the geometric model of demonstration pertaining to mostly mathematical states of affairs. Treating Aristotle's use of teleology in the natural sciences as one homogeneous category would inevitably obscure the richness of his explanatory and demonstrative strategies.

7.3 The Integration of Final Causes and Necessity in Teleological Explanations

Another aspect of the structure of teleological explanations concerns the integration of references to both teleology and necessity in the explanation of living nature. I have argued that in his explanations, Aristotle picks out (roughly speaking) two types of teleology in combination with two types

of necessity: primary teleology in combination with conditional necessity and secondary teleology in combination with material necessity.

Aristotle invokes what I call "primary teleology" in explaining those parts and features of a living being that are the realizations of capacities already given with the kind of soul that being has. The parts and features are the necessary instruments for the performance of the essential and vital functions included in the definition of the substantial being of that living being. In those cases, the formal nature or the soul of that living being is the cause of both the coming to be of those parts and features, and of their presence. The necessity of the coming to be of the part or feature in question (and of its constitutive materials) is conditional upon the need of some essential or vital soul function to be realized; the part and features that are present are then exhibited as the necessary prerequisites of something being what it is and being able to lead the kind of life it does.

However, Aristotle also recognizes that some parts or features that are observed to be present among living beings are not immediately necessitated by the functions specified by the definition of the substantial being of that animal, but do give rise to the performance of functions that contribute to the well-being of the animal. In these cases, Aristotle ascribes the cause of the coming to be of the matter constitutive of those parts and features to material necessity, while ascribing the cause of their structure and presence to the goal-directed actions of the formal nature or soul of the animal. There is no capacity for the performance of a function that conditionally necessitates the realization of luxurious parts, and subsidiary parts are strictly speaking not necessary for the performance of necessary functions. Aristotle believes that, hypothetically speaking, nature could have designed the animals that have subsidiary parts in such a way that they would have been able to function without them, which is evidenced by his observation of other related animals that lack the subsidiary part in question but are nevertheless able to perform the function associated with that subsidiary part. Subsidiary parts are rather present for the animal's well-being or living well. The material processes that take place in the bodies of animals for the sake of generating the necessary parts lead *incidentally* to the generation of residues or other extra materials. These materials are then used by nature – "who, as a good housekeeper, is not in the habit of throwing away things that could be useful" – for the sake of the good of the animal. This latter process is teleological in Aristotle's view, but in a qualified way: the formal nature of the animal attributes a function to a part or to a flow of material, after this part or material has already come to be as the result of material necessity, and does so in accordance with the

available material potentials, which thus have causal priority in generation. The teleology here is secondary on the operation of material necessity.

The integration of material necessity in secondary teleological explanations gives evidence for my view that Aristotle's theory of teleology was not developed for the sake of replacing materialist explanations, which account for everything in terms of material necessity and its coincidental outcomes. In Aristotle's view, material natures usually operate under the constraints of teleology, but not always: sometimes material natures operate according to their own natures without being directed towards the realization of some end, and give rise to structures that can be and often are used for the sake of something. When Aristotle restricts unqualified necessity to the eternal realm of the heavenly bodies he does not thereby deny the existence of material necessity in the sublunary realm. He rather points out that in causal sequences that take place in the heavenly realm the prior always necessitates the coming to be of the posterior, because the coming to be of the posterior is necessary "without qualification." In the sublunary realm the prior in a causal sequence never necessitates the posterior "without qualification," regardless of whether the posterior is necessitated by conditional necessity or by material necessity. The role of material necessity in the sublunary realm is therefore not confined to the "negative" part of constraining the realizations of ends in natural beings. Material necessity also has a more positive role to play, in that it provides extra possibilities ("extra" in the sense that the possibilities are not already given with the soul and the potential for form some living being possesses) for the realization of features and functions that may contribute to the well-being of the animal in which it operates.

The distinction between "primary" and "secondary" teleology also solves some of the problems pertaining to the scope of Aristotle's teleology. For instance, it allows us to attribute an anthropocentric purpose to winter rain (i.e., the growth of crops), without having to conclude that Aristotle's theory of natural teleology is anthropocentric. In the realm of nature, formal natures make good use of what is present of material necessity; in the same way, human beings may – through the application of art – impose secondary functions upon natural phenomena such as winter rain (which occurs regularly due to material necessity), while following the material potentials and natural propensities rain has. It is the application of art that ensures the regular *beneficial* outcomes of winter rain, not a preexisting potential for form that is being realized. Aristotelian teleology pertains strictly to individual kinds of formal natures, and is not in any intrinsic way anthropocentric or cosmic.

7.4 THE EXPLANATORY POWER OF TELEOLOGICAL EXPLANATIONS

The explanatory power of the actual teleological explanations Aristotle provides of natural phenomena derives from the success of his theory of natural teleology in integrating and making intelligible phenomena that would otherwise be dissociated facts of our universe.

Aristotle's theory of natural teleology, in combination with his theory of four causes, allows him to explain natural processes, deliberative action, and artistic production as variations of one and the same basic phenomenon (but, importantly, without trying to reduce them to one abstract model). Aristotle sets up the analogy between agency and nature, and especially between art and nature (where intentionality and deliberation play no significant causal role), in order to bring out the goal-directedness of the latter through our familiarity with the goal-directedness of the former. The analogies thus serve primarily a didactic function: Aristotle reveals the causal frameworks that apply to art and agency and extends those to natural generation as far as the similarities hold. Ultimately, however, the goal-directedness of art and agency are ontologically dependent on that of nature, where goals are asserted to be present most. Living beings (humans, animals, and perhaps in some sense even the heavenly bodies) act goal-directedly, and craftsmen produce artifacts through goal-directed activity, because they *imitate* nature and are themselves endowed with natures.

The force of the analogy between art and nature remains visible also in Aristotle's explanations in the biological works, where the formal, efficient, and final causes are said to coincide in the souls of living beings. Aristotle often depicts these "formal natures" as if they are "internal craftsmen" who make, use, or redirect materials for the sake of realizing the living being's characteristic functions. The theory that nature is goal-directed thus unifies natural beings such as elements, plants, animals, human beings, and even the heavenly bodies under one ontological category. They all become teleologically organized composites of form and matter, but with widely different manifestations of organized complexity. The coming to be and presence of their bodies and features, and the occurrence of their motions and actions all involve goals, ends, and functions that ultimately contribute to their being, life, and living well. The teleological explanations Aristotle provides pick out those goals, aims, and functions, and relate them to the beings, parts, and processes of which they constitute the final cause.

Teleological explanations are most successful in biology. Aristotle provides comprehensive and detailed accounts of why parts belong to the

animals that have them, why they are differentiated in the way they are, and why some animals lack parts that one would expect to have been present. The references to functions Aristotle makes in these explanations are grounded in his theory of soul. In particular, they build upon the classification of the various capacities of the soul to perform life functions and upon the idea that the soul is the final cause of the natural body that is instrumental. Different kinds of living being are demarcated by their characteristic soul functions, and the parts and bodies they have must be necessary for or subsidiary to those functions. Any part of a living being's body is the way it is for the sake of the capacities that characterize its life, because it is causally dependent on and conditionally necessary for these capacities. Capacities and the living bodies in which they are realized are essentially connected.

The success of the use of teleological principles in biology as a heuristic tool for finding final causes where they are not immediately discernible also forms the foundation for Aristotle's use of those very same principles in his cosmology. The lack of empirical data in the latter domain makes the endeavor to explain the heavenly phenomena very difficult. Aristotle tries to integrate the study of the heavens into the science of nature, and he believes that material explanations of the mathematical properties of the heavenly phenomena are insufficient for a complete scientific understanding of them. Aristotle therefore uses teleological principles as a heuristic to find final causes, and by doing so tries to turn his cosmology into a proper natural science. The teleological principles are not a priori postulates, but suppositions derived from the numerous observations Aristotle made in the biological domain. However, because of the lack of empirical data, the teleological explanations that are provided in cosmology amount to – as Aristotle himself keeps pointing out – plausible or reasonable explanations that take away some puzzlement concerning the heavens. They do not constitute explanations that reach the same level of accuracy and necessity as the explanations provided in biology. The use of the theory of natural teleology as a means to generate explanations of natural phenomena is thus limited in those domains where our observations of the phenomena are incomplete. On the other hand, Aristotle's attempt to give teleological explanations of the features and motions of the heavens shows the comprehensiveness of his theory of natural teleology: ultimately he is trying to establish a coherent picture of the whole cosmos and all its natural beings in which (at least for the most part) things are present or absent or differentiated in the way they are for a purpose.

In sum, if my interpretation of the theory and practice of teleological explanations in Aristotle holds, then the explanatory work performed by final causes is significantly different from what has traditionally been thought. Final causes explain the presence of features, but exert no "mysterious pull" from the future. They rather function quite literally as the direction-givers and the ends and limits of developments necessitated by formal-efficient or material-efficient causation. In this way, they provide both the first component of a teleological explanation and the heuristic starting point for investigations that will lead to a statement of the *complete* teleological explanation of the phenomenon in question. This does not mean, however, that final causes have only a heuristic value: since in demonstrations of the teleological type the final causes are part of the conclusion that is being demonstrated, the practice of Aristotle's natural science demonstrates the very existence of natural teleology.

Bibliography

Ackrill, J. L. (1981), "Aristotle's Theory of Definition: Some Questions on Posterior Analytics II.8–10," in E. Berti (ed.), *Aristotle on Science: The Posterior Analytics*, Proceedings of the 8th Symposium Aristotelicum, Padua, 359–384.

Anagnostopoulos, G. (ed.) (2009), *A Companion to Aristotle*, Blackwell Guides to Philosophy, Oxford.

Annas, J. (1982), "Aristotle on Inefficient Causes," *Philosophical Quarterly* 32, 311–322.

Apostle, H. G. (1981), *Aristotle's Posterior Analytics*, translated with Commentaries and Glossary, Grinnell, IA.

Balme, D. M. (1965), "Aristotle's Use of Teleological Explanation." Paper presented at the Inaugural Lecture, Queen Mary College, University of London, London.

(1972), *Aristotle's De Partibus Animalium I and De Generatione Animalium I (with Pages from II.1–3)*, Oxford.

(1980), "Aristotle's Biology was not Essentialist," *Archiv für Geschichte der Philosophie* 62, 1–12; reprinted in A. Gotthelf and J. G. Lennox (eds.) (1987), *Philosophical Issues in Aristotle's Biology*, Cambridge, 291–312.

(1987a), "The Place of Biology in Aristotle's Philosophy," in A. Gotthelf and J. G. Lennox (eds.), *Philosophical Issues in Aristotle's Biology*, Cambridge, 9–20.

(1987b), "Aristotle's Use of Division and Differentiae," in A. Gotthelf and J. G. Lennox (eds.), *Philosophical Issues in Aristotle's Biology*, Cambridge, 69–89.

(1987c), "Teleology and Necessity," in A. Gotthelf and J. G. Lennox (eds.), *Philosophical Issues in Aristotle's Biology*, Cambridge, 275–286.

Barnes, J. (1975), "Aristotle's Theory of Demonstration," in J. Barnes, M. Schofield, and R. Sorabji (eds.), *Articles on Aristotle I: Science*, London, 65–87.

(1981), "Proof and the Syllogism," in E. Berti (ed.), *Aristotle on Science: The Posterior Analytics*, Proceedings of the 8th Symposium Aristotelicum, Padua, 17–59.

(1987), "An Aristotelian Way with Scepticism," in M. Matthen (ed.), *Aristotle Today, Essays on Aristotle's Ideal of Science*, Edmonton, AB, 51–76.

(1993), *Aristotle, Posterior Analytics*, Oxford.

(ed.) (1995), *The Cambridge Companion to Aristotle*, Cambridge.

(1999), "Review of S. Everson, *Aristotle on Perception*," *Classical Review, NS* 49, 120–122.

Barnes, J., M. Schofield, and R. Sorabji (eds.) (1975), *Articles on Aristotle I: Science*, London.

Bayer, G. (1998), "Classification and Explanation in Aristotle's Theory of Definition," *Journal of the History of Philosophy* 36, 487–505.

Bekker, I.(ed.) (1831), *Aristotelis Opera*, Berlin.

Berti, E. (ed.) (1981), *Aristotle on Science: The Posterior Analytics*, Proceedings of the 8th Symposium Aristotelicum, Padua.

(1989–90), "La Finalità in Aristotele," *Fondamenti* 14–16, 8–44.

Bobzien, S. (2002), "The Development of Modus Ponens in Antiquity: From Aristotle to the 2nd Century AD," *Phronesis* 47.4, 359–394.

Bodnár, I. (2005), "Teleology across Natures," *Rhizai* 2, 9–29.

(2006), "Aristotle's Philosophy of Nature," *Stanford Encyclopedia of Philosophy*, 1–12.

Bodnár, I. and P. Pellegrin (2006), "Aristotle's Physics and Cosmology," in M. L. Gill and P. Pellegrin (eds.), *A Companion to Ancient Philosophy*, Blackwell Companions to Philosophy, Malden, MA, 270–291.

Boeri, M. D. (1995), "Change and Teleology in Aristotle Physics," *International Philosophical Quarterly* 34, 87–96.

Bogen, J. and J. E. McGuire (1986–7), "Aristotle's Great Clock: Necessity, Possibility and the Motion of the Cosmos in *De Caelo* I.12," *Philosophy Research Archives* 12, 387–448.

Bolotin, D. (1998), *An Approach to Aristotle's Physics: With Particular Attention to the Role of His Manner of Writing*, Albany, NY.

Bolton, R. (1987), "Definition and Scientific Method in Aristotle's Posterior Analytics and Generation of Animals," in A. Gotthelf and J. G. Lennox (eds.), *Philosophical Issues in Aristotle's Biology*, Cambridge, 120–166.

(1991), "Aristotle's Method in Natural Science: Physics I," in L. Judson (ed.), *Aristotle's Physics, A Collection of Essays*, Oxford, 2–29.

(1997), "The Material Cause: Matter and Explanation in Aristotle's Natural Science," in W. Kullmann and S. Föllinger (eds.), *Aristotelische Biologie: Intentionen, Methoden, Ergebnisse*, Stuttgart, 97–124.

(2002), "Substance and the Definition of Definition in Aristotle," in M. Canto-Sperber and P. Pellegrin (eds.), *Le style de la pensée: recueil des textes en hommage à Jacques Brunschwig*, Paris, 155–181.

(2004), "Causal Explanation and Demonstrative Knowledge in Aristotle," unpublished paper.

(2009), "Two Standards for Inquiry in Aristotle's *De Caelo*," in A. C. Bowen and C. Wildberg (eds.), *New Perspectives on Aristotle's De Caelo*, Leiden, 52–87.

Bonitz, H. (1870), *Index Aristotelicus*, 2nd edn, Berlin (reprinted Graz, 1955).

Bos, A. P. (2001), "Aristotle's *De anima* II, 1: The Traditional Interpretation Rejected," in D. Sfendoni-Mentzou, J. Hattiangadi, and D. M. Johnson (eds.), *Aristotle and Contemporary Science*, vol. II, Frankfurt am Main, 187–201.

Bos, A. P. and R. Ferwerda (2008), *Aristotle, On the Life-Bearing Spirit (De Spiritu) – A Discussion with Plato and his Predecessors on Pneuma as the Instrumental Body of the Soul*, Leiden and Boston.

Bostock, D. (2006), *Space, Time, Matter, and Form: Essays on Aristotle's Physics*, Oxford.

Bowen, A. C. (ed.) (1991), *Science and Philosophy in Classical Greece*, New York.

Bowen, A. C. and C. Wildberg (eds.) (2009), *New Perspectives on Aristotle's De Caelo*, Leiden.

Boylan, M. (1983), *Method and Practice in Aristotle's Biology*, Lanham, MD, and London.

(1984), "The Place of Nature in Aristotle's Teleology," *Apeiron* 18, 126–140.

Bradie, M. and F. D. Miller Jr. (1999), "Teleology and Natural Necessity," in L. P. Gerson (ed.), *Aristotle, Critical Assessments*, London, 75–89; reprint from (1984) *History of Philosophy Quarterly* 1, 133–146.

Broadie, S. (1990), "Nature and Craft in Aristotelian Teleology," in D. Devereux and P. Pellegrin (eds.), *Biologie, logique et métaphysique chez Aristote*, Paris, 389–403.

(1996), "Nous and Nature in *De Anima* III," in J. J. Cleary and W. Wians (eds.), *Proceedings of the Boston Area Colloquium in Ancient Philosophy* 12, 163–176.

Buller, D. J. (ed.) (1999), *Function, Selection, and Design*, New York.

Burnyeat, M. F. (1981), "Aristotle on Understanding Knowledge," in E. Berti (ed.), *Aristotle on Science: The Posterior Analytics*, Proceedings of the 8th Symposium Aristotelicum, Padua, 97–139.

(1992a), "Is an Aristotelian Philosophy of Mind still Credible? (A Draft)," in M. C. Nussbaum and A. O. Rorty (eds.), *Essays on Aristotle's* De Anima, Oxford, 15–26.

(1992b), "How Much Happens When Aristotle Sees Red and Hears Middle C? Remarks On *De Anima* 2.7–8," in M. C. Nussbaum and A. O. Rorty (eds.), *Essays on Aristotle's* De Anima, Oxford, 421–434.

(2001), *A Map of Metaphysics Zeta*, Pittsburgh.

(2002), "*De Anima* II.5," *Phronesis* 47.1, 28–90.

(2004), "Introduction: Aristotle on the Foundations of Sublunary Physics," in F. A. J. de Haas and J. Mansfeld (eds.), *Aristotle's On Generation and Corruption I Book 1*, Symposium Aristotelicum, Oxford, 7–24.

Byl, S. (1971), "Note sur la polysémie d'Organon et sur les origines du finalisme," *L'Antiquité Classique* 40, 121–133.

Byrne, C. (2002), "Aristotle on Physical Necessity and the Limits of Teleological Explanation," *Apeiron* 35, 20–46.

Byrne, P. H. (1997), *Analysis and Science in Aristotle*, Albany, NY.

Cameron, R. (2002), "The Ontology of Aristotle's Final Cause," *Apeiron* 35, 153–179.

Canto-Sperber, M. and P. Pellegrin (eds.) (2002), *Le style de la pensée: recueil des textes en hommage à Jacques Brunschwig*, Paris.

Caston, V. (1996), "Aristotle on the Relation of the Intellect to the Body: Commentary on Broadie," in J. J. Cleary and W. Wians (eds.), *Proceedings of the Boston Area Colloquium in Ancient Philosophy* 12, 177–191.

(2005), "The Spirit and the Letter: Aristotle on Perception," in R. Salles (ed.), *Metaphysics, Soul, and Ethics: Festschrift for Richard Sorabji*, Oxford, 245–320.

(2006), "Aristotle's Psychology," in M. L. Gill and P. Pellegrin (eds.), *A Companion to Ancient Philosophy*, Blackwell Companions to Philosophy Series, London, 316–346.

Catan, J. R. (ed.) (1981), *Aristotle: The Collected Papers of J. Owens*, New York.

Charles, D. (1984), *Aristotle's Philosophy of Action*, Ithaca, NY.

(1988), "Aristotle on Hypothetical Necessity and Irreducibility," *Pacific Philosophical Quarterly* 69, 1–53; reprinted in T. Irwin (ed.) (1995), *Classical Philosophy: Collected Papers*, New York and London, 27–80.

(1991), "Teleological Causation in the *Physics*," in L. Judson (ed.), *Aristotle's Physics: A Collection of Essays*, Oxford, 101–128.

(1994), "Matter and Form: Unity, Persistence, and Identity," in T. Scaltsas, D. Charles, and M. L. Gill (eds.), *Unity, Identity, and Explanation in Aristotle's Metaphysics*, Oxford, 75–105.

(1997), "Aristotle and the Unity and Essence of Biological Kinds," in W. Kullmann and S. Föllinger (eds.), *Aristotelische Biologie: Intentionen, Methoden, Ergebnisse*, Stuttgart, 27–42.

(1999), "Aristotle on Substance, Essence and Biological Kinds," in L. P. Gerson (ed.), *Aristotle: Critical Assessments*, London, 227–255.

(2000), *Aristotle on Meaning and Essence*, Oxford.

Charlton, W. (1970), *Aristotle's Physics I and II*, Oxford.

Cherniss, H. (1935; reprinted 1971), *Aristotle's Criticism of Presocratic Philosophy*, New York.

Code, A. (1987), "Soul as Efficient Cause in Aristotle's Embryology," *Philosophical Topics* 15, 51–59.

(1997), "The Priority of Final Causes over Efficient Causes in Aristotle's Parts of Animals,' in W. Kullmann and S. Föllinger (eds.), *Aristotelische Biologie: Intentionen, Methoden, Ergebnisse*, Stuttgart, 127–143.

Code, A. and J. Moravcsik (1992), "Explaining Various Forms of Living," in M. C. Nussbaum and A. O. Rorty (eds.), *Essays on Aristotle's* De Anima, Oxford, 129–145.

Cohen, S. M. (1989), "Aristotle on Heat, Cold, and Teleological Explanation," *Ancient Philosophy* 9, 255–270.

(1992), "Hylomorphism and Functionalism," in M. C. Nussbaum and A. O. Rorty (eds.), *Essays on Aristotle's* De Anima, Oxford, 57–73.

(1996), *Aristotle on Nature and Incomplete Substance*, Cambridge.

Coles, A. (1990), "Animal and Childhood Cognition in Aristotle's Biology and the *Scala Naturae*," in D. Devereux and P. Pellegrin (eds.), *Biologie, logique et métaphysique chez Aristote*, Paris, 287–323.

Cooper, J. M. (1975), *Reason and Human Good in Aristotle*, Cambridge and London.

(1982), "Aristotle on Natural Teleology," in M. Schofield and M. Nussbaum (eds.), *Language and Logos*, Cambridge, 197–222; reprinted in J. M. Cooper (2004), *Knowledge, Nature and the Good: Essays on Ancient Philosophy*, Princeton, NJ, 107–129.

(1985), "Hypothetical Necessity," in A. Gotthelf (ed.), *Aristotle on Nature and Living Things*, Bristol, 150–167; reprinted in J. M. Cooper (2004), *Knowledge, Nature and the Good: Essays on Ancient Philosophy*, Princeton, NJ, 130–147.

(1987), "Hypothetical Necessity and Natural Teleology," in A. Gotthelf and J. G. Lennox (eds.), *Philosophical Issues in Aristotle's Biology*, Cambridge, 243–274.

(1990), "Metaphysics in Aristotle's Embryology," in D. Devereux and P. Pellegrin (eds.), *Biologie, logique et métaphysique chez Aristote*, Paris, 55–84.

Corcilius, K. (2008a), "Praktische Syllogismen bei Aristoteles," *Archiv für Geschichte der Philosophie* 90.2, 247–297.

(2008b), "Aristoteles' praktische Syllogismen in der zweiten Hälfte des 20. Jahrhunderts," *Logical Analysis and History of Philosophy* 11, 101–132.

(2008c), "Two Jobs for Aristotle's Practical Syllogism?," *Logical Analysis and History of Philosophy* 11, 163–184.

Cornford, F. M. (1975), *Plato's Cosmology*, Indianapolis, IN.

Cummins, R. (1999), "Functional Analysis," in D. J. Buller (ed.), *Function, Selection, and Design*, New York, 57–83.

DeMoss, D. and D. Devereux (1988), "Essence, Existence, and Nominal Definition in Aristotle's *Posterior Analytics* II.8–10," *Phronesis* 33, 133–154.

Depew, D. (1995), "Humans and other Political Animals in Aristotle's History of Animals," *Phronesis* 40, 156–181.

(1997), "Etiological Approaches to Biological Aptness in Aristotle and Darwin," in W. Kullmann and S. Föllinger (eds.), *Aristotelische Biologie, Intentionen, Methoden, Ergebnisse*, Stuttgart, 209–227.

Deslauriers, M. (2007), *Aristotle on Definition*, Leiden.

Detel, W. (1993), *Aristoteles Analytica Posteriora*, Berlin.

(1997), "Why all Animals have a Stomach: Demonstration and Axiomatization in Aristotle's Parts of Animals," in W. Kullmann and S. Föllinger (eds.), *Aristotelische Biologie: Intentionen, Methoden, Ergebnisse*, Stuttgart, 63–84.

(1999), "Aristotle on Zoological Explanation," *Philosophical Topics* 25, 43–68.

(2006), "Aristotle's Logic and Theory of Science," in M. L. Gill and P. Pellegrin (eds.), *A Companion to Ancient Philosophy*, Blackwell Companions to Philosophy, Malden, MA, 245–269.

Devereux, D. and P. Pellegrin (eds.) (1990), *Biologie, logique et métaphysique chez Aristote*, Paris.

Dudley, J. (1997), *The Evolution of the Concept of Change in the Physics and Ethics of Aristotle: A Commentary on Phys II, IV–VI*, Nijmegen.

Düring, I. (ed.) (1969), *Naturphilosophie bei Aristoteles und Theophrast*, 4th Symposium Aristotelicum, Heidelberg.

Eijk, Van Der, Ph. J. (1997), "The Matter of Mind: Aristotle on the Biology of 'Psychic' Processes," in W. Kullmann and S. Föllinger (eds.), *Aristotelische Biologie: Intentionen, Methoden, Ergebnisse*, Stuttgart, 231–258.

(2001), *Diocles of Carystus: A Collection of the Fragments with Translation and Commentary*, Leiden.

Everson, S. (1997), *Aristotle on Perception*, Oxford.

Falcon, A. (2005), *Aristotle and the Science of Nature: Unity without Uniformity*, Cambridge.

(2006), "Aristotle on Causality," *Stanford Encyclopedia of Philosophy*, 1–11.
Ferejohn, M. (1990), *The Origins of Aristotelian Science*, New Haven, CT.
Ferguson, J. (1985), "Teleology in Aristotle's Politics," in A. Gotthelf (ed.), *Aristotle on Nature and Living Things*, Bristol, 259–276.
Fine, G. (1987), "Forms as Causes: Plato and Aristotle," in A. Graeser (ed.), *Mathematics and Metaphysics in Aristotle*, Bern, 69–112.
Fortenbaugh, W. W. (1966), "Nicomachean Ethics I, 1096b26–29," *Phronesis* 11.2, 185–194.
Fortenbaugh, W. W., P. M. Huby and A. A. Long (eds.) (1985), *Theophrastus of Eresus: On his Life and Work*, New Brunswick, NJ.
Fraassen, van, B. (1980), "A Re-examination of Aristotle's Philosophy of Science," *Dialogue* 19, 20–45.
Frede, D. (1992), "The Cognitive Role of Phantasia in Aristotle," in M. C. Nussbaum and A. O. Rorty (eds.), *Essays on Aristotle's* De Anima, Oxford, 279–295.
Frede, M. (1980), "The Original Notion of Cause," in M. Schofield, M. Burnyeat, and J. Barnes (eds.), *Doubt and Dogmatism: Studies in Hellenistic Epistemology*, Oxford, 217–249.
(1992), "On Aristotle's Conception of the Soul," in M. C. Nussbaum and A. O. Rorty (eds.), *Essays on Aristotle's* De Anima, Oxford, 93–107.
Frede, M. and G. Patzig (1988), *Aristoteles, Metaphysik Z*, 2 vols., Munich.
Frede, M. and G. Stricker (eds.) (1996), *Rationality in Greek Thought*, Oxford.
Freeland, C. A. (1990), "Scientific Explanation and Empirical Data in Aristotle's Meteorology," in D. Devereux and P. Pellegrin (eds.), *Biologie, logique et métaphysique chez Aristote*, Paris, 287–320.
(1991), "Accidental Causes and Real Explanations," in L. Judson (ed.), *Aristotle's Physics: A Collection of Essays*, Oxford, 49–72.
(1992), "Aristotle on the Sense of Touch," in M. C. Nussbaum and A. O. Rorty (eds.), *Essays on Aristotle's* De Anima, Oxford, 227–248.
(1995), "Aristotle on Perception, Appetition, and Self-Motion," in M. L. Gill and J. G. Lennox (eds.), *Self-motion from Aristotle to Newton*, Princeton, NJ, 35–63.
Friedman, R. (1983), "Matter and Necessity in *Physics* B 9, 200 a 15–30," *Ancient Philosophy* 1, 8–12.
Furley, D. J. (1985), "The Rainfall Example in *Physics* II.8," in A. Gotthelf (ed.), *Aristotle on Nature and Living Things*, Pittsburgh, PA, 177–182; reprinted in D. J. Furley (1989), *Cosmic Problems*, Cambridge, 115–120.
(1989), *Cosmic Problems*, Cambridge.
(1994), "Self-Movers," in M. L. Gill and J. G. Lennox (eds.), *Self-Motion From Aristotle to Newton*, Princeton, NJ, 3–14.
(1996), "What Kind of Cause is Aristotle's Final Cause?," in M. Frede and G. Stricker (eds.), *Rationality in Greek Thought*, Oxford, 59–79.
(2004), "Aristotle and the Atomists on Forms and Final Causes," in R. W. Sharples (ed.), *Perspectives on Greek Philosophy*, Aldershot and Burlington, VT, 70–84.

Furth, M. (1987), "Aristotle's Biological Universe: An Overview," in A. Gotthelf and J. G. Lennox (eds.), *Philosophical Issues in Aristotle's Biology*, Cambridge, 21–63.

Gaiser, K. (1969), "Das zweifache Telos bei Aristoteles," in I. Düring (ed.), *Naturphilosophie bei Aristoteles und Theophrast*, 4th Symposium Aristotelicum, Heidelberg, 97–113.

Gallop, D. (1988), "Aristotle on Sleep, Dreams, and Final Causes," *Proceedings of the Boston Area Colloquium in Ancient Philosophy* 4, 257–290.

Gerson, L. P. (ed.) (2005), *Aristotle and Other Platonists*, Ithaca, NY, and London.

(1999), *Aristotle: Critical Assessments*, London.

Gentzler, J. (ed.), *Method in Ancient Philosophy*, Oxford.

Gill, M. L. (1980), "Aristotle's Theory of Causal Action in Physics III.3," *Phronesis* 25, 129–147.

(1991), "Aristotle on Self-Motion," in L. Judson (ed.), *Aristotle's Physics: A Collection of Essays*, Oxford, 243–265.

(1997), "Material Necessity and Meteorology IV.12," in W. Kullmann and S. Föllinger (eds.), *Aristotelische Biologie, Intentionen, Methoden, Ergebnisse*, Stuttgart, 145–161.

Gill, M. L. and J. G. Lennox (eds.) (1995), *Self-motion from Aristotle to Newton*, Princeton, NJ.

Gill, M. L. and P. Pellegrin (eds.) (2006), *A Companion to Ancient Philosophy*, Blackwell Companions to Philosophy, Malden, MA.

Goldin, O. (1996), *Explaining an Eclipse: Aristotle's Posterior Analytics 2.1–10*, Ann Harbor, MI.

Gotthelf, A. (1976–7), "Aristotle's Conception of Final Causality," *Review of Metaphysics* 30, 226–254; reprinted with additional notes and a postscript in A. Gotthelf and J. G. Lennox (eds.) (1987), *Philosophical Issues in Aristotle's Biology*, Cambridge, 204–242.

(1980). "Review of M. C. Nussbaum, Aristotle's *De Motu Animalium*," *Journal of Philosophy* 77, 365–378.

(ed.) (1985), *Aristotle on Nature and Living Things (Philosophical and Historical Studies Presented to David M. Balme on his Seventieth Birthday)*, Pittsburgh, PA, and Bristol.

(1987), "First Principles in Aristotle's Parts of Animals," in A. Gotthelf and J. G. Lennox (eds.), *Philosophical Issues in Aristotle's Biology*, Cambridge, 167–198.

(1988), "The Place of the Good in Aristotle's Teleology," in J. J. Cleary and D. C. Shartin (eds.), *Proceedings of the Boston Colloquium in Ancient Philosophy* 4, 113–139.

(1989), "Teleology and Spontaneous Generation: A Discussion," in R. Kraut and T. Penner (eds.), *Nature, Knowledge and Virtue: Apeiron*, Special Issue 22.4, 181–193.

(1997a), "The Elephant's Nose: Further Reflections on the Axiomatic Structure of Biological Explanations in Aristotle," in W. Kullmann and S. Föllinger (eds.), *Aristotelische Biologie: Intentionen, Methoden, Ergebnisse*, Stuttgart, 85–95.

(1997b), "Understanding Aristotle's Teleology," in R. Hassing (ed.), *Final Causality in Nature and Human Affairs*, Studies in Philosophy and the History of Philosophy 30, Washington DC, 71–82.

Gotthelf, A. and J. G. Lennox (eds.) (1987), *Philosophical Issues in Aristotle's Biology*, Cambridge.

Graeser, A. (ed.), *Mathematics and Metaphysics in Aristotle*, Bern.

Granger, H. (1993), "Aristotle on the Analogy between Action and Nature," *Classical Quarterly* 43, 168–176.

Grene, M. and D. Depew (2004), *The Philosophy of Biology: An Episodic History*, Cambridge.

Guthrie, W. K. C. (1939), *Aristotle: On the Heavens*, London.

Hamlyn, D. W. (2001), *Aristotle De Anima, Books II and III (with Passages from Book I)*, translated with introduction and notes, with a report on recent work and a revised bibliography by Christopher Shields, Oxford.

Hankinson, R. J. (1995a), "Philosophy of Science," in J. Barnes (ed.), *The Cambridge Companion to Aristotle*, Cambridge, 109–139.

(1995b), "Science," in J. Barnes (ed.), *The Cambridge Companion to Aristotle*, Cambridge, 140–167.

(1998), *Cause and Explanation in Ancient Greek Thought*, Oxford.

(2002–3), "Xenarchus, Alexander, and Simplicius on Simple Motions, Bodies and Magnitudes," *Bulletin of the Institute of Classical Studies* 46, 19–42.

(2009), "Natural, Unnatural, and Preternatural Motions: Contrariety and the Argument for the Elements in *De Caelo* 1.2–4," in A. C. Bowen and C. Wildberg (eds.), *New Perspectives on Aristotle's* De Caelo, Leiden, 89–132.

Hassing, R. (ed.) (1997), *Final Causality in Nature and Human Affairs*, Studies in Philosophy and the History of Philosophy 30, Washington DC.

Heath, Sir T. L. (1932), *Greek Astronomy*, New York.

Henry, D. (2006), "Understanding Aristotle's Reproductive Hylomorphism," *Apeiron* 39.3, 257–287.

Hett, W. S. (1936), *Aristotle On the Soul, Parva Naturalia, On Breath*, Cambridge and London.

Hintikka, J. (1989), "Concepts of Scientific Method from Aristotle to Newton," in M. Asztalos, J. Murdoch and I. Niiniluoto (eds.), *Proceedings of the 1987 Congress of Medieval Philosophy, Acta Philosophica Fennica*, Societas Philosophica Fennica, Helsinki, 72–84.

Hocutt, M. (1974), "Aristotle's Four Becauses," *Philosophy* 49, 385–399.

Hutchinson, D. S. (1987), "Restoring the Order of Aristotle's *De Anima*," *Classical Quarterly* 37, 373–381.

Ierodiakonou, K. (2005), "Ancient Thought Experiments: A First Approach," *Ancient Philosophy* 25, 125–140.

Irwin, T. (1988), *Aristotle's First Principles*, Oxford.

Johansen, T. K. (1998), *Aristotle on the Sense-Organs*, Cambridge.

(2004), *Plato's Natural Philosophy: A Study of the Timaeus-Critias*, Cambridge.

(2009), "From Plato's *Timaeus* to Aristotle's *De caelo*: The Case of the Missing World Soul," in A. C. Bowen and C. Wildberg (eds.), *New Perspectives on Aristotle's* De Caelo, Leiden, 1–24.

Johnson, M. R. (2005), *Aristotle on Teleology*, Oxford.

Judson, L. (ed.) (1991a), *Aristotle's Physics: A Collection of Essays*, Oxford.

(1991b), "Chance and Always or for the most Part," L. Judson (ed.), *Aristotle's Physics: A Collection of Essays*, Oxford, 73–100.

(2005), "Aristotelian Teleology," *Oxford Studies in Ancient Philosophy* 29, 341–366.

Kahn, C. H. (1985), "The Place of the Prime Mover in Aristotle's Teleology," in A. Gotthelf (ed.), *Aristotle on Nature and Living Things*, Pittsburgh, PA, and Bristol, 183–205.

Katayama, E. G. (1999), *Aristotle on Artifacts: A Metaphysical Puzzle*, New York.

Kelsey, S. (2003), "Aristotle's Definition of Nature," *Oxford Studies in Ancient Philosophy* 25, 59–87.

Kosman, L. A. (1987), "Animals and Other Beings in Aristotle," in A. Gotthelf and J. G. Lennox (eds.), *Philosophical Issues in Aristotle's Biology*, Cambridge, 360–391.

Kraut, R. and T. Penner (eds.) (1989), *Nature, Knowledge and Virtue: Apeiron*, Special Issue 22.4.

Kullmann, W. (1974), *Wissenschaft und Methode, Interpretationen zur Aristotelischen Theorie der Naturwissenschaft*, Berlin.

(1979), *Die Teleologie in der Aristotelischen Biologie: Aristoteles als Zoologe, Embryologe und Genetiker*, Heidelberg.

(1985), "Different Concepts of the Final Cause in Aristotle," in A. Gotthelf (ed.), *Aristotle on Nature and Living Things*, Pittsburgh, PA, 170–175.

(1990), "Bipartite Science in Aristotle's Biology," in D. Devereux and P. Pellegrin (eds.), *Biologie, logique et métaphysique chez Aristote*, Paris, 335–347.

Kullmann, W. and S. Föllinger (eds.) (1997), *Aristotelische Biologie: Intentionen, Methoden, Ergebnisse*, Stuttgart.

Kupreeva, I. (forthcoming), "Causation and Conditional Necessity: *APo.* II 12," in F. A. J. de Haas, M. Leunissen, and M. Martijn (eds.), *Interpreting Aristotle's* Posterior Analytics *in Late Antiquity and the Byzantine Period*, Leiden.

Lang, H. S. (1989), "Aristotelian Physics: Teleological Procedure in Aristotle, Thomas, and Buridan," *Review of Metaphysics* 42, 569–591.

(1998), *The Order of Nature in Aristotle's Physics: Place and the Elements*, Cambridge.

Leggatt, S. (1995), *Aristotle On the Heavens I&II*, with an introduction, translation and commentary, Warminster.

Lennox, J. G. (1982), "Teleology, Chance, and Aristotle's Theory of Spontaneous Generation," *Journal of History of Philosophy* 20, 219–238; reprinted in J. G. Lennox (2001a), *Aristotle's Philosophy of Biology*, Cambridge, 229–249.

(1984), "Aristotle on Chance," *Archiv für Geschichte der Philosophie* 66, 52–60; reprinted in J. G. Lennox (2001a), *Aristotle's Philosophy of Biology*, Cambridge, 250–258.

(1985a), "Plato's Unnatural Teleology," *Studies in Philosophy and the History of Philosophy* 13, 195–218; reprinted in J. G. Lennox (2001a), *Aristotle's Philosophy of Biology*, Cambridge, 280–302.

(1985b), "Theophrastus on the Limits of Teleology," in W. W. Fortenbaugh, P. M. Huby and A. A. Long (eds.), *Theophrastus of Eresus: on his Life and Work*, New Brunswick, NJ, 143–163; reprinted in J. G. Lennox (2001a), *Aristotle's Philosophy of Biology*, Cambridge, 259–279.

(1985c), "Are Aristotelian Species Eternal?," in A. Gotthelf (ed.), *Aristotle on Nature and Living Things*, Pittsburgh, PA, and Bristol, 67–94; reprinted in J. G. Lennox (2001a), *Aristotle's Philosophy of Biology*, Cambridge, 131–159.

(1987a), "Divide and Explain: The Posterior Analytics in Practice," in A. Gotthelf and J. G. Lennox (eds.) (1987), *Philosophical Issues in Aristotle's Biology*, Cambridge, 90–119; reprinted in J. G. Lennox (2001a), *Aristotle's Philosophy of Biology*, Cambridge, 7–38.

(1987b), "Kinds, Forms of Kinds, and the More and the Less in Aristotle's Biology," in A. Gotthelf and J. G. Lennox (eds.) (1987), *Philosophical Issues in Aristotle's Biology*, Cambridge, 339–359; reprinted in J. G. Lennox (2001a), *Aristotle's Philosophy of Biology*, Cambridge, 160–181.

(1990), "Notes on David Charles on *HA*," in D. Devereux and P. Pellegrin (eds.), *Biologie, logique et métaphysique chez Aristote*, Paris, 169–183.

(1991), "Between Data and Demonstration: The Analytics and the *Historia Animalium*," in A. Bowen (ed.), *Science and Philosophy in Classical Greece*, New York, 261–295; reprinted in J. G. Lennox (2001a), *Aristotle's Philosophy of Biology*, Cambridge, 39–71.

(1994), "Aristotelian Problems," *Ancient Philosophy* 14, 53–77.

(1996a), "Material and Formal Natures in Aristotle's *De Partibus Animalium*," in J. J. Cleary and W. Wians (eds.), *Proceedings of the Boston Area Colloquium of Ancient Philosophy* 12; reprinted in J. G. Lennox (2001a), *Aristotle's Philosophy of Biology*, Cambridge, 182–204.

(1996b), "Aristotle's Biological Development: The Balme Hypothesis," in W. Wians (ed.), *Aristotle's Philosophical Development, Problems and Prospects*, London, 229–248.

(1997a), "Putting Philosophy of Science to the Test: The Case of Aristotle's Biology," in W. Kullmann and S. Föllinger (eds.), *Aristotelische Biologie: Intentionen, Methoden, Ergebnisse*, Stuttgart, 163–182; reprinted in J. G. Lennox (2001a), *Aristotle's Philosophy of Biology*, Cambridge, 98–109.

(1997b), "Nature Does Nothing in Vain," in H.-C. Günther and A. Rengakos (eds.), *Beitraege zur antiken Philosophie: Festschrift für Wolfgang Kullmann (mit einer Einleitung von Ernst Vogt)*, Stuttgart, 199–214; reprinted in J. G. Lennox (2001a), *Aristotle's Philosophy of Biology*, Cambridge, 205–223.

(1999), "The Place of Mankind in Aristotle's Zoology," *Philosophical Topics* 27, 1–16.

(2001a), *Aristotle's Philosophy of Biology: Studies in the Origins of Life Science*, Cambridge.

(2001b), *Aristotle on the Parts of Animals I–IV*, translated with an introduction and commentary by J. G. Lennox, Oxford.

(2001c), "Aristotle on the Unity and Disunity of Science," *International Studies in the Philosophy of Science* 15.2, 133–144.

(2004a), "The Place of Zoology in Aristotle's Natural Philosophy," in R. W. Sharples (ed.), *Philosophy and the Sciences in Antiquity*, London, 58–70.

(2004b), "Getting A Science Going: Aristotle on Entry Level Kinds," in G. Wolters (ed.), *Homo Sapiens und Homo Faber (Festschrift Mittelstrass)*, Berlin, 87–100.

(2006), "Aristotle's Biology and Aristotle's Philosophy," in M. L. Gill and P. Pellegrin (eds.), *A Companion to Ancient Philosophy*, Blackwell Companions to Philosophy Series, London, 292–315.

(2009), "*De caelo* 2.2 and its Debt to *De incessu animalium*," in A. C. Bowen and C. Wildberg (eds.), *New Perspectives on Aristotle's* De Caelo, Leiden, 211–243.

Leunissen, M. (2007), "The Structure of Teleological Explanations in Aristotle: Theory and Practice," *Oxford Studies in Ancient Philosophy* 33, 145–178.

(2009), "Why Stars have no Feet: Teleological Explanations in Aristotle's Cosmology," in A. C. Bowen and C. Wildberg (eds.), *New Perspectives on Aristotle's* De Caelo, Leiden, 245–271.

(2010), "Aristotle's Syllogistic Model of Knowledge and the Biological Sciences: Demonstrating Natural Processes," in J. Lesher (ed.), *Apeiron*, Special Issue: "From Inquiry to Demonstrative Knowledge: New Essays on Aristotle's *Posterior Analytics*" 43.2–3.

Leunissen, M. and A. Gotthelf (2010), "What's Teleology Got to Do with It? A Reinterpretation of Aristotle's *Generation of Animals* V," *Phronesis* 55.

Lewis, F. A. (1988), "Teleology and Material/Efficient Causes in Aristotle," *Pacific Philosophical Quarterly* 69, 54–98.

Liatsi, M. (2000), *Aristoteles, De Generatione Animalium, Buch V, Einleitung und Kommentar*, Trier.

Lloyd, G. E. R. (1966), *Polarity and Analogy: Two Types of Argumentation in Early Greek Thought*, Cambridge.

(1978), "The Empirical Basis of the Physiology of the Parva Naturalia," in G. E. R. Lloyd and G. E. L. Owens (eds.), *Aristotle on Mind and the Senses*, Proceedings of the 7th Symposium Aristotelicum, Cambridge, 215–239.

(1983), *Science, Folklore, and Ideology: Studies in the Life Sciences in Ancient Greece*, Cambridge.

(1987), "Empirical Research in Aristotle's Biology," in A. Gotthelf and J. G. Lennox (eds.), *Philosophical Issues in Aristotle's Biology*, Cambridge, 53–63.

(1990), "Aristotle's Zoology and his Metaphysics: The Status Quaestionis; A Critical Review of some Recent Theories," in D. Devereux and P. Pellegrin (eds.), *Biologie, logique et métaphysique chez Aristote*, Paris, 7–35.

(1991), *Methods and Problems in Greek Science*, Cambridge.

(1992), "Aspects of the Relationship between Aristotle's Psychology and his Zoology," in M. C. Nussbaum and A. O. Rorty (eds.), *Essays on Aristotle's* De Anima, Oxford, 147–167.

(1995), "Ancient Greek Concepts of Causation in Comparativist Perspective," in D. Sperber, D. Premack, and A. J. Premack (eds.), *Causal Cognition*, Oxford, 205–233.

(1996), *Aristotelian Explorations*, Cambridge.

Lloyd, G. E. R. and G. E. L. Owens (eds.) (1978), *Aristotle on Mind and the Senses*, Proceedings of the 7th Symposium Aristotelicum, Cambridge.

Löbl, R. (2003), *TEXNH – TECHNE, Untersuchungen zur Bedeutung dieses Worts in der Zeit von Homer bis Aristoteles*, Band II: *Von den Sophisten bis zu Aristoteles*, Würzburg.

Mansfeld, J. (2002), "Deconstructing Doxography," *Philologus* 146, 277–286.

Martin, A. and O. Primavesi (1999), *L'Empédocle de Strasbourg (P. Strasb. Gr. Inv. 1665–1666)*, introduction, édition et commentaire, with an English summary, New York.

Matthen, M. (ed.) (1987), *Aristotle Today, Essays on Aristotle's Ideal of Science*, Edmonton, AB.

(1989), "The Four Causes in Aristotle's Embryology," in R. Kraut and T. Penner (eds.), *Nature, Knowledge and Virtue: Apeiron*, Special Issue 22.4, 159–180.

(2001), "The Holistic Presuppositions of Aristotle's Cosmology," *Oxford Studies in Ancient Philosophy* 20, 171–199.

(2009), "Teleology in Living Things," in G. Anagnostopoulus (ed.), *A Companion to Aristotle*, Blackwell Guides to Philosophy, Oxford, 335–347.

Matthen, M. and R. J. Hankinson (1993), "Aristotle's Universe: Its Form and Matter," *Synthese* 96, 417–435; reprinted in L. P. Gerson (ed.) (1999), *Aristotle: Critical Assessments*, London, 209–226.

Matthews, G. (1992), "*De Anima* 2.2–4 and the Meaning of Life," in M. C. Nussbaum and A. O. Rorty (eds.), *Essays on Aristotle's* De Anima, Oxford, 185–93.

Mayhew, R. (2004), *The Female in Aristotle's Biology: Reason or Rationalization*, Chicago.

McKirahan, R. (1992), *Principles and Proofs: Aristotle's Theory of Demonstrative Science*, Princeton, NJ.

Menn, S. (1994), "The Origins of Aristotle's Concept of Energeia: Energeia and Dunamis," *Ancient Philosophy* 14, 73–114.

(2002), "Aristotle's Definition of Soul and the Programme of the *De Anima*," *Oxford Studies in Ancient Philosophy* 22, 83–139.

Miller, F. D. (1995), *Nature, Justice, and Rights in Aristotle's Politics*, Oxford.

Mirus, C. V. (2004), "The Metaphysical Roots of Aristotle's Teleology," *Review of Metaphysics* 57, 699–724.

Moraux, P. (1961), "La méthode d'Aristote dans l'Étude du Ciel, *De Caelo* I.1–II.12," in S. Mansion (ed.), *Aristote et les problèmes de méthode*, Louvain, 173–195.

Moravcsik, J. M. (1974a), "Aristotle on Adequate Explanations," *Synthese* 28, 3–17.

(1974b), "Aitia as Generative Factor in Aristotle's Philosophy," *Dialogue* 14, 622–638.

(1991), "What Makes Reality Intelligible? Reflections on Aristotle's Theory of *Aitia*," in L. Judson (ed.), *Aristotle's Physics: A Collection of Essays*, Oxford, 31–47.

(1994), "Essences, Powers, and Generic Propositions," in T. Scaltas, D. Charles, and M. L. Gill (eds.), *Unity, Identity, and Explanation in Aristotle's Metaphysics*, Oxford, 229–244.

(1995), "Philosophic Background of Aristotle's *Aitia*," in M. Sim (ed.), *The Crossroads of Norm and Nature: Essays on Aristotle's Ethics and Metaphysics*, Boston, 237–246.

Morison, B, (2002), *On Location: Aristotle's Concept of Place*, Oxford.

Mouracade, J. (ed.) (2008), *Aristotle on Life, Apeiron*, Special Issue 41.3.

Mueller, I. (2006), "Physics and Astronomy: Aristotle's *Physics* II.2, 193b22–194a12," *Arabic Sciences and Philosophy* 16, 175–206.

Mure, G. R. G. (1975), "Cause and Because in Aristotle," *Philosophy* 50, 356–357.

Natali, C. (2001), *The Wisdom of Aristotle*, translated by Gerald Parks, New York.

Nielsen, K. M. (2008), "The Private Parts of Animals: Aristotle on the Teleology of Sexual Difference," *Phronesis* 53, 373–405.

Nussbaum, M. C. (1978), *Aristotle's* De Motu Animalium, Princeton, NJ.

Nussbaum, M. C. and H. Putnam (1992), "Changing Aristotle's Mind," in M. C. Nussbaum and A. O. Rorty (eds.), *Essays on Aristotle's* De Anima, Oxford, 27–56.

Nussbaum, M. C. and A. O. Rorty (eds.) (1992), *Essays on Aristotle's* De Anima, Oxford.

Nussbaum, M. C. and M. Schofield (eds.) (1982), *Language and Logos*, Ithaca, NY.

Ogle, W. (1912), *Aristotle: De Partibus Animalium*, Oxford.

Owen, G. E. L. (1961), "Tithenai ta Phainomena," in S. Mansion (ed.), *Aristote et les problèmes de méthode*, Louvain.

(1986), *Logic, Science, and Dialectic*, ed. M. C. Nussbaum, New York.

Owens, J. (1968), "The Teleology of Nature," *Monist* 52, 159–173; reprinted in J. R. Catan (ed.) (1981), *Aristotle: The Collected Papers of J. Owens*, New York, 136–147.

Pavlopoulos, M. (2003), "Aristotle's Natural Teleology and Metaphysics of Life," *Oxford Studies in Ancient Philosophy* 23, 133–181.

Pellegrin, P. (1986), *Aristotle's Classification of Animals: Biology and the Conceptual Unity of the Aristotelian Corpus*, tranlated by A. Preuss, Berkeley, CA.

(2002), "Les ruses de la nature et l'éternité du mouvement: encore quelques remarques sur la finalité chez Aristote," in M. Canto-Sperber and P. Pellegrin (eds.), *Le style de la pensée: recueil des textes en hommage à Jacques Brunschwig*, Paris, 296–323.

Polansky, R. (1999), "Analogy and Disanalogy of the Soul's Faculties in Aristotle's *De Anima*," *Boston Area Colloquium in Ancient Philosophy* 15, 57–86.

(2007), *Aristotle's* De Anima, Cambridge.

Preus, A. (1975), *Science and Philosophy in Aristotle's Biological Works*, New York.

(1990), "Man and Cosmos in Aristotle: Metaphysics L and the Biological Works," in D. Devereux and P. Pellegrin (eds.), *Biologie, logique et métaphysique chez Aristote*, Paris, 471–490.

Quarantotto, D. (2001), "Ontologia della causa finale aristotelica," *Elenchos* 22.2, 329–365.

(2005), *Causa finale, sostanza, essenza in Aristotele: saggi sulla struttura dei processi teleologici naturali e sulla funzione dei telos*, Naples.

Richardson, H. (1992), "Desire and the Good in *De Anima*," in M. C. Nussbaum and A. O. Rorty (eds.), *Essays on Aristotle's* De Anima, Oxford, 381–399.

Rijksbaron, A., S. R. Slings, P. Stork, and G. C. Wakker (2000), *Beknopte Syntaxis van het klassiek Grieks*, Lunteren.

Rist, J. M. (1965), "Some Aspects of Aristotelian Teleology," *Transactions and Proceedings of the American Philological Association* 96, 337–349.

Ritter, W. E. (1932; 1934), "Why Aristotle Invented the Word *Entelecheia*," *Quarterly Review of Biology* 7, 377–404; 9, 1–35.

Rorty, A. Oksenberg (1992), "*De Anima*: Its Agenda and Its Recent Interpreters," in M. C. Nussbaum and A. O. Rorty (eds.), *Essays on Aristotle's* De Anima, Oxford, 7–13.

Ross, W. D. (1924), *Aristotle's Metaphysics*, Oxford.

(1936), *Aristotle's Physics: A Revised Text with Introduction and Commentary*, Oxford.

(1949), *Aristotle's Prior and Posterior Analytics: A Revised Text with Introduction and Commentary*, Oxford.

(1961), *Aristotle's* De Anima, Oxford.

Salles, R. (ed.) (2005), *Metaphysics, Soul, and Ethics (Festschrift for Richard Sorabji)*, Oxford.

Santas, G. (1969), "Aristotle on Practical Inference, the Explanation of Action, and Akrasia," *Phronesis* 14, 162–189.

Sauvé Meyer, S. (1992), "Aristotle, Teleology, and Reduction," *Philosophical Review* 101, 791–825; reprinted in T. Irwin (ed.) (1995), *Classical Philosophy: Collected Papers*, New York and London, 81–116.

Scaltsas, T., D. Charles, and M. L. Gill (eds.) (1994), *Unity, Identity, and Explanation in Aristotle's Metaphysics*, Oxford.

Scharle, M. (2008), "Elemental Teleology in Aristotle's Physics II.8," *Oxford Studies in Ancient Philosophy* 34, 147–183.

Schofield, M. (1991), "Explanatory Projects in *Physics*, 2.3 and 2.7," *Oxford Studies in Ancient Philosophy, Supplementary Volume 1991*, 29–40.

(1992), "Aristotle on the Imagination," in M. C. Nussbaum and A. O. Rorty (eds.), *Essays on Aristotle's* De Anima, Oxford, 249–277.

Schofield, M., M. Burnyeat, and J. Barnes (eds.) (1980), *Doubt and Dogmatism: Studies in Hellenistic Epistemology*, Oxford.

Schofield, M. and M. Nussbaum (eds.) (1982), *Language and Logos*, Cambridge.

Sedley, D. (1989), "Teleology and Myth in the *Phaedo*," *Proceedings of the Boston Area Colloquium in Ancient Philosophy* 5, 359–383.

(1991), "Is Aristotle's Teleology Anthropocentric?," *Phronesis* 36, 179–197.

(1998), "Platonic Causes," *Phronesis* 43, 114–132.

(2000), "Metaphysics L.10," in M. Frede and D. Charles (eds.), *Aristotle's Metaphysics Lambda*, Symposium Aristotelicum, Oxford, 327–350.

(2003), "Lucretius and the New Empedocles," *Leeds International Classical Studies* 2.4, 1–12.

(2007), *Creationism and its Critics in Antiquity*, Berkeley, CA.

Sfendoni-Mentzou, D. (ed.) (2000), *Aristotle and Contemporary Science*, vol. I, Frankfurt am Main.

Sfendoni-Mentzou, D., J. Hattiangadi, and D. M. Johnson (eds.) (2001), *Aristotle and Contemporary Science*, vol. II, Frankfurt am Main.

Sharples, R. W. (ed.) (2004a), *Philosophy and the Sciences in Antiquity*, London.
(ed.) (2004b), *Perspectives on Greek Philosophy*, Aldershot and Burlington, VT.
Shields, C. (1988), "Soul and Body in Aristotle," *Oxford Studies in Ancient Philosophy* 6, 103–137.
(1990), "The First Functionalist," in J.-C. Smith (ed.), *Historical Foundations of Cognitive Science*, Boston, 19–34.
(1993), "Some Recent Approaches to Aristotle's *De Anima*," in D. W. Hamlyn, *Aristotle De Anima, Books II and III (with Passages from Book I)*, translated with introduction and notes, Oxford, 157–181.
(1999), *Order in Multiplicity: Homonymy in the Philosophy of Aristotle*, Oxford.
Simpson, P. L. P. (1998), *A Philosophical Commentary on the Politics of Aristotle*, Chapel Hill, NC, and London.
Sluiter, I. (1990), *Ancient Grammar in Context: Contributions to the Study of Ancient Linguistic Thought*, Amsterdam.
Smith, R. (1989), *Prior Analytics*, translation with introduction, notes, and commentary, Indianapolis, IN.
Solmsen, F. (1960), *Aristotle's System of the Physical World: A Comparison with his Predecessors*, Ithaca, NY.
(1963), "Nature as Craftsman in Greek Thought," *Journal of the History of Ideas* 24, 473–496; reprinted in F. Solmsen, *Kleine Schriften*, Hildesheim and New York, 332–351.
Sorabji, R. (1974), "Body and Soul in Aristotle," *Philosophy* 49, 63–89.
(1980), *Necessity, Cause, and Blame: Perspectives on Aristotle's Theory*, Ithaca, NY.
(1993), *Animal Minds and Human Morals: The Origins of the Western Debate*, Ithaca, NY.
Sprague, R. K. (1968), "The Four Causes: Aristotle's Exposition and Ours," *Monist* 52, 298–300.
(1991), "Plants as Aristotelian Substances," *Illinois Classical Studies* 56, 221–229.
Suppes, P., J. M. Moravcsik, and H. Mendell (eds.) (2000), *Ancient and Medieval Traditions in the Exact Sciences: Essays in Memory of Wilbur Knorr*, Stanford, CA.
Tierney, R. (2001), "Aristotle's Scientific Demonstrations as Expositions of Essence," *Oxford Studies in Ancient Philosophy* 20, 149–170.
Turnbull, R. G. (1958), "Aristotle's Debt to the 'Natural Philosophy' of the *Phaedo*," *Philosophical Quarterly* 8, 131–143.
Wardy, R. (1993), "Aristotelian Rainfall or the Lore of Averages," *Phronesis* 38, 18–30.
Waterlow, S. (1982), *Nature, Change and Agency in Aristotle's* Physics: *A Philosophical Study*. Oxford.
Whiting, J. (1992), "Living Bodies," in M. C. Nussbaum and A. O. Rorty (eds.), *Essays on Aristotle's* De Anima, Oxford, 76–91.
(2002), "Locomotive Soul: the Parts of Soul in Aristotle's Scientific Works," *Oxford Studies in Ancient Philosophy* 22, 141–200.
Wians, W. (1996), "Scientific Examples in the *Posterior Analytics*," in W. Wians (ed.), *Aristotle's Philosophical Development: Problems and Prospects*, London, 131–150.

Wieland, W. (1975), "The Problem of Teleology," in J. Barnes, M. Schofield, and R. Sorabji (eds.), *Articles on Aristotle*, vol. I: *Science*, London, 141–160; originally published as "Zum Teleologieproblem," in W. Wieland (1962), *Die aristotelische Physik*, Göttingen.

Witt, C. (1994a), *Substance and Essence in Aristotle*, Ithaca, NY.

(1994b), "The Priority of Actuality in Aristotle," in T. Scaltsas, D. Charles, and M. L. Gill (eds.), *Unity, Identity, and Explanation in Aristotle's Metaphysics*, Oxford, 215–228.

(1998), "Teleology in Aristotelian Metaphysics," in J. Gentzler (ed.), *Method in Ancient Philosophy*, Oxford, 253–269.

Woodfield, A. (1976), *Teleology*, London.

Wright, L. (1973–4), "The Astronomy of Eudoxus: Geometry or Physics?," *Studies in the History and Philosophy of Science* 4, 165–172.

(1976), *Teleological Explanations*, Berkeley, CA.

General index

Index locorum

Printed in Great Britain
by Amazon

63057648R00151

Printed in Great Britain
by Amazon

46182732R00175

CAMBRIDGE
UNIVERSITY PRESS

University Printing House, Cambridge CB2 8BS, United Kingdom

Cambridge University Press is part of the University of Cambridge.

It furthers the University's mission by disseminating knowledge in the pursuit of education, learning and research at the highest international levels of excellence.

www.cambridge.org
Information on this title: www.cambridge.org/9781107538856

First published 2010
Reprinted 2011
First paperback edition 2015

A catalogue record for this publication is available from the British Library

ISBN 978-0-521-19774-8 Hardback
ISBN 978-1-107-53885-6 Paperback

EXPLANATION AND TELEOLOGY IN ARISTOTLE'S SCIENCE OF NATURE

MARISKA LEUNISSEN
Washington University in St. Louis

CAMBRIDGE
UNIVERSITY PRESS

EXPLANATION AND TELE(
ARISTOTLE'S SCIENCE OI

In Aristotle's teleological view of the world, natural things come to be and are present for the sake of some function or end (for example, wings are present in birds for the sake of flying). Whereas much recent scholarship has focused on uncovering the (meta-)physical underpinnings of Aristotle's teleology and its contrasts with his notions of chance and necessity, this book examines Aristotle's use of the theory of natural teleology in producing explanations of natural phenomena. Close analyses of Aristotle's natural treatises and his *Posterior Analytics* show what methods are used for the discovery of functions or ends that figure in teleological explanations, how these explanations are structured, and how well they work in making sense of phenomena. The book will be valuable for all those who are interested in Aristotle's natural science, his philosophy of science, and his biology.

MARISKA LEUNISSEN is Assistant Professor of Philosophy at Washington University in St. Louis.

BUCKINGHAM PALACE

As Patron, it is with reflection that I introduce this volume chronicling the history and achievements of The Remembrance Trust.

Founded eight years ago, the Trust was born out of a simple but powerful conviction: that those who gave their lives in the service of our country must not be forgotten. Their names, their stories, and their resting places deserve not only our respect, but our active care.

Since its inception, The Remembrance Trust has worked to restore dignity to neglected war graves, fallen into disrepair or obscurity. These efforts have honoured the memory of the fallen, and rekindled a sense of national responsibility, reminding us that remembrance is not confined to a single day in November, but is a continuous act of gratitude.

I have witnessed firsthand the dedication of those involved in this mission: volunteers who tend forgotten headstones, historians who unearth lost narratives, and communities who preserve the legacy of local heroes.

The Remembrance Trust stands as a testament to what can be achieved when remembrance is pursued with purpose.

Lest we forget.

Anne

Preface

by the Chairman of The Remembrance Trust, Algy Cluff

The late Sir Donald Thompson is the real hero of this heritage story. A Tory MP and Whip, he was a Yorkshire butcher. Above the butcher's shop in Halifax there hung a sign which proclaimed: 'Pleased to meet yer – Meat to Please yer'. He had founded the War Memorials Trust, dedicated to protecting the 60,000 war memorials distributed throughout the United Kingdom. Norman Lamont, a mutual friend, called me one day around fifteen years ago and advised that Donald was unwell and that the Trust was in financial trouble, and asked whether I could take it on. This I did and refinanced it, with the characteristic generosity of Richard Broyd and the support of heritage heroes Gavin Stamp and Colin Amery and the (continued) leadership of Frances Moreton.

After over ten years, I handed over the chairmanship to Peter McCormick. Whilst being concerned for the welfare of war memorials, I became aware of the illogical anomaly concerning war graves. Quite simply, the public is largely ignorant of the fact that the admirable Commonwealth War Graves Commission only kicked in when founded in the First World War by Sir Fabian Ware, and is concerned solely with graves of soldiers, sailors and airmen killed in the Two World Wars. Anyone killed before 1914 is accordingly no one's responsibility.

So I resolved to correct this anomaly – hence The Remembrance Trust, dedicated to restoring graves throughout the world. This was eight years ago. Alas, both Gavin Stamp and Colin Amery are dead, but I assembled a group of Trustees, including the author of this volume, Dr Roger Bowdler, monumentalist.

The Charity received an important boost when HRH The Princess Royal agreed to become our Patron for an initial period of three years, which she has recently extended. How she conjures up the energy to support us and the many other charities with which she is associated I know not, but I am decidedly grateful and welcome the opportunity to pay tribute by dedicating this short history to her, alongside the other dedicatees.

In conclusion, I wish to record my gratitude to my fellow trustees: Richard Kellaway CBE, John May, Brigadier Matthew Maer DSO, MBE, Hubert Picarda KC, Blondel Cluff CBE (my wife) and Roger Bowdler, and to David Wells, the Secretary of the Charity.

Introduction

Since the First World War, the British state has taken full responsibility for the marking of soldiers' graves for those killed in conflict or dying as a consequence. It may come as a surprise to learn that the British were late in this regard: other nations such as the United States had long before concerned themselves with the poignant matter of honouring the dead. So fundamental is the state's role now regarded as being in performing this solemn duty that it is hard to imagine a time when things were different. But they were.

How a nation treats its dead fighting men is a telling barometer of several things. How were soldiers viewed by society? Were lower ranks also thought to be deserving of having honour bestowed on their graves? Was death in battle or in the course of duty worthy of remembrance? Did those who died far from the mother country warrant commemoration – and who at home would ever know? How did the practicalities of campaigning affect the erecting of permanent memorials? There is growing interest in these matters, and the study of the military commemorative experience is still emerging.

This essay is written to give a brisk overview of the long history of martial commemoration and to outline how one charity – The Remembrance Trust (TRT) – has begun to address the issue of caring for these early military memorials. The graves of the majority of those who have died for their country since August 1914 are now the responsibility of the Commonwealth War Graves Commission. This publicly funded body, founded in 1917 as the Imperial War Graves Commission, is internationally admired for its work across the globe. But what of those who fell in previous conflicts – in the Seven Years War, the Revolutionary and French Wars, and the various wars of empire?

The founder of The Remembrance Trust, Algy Cluff, beside the tomb of Col. Robert Ellison, d. 1843, at Kensal Green Cemetery, London 2025.

It was in recognition of this gap that Algy Cluff, a former Grenadier Guards officer, celebrated entrepreneur and the sometime proprietor of *The Spectator*, founded TRT in 2018. Its key aim was to honour the fallen of Britain and the Empire by caring for their tombs, at home and overseas. The Commonwealth War Graves Commission takes care of its own graves supremely well and sometimes looks after post-1914 private memorials too. But for pre-1914 graves there is no equivalent conservation body dedicated to the maintenance and upkeep of commemorative military monuments. There is no shortage of public interest in military commemoration: the National Memorial Arboretum at Alrewas (Staffordshire), opened in 2001 and still expanding, is ample testament to this. But what of earlier generations? How are the tombs and memorials of soldiers and sailors of earlier centuries cared for?

Much has been written about the commemoration of the dead of the First and Second World Wars, and of the work of the Commonwealth War Graves Commission. Much less is known about how earlier soldiers – particularly of the non-officer ranks – were honoured in death, and how they were memorialised. For some periods, such as the Napoleonic Wars, much work has already been done to identify the surviving monuments to the dead. For others, the picture is far less clear. These memorials aren't the same as war memorials, or statues of renowned commanders: the sort of memorials TRT is keen to protect are tributes erected over actual graves. This short study looks at early attitudes to the marking of places where dead soldiers and sailors were laid to rest and shows why the mission TRT has set itself is so worthwhile.

What emerges from a consideration of this poignant topic is that memorials to soldiers other than commanders and officers from the upper echelons of society were uncommon prior to the late Victorian period. This bestows importance on any identified examples, and makes their conservation all the more desirable. Military dignity is a relevant consideration, and the historical interest of these markers warrants their return to a legible state. TRT is committed to the identification of such memorials, at home and abroad, and is keen to work with other partners in delivering this goal.

I

Honouring the Dead of Early Wars

Conflict is as old as time. Who knows what tales lie behind the raising of prehistoric mounds and stones? Early antiquaries were wont to see standing stones and barrows as being the first war memorials – but the truth is that very little is known about how conflict was remembered.

An 18th-century antiquarian view of burial mounds at Ashdon, Essex. These were often believed to be the sites of ancient battles.

The history of the war memorial is generally dated back to the Ancient Greeks: such is the power of the classical tradition that it is no surprise to learn that their commemorative practices deeply influenced modern ones. Homer's *Iliad* has many mentions of the military burial customs accorded to its fallen heroes. The Battle of Marathon (490 BC) saw two tumuli being raised: one 40 feet high, no less, raised over the cremation site of the Athenian dead, and another, just ten feet high, raised over the dead bodies of the Plataeans, their allies. This form of monument resembled the barrows of Northern Europe and probably drew on older forms of memorial to echo the valour of the Trojan War and other early heroes.

The earliest great speech given in honour of fallen warriors was recorded in Thucydides' *History of the Peloponnesian War*. This conflict was fought between Athens and Sparta in 431–404 BC, and Pericles, the Athenian leader, is credited with words of tribute to the fallen warriors of the city state which resonate still today:

> The sacrifice which they collectively made was individually repaid to them; for they received again each one for himself a praise which grows not old, and the noblest of all tombs, I speak not of that in which their remains are laid, but of that in which their glory survives, and is proclaimed always and on every fitting occasion both in word and deed. For the whole earth is the tomb of famous men; not only are they commemorated by columns and inscriptions in their own country, but in foreign lands there dwells also an unwritten memorial

> of them, graven not on stone but in the hearts of men. Make them your examples, and, esteeming courage to be freedom and freedom to be happiness, do not weigh too nicely the perils of war.

This stirring oration set the tone for much that came after. The sense of sacrifice honoured; the enduring nature of remembrance; the idea that to be held in the hearts of the nation was the best of all monuments; and the inspirational nature of their example of giving their lives for freedom: all of these would resonate in subsequent centuries right down to the present day.

For the Greeks, possession of physical remains – generally cremated – was an important consideration: cremation at the battle site enabled the ashes of fallen warriors to be returned to the civic cemetery for public commemoration and when there was no body to be recovered, then the *cenotaph* (or empty tomb) might be raised to stand proxy for the absent corpse. One of the saddest of all ancient Greek memorials to lost soldiers is the Democleides *stela* (or tombstone) in the National Archaeological Museum in Athens, a memorial to a hoplite (or elite citizen-infantryman) who was likely killed in a sea-battle in the late 4th century BC. He is shown seated on the prow of a warship, his pose one of desperate melancholy as though sharing the grief of his disconsolate relicts, denied the consolation of mourning rites over his bodily remains. This idea of absence and distance would be a recurrent one for the soldier in centuries to come.

The funeral *stela* of Democleides, an Athenian soldier lost at sea, late fifth century BC (National Archaeological Museum, Athens).

Warfare is often mobile: possession of the battlefield at the end of the fighting was one of the definitions of victory. Armies in retreat had little opportunity to take care of their dead which were left in the hands of the victorious side. Sometimes, no doubt, truces were struck which enabled the grim business of the recovery of dead and wounded to be attended to. Like so much concerning warfare in the past, there is much that we just do not know. This makes the presence of those military memorials which do survive all the more special. It is the fate of so many fallen soldiers to lie in unmarked graves, forever lost to families and homeland. One of the renowned works of Virgil (70–19 BC), the great epic poet of the late Roman Republic, was the 'Georgics', verses about man's relationship with the earth and its bounteousness which appeared in c.29 BC. This included lines on the disturbance of ancient soldier graves:

> And a time will come, when in those lands,
> The farmer labouring at the earth with curved plough,
> Will come upon spears eaten by scabrous rust,
> Or strike an empty helmet with his heavy hoe,
> And wonder at giant bones in the opened grave.
>
> (*Georgics*, Book 1, lines 493–7)

This inspired Horace Vernet's renowned Romantic painting *The Soldier-Labourer* (1820, Wallace Collection), in which Virgil's poignant scene is transposed to the post-Napoleonic age with the accidental uncovering of the remains of a buried French Cuirassier.

Hidden in the foliage is a wooden cross: such temporary grave-markers must have been the norm for most soldier burials across the ages, and they have invariably disappeared. The whereabouts of dead soldiers is often a tale of mystery.

After Horace Vernet, *Le Soldat Laboureur* (engraving, Metropolitan Museum of Art, New York).

The Roman Army was renowned for its carved tombstones. These tended to be erected at cemeteries outside permanent garrisons, and are remarkable on many counts: for giving us the names of actual soldiers of all ranks, for representing the details of martial trappings, for demonstrating the geographical range of recruitment and deployment, and much else besides. Particularly good examples survive at Chester, Colchester and along Hadrian's Wall. These comprise the single most important category of military tombs prior to the armoured effigies of the medieval period and are in stark contrast to other periods for honouring ordinary soldiers with permanent monuments.

Relief of Roman Auxiliary Cavalryman,
Grosvenor Museum, Chester.

2

Medieval Remembrance

Christian piety and military prowess are entwined in the legion of knightly effigies which emerged from the 12th century onwards. These armoured figures (frequently with their wives) were monuments of clear status: the warrior caste was accorded social respect and worldly authority which ultimately derived from their military power. Just as in later centuries the officer classes would be commemorated, so in medieval times was individual remembrance the preserve of the cleric, aristocrat and knight (and in later medieval times, a growing range of civilians). Ideas of chivalry endured for centuries, and the tombs of medieval knights – sometimes carved, sometimes incised in brass or stone – remain some of the best-loved of all martial memorials. It has been estimated that there are over 1,100 examples of this kind in the British Isles alone.

For the leaders and magnates, individual commemoration was established from the 13th century and spread widely across Europe. One of the most renowned early military brasses is at Elsing in Norfolk, where Sir Hugh Hastings's brass shows the knight set within a damaged canopy, which contains small depictions of his fellow commanders in the Hundred Years' War, who grieve for his loss: Hastings died of dysentery in 1347 at the siege of Calais. For such people, special steps could be taken to ensure that their remains were returned to where they wished to be buried, in dynastic family chapels within churches. Michael de la Pole, 2nd Earl of Suffolk, also died of dysentery, on the Agincourt campaign in 1415, but his will had specified that his bones should be brought back to lie with his ancestors at Wingfield (Suffolk), his body having been excarnated (or boiled, to separate the bones from flesh and enable their transportation home). He and his countess remain there beneath painted wooden effigies (recently rescued from deathwatch beetle), just one example among hundreds of depictions of armoured knights which form a glorious chapter in the history of soldier memorials. The historian Nigel Saul has observed that the great age for military armoured effigies was the 14th century, when they did tend to depict knights who had actually fought in France; during the 15th century, wearing armour was more likely to allude to social status and the possession of land. Even today, not everyone in uniform is a soldier.

Death on campaign rarely ended in such magnificent commemoration. Magnates, knights and squires were more likely to be taken for burial to nearby churches. What happened to the dead of medieval battles remains an elusive topic: the most likely answer is that mass graves were dug close to where the dead had fallen and some form of commemoration then installed at the site of the encounter.

Brass of Sir Hugh Hastings d. 1347, Elsing, Norfolk.
Sir Michael de la Pole, 2nd Earl of Suffolk d. 1415,
Wingfield, Suffolk.

The treatment of the battlefield dead in the Middle Ages is imperfectly understood. Some spectacular archaeological discoveries have shed light on what could take place after a battle, but few markers remain to show where the dead were laid. Outside Shrewsbury is the church of St Mary Magdalene, Battlefield, Shropshire: this unusual name alludes to the Battle of Shrewsbury in 1403, when the relatively newly crowned Henry IV (r. 1399–1413) defeated Henry Percy: out of pious concern for those killed, the local lord caused a church to be raised which was subsequently endowed by the victorious king. Memorial chapels brought a Christian presence to the battlefield, and the saying of masses for the souls of the dead of each side was an important act of piety as well as of thanksgiving for victory. A chapel (long since demolished) was built on the orders of Richard III (r. 1483–5) some years after the Battle of Towton (1461). A similar foundation took place a while after Bosworth (1485) when Henry VIII endowed the church at Dadlington (Leicestershire) in a gesture of remembrance and in gratitude for his father's victory over the House of York. Affording all corpses the dignity of burial was a sacred duty which formed one of the Seven Acts of Mercy, as well as a seemly necessity. Ian Atherton's excellent *The British and Their Battlefields* (2024) describes how the medieval battlefield was commemorated: chapels and crosses were raised, and chantries said prayers for the slain. Few grave markers have come down to us and many of the chapels have been lost. But the battlefields, and their dead, were recognised and sanctified.

St Mary Magdalene church, Battlefield, Shropshire, raised after the Battle of Shrewsbury in 1403.

A powerful discovery was made in 1996 close to Towton Hall in North Yorkshire: a mass grave containing thirty-seven bodies was found, the bones displaying clear evidence of having met violent ends. They lay near the site of the grim Battle of Towton: Britain's bloodiest day, fought on a snowy moor in 1461. Tens of thousands – principally Lancastrians – are thought to have perished, perhaps up to 28,000. These few rediscovered dead stand for the legion of lost fatalities: unmarked oblivion was the lot of the medieval soldier, save for magnates and associates. As proof of this, one sole monument exists to the dead of Towton: in the churchyard of Saxton, south of the battlefield, stands an exceptionally rare outdoor tomb to an aristocrat – Ralph, 1st Lord Dacre of Gilsland who fell in the Lancastrian cause. It is the only memorial to a magnate from the Wars of the Roses located close to where they perished on the field of battle, and an exceptionally rare outdoor aristocratic tomb. But for rank and file fatalities, the reality was wholly unceremonious battlefield burial. Truces were sometimes declared to permit both sides to recover the bodies of prominent men and to bury the rest: this happened after the slaughter at Crécy in 1346. On other occasions, the pressures of the military situation could rule this out. After Agincourt (1415), despite being victorious, Henry V was so fearful of a second French attack and so eager to withdraw that he is alleged to have had the bodies of the English and Welsh dead brought inside a barn which was then set alight. Cremation was unthinkable in a medieval Christian context: this report (from a single foreign source, admittedly) demonstrates the practical issues surrounding burial in a war context and the extreme measures allegedly taken.

Tomb of Lord Dacre of Gilsland d. 1461, Saxton, Yorkshire West Riding.

Medieval military burial was characterised by an extreme polarity between burials of the great and the mass interments of all other fighting men. This was part of what social status was all about. The foundation of battlefield chantry chapels to say prayers for the souls of the dead went some way to providing a measure of remembrance, even if these were not specific to the fallen men. Among the most remarkable commemorative institutions was All Souls College at Oxford, founded by Archbishop Chichele and Henry VI in 1438 in memory of those killed fighting in France in the Hundred Years War. Medieval remembrance was not specific to the individual unless they were of very high social standing. The armoured effigies of the period must stand proxy for all the others killed in battle in this period.

3

The Early Modern Period

Thus far, memorials to individual soldiers have yet to emerge as a common response to death in battle or on campaign. The Reformation of the 16th century made a big difference in the way the battlefield dead were treated, according to Ian Atherton. Out went the chantry chapels, the crosses, the masses for the dead: a whole system of remembrance was dissolved and battlefields lost something of their sanctified recognition which had sought to offset the oblivion of their dead. A new emphasis on individual remembrance took its place, with the dead being offered up as exemplars for the living. Monuments celebrating valour would begin to appear, and the rise of individual memorials to those lost on land and at sea can be traced.

The English Civil War (1642–51) witnessed the last prolonged period of fighting on English soil. Church monuments and churchyard memorials commemorate both victims and veterans of the fighting: most, inevitably, were to officers. Best known is the 'Golden Cavalier' in Lydiard Tregoze church, Wiltshire which depicts the Royalist cavalryman Edward St John, who died in 1645 of wounds sustained at the 2nd Battle of Newbury the previous year: underneath his gilded armoured effigy is a relief of him leading his cavalry troop into action.

Edward St John d. 1645, Lydiard Tregoze, Wiltshire.

Oxford became Charles I's headquarters during the early years of the Civil War, and the south transept of Christ Church (now Oxford Cathedral) became a preferred resting place for the upper echelons of Royalist dead and a number of memorials are to be found there.

Memorial to Sir Bevil Grenville, killed in the Battle of Lansdown 1643, erected in 1720. Lansdown, Bath.

Understandably, monuments to soldiers on the Parliamentarian side are far rarer: some, like General Henry Ireton's in Westminster Abbey, were removed at the Restoration in 1660 and destroyed. The bodies of the regicides Oliver Cromwell, Ireton and John Bradshaw were exhumed and ritually 'executed' on the 12th anniversary of Charles I's execution in 1661 as a mark of posthumous vengeance.

Battlefield monuments of the English Civil War only came later. Initially these continued to honour commanders rather than commemorate all who fought and fell in battle. Outside Bath, the monument to Royalist general Sir Bevil Grenville, killed in a bloody assault at Lansdown in 1643, was raised in 1720 by his grandson (who also caused a monument to be erected over Grenville's resting place in Kilkhampton church in 1714, his body having been returned to Cornwall after the battle). The earliest of all field memorials to fallen officers is the pedestal in Wigan (Lancs.) to the Royalist Major General Thomas Tyldesley, killed at the Battle of Wigan Lane in 1651 which was raised in 1679. 'The Soldier Stone' outside Falkirk may – or may not – mark the place where a young member of the Gordon family was killed, fleeing from the Battle of Kilsyth in 1645: a plain slab with incised initials and a date, it has been moved but it still hints at early endeavours to preserve the memory of the slain.

The dead of the Civil War are elusive: very few mass burials have been identified and there are no early markers on battlefields. A perplexing discovery was made in 1818 of a mass grave outside Aylesbury

Memorial to Major General Thomas Tyldesley, killed in the Battle of Wigan Lane 1651, erected 1679. Wigan, Lancs.

(Buckinghamshire) of 247 skeletons which led the local MP, Lord Nugent, to raise a monument at Hardwick churchyard in Buckinghamshire in their memory, connecting them with a skirmish in 1642. The inscription concludes: 'They were buried in one common grave, close to the spot where they had lately stood in arms against each other. May the memory of the brave be respected, and may our country never again be called upon to take part in contests such as these which this tablet records.' This memorial highlights the tendency for later periods to overlay their own take on the alleged sites of battles: nothing is known about such a clash ever taking place, which challenges the plausibility of Lord Nugent's memorial. Elsewhere, inquiry explains mystery. Archaeological investigation has successfully identified the remains of twenty-eight skeletons in two mass graves, discovered close to Durham Cathedral in 2013. They were Scottish soldiers taken prisoner by Cromwell's forces at the Battle of Dunbar in 1650 and incarcerated in the cathedral; they were unceremoniously dumped in pits when they succumbed to dysentery. Hitherto unmarked and forgotten, these burials sum up the forlorn lot of most battlefield casualties.

Monuments to soldiers and sailors were becoming more common in later Stuart times. Many of them commemorated Royalist officers, like the magnificent Baroque memorial in Bath Abbey to Col. Philip Frowde (d. 1674). At Ampthill, Bedfordshire, Col. Richard Nicolls is remembered with a classical monument recalling his death at the Battle of Solebay in 1672, fighting the Dutch off the Suffolk coast. It is extremely unusual in one macabre respect: within the pediment at the top is the actual cannon ball which killed him. Other naval memorials were beginning to appear in Westminster Abbey too. These personal tributes mirrored the emergence of visual celebrations of martial glory, best seen in royal building projects like William and Mary's enlargement of Hampton Court or within the Painted Hall at the Greenwich Naval Hospital.

Monument to Col. Sir Philip Frowde d. 1674, Bath Abbey.

Monument to Col. Richard Nicholls, killed in the Battle of Solebay 1672, Ampthill church, Bedfordshire.

The founding of the Royal Hospital Chelsea in 1682 and its naval equivalent at Greenwich in 1694 each embodied a new considerateness for the common soldier or sailor, and a recognition of their service and sacrifice. Undoubtedly inspired by Louis XIV's Les Invalides (opened in 1674), this foundation embodied Charles II's awareness of the debt the Crown owed to the fighting men who had suffered for the Royalist cause and for England in later conflicts. It marked a new stage in the public honouring of rank and file soldiers.

Royal Hospital Burial Ground, Chelsea: this burial ground was first used in 1692.

Fittingly, each was provided with a detached burial ground in which the Pensioners would be laid to rest. These were the first specifically military cemeteries in Britain. Here were to be found tombstones to ordinary soldiers: to Corporal Theophilus Cecil (who died in 1695) and Serjeant James Ford of Villiers' Regiment of Foot, who died in 1698. These are very early examples indeed of memorials to soldiers, not officers, and are of considerable importance as such. One inscription stands out among the memorials at Chelsea, which were mainly to officers and officials attached to the Hospital. This was a ledger slab to William Hiseland, 'A Vetran [*sic*] if ever Soldier was', who died in 1732 at the alleged age of 112. Hiseland fought for the King at Edgehill in 1642 and is alleged to have served under Marlborough in the War of Spanish Succession (1704–13). The epitaph demands to be quoted as the earliest lapidary pen-portrait of a veteran soldier:

> Who merited well a Pension
> If Long Service be a Merit
> Having served upwards of the Days of Man
> Antient but not Superannuated
> Engaged in a series of Wars
> Civil as well as Foreign
> Yet not maimed or worn out by either
> His Complexion was fresh & florid
> His Health hale & hearty
> His Memory exact & ready
> In Stature
> He exceeded the Military size

In Strength
He surpassed the prime of Youth, and
What rendered his Age
Still more Patriarchal
When above One Hundred Years Old
He took unto him a Wife
Read Fellow Soldiers and Reflect
That there is a Spiritual Warfare
As well as a Warfare Temporal.

George Alsop: portrait of William Hiseland, 1730
(reproduced by permission of the Royal Hospital Chelsea).

Equally unusually for a private soldier, Hiseland's portrait was painted in 1730 and it is still on display in the Royal Hospital. This burial ground at Chelsea can be seen as London's equivalent of the Invalidenfriedhof in Berlin, which become something of a Prussian Valhalla after opening in 1748. Chelsea's naval equivalent, the burial ground at Greenwich Hospital, has largely been cleared of its 20,000 dead, and the few naval memorials which do remain are to officers. Many of the Royal Navy's dead were buried at sea, and hardly any stones remain at the naval hospitals at Haslar (Gosport) or Devonport. Ordinary seamen have left very little commemorative trace on British soil.

4

The Eighteenth Century

Where were dead of Marlborough's Wars, the dead of Blenheim (1704) and bloody Malplaquet (1709)? Robert Southey's poem of 1796, 'The Battle of Blenheim', looked at Marlborough's great victory through a radical lens: its mouthpiece is that of a local peasant who encounters the bones of fallen soldiers in his daily business while pondering why so many had to die, and in what cause. Southey used the strewing of human remains after a battle as the measure of the cruel irony of glory: what is hailed as a martial triumph, derived from soldiers' sacrifice, comes to be forgotten in the course of time:

> 'I find them in the garden,
> For there's many here about;
> And often when I go to plough,
> The ploughshare turns them out!
> For many thousand men,' said he,
> 'Were slain in that great victory.'

The Age of Marlborough was a triumphalist one, culminating in glory-laden Blenheim Palace and its huge

Column of Victory, raised after the Duke's death in 1722. This was the zenith of the cult: the fallen troops who delivered such glory continued to be disposed of without any fanfare whatsoever. But if attention is paid to the grand monument to the Duke in the private chapel at Blenheim Palace by Rysbrack, it is notable that the suffering and sacrifice of his soldiers is not entirely forgotten: the relief of the aftermath of the battle on this magnificent tomb shows the wounded and the dead alongside the triumphant general. These victories came at a price.

Michael Rysbrack: detail of relief from monument of John Churchill, 1st Duke of Marlborough d. 1722, Blenheim Palace, Oxfordshire.

Britain's rise to world power exacted a growing toll from soldiers and sailors: but individual tombs remained only for the few. The first martial monument to be sanctioned by Parliament was raised in Westminster Abbey to Captain James Cornewall, an MP as well as a naval officer who was killed at the Battle of Toulon in 1744. Made by Robert Taylor, this was the first of a sequence of grand memorials in the Abbey (and later in St Paul's Cathedral) to fallen commanders, paid for out of public funds. General James Wolfe, killed at Quebec in 1759, was the next recipient of a state-funded monument in the Abbey: made by Joseph Wilton, it was finally installed in 1772.

Monument to Cornet Francis Geary, killed in an ambush in New Jersey in 1776. Great Bookham church, Surrey.

Families tended to put up monuments in their local church. At Great Bookham (Surrey) is an exceptional memorial to Cornet Francis Geary, killed in an ambush in New Jersey in 1776, early in the American War of Independence: a bas-relief on the tomb shows the Queen's Light Dragoon officer being unhorsed by a volley fired from behind a fence. It was a vivid depiction of contemporary warfare erected by grieving parents: his father was an Admiral. Geary's body was not returned to the British for burial, as would have been customary, but buried in secrecy by his foes: in 1891 the local historical society at Hunterdon (New Jersey) carried out a dig at the reputed burial spot and duly found a skeleton with Light Dragoon buttons and fragments of silver lace. In 1907 the Geary family placed a stone over his rediscovered grave, but left his bones in their American resting place.

Headstones in churchyards were becoming more common in the 18th century: this can be explained in various ways, including improvements in transport making the shifting of stone more manageable; in the growth of literacy; in the emergence of raising tombstones as a social custom; and in the rise of levels of disposable income. The period was a golden age for tombstones, and at their finest they combined elegant lettering with arresting shallow relief carving. For soldiers and sailors from modest backgrounds, such memorials remained out of reach. One tragic exception is found at Thursley, where in 1786 an unknown sailor, on his way from London to Portsmouth, fell in with three other sailors and was murdered for his money; the celebrated tombstone shows the killing. This was death at home, and local shock at this dastardly deed led to the raising of the memorial.

Postcard c.1900 of the headstone to the Unknown Sailor, murdered in 1786, in Thursley churchyard, Surrey.

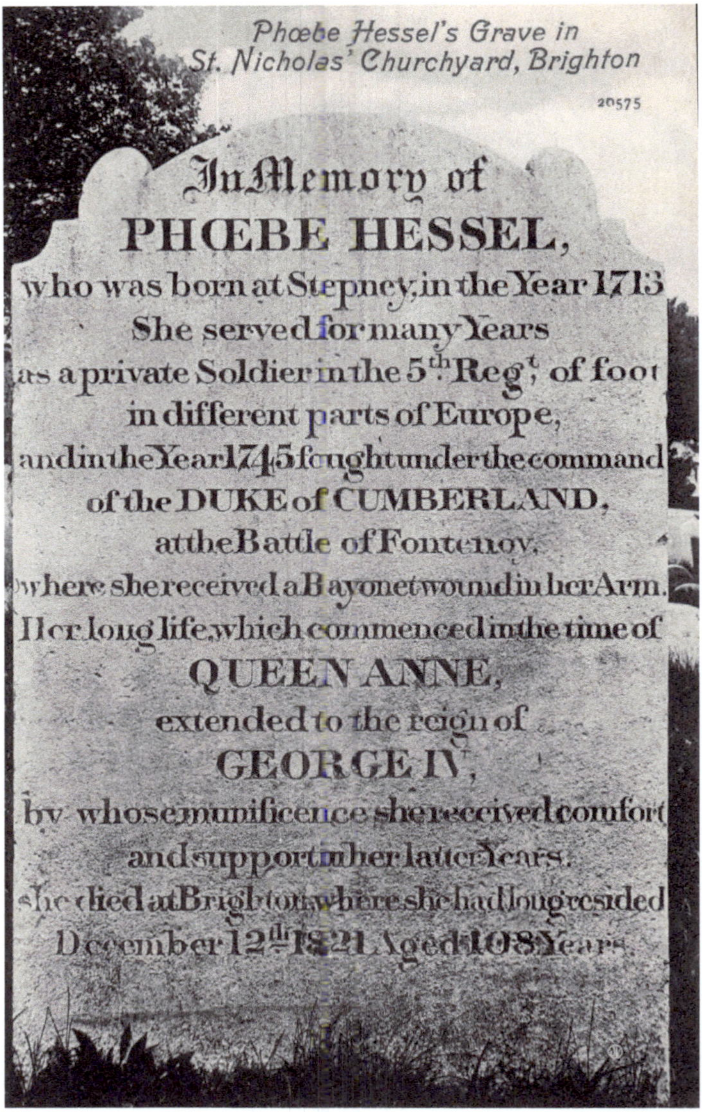

Postcard c.1910 of the headstone to Phoebe Hessel, d. 1821,
St Nicholas' churchyard, Brighton, Sussex.

As tombstones became more numerous, some began to be erected to remarkable soldiers and sailors. One of the few non-officer veterans of the War of Austrian Succession (1740–48) to warrant a memorial is also one of the most surprising. This was the redoubtable Phoebe Hessel, who died in 1821 and was buried in St Nicholas' churchyard, Brighton at the grand old age of 108 (if her headstone is to be believed). It relates how 'She served for many years as a private Soldier in the 5th Regt. of foot in different parts of Europe and in the year 1745 fought under the command of the DUKE OF CUMBERLAND at the Battle of Fontenoy where she received a Bayonet wound in her Arm.' Her longevity and her gender-defying soldiering each won her renown (and the receipt of a royal pension) and the epitaph relates a remarkable tale of concealed identity. Old age and long service occur again at Longnor, Staffs. where William Billinge (1679–1791) lies underneath a stone which relates how he joined the Army in 1703: 'and was at the taking of the Fortress of Gibralta [*sic*] in 1704. He afterwards served under the Duke of Marlborough at the ever Memorable Battle of Ramillies, fought on the 23 May 1706 where he was wounded by a musket shot in the thigh.' His epitaph closes with this rousing couplet:

> Billeted by Death I quartered here remain
> When the trumpet sounds I'll rise and march again.

Old soldiers who had made it back home were of course easier to commemorate than those lost on campaign and who were lost for ever. These few early soldier monuments stand proxy for very many others.

Gravestones were one way of appealing to public feelings (especially in an Age of Sensibility). And towards the end of the 18th century it became evident that the public was becoming more compassionate about the soldier's lot, and the welfare of their dependants. This shift is nicely demonstrated in a painting. One of Joseph Wright of Derby's most successful works, known from a number of versions, was called *The Dead Soldier* (1789; examples can be found in Bath, New Haven, San Francisco and Ann Arbor). It depicted a woman with babe, weeping over the corpse of her recently killed redcoat husband, and was inspired by the Rev. John Langhorne's 1774 verse 'The Country Justice':

> …Cold on Canadian Hills, or Minden's Plain,
> Perhaps that Parent mourn'd her soldier slain;
> Bent o'er her Babe, her Eye dissolv'd in Dew,
> The big Drops mingling with the Milk He drew,
> Gave the sad Presage of his future Years,
> The Child of Misery, baptiz'd in Tears!

Dead soldiers were out of sight and out of mind, but from this period can be traced the beginnings of a more compassionate approach to the victims of war and what would now be termed the 'Army family'.

Joseph Wright, *The Dead Soldier*, c.1789. Yale Center for British Art, New Haven, Connecticut.

5

Soldier Memorials in the Revolutionary and Napoleonic Age

Britain was at war with France and her allies from 1793 to 1815, with a pause in 1802–3. 300,000 lives are estimated to have been lost. The wars gave rise to a remarkable group of public monuments to prominent commanders killed in the fighting, and to the beginnings of the practice of marking soldiers' graves as well.

The most prestigious memorials were raised at Parliamentary expense to fallen commanders: thirty-one were erected in St Paul's Cathedral, and two in Westminster Abbey, costing the vast sum of £110,575 between 1793 and 1824, the equivalent of over £10m today: commemorating at least some of the dead was thus regarded as a government duty, but not one which was spread across the ranks. One of the first to be raised was to Major General Thomas Dundas (d. 1794), Governor of newly captured Guadeloupe: he died of fever, and when the French re-took the island at the end of that year, a decree was issued, ordering his body to be dug up and 'given as prey to the birds of the air'. This was a rare instance of the abuse of the dead, echoing the vengeful treatment of the Cromwellian regicides' corpses back in 1661.

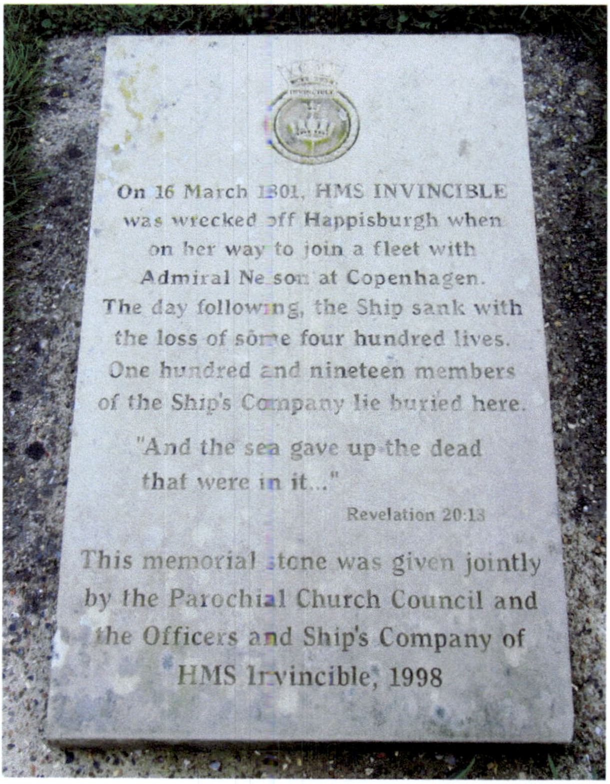

Memorial stone to the sailors of HMS *Invincible*, lost off Happisburgh, Suffolk in 1801, laid in 1998 over their mass grave.

As earlier, the military and naval dead were usually left unremembered, even when their bodies were on home soil, and even when major losses occurred.

HMS *Invincible* was lost on a sandbank in a storm off the Suffolk coast in 1801: some 400 sailors perished, and 119 bodies were washed ashore. These were laid in a mass grave just outside Happisburgh churchyard without any memorial, and only in 1998, when a trench was being dug, were they rediscovered. An inscribed stone slab was placed as a permanent marker over their resting place, partly funded by the crew of the modern HMS *Invincible*, an aircraft carrier. By contrast, the loss of one single man in the ranks could sometimes be marked with a memorial. At Bexhill, in 1804, Robert White of the 11th Light Dragoons was given a headstone by his comrades, having drowned while stationed there: his epitaph reads 'On Duty Cheerful and in Battle Brave / Yet fell a Victim to the foaming Wave.'

At Dover, a noted garrison, tombstones began to be

One of the 22 headstones in Shorncliffe Cemetery, Kent to soldiers who died in 1802–4, recently restored by The Remembrance Trust.

raised to rankers: The Remembrance Trust has in recent years conserved several of these notable memorials to ordinary soldiers which were relocated to Shorncliffe Cemetery in the 1990s. Honouring the dead was of course easier when stationed at home than when abroad on campaign. Fighting in defence of the homeland was a prospect the British – with rare exceptions, as in Ireland – did not have to confront. On the continent, where campaigning was intensive, some places developed a different approach to the graves of fallen soldiers. In the German lands, those who fell in the Wars of Liberation against Napoleon were kept firmly in mind. In George Mosse's words, 'The cult of the fallen provided the nation with martyrs and, in their last resting place, with a shrine of national worship.' The woodland memorial to the Saxon poet and soldier Theodor Körner (killed in 1813) at Wöbbelin in North Germany became one such site of Romantic memory.

Cast-iron memorial to the soldier poet Theodor Körner (killed 1813), Wöbbelin, North Germany (from *Die Gartenlaube* 1863).

Prussia was in the vanguard of encouraging memorials to the dead: Kaiser Friedrich Wilhelm III issued a decree in 1813 which obliged each parish to honour its fallen men.

The best-known poem in English about a soldier's burial is Charles Wolfe's 'The Burial of Sir John Moore', first published in 1817:

Not a drum was heard, not a funeral note,
As his corse to the rampart we hurried;
Not a soldier discharged his farewell shot
O'er the grave where our hero we buried.

We buried him darkly at dead of night,
The sods with our bayonets turning;
By the struggling moonbeam's misty light
And the lantern dimly burning.

No useless coffin enclosed his breast,
Nor in sheet nor in shroud we wound him,
But he lay like a warrior taking his rest
With his martial cloak around him…

The final verse is particularly apt:

Slowly and sadly we laid him down,
From the field of his fame fresh and gory;
We carved not a line, and we raised not a stone,
But left him alone with his glory.

Moore, who was killed in January 1809 as his retreating

army repulsed a French assault, would subsequently receive one of the most imposing of all battlefield monuments: a large sarcophagus in a park in the centre of La Coruña, erected in 1839, replacing a smaller granite memorial erected not long after his death. He was also remembered with a moving memorial in St Paul's, showing his corpse being lowered into his tomb.

John Bacon Junior: Memorial of General Sir John Moore d. 1809, St Paul's Cathedral, London (1815).

The rigours of campaigning seldom permitted soldiers to erect memorials to their dead. A notable exception to this can be found, interestingly enough, on French territory. At the very end of the fighting in 1814, Wellington's forces had crossed the Pyrenees and were advancing into France itself. The futile French sortie out of Bayonne in April 1814 was one of the very last actions of the war, carried out ten days after Napoleon's first abdication: fiercely contested and wholly pointless, it led to 157 Allied deaths, including Major General Andrew Hay (honoured with a memorial in St Paul's). Perhaps because this encounter came at the very end of the war, there was time to mark the graves of the fallen with some care. As a result Bayonne boasts some exceptional monuments to British soldiers: two cemeteries were created at Saint Etienne for the dead of the First and Third Foot Guards, and stone monuments raised to officers and men. One tablet commemorated Colour Sergeant William Yuill, 'Killed by a Grape Shot 7th April Belov'd by the Regt. in which he served 20 Years. A FRIEND TO TRUTH He loved his King, Zealous for his Country And in its just Cause he Breath'd his last. Adue My Friend.' Remarkably, the stone then states that 'This stone recovered from a washing fountain in a wood where the 1st Foot Guards were encamped in 1814 was removed to this cemetery May 28th 1881.' Was there a stonemason in his battalion? Was a French artisan co-opted? The Yuill stone marks a special development: the appearance of a stone grave-marker to a much-lamented senior NCO. The war was at an end, permitting regiments to pause and re-group. This included the unusual step of establishing permanent cemeteries: and in enemy territory too. A monument to fallen British officers was also raised in 1815 at Bergen-op-Zoom, the scene of a disastrous siege of a port on the Dutch coast in the previous year.

Memorial tablet to Sergeant William Yuill d. 1814, St Etienne Cemetery, Bayonne.

The epic Battle of Waterloo led to a battlefield landscape which was to be populated with monuments in a way only rivalled by the field of Borodino (and later Gettysburg). Among the earliest was a broken column designed by Papworth, raised in memory of Wellington's favourite ADC, Lt-Col. Alexander Gordon, who died of wounds sustained at the close of the day. There are numerous mural tablets to fallen officers in Waterloo church, and one which precociously lists the names of all ranks, erected by the 12th Light Dragoons. Some officers' bodies were brought back to rest in family vaults in England. That of Major the Hon. Frederick Howard of the 10th Light Dragoons was brought back to rest in the grandeur of Hawksmoor's mausoleum at Castle Howard: a tablet raised by his regiment in Waterloo church states that 'His mutilated remains were removed from the field of battle by order of his affectionate Father Frederick Earl of Carlisle to be deposited in the family Mausoleum.'

Monument to Lt-Col. Alexander Gordon d. 1815, designed by J.B. Papworth, at Waterloo. Gordon, Wellington's ADC, was fatally wounded in the battle and was one of the very few individuals to be commemorated with a battlefield memorial.

Until recently it was a mystery what had happened to the thousands of dead soldiers of Waterloo. That the bodies on the field were ransacked for their teeth has long been known; it now emerges that the dead underwent even greater post-mortem indignity: their bones were systematically dug up and ground up for industrial use in processing sugar beet and other purposes. In today's age when the discovery of the remains of a single soldier from the Great War makes the news, and when even the display of actual human remains comes in for curatorial censure, it comes as something of a shock to learn how disrespectful the treatment of the remains of the fallen actually was. This was an age of sentiment and of the cult of military valour after all. Limited recompense was made in 1890, when an opulent bronze monument to the British dead of the campaign was unveiled in Evere Cemetery, Brussels. Another instance of retrospective martial remembrance took place in 1914 when the 'Entente Cordiale Society' raised an eagle-topped column at Norman Cross in Cambridgeshire to honour the 1,770 French prisoners of war who had died in the camp established there in 1797. Former enemies were now allies, and the move towards remembering the forgotten dead was well underway.

The wave of commemoration which grew around those who served in the British Army in the Peninsular Wars and at Waterloo has been heroically chronicled in a two-volume study by Janet and David Bromley, *Wellington's Men Remembered* (2012–2015), compiled on behalf of the Association of Friends of the Waterloo Committee. Thousands of monuments were raised on church walls and in cemeteries, recording past involvement in the great actions of the wars with France. These two volumes offer clear evidence of the rise of commemorating soldiers, and while the majority of its entries are to officers from the monument-raising classes, there are also numerous instances of soldiers from the ranks who were starting to be given tombstones. Partly this reflects the growth in memorial raising generally during the 19th century: but it is also clear evidence of the rising prestige being accorded to veterans. One of the hundreds of tombstones raised in memory of Wellington's men is in Penrith (Cumbria): it honours Private Levi Grisdale of the 10th Hussars who played a major part in the capture of General Charles Lefebvre-Desnouettes, commander of the Chasseurs à Cheval of the Imperial Guard, Napoleon's bodyguard. This took place during the retreat to La Coruña in December 1808 at Benavente, northern Spain. This bold cavalry action was mentioned in Grisdale's epitaph; in later years he ran an inn called the General Lefebvre. A headstone at Beaulieu (Hampshire) to Sergeant William Philips of the 15th Hussars (now badly eroded, and a deserving candidate for conservation) included a cast of his Waterloo Medal, the first medal awarded to all who served in the campaign, irrespective of rank, and to their next-of-kin as well. This was issued in 1816–7, and shows how far attitudes were shifting towards the greater recognition of the service of all ranks. Some veterans of the Napoleonic Wars lived abroad and the remarkable story of Captain Matthew Latham of the Buffs, hero of Albuera, will be considered in Chapter 8 below.

Headstone of Sergeant William Philips, Beaulieu, Hampshire showing a cast of his Waterloo medal.

6

Remembering Soldiers in the Victorian Age

Shifting attitudes can be seen also in the rise of regimental memorials which, from the 1840s onwards, started to list the names of the dead of all ranks, and not just those of officers. The 24th Foot raised an obelisk outside the Royal Hospital, designed by Charles Cockerell, which commemorated by name all of the many fatalities of the Battle of Chillianwala (1849) in the Punjab (Pakistan). The dead were buried on the battlefield, and a tablet in Cork's Protestant Cathedral, to Capt. Robert Travers, simply states 'There fills, on the field of battle, a soldier's grave.' Something is known about the actual burials of the dead of the 24th from a letter published in *The Times* on 10 January 1902. It related how a Deputy Commissioner visited the battlefield in 1864 and asked to be shown the British graves: the site was by then under plough, but digging a few feet revealed bones and among them brass buttons inscribed '24'; a monument was subsequently raised and the place of burial enclosed with a stone wall and planted with trees. Right across the globe, memorials and military cemeteries were arising wherever British garrisons and naval stations were established. Bermuda has a number of military cemeteries, primarily to receive the bodies of victims of yellow fever, which are now cared for by the Bermuda National Trust: of the eight, the earliest is St George's Military Cemetery on Grenadier Lane. On Antigua, on Shirley Heights above the important naval base of English Harbour, is an enclosed cemetery containing a number of 19th-century memorials, the largest of which is an obelisk to the soldiers of the 54th Regiment who died in the course of their posting to the Caribbean in 1848 to 1851. The Remembrance Trust is currently working on the restoration of this site.

Obelisk to the men of the 24th Foot, killed at the Battle of Chillianwala (1849), listing the names of all ranks of the dead. Royal Hospital, Chelsea.

Memorial to the men of the 54th Foot who died in the West Indies in 1848–51. Shirley Heights Cemetery, Antigua.

There was an undoubted pride among soldiers about the comradeship of burying their dead in a dignified and identified way – especially if it was across the globe and far from home. Both Army and individual families had a claim on the dead, but for practical reasons this rarely resulted in the return of bodies. The rise of regimental memorials in the mid-19th century is a reflection of heightened domestic appreciation of soldiers in society and the identification of localities with specific units. They began to appear in cathedrals across Britain and were often joined by regimental standards being laid up alongside them. In St Paul's Cathedral the 77th (East Middlesex) Regiment raised a monument by Matthew Noble to their dead of the Crimean War, with a relief showing an angel hovering over an open grave in which the coffined bodies of the fallen soldiers lie. This recreated the far-off scene of burial for a home audience and added a note of religious comfort for good measure. It also depicted comradeship in death: a sentiment which lay behind the erection of a tombstone in Heston churchyard (London Borough of Hounslow) to Private Frederick White of the 7th Hussars, who died in 1846 shortly after being flogged. White's death was a provocative case at a time when soldier welfare was beginning to receive rather more attention than had hitherto been paid: the headstone, regularly renewed by the regiment, stood as a reproach to ill treatment and a coarse system of martial discipline.

The Crimean War (1853–6) was the most significant conflict to involve British forces since Waterloo. Thanks to the emerging profession of the war reporter, the public knew more about this campaign – its battles, its hardships and its failures of administration – than any other to date. A remarkable compilation of British monuments in the Crimea was published in 1857. This was entitled *The Last of the Brave; or Resting Places of our Fallen Heroes in the Crimea and Scutari*, prepared by Captains Colborne and Brine and published by the celebrated firm of Ackermann and Co in 1857. This was the first printed collection of military epitaphs from a battle front, and included lithographs showing the battlefield cemeteries at Alma, Inkerman and elsewhere. New levels of sepulchral effort were reached, perhaps in keeping with the early Victorian age's taste for landscapes of feeling, embodied in the growing numbers of cemeteries being opened at home.

Cemetery of the British 2nd Brigade, Light Division, outside Sebastopol, Crimea: lithograph from Colborne and Brine, *The Last of the Brave* (1857).

Comparisons were even made between the military cemeteries of the Crimea and Europe's leading gardens for the dead:

> Of the burial grounds in general, the one most remarkable for its picturesque beauty was that of the Second Brigade, Light Division, Woronzoff Road, to which was imparted a certain foreign character from its being laid out in walks and alleys somewhat after the manner of 'Père la Chaise.' Cathcart's Hill might be termed an humble imitation of Kensal Green, and contains some handsome monuments, in design and execution far from inferior to many in England, as does also the graveyard of the First Brigade, Light Division. To the burial grounds of the Naval Brigade and those of the sailors at Balaklava and Kazatch must be assigned a touching grace peculiar to themselves.

Many monuments were built by the Royal Engineers: others by the regiments themselves. These were made possible by the static nature of the campaign: a war of movement would have prevented elaborate permanent cemeteries from being laid out. It was as well that Colborne and Brine went to such trouble in recording the memorials: after much agitation (and the deterioration of relations with Russia) the War Office decided to abandon all cemeteries in the Crimea save for that at Cathcart Hill in 1884. Savage fighting on the Eastern Front in the Second World War further damaged what was left, and further removals took place in the 1950s. The modern obelisk there is a quiet echo of the 120 cemeteries which once existed in the Crimea and which marked a new phase of military commemoration.

Scutari Hospital and Cemetery, Haydarpasa, Constantinople.
Lithograph by J. Needham after W. Simpson, 1856.

At Scutari, across the Bosphorus from Constantinople, the Selimiye Barracks were used as an allied hospital: inevitably a cemetery was needed and at Haydarpasa, overlooking the Sea of Marmara, ground was given by the Turkish authorities to provide just such a place. This was depicted many times over in paint, print and even photography: a real contrast to the oblivion of earlier military graves. Soldiers' graves lay beneath mounded earth: for some, a simple inscribed wooden board sufficed as a marker but for others – including some women nurses, working alongside Florence

Nightingale – a monument imported from the mother country would be raised as a more permanent tribute. Almost all the surviving inscriptions recall officers. Back home, the survivors of the war – and especially survivors of the Charge of the Light Brigade – were often later remembered with headstones which alluded to their taking part in one of the great cavalry actions in British history. Many of these have been identified by Gavin Hughes and Jonathan Trigg in a specialist study; others continue to emerge, such as the memorial in Kettering Cemetery (Northants.) to James Dray of the 4th Hussars, a veteran of the Crimea who died in the workhouse in 1894: 'This stone was erected by patriotic & sympathising friends', stated his epitaph, a reminder that the Crimea lodged in the British memory, and that honouring veterans was becoming an expression of imperial loyalty. Later, one of the veterans of Rorke's Drift (1879) would be granted an extravagant memorial in Chiswick Cemetery (London Borough of Hounslow): Private Fred Hitch VC died in 1913, and the granite rock, draped with a Union flag and topped with a pith helmet, was paid for by public subscription. In some ways it echoed the whitewashed cairns which were raised over the gathered bones of the dead of Isandlwana close by.

The rise of the volunteer movement from the 1850s was a further step towards a quicker social acceptance of the soldier in society. Citizen-soldiers would come to play an increasingly important role in Britain's armed forces, which was another reason behind the growing number of memorials to fighting men. Elsewhere, major conflicts such as the American Civil War (1861–5) and the Franco-Prussian War (1870–1) saw the mobilisation of the nation and the emergence of state-funded

left: Headstone of Private James Dray d. 1894, Kettering Cemetery, Northants. Dray, a veteran of the Charge of the Light Brigade, ended his days in the workhouse.
right: Monument to Private Frederick Hitch VC d. 1913, Chiswick Old Cemetery, London Borough of Hounslow.

programmes of remembrance and the creation of military cemeteries. Congress passed an Act in 1862, stipulating that all those who gave their lives in the cause of protecting the Republic should be placed in securely enclosed cemeteries with individual grave markers provided by the state: by 1866 there were 74 national cemeteries for the Union's dead, housing 303,536 men (54% of whom were identified); the burial of the defeated Confederates was a much more protracted affair. This programme cost the US War Department over $4 million: as the poet Walt Whitman expressed it,

'Such a consecration of a nation's power and resources to a *sentiment*, the world has never seen.' Arlington Cemetery, developing out of a military hospital on the edge of Washington DC, remains the national shrine for the burial of American soldiers. Nowhere in Europe, Britain included, followed this model of national remembrance for the fallen. That would have to wait until the enormous losses of the Great War demanded a response of appropriate magnitude.

Part of the Antietam National Cemetery, Maryland, USA showing the marble grave-markers erected over the Union dead of the 1862 battle.

As British naval operations spread ever further across the globe, the concept of the dispersed dead became ever more relevant. Those who made it back to shore-side hospitals might be buried in naval cemeteries like that on Bermuda: land for a burial ground on Ireland Island South was purchased by the Admiralty in 1809 and consecrated in 1812. Small cemeteries began to be formed wherever the British imperial effort made itself felt. Off Zanzibar is Chapwani Island, better known to some as Grave Island: the Commonwealth War Graves Commission now cares for it but there are earlier markers here dating from the 1870s, primarily to sailors. The fate of many of them was burial at sea. Robert Louis Stevenson's 1878 essay 'The English Admirals' was included in his celebrated collection *Virginibus Puerisque* (1881), and expressed most memorably the idea that the sea itself became a sepulchre:

> We should consider ourselves unworthy of our descent if we did not share the arrogance of our progenitors, and please ourselves with the pretension that the sea is English. Even where it is looked upon by the guns and battlements of another nation we regard it as a kind of English cemetery, where the bones of our seafaring fathers take their rest until the last trumpet; for I suppose no other nation has lost as many ships, or sent as many brave fellows to the bottom.

This idea of the sea as a naval cemetery would have resonated with families whose dead lay far away. At home, military burial grounds had hitherto been confined to hospitals. In later Victorian times, more memorials to soldiers and sailors were being erected in public cemeteries. Partly this just reflected the democratisation of remembrance, as a widening social range raised family tombs. But there was another development underway too: the specific honouring of the military dead. The Army itself opened a cemetery at Aldershot in the mid-1850s which offered a distinctive resting place for those who died while serving at this important garrison: the memorials here include a striking cross of terracotta, made by the Compton Potters' Arts Guild, in memory of a young Canadian officer called Lieut. Roy Gzowski who died in 1910 of typhoid and pneumonia after observing British Army exercises.

Compton Potters' Arts Guild: memorial cross of Lieut. Roy Gzowski d. 1910, Aldershot Military Cemetery, Hampshire.

The Royal Navy's Haslar Hospital at Gosport (Hampshire) had had a burial ground since its foundation in the 1740s: in 1859 the Clayhall Royal Naval Cemetery was opened close by and a homogenous form or memorial (albeit of concrete) was introduced which can be seen as a forerunner of the uniform headstones of the Imperial War Graves Commission. Norwich's Earlham Cemetery established a plot dedicated to military burials in 1878: at its centre was a giant figure referred to as 'The Soldier's Memorial' (originally named 'Armed Science', and also known as 'Spirit of the Army'), executed in terracotta by Doultons and modelled by John Bell.

John Bell, 'The Soldier's Memorial', Earlham Cemetery, Norfolk, 1878. An early creation of a military section in a civilian cemetery.

Guards Memorial, Brompton Cemetery, Royal Borough of Kensington and Chelsea, London.

In 1889 the Brigade of Guards erected an imposing marble cross in Brompton Cemetery to those Guardsmen who died on duty in London since 1854: individual names were inscribed in lead letters on a series of headstones arranged around the memorial. The Remembrance Trust has recently undertaken its restoration, including the replacement of missing letters. The dead of the Royal Hospital had been buried nearby in Brompton Cemetery since 1855: by 1893, 2,625 In-Pensioners had been buried there. The call for a fitting memorial led to the erection in 1901 of an elaborate memorial by John Whitehead and Sons, monumental sculptors, which listed the many campaigns they had fought in, and included stirring tributes which sum up patriotic appreciation of the soldier:

THESE VETERANS/ HAVING FOUGHT/ FOR KING/ FOR QUEEN/ FOR ENGLAND/ FOR EMPIRE/ IN ALMOST EVERY/ PART OF THE WORLD/ CAME HOME TO DIE/ IN PEACE/ HONOURED/ AND RESPECTED/ BY THEIR/ FELLOW-COUNTRYMEN

ERECTED/ BY THE/ CHELSEA/ COMMISSIONERS/ ON BEHALF OF/ AN ADMIRING NATION/ AS A TESTIMONY/ AND TRIBUTE TO/ VALOUR ENDURANCE/ SUFFERINGS & DEVOTION

A stronger military and naval presence was making itself felt in the later Victorian commemorative scene, and overdue respect was being paid to British soldiers and sailors.

Guards Memorial, Brompton Cemetery after conservation by TRT.

Chelsea Pensioners Monument, 1901, Brompton Cemetery.

7

Soldier Graves in Edwardian Times

Some public monuments in cemeteries had been raised to the dead of the Crimean War (at Lancaster, Bath, Mansfield and elsewhere) but it was the Second Boer War (1899–1902) which really saw the take-off for civic war memorials, laying the way for the legion of tributes which would arise for the Great War's dead. Peter Donaldson's study of the subject cites the example of Halifax, where the local newspaper in June 1902 referred to the forty dead who 'lie buried 'neath the veldt in that far off clime, their graves marked by crude monuments erected by sorrowing comrades' and urged the raising of 'something permanent at home … to show [the fallen] some honour'. Some of the ensuing monuments to the far-off dead were spectacular, a prelude to those raised after the First World War. Thomas Hardy's celebrated poem 'Drummer Hodge' (published in 1899 as 'The Dead Drummer') also dealt with this sense of distance:

> They throw in Drummer Hodge, to rest
> Uncoffined – just as found:

His landmark is a kopje-crest
That breaks the veldt around;
And foreign constellations move west
Each night above his mound.

Boer War Memorial to Northumberland Regiments, Newcastle (1908 postcard). Designed by T. Eyre Macklin, this was one of the most elaborate war memorials from this conflict.

In a prefiguring of Rupert Brooke's celebrated verse from 1914, 'The Soldier', Hardy ends the poem with a reverie about an English body beneath the southern skies:

> ... Yet portion of that unknown plain
> Will Hodge for ever be;
> His homely Northern breast and brain
> Grow to some Southern tree,
> And strange-eyed constellations reign
> His stars eternally.

By 1900 the attachment Britons felt to the posthumous treatment of their war dead – many of whom came from Territorial units, and were therefore regarded as citizen-soldiers – was much stronger than it had been before. Battlefield burials at the front were later embellished with permanent memorials, such as the cross placed over the trench at Spion Kop, where a British contingent was badly mauled in January 1900. There were 22,000 fatalities (14,000 from disease) in the conflict, but no comprehensive military response to the provision of war graves, which continued to be left to individual units, and then to private initiatives, to arrange. A letter to *The Times* on 24 October 1903 from the South African Graves Fund Committee of the Victoria League (a patriotic women's association) assured readers that 'The Guild of Loyal Women of South Africa' would tend any grave needing attention. At the zenith of British imperial power, the solemn business of honouring those who gave their lives for their country was still a random affair without state oversight.

View of grave markers at Spion Kop, South Africa. This 1900 action led to heavy British losses: many were buried in the trenches where they fought.

It took the sheer carnage of the Great War to put a central co-ordinated system in place to oversee the marking of graves of Britain's fallen. Perhaps the most famous poem from the outset of the war was Rupert Brooke's 'The Soldier', published in his posthumous collection *1914 and Other Poems* after the writer had died of sepsis and been buried on the Greek island of Skyros in the Aegean, on his way to Gallipoli. Brooke's patriotic message of the enduring identity of the distant dead came right at the end of the ages-long period of the anonymous soldier grave. Brooke could not know that within three years a state organisation would be founded to mark and honour the resting places of all who gave their lives for the nation. His verse thus stands for the all the dead warriors of earlier centuries, whose lot was a remote rushed grave and for whom enduring memorials were denied.

> If I should die, think only this of me:
> That there's some corner of a foreign field
> That is for ever England. There shall be
> In that rich earth a richer dust concealed;
> A dust whom England bore, shaped, made aware,
> Gave, once, her flowers to love, her ways to roam,
> A body of England's, breathing English air,
> Washed by the rivers, blest by suns of home.
> And think, this heart, all evil shed away,
> A pulse in the eternal mind, no less
> Gives somewhere back the thoughts by England given;
> Her sights and sounds; dreams happy as her day;
> And laughter, learnt of friends; and gentleness,
> In hearts at peace, under an English heaven.

Brooke lies beneath a bespoke marble monument on Skyros, commissioned by his family and raised in the 1920s at a time when the Imperial War Graves Commission was assuming responsibility for the commemoration of the dead of the Great War. A coped ledger slab, very Christian in character, it was one of a very select group of private battlefield memorials. For the vast majority of the fallen, the nation now cared for their graves and provided the memorials which marked them.

8

The Work of The Remembrance Trust

More interest is taken today in the graves of fallen soldiers of all periods than at any time since their deaths. There are many possible explanations for this: the growth in travel generally, and the rise of battlefield tourism; the ease with which historical information can be accessed, thanks to the internet; the rise of family history as a hobby; higher levels of education; and the perennial fascination with the fallen of the World Wars, which reflects its melancholy light backwards into the dead of earlier conflicts.

There is also an awareness that these memorials won't look after themselves: active conservation is needed if they are to survive into the future in a suitably dignified state, striking the right balance between legible smartness and the mellowness of age. Dignity is the watchword of The Remembrance Trust (TRT), which aims to reverse the disfiguring marks of time while respecting the historic character of these memorials. Legibility is a key issue: memorials are there to summon up past lives, and the readability of epitaphs is an essential goal.

Tyne Cot Cemetery, Passchendaele, Belgium. The largest CWGC cemetery anywhere, it contains just under 12,000 dead from the Ypres sector and was designed by Sir Herbert Baker.

There are numerous initiatives, current and recent, which pursue research into the graves and monuments of British soldiers and sailors. The leading organisation is the Commonwealth (formerly Imperial) War Graves Commission (CWGC): established in 1917, it is perhaps the pre-eminent state organisation charged with the upkeep of military burials from the World Wars; the work of the American Battle Monuments Commission comes closest. Sometimes the CWGC takes earlier burials into its care – there are examples of this in Africa – but its already huge responsibilities of caring for the dead of the First and Second World Wars, spread across the globe in 23,000 locations, prevent it from easily reaching backwards to assume responsibility for all earlier British military burials. It was established under Royal charter with the deliberate purpose of caring for the fallen of the Great War, which was later extended to those of the Second World War (up to 1947). Because the CWGC does such a fine job of caring for its cemeteries, it has set an example which places earlier military memorials at a distinct disadvantage. It was to fill this gap that Algy Cliff resolved to found The Remembrance Trust.

Amongst private initiatives in the realm of caring for historic military memorials, in the vanguard is BACSA, the British Association for Cemeteries in South Asia: not exclusively military, this charity was founded in 1977 by Theon Wilkinson and combines research and restoration with vigour. The War Memorials Trust, founded in 1997, covers periods prior to the First World War, but its efforts tend to be concentrated on monuments from that conflict. It gives out grants and advice on conservation issues. Younger, and devoted to the specific period of 1776–1815, is the Napoleonic and Revolutionary War Graves Charity which was founded in 2021 and concentrates on the sharing of understanding about fighting personnel of the American revolutionary wars through to Waterloo, and about the upkeep of graves ('Any nationality, Any branch of the armed forces, Anywhere in the world'). It has recently undertaken some tidying of the Napoleonic French officer prisoner-of-war headstones at Alresford, Hampshire. Individual regiments have been involved in restoration projects for their own dead: at Blingel, close to the site of the Battle of Agincourt in the Pas de Calais, is the obelisk to Capt. Matthew Latham (d. 1865), hero of the Battle of Albuera (1811), who protected the colour of the 3rd Foot (the Buffs) from fierce French assault, becoming dreadfully wounded in the process and losing an arm and his nose. The successor regiment, the Princess of Wales's Royal Regiment, has recently undertaken the restoration of the obelisk with the assistance of TRT and installed interpretation panels to explain Latham's remarkable courage and the reason why he ended up living in France (he had married a French woman).

Monument to Capt Matthew Latham, Blingel, Northern France. Latham was gravely wounded defending the colours of the 3rd Foot (The Buffs) at the Battle of Albuera in 1811. Recently restored, with the support of The Remembrance Trust. Photo courtesy of Lieut-Col. Martin Neame, project officer for the restoration.

Plaques on a conserved Napoleonic memorial in Père Lachaise, Paris showing the participation of Le Souvenir Français and the Association pour la Conservation des Monuments Napoléoniens.

Memorials relating to the age of Nelson are fortunate to be within the remit of the 1805 Association which, since its foundation in 1990, has undertaken the restoration of a number of naval monuments. Other bodies like the Mausolea and Monuments Trust (founded in 1997) existed to take on abandoned mausolea and support some tomb restorations but it does not have a military focus. Over in France the organisation Souvenir Française has existed since 1887, its aim being to commemorate the fast-disappearing veterans of the Napoleonic periods and to promote other memorials of French valour, ranging from Vercingetorix the Gaul to the soldiers of the Franco-Prussian War of 1870–1. In recent times their conservation efforts are readily recognised through the enamel cockades which are affixed to memorials they have worked on. It sometimes works with a younger body, established in 1995, the Association pour la Conservation des Monuments Napoléoniens: many examples of their work are to be found in Père Lachaise Cemetery in Paris. The restoration of martial memorials in France is undertaken with impressive vigour.

The Remembrance Trust was established in 2017 by Algy Cluff to undertake what no other British body was then doing: the restoration of older neglected military graves. The centenary of the First World War was gathering much attention and efforts were being concentrated on war memorials. The plight of earlier martial memorials was getting worse.

One of Algy Cluff's initial campaigns for monuments had taken place in South Africa. During 2005 there was much public concern about the poor state of repair of the graves of the British soldiers who died in the Anglo-Boer Wars, later known as the South African Wars. The graves had not been maintained for years and there had been theft of the metal crosses which marked the graves and many cases of vandalism. The British casualties lay in 223 burial sites, ranging from isolated sites on farms or scattered in unmaintained municipal cemeteries, to graves in military cemeteries or in dedicated military plots. Algy became involved and quickly but determinedly raised sufficient funds to help commence the restoration of these graves. The money raised was matched by the UK Ministry of Defence (MOD) but Algy persevered and persuaded the MOD to complete the restoration and to fund future maintenance by the CWGC.

Monument to Maj. Gen. William McBean VC d. 1878, Grange Cemetery, Edinburgh before and after cleaning.

TRT's only project in Scotland so far has been in Edinburgh's Grange Cemetery, where the marble pedestal tomb to Major General William McBean VC (1819–78) was cleaned and returned to a legible state: these represent a particularly pleasing 'before and after' result. McBean, the son of an Inverness shoemaker, rose through the ranks and won his VC at Lucknow in the Indian Mutiny. Its first transatlantic project was undertaken in Bermuda, where commemorative brasses at St Peter's Church to soldiers of the Grenadier Guards who died of disease in 1890–1 were conserved. Similar items in the Guards Chapel on Birdcage Walk, London, which were damaged in the tragic V1 strike in 1944, have just been restored with TRT's help.

Victoria Cross winners are clear priorities for

restoration. At Great Chart churchyard near Ashford (Kent), the marble headstone to Major General William Knox Leet VC (1833–98), gallant hero of the Zulu War of 1879, was returned to a pristine state through the dogged work of Corporal Steve Davis, a regular partner of TRT in this area who has devoted himself to the restoration of military graves. One particularly poignant winner of this supreme award for gallantry was Lance Corporal William House VC (1879–1912) of the Royal Berkshires: he won his VC rescuing wounded comrades in the Boer War in 1900, but was traumatised by the experience and took his own life in 1912 while serving in India. He was only recently granted a headstone by his old regiment (now part of The Rifles): as this case falls within the pre-1914 remit of TRT it was felt appropriate to smarten up its appearance as part of a wider project in St George's Cemetery, Dover, which contains many military memorials. In 2023 the cemetery was graced with a visit from HRH The Princess Royal, the Trust's patron, who was shown the work being carried out there by the Trust.

A more recent headstone at Elmers End Cemetery (London Borough of Bromley) was similarly overhauled: it marked the resting place of Company Sergeant Major William Evans VC (1876–1937) who worked as an inspector for the National Society for the Prevention of Cruelty to Children before returning to the Army and winning his award during the Battle of the Somme. If some object that his date of death falls outside the TRT's remit of pre-1914, then the only proper response must be that sometimes rules are made to be broken.

HRH The Princess Royal inspecting a monument being conserved by Martin Gwilliams at Dover Cemetery, 2023.

Part of the reason for TRT's existence is to offset the waning custom of tending graves. When memorials were regularly visited by family and comrades, as was once customary, trouble would be taken to ensure the grave was in good condition. If necessary a mason might be brought in to touch up an inscription which was fading, or clean away lichen and algae from the stone. In recent times this tradition has fallen away and visits to family graves are far less common. Deterioration can build up to the point of rendering an epitaph illegible, making the task of reinstatement more of a challenge. A further drawback is the ageing of natural stone. Some are very enduring and resilient: particularly granite. But other popular kinds of stone such as sandstone and marble frequently decay, losing their finished surface smoothness and losing their inscriptions too. Cleaning stone needs care: an experienced eye is required to estimate whether a headstone which shows signs of deterioration can withstand pressurised water treatment or harsh brushing, as limestone and sandstone memorials lack the durability of granite and other preferred modern materials. Older historic memorials are best left to qualified conservators, but benign intervention such as the removal of plant growth, the cleaning of algae staining and the freshening of inscriptions is possible.

Sometimes the TRT can salvage the legibility simply by renewing the painted infilling to the sunken lettering: this is shown on the stone at Dover Cemetery to Quartermaster Charles Wooden VC (1829–76), or by replacing lost lead letters (as at the Guards Memorial at Brompton Cemetery). Soldiers take pride in their appearance – Guardsmen especially so – and it is distressing to encounter their memorials in a neglected state. TRT was pleased to be able to tackle over seventy tombs in the Grenadier Guards section of Caterham Cemetery, Surrey and return them to a fitting state. The appearance of five monuments in Fairlight Cemetery (East Sussex) was greatly improved through a programme of cleaning in 2021. But the biggest single campaign has been in Hove Cemetery (West Sussex) where no fewer than 23 marble monuments have been transformed through cleaning and are now as spick and span as their recipients would have wished them to be.

Quartermaster Charles Wooden VC, d. 1876. A survivor of the Charge of the Light Brigade, his headstone in Dover Cemetery was recently restored by TRT.

TRT is committed to working with others who share their vision of reinstating the original dignity of martial memorials. Some are simply too delicate and complicated to be tackled by any but a conservator, and TRT is lucky to have been able to call on the services of Martin Gwilliams, a qualified stonemason and skilled letter-cutter who now works at St Paul's Cathedral. Working in partnership with military and naval units, with cemetery friends, with descendants and with other bodies, TRT looks forward to delivering more projects in the future. It is also eager to work abroad, wherever there are monuments to British personnel from the pre-1914 period. With the help of generous donors, TRT is able to reinstate the dignity of these memorials and thereby pay tribute to their memory.

Tomb of Commander James Pitt RN (1761–80), St Paul's Parish, Falmouth, Antigua. The TRT is eager to restore surviving memorials across the globe. Pitt was the youngest son of Pitt the Elder, Earl of Chatham, and brother of Pitt the Younger.

Contact Details

The Remembrance Trust can be contacted via its website:

https://www.theremembrancetrust.com

or by post at:

Rooms M22–24, Lord Warden House,
Lord Warden Square,
Dover, Kent CT17 9EQ

Telephone: 01304 448900

The Trust is a registered charity, No. 1177492

Further Reading

This essay has drawn on numerous books and articles and there is a growing profusion of online sites covering the topic too.

Alan Borg's *War Memorials: From Antiquity to the Present* (1991) is unbeaten as a clear introduction. The present author's *War Memorials* (Amberley, 2019) provides a short, illustrated survey of British examples. Ian Atherton's *Britons and their Battlefields: War, Memory, and Commemoration since the Fourteenth Century* (Oxford University Press, 2024) looks at burial and monuments alongside much else and is highly recommended. The Battlefields Trust has a useful website (https://www.battlefieldstrust.com/) which includes registers of memorials from the Wars of the Roses and English Civil War as well as detailed gazetteers of all battlefield sites in the UK. The Imperial War Museum's War Memorials Register (https://www.iwm.org.uk/memorials) is a digital archive covering several centuries which includes some military graves as well as war memorials.

Glenn Foard and Richard Morris's *The Archaeology of British Battlefields: Conflict in the Pre-Industrial Landscape* (English Heritage/Council for British Archaeology, 2012) presents the evidence from past excavations and covers burials. The question of their whereabouts is presented in Anne Curry and Glenn Foard's article 'Where are the dead of medieval battles? A preliminary survey',

Journal of Conflict Archaeology, vol. 11 (2017), pp. 61–77, available at https://doi.org/10.1080/15740773.2017.1324675. Nigel Saul's *English Church Monuments in the Middle Ages* (Oxford University Press, 2009) gives a clear overview of the military effigy. The Towton mass grave is comprehensively analysed in Veronica Fiorato et al. ed., *Blood Red Roses: The Archaeology of a Mass Grave from the Battle of Towton AD 1461* (Oxbow Books, 2000).

Memorials to the British soldier dead of the two key campaigns of the Napoleonic Wars are gathered together in an epic two-volume study by Janet and David Bromley, *Wellington's Men Remembered: A Register of Memorials to Soldiers Who Served in the Peninsular War and at Waterloo 1808–1815* (Praetorian Press, 2012–15). Organised under the aegis of the Waterloo Association, this monumental work nonetheless excludes those who served in other campaigns and perforce concentrates on the Army alone. The Guards Cemetery at Bayonne was described in a book of that title by Philip A. Hurt in 1887. The sorry post-mortem fate of the bones (and teeth) of the dead at Waterloo is explained in Bernard Wilkin and Robin Schäfer's *Bones of Contention: The industrial exploitation of human bones in the modern age* (Archives générales du Royaume, Brussels, 2024). Crimean War memorials are covered in an article by Gavin Hughes and Jonathan Trigg in *The Journal of Conflict Archaeology* vol. 4 (2008), pp. 39–58. Naval memorials are covered by Barbara Tomlinson's *Commemorating the Seafarer: monuments, memorials and memory* (Boydell and Brewer, 2015).

George L. Mosse's *Fallen Soldiers: Reshaping the Memory*

of the World Wars (Oxford University Press, 1990) looks back to the emergence of national responses to military losses from the Napoleonic period onwards. Andrew Keating's 2011 PhD thesis *The Empire of the Dead: British Burial Abroad and the Formation of National Identity* discusses overseas military burials, especially those in the Crimea (available at https://escholarship.org/uc/item/33r4g0gj). Drew Gilpin Faust's *This Republic of Suffering* (Knopf Doubleday, 2008) discusses the burial and remembering of the dead of the US Civil War. Peter Donaldson's *Remembering the South African War: Britain and the Memory of the Ango-Boer War, from 1899 to the Present* (Liverpool University Press, 2012), available at https://library.oapen.org/handle/20.500.12657/31644, discusses the issue of the absent dead and the need for war memorials at home. Barrie Thorpe's *Private Memorials of the Great War on the Western Front* (Western Front Association, 1999) describes the few such tributes erected in that theatre of war.

In terms of conservation, the Historic England website contains helpful guides to the care of war memorials:

https://historicengland.org.uk/images-books/publications/conserving-war-memorials-structural/heag169-conserving-war-memorials-structural

and of cemetery monuments:

https://historicengland.org.uk/advice/caring-for-heritage/cemeteries-and-burial-grounds/monuments/

A useful guide to memorial conservation is also found on the website of the 1805 Association:

https://www.1805club.org/conservation-projects

The restorer of military memorials, Steve Davis, updates his latest work at:

https://www.facebook.com/MilitaryGraveRestorer

The work of the Napoleonic and Revolutionary War Graves Charity can be seen on their website at:

https://www.nrwgc.com

All URLs retrieved in September 2025.

Illustration Credits

2. Ashdon, Essex: Metropolitan Museum of Art, New York via Creative Commons.

3. Democleides: National Archaeological Museum, Athens, via Creative Commons.

6. Sir Hugh Hastings: British Museum.

7. Sir Michael de la Pole: David Carrington.

8. St Mary Magdalene church: Paul Stamper.

9. Lord Dacre: Geograph via Creative Commons.

12, 24, 26. Major General Thomas Tyldesley, Theodor Körner, Sergeant William Yuill: Wikipedia via Creative Commons.

16. William Hiseland: Royal Hospital Chelsea.

21. Joseph Wright, *The Dead Soldier*: Yale Center for British Art.

23, 39, 46, 47, 49. Shorncliffe; Guards Memorial, Brompton Cemetery; Maj. Gen. William McBean VC; Quartermaster Charles Wooden VC: The Remembrance Trust.

32. Haydarpasa: Wellcome Collection.

44. Capt. Matthew Latham: Lieut-Col. Martin Neame.

All other photographs are by the author.